THE WESTERN PERSPECTIVE

A History of Civilization in the West

Volume C: 1789–Present

Philip V. Cannistraro
Queens College, The City University of New York

John J. Reich
Syracuse University in Florence, Italy

THE WESTERN PERSPECTIVE

A History of Civilization in the West

Volume C: 1789–Present

Harcourt Brace College Publishers

Fort Worth Philadelphia San Diego New York Orlando Austin San Antonio
Toronto Montreal London Sydney Tokyo

Publisher   Earl McPeek

Acquisitions Editor   David Tatom

Product Manager   Steve Drummond

Project Editor   Laura J. Hanna

Art Director   Garry Harman

Production Manager   Kathleen Ferguson

Cover Credit   *Three Musicians* by Pablo Picasso. Philadelphia Museum of Art.

Address for Orders: Harcourt Brace College Publishers, 6277 Sea Harbor Drive, Orlando, FL 32887-6777. 1-800-782-4479

Address for Editorial Correspondence: Harcourt Brace College Publishers, 301 Commerce Street, Suite 3700, Fort Worth, TX 76102

Web Site Address: http://www.hbcollege.com

Harcourt Brace College Publishers will provide complimentary supplements or supplement packages to those adopters qualified under our adoption policy. Please contact your sales representative to learn how you qualify. If as an adopter or potential user you receive supplements you do not need, please return them to your sales representative or send them to: Attn: Returns Department, Troy Warehouse, 465 South Lincoln Drive, Troy, MO 63379.

ISBN: 0-03-045763-7

Library of Congress Catalog Card Number: 98-72311

Printed in the United States of America

8 9 0 1 2 3 4 5 6 7 048 9 8 7 6 5 4 3 2 1

To accommodate teachers at institutions with different versions of Western Civilization courses, this book has been produced in seven different formats.

A complete, one-volume edition containing the entire text
Volume I: To 1715
Volume II: Since 1500
Volume A: To 1500
Volume B: 1300–1815
Volume C: 1789–Present
Alternate Volume: Since the Renaissance

PHILIP V. CANNISTRARO. Born in New York City, Philip V. Cannistraro is an authority on modern Italian history and the Italian American experience. He studied in both the undergraduate and graduate programs at New York University and is now Distinguished Professor at Queens College and at the Graduate School, the City University of New York. Professor Cannistraro serves on the boards of several journals and is editor of *The Italian American Review.* He has written or edited a number of books, including *Civilizations of the World* (with R. Greaves, R. Murphey, and R. Zaller, 3rd ed., 1997), *La fabbrica del consenso: Fascismo e mass media* (1975), *Fascismo, Chiesa e Emigrazione* (with G. Rosoli, 1979), *Historical Dictionary of Fascist Italy* (1981), and *Il Duce's Other Woman,* a biography of Margherita Sarfatti (with B. Sullivan, 1993).

JOHN J. REICH. A native of England, John Reich was trained as a classical archaeologist and did both his undergraduate and graduate work at the University of Manchester. He is an authority on Minoan civilization, pre-Roman Italy, and music. Professor Reich is associated with the Syracuse University study program in Florence, Italy. Reich lectures frequently in Europe and the United States on history, art, and the humanities and is the author of many scholarly articles and several books, including *Italy Before Rome* (1979) and the widely acclaimed *Culture and Values* (with Lawrence S. Cunningham, Harcourt Brace, 4th ed., 1998). He lives in a Medieval castle in the hilltop town of Panzano in Chianti in Italy.

Perspectives on History:
The Historians' French
Revolution, Jack R.
Censer, *George Mason
University*   *752*

*Documents on
History:*
The Rights of Women
796

*Public Figures and
Private Lives*
Mary Wollstonecraft
and Percy Bysshe
Shelley   *812*

Documents on History:
The Drive for Empire
952

Perspectives on History

Public Figures/Private Lives

Tables and Graphs

Acknowledgments

This project began what seems like centuries ago, when Ted Buchholz, now President of Harcourt Brace College Publishers, asked us to write what has evolved into *The Western Perspective*. Since then he exhibited unfailing faith in our ability to carry this project to conclusion and gave us the full support of Harcourt Brace's extensive publishing resources. Immediately after we agreed to undertake the book, we had the good fortune of working under the close direction of David Tatom, senior editor for history, who over many years worked with us on the planning and development of the book, bolstered our spirits, and encouraged our work at every turn. Over the last several years, Kristie L. Kelly has been our developmental editor, in which capacity she has helped to put the manuscript into final form and skillfully managed the details of what became an increasingly complex undertaking. Laura Hanna moved the book through the last stages of creation as senior project editor; Kathy Ferguson and Garry Harman served as production manager and art director. Elsa Peterson was the photo researcher.

A number of friends and colleagues have contributed to this book in many important ways, and we wish especially to thank the following individuals: Eric D. Brose, Robert S. Browning, H. James Burgwyn, Elisheva Carlebach, Peter Carravetta, Jennifer Cook, Patricia A. Cooper, Alexander DeGrand, Spencer DiScala, Karen Dubno, Monte Finkelstein, Elisabeth Giansiracusa, Charles L. Killinger, Julie Mostov, David Nasaw, Nunzio Pernicone, Ben Reich, Cecil O. Smith, Donald F. Stevens, David Syrett, Elena Frangakis-Syrett, Frank Warren, and M. Hratch Zadoian.

In addition, we are indebted to our colleagues who generously shared with us their wealth of experience and knowledge. Our sincere thanks to the following instructors:

Phillip Adler, East Carolina State University

Gerald Anderson, North Dakota State University

Jay P. Anglin, University of Southern Mississippi

Martin Arbagi, Wright State

Patrick Armstrong, Jefferson State Community College

Frank Baglione, Tallahassee Community College

Carol Bargeron, Louisiana State University

Ed Beemon, Middle Tennessee State University

Alan Beyerden, Ohio State University

Lawrence Blacklund, Montgomery County Community College

Stephen Blumm, Montgomery County Community College

Melissa Bokovoy, University of New Mexico

Paul Bookbinder, University of Massachusetts at Boston

Darwin Bostick, Old Dominion University

James Brink, Texas Tech University

Daniel P. Brown, Moorpark College

Tom Bryan, Alvin Community College

Gary Burbridge, Grand Rapids Community College

Thomas Burns, Emory University

Elizabeth Carney, Clemson University

Lamar Cecil, University of North Carolina at Chapel Hill

Thomas Christofferson, California State University at Northridge

Orazio Ciccarelli, University of Southern Mississippi

Franz Coetzee, Yale University

Fred Colvin, Middle Tennessee State University

William Connell, Rutgers University

John Contreni, Purdue University

Jessica Coope, University of Nebraska

Marc Cooper, Southwest Missouri State University

Frederick M. Crawford, Middle Tennessee State University

Gary Cross, Pennsylvania State University

Paige Cubbison, Miami Dade Community College

Nancy Curtin, Fordham University

Maribel Dietz, Louisiana State University

Michael Doyle, Ocean Community College

Charles Endress, Angelo State

Thomas Fabiano, Monroe Community College

Gary Ferngren, Oregon State

Monte Finkelstein, Tallahassee Community College

Edward W. Fox, Cornell University

Carl Frasure, University of Alaska

Elizabeth Furdell, University of North Florida

Alan Galpern, University of Pittsburgh

Richard Golden, Clemson University

Seella Gomezdelcampo, Roane State Community College

Karen Gould

David Gross, University of Colorado at Boulder

Alan Grubb, Clemson University

James D. Hardy, Louisiana State University

Jeanne Harrie, California State University at Bakersfield

Stephen Hauser, Marquette University

Peter Hayes, Northwestern University

Neil Hayman, San Diego State University

Susan Holt, Houston Community College

Robert Houston, University of the South

Bill Hughes, Essex Community College

Laura Hunt, University of Dayton

Frances Kelleher, Grand Valley State University

George Kelner, Rhode Island College

Susan Kent, University of Colorado at Boulder

Charles Killinger III, Valencia Community College

Lloyd Kramer, University of North Carolina at Chapel Hill

Thomas Kselman, University of Notre Dame

David Large, Montana State University

Frederick Lauritsen, Eastern Washington University

Ron Lesko, Suffolk Community College

Mary Ann Lizondo, Northern Virginia Community College

Paul Lockhart, Wright State

Gary Long, Methodist College

Leo Loubere, SUNY at Buffalo

Gladys Luster, John C. Calhoun College

David MacDonald, Illinois State University

Paul Maier, Western Michigan University

James Martin, Campbell University

William Mathews, Ohio State University

John Matzko, Bob Jones University

John McFarland, Sierra College

James Mini, Montgomery County Community College

Thomas Mockaitis, DePaul

Marjorie Morgan, Southern Illinois University

Rex Morrow, Trident Technical College

Pierce Mullens, Missouri State University

Francis J. Murphy, Boston College

Martha Newman, University of Texas at Austin

Bill Olsen, Marist College

Fred Olsen, Northern Virginia Community College

Thomas Ott, University of North Alabama

Neil Pease, University of Wisconsin at Milwaukee

Jack Pesda, Camden County College

Donald Pryce, University of South Dakota

Herman Rebel, University of Arizona

Marlette Rebhorn, Austin Community College - Rio Grande Campus

Larry Rotge, Slippery Rock University

John Rothney, Ohio State University

Jose Sanches, St. Louis University

Lura Scales, Hinds Community College

Robert G. Schafer, University of Michigan at Flint

Ezel Kural Shaw, California State University at Northridge

Susan Shoemaker, University of Delaware

Ronald Smith, Arizona State University

Eileen Soldwedel, Edmonds Community College

William Stiebing, University of New Orleans

David Tait, Oklahoma State University

Maxine Taylor, Northwestern State University

Janet TeBrake, University of Maine

David Tengwall, Anne Arundel Community College

Jack Thacker, Western Kentucky University

Richard Todd, Wichita State University

Spencer Tucker, Texas Christian University

Thomas Turley, Santa Clara University

Jeffry von Arx, Georgetown University

L. J. Worley, University of Washington

Finally, the authors would like to thank each other: their long friendship over many years not only survived the close and constant working together on this project, but actually strengthened. All collaborations should be this good.

To vary a cliche, each generation rewrites the history textbooks. As a result, there are today about a dozen books on the market that are suitable for use as texts in college-level Western Civilization courses.

Why, then, still another one?

We have each taught Western Civilization or similar courses at large universities for more than 25 years and, like countless colleagues, have wished for a book that we felt met the needs of our students as well as our own requirements as teachers. Existing books run the full range, from traditional works that emphasize political, diplomatic, and military history and look at developments largely from the point of view of leaders and élites, to more recent books that emphasize one approach, particularly social history, and try to present historical change as experienced by ordinary people.

Traditional treatments reinforce the views of earlier generations but do not stress the trends in more recent scholarship, while the new texts can leave students confused about how history changes and civilizations evolve. Another characteristic in recent textbook writing has been the tendency to underrate students and to "unclutter" the picture by omitting the kind of detail that is the guts of history. The stress on analysis and pattern, rather than on facts, of necessity emphasizes broad economic and social forces to the exclusion of human agency and, yes, even of historical accident.

We believe the best approach is one that conveys the full range of human experience and that considers both the material processes and spiritual values of historical development. We have sought to achieve a genuine balance between narrative and analysis. The writing of history at its best has always been the ability to tell a story—by which we mean a narrative of the record of human struggle and achievement, of conflict and community, of cultural diversity and social change. It is not always an easy or pleasant story to relate, but it should be told as much as possible as it unfolded rather than as we would have wanted it to. Moreover, history without detail may leave students bored and deprive them of the kind of vivid images that give life and breath to the story. Abstract analysis, while important to critical thinking, is not a substitute for factual knowledge. Both are necessary to our understanding of history and vital to navigating the ever more complex world in which we live.

Our Structural Design. A textbook is a learning and a teaching tool and should reflect the realities of the classroom. It occurred to us early on that our text should correspond to the needs and interests of today's teachers. A major case in point is the fact that the 30 to 35 chapters into which most books are divided do not conform to the number of class sessions usually available to the instructor. As teachers we must constantly think about how to break up and present material in topics that can be handled in one class period and that students can digest. This means, inevitably, dividing the conventional, large textbook chapters into smaller units.

To correct this longstanding pedagogical problem, we have given our book a unique—although not a startlingly different—structure by arranging the story of Western Civilization in 95 smaller "Topics," corresponding to the approximate number of class sessions in an academic year. Most of our Topics are appropriate for a single class period.

At first glance instructors might assume that this structural design artificially separates material that should be presented in an "integrated" manner. But a closer look will reveal that we have simply divided the overly large chapters of conventional texts into logical, teachable units. The result provides the instructor with a great deal more flexibility in terms of assigning student reading, syllabus design, and in-class analysis. We have also taken pains to provide students with ways to connect these smaller topics in the larger stream of historical narrative as well as with methods to focus on important themes. Furthermore, we grouped the 95 topics into eight broad chronological "Parts," corresponding to the traditional divisions of Western history. Each Part is introduced by an essay discussing the broad trends and patterns that characterize the period.

Our approach has been to provide full coverage of all major aspects of historical experience. In addition to the political, diplomatic, and military events of the more traditional texts, each Part contains Topics that deal individually with social, economic, cultural, and intellectual history. Our treatment of cultural history is unusually rich, including a full discussion of art and music. We have also written Topics that deal fully with regions that are generally neglected or given only brief mention, such as eastern and southern Europe, and we have included Topics that examine economic and technological developments in depth. Our discussion of social trends seeks to offer students an understanding of daily life and the broad patterns of social change, as well as of the status of slaves, Jews, and other ethnic, religious, or sexual minorities. We have, of course, tried to incorporate the most recent findings from the burgeoning world of women's history into our narrative.

The title of our book, *The Western Perspective*, reflects the fact that while our focus is the Western experience, we believe it is important to place that experience in the wider context of world history. We therefore discuss developments in Africa, Asia, the Americas, and the Pacific when they had an impact on, or were affected by, Western history.

Special Features. In addition to the overall structure of our book, we have designed a number of innovative special features that we believe lend both deeper insight and immediacy to the narrative.

Each Part contains a number of essays called "Perspectives on History," written especially for this book by leading experts in the field. These essays furnish students with a sense of the clash of scholarly opinion about particular subjects, such as the French Revolution and Fascism, or shed special light on a particularly interesting and unusual aspect of historical experience, such as the status of women in ancient Mesopotamia or the earliest Africans in Europe.

Each Part also contains sections entitled "Public Figures and Private Lives." These consist of portraits of the private and public lives of couples in which one or both partners played an influential part in culture, society, or politics. Such sketches serve a number of useful purposes: by relating larger trends to individuals, they give students immediate and easily understandable insight into an important era or development; they provide specific examples of the different roles of, and the interaction between, men and women in various historical periods, and suggest the impact of gender on social and private lives.

Most texts print short quotations from primary sources to add flavor to the narrative. Our "Documents on History" sections are designed with a specific pedagogical purpose in mind. Each one of these document sections consists of several pages that provide a variety of readings from primary sources on a selected issue. In this way students are able to gain a serious, in-depth insight into historical method, to analyze conflicting documents, and to engage in genuine class discussion.

Each of our 95 Topics begins with an overview, which provides a brief look at the major themes and subjects to be discussed. Where appropriate, the Topics contain one or more boxes of "Significant Dates" of principal events. Each Topic ends with a conclusion, set off from the text, a series of questions for further study, and an up-to-date bibliography.

To make this book a vivid visual experience, it has been designed as a full color production, with hundreds of illustrations and maps, as well as charts and tables.

Test Manual to accompany *The Western Perspective*   Marlette Rebhorn   Austin Community College

This test bank provides the instructor with a variety of question styles. In addition to multiple choice questions, there are identification questions, essay questions, and book report questions. Free to instructors.

Computerized Test Banks   Available in four formats
IBM® 5.25"   IBM® 3.50"   Macintosh®   MS Windows®

Study Guide to accompany *The Western Perspective*   Gerald Anderson   North Dakota State University

This student guide includes a brief overview of each Topic, as well as identifications, geographical identifications, map exercises, timeline questions, short-answer exercises, and essay questions.

Computerized Study Guide   This new student supplement is designed specifically to accompany *The Western Perspective*. It offers students, at an affordable price, a variety of interactive exercises tied to the chapter organization of the text. Free preview for instructors. Available in Windows® format from Educational Software Concepts, Inc. To order, or for more information, call toll free 1-800-748-7734.

Instructor's Manual to accompany *The Western Perspective*   This manual includes a summary of chapter topics, lecture notes, suggested readings, and discussion questions which will spark debate among your students.

Overhead Transparency Package   A comprehensive collection of 183 full color acetates including 128 maps, 35 transparencies of major works of art, tables, and charts.

Western Civilization Videos/Films for the Humanities   Choose from a wide variety of videos from the extensive Films for the Humanities history catalog. Contact your local Harcourt Brace sales representative for a complete listing of available videos. Adoption requirements apply.

Arts & Entertainment History Videos   Many outstanding selections are available from the Arts & Entertainment video library which include selections from A & E's extensive *Biography* collection. Contact your local Harcourt Brace sales representative for a complete listing of available videos. Adoption requirements apply.

PBS Video Series   Several outstanding videos are available from the PBS video series written and narrated by David Macauley. Contact your local Harcourt Brace sales representative for a complete listing of available videos. Adoption requirements apply.

The Western Civilization Videodisc   This disc provides the instructor with a wide-ranging resource, organized in a unique, flexible format, which makes it easy to prepare illustrated lectures and tailor-made presentations. Adoption requirements apply.

Harcourt Brace's *The Western Perspective* **Web Site**   This Web site provides access to many online resources for instructors and students.

Students have access to topic summaries, primary sources, annotated Internet links relevant to each topic, links to topic-relevant search engines, Web-based exercises, online practice quizzes, and a bulletin board that allows students taking the course to communicate with each other.

Instructors have access to all student material plus overhead transparencies, answers to the Web-based exercises, a downloadable computerized test bank with answer key, lecture outlines, and a mail list for instructors using *The Western Perspective* to correspond with each other.

Start your tour with our home page at www.hbcollege.com.

PART VI

THE OLD REGIME

The term "Old Regime" describes the period of transition in European history that led up to the French Revolution of 1789. On the surface, life in Europe continued to follow patterns established in the Middle Ages. Agriculture remained the chief occupation and economic activity. Most Europeans lived in farming communities, and while peasants in Western Europe were free, many still owed feudal obligations to land owners; in Eastern Europe the majority were still serfs.

Political and economic power remained in the hands of a hereditary aristocracy, and, to a lesser extent, of the religious authorities. Whether in the Dutch republic, in England—a constitutional monarchy—or absolute monarchies such as France or Prussia, participation in government was limited to a tiny section of the population, who used their influence to protect their own interests. Moreover, in

France as well as in Central and Eastern Europe government evolved in the direction of royal absolutism.

Throughout Europe a legally recognized social hierarchy concentrated privilege and status among traditional élites, while the bulk of society—the peasantry, urban workers, and the middle classes—remained excluded from government but bore the brunt of taxation. The trade in African slaves, and the institution of slavery itself, continued to be condoned and advanced by European states.

Yet behind the apparently permanent façade, there were signs of instability. The scientific revolution of the 17th century and the intellectual movement known as the Enlightenment of the 18th century led slowly but inevitably to dissatisfaction with old ways and beliefs. Out of the English political experiment of the 17th century and the ideas of the Enlightenment there emerged theories of political sovereignty that recognized the right of ordinary citizens to resist oppression and overthrow despots. As traditional political patterns came under question, an economic system that had lasted for centuries began to erode. Sectors of the middle class, especially the educated professional groups, became increasingly interested in the issue of political representation. With the growth of cities, an increasing proportion of the population was within reach of education, and ideas began to spread far more rapidly. One of the major factors in the development of urban life was the industrial revolution that began in the late 18th century.

In international affairs, the traditional rivalry between the two great powers of Europe, England and France, continued to dominate politics, while in the 18th century two new continental contenders began to emerge: the German state of Brandenburg-Prussia and Russia. Furthermore, with Europeans busily colonizing in Asia and the Americas, competition among the great powers resulted in military clashes on a global scale.

The buildup of a century and a half of pressure for change exploded in 1789 in the French Revolution. It was a sign of the new world which the revolutionary leaders hoped to create that they took inspiration from a revolution halfway across the globe: that of the Americans against their British colonial rulers.

Topic   11

THE AGE OF REASON

oward the end of the 17th century, scientists and intellectuals began to circulate to a wider public the ideas and principles behind 17th-century science. During the 18th century, philosophers applied the same scientific attitudes to broader questions of human behavior. The school of thought that developed was called the Enlightenment, and the period during which it flourished—1740–1790—is often known as the Age of Reason.

The origins of Enlightenment thought lay in the emphasis placed on reason and order by 17th-century thinkers such as Isaac Newton and John Locke. The latter, in particular, advocated the virtues of political and religious freedom, and claimed that human beings were essentially good.

The center of Enlightenment thinking was France, where a group of intellectuals known as the *philosophes* developed a consistent view of the world. The highest power, they believed, was reason used critically, since only by its means could true knowledge be gained. Reason, in turn, reflected the rational essence of Nature, which is ordered, and operates according to logical and unchanging laws. If humans would only follow reason, and abandon the superstitions of traditional religion, with its emphasis on original sin and divine prescription, they could create personal and social progress.

At the same time, Enlightenment thinkers were believers in practical information and experiment. The chief expression of this conviction was the *Encyclopédie*, a vast multi-authored work describing the contemporary state of science, technology, and philosophy. The project's editors were Denis Diderot and Jean Le Rond d'Alembert. In spite of government interference, Diderot managed to bring out 17 volumes of the *Encyclopédie* between 1747 and 1771, and its sales throughout Europe helped to spread the ideas behind the Enlightenment.

The leader in the Enlightenment battle against organized religion was Voltaire. Poet, novelist, historian, Voltaire also wrote on science and philosophy. The most famous intellectual of his time, in the last 25 years of his life Voltaire constantly attacked organized religion—he called it "the infamous thing"—which he believed caused so much bigotry and fanaticism.

Other thinkers dealt with scientific and social issues. Georges Buffon was the first modern classifier of the animal world, while Marie-Jean Condorcet used his work as a mathematician to reinforce his belief that the human race was capable of systematic progress. In Italy, Cesare Beccaria studied new approaches to criminals and their punishment. The Scottish economist Adam Smith, in writing *The Wealth of Nations* (1776), founded economics as a social science.

Although he was one of the contributors to the *Encyclopédie*, Jean-Jacques Rousseau strongly contested the philosophes' notion that civilization would lead to an improved society. On the contrary, he held that humans were good but civilization evil. The way to happiness, therefore, lay in a return to a simple, natural life. An advocate of free love and unrestrained emotion, Rousseau devised a social contract which proposed a new kind of relationship between individuals and their government.

THE SEEDS OF THE ENLIGHTENMENT

The intellectual movement known as the Enlightenment, which reached its peak in the latter part of the 18th century, represented the fusion of several currents of thought from the late 17th century. The scientific revolution had led the way in seeking to understand how the world works, revealing in the process that many of the teachings of traditional Christianity about natural science and astronomy were simply wrong (on the scientific revolution and Isaac Newton, see Part VI, Topic 1). In particular, the works of the great physicist Sir Isaac Newton demonstrated that the universe operated along orderly lines, which the power of human reason was capable of perceiving.

The Philosophy of John Locke

One of the heroic fathers of the Enlightenment was the English philosopher John Locke (1632–1704). In *An Essay Concerning Human Understanding* (1690), Locke discussed the origin and nature of knowledge. At birth, he argued, the human mind was a blank tablet—a *tabula rasa*—that was filled up by sense impressions gained through direct experience. As a result, all human beings were born as equals, whereas status and privilege usually determined the kind of experiences that each person underwent. Education was, therefore, of prime importance in creating a just and equitable society. Locke's empiricism was clearly inspired by the scientific method of Galileo and others.

In a truly revolutionary move, Locke rejected the traditional Christian teaching of original sin, and the traditional political system of monarchy. Instead, he believed in the essential goodness of humanity, and argued that political power should have a broad popular base. In his *Two Treatises on Civil Government* (1690), written in the wake of the English Revolution, Locke posited the contract theory of government, according to which individuals living in a state of nature entered freely into a political compact in order to protect the essential individual rights of life, liberty, and property. Citizens would act loyally toward government, but if government broke its part of the contract by undermining these liberties, then the people had the right to change it (for a selection from Locke's *Second Treatise* see Part VI, Topic 4).

As the scientific revolution had demonstrated, by the use of reason it was possible for humans to make progress in understanding the workings of nature. Similar beneficial change could be created in society by following the same positive course. Although many of the rationalists who followed him abandoned all belief in God, Locke himself was not an atheist and strongly advocated a degree of religious freedom—although not for Catholics, Jews, or atheists.

By the early part of the 18th century, these ideas had begun to crystallize. Thinkers increasingly rejected the past, and looked forward to social and political reform. Custom and tradition, far from being valuable, were the shackles that bound the human race and prevented progress. Hope for humanity lay not in contemplating the rewards of the next life—the existence of which in any case could not be objectively demonstrated—but in concentrating on improvements in the real world. With this optimistic attitude, civilization could reach new heights, and redress many of the existing injustices.

THE PHILOSOPHES: THE BATTLE AGAINST SUPERSTITION

The center of Enlightenment thought was France, where its representatives fought a constant battle against the weakening absolutism of Louis XV and the power of the Catholic Church. Important Enlightenment movements developed in Germany and Italy, and Enlightenment ideas also circulated in North America, especially toward the end of the century, where they influenced the first pronouncements of the founding fathers. Eastern Europe was relatively little affected, its rulers being fully aware of the subversive character of Enlightenment doctrines.

In France, the movement's leaders were the *philosophes* (the word means "philosophers" in French). The philosophes were not so much original thinkers as popularizers and propagandizers, who circulated the ideas of others in the form of pamphlets, plays, novels, or works of history.

Few Enlightenment thinkers completely ruled out the possibility of the existence of a divine force in the universe; even the highly skeptical Edinburgh philosopher David Hume (1711–1776) argued only against the provability of such a power. Most of them, however, attacked the power of the clergy and all traditional religious superstition.

In place of the Christian God stood nature—or Nature—whose natural laws benevolently governed the universe. The same order that existed in astronomy and physics could be found in morality, or politics, or even economics. Only by seeking to understand these natural laws and following them could humans achieve happiness. By emphasizing happiness, rather than salvation, the philosophes rejected the traditional Christian view that misery in this life would receive compensation in the next; the Jeffersonian belief in the right of all humans to "the pursuit of happiness," as well as life and liberty, was a typical Enlightenment concept derived from Locke.

The concern with general well-being led to protests at the ill-treatment of prisoners and the insane, and condemnation of slavery. Most Enlightenment thinkers were pacifists and internationalists, who saw patriotism—along with religion—as the cause of most wars. Above all, they believed in freedom. The France of Louis XV, although less repressive than that of his predecessor, still maintained restrictions on freedom of speech, religion, trade, and work.

For all their fervor, however, the philosophes were not revolutionaries. They advocated not immediate democracy, but a gradual transition by means of rulers who were "enlightened despots" such as Friedrich II of Prussia (on the Enlightened Despots, see Part VII, Topic 1). They did not aim at radical change, even though many of their ideas inspired the leaders of the French Revolution. Furthermore, Enlightenment thought circulated chiefly among the urban aristocracy and educated middle classes.

In addition, few of the philosophes had much time for women's rights, even though a number of them reached their audience by means of the salons of the more advanced women of the day. By contrast with centuries of earlier thinkers, they acknowledged women's ability to reason, and encouraged female education, but on the whole they accepted the conventional notion of women as inferior to men. The only real attempt to argue for fundamental change, Mary Wollstonecraft's *Vindication of the Rights of Women* (1792), found few sympathizers.

Diderot and the *Encyclopédie*

One of the leading French philosophes, Denis Diderot (1713–1784), sought to provide an organized basis for Enlightenment thought by preparing an immense encyclopedia. He intended the work to describe the contemporary state of science, technology, and philosophy, and at the same time to establish a classification system for human knowledge.

Working with the physicist and mathematician Jean Le Rond d'Alembert (1717–1783) as his co-editor, Diderot began work on the project in 1747; the last of its 17 volumes of text and 11 of engravings appeared in 1771. The *Encyclopédie*, with its articles by various contributors, provided a wealth of information on a

Denis Diderot, editor of the *Encyclopédie*.

The *philosophes* at supper. They include Voltaire (with left hand raised), Diderot, and Condorcet.

bewildering range of subjects, from metallurgy to political economy to the raising of asparagus.

Implicit in this philosophy was the idea that no political or religious system should try to limit or control the minds of individuals. The authors of the *Encyclopédie* opposed all corporate privilege, in fact, and believed that no group — the guilds, for example — had exclusive rights to any area of knowledge. As the leading German philosopher of the Enlightenment, Immanuel Kant (1724–1804), pointed out, the very essence of the Enlightenment was to "dare to know." If this meant rejecting established wisdom or resisting authority, then the philosophes were prepared to do so. Voltaire had to leave France, Hume was threatened with excommunication (and thus ostracism), and Diderot spent time in jail. Church and government authorities both tried to stop publication of the *Encyclopédie,* or at least censor it, but Diderot succeeded in bringing his project to completion.

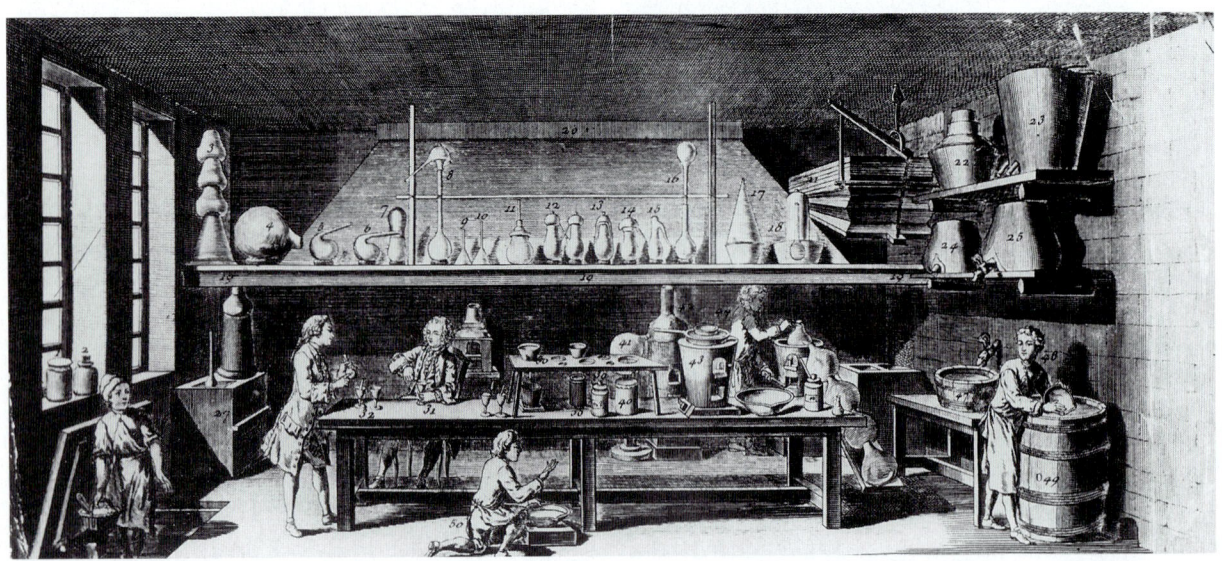

An illustration of a laboratory from the *Encyclopédie* of Diderot.

The *Encyclopédie* sold not only in Europe's great cities, but in small provincial towns. It helped an entire generation to see their lives in an entirely fresh way, and led them to challenge hitherto unquestioned assumptions. Its tone of optimism, and its conviction that humans had their destiny in their own hands, powerfully influenced the Declaration of Independence of the new American nation.

Charles-Louis Montesquieu

A more specific influence on the political growth of America was the political philosophy of one of the contributors to the *Encyclopédie*, Charles-Louis Montesquieu (1689–1755). Aristocratic by birth, Montesquieu argued against the abolition of monarchy. His ideal system of government was based upon a division of powers between king, lords, and commons. This separation of powers would, he believed, create a series of "checks and balances" capable of safeguarding personal liberty. The framers of the American Constitution adapted the principle, transforming Montesquieu's three divisions into the executive, judicial, and legislative branches of government.

Montesquieu's other important contribution to the study of politics was his book *The Spirit of the Laws* (1748). In it he claimed that different forms of government were appropriate to different geographical conditions. Small states such as Venice or 5th-century B.C. Athens were best suited by a republican government, whereas vast countries like Russia required an absolute monarchy. Pioneering in its aims, Montesquieu's work was the first serious attempt to examine the relationship between politics and environment.

"THE INFAMOUS THING": VOLTAIRE AND NATURAL MORALITY

Perhaps the most versatile genius produced by the Enlightenment—if less original than Diderot—was François-Marie Arouet (1694–1778), best known to us as Voltaire, his pen name. As a writer, Voltaire moved with ease from drama to satire to history. His studies included science and politics. He was an honored guest at the courts of Louis XV and Friedrich II, but also spent time in prison. Above all, Voltaire was fully committed to the great issues and battles of his times. An enemy of all forms of tyranny, he spent most of his life in exile.

His early satirical writings pilloried French aristocratic society, and won him a jail sentence in the Bastille (1717–1718). Undeterred, he continued with an epic poem on Henry IV of France, which he published in 1723. After he spent another few months in prison in 1726, the authorities released him on the condition that he left France.

Voltaire chose to spend his exile in England, where the system of government seemed to him far more just and liberal than that of France. Returning home in 1729, he wrote his *Letters on the English* (first published in English in 1733; in French in 1734), extolling English social and political liberalism and religious toleration, and praising the ideas of Newton and Locke. In advocating the experimental approach to science, he held that doubt is the beginning of wisdom and the basis of tolerance. Humans should limit themselves to observing and measuring, and to trying to improve the lot of their fellow mortals, a theme to which he constantly returned.

His contemporaries were enraged by the book's attack on French society and political institutions, and the uproar it created drove him out of Paris into the

The French writer and philosopher Voltaire, perhaps the leading figure of the Enlightenment.

DOCUMENTS ON HISTORY

The Age of Reason

The Enlightenment was known as the Age of Reason because the philosophes argued that superstition, faith, and tradition should be replaced by logic, scientific inquiry, and a secular spirit of the quest for knowledge of the natural laws that governed the universe. These principles informed the works of all the major writers of the era.

THE NATURE OF ENLIGHTENMENT

The German thinker Immanuel Kant, whose complex philosophical system rejected a simpleminded mechanistic understanding of truth and skepticism, explained the meaning of "enlightenment" in an essay of 1784, in which he stressed the fundamental importance of freedom of discussion.

Enlightenment is man's release from his self-incurred tutelage. Tutelage is man's inability to make use of his understanding without direction from another. Self-incurred is this tutelage when its cause lies not in lack of reason but in lack of resolution and courage to use it without direction from another. *Sapere aude!*[1] "Have courage to use your own reason!"—that is the motto of enlightenment.

Laziness and cowardice are the reasons why so great a portion of mankind, after nature has long since discharged them from external direction . . . , nevertheless remains under lifelong tutelage, and why it is so easy for others to set themselves up as their guardians. It is so easy not to be of age. If I have a book which understands for me, a pastor who has a conscience for me, a physician who decides my diet, and so forth, I need not trouble myself. I need not think, if I can only pay—others will readily undertake the irksome work for me.

That the step in competence is held to be very dangerous by the far greater portion of mankind (and by the entire fair sex)—quite apart from its being arduous—is seen to by those guardians who have so kindly assumed superintendence over them. After the guardians have first made their domestic cattle dumb and have made sure that these placid creatures will not dare take a single step without the harness of the cart to which they are tethered, the guardians then show them the danger which threatens if they try to go alone. Actually, however, this danger is not so great, for by falling a few times they would finally

---

[1] "Dare to know!", the motto of the Society of the Friends of Truth.

learn to walk alone. But an example of this failure makes them timid and ordinarily frightens them away from all further trials.

For any single individual to work himself out of the life under tutelage which has become almost his nature is very difficult. He has come to be fond of this state, and he is for the present really incapable of making use of his reason, for no one has ever let him try it out. Statutes and formulas, those mechanical tools of the rational employment or rather misemployment of his natural gifts, are the fetters of an everlasting tutelage. Whoever throws them off makes only an uncertain leap over the narrowest ditch because he is not accustomed to that kind of free motion. Therefore, there are few who have succeeded by their own exercise of mind both in freeing themselves from incompetence and in achieving a steady pace. . . .

From Immanuel Kant, "What Is Enlightenment?" in L. W. Beck, ed. and trans., *Immanuel Kant on History.* Macmillan, Copyright © 1963.

ON METHOD

René Descartes (1596–1650) *was one of the leading figures of the scientific revolution. Perhaps his greatest contribution to the Enlightenment is the set of principles he enunciated in 1637 on the proper method to be followed in pursuing "scientific" truth.*

I believed that the four [principles] following would prove perfectly sufficient for me, provided I took the firm and unwavering resolution never in a single instance to fail in observing them.

The *first* was never to accept anything for true which I did not clearly know to be such; that is to say, carefully to avoid precipitancy and prejudice, and to comprise nothing more in my judgment than what was presented to my mind so clearly and distinctly as to exclude all ground of doubt.

The *second*, to divide each of the difficulties under examination into as many parts as possible, and as might be necessary for its adequate solution.

The *third*, to conduct my thoughts in such order that, by commencing with objects the simplest and easiest to know, I might ascend by little and little, and, as it were, step by step, to the knowledge of the more complex; assigning in thought a certain order even to those objects which in their own nature do not stand in a relation of antecedence and sequence.

And the *last*, in every case to make enumerations so complete, and reviews so general, that I might be assured that nothing was omitted.

The long chains of simple and easy reasonings by means of which geometers are accustomed to reach the conclusions of their most difficult demonstrations, had led me to imagine that all things, to the knowledge of which man is competent, are mutually connected in the same way, and that there is nothing so far removed from us as to be beyond our reach, or so hidden that we cannot discover it, provided only we abstain from accepting the false for the true, and always preserve in our thoughts the order necessary for the deduction of one truth from another. . . .

From Brian Tierney, Donald Kagan, and L. Pearce Williams, eds., *Great Issues in Western Civilization*, 4th ed., Vol. II. McGraw-Hill, Copyright © 1992.

NATURAL LAW

Most of the philosophes believed that the universe and the human condition were based on natural law, and that a discovery of truth could be achieved by understanding those laws. The following extract is from an article by Denis Diderot written for his Encyclopédie.*

continued next page

In its broadest sense the term [natural law] is taken to designate certain principles which nature alone inspires and which all animals as well as all men have in common. On this law are based the union of male and female, the begetting of children as well as their education, love of liberty, self-preservation, concern for self-defense.

It is improper to call the behavior of animals natural law, for, not being endowed with reason, they can know neither law nor justice.

More commonly we understand by natural law certain laws of justice and equity which only natural reason has established among men, or better, which God has engraved in our hearts.

The fundamental principles of law and all justice are: to live honestly, not to give offense to anyone, and to render unto each whatever is his. From these general principles derive a great many particular rules which nature alone, that is, reason and equity, suggest to mankind. . . .

It would not be proper for men to live without rules; rules presuppose a final goal; that of man is to aspire to happiness; this is the system of Providence; it is the essential desire of man, inseparable from reason which is man's basic guide. Since true happiness cannot be incompatible with the nature and condition of man, rules of conduct consist in a distinction between good and evil, in a comparison of past and present, in not seeking a good that may give rise to greater evil, in accepting a small evil if it is followed by a great good, in giving preference to the greatest good, in certain cases in being persuaded only by probability or verisimilitude and finally in acquiring the inclination toward the truly good.

In order really to know natural law, one has to understand what is meant by obligation in general. Law taken as power produces obligations; rights and obligations are several: some are natural, others are acquired; some are such that they cannot be rigidly fulfilled, others cannot be renounced. These obligations are also distinguished by their object. For instance, there is the right we have over ourselves, which is called liberty; the right of property or estate over things that belong to us; the right one has over the person or actions of another, which is called sovereignty or authority; finally the right one can have over things belonging to someone else, which is also of several kinds.

Man, by nature a dependent being, must take law as the rule of his action, for law is nothing other than a rule set down by the sovereign. The true foundations of sovereignty are power, wisdom, and goodness combined. The goal of laws is not to impede liberty but to direct properly all man's actions.

From *Encyclopedia:* Selections by Denis Diderot, D'Alembert.

THE PRINCIPLES OF MORALS

avid Hume (1711–1776), perhaps the most important English philosopher of the 18th century, sought to understand the world beyond the senses. In this essay from 1751 on the nature of morals, he revealed his belief that morality was capable of scientific, rational analysis.

There has been a controversy started of late, much better worth examination, concerning the general foundation of MORALS; whether they be derived from REASON or from SENTIMENT; whether we attain the knowledge of them by a chain of argument and induction, or by an immediate feeling and finer internal sense; whether, like all sound judgment of truth and falsehood, they should be the same to every rational intelligent being; or whether, like the perception of beauty and deformity, they be founded entirely on the particular fabric and constitution of the human species. . . .

It must be acknowledged, that both sides of the question are susceptible of specious arguments. Moral distinctions, it may be said, are discernible by pure *reason*: else, whence the many disputes that reign in common life, as well as in philosophy, with regard to this subject; the long chain of proofs often produced on both sides, the example cited, the authorities appealed to, the analogies employed, the fallacies detected, the inferences drawn, and the several conclusions adjusted to their proper principles? Truth is disputable; not taste: what exists in the nature of things is the standard of our judgment: what each man feels within himself is the standard of sentiment. Propositions in geometry may be proved, systems in physics may be controverted; but the harmony of verse, the tenderness of passion, the brilliancy of wit, must give immediate pleasure. No man reasons concerning another's beauty; but frequently concerning the justice or injustice of his actions. . . .

The end of all moral speculations is to teach us our duty; and, by proper representations of the deformity of vice and beauty of virtue, beget correspondent habits, and engage us to avoid the one, and embrace the other. But is this ever to be expected from inferences and conclusions of the understanding, which of themselves have no hold of the affections, or set in motion the active powers of men? They discover truths: but where the truths which they discover are indifferent, and beget no desire or aversion, they can have no influence on conduct and behaviour. What is honourable, what is fair, what is becoming, what is noble, what is generous, takes possession of the heart, and animates us to embrace and maintain it. What is intelligible, what is evident, what is probable, what is true, procures only the cool assent of the understanding; and gratifying a speculative curiosity, puts an end to our researches.

Extinguish all the warm feeling and prepossessions in favour of virtue, and all disgust or aversion to vice; render men totally indifferent towards these distinctions; and morality is no longer a practical study, nor has any tendency to regulate our lives and actions.

These arguments on each side (and many more might be produced) are so plausible, that I am apt to suspect they may, the one as well as the other, be solid and satisfactory, and that *reason* and *sentiment* concur in almost all moral determinations and conclusions. The final sen-

tence, it is probable, which pronounces characters and actions amiable, or odious, praiseworthy or blameable; that which stamps on them the mark of honour or infamy, approbation or censure; that which renders morality an active principle, and constitutes virtue our happiness, and vice our misery: it is probable, I say, that this final sentence depends on some internal sense or feeling, which nature has made universal in the whole species. For what else can have an influence of this nature? But in order to pave the way for such a sentiment, and give a proper discernment of its object, it is often necessary, we find, that much reasoning should precede, that nice distinctions be made, just conclusions drawn, distant comparisons formed, complicated relations examined, and general facts fixed and ascertained. Some species of beauty, especially the natural kinds, on their first appearance, command our affection and approbation; and where they fail of this effect, it is impossible for any reasoning to redress their influence, or adapt them better to our taste and sentiment. But in many orders of beauty, particularly those of the finer arts, it is requisite to employ much reasoning, in order to feel the proper sentiment; and a false relish may frequently be corrected by argument and reflection. There are just grounds to conclude that moral beauty partakes much of this latter species, and demands the assistance of our intellectual faculties, in order to give it a suitable influence on the human mind.

David Hume, *An Inquiry Concerning the Principles of Morals,* Section I.

THE IDEA OF PROGRESS

Marie-Jean Caritat, *the marquis de Condorcet, was one of the leading French philosophes. In the essay that follows, he explains the idea of progress, a fundamental principle of Enlightenment thought that explained history and the future of humankind.*

continued next page

The aim of the book that I have undertaken to write, and what it will prove, is that man by using reason and facts will attain perfection. Nature has set no limits to the perfection of the human faculties. The perfectibility of mankind is truly indefinite; and the progress of this perfectibility, henceforth to be free of all hindrances, will last as long as the globe on which nature has placed us. Doubtless his progress will be more or less rapid, but it will never be retrograde, at least as long as the globe occupies its present place in the system of the universe; and unless the general laws that govern this system bring to pass a universal cataclysm, or such changes as will prevent man from maintaining his existence, from using his faculties, and from finding his needed resources. . . .

Since the period when alphabetical writing flourished in Greece the history of mankind has been linked to the condition of men of our time in the most enlightened countries of Europe by an unbroken chain of facts and observations. The picture of the march and progress of the human mind is now revealed as being truly histori-cal. Philosophy no longer has to guess, no longer has to advance hypothetical theories. It now suf-fices to assemble and to arrange the facts, and to show the truths that arise from their connection and from their totality. . . .

If man can predict with almost complete certainty those phenomena whose laws he knows; and if, when he does not know these laws, he can, on the basis of his experience in the past, predict future events with assurance why then should it be regarded as chimerical to trace with a fair degree of accuracy the picture of man's future on the basis of his history? The sole foundation for belief in the natural sciences is the principle that universal laws, known or unknown, which regulate the universe are nec-essary and constant. Why then should this prin-ciple be less true for the development of the intellectual and moral faculties of man than it is for the other operations of nature? Finally, since beliefs, based on past experience under like con-ditions, constitute the only rule according to which the wisest men act, why then forbid the philosopher to support his beliefs on the same foundations, as long as he does not attribute to

---

country. He spent most of the next 15 years living in isolation with his mistress, Madame du Châtelet (1706–1749). A woman of considerable learning, and a prolific writer on scientific subjects—among her works was a translation of Newton's *Principia*—she ex-ercised an important intellectual influence on Voltaire. The two of them returned briefly to Versailles in 1744, but life at the court of Louis XV was sterile and frus-trating, and they soon withdrew.

The death of Madame du Châtelet in 1749 came as a bitter blow, and the following year Voltaire ac-cepted an invitation to visit the court of Friedrich II at Potsdam. At first he established a close friendship with the king and worked on a history of the age of Louis XIV, his most important historical work. Two such powerful temperaments were probably bound to clash before long, however. The king made it clear that royal friendship had its limits: when Voltaire dared to criti-cize his patron's verse, the king abruptly dismissed him. In 1753, Voltaire left Prussia in disillusionment, and circulated throughout Europe his own version of the falling-out.

The last 20 years of his life were spent in the village of Ferney, near Geneva, where he set up his own court. A procession of the leading figures in European political and intellectual life came to visit him, to discuss, and above all to listen to the sage of Ferney. Voltaire returned to Paris only in 1778, but the hero's welcome he received proved too much for his poor health and the excitement probably hastened his death.

"The Infamous Thing"

Voltaire's writings touched on all the great questions raised by Enlightenment thinkers, but the most fre-quently recurring theme is the importance of freedom

them a certainty not warranted by the number, the constancy, and the accuracy of his observations. . . .

From J. Salwyn Schapiro, ed., *Liberalism: Its Meaning and History*. D. Van Nostrand, Copyright © 1958.

A CALL FOR TOLERATION

*V*oltaire used his brilliant style and sense of irony to debunk many aspects of the Old Regime and its dependence on superstition. In the following essay, he tried to point out that a major step toward toleration was often just a matter of putting oneself in the other person's place.

One does not need great art and skilful eloquence to prove that Christians ought to tolerate each other—nay, even to regard all men as brothers. Why, you say, is the Turk, the Chinese, or the Jew my brother? Assuredly; are we not all children of the same father, creatures of the same God?

But these people despise us and treat us as idolaters. Very well; I will tell them that they are quite wrong. It seems to me that I might astonish, at least, the stubborn pride of a Mohammedan or a Buddhist priest if I spoke to them somewhat as follows:

This little globe, which is but a point, travels in space like many other globes; we are lost in the immensity. Man, about five feet high, is certainly a small thing in the universe. One of these imperceptible beings says to some of his neighbours, in Arabia or South Africa: "Listen to me, for the God of all these worlds has enlightened me. There are nine hundred million little ants like us on the earth, but my ant-hole alone is dear to God. All the others are eternally reprobated by him. Mine alone will be happy."

They would then interrupt me, and ask who was the fool that talked all this nonsense. I should be obliged to tell them that it was themselves. I would then try to appease them, which would be difficult. . . .

From Lynn Hunt, Thomas R. Martin, Barbara H. Rosenwein, R. Po-chia Hsia, Bonnie G. Smith, eds., *Connecting with the Past*, Vol. I. D.C. Heath, Copyright © 1995.

of thought. From the beginning of his career he castigated bigotry and intolerance, and to the end of his life he poured out a stream of pamphlets condemning prejudice and fanaticism: "The superstitious man is ruled by fanatics and he becomes one himself." Many of the letters in his vast correspondence ended with the phrase he made famous: "Crush the infamous thing!" The "thing" in question is organized religion, together with the intolerance bred of superstition.

The chief agents of prejudice, he believed, were the Christians, both Catholic and Protestant. Voltaire ridiculed the notion of the Bible as the inspired word of God. Rather, he saw it as a collection of anecdotes and contradictions that had no relevance to the modern world. Furthermore, it had provided the basis for centuries of disputes and persecutions that were as violent as they were pointless. The results, he said, were self-interested priests and false traditions.

Voltaire's attacks on organized religion were particularly bitter. His book *Candide* contains a famous scene based on an actual historical event—after the earthquake that destroyed most of Lisbon in 1755, killing over 30,000 people, some of the victims who managed to survive the devastation were solemnly burned alive by the "wise men," the priests and monks, in a superstitious attempt to avert further disaster. Yet his position was fully in line with the Enlightenment's chief aims and goals, and most Enlightenment thinkers actively campaigned against the outward manifestations of organized religion.

Yet Voltaire was no atheist. The God in whom he believed created the world, but could not be tied down to any single religion. Like many of the philosophes, the sage of Ferney held that only natural morality—the true religion common to all humans—could cure the ignorance and arrogance that plagued the world: "The only book that needs to be read is the great book of Nature."

Candide

Voltaire's most famous work, the tale *Candide* (1759), presents a rather darker vision of human life. The constant barrage of disasters and suffering to which the good-natured Candide, the story's hero, is subjected make a mockery of the optimism of philosophers such as Gottfried Leibnitz (1646–1716). Leibnitz preached philosophical optimism (the belief in an inherently just world) and wrote of the "pre-established harmony of the universe." Voltaire reduces this to the trite belief that "everything is for the best in the best of all possible worlds," and illustrates its absurdity with bleak humor.

As the innocent Candide travels from Germany to Portugal to the New World and back again to Europe, he finds nothing but evil and ignorance. Candide has to learn the hard way that experience is a better teacher than philosophy, even if its lesson is that pain and disillusionment are unavoidable.

By the book's end, Candide manages to temper the complete despair induced by this message with a note of comfort. The hero's last words of advice to his friends are that "we must cultivate our gardens." Even this suggestion is ambiguous. Many readers have concluded that Voltaire sees the world as cruel and indifferent to our suffering, but advises us not to give way to hopelessness. We should try to find some small, constructive activity we can perform in seclusion, and make an island of sanity and peace in a hostile universe. Others, however, interpreting Voltaire's message as far more positive, believe that the "garden" stands for Europe, or even the world. The instruction to cultivate it is thus a call for a life of political and social activism.

SCIENCE AND SOCIETY: SOCIAL AND ECONOMIC THOUGHT

Many of the philosophes, including Voltaire, took an active interest in science and mathematics. Marie-Jean Condorcet (1743–1794), who helped in the preparation of the *Encyclopédie*, was a mathematician with a special interest in probability theory. Believing as he did in the inevitability of human progress, Condorcet looked forward to a time when even human biology might improve. Like Candide, Condorcet found his optimism tested by his experience. He played an important role in the French Revolution, but incurred the hostility of the extremists for his moderate opinions.

After two years in hiding, he was arrested and thrown into prison, where he committed suicide.

The naturalist Georges-Louis Buffon (1707–1788) also believed in the possibility of physical progress. He ran a series of experiments to try to extend the human life span to 120 years or more. Buffon is best known for his work on the classification of the animal kingdom, and he also directed the royal gardens in Paris (the present Jardin des Plantes). The 44-volume *Natural History* (1749–1804) whose production he led was one of the major scientific achievements of the 18th century.

Cesare Beccaria and Prison Reform

The center of the Enlightenment in Italy was Milan, where the brothers Alessandro (1741–1816) and Pietro (1728–1797) Verri headed a group of liberal intellectuals and published the influential journal *Il Caffè* (*The Cafe*). Among the younger members of the group was the economist and criminologist Cesare Beccaria (1738–1794), who derived an interest in political and social issues from his reading of Montesquieu.

In 1764, at the age of 26, Beccaria published *On Crimes and Punishments*, the first systematic treatment of rational criminal punishment. The work was an instant success, and was translated into a variety of languages. Eventually its ideas led the way to criminal reform in many European countries, including Russia, and helped in the shaping of the United States' system of criminal justice. Beccaria's main thesis was that his contemporaries' attitude to criminals was unreasonable and inefficient. The harsh system of punishments, with long prison terms or death sentences for relatively minor crimes, was based on the belief that criminals were hopelessly evil. Since they were believed incapable of repentance, they deserved no mercy. Furthermore, the penalties were applied inconsistently.

As a child of the Enlightenment, Beccaria believed that all humans were capable of improvement. Prisons should thus be places for rehabilitation, whose occupants were adequately housed and fed and given the chance to work, rather than centers of futile and vindictive punishment. His book argued passionately against the death penalty and torture, pointing out that such savage penalties do not stop crime; in any case, torture was uncivilized, and capital punishment was an abuse of the natural rights of humans.

Adam Smith and Free Trade

In his economic lectures, Beccaria anticipated the ideas of the leading economist of the 18th century, the Scot, Adam Smith (1723–1790). While traveling in Europe,

Smith met and was influenced by members of a French school of economists known as the *physiocrats*. Their most famous principle was *"laissez faire"*—"let it be": the natural laws of economics require only noninterference to be successful. Smith also visited Voltaire at Ferney.

On returning home, Smith retired to his native town of Kirkcaldy, near Edinburgh. He spent the next ten years working on his most famous publication, *The Wealth of Nations* (1776), while involving himself on an almost daily basis in Edinburgh's intellectual and cultural life. In *The Wealth of Nations* he worked out his theory of the division of labor, money, prices, wages, and distribution; the classic system of economics he described laid the foundations of the science of political economy. The book had a worldwide influence on politics as well as economics, and inspired the 19th-century Free Trade movement.

Like the physiocrats, Smith argued that if market forces were allowed to operate without state intervention, an "invisible hand" would guide self-interest for the benefit of all. This was another example of Enlightenment optimism. He was in favor of open competition and strongly opposed to price rings (the predecessors of the modern cartels), observing: "People of the same trade seldom meet together even for merriment or diversion, but that the conversation ends in some conspiracy against the public, or in some contrivance to raise prices." Smith thus rejected the government regulations, monopolies, and protective tariffs that characterized the policy of mercantilism. Like the other philosophes, he urged that "natural laws"—in this case, those affecting production and exchange— be allowed to unfold freely.

Later political economists, including Thomas Malthus (1766–1834) and David Ricardo (1772–1823), constituted the so-called "Manchester School" of economic theory, which significantly differed from the ideas of Smith. While their enemies labeled their ideas "laissez faire," they also form the basis of what is known as classical economics. The essential point of this doctrine is that economic relationships are separate and autonomous from government and politics. Instead, the free market regulates itself by laws of supply and demand. Extended beyond the economic realm, they held that all individuals should follow their own self-interest, whereas government should do only those things that are absolutely necessary, such as protecting life and property. Private initiative, not government assistance, should take care of social, cultural, and economic matters. A generation earlier, Adam Smith had advocated the increase of state education, and had deplored the effects on individuals of repetitive industrial work. The severe doctrines of the Manchester School reflected the grim realities of life in 19th-century industrial Europe.

THE OUTSIDER: ROUSSEAU AND THE SOCIAL CONTRACT

Enlightenment belief in the blessings of civilization found one eloquent dissenter: Jean-Jacques Rousseau (1712–1778). Tormented and quarrelsome, Rousseau's unstable temperament shaped most of his life. He lost his mother at birth and was separated from his father at the age of ten. After a brief period as an engraver's apprentice, he met and fell in love with a French noblewoman, Madame de Warens (1700–1762). The two settled down in the country for almost ten years (1732–1741), a period Rousseau later recalled in his autobiographical *Confessions* (1765–1770) as idyllic.

In 1741 he set out for Paris, where he devoted himself to music. In the 1750s, Diderot commissioned him to produce some articles on music for the *Encyclopédie*, and his short opera *The Village Soothsayer* (1752) was an instant success. In 1745 he began an affair with an illiterate servant girl, Thérèse Levasseur.

The first of his major philosophical works, *Discourse on the Sciences and the Arts*, appeared in 1750. It

Jean-Jacques Rousseau, writer, composer, and philosopher.

laid out one of his basic principles: the savage, "natural" condition is superior to civilization. Rousseau was convinced that the growth of society had corrupted the natural goodness of the human race and destroyed the freedom of the individual. Humans, in short, were good; society was bad.

The Social Contract

Rousseau soon became identified with the notion of the "noble savage," but he never advocated a return to some form of primitive existence. Instead he urged the creation of a new social order. In 1762 he published *The Social Contract,* one of the most radical political works of the 18th century, and one which proved immensely influential on modern political theory.

The issue at the heart of *The Social Contract* is how to reconcile individual freedom and the government of society: "The problem is to find a form of association in which each, while uniting himself with all, may still obey himself alone, and remain as free as before." Rousseau's solution was vague and unsatisfactory: a state governed by the "general will" of its citizens, who would delegate power to their rulers when necessary.

Rousseau's ideal was a society in which there was no hereditary, privileged aristocracy. All members should have joined freely, surrendering their individual rights to the group. The "rulers" would be the servants of the community, answerable to the people's will, and instantly removable if the people so decided. Unlike his contemporaries, Rousseau claimed that if the people really governed themselves, there would be no need for checks and balances, separation of powers, or protection of rights.

Clearly such a system could operate only in a small society. In any case Rousseau did not intend *The Social Contract* to be taken as a practical program, although in the bloodiest days of the French Revolution, the extremist Robespierre claimed to be following Rousseau's recommendations in unleashing the Reign of Terror. Its purpose was to set out the basic theory of democratic government. For conservatives, Rousseau was a dangerous emotionalist and an anarchist, while for liberals and democrats, a forerunner of totalitarian dictatorship. Few political thinkers have inspired more controversy.

Rousseau and the Role of Women

For all the importance of *The Social Contract,* most of Rousseau's readers were more interested in the social ideas expressed in his novels than in his political philosophy. His two most popular books, *The New Heloise* (1761) and *Émile* (1762), were best-sellers throughout Europe. These works reveal Rousseau's ideas about education, society, and the role of women. The first of them owed much of its popularity to its praise of the open display of emotion, while the other dealt with education, recommending that children be protected from the harmful effects of civilization, and exposed instead to the moral influence of nature.

In both books, women are assigned specific social roles as nurturers and educators. Julie, the heroine of *The New Heloise,* inspires her children with a sense of right and wrong—law enforcer rather than law maker. In *Émile,* the two children who are the tale's principal characters are both given unconventional educations, but their training is not the same. Émile, the boy, learns knowledge and self-control so that he can become confident and in charge of his own destiny in the wider world. Sophie, his future partner, is educated for the domestic sphere, where she will serve as Émile's faithful and obedient companion. For all Rousseau's revolutionary political thinking, he was quite prepared to institutionalize the traditional "separate spheres" for women and men. Women, he believed, far from receiving a natural education, should be kept away from nature lest they became disruptive.

For many Enlightenment thinkers, their movement marked humanity's coming of age. The power of pragmatism and critical reason had replaced the childish superstitions of the Middle Ages. Their strenuous opposition to the Old Regime and all its works was to help to bring it crashing down, and by undermining respect for established authority they laid the foundations for the increasing intellectual freedom of the 19th century. Some of their ideas, such as Rousseau's praise of open emotional expression, were taken up by the romantics.

On the other hand, most of the philosophes fully realized that further human progress would be neither smooth nor painless. Many of them were concerned at the desperate state in which the vast majority of Europe's population lived. Smith and Hume both wrote about the conditions of the rural and urban poor, and the French physiocrat Jacques Turgot tried to redistribute taxes more fairly and abolish compulsory labor. Hume even argued on his deathbed that "man will never be enlightened." Most Enlightenment thinkers, in fact, aimed to bring about progress on a limited scale, through their local societies and academies, in the hope that someday the total accumulation of their efforts might produce significant change.

The upheavals of the French Revolution and the subsequent Napoleonic era seemed to bear out Hume's skeptical conclusion. Yet in the long run the Enlightenment proved decisive in changing basic attitudes in Western culture. Never again did traditional religion occupy the position it held before the 18th century. From the end of the 18th century, democracy became an increasingly admired political ideal, even if it could not be attained in practice. Science and technology maintained their role as catalysts of social change, while the Encyclopédie *illustrated the immense value of knowledge and practical information.*

Condorcet once described the intellectuals of his time as a "class of men less concerned with discovering the truth than with propagating it." For all the immensity of the task, the leaders of the Enlightenment led the way to the social and political revolutions of the 19th century.

Questions for Further Study

1. What were the main goals of the Enlightenment? How did its philosophers set about achieving their aims, and how successful were they?

2. What effect did Enlightenment thinking have on European economic development?

3. How did the ideas of Voltaire and Rousseau differ? Which of the two was closer to the ideals of the Enlightenment?

4. How far did Beccaria's attitude to prison reform anticipate or inspire modern approaches?

Suggestions for Further Reading

Behrens, C. *Society, Government, and the Enlightenment: The Experiences of Eighteenth-Century France and Prussia.* New York, 1986.

Besterman, T. *Voltaire.* Chicago, 1976.

Hampson, N. *The Enlightenment.* London, 1982.

Rendall, J. *The Origins of Modern Feminism: Women in Britain, France and the United States.* New York, 1984.

Sklar, J. *Montesquieu.* Oxford, 1987.

Scott, H. M. *Enlightened Absolutism.* Ann Arbor, MI, 1990.

Spencer, S. *French Women and the Age of Enlightenment.* Bloomington, IN, 1984.

Wilson, A. M. *Diderot.* Oxford, 1972.

The Modern Age

The 18th century produced two revolutionary transformations with profound historical consequences—the industrial revolution and the French Revolution of 1789. Each in its own way led to fundamental structural and ideological changes in European and world civilization and gave birth to the modern age. From these and other events—including startling population growth and major advances in agricultural production—flowed much of the developments in the Western experience for the next two centuries.

In its simplest form, the industrial revolution saw machines and steam power assume functions that had always been the exclusive province of human and animal labor. As a result, the West entered a long period of unprecedented economic growth in which living standards for the vast majority of people improved. The social structure

that came to characterize modern Europe was no longer determined solely by birth and inherited privilege, although these factors continued to be important. Instead, under the dual impact of industrialization and the French Revolution, economic class, defined by the relationship of individuals to labor and capital, now became an increasingly important social determinant. By the opening of the 20th century, Western European civilization had become a predominantly urban, industrial, and secular culture that was able to seize world power as a result of its mastery of science and technology.

Europe's transition from tradition to modernity was accelerated at the end of the 18th century by the French Revolution. Historians often mark the beginning of "modern" history with the start of the French Revolution, for it radically altered centuries of political and social tradition. The revolution swept away the remnants of feudalism in France and the social system of the Old Regime that had rested on the hereditary privilege of the nobility. The events that took place in France from the late 1780s to the mid-1790s ushered in the age of "mass politics," in which social elements that had never been active in politics, such as the peasantry, workers, women, and the urban poor, now became participants in the making of history. The famous rallying cry of those who made the Revolution—

"liberty, equality, fraternity"—entered the Western political consciousness as the ideal slogan of liberal political systems.

In the aftermath of the revolution, three sets of ideas vied with each other in Europe: nationalism, liberalism, and socialism. Nationalism eventually took hold throughout the West, culminating in the process of nation building and, in our own times, in the struggle for decolonization. Liberalism became the political and social doctrine of the emerging middle classes which would dominate the modern era and become the chief form of political system for most of Europe. Socialism, on the other hand, would offer the new urban working classes both a philosophy of emancipation from economic exploitation and a political strategy for seizing power.

At the end of the 19th century, two events of global importance were rapidly making themselves felt in Europe: the last stage of Western imperialism, which resulted in the European conquest of most of Asia and Africa; and the emergence of the United States as an economic and political world power.

By the opening of the 20th century, European civilization was moving rapidly toward a critical phase in its history. Increasing nationalist tensions and imperial competition had divided its great powers into competition with alliance systems, while social tensions and extremist political programs—anarchist, syndicalist, and Marxist—raised serious questions about future stability. Responding to the doubts and uncertainties of the age, artists and intellectuals forged a modernist culture that was at once revolutionary, experimental, and often irrational in its appeal. The outbreak of World War I in 1914 signaled the end of the era of European dominance in world history.

T o p i c 1

THE POLITICS OF ENLIGHTENMENT: EUROPE AND AMERICA

he Enlightenment had a far-reaching impact that extended beyond Western Europe—the ideas of the Enlightenment spread as far west as the New World and as far east as the steppes of Russia. Nor was the Age of Reason only an intellectual revolution. In the course of the 18th century, the thought of the *philosophes* also affected political developments and lay behind a variety of reform impulses in states as diverse as Russia, Prussia, and Austria.

The philosophes were practical people who wanted to see improvement in the condition of human society through meaningful reforms. Despite the legacy of Rousseau, however, few philosophes were democrats who trusted the common people to rule themselves. Some philosophes, who evolved the principles of what was once known as "enlightened despotism" (historians now prefer the term "enlightened absolutism"), were convinced that strong—although not absolute—rulers were needed to maintain order, protect the "natural rights" of individuals, and implement reforms. In this sense, the ideal ruler was one who exercised authority fairly and impartially, permitted domestic tolerance for religious beliefs and free expression, and created conditions in which science and the arts would flourish. Other philosophes looked to the educated, reasonable members of the mercantile classes, who gathered in the academies and literary societies. For most reformers of the period, whether supporters of monarchs or the enlightened middle class, change should come from above, not from below.

To what degree did the monarchs of the 18th century fulfill such expectations and qualify as "enlightened despots"? The question has been often debated by scholars, who have examined the policies of the leading monarchs of the age in order to test the theory. Were Josef II of Austria, Friedrich the Great of Prussia, and Catherine the Great of Russia genuinely inspired by the philosophes and did they actually apply the principles of the Enlightenment in ruling their states?

THE POLITICAL THOUGHT OF THE *PHILOSOPHES*

Political ideas stemmed from the same set of intellectual assumptions that inspired other aspects of the Enlightenment. Whereas scientists such as Sir Isaac Newton and economists such as Adam Smith emphasized adherence to natural laws, in politics the equivalent concept was natural rights. In the 17th century, John Locke had identified these rights broadly as life, liberty, and property—rights which no legitimate ruler should abridge or deny. Should a monarch cease to

Significant Dates

The Politics of Enlightenment

1748	Montesquieu's *The Spirit of the Laws*
1762	Rousseau's *The Social Contract*
1774	First Continental Congress meets in Philadelphia
1775	Cossack rebellion in Russia under Pugachev
1776	American War of Independence begins
1781	Josef II issues the Edict of Toleration
1783	Treaty of Paris
1740–1786	Friedrich II rules as king of Prussia
1789	U.S. Constitution adopted
1765–1790	Josef II rules as Austrian emperor
1765–1790	Leopold II rules as grand duke of Tuscany, and as emperor 1790–1792
1762–1796	Catherine II rules as empress of Russia
1743–1826	Life of Thomas Jefferson

separation of powers and checks and balances at work: Parliament checked the powers of the monarch, while within Parliament the House of Lords and the House of Commons checked each other. In the government as a whole, the balance was maintained by means of the separation of powers. Montesquieu could not have known, of course, that over the next century and a half the principle of separation of powers would decline in Britain as the House of Commons gathered more power unto itself, including control over the cabinet, which was becoming an instrument of legislative authority.

More radical in nature were the theories of Jean-Jacques Rousseau, which had a great influence on Enlightenment political ideas. Nature, he believed, dignified people, whereas civilization corrupted them. Hence, social and political institutions should adhere more closely to nature. In *The Social Contract* (1762), Rousseau sought to establish a new version of government by contract by reconciling individual liberty with government. Whereas Locke and other contract theorists had stressed agreement between a ruler and the people's willingness to be governed, Rousseau emphasized the agreement of society as a whole to be ruled by its "general will," to which every person submits. "In our corporate capacity," he argued, "we receive each member as an indivisible part of the whole." When an

protect such inalienable rights, the people had a further right to change their government, for the monarch had violated the compact formed between ruler and ruled.

Political Ideas in the Age of Reason

Those philosophes who thought most consistently about political reform stressed not only toleration but the practical fact that no one system of government was best for all countries. In *The Spirit of the Laws* (1748), Montesquieu insisted that tradition and environment helped to determine the form of government best suited for a particular society. He argued that the larger the political unit, the more power had to be exercised by the monarch. In Britain, a state of moderate size, the hereditary nobility in the House of Lords was balanced by the elected representatives in the House of Commons. Like most other enlightened thinkers of his age, Montesquieu believed that by themselves the common people were "extremely unfit" to govern a nation. In the case of his own country, he suggested that France might have been better off if the Bourbon monarchs had kept the political power of the aristocracy intact. In Britain, Montesquieu also saw the principles of the

The political ideas of the French philosopher Montesquieu were the basis of Enlightenment thought about government.

individual puts selfish interests before the needs of the community, that individual is forced to obey the general will—"forced," in Rousseau's words, "to be free."

Rousseau insisted that determining the general will was the responsibility of all the people and should not be left to an elected body, while the power to implement the general will could be delegated to a smaller group. He did not believe that any society could be governed by a genuine democracy, in which the people themselves both made and carried out the laws. Yet Rousseau's ideas were idealistic, and he maintained a deep personal dislike for royal absolutism. Holders of executive power, he argued, were the officers of the people, not their masters, and could be removed. Placed in the perspective of later history, however, his notion of the general will may appear to offer a justification for totalitarian government. He seems, for example, to be insisting that the whole of the general will is more precious and moral than its individual parts. Some later critics have argued that for Rousseau the welfare of the nation was greater than that of its citizens—an argument used, for example, by 20th-century dictators who claimed that they had a superior understanding of the general will and could set it above individual interests. In any case, this concept of the general will provided a rationale for some rulers who wanted to implement reforms.

Many of the English and Scottish intellectual colleagues of Montesquieu and Rousseau shared their concern for the nature of legislative authority. Those who did not agree believed that the only real responsibility of government was to administer the laws of nature instituted by God and that such authority was too often in the hands of individuals whose personal interests conflicted with the general welfare of society. Only hereditary monarchs, argued some philosophes, could reconcile their personal interests with those of the nation. Legitimacy—the right to rule—was maintained as long as royal policies were both reasonable and natural, and many monarchs of the period saw in the concept of enlightened despotism a useful justification for their powers, a more modern justification than divine right theory.

JOSEF II AND THE FAILURE OF THE AUSTRIAN ENLIGHTENMENT

The victory of Friedrich the Great in the War of the Austrian Succession exposed the weaknesses of the Hapsburg empire (see Part VI, Topic 9). The young and

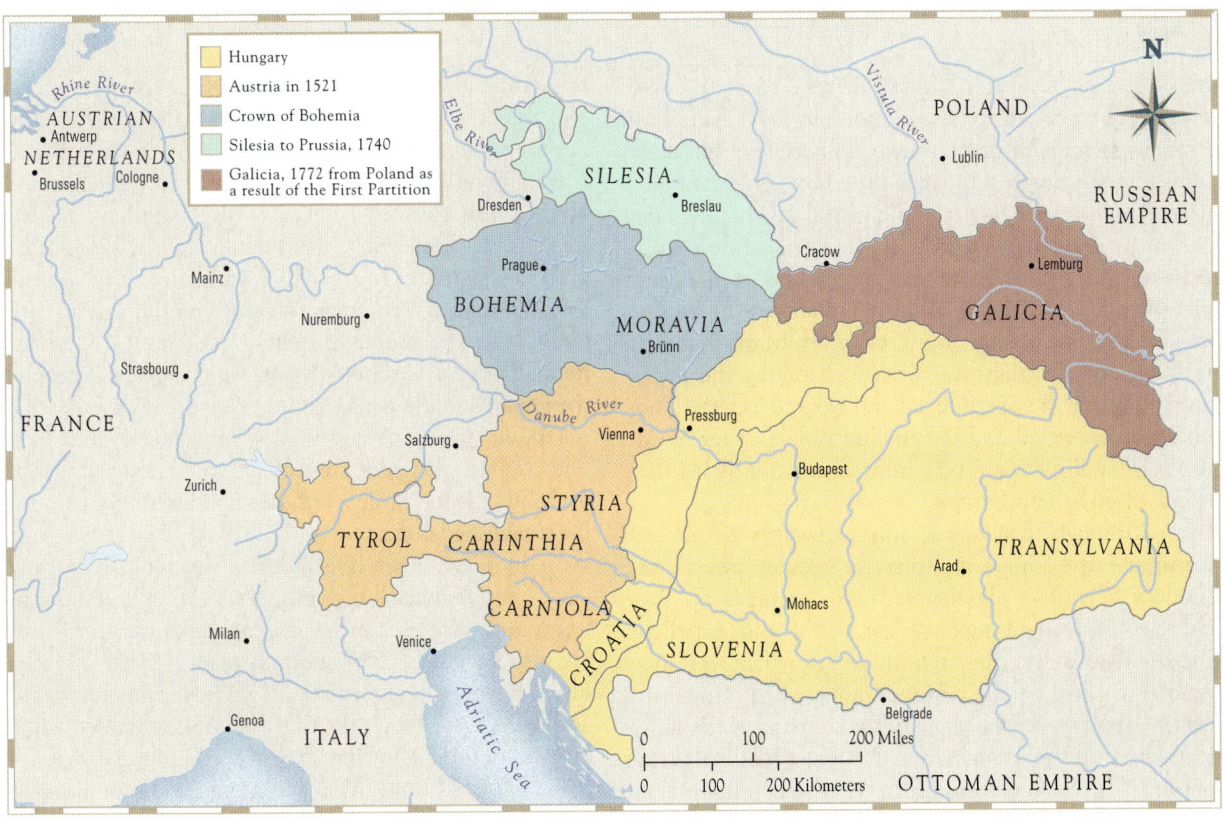

Map 1.1 The Austrian Empire, 1521–1772

The Empress Maria Theresa and Her Family by Martin van Maytens. Maria Theresa (right, seated) and her husband Francis I (left, seated) had 16 children. Their oldest son (the tall boy on his mother's right) became Josef II, and their youngest daughter, Marie Antoinette (center), married Louis XVI of France.

inexperienced Empress Maria Theresa proved, however, to be a practical champion of reforms designed to strengthen imperial government. Advised by talented ministers, the empress increased the taxes on the nobility and reduced the power of their local assemblies. The central bureaucracy was modernized and staffed with experts, and the non-German populations of the empire were forced to accept both German administrators and language. Most important, however, Maria Theresa took measures to improve conditions among the peasantry, most of whom still lived and worked as serfs. The taxes peasants paid and the amount of labor they owed to their landlords were now limited, in contrast to the trends elsewhere in Europe.

Although the empress was a devout Catholic—Catherine the Great of Russia scornfully called her "Lady Prayerful"—she imposed heavier taxes on the church, confiscated monastic property, and expelled the Jesuits. Despite these reforms, all of which were intended to increase the power of imperial government, Maria Theresa was not sympathetic to many of the critical ideas of the Enlightenment. She prohibited the publication or circulation of the works of Voltaire and Rousseau and suppressed all books that she deemed dangerous to the established order.

Josef II and the Austrian Empire

Not Maria Theresa but her eldest son, Josef II, was the Austrian monarch most responsible for bringing "enlightened absolutism" to the Hapsburg realm. Josef (ruled 1765–1790) ruled as coregent with Maria Theresa but was constantly held back and dominated by his mother until her death in 1780. Stricken with grief when his wife died, Josef became a compulsive worker, impatient with bureaucratic delay and entrenched interests. A serious-minded man, he declared that he would make philosophy the guide for all imperial laws. During the decade that he ruled alone, he promulgated some 17,000 measures. Although his policies were more often than not similar to his mother's, Josef ruled with less caution or concern for the established order.

In 1781, Josef II issued the Edict of Toleration, which gave Lutherans, Calvinists, and Orthodox Christians freedom to worship for the first time in Austrian history. He also improved the condition of his Jewish subjects, lifting the requirement that they live within the ghetto and wear the yellow star that had once branded them as inferior, and allowing them to enter universities—these reforms he regarded not as just and moral but as practical, for he hoped to make the Jews useful to the empire.

Josef reinforced his mother's policy of making the Catholic Church subservient to the authority of the empire. The emperor insisted that he, not the pope, was the final ecclesiastical authority within Hapsburg lands. He reduced the number of religious holidays and the number of nuns and monks, calling the latter "useless." He suppressed a third of all monasteries and convents, selling or renting these lands for the support of hospitals in Vienna, but encouraged those orders dedicated to education and charity.

In dealing with the plight of the peasantry, Josef took the policy of reform initiated by his mother to its logical conclusion. He emancipated the serfs and abolished most of their feudal obligations to the landowners, and also removed the traditional noble right to administer justice among the peasants. Following the suggestion of the physiocrats, he tried collecting a single tax on agricultural land, a revolutionary step because the large noble estates were to be taxed on the same basis as the small peasant holdings.

Like the philosophes, Josef II believed in the leveling effect of popular education, and provided teachers and textbooks for all primary schools. By the end of the century, more children attended school in Austria—about one out of four—than in any other European state. The emperor also accepted, at least in symbolic fashion, the concept of social equality, and opened a large public park in Vienna, known as the Prater, to citizens of every social status. A new legal code reflected the ideas of the Italian reformer Cesare Beccaria (see Part VI, Topic 11) about equality before the law, and abolished both capital punishment and the use of torture. Noblemen found guilty of crimes, like commoners, were often sentenced to sweep the streets of the capital.

The Limits of Austrian Reform

Other aspects of Josef's policies often reflected an unenlightened absolutism. He rejected the economic theories of the physiocrats in favor of old mercantilist policies such as high protective tariffs on imports. In other ways, he continued many of his mother's programs—weakening the influence of the nobility by appointing commoners to important positions and furthering the Germanization of the empire by speaking German and patronizing German writers. Josef also tried to reduce the administrative and cultural autonomy of non-German areas of the empire such as Hungary and Bohemia.

Josef's enlightened reforms and centralizing policies sparked domestic opposition from all directions. The nobility spoke out bitterly against laws enforcing equality and forced him to revoke the single-tax decree. The religious faith of the peasants, who remained oblivious to most of his other reforms, led them to resent his suppression of the Catholic Church. The Hungarians and Bohemians resorted to rebellion to protect their local rights against encroachments from Vienna. Josef was both an absolutist and a realist. More often than not, he dealt with his opponents simply by insisting on having his way.

Josef II died of exhaustion and overwork, believing that his policies had been right but that he had failed to accomplish great things. The judgment of one contemporary was that he had "governed too much and reigned too little." Certainly not all of Josef's reforms succeeded—some of them, such as the abolition of serfdom, were repealed after he died—but many others remained intact.

Josef's lasting reforms were reinforced by the policies of his younger brother, Leopold II (ruled 1790–1792), Grand Duke of Tuscany, who succeeded

One of several paintings and prints intended to show Josef II of Austria as promoter of agricultural reform.

to the imperial throne and proved to be an enlightened absolutist in much the same tradition. In the 25 years that he served as ruler of Tuscany, he had made considerable reforms in the government of the Italian duchy, including economic reforms advocated by the physiocrats and legal reforms suggested by Cesare Beccaria. Leopold sought to bring his subjects into public affairs and, unlike the other enlightened monarchs of the day, was interested in representative government as it was unfolding in the newly created United States of America.

"FIRST SERVANT OF THE STATE": FRIEDRICH THE GREAT OF PRUSSIA

In many ways, Prussian King Friedrich II (ruled 1740–1786), known as "the Great," appeared to be the

Friedrich the Great of Prussia as shown in an 18th-century engraving.

best example of an enlightened despot. In his youth he had tried to escape from the harsh discipline of his father, Friedrich Wilhelm I (see Part VI, Topic 5), who tried his son as a deserter and executed his son's companion and probable lover. A young man of sensibility and studious habits, he devoted the next ten years of his life to literary pursuits and music. His flute, which he carried with him everywhere, remained one of his favorite pastimes. He studied the writings of the philosophes and corresponded with many of them, favored French writers, and in 1750 invited Voltaire to live for three years at Potsdam Palace, outside Berlin.

Like Josef II of Austria, Friedrich worked hard at being king and drove his ministers and servants relentlessly. He avoided luxury and overindulgence, often wore dirty, ill-fitting clothing, and appeared obsessed with achieving success. In the conduct of foreign affairs and warfare he proved to be a man of genius and cunning. Friedrich was one of the most efficient and successful monarchs of the 18th century, but there is no doubt that he practiced the art of despotism as much as he believed in the ideas of the Enlightenment.

The Contradictions of Enlightened Absolutism

In economic affairs, Friedrich's policies were marked by deep-seated contradictions. He improved Prussian agriculture by importing from Western Europe crop rotation and the iron plow as well as new crops such as the potato and clover. He reclaimed land from swamps and after the conquest of Silesia established farms there and settled the region with immigrants from other German states. In the aftermath of the Seven Years' War, Friedrich worked to restore ruined forests and supplied the peasants with tools, seed, and animals. Also, like his Austrian counterpart, Friedrich did not accept the physiocratic doctrine of a laissez-faire (free market) economy and resorted to mercantilist protectionism to stimulate Prussian industry, especially for such items as metals and textiles needed by the army. In Prussia, as elsewhere in Europe, the consumption of coffee grew rapidly in the 18th century. When it became apparent, however, that this new consumer fad required the export of Prussian currency, he put a heavy import duty on coffee beans and set up a corps of special agents to stop coffee smuggling. Moreover, Friedrich considered coffee and tea signs of the degeneration of modern society and insisted that his soldiers drink beer instead. Friedrich's military ambitions imposed a heavy tax burden on his subjects.

Despite his adherence to Enlightenment notions of equality, Friedrich believed in the maintenance of social hierarchy. At the same time, he was convinced that the same patriotic duties were expected of both

Map 1.2   Prussia, 1440–1786

monarch and subjects—the king, he said, was merely "the first servant of the state." The elite *Junker* class of landowners exercised a monopoly of social prestige in Prussia but Friedrich did not spare them from the consequences of his absolutism. Only Junkers received appointments as army officers, but he discouraged marriage among them in order to avoid having to pay their widows military pensions. He abolished serfdom on the royal estates but not elsewhere in his realm, although in 1773 he did prohibit the sale of landless serfs in East Prussia. For practical reasons, he supported a minimum rural literacy and gave the peasants considerable economic assistance. The middle class he generally held in contempt, although he recognized their usefulness as tax payers. After the Seven Years' War, middle-class officers were forced out of the army and made exempt from military service.

Friedrich was a deist who took pride in his religious tolerance, yet his religious policies were also riddled with contradictions. When the Jesuits were expelled from other states, he invited them to his own Lutheran country. Throughout his realm, the king granted his Catholic subjects almost full equality, and even built an impressive Catholic church in Berlin. On the other hand, in 1779, when the writer Gotthold Lessing (1729–1781) made a Jew the hero

of his play *Nathan the Wise*, Friedrich kept him out of the royal academy. Whereas Josef considered his Jewish citizens useful, Friedrich pronounced Prussia's Jews to be useless and levied special taxes on them, and discouraged them from entering the professions and the civil service.

Friedrich made sweeping reforms in the Prussian legal system, freeing the courts from political pressures and reducing the use of torture. He also created a system of appellate courts to replace the strange tradition of allowing university faculties to hear appeals from the courts. Finally, he tried to eliminate the widespread practice of bribery by setting up a special gratuities fund for the purpose of supplementing judicial salaries.

Was Friedrich's enlightened absolutism little more than a clever deception to hide his will to dominance behind the fashionable intellectual discourse of the day? In his last testament, Friedrich insisted that he be buried beside his pet dogs. Some historians, like a number of Friedrich's contemporaries, have seen this gesture as a symbol of his contempt for his fellow human beings. Perhaps that scorn was a result of the difficulties of Friedrich's own life, torn as he was between the severe military traditions of his own Hohenzollern dynasty and the gentler doctrines of the Age of Reason.

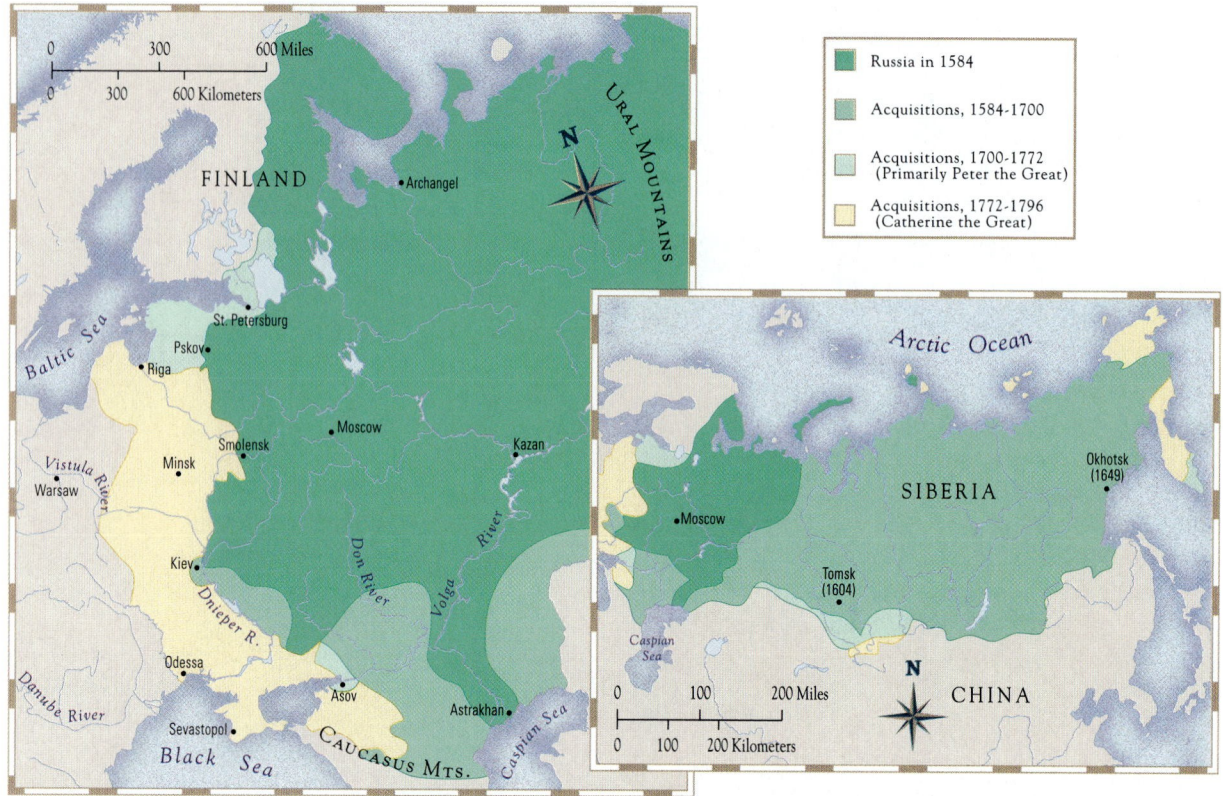

Map 1.3   Russian Expansion, 1584–1796

ENLIGHTENMENT IN THE EAST: RUSSIA FROM CATHERINE TO ALEXANDER

Like the Austrian Empire, Russia had two monarchs whose policies conformed to the general pattern of enlightened absolutism: Catherine II (ruled 1762–1796) and her grandson Alexander I (ruled 1801–1825). The empire that they ruled was a vast country in which feudal traditions were still very strong. In the decades following the death of Peter the Great in 1725, the monarchy suffered from a series of weak and ineffective leaders and the nobility reemerged as a dominant force.

Having chafed under the harsh reign of Peter the Great, the deeply dissatisfied nobles sought to regain their former status and privileges. In 1730 the gentry began to extricate themselves from servitude to the tsar, and by 1762 the nobles gave military service to the tsar only by choice. At the same time, the noble landowners extended their power over the serfs, serving as agents for collecting the poll tax. Masters could still exile their serfs to Siberia and mete out physical punishment at will. Serfs lost the right to gain their freedom by joining the army, and could neither buy land nor engage in commercial activities without permission from their masters.

Catherine the Great

Brought up in a German court, Catherine was married at the age of 15 to the Russian Grand Duke Peter. In St. Petersburg, she ingratiated herself quickly with the Russians, learning their language and embracing the Orthodox religion. She soon came to detest her husband, took on a succession of lovers, and conspired to become empress in her own right. In 1762, a palace coup dethroned and assassinated Peter in a plot that probably involved Catherine, who was proclaimed Empress Catherine II, known as "the Great." The new ruler was a devoted student of the Enlightenment, who wrote plays, edited a journal, and read the works of the philosophes with great eagerness. Catherine wanted a good press in Western Europe both for herself and for the country she ruled, and used the philosophes for that purpose. She invited Diderot, whose library she purchased, to visit St. Petersburg and granted him a pension. Catherine also corresponded with Voltaire, who did not visit Russia but did accept her financial support, praising her in return as "the north star."

Reform and Its Constraints

The empress was no doubt inclined to institute sweeping reforms in Russia, but a combination of personal liabilities—principally the fact that she was both a woman and a foreigner—made it difficult for her to move swiftly or decisively. Because she relied heavily on the support of the nobility, she felt she could not work to eliminate serfdom. On the contrary, in granting huge estates to her supporters, she converted many thousands of state peasants to privately owned serfs.

Like Montesquieu, Catherine believed that a country as large as Russia had to be ruled by an autocrat. Once on the throne, however, Catherine appointed a Legislative Commission to codify the complex laws implemented over the previous century. Catherine personally helped to write the Commission's guidelines, which were replete with theories taken from Montesquieu's *Spirit of the Laws* and Beccaria's *Crimes and Punishments*. In addition, the more than 500 members of the Commission were elected by all social classes except the serfs and had to compile written statements of grievances from their districts. After a year and a half of inconclusive debate, Catherine closed down the Commission without having codified the laws. This was the last attempt by the Russian monarchy to consult its subjects until the 20th century.

Catherine the Great of Russia in a painting depicting the empress as a warrior (1762).

Rebellion and Repression

In 1775, Catherine faced a great Cossack rebellion under the leadership of Yemelyan Pugachev (1726–1775). With a coalition of soldiers and peasants, Pugachev led a revolt against Catherine. The Cossack leader claimed to be Peter III, the murdered husband of the empress, and promised freedom and land to the serfs. Pugachev moved across southeastern Russia toward Moscow, burning and killing, and slaughtering landlords and priests. The outbreak of famine along the Volga River and betrayal by some of his followers brought an end to the rebellion. Pugachev was taken in an iron cage to Moscow in 1775, where he was tried and executed. Like similar revolts in the 17th century, Pugachev's rebellion—which Catherine brutally crushed—reflected the depth of discontent felt for the monarchy as well as for landowners and government officials.

Catherine moved immediately to increase imperial centralization and further repress the serfs. In a major restructuring of local government, she increased the number of provinces from 20 to 50, hoping that the smaller provinces would prove easier to govern. She appointed nobles to most of the new provincial offices while imposing close government supervision on their activities. In 1785, Catherine issued two imperial charters. One charter granted the nobles exemption from taxation and military service and gave them complete control over their serfs. The other charter, which permitted self-government for cities, revealed Catherine's support for the small but growing middle class.

When the empress died in 1796, her son succeeded her as Paul I (ruled 1796–1801). Catherine had always feared that her son might lead a conspiracy against her, so that when Paul became tsar many thought he would eliminate his mother's reforms. Paul proved, however, to be unpredictable. In his more reactionary moments, he placed the population of St. Petersburg under a strict curfew and prohibited Western sheet music, fearing that it would spread revolutionary sentiments among his subjects. He also continued the practice of giving state lands to his supporters, thereby transforming hundreds of thousands of peasants into private serfs. In 1797 he prohibited serfs from working on Sunday but permitted landlords to increase the amount of their labor.

Paul's policy toward the nobles proved to be his undoing. Attempting to reverse the developments of decades, he made the aristocrats once again subject to imperial service and limited their local powers. He also forced them to subsidize the construction of public buildings and to pay new land taxes. In a different area of reform, Paul wanted to modernize his army along Prussian lines, instilling in the officers a sense of responsibility for ordinary soldiers. The élite guards'

PERSPECTIVES ON HISTORY

How Enlightened Were the Enlightened Despots?

John G. Gagliardo
Boston University

A vigorous debate on this question has occurred since the term "enlightened despotism" (now, more commonly "enlightened absolutism") first came into historical usage in the 19th century. The debate has revolved mostly around the motivation and purposes of the domestic policies and programs of those European monarchs of roughly the last half of the 18th century to whom the term has been applied. Over the years, many historians have argued that the reform programs of the so-called "enlightened despots" were neither chiefly called forth by nor primarily intended to serve the higher humanitarian ideals usually associated with the Enlightenment. Such policies were instead not much more than updated versions of periodic earlier efforts to strengthen the political power of absolute monarchy and to improve the economic and military position of their states in the dangerous climate of the 18th-century international system.

These historians hold that the cultivation of power rather than service to the spiritual and material welfare of their peoples was the prime motivator of the "enlightened despots." Their frequent appeal to Enlightenment ideals and principles is seen as rhetorical camouflage designed to justify in the name of philanthropic necessity what was in fact a self-interested campaign to regiment and control their societies more tightly in the service of goals that had little to do with social welfare. At the risk of some simplification, the evidence produced for this interpretation points to the fact that nearly all reforms launched by these princes, including those that did bring some humanitarian benefit, also strengthened the fiscal or governmental apparatus of the monarchical state. Moreover, the programs with the strongest "purely" humanitarian content—popular education, charitable enterprises, reform of the brutal criminal justice system and of prisons, and so on—were persistently underfunded and always the first to be abandoned when money got tight. Some rulers did successfully move to abolish serfdom, and many more to alleviate its burdens, but the record is a very mixed one; and while noble privilege was invaded and curtailed in some respects, no ruler undertook to overthrow the traditional "society of orders" to which the concepts of privilege and legal inequality were fundamental. Even the two reforms most universally demanded by the enlightened community—religious toleration and freedom of the press—were not everywhere realized or well enforced, and some degree of censorship continued to exist in even the most "enlightened" states. This negative interpretation does not deny the achievement of some practical benefits for these monarchs' peoples; it simply asserts that the humanitarian ideas of the Enlightenment were not an important source of their policies, that any popular benefits resulting from those policies were more incidental than purposeful, and that an "enlightened absolutism" therefore did not really exist at all.

Even without disputing the historical facts of this interpretation, however, it is possible to approach the question from a different perspective—one which puts far more weight on the judgment of those contemporaries who first termed these monarchs "enlightened," and who persisted in doing so through all of the failures, partial successes, and supposedly hypocritical rhetoric of their undertakings. Unless we assume stupidity or willful naiveté in a very large part of the enlightened community, we have to believe on their own testimony that they perceived the "enlightened despots" as actual executors of many of their hopes for mankind, and applauded them for the overall direction of their regimes (without necessarily keeping detailed lists of every success or failure). Most enlightened thinkers and publicists, after all, were not dreamers or utopians, but informed and intelligent people living in a real world of real problems they wanted corrected. Almost none of them developed schemes for anything resembling a completely new political or social system; and in spite of much grumbling about the pace or depth of reform, or about the foreign and military policies of even those states they regarded as most enlightened, they also recognized the difficulties of reform. Consequently, they were not uncomfortable with incrementalist approaches to reform as long as they were persistent and real in terms of identifiable progress, however partial. They were, in general terms, "possibilists" rather than revolutionaries, who judged rulers and regimes by their *tendencies* rather than by comparison to some finished blueprint of a perfect society.

The fact that various reform projects corresponding to their own desires also served the self-interest of monarchs by bringing new power and efficiency to their governmental apparatus was not uniformly worrisome to the philosophes of Europe, and indeed had positive aspects: it not only illustrated a favorite truth discovered by the Enlightenment—the cunningly beneficial relationship between self-interest and public utility—but also improved the power of rulers to do good; we should not forget, after all, that most enlightened thinkers supported a powerful absolute monarchy as the form of government best able to reform a stubbornly traditional society, *when animated by enlightened rulership.*

What the philosophes sought, in broadest terms, was a society more tolerant of diversity (especially in matters of religious faith, with all their secondary social consequences); more humane (in caring for the disadvantaged of all sorts, including accused and convicted criminals); and more efficient and less wasteful (quicker and less expensive justice, rationalized civil codes, and elimination of arbitrary and capricious administrative practices through the greater regularity of a government operating under known and comprehensive laws). Even a brief review of the history of the "enlightened despotisms" will reveal much dedicated attention to this agenda—an attention more persistent and successful in some places than in others, but real nonetheless. By the standards employed by the philosophes themselves, therefore, the record of reform achievement in these areas, while not of revolutionary proportions, is undeniable, and suggests that their positive view of these

princes was based on observed fact, not on wishful thinking or on such enlightened rhetoric as the latter employed. (A strong case can be made for the personal adherence of many of the "enlightened despots" to the basic premises of the Enlightenment—natural law doctrine, for example—which they knew well through some combination of both formal education and their own reading, and personal contacts with leading literary exponents of Enlightenment. This personal culture cannot be ignored in approaching the question of motivation.)

Another and extremely important objective of the Enlightenment as a whole was a *fairer* society. The abundant social criticism arising from this demand was directed chiefly at the privileges and immunities of both clergy and nobility, but especially the latter, that were built into the Old Regime's "society of orders." Moreover, no government moved to abolish this class-based system. Some historians, seeing in this the *decisive* criterion of monarchs' entitlement to true enlightenment, have denied it to them almost on these grounds alone. But this position ignores the real objection of contemporaries, which was not to the *existence* of privilege but to the current standards of *access* to it. What most of them wanted was certainly not abolition of the traditional social order, but a reformulation of it in which privilege would be accessible to all men on the basis of meritorious achievement, not just by birth or money alone. Nobility (and privilege, and the whole "society of orders" along with it) was perfectly acceptable, in other words, as long as it was justified by merit or, to the extent that merit was not present in already existing aristocracies, would be modified by removal or reduction of privileges and immunities. The "enlightened despots" concurred with the philosophes in this desire. From that arose not only a strengthening of the public service ethic of the "service nobilities" already in place in some countries, as well as new taxes on the nobility, but also a new insistence on performance as the criterion for appointment and promotion in the civil and military bureaucracies. The fact that these developments did not in fact or by intention move in the direction of 20th-century social

continued next page

egalitarianism is irrelevant, since no one at the time either expected or wanted them to. And again, that these reforms were slow, sporadic, and partial, or that the monarchs derived advantage as rulers from them, rendered them no less attractive to the enlightened community, which recognized the great value of the *tendency*—public recognition of the larger principle of social advancement for merit.

In the final analysis, to be sure, it is necessary to recognize several facts that may qualify the degree of enlightenment of the "enlightened despots." Motive, to begin with, is always a murky and perhaps in the end impenetrable question; some of the reforms of the period clearly were continuations of earlier policies more than wholly new initiatives; there was often a considerable gap between announced intentions and results achieved, and what did not get done was at least as impressive as what did; and, finally, there is little evidence that the monarchs of the time had any vision of a breakthrough to an entirely new kind of society that might be made possible by their own efforts. The removal of all these reservations might be necessary to qualify these rulers as "enlightened" by today's standards. Nonetheless, shrewd and critical observers in their own time clearly believed not only that their intellectual receptivity, openness to experimentation, and intentions conformed to the enlightened spirit of the age, but also that their regimes represented a sufficiently progressive chapter in the history of monarchy itself as to justify dubbing them "enlightened."

In the end, then, if one can accept the reality of mixed motives—a genuine degree of humanitarian concern, combined with the imperative to keep the state both solvent and militarily strong—and if one can recognize the numerous and severe obstacles to all reform in societies that were economically marginal and stubbornly traditionalistic, with much ability to resist change, then a reasonable case for a genuine "enlightened despotism" can be made. In all essentials, it is the case made by the Enlightenment itself, and it remains a compelling one today.

regiments resented these changes and hatched a conspiracy that murdered Paul in 1801.

The Liberal Tsar

Alexander I (ruled 1801–1825) was educated by a liberal Swiss tutor who instilled in him a respect for the teachings of the Enlightenment. Despite his liberal leanings, however, Alexander made such extensive compromises that his accomplishments were limited. Perhaps one of his most ambitious reforms was a law that created a class of landowning farmers from former serfs freed by their masters. This measure had only limited success, however, since emancipation by landlords was voluntary—less than 40,000 serfs were freed out of many millions.

The liberal but hesitant Alexander had the benefit of an exceptionally talented adviser, Michael Speransky (1772–1839), the intelligent and well educated son of a priest. Inspired by Montesquieu's doctrine of the separation of powers, Speransky presented Alexander with a plan for constitutional government. It provided for a number of elected provincial assemblies and a Duma, or national parliament, which would approve all laws presented by the tsar. These bodies would be elected by the nobility and the middle classes, with the exclusion of the serfs.

Had it been implemented, Speransky's far-reaching plan would have ended absolutism in Russia, but Alexander refused to put it into effect. Speransky had made powerful enemies in his effort to reform the civil service by requiring examinations and promotion based on merit, a system opposed by the many nobles and illiterates who held government office. He had also proposed an income tax for the nobility. Speransky's enemies found an opportunity to undermine him in 1812, when Napoleon invaded Russia—Speransky, who had arranged an alliance with the French ruler, was exiled. The constitutional scheme was abandoned, but two provisions that did not weaken the tsar's power were implemented. Alexander established a purely advisory council of state, whose members he appointed and dismissed, a measure that increased imperial efficiency. By reorganizing the government ministries and defining their responsibilities, Alexander eliminated overlapping jurisdictions.

During his last years, Alexander was influenced by Count Alexis Arakcheev (1769–1834), a conservative landowner and military officer who was given free reign over most domestic affairs. He instituted a series of "military colonies" in farming communities that it was hoped would pay for the army. When not fighting or training, the soldiers could live with their families and work the farms, although in practice these were staffed by drafting local populations and run by brutal officers. By the end of Alexander's reign, some 400,000 soldiers—about a third of the army—were living in these camps.

Ironically, Alexander proved to be a more liberal tsar in the territories he ruled beyond Russia's borders. In 1809, after he had annexed Finland from Sweden, the tsar allowed the Finns to keep their law codes and a degree of local government. Similarly, when he became king of Poland in 1815, he granted the Poles a constitution and permitted them to have their own army and government officials, as well as to use their own language. It was in Russia itself that tsarist absolutism failed to temper the repressive regime with the political doctrines of the Enlightenment.

THE GREAT EXPERIMENT: THE ENLIGHTENMENT AND THE AMERICAN REVOLUTION

In the context of the Age of Reason, the American Revolution was an important event in European history. Its immediate causes lay in specific fiscal problems between Great Britain and its North American colonies, but the political ideals that undergirded the American revolt were part of the Enlightenment tradition. Inspired by the thought of John Locke, Rousseau, and

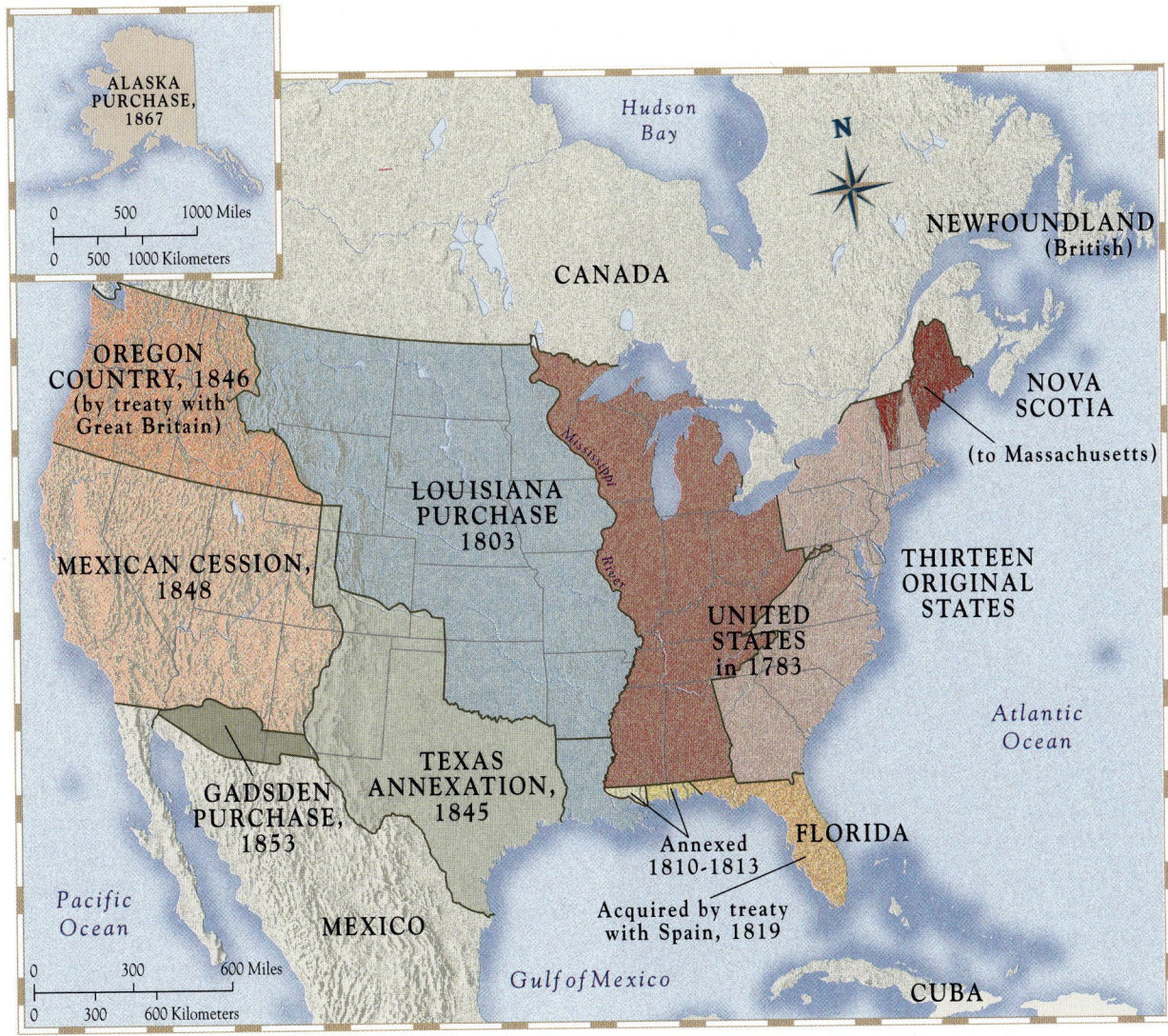

Map 1.4   The United States, 1776–1867

other political theorists, colonial leaders such as Benjamin Franklin and Thomas Jefferson posed basic questions about the advantages of monarchy versus constitutional government and about the sources of political authority.

The Roots of Revolution

After the end of the Seven Years' War in 1763, a victorious Great Britain had to deal with several pressing problems in America. London quickly discovered that its much enlarged empire required considerable financial expenditures, and insisted that these be shared with the American colonists, who had benefited most from the war. The problem lay, however, in the fact that the colonists opposed all efforts to tax them, mainly because their economy was no longer suited to Britain's mercantilist policies.

In 1764 Parliament passed the Sugar Act, which aimed to raise revenue through import duties, followed in 1765 by the Stamp Act, which put a tax on such items as legal documents and newspapers. The American

Thomas Jefferson was perhaps the most important philosophe of the American Enlightenment.

response was that since they were not represented in Parliament, they should not be taxed by that body—"no taxation," they insisted, "without representation." That October, the so-called Stamp Act Congress agreed not to import British goods and issued a protest to the king. In the face of this resistance, Parliament repealed the Stamp Act, while asserting its right to legislate for the colonies.

Over the next decade, a familiar pattern repeated itself: whenever Parliament passed a revenue measure or an administrative act affecting the colonies, the Americans resisted it, often with violence, and the British would then back down. Relations between colonies and mother country deteriorated steadily. When the colonies resisted a set of four import duties sponsored by Chancellor of the Exchequer Charles Townshend (1725–1767), the British sent special customs agents and soldiers to Boston in 1768 to enforce the laws. Tensions rose and in March 1770 British troops killed five civilians in what came to be called the Boston Massacre. Parliament repealed all but one—that on tea—of the Townshend duties.

In May 1773 Parliament permitted the East India Company to sell tea directly to American distributors, thereby avoiding American wholesalers. Although the measure lowered the price of tea, colonial merchants viewed it as an oppressive act against American merchants. Some American cities refused to permit the unloading of tea in their ports, and in Boston a cargo of tea was dumped into the harbor. In 1774, British Prime Minister Lord North (1732–1792), determined to assert British authority over the colonies, passed the so-called Intolerable Acts. These laws closed the port of Boston, suspended many rights, and permitted soldiers to be quartered and fed in private homes.

Crisis was at hand. Incensed by what they considered high-handed and unjust treatment, colonists critical of Britain formed committees to discuss their common problems. In September 1774 the First Continental Congress met in Philadelphia, where the 56 delegates demanded redress as British citizens, denounced taxation without representation, and agreed to boycott trade until their rights were restored. The result, however, was war rather than negotiation. By May 1775, when the second Congress met, battles had already been fought at Lexington and Concord. Although the colonists met defeat at Bunker Hill in June, the assemblies of each colony began to meet as sovereign bodies instead of under the king's authority. The revolution had begun.

Franklin, Jefferson, and the American Enlightenment

When the Second Continental Congress met that spring, it could boast among its members two of the most illustrious intellects in the American colonies: Benjamin Franklin (1706–1790) and Thomas Jefferson (1743–1826). Both men epitomized the American Enlightenment, and their ideas made important contributions to the course of the revolution and to the political development of the future United States.

Franklin was born in Boston of modest background, the son of a soap and candle maker, and learned the printing trade as a young man. In Philadelphia, he ran his own print shop and published the *Pennsylvania Gazette* as well as *Poor Richard's Almanac.* At the age of 42, he retired from business with enough money to devote his energies to the sciences and public affairs. He had already helped to set up a library, an academy that eventually became the University of Pennsylvania, and a discussion group that gave rise to the American Philosophical Society. He published the influential book *Experiments and Observations on Electricity* in 1751 and was a prolific inventor. The embodiment of a trained observer of natural phenomena in the Age of Reason, Franklin's scientific knowledge included astronomy, medicine, geology, and physics. Serving as Pennsylvania's agent in London from 1764 to 1775, he had been an important voice for conciliation with Britain before becoming a member of the Second Continental Congress.

In contrast to Franklin's humble origins, Jefferson was the son of a Virginia planter and educated as a lawyer. The breadth of his interests and learning was even greater than that of Franklin, who had little interest in aesthetics. Jefferson read widely in the arts and humanities as well as in the sciences, played the violin, and read or spoke seven languages. He was an accomplished architect, and knowledgeable in mathematics and engineering. His book *Notes on Virginia* (1785) showed him to be familiar with botany, zoology, geography, and archeology. Later in his life, one of the contributions of which he was most proud was the founding of the University of Virginia. Jefferson first entered politics in 1769 as a member of the Virginia House of Burgesses. In 1774, in response to the Intolerable Acts, Jefferson wrote *A Summary View of the Rights of British America,* in which he rejected Britain's right to govern in America.

Although the Second Continental Congress sought conciliation with Britain, events led the body to plan for self-government, for King George III had declared the colonies to be in rebellion. In the winter of 1775, an impassioned and immensely influential pamphlet by Thomas Paine (1737–1809) entitled *Common Sense* influenced many Americans toward independence. A colonial army was created under the command of George Washington (1732–1799).

In June 1776, the Continental Congress appointed a five-man committee, including Franklin and Jefferson, to write a Declaration of Independence. Jefferson drafted the document, to which Franklin contributed much discussion and some changes of language. The final version was a moving statement of the essential principles of Enlightenment political thought. Both Franklin and Jefferson were familiar with the works of Locke and the French philosophes, and the emphasis on natural rights embodied in it could not have been more clear: "We hold these truths to be self-evident, that all men are created equal; that they are endowed by their creator with certain inalienable rights; that among these are life, liberty and the pursuit of happiness." The colonies had invoked the notion of contract theory, in which subjects were free to overthrow an unjust monarch. On July 2, the Continental Congress declared the independence of the colonies and on July 4 adopted the Declaration of Independence.

The War of Independence raged on, widening in 1778 into a European conflict when Franklin, then serving as rebel minister to France, persuaded the government of Louis XVI to support the Americans. In 1779–1780 Spain and the Dutch Republic also joined the war on the side of the colonies. In 1781, after Washington's army decisively defeated British forces at Yorktown, the British agreed to sue for peace. Franklin led the negotiations, which culminated in the Treaty of Paris (1783). The thirteen American colonies had won their independence.

The Early United States

Perhaps the most successful application of Enlightenment principles to the world of politics in the 18th century took place not in Europe but in the United States. Between 1781 and 1789, the Americans governed themselves through the Articles of Confederation, which provided for a weak central authority in recognition of the difficulties they had experienced at the hands of the British monarchy. In 1787, however, a convention meeting in Philadelphia drafted an entirely new constitution for the United States. A national government was created with powers that transcended those of the individual states, such as the authority to tax, conduct foreign policy, and raise an army. Montesquieu's dual principles of separation of powers and checks and balances inspired the creation of an executive (an elected president), a legislature (a two-chamber Congress, consisting of a Senate elected by the states and a House of Representatives chosen directly by popular vote), and a Supreme Court.

During the early decades of their republic, Americans were as divided over political ideology as their European counterparts. In the United States, political leaders split between Federalists and Democrats, much as Europeans chose conservatism or liberalism. The

Federalist party, founded by Alexander Hamilton (1755?–1804), was the first true American political party. Hamilton's support came mainly from prosperous business groups and landowners from the northern states; they wanted a strong central government run by the educated and wealthy élite. They were the strongest supporters of the new constitution and pushed for the addition of the Bill of Rights to the document, which were ratified as ten amendments in 1790. These guaranteed such basic rights for citizens as freedom of speech, press, assembly, and worship, and trial by jury. The Democratic Republican party, on the other hand, represented small independent farmers, largely from the south. The titular leader of the Democratic Republicans was Jefferson (president from 1801 to 1809), who preached popular control of government.

Enlightened absolutism had many weaknesses, not the least of which was the fact that a good monarch ruled as an accident of birth, not by the choice of the people. Nor were there any devices built into the system in the event that these monarchs acted as despots without the benefit of enlightened sensibilities. Josef II of Austria proved to be too rigid and wedded to centralized control of an empire that incorporated too many diverse ethnic groups. The Prussian king, Friedrich the Great, was determined to increase the power of the monarchy and reinforced the status and power of the Junkers, who generally opposed the Enlightenment. In Russia, Catherine the Great compromised her reformist principles to satisfy the power of the nobility. Only in the United States, where the political principles of the Enlightenment were applied without a monarch, did democracy thrive.

Questions for Further Study

1. To what degree did the monarchs of the 18th century qualify as "enlightened despots"?

2. What were the political goals of monarchs in Prussia, Austria, and Russia? How did enlightened reforms help them to achieve those goals?

3. What cultural and intellectual connections existed between 18th-century Europe and the American colonies?

Suggestions for Further Study

Beales, Derek. *Joseph II*. Vol. I. Cambridge, MA, 1987.

Blanning, T. C. W. *Joseph II and Enlightened Despotism*. New York, 1970.

Gagliardo, John. *Enlightened Despotism*. Arlington Heights, IL, 1967.

Krieger, Leonard. *An Essay on the Theory of Enlightened Despotism*. Chicago, 1975.

Madariaga, Isabel de. *Russia in the Age of Catherine the Great*. London, 1981.

Palmer, R. R. *The Age of Democratic Revolution: A Political History of Europe and America, 1760–1800*. 2 vols. Princeton, NJ, 1964.

Ritter, Gerhard. *Frederick the Great: A Historical Profile*. Berkeley, CA, 1968.

Scott, Hamish M. *Enlightened Absolutism*. Ann Arbor, MI, 1990.

Topic 2

The Industrial Revolution

eginning in the 18th century, life in the West underwent a gradual transformation so far-reaching that the term "revolution" has been employed to describe it. The new era, in which machines and steam power took over functions previously the exclusive province of human and animal labor, produced unprecedented and continuing economic growth. Living standards for the vast majority of Europeans improved, while much smaller numbers of entrepreneurs accumulated huge fortunes. The social structure that came to characterize modern Europe was no longer determined by birth and inherited privilege but by economic class, defined by the relationship of individuals to labor and capital. This "revolution" gave rise by the 20th century to the western European civilization with which we are familiar today—a predominantly urban, industrial, and secular culture that was able to seize world power as a result of its mastery of science and technology.

Europe's transition from tradition to modernity was accelerated at the end of the century by the French Revolution (see Part VII, Topic 3). That political upheaval was, however, largely independent of this wider transformation. Three other sweeping changes had been at work in Europe before 1789: revolutions in population growth, in agriculture, and in the means of production. While the industrial revolution—a process rather than an event—unfolded more slowly across a longer period of time than the French Revolution, its consequences were even more crucial to the way in which most Europeans lived.

THE ORIGINS OF THE INDUSTRIAL REVOLUTION

Industrialization required certain preconditions: a labor supply, markets, investment capital, raw material, and technological innovation. The rate of industrial development also depended on the political, social, and economic circumstances that prevailed in a given country. The industrial revolution began in the 1760s in England, where the prerequisites were present at more or less the same time, and spread to the Continent after 1815.

The Agricultural Revolution

The great population explosion that began to unfold in the 18th century provided one essential element in the complex of factors behind the industrial revolution. This development was, in turn, closely linked to the improvement in farming and stock breeding that constituted an "agricultural revolution" in the 18th century.

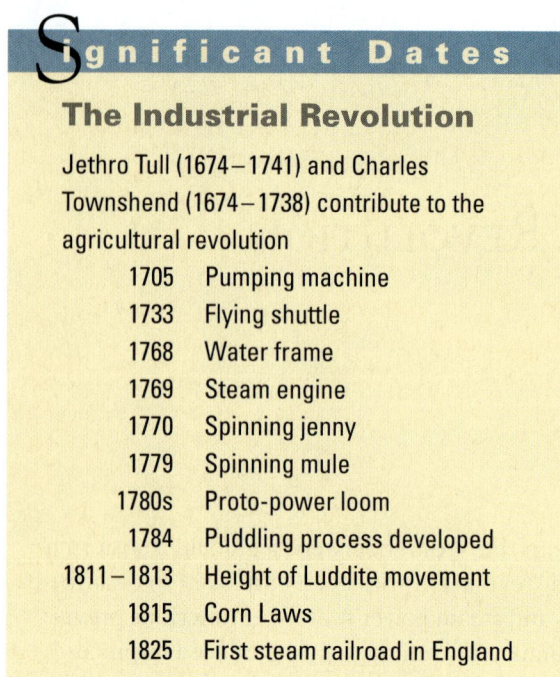

The Industrial Revolution

Jethro Tull (1674–1741) and Charles Townshend (1674–1738) contribute to the agricultural revolution

1705	Pumping machine
1733	Flying shuttle
1768	Water frame
1769	Steam engine
1770	Spinning jenny
1779	Spinning mule
1780s	Proto-power loom
1784	Puddling process developed
1811–1813	Height of Luddite movement
1815	Corn Laws
1825	First steam railroad in England

The tremendous increase in Europe's population had the effect of pushing the price of food higher, and this in turn made life difficult for the poorer peasants. The larger landowners who marketed their crops, however, earned more. As profits grew, so too did the inclination to increase income even further by improving cultivation methods. In the crowded Netherlands, where farmable land was in short supply, the Dutch had pioneered in planting new money crops, particularly turnips, and in reclaiming land through drainage and the construction of dikes.

In the 18th century, English landlords began copying these methods for consumption crops and became enthusiastic proponents of agricultural innovation. There, as on much of the Continent, two Medieval practices mitigated against the widespread adoption of new methods and crops: the three-field and the open field systems. The first consisted of the planting of crops on a rotating basis in which one field was planted with a winter crop, followed by a spring crop, and then allowed to lie fallow for a year in order to restore fertility (the three-field system was used in northern Europe; in the dryer regions of the south, where rainfall was limited in the summer, a two-field system was used). Under that system, a third of the land was unproductive each year. Although manure could alleviate the need for fallow land, the large number of animals needed for the purpose made this method prohibitively expensive.

In England, a number of landowners sought to overcome these problems by diversifying crops, trying other kinds of fertilizer, and developing new techniques and equipment. Jethro Tull (1674–1741), an agricultural inventor, developed a mechanical wheat seeder and used iron plows to dig deeper furrows. Tull's work in agricultural experimentation encouraged others. Charles "Turnip" Townshend (1674–1738) successfully used turnips and other crops on a rotating system—this was a crucial contribution, for by rotating crops that required different nutritional properties from the soil, the fallow field could be eliminated. His innovations were interconnected, for the new methods increased the quantity of animal feed produced per acre, and the resulting larger livestock herds were a source of manure for wheat and barley planting.

Such ideas were disseminated on the Continent through the writings of the French physiocrats. In England, where King George III (ruled 1760–1820) took a personal interest in agricultural improvements, special journals such as the *Farmers' Magazine* and the *Annals of Agriculture* were published. Similar magazines, filled with reports of experiments and practical advice, appeared later on in Italy, France, and other places on the Continent. The influence of British agricultural innovation on the rest of Europe is shown by the publication between 1798 and 1800 of a book by a German professor named Albrecht Thaer, *Introduction to the Knowledge of English Agriculture*.

The "open field" system of landholding was the other impediment to the modernization of agriculture. Traditionally, farmers owned property in the form of small, narrow strips of unconnected land. These strips were not fenced in, but rather open to those of other landowners. In addition, villages usually shared common lands on which animals grazed, while the entire community decided what crops to plant as well as the rotation plan. This splintered pattern of landholding, together with the communal decision-making process, made it virtually impossible for innovative cultivators to apply the new methods on a large scale.

The Enclosure of the Land

In order to create more productive, successful farms that could be effectively managed, some British landowners sought to put together large tracts made up of many contiguous fields that could be enclosed with hedges or fences. This tendency had begun in the 16th century, when farms were converted to sheep pastures and enclosed, in response to the growing wool trade. To achieve this purpose, lands formerly rented to peasants were taken back and consolidated with other small parcels to make larger units. Sometimes common lands and entire villages were enclosed. When poor farmers, who had benefited from the open field system, objected, the landowners secured the legalization of enclosures through the passage of special acts of Parliament. In the

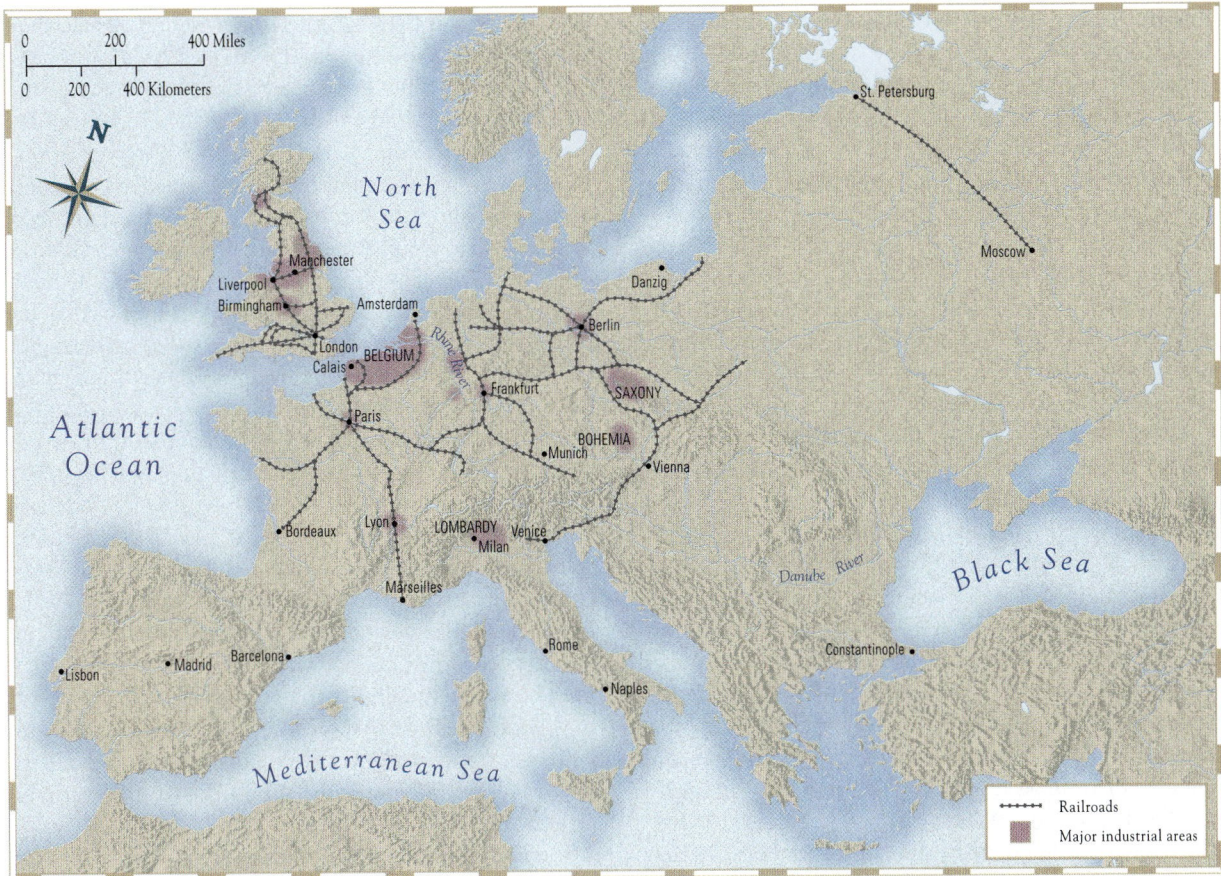

Map 2.1   Industrialization, c. 1850

second half of the 18th century alone, more than half a million acres of English farm land were enclosed in this manner.

The enclosure movement eliminated the open field system and altered English rural life. The small farmer was not only barred from the common fields but often relegated to unproductive pieces of land. Many lost the use of their plots and become workers without property, so that the English yeoman, or independent free landowner, became practically a thing of the past. At the beginning of the 18th century, most people in Great Britain had made their livelihoods in agriculture, but by 1800 less than half did so. And while some displaced peasants did move to the cities to seek employment, it is important to stress that the enclosure movement did not result in the widespread emigration of people from the countryside.

If the enclosure movement did not provide the workforce for the industrial revolution, it did have an impact on industrialization. Profits made from commercial agriculture increased the supply of capital available in England, and the example of rational farming managed by entrepreneurial criteria was increasingly followed in much of Western Europe in the 19th century.

Moreover, the agricultural revolution, of which enclosure was a feature, increased productivity so significantly that for the first time food could be produced in sufficient quantity to feed both the countryside and the cities—at lower cost, with less labor, and on a consistent basis.

TECHNOLOGY AND INVENTION IN THE AGE OF STEAM

In its initial stages, the industrial revolution primarily affected three critical industries, textiles, mining, and metals, and was specifically concerned with the most important products of each: cotton, coal, and iron. At the heart of the transformation in these industries were two essential developments: the invention of machines that could make products or exploit raw materials faster, more efficiently, and in greater quantity; and the harnessing of forms of energy other than muscle power to drive the machinery. Together, these two features of industrialization resulted in the transfer of production from homes and small shops, chiefly in the countryside, to urban factories. The factory system, both a new means of production and a social factor of great significance, radically transformed the daily lives and the quality of existence for millions of people. The factory remains to our own day the primary unit of industrial production.

The Textile Industry

The English had been manufacturing wool for centuries. Next to agriculture, wool production employed more people and accounted for a greater volume of trade than any other industry. Wool, made in virtually every county in England and Wales, provided secondary work and income for farmers and agricultural workers. Yet the first significant technological innovations occurred in the manufacturing of cotton rather than wool. The demand for cotton had increased as a result of the India trade, which supplied most of the muslin and calico used in England. It was not only cheaper than wool, but was lightweight and could be cleaned by washing. Moreover, unlike wool, cotton could be dyed or printed by machine in bright, appealing colors. English spinners were unable, however, to make a cotton thread of sufficient strength or quantity, so that production was limited.

Encouragement for the development of new methods of cotton manufacturing came in 1700 when wool merchants, alarmed at the popularity of the competing fabric, secured the passage of import restrictions on printed cottons from India. In 1733, a clock maker from Lancashire named John Kay made an important improvement in the loom called the "flying shuttle," by which one worker could move the shuttle with wooden arms controlled by strings, instead of by hand. This speeded up the weaving and resulted in a much wider fabric at lower cost, although it was slow to be adopted.

Kay's shuttle improved the weaving process but the problem of spinning still remained. In 1738 Lewis Paul of Birmingham developed a device intended to do for spinning what Kay tried for weaving. Technical defects in both Kay's and Paul's inventions, as well as opposition from the spinners and weavers, created difficulties, and it was only in the 1760s that improved versions of these machines came into widespread use.

In 1770 James Hargreaves (?–1778), a weaver and carpenter, patented the *spinning jenny*, which he had developed several years earlier. With this simple machine, a worker could spin up to eight—and, with further improvements, many more—threads at once. The jenny spread rapidly, and by 1788 there were an estimated 20,000 machines in use in England. In 1768, Richard Arkwright (1732–1792), a barber by trade, invented the *water frame*, a device similar to Paul's early spinning machine. The frame required less skill than the jenny but more power than human hands could provide, so that a large installation with water power was needed. In 1771, therefore, Arkwright built a factory that eventually employed some 600 workers, mostly children. The water frame provided a major impetus to the creation of the factory system, its rollers and weights automatically spinning out the yarn at proper tension.

Two additional inventions made it possible for English entrepreneurs to produce cotton fabric on a massive commercial basis. In 1779 Samuel Crompton (1753–1827) invented the *spinning mule*, a steam-powered hybrid of the jenny and the frame that was able to produce high-quality thread. Crompton, a poor weaver, sold his patent rights for a mere £60, although many years later Parliament awarded him a settlement. In the 1780s, when the demand for cotton increased tremendously, Edmund Cartwright (1743–1822), a clergyman, developed a proto-power loom, which could be driven

Spinning mules in an English factory, 1834.

by horse, water, or steam, although it was not widely used until the 1820s.

As cotton factories and the new technology spread, centers that had once been sparsely populated burgeoned into urban communities. The city of Manchester, located in the county of Lancashire, became the first important center of urban industry, having the advantage of water supply, coal deposits, and the nearby port of Liverpool for shipping goods to customers abroad. By the late 1830s, cotton fabric accounted for half of all British exports. Moreover, in order to capture the Indian market entirely, the British made it illegal for Indians to produce cotton textiles, and between 1820 and 1840 exports to India rose from 11 million yards to 145 million yards.

The Industrial Matrix:
Coal, Steam, and Iron

The British textile industry did not grow in a technological vacuum, for advances in factory production were dependent on metal processing to build the machines and on the availability of inexpensive energy to power them. This interdependency can be clearly seen in the development of the coal and iron industries, and the steam engine.

For many centuries the fuel for such tasks as heating, brewing, and firing furnaces had been wood or coal, but by the start of the 18th century English forests were depleted. Yet water power, on which the early industrial revolution had been based, also had its limitations, for the supply of water—and therefore its force—varied with the seasons. Moreover, factories had to be located at particular water sources, which were often far from markets, raw materials, and ports.

Coal, of which Britain had immensely rich deposits, provided a solution to the fuel problem. As the demand for coal increased, however, technical obstacles arose. Deep mining required shafts as deep as 200 feet below the surface, and the extensive networks of underground tunnels needed pumps for removing water and for ventilation. In 1698 Thomas Savery invented his "fire engine," a steam pump consisting of a boiler and a condenser. When the steam condensed, it created a vacuum that collected the water; more steam then forced the water up a pipe to the surface. Although it was a successful if primitive prototype of a steam engine, Savery's pumping device wasted energy. The first effective pumping machine was invented in 1705 by a blacksmith named Thomas Newcomen. Here steam was condensed inside a cylinder housing a piston, which was connected to a cross beam. When the steam condensed, producing a vacuum, the piston was driven down by atmospheric pressure and moved the beam, thus pulling up the pump player attached to the other end. Newcomen's engine was only slightly more efficient, but some 100 of them were in use by 1765 in coal mining, where fuel was cheap.

Newcomen's steam pump increased coal production, but it could be used only for pumping, not for turning wheels, so that it had little application in factories. It was James Watt (1736–1819), a mechanical engineer from Scotland, who succeeded in designing the first steam engine capable of operating factory machinery. He came to his discovery by accident when he was asked to repair one of Newcomen's machines for the University of Glasgow. Realizing the great waste of energy in heating and cooling the cylinder for every stroke, Watt made a simple but important design change: he installed a separate condenser in order to save heat. Watt received a patent for his steam engine in 1769, but continued to improve it. In 1782 he developed an even more effective engine that used the pressure of steam itself, rather than atmospheric pressure.

In perfecting the steam engine, Watt, a mechanical genius, would not have succeeded without the entrepreneurial daring and business sense of Matthew Boulton (1728–1809) of Birmingham. Watt moved to that city—the center of Britain's metal crafts and iron manufacture industry—and developed his invention with Boulton's capital. John Wilkinson, a local weapons maker, and other skilled technicians helped Watt to design further improvements, including a gear mechanism that turned the back and forth motion of the piston into the rotating motion of machine shafts.

Watt's new prime mover, twice as efficient as Newcomen's, was the great breakthrough in the industrial revolution, and intensified the interdependency of the various industrial sectors. The rotation device enabled the steam engine to power new iron industrial machinery as well as coal mining pumps. Its first widespread application was in the cotton factories, the rapid growth of which required both ever larger quantities of coal and more machines. In turn, the increased demand for steam engines and the machinery they powered provided the impetus behind the takeoff of the British iron industry and machine tools.

The manufacture of iron, however, faced technological problems of a different sort. The steam engine enabled the blast furnaces used in iron smelting to achieve higher temperatures—an important factor in determining the kind of fuel that could be used and, as a result, the purity of the iron. In smelting, the fuel was burned together with the iron ore. Coal could not be used for this purpose because its impurities mixed with and contaminated the iron. Consequently, charcoal, with less impurities, had always been used to smelt iron ore. This presented another problem, however, because charcoal was made from wood, which was becoming scarce and expensive. The first breakthrough was achieved by Abraham Darby (1678?–1717), who founded the Bristol Iron Company in 1708 and the next year succeeded in using coke—coal from which most of the gases have been removed—to smelt iron ore. In 1784, Henry Cort (1740–1800) took the process another major step forward with his "puddling process." As fuel for this method of melting and mixing the ore Cort used coke. In addition, iron made by the puddling process had a greater purity.

Once England's plentiful supply of coal could be used as a source of fuel for smelting, the iron industry began to expand. Other innovations followed quickly. Cort himself designed the rolling mill, which eliminated the need for ironmasters to beat the semi-molten iron into industrial shapes and thereby dramatically increased productivity while lowering costs. In 1815, James Neilson overcame the last obstacle to the unfettered use of coal with his "hot blast" process, which eventually enabled coal instead of coke to be used in smelting. This, in turn, produced a critical need for cheap transportation, a problem solved between 1770 and 1800 by the extensive network of canals built by the British.

FROM COTTAGE TO FACTORY: THE GROWTH OF INDUSTRIAL CAPITALISM

Until the industrial revolution introduced the factory system, textile manufacturing had been largely a rural affair, an important offshoot of the peasant economy.

The rise of the factory toward the end of the 18th century transformed not only the system of production and the pattern of daily life for millions of workers, but the size and appearance of Europe's cities. Moreover, the large amounts of investment capital required to build the industrial system created a new form of capitalist enterprise and altered the relationship between business, finance, and government. It also expanded the distance between worker and management.

The Cottage System

Traditionally, poor farmers added to their incomes by processing, spinning, and weaving linen, wool, and later cotton cloth in their homes. All members of the peasant family—husbands, wives, children, and grandparents—participated in the various stages of the work. The cloth thus produced was not intended for domestic consumption, but for commercial markets. This so-called "cottage industry" spread widely in the 18th century, especially as unemployment increased as a result of population growth in the countryside.

The link between the peasant workers and the marketplace was provided by the merchant middlemen, who operated the "putting out" system as primitive capitalists. The merchants provided (or "put out") the raw wool to the peasant families, who worked it in their cottages with simple hand tools that included combing brushes, washing and dyeing vats, spinning wheels, and looms. The labor itself was generally divided along gender lines, with women and children processing the raw wool and spinning the thread and the men weaving the cloth. The workers received payment by the piece from the merchant, who traveled from village to village to put out the raw material and collected the finished product, which he then sold at regional marketplaces.

The cottage industry of the preindustrial age was a complete production unit. Here an Irish family works flax into cloth.

An illustration from Gustav Doré and Blanchard Jerrold's *London* (1872) showing crowded conditions in a working-class neighborhood.

Enterprising peasants occasionally altered the merchant-worker relationship. Some would buy their own raw wool and then sell the finished cloth to the merchants for a higher profit than the wages would bring, while others in effect acted as subcontractors, putting out the wool or thread to other peasant families. Because the slower spinning process could not keep up with the weaving, unmarried aunts, female cousins, and widows—"spinsters"—were often hired to work additional spinning wheels.

Cottage industry became a vital part of the British rural economy, but was not without its problems. Merchant-worker relations varied according to local practice and custom, and the distribution of the process across the countryside prevented the adoption of standardized procedures or quality control, so that the final product varied greatly. Since cloth making was a secondary occupation for most peasants, who worked long, hard hours tilling the soil, they were not inclined to keep to production quotas. Quantity remained low and, especially after cotton came into vogue, could not keep up with the rising demand.

The Rise of the Factory

The textile industry was the first sector to be affected by the factory system in a major way, but in all industries conversion to factory production was slow, both because of the enormous capital required and worker resistance to the machines and the work environment outside the home. It was also impossible before the age of Watt, cheap iron, and machine tools.

At first, most factories remained modest in size and number. In 1782, Manchester had only two cotton mills, while 20 years later the city boasted 52. In the late 1830s, by which time there were 100,000 power looms operating in England, Manchester had the largest cotton factories, which employed an average of 300 workers each. Between 1800 and 1850, the city's population rose from some 75,000 to more than 300,000.

The growth in population had reduced the scarcity of labor by the end of the 18th century. Nevertheless, though rural laborers were attracted by the higher pay, they moved to the urban factories with some reluctance, and only during periods of unemployment. Indeed, most factory equipment required little or no skill or muscle to operate, and many of the early factory workers seem to have been drawn from the unskilled urban classes. Only later, in the first decades of the next century, did large-scale migration from the countryside to the cities take place.

The concentration of labor under one roof and the new machinery not only increased productivity, but brought an entirely different mode of work and labor organization. "Factory discipline" was imposed on the independent-minded workers who, especially in the countryside, had controlled their own work pace, schedules, and leisure time. Time, once measured by the rising and setting of the sun for rural laborers, was now determined by precise rules laid down by employers. Most factories had bell towers, and later clocks, over their entrances to control the rhythm of life for industrial workers. Starting before sunrise, often at 5:30 A.M., factory employees usually worked for twelve to fourteen hours, and sometimes more, until British factory legislation in the 1840s lowered the workday to ten hours. Workers who arrived late were either locked out or fined.

Women and children were widely employed in coal mines because they were cheaper and less troublesome.

Factory conditions were inflexible, grueling, and dangerous. The long hours and monotony of tasks often led workers to fall asleep or collapse, and the incidence of industrial accidents was high, especially among children. Extremes of temperature from summer to winter, together with high humidity, filth, and polluted air, made the factories unhealthy places for workers. Foremen controlled the discipline inside the factories, imposing fines and layoffs on unruly or slack workers and sometimes meting out physical punishment. During the 19th century, such harsh working conditions were exposed and criticized by social reformers and government investigators, but improvements came slowly (see Part VII, Topic 13).

In the factories, as in the cottage, work was divided according to gender and age. Men did not only the heavier tasks, but were usually assigned the more skilled technical work. Women and children, on the other hand, were relegated to the simpler, repetitive work. In the early stages of the industrial revolution the majority of factory workers were women and children—indeed, even in the late 19th century, women continued to represent some 30 to 40 percent of the industrial workforce. Employers paid women and children less than men, and preferred them because of the assumption that they would conform more easily to discipline. Often workers secured employment for their entire family in the same factory. The division of labor into specialized tasks speeded up productivity and required less worker training. Artisans and skilled craftsmen who were drawn to the factories in hard times resented this simplification of the production process, but when they protested they were usually replaced with women and children (see Part VII, Topic 6).

INDUSTRIALIZATION AND THE EUROPEAN ECONOMY

Although industrialization proceeded slowly, it changed the means of production, the lives of workers, and the general European economy so radically that it has been called a "revolution." In those industries that it affected, productivity increased at an ever-accelerating pace, and in the first half of the 19th century industrialization spread from England to parts of continental Europe.

Industrialization proved to be particularly sensitive to political developments. Periods of war and peace, as well as government tariff regulation, affected markets and prices. Such fundamental transformation destabilized long-established social arrangements and intensified the impact of business and financial cycles on the immediate lives of ordinary people.

The Pace of Industrialization in Great Britain

At the end of the Napoleonic Wars, three-fourths of the population of Europe continued to earn their living from agriculture, and some 90 percent of the world's energy was still generated by human or animal muscle. Even in England, where industrialization was most advanced, two-thirds of the people lived and worked in rural areas. There, as late as 1815, more spinning was being done by hand than by machinery, and half the cotton mills were still powered by water. It was not until the 1820s that England developed a full-fledged industrial system.

Production figures for major industrial sectors reveal the pace of British industrialization. The output of pig iron, for example, jumped from a mere 17,000 tons in 1740 to 127,000 in 1786, and then rose to 248,000 in 1806. Thereafter, iron production generally registered steady increases, so that by 1835 it had reached more than 1 million tons, and by 1850 more than doubled to 2.285 million tons. Between 1815 and 1840, the mining of coal doubled, from 16 to 34 million tons a year, and in 1850 had increased to over 50 million. Similarly, the amount of raw cotton consumed by England's textile mills almost doubled every ten years between 1820 and 1850. In 1852, when the cotton consumption figure stood at 336,000 tons, cotton factories contained more than 20 million spindles and employed 500,000 people. By 1840, half of British workers were industrial.

Technological innovations also continued to multiply. The number of patents issued by the British government rose from less than a dozen a year before 1760 to 250 in 1825 alone. Technological innovations, originally developed for particular purposes, were quickly applied to other tasks—the high-pressure steam engine made it possible to power ships and railways, while the cheap iron was used to make bridges, weapons, buildings, and railway tracks.

In 1825 the British built the earliest steam railway that carried passengers; France followed in 1828, Belgium in 1835, and the German Confederation in 1839. The railroads provided a major stimulus to industrial and financial expansion. Private investors made huge fortunes by speculating in railroads, which also stimulated the demand for machinery, engines, and iron. Together with improved roads, canals, and bridges, the railroads created national—and international—markets, speeding up the movement of raw materials and finished goods as well as increasing worker mobility. Railroads made the industrial process itself more efficient, for they linked factories with mines and ports and the countryside with urban centers. British rail construction reached almost 10,000 kilometers by 1850.

By midcentury, Britain had become the wealthiest nation in the West—not only the "workshop of the world," but also its shipper, for it carried a third of the world's trade on its ships. Its output of coal, iron, and textiles exceeded the total production of all other European countries combined. Britain's role as the world's leading industrial power was maintained until late in the 19th century.

The Expansion of Industrialism

The industrial revolution spread to a number of other European states during the early part of the century. On the whole, industrialization moved more slowly on the Continent than it had in Britain, and it varied widely from country to country because of differences in social mobility, political cohesiveness, and resources. Moreover, most continental societies faced greater resistance to industrialism from traditional values. Nevertheless, industrial development began to transform Europe in the 1830s.

Belgium, which had won its independence from the Netherlands in 1830, led the way. The small country had coal and iron deposits of its own as well as a long tradition of textile manufacturing and trade with Britain. Moreover, its entrepreneurs readily received English technological innovations. The British machine firm of Cockerill, which had a factory branch in Belgium early in the industrial revolution, sold machinery and steam engines to neighboring countries. France, the German Confederation, Russia, and even Sweden outproduced Belgium in charcoal pig iron, but between 1815 and 1850 Belgium mined more coal than they did. The new nation-state planned and built its railroads with lines linking it to France, the German Confederation, and the Netherlands. In 1840,

The Stockton-Darlington Railway opened in England in 1825.

Engraving of a steelworks in Paris in 1800.

10 percent of its population of 4 million were industrial workers, making Belgium the first industrialized country on the Continent.

France ranked as the major industrial power on the Continent throughout the first half of the 19th century, second only to Britain in iron and textile production. Its familiarity with technology dated to the late 18th century, when drawings and entries on traditional machines and industrial processes were published in Diderot's *Encyclopedie*. Napoleon had encouraged scientific inquiry and technological experimentation, and by 1810 the Creusot works were using coke for iron smelting. Lille in northeastern France contained rich coal and iron deposits, and it was there that much of the country's industry developed.

Under the liberal monarchy of Louis Philippe after 1830, private business received some encouragement and support. Railways, roads, and canals were built and improved with capital from private banks. Along with cotton mills in Normandy and Alsace, France also had an important silk manufacturing center at Lyon, and almost doubled its cotton and iron production between 1830 and 1850. Moreover, by midcentury the country had more steam engines than the

rest of continental Europe combined. Despite such gains, however, the Prussians were already generating more horsepower, and although more than a million French workers were employed in large-scale industries, half of all Parisian workers—where a total of 400,000 were employed by midcentury—were still in small preindustrial shops.

The German states, which after unification became Europe's new industrial giant in the late 19th century, were hampered by political division. The Prussians took the lead in trying to overcome this disability by eliminating all internal tariffs within their borders in 1818. More important for long-range development, Prussia advanced the 1834 tariff union, which included most of the important German states and did much to increase trade and industry. The coming of the railroads in the mid-1830s was the major factor in sparking industrialization, for a common market was of little use without cheap transportation. The Prussian industrialist August Borsig manufactured locomotives outside Berlin with the support of the future King Friedrich Wilhelm IV, and, between 1835 and 1850, German railway lines grew from 6 to almost 6000 kilometers—half of which were in Prussia alone. The German states had laid the foundations for becoming a center of the continental network of transport and distribution.

The German Confederation was rich in mineral resources, but its early industries imported much of their iron from the French region of Lorraine. German coal and iron mines in the Ruhr, the Saar, and in Silesia were first developed in the 1830s. In the Ruhr a coal merchant named Franz Haniel had pioneered deep shaft mining and then expanded into manufacturing. The firm of Friedrich Krupp (1787–1826), founded in 1810, developed iron and machine factories in Essen in the same period, although at the time the company first used steam engines in the 1840s, it employed less than 200 people. The Krupp Works later went into armaments manufacturing. Nevertheless, during the first half of the 19th century the German states lagged behind France and Russia in pig iron production and were only slightly ahead of Belgium in coal mining. Despite such limited beginnings, before the achievement of national unification in 1870–1871 the Germans had begun to challenge Britain's industrial supremacy.

Instability and Crises in the European Economy

During the first years of the industrial revolution, the profit margin was extremely high in Britain for those enterprises that did not fail, for although wages rose steadily, prices for food and manufactured goods had kept ahead of them. The Napoleonic Wars had helped to create an artificial demand for arms and other industrial goods, but this situation collapsed in 1815 with the coming of peace. Prices dropped, reducing profit and investment. The results were especially harsh for the working class. Some 300,000 veteran soldiers were suddenly added to the labor market. To make matters worse, in 1815 the powerful landowners had secured passage of restrictionist tariffs on grain, known as the Corn Laws. This legislation increased the cost of food and kept it high, thereby reducing spending power for manufactured goods. Across the English Channel, where the economy had been artificially sustained by Napoleon's Continental System, the end of hostilities brought similar distress, with conditions in southern Italy possibly the worst in Europe.

The European economy recovered temporarily in 1820. Britain established its currency on the gold standard and good harvests drove down the price of food. But the rapid expansion of industry in the early 1820s led to uncontrolled speculation and a bust. For the next several decades, economic depressions and bad harvests followed each other in succession in 1825–1826, 1838–1839, and 1846–1847.

The response from manufacturers was to keep profits up by cutting costs. Despite the periods of eco-

nomic crisis, real wages for British workers had risen during most of the first half of the 19th century, and it was in the area of wages that the savings came. The lowering of wages, the extension of factory work hours and discipline, and cyclical unemployment constituted a general trend in labor-management relations. Factory owners also redoubled their efforts to introduce labor-saving devices, expecting that increased mechanization would reduce production costs.

WORKERS, MACHINES, AND LABOR PROTEST

As machines found their way into more and more factories and industrial sectors, their impact on the lives of workers became more evident. To the workers themselves it was clear that technology and factory production represented elements of a new economic system that would deeply alter their daily lives. The response came in the form of a radical worker movement that sought to destroy the machine and hold back the tide of what they regarded as the increasing repression of the industrialists.

The Machine and the Worker

The factory system was a social institution of major significance as well as a unit of production. As we have seen, workers who took employment in factories during the industrial revolution experienced a degree of regimentation unknown in agrarian society.

As the major component in the factory system, machines were central to the work process. Their introduction caused a serious psychological impact on those operating them. Machine technology created a routine of monotonous dehumanization, in which the workers were removed from what had once been a creative process over which they had exercised control. Now, for the sake of greater productivity and cheap consumer goods, laborers would lose control over their own labor.

Nor were workers themselves alone in seeing the problem of technology in these terms. In 1819, a report issued by inspectors of the Prussian government observed that:

> Factory owners . . . have become accustomed to consider the productive workers and their subordinates and children to be incidental appendages to the machines, and that it is sufficient for them . . . that their bodies go through the appropriate motions.[1]

In 1832 Charles Babbage (1792–1871), who invented a primitive form of the computer, argued in *On*

---

[1] Quoted from John R. Gillis, *The Development of European Society, 1770–1870* (Boston: Houghton Mifflin Company, 1977), 163.

Economy of Machines and Manufactures that the principles of mathematical precision and the calculating machine could be applied to the factory system.

Some workers of the early 19th century saw the machine as a means of restructuring social relations between the working class and the property-owning middle class to their disadvantage. They realized that layoffs and lower wages were the result of machine-based industry. As one historian has observed, "people at the point of production were the first to comprehend the full significance of the first Industrial Revolution."[2]

The Luddites and Labor Resistance

Workers were no mere passive observers of the process of mechanization. Indeed, as early as the Middle Ages there had been examples of workers who took action to oppose the introduction of new machinery. In 1753, the home of John Kay was destroyed by spinners protesting his flying shuttle. Similarly, Hargreaves' spinning jennies and Arkwright's water frame had also been subject to industrial sabotage by workers.

The most celebrated incident in the movement to smash machines took place in 1811, when stocking knitters in Nottingham began protesting wage cuts. Calling themselves followers of the mythical Ned Ludd, the "Luddites" organized themselves into groups of 50 or so men and wrecked knitting frames with heavy hammers and metal pikes. In January 1812, after the passage of a law making machine breaking an offense punishable by hanging, the Luddites issued a statement from "Ned Ludd's Office, Sherwood Forest," declaring their intention to continue their operations. That year the movement spread to the woolen trade and cotton towns, where William Cartwright's factory was attacked. In all, perhaps as many as 1000 mills were destroyed in the Nottingham area, and some factory owners killed.

The British authorities saw the Luddite movement as a plot against the government and an "insurrection of poor against the rich." A parliamentary committee investigating the uprisings agreed to the use of troops, despite the eloquent appeal of the English poet Lord Byron (1788–1824) in the House of Lords that the machine breakings "have arisen from circumstances of the most unparalleled distress." In January 1813, 17 Luddites were hanged in York. Although the machine breaking continued sporadically over the next several years, including a major incident near Manchester as late as 1829, the movement was eventually crushed.

Later, the Luddites were viewed as irrational primitives intent on holding back progress. More recently, however, some historians have concluded that these workers were not against technology as such, but rather against the social changes that the new technology reinforced. Along with their violent assaults on the factories and machines, the Luddites issued rational statements about wages, market conditions, and other technical issues that affected their livelihoods. In a period when trade unions were outlawed as conspiracies by association, the Luddite movement constituted a form of organized protest against employers and their efforts to replace labor with machines in order to lower costs of production. Against this desperate but deliberate campaign, in which machine breaking was not just a tactic but the central purpose, later critics devised what has been called "an ideology of technological progress" which regarded machines as both inevitable and essential to human welfare.

The Luddites in England were not an isolated case. Throughout the 19th century, similar worker movements incorporated machine breaking in their labor tactics in other countries, including those of the silk weavers in Lyon in 1831 and linen weavers in Silesia in 1844. Yet the labor movement was to take quite another direction, especially after the rise of socialist parties and trade unions in the second half of the century. In the plight and the protests of the Luddites, however, there came together the central issue: the human consequences of the industrial revolution.

On one level, the term "industrial revolution" refers to a series of technological innovations between the mid-18th and the early 19th centuries that enabled human beings to produce food and manufactured goods faster, in greater quantity, and more cheaply. The revolution in production was possible because the new machines were made of cheap iron and run by a new form of energy—the use of coal to produce steam power. In industry proper, these advances were applied first to the making of textiles and iron.

In another sense, however, the industrial revolution is associated with a complex set of social and economic changes that transformed European civilization. These changes involved not only population growth, but the way in which millions of ordinary men and women led their daily lives. The shift from the cottage industry to the factory system altered the relationship between worker and work as well as between worker and entrepreneur. The formation of an industrial labor force affected how society was structured and had important implications for gender relations, family structure, and sexuality. The revolution in industry also brought a radical change in how and where people lived, drawing people from country to city, and affecting housing, health, and general living conditions.

For two centuries after the start of the industrial revolution, the West—Europe and the United States—exercised unchallenged economic and political hegemony over

---

[2] David F. Noble, "Present Tense Technology," in *Democracy*, vol. 13 (1983), 10.

the rest of the world. This unique position was due above all to technological achievements and industrialization.

Questions for Further Study

1. What did population growth and agriculture have to do with the industrial revolution?

2. Which were the most important inventions of the industrial revolution? How did one invention stimulate a demand for still more inventions?

3. How did the factory system change labor and social life?

4. By what process did industrialization spread from England to the Continent?

Suggestions for Further Reading

Ashton, Thomas S. *The Industrial Revolution, 1760–1830.* London, 1961.

Chambers, Jonathan D., and G. E. Mingay. *The Agricultural Revolution, 1750–1850.* New York, 1966.

Cipolla, Carlo M., ed. *The Industrial Revolution, 1700–1914.* London, 1973.

Crafts, N. F. R. *British Economic Growth During the Industrial Revolution.* New York, 1986.

Dennis, Richard. *English Industrial Cities of the Nineteenth Century.* Cambridge, MA, 1984.

Henderson, William O. *The Industrial Revolution in Europe.* Chicago, 1961.

Hobsbawm, Eric J. *Industry and Empire.* Harmondsworth, England, 1970.

Landes, David. *The Unbound Prometheus: Technological Change and Industrial Development in Western Europe.* Cambridge, MA, 1969.

Mathias, Peter. *The First Industrial Nation: An Economic History of Britain, 1700–1914.* New York, 1969.

Mokyr, Joel, ed. *The Economies of the Industrial Revolution.* London, 1985.

Perkin, Harold. *The Origin of Modern English Society, 1780–1860.* London, 1969.

Thompson, Edward P. *The Making of the English Working Class.* Harmondsworth, England, 1964.

Topic 3

REVOLUTION IN FRANCE:
LIBERTY, TERROR, REACTION

efore 1789, no one had foreseen anything like the French Revolution, a political and social upheaval so vast in its repercussions as to be judged the most important event in Western history in the modern era.

The Revolution swept away the social system of the Old Regime that had rested on noble privilege (on the Old Regime, see Part VI, Topic 10). Thereafter, feudalism ceased to exist in France while power and influence were opened to those with wealth and ability. The events that took place in France from the late 1780s to the mid-1790s gave shape, through trial and error, to the very concept of "revolution" as a means of solving fundamental political and social problems. It ushered in the age of "mass politics," in which once politically passive social groups, such as the peasantry, workers, women, and the urban poor, now became active participants in the making of history. The revolutionary slogan, "liberty, equality, fraternity," became a permanent part of the Western political vocabulary as the ideal expression of political liberalism.

In France itself, the Revolution gave birth to the nation-state, whose sovereignty was seen not as the will of a divine right king, but as the expression, first, of the nation and then of the people. The new state mobilized and claimed the allegiance of all citizens. Beginning in 1793, citizen soldiers extended these revolutionary ideals, together with French conquest and occupation, beyond the borders of France. The Napoleonic Wars provoked staunch resistance that helped to stimulate nationalism throughout the Continent. In less than a generation, the Revolution profoundly and permanently changed the face of Europe.

THE THIRD ESTATE AND THE "RIGHTS OF MAN"

The Revolution had its distant roots in the underlying social trends that had characterized the Old Regime. In a more immediate sense, however, it came as a result of a fiscal crisis that was mishandled by an inept king and his ministers.

The Calling of the Estates General

By the end of the 18th century, the Seven Years' War and intervention in the American Revolution, together with the high costs of the royal court, had brought the French government to the edge of bankruptcy. When he came to the throne in 1774, King Louis XVI (ruled 1774–1792) had appointed the physiocrat Jacques Turgot (1727–1781) as his finance minister. But Turgot's plan to extract revenue from the nobility, together with the opposition of Queen Marie

Significant Dates

The French Revolution

1774–1793	Louis XVI rules as king of France
May 5, 1789	Estates General meets
June 17, 1789	National Assembly formed
July 14, 1789	Bastille stormed
August 4, 1789	Feudalism abolished
August 26, 1789	Declaration of Rights of Man and Citizen
October 5, 1789	March to Versailles
1790	Civil Constitution of the Clergy
June 1791	Flight to Varennes
April 20, 1792	War against Austria
August 10, 1792	Attack on Tuileries Palace
September 1792	"Massacres" in Paris
January 21, 1793	Louis XVI executed
March 1793	Vendeé uprising begins
June 1793–July 1794	Reign of Terror
October 1793	Marie Antoinette executed
February 4, 1794	Slavery abolished
March 1794	Widespread arrests and executions, including Danton
July 27, 1794	Thermidor
November 1799	Coup by Napoleon Bonaparte

and prelates, to endorse Calonne's measures. The assembly insisted on preserving the basic distinctions between the three social orders. Louis then replaced Calonne with the former archbishop of Toulouse, Loménie de Brienne (1727–1794), hoping that he would be able to convince the stubborn nobility and his fellow clergymen to accept the taxation. Brienne took the tax reform to the Parlement of Paris, the judicial body empowered to approve new laws, but he, too, failed to win the backing of the notables. Instead, Parlement demanded the convocation of the Estates General.

Exasperated by the intransigence of the privileged orders, Louis then declared that royal prerogative alone made the new taxes legal, and ordered the closing of the Parlement. Nobles protested and some of the lawyers from the Parlement stirred up provincial riots. It was, however, the middle-class bankers who forced Louis to capitulate by refusing to lend the government any more money. Finally, in 1788 the king recalled Necker and that August agreed to the demand of the nobles and clergy to call the Estates General.

The Estates General represented the three traditional principal social orders of clergy, nobles, and the Third Estate of peasants, workers, and bourgeoisie. The principles of absolutism had led Louis XVI's predecessors to rule without consulting the Estates General, which had not met since 1614. The convening of the assembly was decisive in the coming of the French Revolution, for it brought the less privileged middle classes into the political process.

Delegates were elected in the winter and spring of 1789. The elections provided an opportunity for a public analysis of national problems, for the delegates circulated lists of ills that reflected regional concerns. Most of these documents, called *cahiers de doléances* (grievance reports), were not statements of revolutionary principle. Rather, they were specific complaints concerning provincial abuses, corruption, and administrative waste. Only in Paris and other principal cities did some of the cahiers reflect such Enlightenment ideas as social justice and legal equality.

As the Estates General prepared to meet, Louis XVI reacted ineptly, attempting unsuccessfully to maneuver between the interests of two increasingly competing social groups, the nobility and the bourgeoisie. The nobles, intent on regaining a role in government and preserving their privileges against the monarchy's encroachments, fully expected to dominate the proceedings. The middle classes, aspiring to share power and status as they grew in wealth and numbers, sought to end the monopoly of special privileges enjoyed by the other two orders; more specifically, the bourgeoisie wanted to be certain that the national debt was not repudiated so that their investments would be safeguarded.

Antoinette (1755–1793), led to his downfall. Most of Turgot's replacements followed the same approach and, as a result, fared no better. Jacques Necker (1732–1804) pushed the government further into debt by borrowing heavily at high interest rates and in 1783 he, too, was dismissed. Charles Alexandre de Calonne (1734–1802), Necker's eventual successor, revived Turgot's plan by proposing a single land tax on the First Estate (the clergy) and the Second Estate (the nobility). Both estates had been largely exempt from direct taxation but together controlled perhaps a third of all French agricultural land and a comparable portion of French income.

In February 1787, Louis XVI called a special Assembly of Notables, consisting mainly of great lords

The opening of the Estates General in May 1789.

The Tennis Court Oath and the National Assembly

Each estate had roughly the same number of representatives, but the Third Estate, led by lawyers and business groups, represented 98 percent of the population of France, including workers and peasants. It asked, therefore, for double the number of representatives and to vote by head—this would have enabled the Third Estate to control the outcome, since some clergy and liberal nobles wished to support reforms. The aristocrats, on the other hand, had demanded that each estate have one vote, which would have given the First and Second Estates the ability to determine all decisions. Persuaded by Necker to make concessions to the Third Estate, the king agreed to double the number of representatives, but did not give in on the issue of voting by head rather than by order. In January 1789 the Abbé Emmanuel Sieyès (1748–1836) published a pamphlet entitled *What Is the Third Estate?*, proclaiming the political agenda of the middle classes in this way: "What is the Third Estate? *Everything.* What has it been in the political order up to the present? *Nothing.* What does it ask? *To become something.*"

When the approximately 1700 deputies (including alternates) gathered at Versailles in May, the hostility of the court was made clear to the delegates of the Third Estate. After the opening ceremonies, each order was assigned its own chamber. Louis' refusal to bend on the voting issue provoked the first major act of revolutionary defiance on the part of the Third Estate, which found another spokesman in the skillful and persuasive politician Honoré Gabriel de Mirabeau (1749–1791), a renegade noble who had won election as a deputy for the Third Estate. On June 17, with Sieyès and Mirabeau to guide it, the Third Estate, along with some clergy, constituted itself as the National Assembly and called upon the other two orders to meet with it as a single body. This prompted the king to act, and the delegates of the Third Estate found themselves locked out of their meeting hall. The outraged deputies gathered instead in a tennis court and swore not to disband until they had written a constitution for France.

The so-called "Tennis Court Oath," taken on June 20, forced the weak-willed monarch to back down again, especially after many of the clergy and liberal nobles joined the middle class. Louis remained indecisive, but at a special session of the Estates General on June 23, he declared that the deputies could discuss constitutional matters only in separate chambers, and warned them not to tamper with the army or property rights. Threatening to dismiss the Estates General if he were not obeyed, he commanded the deputies to separate immediately into the three traditional orders. To the king's aide, who repeated the royal command at the end of the session, Mirabeau is said to have responded for the National Assembly, "Go and tell those who sent you that we are here by the will of the people, and that we will go only if we are driven at the point of the bayonet." On the 27th, the ever-hesitant Louis announced that the three estates would meet together as the National Assembly in order to draft a constitution (the National Assembly later renamed itself the National Constituent Assembly). The king had sanctioned the demise of absolute monarchy in France.

The People and the Revolution

The creation of the National Assembly was the first real revolutionary event, for the inclusion of the middle classes constituted the end of government controlled exclusively by the nobility and the monarchy. Despite the domination of the Third Estate, the National Assembly was a rather conservative body. Its members, drawn from a minority of the French people, were wedded to the protection of property, the maintenance of social order, and the preservation of the monarchy, but they also wanted a role in government decisions that they had lost under absolutism. The summer of 1789, however, saw the entrance of two genuinely revolutionary forces into the already complex political situation—the peasantry of the countryside and the lower classes of the cities. These forces, perceived as a common threat by most of the delegates to the National Assembly, would push the Revolution in a more radical direction.

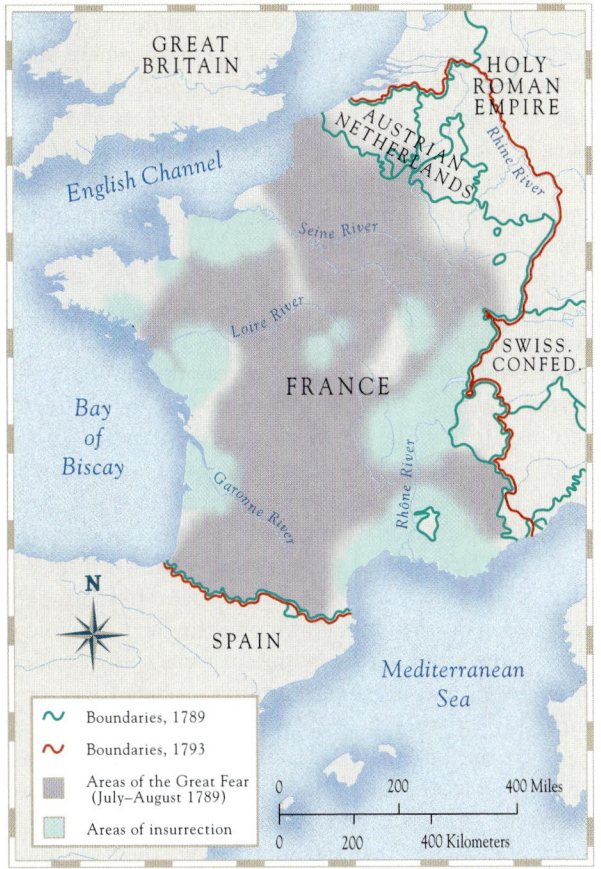

Map 3.1   France in Revolution

The Tennis Court Oath. An oil sketch attributed to Jacques-Louis David depicts the Tennis Court Oath, June 20, 1789.

Food shortages and economic hardship sparked social unrest in the rural regions of France, where farm prices had fallen and taxes had increased during the last 20 years. A disastrous harvest in 1788 had produced severe grain losses and a spiraling rise in the price of bread, the basic staple of most French households. In the countryside the peasants stopped paying taxes and the "seignorial dues" which they had been obliged to render to their landlords, the church, and local nobles since Medieval times. The peasants regarded the local nobility as their enemy. Acts of organized violence erupted as early as May as peasants burned local castles and town halls in order to destroy tax and dues records. In July, these revolts merged with the "Great Fear," a series of panics that swept the countryside. These panics were fueled by rumors that the nobles and their hired brigands were killing peasants and destroying the new crop about to be harvested. As the rural social order deteriorated, peasants sought not only to seize the food they had grown and the land on which they worked, but to destroy the manorial system under which they and their ancestors had suffered for centuries.

In the cities, where food shortages and the increase in bread prices coincided with growing unemployment, demonstrations and riots broke out. In Paris, a city of more than half a million people, the royal government had 5000 troops and police to maintain public order, but as unrest grew, Louis XVI gathered another 20,000 soldiers outside the city. Groups of citizens, consisting mainly of artisans, small shopkeepers, housewives, and wage earners, had been organizing themselves on the ward level ever since the elections to the Estates General. Now, fired by signs that the king was turning against the Revolution, they formed a citizen

militia and attacked barracks in search of weapons. Later the militia became the National Guard, commanded by the Marquis de Lafayette (1757–1834), a liberal and respected hero of the American Revolution. Lafayette designed a flag that combined the red and blue of Paris with the white of the royal family, thus producing the "tricolor."

On July 11, Louis suddenly dismissed Necker, the only nonnoble minister in the government and a man who had been regarded as protector of the people. Parisian crowds, intoxicated by alcoholic beverages and revolutionary oratory, erupted in anger. This insurrection, which was also a food riot, climaxed on July 14 with the storming of the Bastille. Rumor spread that arms were stored in the Bastille, an old fortress used to house special prisoners and defended only by 80 retired soldiers and 30 Swiss guards. When the crowd broke into the courtyard of the Bastille, about 100 citizens were shot and killed. With help from renegade government troops who joined the insurgents with cannon, the fortress surrendered. The enraged mob massacred the commander and several guards, cutting off their heads and parading them through the city on pikes. The fall of the Bastille became a powerful symbol of the unfolding revolution.

The peasant violence and the fall of the Bastille were dramatic evidence of the revolutionary spirit of the common people. Radical delegates in the National Constituent Assembly, heeding the temper of the people, seized the initiative. Late on August 4, an exceptionally hot and humid night, a liberal aristocrat who himself owned no land called upon the nobles and clergy to renounce all their feudal rights and dues. Frightened by the growing disorder in the country, and caught up in the passionate scene, the delegates of the

Map 3.2 Revolutionary Paris

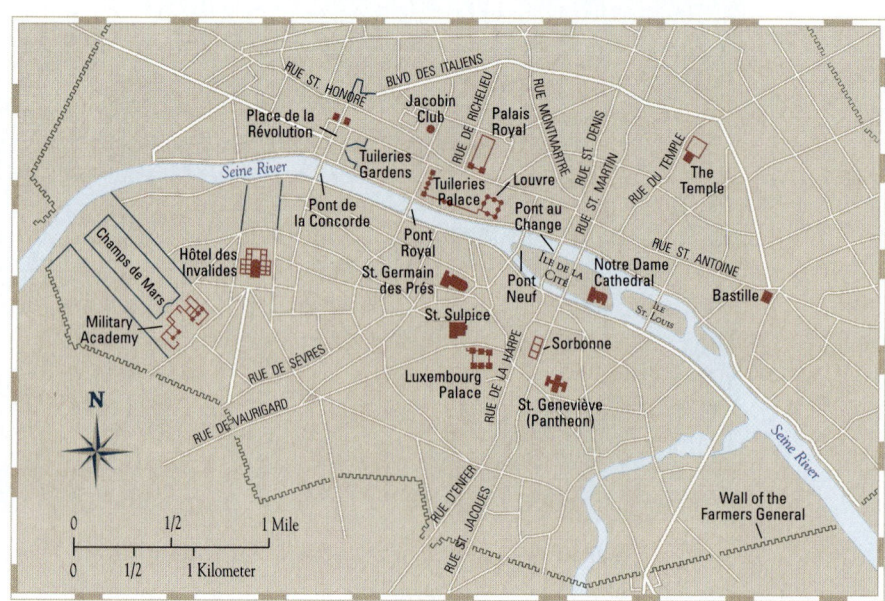

Depart des Heroïnes de Paris pour Versailles le 5 Octobre 1789.

A sketch of the armed women of Paris marching on Versailles, October 5, 1789.

First and Second Estates rose one by one to surrender their ancient privileges. Later, the assembly thought more carefully about what it had done and tempered its action by declaring forms of compensation for lost rents. By the next morning, however, feudalism had been all but eliminated in France.

Later that month, the National Assembly issued a set of general principles on which to base the constitution that it was drafting. The "Declaration of the Rights of Man and of the Citizen," issued on August 27, reflected Enlightenment thought as well as the ideas that had inspired the leaders of the American struggle for independence. Proclaiming that all people were born "free and equal in rights," the document identified "liberty, property, security, and resistance to oppression" as the most important of these rights. Citizens were to enjoy freedom of worship, equal access to public office, and equality before the law, while government was to protect these rights and tax its citizens only according to their income.

The framers of the Declaration assumed that laws and government were the expression of popular will—that is, that "sovereignty" resided in the nation. This assertion was to have important European consequences. In defining political sovereignty in national terms, the Declaration elevated nationalism to a sacred doctrine that, in its extreme form, claimed blind devotion and loyalty. Under the threat of foreign invasion, the doctrine of revolutionary nationalism would succeed in mobilizing millions of Frenchmen.

Popular unrest continued unabated through the fall, despite the Declaration and reform decrees issued by the National Assembly. In Paris the supply of grain from the bad harvest of the previous year had all but run out. Hunger, together with encouragement from radicals and suspicions against Louis XVI and the unpopular Marie Antoinette, aroused the people to action. On the morning of October 5, a large group of housewives demanding bread caused a disturbance at a baker's shop. After being joined by more women from the market, they moved on to the municipal hall, which they ransacked. Eventually a force of several thousand women began marching to Versailles, their ranks swelled along the way. Lafayette followed them with the National Guard. The next day, after a violent skirmish with palace guards, the mob forced Louis, Marie Antoinette, and their son to follow them back to Paris, where they took up residence in the Tuileries. The crowd chanted, "we have the baker, the baker's wife, and the baker's child." A few days later, the National Assembly also moved to Paris. The king had become a virtual prisoner of the Revolution, and the mob could now keep a watchful eye on both the royal family and the National Assembly.

THE ASCENDANCY OF THE MODERATES

In the two years between the Declaration of the Rights of Man and the adoption of the constitution in 1791, the National Assembly governed the nation. Its policies changed France in a number of fundamental ways that reflected the interests and values of the middle classes that dominated the assembly.

Property and the Church

Economic issues were at the center of the assembly's actions. The Declaration of the Rights of Man had stressed that "Property being a sacred and inviolable right, no one can be deprived of it unless a legally established public necessity evidently demands it, under the condition of a just and prior indemnity." Having made private property secure, however, the assembly still had to deal with the huge debt that had brought the royal government into crisis in the first place. Rather than repudiate the debt—which was owed to the middle-class bankers and merchants—the bishop of Autun, Charles Maurice de Talleyrand (1754–1838), proposed another solution. In November 1789 the assembly endorsed his proposal to confiscate and sell off all lands belonging to the Catholic Church.

With the anticipated revenue from the sale of church property as backing, the assembly issued bonds, called *assignats*, to finance the debt, despite urgent warnings from Necker. The assignats were so popular that they were soon used as currency, and the assembly issued even more, thus fueling inflation. Nevertheless, the sale of church land had a long-range stabilizing effect, for it enlarged the number of property owners in France. Buyers of the land, mainly the middle class and the wealthier peasants, were thereby tied more closely to the successful outcome of the Revolution. Petitions from the landless peasantry for the division of the large estates were ignored.

The church found further reason for declaring itself an enemy of the Revolution. The abolition of ecclesiastical tithes and the confiscation of the land made the Catholic Church in France financially dependent on the government. The following July, therefore, the assembly passed the "Civil Constitution of the Clergy," a measure that placed the church under the jurisdiction of the state. The act reduced the 139 bishoprics in France to 83, and parishes and dioceses were redivided into simpler, more uniform units, the latter conforming in territory to the new administrative *départements* into which the assembly had already divided France itself (see below). Priests and bishops were henceforth popularly elected—even by Protestants and Jews—and paid government salaries.

The Civil Constitution, which undermined the independence of the church and the authority of the pope in the most fundamental ways, generated considerable controversy. When it became clear that some bishops and priests would resist, the assembly went even further by requiring the clergy to swear an oath to abide by and support the constitution. Half of all French priests—the more affluent—and most bishops refused to take the oath, earning them the designation of "nonjuring" or "refractory" clergy. The papacy naturally supported the protests of the clergy. With these

and other measures the Revolution had created a rift between the state and the church in France that continued into the next century.

Economic liberalism, together with the interests of the middle classes, influenced the assembly's policies. A number of direct taxes—on land, on income from commerce and manufacturing, and on rents—were voted, but they proved difficult to collect. In order to stimulate trade and business, the assembly abolished internal tariffs and monopolies granted by the crown, and standardized weights and measures by the introduction of the metric system. The old guilds were abolished so as to lift restrictions on professions and crafts, but the assembly passed the so-called Le Chapelier Law (June 14, 1791), which outlawed worker unions and the right to strike in accordance with the principles of 18th-century economic liberalism.

The Constitution of 1791

It was not until September 1791 that the assembly completed the constitution under which France was to be governed. While it did not address all the ills of the Old Regime, the constitution did reflect the theories of Enlightenment reformers who wanted government to be rational, efficient, and just. Local administration was standardized and a simplified judicial system with elected judges and prosecutors introduced. The former patchwork of provincial subdivisions was replaced by 83 départements of roughly equal size, each further subdivided into smaller administrative units in which local assemblies were elected.

The Constitution of 1791 transformed the French government into a limited, rather than an absolute, hereditary monarchy. The king still appointed and dismissed his ministers at will, but the power to legislate was invested in a body called the Legislative Assembly, chosen by indirect election. The king could temporarily veto its measures, although the Legislative Assembly could override the royal veto by approving a bill in three successive assemblies. No one who had served in the National Assembly was permitted to participate in the new body, with the result that its members were more radical and less experienced.

The Constitution was by no means a radical democratic document. The Declaration of the Rights of Man had proclaimed that all citizens were free and equal, but the right to vote was limited in a number of important ways. The population was divided into two categories, "active" and "passive," a distinction based on wealth. Only French males who were 25 years of age or older, and who paid taxes equivalent to three days' wages, had the franchise. A voluntary tax also enabled a passive citizen to become an active one. These men voted for electors, who in turn chose the deputies.

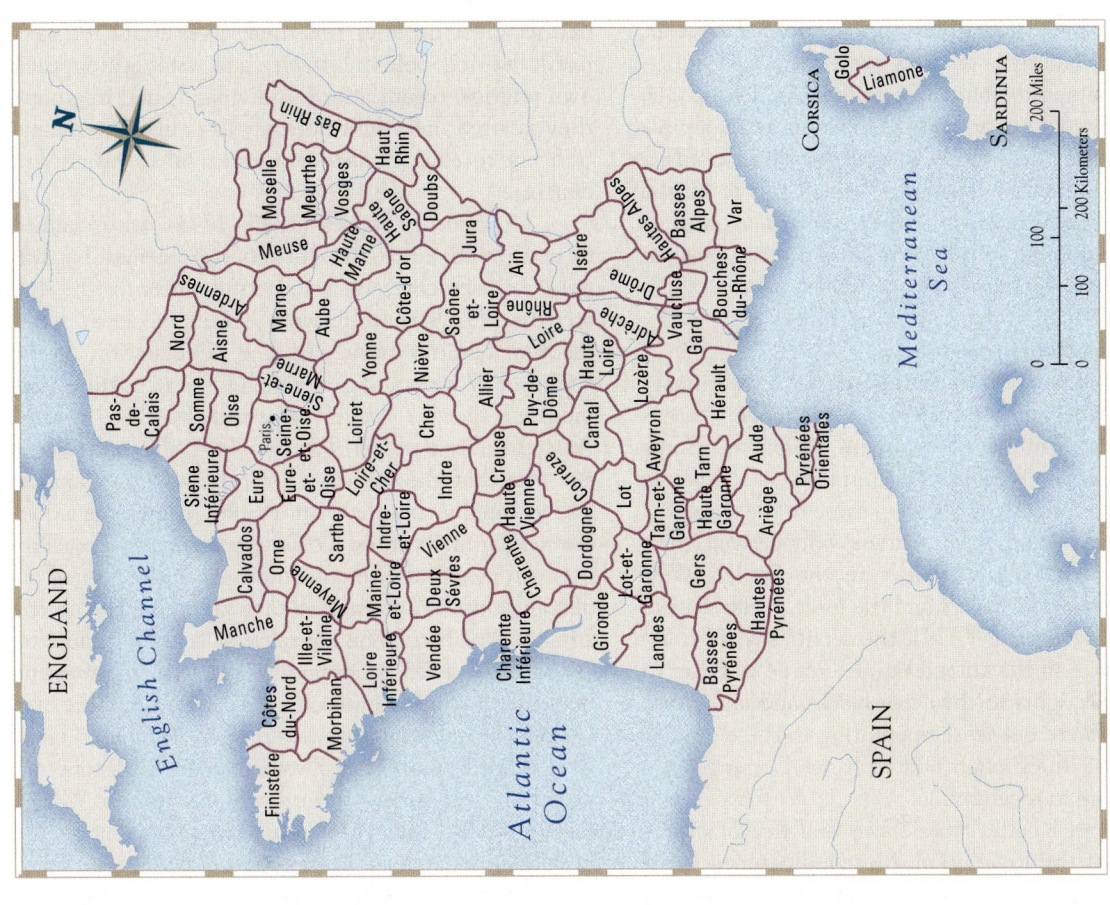

AFTER 1789

BEFORE 1789

Map 3.3   Administrative Changes in France

Higher income qualifications were required of electors, and deputies had to be property owners.

Of the approximately 26 million French people, 4.25 million could vote, only 50 thousand were eligible to serve as electors, and even fewer as deputies. This formula of limited male suffrage, which was to be the pattern of European constitutions throughout most of the 19th century, essentially placed political power in the hands of men of property.

Women and Minorities

The status of women and minorities in revolutionary France provides further evidence of the moderate outlook of the National Constituent Assembly. Some deputies had, for example, argued in favor of abolishing slavery, but economic interests—those of the shipowners, merchants, and sugar refiners who derived their profits from the sugar colonies in the French West Indies—prevailed. Slavery and the trade in slaves were preserved. In September 1791, the deputies voted to allow assemblies in the colonies to determine whether to give political rights to their free blacks and mulattoes. The results were deeply disappointing to these groups, and in Haiti, the French part of Santo Domingo, the blacks rose up in rebellion.

Jews fared better than slaves and free blacks at the hands of the Revolution. Most Enlightened monarchs had taken steps to integrate Jews into the state in the 18th century, but in France their status varied from region to region. The National Assembly had first debated Jewish rights as part of efforts to define "active citizenship" for voting purposes, but without result. In January 1790, an exception was made for the Jews of Bordeaux, Bayonne, and Provence, whose economic status and social contacts enabled them to claim "élite" status among their people. Some Parisian Jews, rigorous supporters of the Revolution, then succeeded in securing the endorsement of voters for emancipation from most of the city's districts. In September 1791 the assembly passed a law enfranchising all Jews.

As we have seen, women played an active role in some of the leading events of the Revolution. Yet the Declaration of the Rights of Man was just that—a document that proclaimed civil equality among men. The Enlightenment philosophes had been divided on the question of women's rights. A few, such as the Marquis Marie Jean de Condorcet (1743–1794), supported the "admission of women to the rights of citizenship" on the basis of natural rights; most either ignored the issue or, like Rousseau, saw women as childbearers and incapable of participating in public affairs.

Frenchwomen, inspired by the ideals of the Revolution, seized the initiative by taking their demands into the streets, presenting their arguments before the National Assembly (to which they could neither elect deputies nor themselves stand for election), writing political tracts, and establishing their own political organizations. Individually and in groups, they asserted their right not only to political participation but to education, to property, and to equality in marriage.

Olympe de Gouges (1748–1793), who claimed to be the illegitimate daughter of a nobleman but was raised by a butcher, was a successful writer for the theater. In 1791, she wrote what became a classic statement of feminist principles, the "Declaration of the Rights of Woman and the French Citizen," deliberately modeled on the document issued by the National Assembly (see Part VII, Topic 6). In it, she underscored the fact that the framers of the original Declaration had violated revolutionary principles by creating a double standard in politics. De Gouges argued that equality between men and women conformed to the natural order, and urged all women to take an active part in the struggle for liberty. She appealed to Marie Antoinette, "mother and wife," to assume leadership in the women's movement, a mistake which later caused her to be executed as a royalist sympathizer. In 1792, de Gouges' views were echoed by an Englishwoman, Mary Wollstonecraft (1759–1797), in her *Vindication of the Rights of Women* (see Part VII, Topic 6). Basing her argument on the Enlightenment belief in reason, Wollstonecraft chastised the framers of the Constitution of 1791 for limiting the rights of citizenship to men and lectured them that women were equal to men as rational beings. She replied in detail to Rousseau's position on female inferiority, stressing the need for educational equality.

Between 1790 and 1793, legislation partially corrected what the Declaration of the Rights of Man had ignored. Illegitimate children and their mothers were now able to sue fathers for support, and the ancient system of primogeniture was abolished by giving all children the right to inherit equally. New laws enabled wives as well as husbands to seek legal remedy in divorce, while another law permitted civil marriage and lowered the age of legal consent for women to 21. Despite these gains, the Jacobin leaders, inspired by Rousseau, did not admit women to the category of "active" citizens.

THE RADICALS IN POWER: THE REIGN OF TERROR

Within two years of the meeting of the Estates General, the social order and political structure of France had been radically changed. Yet this period represented only the first, more moderate phase of an ongoing revolutionary process. The upheaval grew more extreme over the next several years as conservative opponents, whose world of privilege, monarchy, and tradition had collapsed, and radical patriots, who felt that change had not gone far enough, pressed the Revolution from both sides. Meanwhile, the Revolution also aroused active opposition from the conservative powers of Europe, especially Austria and Prussia.

Revolution Within a Revolution

The crisis of the Revolution had actually begun as a result of a failed effort by Louis XVI to leave the country. Escape plans had been under way ever since October 1789, when the royal family had been forced to leave Versailles and move to Paris. In June 1791, Louis XVI, encouraged by French emigrés, attempted to flee with his family to Belgium but was caught at Varennes and brought back to the capital. Louis, who had maintained secret contacts with monarchist supporters in the National Assembly as well as with emigré nobles and the Austrian government, had thus proven himself an enemy of the Revolution.

The constitution that was then being drafted rested on the premise of a monarch committed to the constitution. Louis' actions had the effect, therefore, of undermining the document even before it was adopted. The king's capture, together with radical threats against the monarch, drew a sharp reaction from abroad. On August 27, 1791, Emperor Leopold II (ruled 1790–1792) of Austria (Marie Antoinette's brother) and King Friedrich Wilhelm II (ruled 1786–1797) of Prussia issued the Declaration of Pillnitz, in which they threatened to intervene in France if the royal family or the monarchy were in danger. Both radicals and moderates began clamoring for war against these external enemies of the Revolution.

The flight to Varennes aroused the ire of the Parisian radicals, who condemned the king as a traitor to the Revolution. The moderates in the assembly, on the other hand, had been weakened by the death of Mirabeau. They spread the story that the king, whom they regarded as a force for stability, had been kidnapped. Indeed, the split between radicals (the "left") and moderates (the "right")—the terms *left* and *right* derived from the seating arrangements in the assembly—had grown sharper ever since 1789. For some time the radicals had been organizing political clubs through which to discuss and spread their ideas. The most influential of them, the Jacobin Club (which took its name from its meeting place, the former St. Jacques monastery of Dominican friars, who were known as Jacobins), consisted chiefly of educated members of the Third Estate such as the physician-turned-journalist

Jean Paul Marat (1743–1793) and the lawyer Georges-Jacques Danton (1759–1794). The views of the Jacobins, who corresponded with branches in the provinces, grew increasingly radical. The political clubs provided opportunities for leadership, maintained contact with the deputies, and explained the actions of the assembly to the people. The Jacobins gained control of the municipal government of Paris and began to forge an alliance with the common people of the city. Now, in the face of Louis' attempt to flee, they insisted that France needed a republic instead of a monarchy. An influential radical press controlled by members of these clubs, chief of which was Marat's *L'Ami du Peuple* (*Friend of the People*), incited the Parisians.

The more radical Legislative Assembly elected in 1791 pushed through laws against the noble emigrés and the refractory clergy and spearheaded the call for a declaration of war against Austria, which was passed on April 20, 1792. Soon France was at war with Prussia as well. Over the king's veto, the Legislative Assembly voted to create a force of 20,000 national guardsmen to defend Paris.

The war, depicted at home as a crusade against the enemies of the Revolution, started out poorly. A Prussian army repelled the French troops and pushed their way across the border. Proclaiming the nation to be in mortal danger, the assembly pleaded for citizen volunteers. From abroad, the duke of Brunswick, the Prussian commander, announced on July 15 that he would take any action, including the destruction of Paris itself, in order to prevent harm from befalling the royal family.

Brunswick's threat both energized the spirit of resistance and emboldened the radicals. On August 10, the communal leaders of the capital staged an uprising that changed the course of the Revolution. A large crowd, angry at the king's attempt to escape, broke into the Tuileries. While the Parisians fought a bloody battle with the king's Swiss guard, Louis and Marie Antoinette fled to the Legislative Assembly for safety. The wrath of the people frightened the deputies, and after suspending the king's powers, many of them left the city. Parisian militants forced those deputies who stayed behind to schedule elections to a new body, known as the National Convention, and to dissolve the Legislative Assembly.

Jacobins, Sans-culottes, and the National Convention

In the aftermath of the dethroning of Louis XVI, the Revolution faced three serious problems: a dangerous and expanding war, deepening economic crisis, and the growing anxieties of the Parisian masses. To these dangers were soon added a royalist uprising and a widening factional division within the ranks of the Jacobins.

Under these combined pressures, the temper of the Revolution accelerated and reached its most extreme form in the "Reign of Terror" that engulfed France.

The majority of deputies elected to the Legislative Assembly had originally called themselves royalists or constitutionalists, but leadership soon passed into the hands of two radical groups that emerged out of the Jacobin Club—the Girondists and the Mountain. A group of deputies around Jacques Brissot (1754–1793) and the philosophe Condorcet, known as Girondists, after the region of France from which many had come, formed a fiery cadre of brilliant orators. The Girondists had supported the war and extreme measures against the nobles and the clergy, but they began to draw back from popular violence and feared that the radicalization of the Parisian masses would result in anarchy. The Girondists were soon forced out of the Jacobin Club by more extremist radicals.

In early September 1792, as Paris was rife with rumors of counterrevolutionary plots, common citizens unleashed a startling massacre. Crowds of workers, shopkeepers, and artisans stormed the prisons, from which it was believed that thousands of royalists would break out in the event of foreign invasion. Popular courts were improvised and in ritual fashion they condemned and brutally ordered the executions of more than 1000 prisoners, many of whom were common criminals and prostitutes. These "September Massacres," for which no rational explanation can be adduced, set the tone for the next two years of the Revolution.

News of a French victory at Valmy on September 20 helped to calm the atmosphere of tension in Paris. The National Convention, elected on the basis of universal male suffrage, met for the first time the following day. Among its deputies was a group of extremist Jacobins elected from Paris that included Danton, who had helped to incite the storming of the Tuileries; Marat, who had cheered on the September Massacres; and Maximilien de Robespierre (1758–1794), who became the principal architect of the terror that was to come.

These men formed a nucleus of radical Parisian Jacobins known as the "Mountain," so-called because its members sat high up in the chamber of the convention. The Mountain believed the war would consolidate support at home for radical domestic measures against the counterrevolution. The Girondists outnumbered the Mountain, but Robespierre and his colleagues quickly learned to outmaneuver opponents with help from the crowds of Paris. The Mountain and the Girondists, who attacked each other with increasing bitterness, were soon locked in a deadly battle for control of the convention and the support of the several hundred deputies in the center, known as the Plain.

Neither group, however, represented an organized party with consistent ideas.

The fate of Louis XVI was the first major issue over which the Mountain and the Girondists fought their struggle for mastery of the Revolution. As one of its first acts, the convention abolished the monarchy and declared France a republic. But what was to be done with the deposed king? While the Girondists sought to spare Louis, the Mountain demanded his execution. In the trial that took place in December, the Mountain prevailed. Louis XVI was found guilty by an overwhelming margin, although he was then condemned to death by a vote of 361 to 360. He was beheaded by guillotine on January 21, 1793. Marie Antoinette's turn followed in October, after a trial in which her allegedly promiscuous sexual conduct formed part of the charges against her.

The leaders of the Mountain, men skilled in oratory and the manipulation of popular sentiment, had understood from the beginning that the radicalization of the Revolution was the result of direct action by the common people of Paris—the *sans-culottes*, or people "without breeches," so-called because, unlike the aristocrats who wore knee breeches, the working populace wore long trousers. In the sans-culottes the Mountain recognized a unique political force that, if properly guided and manipulated, could be used as an avenue to power. Since the fall of 1789, men like Danton and

An anonymous portrait of Robespierre.

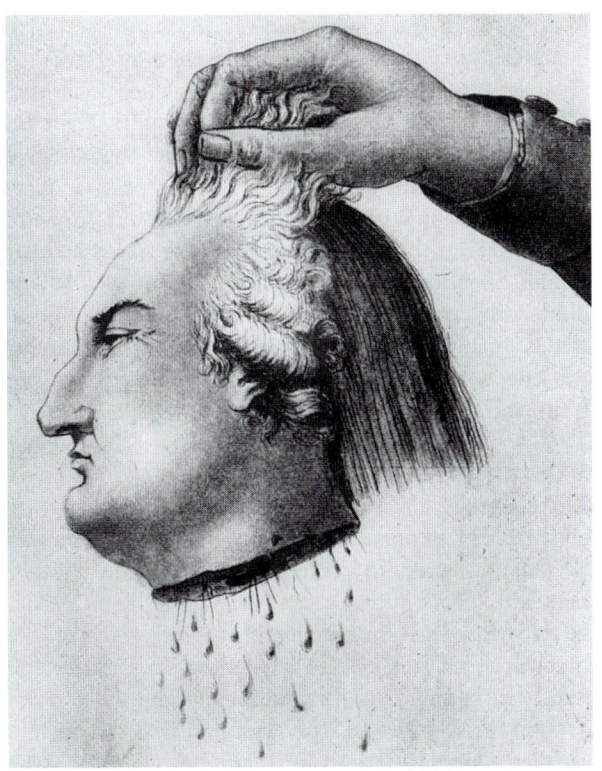

The head of Louis XVI shown to the monarchs of Europe.

promised to export. The conflict, with frequent changes in alliances and brief periods of peace, dragged on for the next 20 years.

In the offensive launched by Austria and Prussia in 1793, French troops suffered serious reverses after initial victories. In March their commander, General Charles Dumouriez, defected to the enemy. Unrest at home worsened the crisis. The convention voted to impose a military draft, just as food riots erupted once again in Paris. That same month the peasants of the Vendée, in western France, rose in revolt against the Parisian leaders of the anticlerical Revolution. In the spring and summer, Lyon, Marseilles, and Bordeaux followed suit. In all cases, royalist agitators channeled local discontent into counterrevolutionary insurrections.

The Mountain and the sans-culottes drove the convention into action to deal with these challenges. In March "surveillance" committees were set up in towns and villages to crush counterrevolutionaries. The following month saw the establishment of the twelve-member Committee of Public Safety, which functioned as the executive branch of government. The committee was quickly dominated by Robespierre and his fellow

Robespierre had been encouraging the Parisian masses with their democratic rhetoric. In the National Constituent Assembly and the Legislative Assembly, they had railed against the moderates for their pro-royalist position and the economic problems that beset the nation; now, in the National Convention, they continued to play to the crowds, charging the Girondists with responsibility for the continuing economic hardships and chronic food shortages. Over the next year and half, the Mountain regarded the sans-culottes as its constituency, implementing extremist policies in their name and, in turn, being goaded on by them to impel the Revolution further.

The Jacobins in Power

The National Convention came into being as the fate of the Revolution hung in the balance. A week after the execution of the king, the convention declared war on Great Britain. By April, revolutionary France was also at war with Austria, Prussia, the Netherlands, Spain, and Piedmont-Sardinia. At stake, however, were not the traditional issues of power politics. In December 1792 the convention had proclaimed its intention of helping the other peoples of Europe to free themselves from the tyranny of kings and the oppression of the Old Regime. The monarchs of Europe responded, therefore, not only to French military aggression, but to the dangerous ideology of revolution that its armies

Marie Antoinette on the way to the guillotine as sketched by David.

radicals, and for the next year or so they acted as the real government of France. In late May, the leaders of the Mountain prepared to assume all power. They charged the Girondists with treason and complicity with the enemy, while the sans-culottes staged a massive demonstration before the convention. On June 2, under the combined pressures of the Mountain and the crowd, the convention voted to expel and arrest some two dozen Girondists. The extremists were now in control of both the convention and the Committee of Public Safety.

With domestic power secured, the committee turned its attention to the war, which was going against the French. The military effort was now placed under the direction of Lazare-Nicolas Carnot (1753–1823), a military engineer who had served in the Legislative Assembly and was now appointed to the Committee of Public Safety. In August, Carnot proclaimed the mobilization of the entire nation—a *levée en masse* that drafted all single males, from every social class, between 18 and 25. Since most high-ranking officers had been nobles, the Revolution produced a critical shortage of military leaders. To solve this problem, as well as to instill patriotic spirit among the conscripted soldiers, noncommissioned officers were elected, while higher ranks were to be appointed on the basis of talent. Within six months, more than 800,000 soldiers were raised and France seized the military initiative once again.

On the home front, civilians were mobilized by propaganda to support the war effort and to produce war materiel. The levée en masse also called upon women, children, and the aged to contribute their skills, from farming to cooking, to the victory. On September 5, following another large demonstration of the sans-culottes, the committee imposed stringent economic policies, including price controls and measures to prevent the hoarding of food. In this unprecedented manner, the entire French nation went to war.

The 1793–1794 period, during which the "Reign of Terror" triumphed, has gone down in history as the most infamous phase of the French Revolution. Under the rule of the Mountain, the government was rigidly centralized and all internal dissent silenced. Along with the economic controls imposed that September, the committee passed the "law of suspects," whereby the local surveillance committees were given authority to arrest citizens suspected of disloyalty and, in turn, try them by revolutionary tribunals. Local branches of the Jacobin Club, reporting back to the central club in Paris, acted as watchdogs of the Revolution in the provinces. Over the following months, domestic revolutionary armies were created to crush the peasant uprisings in the Vendée and put down the rebellion of the southern cities. All local committees were made directly responsible to the Committee of Public Safety, which demanded total unity and obedience to its directives.

In July 1793, a young woman named Charlotte Corday (1768–1793), inspired by Girondist rhetoric, assassinated Marat in his bath, convinced that she had rid France of an evil influence. For her deed, Corday was guillotined. With Marat dead, Robespierre came to be regarded as the leader of the Mountain and now assumed direction of the Committee of Public Safety. Under his command, the committee not only orchestrated a campaign of systematic terror aimed at purging the enemies of the Revolution but also undertook to transform the everyday life of all citizens.

Robespierre and the Republic of Virtue

Robespierre was a complex man, selfless in his absolute commitment to preserve the republic, single-minded in his determination to protect the Revolution. A self-righteous, ascetic young bachelor, a lawyer by profession, he had earned a reputation among his colleagues as "the Incorruptible." Yet despite his radicalism, Robespierre refused to alter his elegant prerevolutionary dress. An admirer of Rousseau's *Social Contract,* he claimed to speak for oppressed humanity and made himself the spokesman of the sans-culottes. Robespierre asserted that revolutionary times required two qualities—virtue and terror. The republic created by the Revolution would, he believed, engender civic virtue in all citizens, who should devote themselves to the service of the nation and their fellow citizens. He took from Rousseau the vision of an ideal republic—a "Republic of Virtue"—in which both poverty and excessive wealth would be eliminated, and in which reason, trust, and justice would reign.

For all his idealism, Robespierre was cold-blooded in ordering the execution of the Revolution's enemies—or his own. His fanaticism led him to believe that terror was another name for revolutionary justice. The purpose of the Terror was to purify the nation and impose obedience on it by impressing citizens with the severity of republican discipline. The justification for the Terror was that immediate liberties had to be sacrificed to the future of a free republic.

The Terror was used against a wide variety of people, many of whom simply disagreed with the policies of the Committee of Public Safety. The victims of the guillotine included former nobles and priests, peasants and workers, members of the convention and some of Robespierre's own colleagues in the government. By the winter of 1794 the Terror was turned against republican politicians, both on the right and the left. In March, extreme radicals in Paris known as the *enragés* (the "wild men"), led by Jacques Hébert, were beheaded for plotting to destroy the republic. The next month came executions of conservative republicans,

A contemporary print satirizing the Reign of Terror—Robespierre executing the executioner.

dechristianize the nation. In place of established religions the Revolution now proclaimed the worship of Reason. Churches were systematically closed and the clergy persecuted, and the Cathedral of Notre Dame in Paris was turned into a "Temple of Reason." In May 1794, Robespierre abandoned the worship of Reason because he believed it too difficult for common people to understand. In its place he substituted the deistic Cult of the Supreme Being, which he hoped would promote civic morality.

The transformation of everyday life went further. New forms of public discourse were adopted—"citizen" became the proper term of address for all French people—and streets, buildings, and even cities were renamed according to the revolutionary vocabulary. In dress, trousers of the sans-culottes were adopted by men, while more severe dresses with high necklines and flattened skirts became the style of female attire. Prostitution and gambling, identified by revolutionary propagandists as typically aristocratic vices, were repressed, and a cult of veneration for the virtuous mother became the order of the day. Even chess pieces and playing cards were changed in order to eliminate references to such vestiges of the past as kings, queens, and knights.

If the Revolution had proclaimed the general will as the basis for French politics, the Terror and the changes in social custom and mentality were part of a program to create a particular kind of public will, not to allow for free expression. As expressed through the Jacobin Clubs of the cities, these policies represented the high point of the influence of the sans-culottes and those who claimed to speak for them. When the inevitable reaction to these policies came, the Revolution shifted course once again.

including Danton himself. In June, Robespierre had a law approved that allowed for the conviction of suspects without evidence. In all, nearly 30,000 people were executed before the Terror was over.

Along with the Terror came deliberate efforts to demonstrate in tangible ways that the Revolution had remade history and created an entirely new world. Beginning in September 1792, government documents were dated from "Year I of the French Republic." In October 1793, a new calendar was put into effect (used until 1806), based on "reason" and "nature." The new dating system began with the first day of the republic. There were ten days in a week, three weeks in a month, and twelve months in a year. The remaining five days were declared republican holidays. The months were named after seasons and the weather, such as Brumaire (fog) and Thermidor (heat).

Not only did the calendar symbolize a new era in human history, but it was also part of a larger effort to

RETURN FROM THE BRINK: FROM THERMIDOR TO THE DIRECTORY

The dictatorial rule of Robespierre and the Committee of Public Safety was sustained by the need for strong government in the midst of the war and domestic instability. In 1793–1794, following the levée en masse, the French armies once again went on the offensive and won a series of important victories. In June 1794, French troops occupied the Austrian Netherlands, as they had done once before, and annexed the territory. Similar successes on the Rhine frontier and the Pyrenees led to the negotiation of peace terms with Prussia, Spain, Piedmont-Sardinia, and Austria. Having also crushed provincial rebellions against the republic, by

PERSPECTIVES ON HISTORY

The Historians' French Revolution

Jack R. Censer
George Mason University

The tumultuous political storms of the French Revolution as well as the complexity of the event itself have made agreement among historians extremely elusive. To understand the current controversies requires a survey of how earlier scholars interpreted its causes and development. Early in this century the most visible battle was the struggle between two French historians, Alphonse Aulard (1849–1928) and Albert Mathiez (1874–1932). Like many other scholars of his day, Aulard ignored social and economic factors and focused on ideas and politics. In his best-known book, *The French Revolution: A Political History* (1901), he approvingly chronicled the rise of republicanism. But what is most notable about Aulard's work was his overwhelming commitment to the moderate Georges Danton rather than to the Jacobin Maximilien Robespierre as the representative man of the Revolution. Aulard and his followers were especially concerned about rescuing Danton's reputation from charges of corruption. By cheering on revolutionary republicanism and embodying it in Danton, Aulard could praise a government vaguely similar to the moderate reformist Third Republic—the regime of his own day to which he wished to lend support (on the Third Republic, see Part VII, Topic 15).

Mathiez, who had been Aulard's student, broke with the older man in nearly every way. Interested more in social and economic than political factors, Mathiez also glorified Robespierre and the Jacobin dictatorship. Mathiez's politics—sometimes socialist, occasionally communist—doubtless influenced this perspective, so contrary to his mentor's. In particular, in Robespierre's speeches about equality Mathiez could find forerunners of his own 20th-century positions.

Although Aulard and Mathiez both demonstrated extraordinary knowledge of the historical sources, the tendency of each to praise his personal hero often made their work unconvincing. Such history seemed to approach propaganda and encouraged the emergence of an entirely new focus. It was mainly the avowedly Marxist Georges Lefebvre (1874–1959) who supplied a fresh perspective in the 1930s. This historical vision, whose later champions would include Albert Soboul (1914–1982), generally maintained—like other Marxists—that antagonisms among different social classes led to the founding of a new order. But even earlier during the Old Regime, argued Lefebvre, a political competition between the monarchy and nobility had demolished the solidarity of the elite. Social tensions then intervened. Peasants, workers, and particularly the middle class, or bourgeoisie, went into the Revolution hoping to redress their long-term grievances against the aristocracy. Class conflict likewise explained revolutionary developments. Once in charge, the bourgeoisie forgot its alliance with the other two classes and pursued its own interests until the summer of 1793, when middle-class radicals came to power assisted by the Parisian working class. From this point on, revolutionary governments mainly reflected how power-hungry bourgeois politicians capitalized upon the lower classes' social and economic problems. Politics moved leftward as leaders increasingly sought the support of urban workers; and it reversed direction after the summer and fall of 1794 when politicians, stunned by growing working-class independence, drew back from the demands of the poor. The middle class found the only sure protection against both the working class and nobility to be an agreement with the military in general and Napoleon in particular. Finally, this class conflict interpretation used the dominance of the bourgeoisie to explain the consequences of the Revolution.

But by the beginning of the 1980s new findings of North American and English historians had largely undermined this widely accepted view. First, it seems that prior to 1789 there may have been little social conflict between aristocracy and bourgeoisie. Furthermore, under the Old Regime, nobles proved as likely as commoners to support Enlightenment notions that challenged, at least in theory, both the absolute monarchy and the social organization of the Old Regime. Such positions suggested that an independent revolutionary middle class, vital to Lefebvre's position, did not exist. And historians also found problems in the Marxist interpretation of the revolutionary decade itself.

In the last 20 years new general interpretations have come along to replace Lefebvre and Soboul's. Of all these overviews of the French Revolution, François Furet's remains the most influential. To Furet, ideas possessed the power that Lefebvre attributed to social class. Thus he presented a story of competing ideologies. Ways of thinking—not class interests—played the determining role. Furet began by describing (and defending) the ideology that undergirded the French Old Regime. Although revolutionaries criticized this philosophy for protecting a system of special privileges, Furet argued that they did not understand the benefits of such privileges. Under the Old Regime, he claimed, residency in a city or participation in a craft guild, just like the rank of nobility, served to guarantee individuals' freedom (here defined as lack of oppression). But such traditional privileges came under attack, ironically, from the monarchy, and French society became particularly interested in the appeals of new political ideologies. In this changeable situation, Rousseauian notions of equality, best explained in *The Social Contract*, emerged as the strongest competitor to tradition according to Furet, and gradually upstaged defenders of the system of privileges.

According to Furet, the events of the Revolution settled this ideological conflict. First, the financial crisis in 1787 had undermined royal authority, but it took two years for the people to appreciate fully what had happened. Then, in the midst of the Revolution, with the exercise of power believed to be responsible for the ills of society, "language was substituted for power, for it was the sole guarantee that power would belong only to the people, that is, to nobody." With politics reduced to a struggle over language, Rousseauian thinking, already ascendant, emerged

dominant. In these circumstances, politicians could no longer wield power in the traditional sense. Although some resisted, in the end they were forced to compete in the arena of ideas and language. The most influential revolutionary leaders clearly understood that if they were to play the game of politics, they had no choice about its rules. Leadership passed to those who promised the greatest subservience to the people and the greatest equality. Once extreme notions of equality that denied individual differences dominated political debate, the coming of the Terror seemed inevitable. Fortunately, Furet went on, the Thermidorians broke the tyranny of language and returned politics to competition among classes and political groups.

Like Furet, Lynn Hunt is interested in language and owes much to him, but she tends to focus on subtle shifts in word usage and grammar rather than on the clash of ideas. For Hunt, language and image serve as barometers of revolutionary sentiment. In her pathbreaking work *Politics, Culture, and Class in the French Revolution* (1984), Hunt scrutinized the everyday language used to express the ideology of "democratic republicanism," which she found at the core of the revolutionary spirit. Her concern was first to uncover and then to explain its underlying structure, which she calls grammar. To do so, she turned to a range of theoretical writings, particularly those regarding theatricality. She also borrowed insights from the works of literary critics, anthropologists, and linguists. She used their theories to help her arrange and rearrange the content of revolutionaries' language, to uncover their basic values, the deeply imbedded categories of revolutionary thinking. Revolutionaries' intentions, she argued, could be inferred especially well from their symbolic usages. Hunt's interest in discourse analysis strongly shaped her overview of the French Revolution. Within revolutionary thought, she argued, there was no past, only a "mythic present," composed of belief in the nation and the Revolution. Revolutionaries, ever fearful of conspiracies, spoke and wrote first as if actors in a comedy, cheering their successes; then as if in a romance, struggling with good and evil; and finally as if in a tragedy,

continued next page

watching things fall apart. In all three stages, Hunt believes their thought to be transparent, that is, hostile to artificiality. It was also ever vigilant and always subservient to the people. Through the revolutionaries' use of symbols, they developed this litany of new beliefs.

Another important tendency emerges collectively in the works of four recent historians: William Doyle, D. M. G. Sutherland, Simon Schama, and John Bosher. Although they do not constitute a formal school, these historians share common concerns, including similar strategies to describe and explain the Revolution. Politics take center stage, and extensive political chronologies fill their works. Yet they also consider social, intellectual, and economic factors, a commonsense approach typical of historians for whom political and literary theories are relatively unimportant. In particular, they make no attempt to deal with current debates about the relation of discourse to reality. They simply accept that these factors coexist, one alongside the other. Although these authors differ about some specific aspects of the Revolution, their views accord on some important issues. They all find redeeming value in the Old Regime and also believe that overall the Revolution failed to advance the good of humanity. This simultaneous praise for the Old Regime and attack on the new provides an especially strong blast against the claims of many participants and later historians. Such considerable concurrence of opinion should not obscure considerable disagreements over the Revolution. For example, Schama and Bosher argue that France experienced its problems in large part because of the machinations of ruthless and unscrupulous Jacobins. To the contrary, Sutherland and Doyle tend not to blame the revolutionaries but to point to outside problems, especially those of the war and counterrevolution.

To some degree the variations in these four interpretations matter less because of their distance from Furet's and Hunt's emphasis on ideas. But the interpretations mentioned here hardly exhaust the list of new approaches that continue to tumble forward. Fertile as the Revolution was for contemporaries, it also shows no sign of withering for historians.

the late summer of 1794 the government of the radical Jacobins had achieved its most important success.

Thermidor: The Revolution in Reverse

Ironically, the end of the military crisis proved to be the undoing of the rule of the radicals. Once relieved of its foreign enemies, many leaders of the Revolution began calling for relief from the stringent domestic policies of the Committee of Public Safety. Moreover, Robespierre and his colleagues had alienated far too many political forces and social groups on the right and the left, and by mid-1794 found themselves isolated. Even the sans-culottes, whose power base in Paris had been curbed, were alienated from the Jacobins. The moderates in the National Convention, who once cowed before the Terror, now reasserted themselves.

It was Robespierre himself who pushed the growing discontent to the breaking point and provoked his enemies into the "Thermidorian Reaction" that at last ended the Terror. On July 26 he went before the convention to denounce unnamed conspirators in the government who were plotting against him and against the Revolution. Robespierre had followed the tactic in the past in preparation for purging opponents. This time, however, members of the convention organized against him. The next day, the ninth of Thermidor, as Robespierre rose to speak again, he was shouted down and a special decree ordering the arrest of the Robespierrists was pushed through. On the tenth of Thermidor, Robespierre and 60 of his colleagues were guillotined. The Revolution had devoured its most fanatical children.

The Thermidorian Reaction was much more than a political coup against a group of leaders—it reversed many of the trends and policies that had marked the Revolution since the purge of the Girondists. The Committee of Public Safety was stripped of much of its authority and the instruments of the Terror, such as the revolutionary committees and their tribunals, were eliminated. A general amnesty for political prisoners was declared and even the Jacobin Club of Paris closed down.

The social policies of Thermidor also altered the general atmosphere of the nation. The emphasis on civic morality, with its attendant campaigns against gambling, pornography, and prostitution, disappeared, while the middle classes reverted to their former styles of dress and speech. Many Catholic priests returned to France as freedom of worship was restored.

Even Thermidor, however, was not without its own violence, for a "white terror" in the form of street fighting and massacres now struck the Jacobins and their supporters as well as the sans-culottes. Along with the reaction came an extremely poor harvest in 1795 that resulted in food shortages worse than those of 1789. The Thermidorians were, however, unwilling to intervene in the economy despite widespread misery and the result was an abortive uprising followed by a bloody repression.

The Directory

Following the fall of Robespierre, the convention issued a third constitution, which operated from 1795 to 1799. The system of universal male suffrage adopted in 1793 was now abandoned and the country returned to a franchise similar to that incorporated in the 1791 Constitution, based on property and wealth—an exception was made for soldiers, who were entitled to vote regardless of whether they owned property. A two-chamber legislature was established, consisting of a Council of Elders and a Council of Five Hundred. The new document created a five-person directory to function as a plural executive branch of government.

On October 5, a royalist-supported insurrection rose against the government, which had only 4000 soldiers available, but a young artillery officer, General Napoleon Bonaparte (1769–1821), put down the rebellion by ordering his troops to fire cannon point-blank into the crowd. Thermidor effectively ended the active role of the crowd in the Revolution (see Part VII, Topic 4).

The Directory sought to reestablish political consensus by assuming a moderate position that eschewed extremists on both sides. Thus, while it eliminated the popular democracy of the radical phase of the Revolution, it also opposed a complete resurgence of either royalism or Jacobinism. With stability as the goal, the directors refused to tolerate any organized political opposition that could threaten their rule, although their efforts to repress the extremists did not include a return to wholesale terror. In the spring of 1796, François "Gracchus" Babeuf (1760–1797) led the last real effort at mobilizing the crowds of Paris. Babeuf, who espoused a society based on agrarian communism, attempted to stage a "Conspiracy of Equals," but it failed miserably and he was executed.

Despite its aim of restoring stability to the French body politic, the Directory's rule proved to be unstable. Coups and plots continued to challenge the new government, and a wide range of political ideologies flourished just below the level of organized political opposition. The renewal of war with the monarchs of Europe once again brought reliance on the army. When elections in the spring of 1799 went against the candidates sponsored by the Directory, the legislature replaced four of the Directory's five members with a group led by the Abbé Sieyès, who had championed the middle classes in 1789. In turning to the ambitious and brilliant General Bonaparte for support, Sieyès introduced a new factor into the ever-changing course of the French Revolution.

The importance of the Revolution transcended France, for its repercussions would be felt for many decades to come throughout Europe and, indeed, on a worldwide scale. In its aftermath, the society of the Old Regime was increasingly undermined and eventually replaced in most of Western and Central Europe. The social changes that the Revolution had introduced with such drama and violence were reinforced by the long-range repercussions of industrialization. In the 1790s, France had joined Great Britain as the second major European state to apply the ideas of resistance and to depose—indeed, behead—its ruler. Coming on the heels of the recent American Revolution, the revolution in France had forever altered politics in the West. By the late 19th century, the liberal ideas of the French moderates characterized most European governments, while the radical experiment with mass politics would become the predominant pattern of political discourse as the 20th century opened. Perhaps more than anything, however, the French Revolution had given vivid and tangible proof of the Enlightenment belief in the possibilities of change for the human condition.

Questions for Further Study

1. What were the causes of the French Revolution?

2. What role did the bourgeoisie play in the Revolution? Why was the concept of property important to the revolutionary leaders?

3. How did the sans-culottes affect the course of the Revolution? What was their relationship to the Jacobins?

4. What caused the reaction against the Reign of Terror?

Suggestions for Further Reading

Blanning, T. C. W. *The French Revolution: Aristocrats Versus Bourgeois?* Atlantic Highlands, NJ, 1987.

Cobban, Alfred. *The Social Interpretation of the French Revolution.* Cambridge, MA, 1964.

Furet, François. *Interpreting the French Revolution,* trans. E. Forster. New York, 1981.

Hunt, Lynn. *Politics, Culture, and Class in the French Revolution.* Berkeley, CA, 1984.

Jones, P. M. *The Peasantry in the French Revolution.* Cambridge, MA, 1988.

Jordan, David. P. *The King's Trial: The French Revolution Versus Louis XVI*. Berkeley, CA, 1979.

Landes, Joan. *Women and the Public Sphere in the Age of the French Revolution*. Ithaca, NY, 1988.

Lefebvre, Georges. *The Coming of the French Revolution*, trans. R. R. Palmer. Princeton, NJ, 1947.

Palmer, R. R. *Twelve Who Ruled: The Year of the Terror in the French Revolution*. Princeton, NJ, 1970.

Schama, Simon. *Citizens: A Chronicle of the French Revolution*. New York, 1989.

Soboul, Albert. *The Sans-Culottes: The Popular Movement and Revolutionary Government, 1793–1794*, trans. R. Hall. Princeton, NJ, 1980.

Sutherland, Donald M. G. *France, 1789–1815: Revolution and Counterrevolution*. Oxford, 1986.

T o p i c 4

EUROPE IN THE NAPOLEONIC ERA

he Directory brought welcome relief from the excesses of the Revolution, but it did little to solve France's underlying political problems, or the dependence of the economy on war booty and government military contracts. In turning to the young general, Napoleon Bonaparte, to overturn the results of the elections of 1799, its moderate leaders launched the final stage of revolutionary transformation.

Napoleon's rapid ascent to power, based like much of his career on a potent combination of military virtuosity and personal charisma, saw him assume the title of first consul in 1799. His Consulate brought about widespread domestic reform in France. He reorganized the institutions of law, religion, education, and the economy. Peace at home was generally restored, together with public self-esteem.

With his coronation as emperor in 1804, Napoleon moved to the wider stage of continental Europe. Britain was protected by its superior naval power, but virtually the whole of the rest of Europe fell more or less under Napoleonic rule. Even Russia had to negotiate an alliance that reduced the tsar to the status of a junior partner.

The Napoleonic empire was short-lived. The attempt to blockade all trade with Britain was a predictable failure, and French domination of Spain proved costly in men and resources. In 1812, while still embroiled with the Spanish rebels, Napoleon launched an expedition to the other end of Europe, against Russia, where massive losses, combined with the blizzards of the harsh winter, devastated the French Army. Other European nations were emboldened to unite with Russia in a war of liberation.

The end came quickly. In 1813, after the inconclusive Battle of Leipzig, Napoleon retreated back to France. The following year the European allies invaded Paris, forced the emperor to abdicate, and shipped him off to the island of Elba. His last attempt to return to power lasted no more than 100 days. He escaped back to France in March 1815 and gathered an army, but was finally defeated at the Battle of Waterloo that June.

With the triumph of the European powers and a Bourbon monarch once more on the throne of France, the forces of the Revolution seemed exhausted. Yet by the end of the Napoleonic period, Europe had been transformed. Revolutionary political and social concepts permeated all levels of society throughout the Continent. Furthermore, the desire for national independence, born out of resistance to Napoleon, was to become a dominating theme in the history of the 19th century.

THE RISE OF BONAPARTE: FROM CONSUL TO EMPEROR

Napoleon (ruled as first consul 1799–1804 and as emperor 1804–1814) was unquestionably a figure whose decisions and actions irrevocably changed the lives of countless people. He was known to many of his contemporaries, both admirers and enemies, simply as "The Man"; decades after his death in exile, English children were scared into obedience by the mere mention of his name—"Old Boney."

Many believed that they had reason to be grateful to him. In Italy and the Rhineland his troops threw down the walls of the ghettoes and allowed the Jews to emerge into freedom for the first time since the Counter-Reformation. In other cases his social and political policies undermined some of the achievements of the Revolution: the civil liberties of women, to which revolutionary legislators had been more sympathetic, were removed by the Napoleonic Code of Law. Nor did his many opponents, from Spain to Russia, hesitate to characterize him as a bloodthirsty dictator.

Napoleon the Administrator

It is misleading to look for a broad, consistent philosophy behind the details of Napoleon's actions. Indeed, some of the contradictions that marked his rise and fall were present in his childhood and early career. He was born in 1769 in Corsica, an island ruled by France but predominantly Italian-speaking; the Genoese sold it to France in 1768, and Napoleon himself never managed to speak French without an accent. In his youth, moreover, the first political ambitions of the future emperor of France were to free Corsica from French control.

At the military academies he attended in France (he was sent to his first at the age of nine), he set out to shock his aristocratic fellow students by spectacular displays of bad behavior, which were intended to show his contempt for their genteel world. His own family was noble but impoverished, and throughout his life he was proud of the fact that he had achieved success by his own merits rather than by family influence. Yet his career was one of contradictions: once in power, he introduced reforms that helped others of ability to overcome the disadvantage of their nonaristocratic birth and rise to positions of influence, yet he also created a new aristocracy and made family members the rulers of states throughout Europe.

For all his love of the unconventional, Napoleon's intellectual interests marked him as a child of the Enlightenment. Like many of his contemporaries, he was an enthusiastic reader of history and a keen student of mathematics. His distinction lay in the imagination and speed with which he was able to transform theoretical ideas into practice: even Napoleon's enemies recognized his outstanding administrative gifts.

His talent for organization and demand for efficiency were formidable, and he was famous for his ability to dictate three letters on different topics to three secretaries simultaneously, without losing concentration or creating confusion. When he applied these skills to major issues, he produced rapid and significant results. Thus his interest in law culminated in the Napoleonic Code, a massive program of legal reform that was destined to have wide-reaching effects—both for better and for worse—far beyond the borders of France.

Napoleon's Early Career

His rise in the army was helped by the need for talented officers, since many former commanders, drawn from aristocratic families, had either fled or had been demoted during the Revolution. Nonetheless his astonishing ability to make a rapid decision and then act on it soon drew attention.

Among those impressed was General Paul Barras, one of the five leaders of the Directory. In 1795, at the National Convention to set up the Directory's constitution, monarchist leaders mounted a huge public demonstration against the convention. When called upon to deal with the emergency, Barras summoned Napoleon, whom he had seen in action at the siege of Toulon in 1793, and the crowds were scattered by cannon fired by troops under Napoleon's orders.

In return for his help, Napoleon asked for command of the French forces in northern Italy, which offered the chance of winning military glory in more conventional style. With a dazzling series of moves he defeated the Austrians and occupied Milan. Exceeding his orders, he pushed into north-central Italy and in October 1797 he personally negotiated the Treaty of Campo Formio, whereby Austria recognized the new state of the Cisalpine Republic, made up of Lombardy, Genoa, and several smaller duchies, in return for control over Venice.

Within the next two years, as French armies moved through Italy, French-controlled republics also sprang up in the Papal States, Naples, and Tuscany. The strategically important Kingdom of Piedmont was occupied and eventually annexed to France. By the end of his command, Napoleon had demonstrated his abilities as statesman, as well as military leader.

Napoleon's sense of drama and love of excitement had a great appeal for the Italians, whose own dreams of independence he astutely encouraged. The leaders of the Directory back in Paris were less enthusi-

Jacques-Louis David, *Napoleon in His Study*, 1812.

astic at the growing popularity of the young hero (to say nothing of the prospect of a liberated and united Italy), and Napoleon's next move was cunningly designed to enhance his domestic standing. France's greatest enemy was Britain. Even Napoleon was not yet prepared to undertake an armed invasion of the British Isles, but why not attack British interests elsewhere?

The Egyptian Campaign

The expedition he led to Egypt in the spring of 1798 was aimed at interfering with British colonial trade and striking a symbolic blow at the British Empire. Furthermore he hoped to find in North Africa an appropriate setting for sensational new heroic exploits, while avoiding the full might of the British Navy.

In the end, the expedition proved disastrous. The French fleet was destroyed by British forces under Admiral Nelson (1758–1805) at the Battle of the Nile on August 1, 1798, and the French army was left stranded. Napoleon hastily abandoned his troops in order to return to France as quickly as possible, and try to limit the damage to his reputation. He and his supporters concealed the military catastrophe as best they could by adroit manipulation of the news from Egypt, and by circulating information about the expedition's various scientific exploits. Among the most valuable of these was the discovery of the Rosetta Stone, a carved stone inscription, which made it possible in 1822 to decode the ancient Egyptian hieroglyphic script.

The ease with which he succeeded in reinstating himself was due in large measure to the chaotic political situation he found in Paris on his return. During his absence, further French moves in Italy had provoked Britain, Austria, and Russia into forming a coalition against France. The subsequent military crisis, which led to a series of French setbacks in Italy, undermined the credibility of the Directory and led to violent conflict between conservatives and democrats. Napoleon's reappearance on the scene provided the conservatives with a popular hero to lead a political coup.

The Brumaire Coup

On November 9, 1799, Napoleon seized power and appointed himself first consul, with virtually dictatorial powers; two other consuls were named, but they were never given any real authority. This act is generally known as the "Brumaire Coup," since its date, according to the revolutionary calendar, was 18 Brumaire VIII. Among the coup's supporters was the Abbé Sieyès (see Part VII, Topic 3), the former revolutionary and advocate of national sovereignty, who now called for "Confidence from below, authority from above."

The conservatives had intended the takeover to institute a republican oligarchy, but the first consul had other ideas. He maintained control of the armed forces, and thereby of both internal security and foreign affairs. A carefully picked Council of State was put in charge of all national legislation. Regional governments, corresponding to the departments established by the revolutionary government, became subject to strict surveillance by the appointment of prefects, officials sent from Paris to act as agents of the central government, and report back to Napoleon.

Like many another dictator, Napoleon did what he could to obtain the appearance of popular support, using censorship where necessary to block the circulation of opposing views: for all the rhetoric of his public statements, Napoleon was, in his own way, as repressive as the Old Regime. The constitution he and his advisers drafted included two national legislative bodies with vague general powers, for which all French adult males could vote (women lost the rights which they had gained under the Revolution). In reality these two councils had no power to introduce new laws, but when Napoleon's proposed reforms were submitted to a popular referendum, approval was overwhelming.

The Consulate

The years of the Consulate—1799–1804—saw a return to stability in France. The authority of the central government was restored and citizens could count on the protection of the law. The achievement of a balanced budget and the efficient collecting of a more justly assessed tax burden (there were no more exemptions for the aristocracy and the clergy) reestablished the economy on a sound footing. By 1802, the average Frenchman paid less taxes than in 1789, and received more and better services. The Bank of France, an institution founded by Napoleon, was privately owned but state controlled; it took charge of government funds and the distribution of paper currency and proved a strong centralizing force.

Napoleon put an end to the Revolution's battle with the Catholic Church by negotiating a concordat, signed by the first consul and Pope Pius VII in 1801. This agreement proclaimed Catholicism the "preferred" religion in France, but maintained the freedom of religion established during the Revolution. Among its provisions, it held that the church would renounce its claims to the land and other church property confiscated by the National Assembly. Napoleon's own attitude to religion was practical, to say the least: he is said to have claimed that "God is always on the side of those with the most cannon." The concordat was intended to reassure traditional Catholics in France, who had been shocked by the atheism of many of the revolutionary leaders. On the whole, however, it strengthened the power of the state and was never popular with the Catholic clergy. The pope later renounced it.

The Code Napoleon

Amid this whirl of reform, the foundations were laid for radical changes in law and education, two areas which had been of particular interest to Napoleon in his youth. With his customary genius for bureaucratic efficiency, he supervised the drawing up of a systematic and consistent body of laws, the Code Napoleon. Among the code's aims was the creation of a rational system for the buying, selling, and holding of property, which established sound general principles and yet did not interfere with individual rights.

On the other hand, in dealing with family questions, the code was far less egalitarian: it awarded husbands complete control over their wives, children, and possessions. Furthermore, women's occupations were to be limited as far as possible to the marital, maternal, and domestic spheres, with men in complete charge of public matters. Those women who worked were required to give their wages to their husbands; any woman operating a business—selling in a market, for example—could do so only with the permission of her husband, who had a legal right to all her profits.

The code's bias did not go unnoticed: as one woman wrote in the early 19th century, "From the way the Code treats women, you can tell it was written by men." Its effects spread far beyond France. Many new nations, both in the Old and New Worlds, which came into being in the 19th century adopted the Code Napoleon as the basis of their own legal systems. In the process its attitude to gender roles became widely diffused and enforced.

In education as elsewhere, Napoleon was concerned to strengthen the power of the central authority. The University of France was founded to supervise educational institutions throughout the country, and new categories of schools were introduced: professional and technical academies, and a nationwide high school (or *lycée*) system. As in the case of financial and legal reform, the chief beneficiaries of these new schools were the middle classes and their families; they had begun to win a new status for themselves before the Revolution, and now their progress was confirmed.

The return of law, order, and prosperity ensured Napoleon's popularity, and in 1802 he was acclaimed "consul for life"; the popular vote gave him over 95 percent support. So far his achievements had been principally limited to France, but early in his Consulate he had staged a highly successful campaign against Hapsburg forces in northern Italy and Germany. The Treaty of Luneville, signed in 1801 as a result of his victories, returned to French control the territory lost in 1799, and, more importantly, France's self-esteem.

The only real failure of the Consulate occurred far enough away from France to make little impact. Although Napoleon won back the North American territory of Louisiana from Spain, he was unable to occupy and develop it and eventually sold the territory to the United States for $15 million.

With security and stability ensured at home, wider horizons beckoned again: the dream of European conquest. For this enterprise, however, a more grandiose title was in order. In 1804, in the cathedral of Notre Dame, he crowned himself emperor with a laurel wreath, symbol of ancient Rome, before crowning his wife, Josephine, in more opulent style. His goal was to recreate the Roman Empire and unite Europe under his rule. The artistic legacy of the Napoleonic period, produced in a style known as *Empire*, provided an

Jacques-Louis David, *The Coronation of Napoleon in the presence of Pope Pius VII in 1804.*

appropriate background for these conquests, with its triumphal arches, columns, and "antique" dresses.

EUROPE AND THE FRENCH IMPERIUM

Within a few months of Napoleon's coronation, France was faced for a third time by a hostile coalition of Britain, Austria, and Russia, an alliance formed the previous year to combat the spread of French influence. The most potentially threatening of these three were the British, who joined the coalition even though Napoleon had, in fact, signed a peace treaty with them in 1801. This treaty, the Peace of Amiens, had been negotiated unenthusiastically on both sides. Both Britain and France refused essential concessions—a British withdrawal from Gibraltar and Malta in return for a French evacuation of the Low Countries—and the treaty soon collapsed.

Napoleon's first strategy for undermining his opponents was to eliminate their strongest member by direct attack. The invasion he launched against England, however, was soon discouraged by the presence of the massed forces of the British Navy in the English Channel. Furthermore, in October 1805 any future threat of a French naval offensive was eliminated by British victory over the combined French and Spanish fleets at the Battle of Trafalgar. Under the command once again of Admiral Nelson, a tactician as brilliantly unorthodox at sea as Napoleon was on land, the British Navy devastated the French and Spanish forces. The battle cost Nelson his life, but effectively guaranteed the security of the British Isles from invasion, and limited Napoleon's enterprises to continental Europe.

The Conquest of Continental Europe

With characteristic boldness, Napoleon was quick to regain the offensive. French troops moved across Europe at astonishing speed. After occupying Vienna, they took on the combined Austrian and Russian armies at Austerlitz and crushed them; in the battle the French pretended to retreat, only to trap their enemies into taking up an overexposed position, and Napoleon won one of his most famous victories. The Austrians had little choice but to negotiate a peace settlement, the terms of which were distinctly unfavorable to them, while favoring the French position in central Europe. The Russians, badly shaken, retreated back east in the hope of better luck in the future.

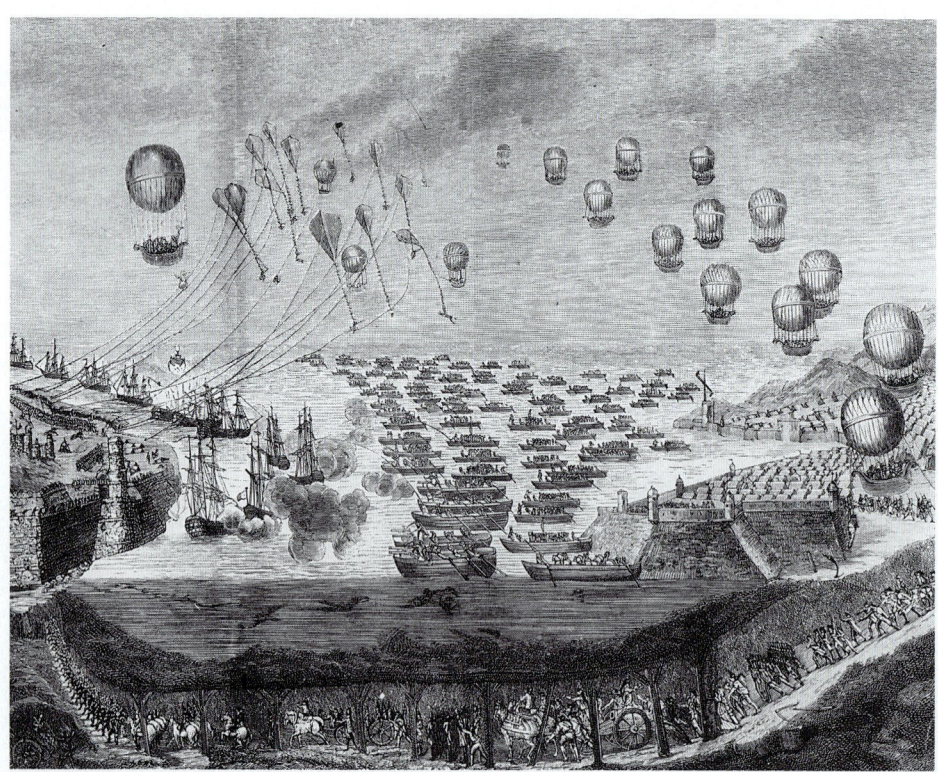

Engraving of a supposed plan by Napoleon to invade England by a combination of ships, balloons, and an underground tunnel.

Napoleon's imperial seal.

Throughout the hostilities the Prussians had remained neutral, unwilling to come to the aid of their Austrian neighbors and unable to see that their turn was next. With Austria disposed of, Napoleon could turn his attention north and by the time the Prussians finally declared war it was too late for them to put up much resistance. The legendary Prussian army, a mere shadow of its former glory, was soundly whipped in October 1806, at the Battle of Jena. Napoleon was master of central Europe.

Formally declaring the end of the Holy Roman Empire, he reorganized its many kingdoms and principalities into a series of new states. Some of these were placed under the rule of family members: his youngest brother, Jerome, was given Westphalia, while Marshal Joachim Murat, the husband of his sister Caroline Bonaparte, became ruler of the Grand Duchy of Berg. Napoleon's purpose in dividing up his conquests among the family was partly to establish dynasties, while at the same time it enabled him to retain control in his own hands. His brother Louis became king of Holland, but when he began to show too much interest in the welfare of his Dutch subjects, Napoleon deposed him and made Holland French territory.

The French in Eastern Europe
Among the newly created states was the Grand Duchy of Warsaw, made up of that part of Poland which had been carved out by the Prussians. By appearing to favor the cause of Polish independence, Napoleon could claim to be the champion of national aspirations, as he had in his earlier days in Italy.

More to the point, he provided himself with a base from which to move against his last unconquered enemy, Russia. After an indecisive battle at Eylau, which was fought in a raging blizzard and produced terrible casualties on both sides, the Russians were finally defeated at Friedland in June 1807. Within weeks Tsar Alexander I and Emperor Napoleon I met at Tilsit to sign an agreement which divided Europe into two halves. In return for a relatively free hand in extending Russian influence into the Ottoman-controlled Balkans, Alexander accepted Napoleon's annexation and reorganization of Western Europe, and agreed to restrict trade and other contacts with Britain. The terms were in France's favor, but the tsar had little choice.

Italy and Spain
With eastern and central Europe reshaped, it was then the turn of the Mediterranean region to provide thrones for the Bonaparte family. Parts of Italy, including Piedmont, Tuscany, the Papal States, and several smaller duchies, had already become French territory. Napoleon merged the former Cisalpine Republic, together with a recaptured Venice and the remaining central parts of the peninsula, into the Kingdom of Italy, governing himself as king through his stepson. In southern Italy, his brother Joseph became king of the Kingdom of Naples in 1806.

In 1808, Napoleon sent Murat to Naples and transferred Joseph to Spain in an attempt to secure power in Iberia. Since 1795 the Spanish had been only fitful allies of the French in their joint attempt to undermine British influence in Europe and the colonies. The destruction of a considerable portion of the Spanish Navy at Trafalgar further reduced Spain's enthusiasm for the French cause. To complicate matters even more, the Spanish royal house was racked by bitter in-fighting and scandal. Napoleon's solution to dealing with his supposed allies was, as might be expected, radical and direct. In 1808 the Spanish king and his son were paid off, and Joseph led French troops to Madrid to oversee the introduction of the new regime.

For once, Napoleon's political instincts had deserted him. By this blatant takeover the former supporter of nationalist causes provoked a nationalist uprising that was to last for several years. The popular riots of early May 1808 were soon put down by bloody and brutal troop action on the part of the French, but the very memory of the repression served to galvanize the forces of rebellion. Regular Spanish troops combined with local civilian forces to challenge French occupation of their country, and bitter fighting dragged on until the French were finally driven out of Spain in 1814.

Francisco Goya's dramatic depiction of *The Executions of May 3, 1808,* when Spanish resistance fighters were gunned down by Napoleonic troops.

Napoleon's move backfired in a number of ways. He had provoked genuine popular resistance among the Spanish. This in turn encouraged nations elsewhere in Europe to resist French strongarm tactics; while the conflict in Spain itself provided a golden opportunity to Napoleon's greatest enemies, the British, who despatched a force to drive the French out of the Iberian peninsula, in a campaign known as the Peninsular War.

The war trapped a large part of the French Army in a hopeless struggle against a mixture of British troops, the local anti-French forces, and several thousand Spanish guerrilla fighters, these latter inspired by memory of the horrors of the May brutalities. The term *guerrilla* is the Spanish word for "little war"; the development in the Peninsular War of "guerrilla tactics"—hit-and-run, ambush, sabotage, surprise attack—against larger and better-equipped forces proved highly influential in many subsequent conflicts around the globe.

In 1808, with all western and central Europe at Napoleon's command, the problem of Spain must have seemed relatively unimportant; in the end it proved one of the chief causes of his downfall, since over 200,000 troops embroiled in the fighting there were urgently needed elsewhere.

THE GRAND EXPERIMENT: OCCUPATION AND REFORM

The Napoleonic empire lasted for a shorter time than just about any empire of comparable size in Western history. In 1808 the French controlled, in one way or another, much of Central and Western Europe (with the exception of the British Isles). By 1813 Napoleon's domination was over. Yet for all the brevity of its duration, French imperial rule had a profound and lasting effect on European life.

The Imperial Administration

In order to administer these vast territories, Napoleon introduced throughout Europe many of the reforms that had succeeded so well in France. The old ranks and privileges were abolished, and family status no longer assured a successful career: the Napoleonic bureaucracy offered the possibility of advancement in public life to those of talent and ability, regardless of their origins. Many of the special powers of the church were curtailed, or—as in the case of church courts—abolished. Under the Code Napoleon, which was valid in the conquered territories, all were equal in the eyes of the law.

Financial reorganization and the implementation of a coherent tax system helped improve local

Map 4.1   Europe at the Height of the Napoleonic Empire

economies. In the process, those involved in trade and commerce were more able to pursue their business and advance their interests. In one area, however, even the emperor failed to remove old barriers. In spite of his attempts to abolish customs tariffs for the importation of goods across national boundaries, the various European economic groups maintained their rival tariff systems. With the end of Napoleonic rule, the concept of European free trade disappeared, until it was revived almost 150 years later in the years of rebuilding after World War II.

All these various reforms were, of course, principally intended to strengthen French rule over her empire. The local populations were free to pursue their own careers, protect their property rights, work as they pleased. They were not free to govern themselves. The efficient working of the system was intended to maintain control by a centralized government in Paris that, in turn, was responsible to the emperor. A prosperous Europe, in addition, would pay taxes to pay for the French armies of occupation and finance future military adventures.

Napoleonic Rule in Practice: The Case of Pauline Borghese

The internal contradictions of Napoleon's occupation policies, with all of their much-needed reforms and blatant exploitation, and their cultural and social brilliance and personal intrigues, can be seen in microcosm in the life of his sister Pauline.

Pauline Bonaparte (1780–1825), whom Napoleon once called "the most beautiful woman of her time," grew up spoiled, rebellious, and strong-willed. Although she constantly fought his efforts to control her life, she was devoted to her brother. After an early marriage to one of his favorites, General Charles Leclerc, she reluctantly accompanied her husband to Santo Domingo when he was sent there to assert French control over the island's black population. When Leclerc died in 1802 of yellow fever, Pauline returned with relief to Paris.

The role of a general's widow ill-suited Pauline's vivacious temperament. In 1803, in order to avoid the scandal her illicit affairs were causing, Napoleon allowed her to marry Camillo Borghese (1775–1832), the handsome, outgoing heir to one of Rome's oldest and most distinguished noble families. Pauline, together with a sumptuous wardrobe, valuable jewels, and her new husband, moved to the Villa Borghese in Rome. Pauline soon tired of Rome's staid, monotonous social life, however, and began a series of liaisons with writers, actors, and intellectuals. Between 1804 and 1805, the neoclassical sculptor Antonio Canova (1757–1822) executed a sensuously lifelike statue of Pauline depicting her as a semi-nude Venus lounging alluringly on a bed while holding an apple of temptation. When Borghese saw the statue, he was so scandalized that he banished it to the basement.

In 1808 Napoleon appointed Borghese governor general of the French-annexed territories of northern Italy, and the couple moved to Turin, the capital of Piedmont. Borghese's work as administrator was efficient if unspectacular, but he did implement Napoleon's reforms. Pauline, bored with politics, was

A sculpture by Canova of Napoleon's sister Pauline as Venus.

soon ready for a change. Leaving Borghese, she returned to Paris, bringing glamour to the social life of the court and, in an age noted for its amorous liaisons, outdoing most women of the empire.

After Napoleon's defeat and abdication in 1814, the last years of Pauline's life were filled with sadness and depression. Borghese rapidly divested himself of his association with the former emperor. He attempted to have his marriage annulled, but Pauline managed to obtain a legal separation and a generous annual stipend. She visited her brother in exile on the island of Elba and later tried without success to join him at St. Helena.

Her beauty and her health rapidly fading, Pauline returned to Italy in 1816 and, after a last affair with the young composer Giovanni Pacini (1796–1867), asked for a reconciliation with Borghese. Wounded by her past infidelities, however, the prince spurned her. Only in 1824, after she had fallen gravely ill and had written countless letters of entreaty, did Borghese agree to be reunited. She died a few months later and was buried in the Borghese chapel in Rome.

In retrospect, Pauline Bonaparte and Camillo Borghese were each victims of the lure of the Grand Empire—Borghese, an opportunist who rose to fame and influence by siding with the French against both the ruler of Italy and the pope, and who then just as astutely abandoned his fallen protector; Pauline, a spirited woman who, while living in the shadow of her egoistic brother, used his power for her own ends while seeking personal freedom from the men who had wanted to possess her.

Napoleon and Liberty

While the reasons for the Napoleonic reorganization of Europe were practical, they were underpinned by broader philosophical principles. Napoleon had, after all, come to power with the claim that he would implement some of the ideals of the Revolution, with its doctrines of liberty and equality. Many of his reforms, both in France and throughout the empire, did produce a more free and just society.

In many cases, even after his fall, the old vested interests of the aristocracy were unable to impose themselves again. Furthermore the spirit of national independence and self-determination, which both the Revolution and Napoleon claimed to support, was an intoxicating one; in Germany, in particular, resistance to Napoleon played an important role in stimulating nationalism. The very peoples who finally united to overthrow the empire did so following the vision of freedom which the Revolution seemed to offer, and which the Napoleonic reforms made at least partly real. After Napoleon, Europe could never return to the old social and political ways.

The Jews Under Napoleon

In the case of one people, however—the Jews—progress did not survive the end of the Napoleonic era. As early as 1791 the National Assembly had decreed that French Jews possessed the rights of full citizens. Napoleon, with his enlightened attitude to religious tolerance, continued to work for the integration of the Jews into society. The constitution of the Cisalpine Republic that he founded in 1797 in northern Italy provided for their freedom of worship, and the concordat signed with the Catholic Church in 1801 contained nothing to undermine the Jews' new civic status in France.

In the years of conquest, as French armies moved through Europe, they freed Jews from their ghettoes and extended full rights to them, although the Jews were often required to pay heavy taxes in return. Jewish candidates were able to stand as candidates for election to public office, and Jewish intellectuals were nominated as members of learned societies such as the Italian Academy of Sciences.

With a characteristic care for detail, Napoleon tried to regularize the position of the Jews, a people who transcended national boundaries, by convening an international congress. In 1806 Jewish representatives were summoned to Paris from all parts of the empire to discuss such questions as divorce and mixed marriages, and Jewish difficulties in entering the professions. A Napoleonic decree emerged two years later; it established local administrative councils in Jewish communities throughout the empire, which were answerable to a central council in Paris.

With the defeat of Napoleon, however, the entire system collapsed. In France the Jews retained their rights, but elsewhere in Europe they were repressed even more ferociously, precisely because they had been set free by the hated French conquerors, and in gratitude had exchanged their yellow stars for the French *tricouleurs*. The walls of the ghetto at Rome were thrown up again and the Jews confined there as soon as Napoleon's downfall seemed assured. The Jews of Italy finally won their freedom in the mid-19th century, following the Italian struggle for independence, but many of those in central and eastern Europe could only hope to find theirs by emigrating to the New World at the end of the century.

THE EUROPEAN COALITION AND THE COLLAPSE OF FRANCE

Napoleon was finally overthrown by a third coalition of the European powers, although their success was due as much to the emperor's miscalculations as to their own military prowess. Both in economic and foreign policy, the French undermined their own strength.

The Continental System

In the aftermath of the disastrous defeat at Trafalgar, with the British unshaken in their naval power, Napoleon tried to find a way to undermine Britain economically. His device was the Continental System, introduced for the first time in 1806; among its other policies, it prohibited the importation of British goods into continental Europe. The aim was to destroy the commercial life of a country which Napoleon himself referred to as "a nation of shopkeepers." When the British in turn imposed their own countermeasures, the ensuing naval blockade and counterblockade involved virtually all trading nations, including neutral powers such as the United States. Indeed, American irritation at being drawn into the conflict contributed to the brief and inconclusive War of 1812 with Britain.

Although the barriers created by the Continental System stimulated the British to exploit alternative markets, including a number in South America, they undoubtedly proved disruptive to business. The riots and popular demonstrations that racked England in 1811 were a direct result of the unemployment caused by the trade war. In the end, however, the consequences for the economies of continental Europe were much more disastrous. It became increasingly difficult to obtain the raw materials essential for manufacturing. The economic life of great ports and business centers such as Amsterdam was paralyzed. Production declined and unemployment rose. The Continent—including France—lost more than Britain by the boycott, and the general resentment at French interference did much to fuel the European powers' final military resistance to Napoleon.

The Russian Campaign

It was against a background of developing restlessness that the emperor made his fatal mistake—he launched a campaign against the Russians. The most obvious pretext for his invasion was revenge for Alexander's flouting of the Continental System. The Russian economy was heavily dependent on the export of agricultural produce in exchange for manufactured goods, and one of Russia's most important trading partners was Britain. The French demand that the Baltic ports remain closed to British ships caused a serious economic crisis in Russia, and Alexander gradually began to break the embargo.

Napoleon's response was to muster the *"Grande Armée,"* the largest army the world had seen—over 600,000 in number; many of the troops were conscripts from countries under French rule and thus neither professional soldiers nor enthusiastic supporters of the French cause.

In the spring of 1812, the emperor and his army set out to conquer Russia. After the long march to the Russian border, the French force advanced into the heart of the country. The Russians avoided battle and retreated toward Moscow, destroying their own spring crops as they went. The French lines of communication

A contemporary depiction of Napoleon's retreat from Moscow, 1812.

became ever longer and more tenuous, and supplies increasingly difficult to obtain.

The Russians finally took a stand at Borodino, some 70 miles southwest of Moscow. In the battle that followed, both sides suffered terrible losses. Although Napoleon pushed on to Moscow, the Russian army maintained its discipline. The tsar refused to sue for peace, and retreated to positions east and south of Moscow. On the evening after the French entered the ancient Russian capital, a mysterious fire broke out, destroying many of its buildings, and leaving the French soldiers with little in the way of shelter. The city's population had fled, taking with them all available supplies.

For once Napoleon's decisiveness deserted him. Weeks passed as he waited in vain for signs that Russian resistance was crumbling. Only toward the end of October did he finally order the retreat of the Grande Armée, and the delay proved fatal. Loaded down with plunder, his troops trudged into the depths of the Russian winter. As rivers overflowed, swollen by the seasonal rains, the French army was engulfed in mud and battered by blizzards. Disease and hunger ran rampant, while the weary soldiers were harried by bands of mounted Russian Cossacks, who rode out of the storms to wreak yet more havoc.

Six weeks later the survivors staggered back across the border into Germany, the pitiful remnants of the mighty expedition—of the original force of over 600,000, only 100,000 were left. Napoleon hastened back to Paris to build a new army, apparently neither discouraged by the horrors of the retreat nor deterred by the human misery his campaign had inflicted on so many. The Prussian conscripts deserted.

The End of the Empire

At last the spell was broken, and European statesmen began to plan a war of liberation that would see the end of French domination; one of their leaders was Prince Klemens von Metternich of Austria, a figure to play a crucial role in the post-Napoleonic era. In March 1813 a treaty was signed between Russia and Prussia, and Europe waited in suspense to see whether Austria would join the allied coalition against France or remain neutral. The news that the Austrian emperor had finally declared war on France was accompanied by tidings of further French losses in Spain, where the Peninsular War still dragged on.

Faced with the collapse of his empire, Napoleon succeeded in mounting an army, but only by recruiting conscripted troops who were underage. In October 1813 at Leipzig, in central Germany, his forces were defeated, and he was driven back to France. As the European powers began to close in, the British joined the coalition. Terms were offered to Napoleon which

allowed him to remain emperor, but required France's return to her "normal borders"—the term was deliberately vague. When the conditions were rejected, the allies invaded France.

In March 1814 Paris was taken and Napoleon forced to abdicate. A brother of Louis XVI was recognized as king of France, and took the title of Louis XVIII (ruled 1814–1824). Meanwhile the allied powers summoned a congress to meet in Vienna a few months later, to negotiate a settlement for the rest of Europe. Somewhat at a loss as to what to do with the former emperor, they exiled him to Elba, a tiny island off the coast of Italy.

He was set up as ruler of the island in a modest villa, and permitted to organize a miniature court, for which he designed the uniforms and prescribed the ceremonials. Among those who attended receptions there was his redoubtable sister Pauline. The rooms of the villa were decorated with paintings showing scenes from his campaigns; on the wall of one of them visitors can still see an inscription, in the former emperor's handwriting, which says: "Napoleon can be happy everywhere."

His happiness seems to have lasted no more than ten months. As the allies gathered at Vienna and bickered amongst themselves about the reshaping of Europe, "The Man" escaped and returned to France, where in the famous "Hundred Days" he reawakened popular enthusiasm and raised an army. Only on June 18, 1815, was he finally defeated at the Battle of Waterloo, in Belgium. At one stage in the fighting Napoleon's army came within sight of victory, and afterwards he bitterly blamed his marshals for the loss.

This time the allies were taking no chances. He was shipped out to the remote island of St. Helena far off in the south Atlantic, where he lived out the last six years of his life in seclusion.

During the Napoleonic period Europe underwent a transformation. In France, the confused and often brutal measures of the Revolution and its aftermath gave way to the relative order of the Consulate. Even before the Revolution the middle classes had demonstrated their special role in French society, and the effect of Napoleonic reform was to strengthen their position. Preservation of the land settlement, reform of secondary and higher education, and the establishment of a civil service all played a crucial role in middle-class achievements later in the 19th century.

As Napoleon's power spread throughout continental Europe, it brought to an end the rule of the Old Regime. A system of states that was the product of centuries of development became irrevocably dismantled. The period immediately following his overthrow saw a strongly conservative reaction, but the ideas of individual and national freedom released into the mainstream of European thought remained a powerful force in 19th-century politics. Even some of the most reactionary rulers were forced to compromise with the advocates of liberty.

Britain, Napoleon's bitterest enemy, was the only country in Europe to have no firsthand experience of his reforms. Nonetheless the Napoleonic Wars produced major changes in British life. During the years of war the country's economy suffered the strains imposed by the Continental System, but industrial production was high, and on the whole hatred and fear of Old Boney kept internal divisions within bounds. With the coming of peace, Britain plunged into a period of economic depression. As a consequence of the trade blockade, manufactured goods had piled up unsold. The return home of soldiers from the Peninsular War and other campaigns flooded the market with workers for whom there were no jobs. The social unrest that followed introduced elements of revolutionary struggle into British life and politics.

As for the Russians, the Napoleonic Wars succeeded in introducing them into the mainstream of European events, and they played a decisive role in liberating the Continent. Yet the spirit of revolution had little immediate effect on Russian society. Even Tsar Alexander I, who flirted briefly with liberal notions, soon returned to conservative orthodoxy. The chief memory left by Napoleon's invasion was that of the heroic Russian resistance. Whether in Tolstoy's epic narrative of War and Peace, *or in the clashing national anthems of Tchaikovsky's* 1812 Overture, *future Russians commemorated the victory against Napoleon as one of their country's proudest achievements.*

Questions for Further Discussion

1. What were the main features of Napoleon's administrative and legal reorganization in Europe? How many of them had a permanent effect?

2. What were the chief economic consequences of the Napoleonic Wars? Which European countries were most affected by them?

3. To what extent did Napoleon undermine his own achievements by his miscalculations? What were his principal mistakes?

Suggestions for Further Reading

Applewhite, H. B., and D. G. Levy. *Women and Politics in the Age of the Democratic Revolution.* Ann Arbor, MI, 1990.

Bergeron, L. *France under Napoleon.* Princeton, NJ, 1981.

Chandler, David G. *The Campaigns of Napoleon.* New York, 1973.

Connelly, O. *Napoleon's Satellite Kingdoms.* New York, 1970.

Godechot, J., B. Hyslop, and D. Dowd. *The Napoleonic Era in Europe.* New York, 1971.

Hesse, Carla. *Publishing and Cultural Politics in Revolutionary Paris, 1789–1810.* Berkeley, CA, 1991.

Holtman, R. *The Napoleonic Revolution.* Baton Rouge, LA, 1979.

Woloch, Isser. *The French Veteran from the Revolution to the Restoration.* Chapel Hill, NC, 1979.

RESTORATION AND RESISTANCE IN THE AGE OF METTERNICH

The years following Napoleon's defeat saw conflicting attempts to remodel European politics and society. Conservative statesmen aimed to construct a balance of power which left no single state in a dominant position. At the same time, they tried to restore the social patterns of prerevolutionary life and stamp out the vestiges of revolutionary ideology.

Set against this were two important new forces in European political thought: liberalism and nationalism. For liberals, successful government required that an increased portion of those being governed play some part in the process of political decision making. The liberal state, the ideal form of which was a constitutional monarchy, should protect the rights of the individual, encourage the development of business and industry, and establish friendly relations with other nations. Those who most eagerly took up the liberal cause were those most likely to benefit from it: the middle classes.

Many liberals, especially in central Europe and Italy, believed that their goals could best be obtained by the creation of self-ruling nation-states to replace the tangled network of principalities, monarchies, and empires typical of pre-Napoleonic Europe. Nationalism thus served the liberal interest; indeed many saw a nationalist revolution as the essential prelude to the formation of a liberal government.

At the Congress of Vienna, the five chief European powers—Austria, Britain, France, Prussia, and Russia—agreed to redistribute territory while paying little heed to the interests of those whose frontiers were being redrawn. The results came under almost immediate fire from reformers and revolutionaries. Yet however high-handed the settlement, its provisions helped to keep widespread international conflict at bay up to World War I.

The conservative statesmen at Vienna believed that society could be successfully governed only by maintaining the distinctions and privileges that had evolved over time. The country where this ideology was most rigidly enforced was Russia, where the still absolutist tsar exercised virtually complete control over social and political life.

Elsewhere, conservative rulers struggled to maintain their positions intact. The ethnically complex Hapsburg empire tried to protect itself against nationalist revolts by the formation of a police state, and in the German states student demonstrations were suppressed. Only intervention by foreign powers reestablished reactionary governments in Spain and Italy, where military uprisings against Bourbon rulers had introduced liberal reforms.

The purpose of these interventions was to enforce the agreements reached at the Congress of Vienna, where Britain, Prussia, and Russia had joined with Austria in acting as guarantors of the new map of Europe. France was admitted to the alliance in 1818. The concept of united action against the forces of revolution is known as the Concert of Europe. Far from strengthening the unity of the allies, however, the Concert of Europe soon proved discordant, with the British opposed to the idea of "superintending" the Continent. When the concept was extended by Russian intervention on behalf of Spain in the New World colonies, the president of the United States issued the Monroe Declaration (which established the policy known as the Monroe Doctrine), warning the Europeans not to interfere in the Western Hemisphere. The political scene in France after Napoleon was shaped by conflict between Louis XVIII's cautiously reforming conservatism and the ultra-right wing. Although the restoration of the Bourbons began with a return to relative peace and prosperity, tension between the two extremes soon began to wreck the compromise which Louis XVIII sought. Louis was succeeded by his arrogant younger brother, who reigned as Charles X until his ultra-royalist policies and political maneuverings forced him into exile in 1830. His replacement, Louis Philippe, avoided making the same mistake. Increasing the power of the middle class, he was generally successful in rebuilding order and prosperity.

In Britain there was no need to restore the old order, because it had never been seriously challenged. The number of those eligible to vote was severely limited and tied to property. Both houses of Parliament were predominantly aristocratic, as were members of the two political parties, the ruling conservative Tories and the slightly more liberal Whigs, who thus came essentially from the same class. Popular unrest provoked by the economic depression following the Napoleonic Wars led to demands for parliamentary reform. From 1829 to 1835, Parliament passed a series of reform bills that, while far from radical, marked a significant change.

THE CONGRESS OF VIENNA AND THE SEARCH FOR STABILITY

Against a background of pomp and ceremony, the leaders of the great powers of Europe gathered in Vienna to restore the Continent to what they conceived to be its rightful order.

Leaders at the Congress of Vienna

The central figure in the deliberations was Prince Klemens von Metternich (1773–1859), Austrian foreign minister from 1809 to 1848. An urbane aristocrat whose name has become synonymous with cunning intrigue and the manipulation of power, Metternich's aim at the Congress was to return Europe as far as possible to its pre-Napoleonic state, and do whatever possible to prevent any future outbreaks of "the virus of revolution." For decades Metternich's political and social views made him the chief spokesman of European conservatism, while some of his policies justifiably earned him the label of reactionary.

His only equal as a diplomat was the French representative, Prince Talleyrand, whose years of service to a bewildering variety of masters—the church under the Old Regime, then the various revolutionary governments, and most recently Napoleon—had made him a wily negotiator. Talleyrand was sent to Vienna to secure a deal for France that would not only involve the fewest possible penalties for his former master's misdeeds, but would restore French influence on the European political scene.

The participants in the Congress of Vienna, 1815.

The British spokesman, Lord Castlereagh (1769–1822), was, like the other two, his country's foreign minister. Less occupied with the finer details than his colleagues, Castlereagh's chief concern was to see that the final agreement posed no threat to Britain's position as the leading European power. Although a less dominating figure than Metternich, Castlereagh was probably the most influential in framing the final decisions of the Congress.

In such professional company the Prussian king, Friedrich Wilhelm III (ruled 1797–1840), played a lesser role. The remaining great power, Russia, was represented by its ruler, Tsar Alexander I. In the early part of his reign, the tsar demonstrated some interest in the ideas of the Enlightenment, but after the defeat of Napoleon he turned to mystical visions of converting his fellow rulers to Christian virtue. By the time of the Congress he was as staunchly conservative as Metternich, but the Austrian, more interested in balancing self-interest and expediency, and violently anti-Russian, had little patience with Alexander's grandiose and incoherent notions.

The Reshaping of Europe

The guiding principle at Vienna was "legitimacy." This referred to the idea that the status of rulers and their borders should revert to that of 1789, before the Revolution. The concept was actually suggested by Talleyrand and accepted by Metternich and Alexander for two reasons: it legitimized the return of a Bourbon

monarch to France, and it avoided the loss of any French territory as punishment for Napoleon's aggression. Metternich adopted the idea of legitimacy as a means of justifying his reactionary policies, but it was applied selectively. In the case of France, Talleyrand obtained what he wanted, together with the restoration of Bourbon monarchies in Spain and Naples and the kingdom of Piedmont-Sardinia.

Even though France retained its territory, the other participants were concerned with other issues than the simple one of legitimacy. The redrawing of frontiers aimed to compensate France's conquerors, while providing a secure balance of power. Furthermore, Metternich and his colleagues were determined to block any future French attempt at expansion. To that end the Dutch Republic was combined with the Austrian Netherlands (Belgium), to form the Kingdom of the Netherlands. This arrangement also satisfied the British concern that the vital North Sea ports remain in neutral hands.

In return for their giving up the Netherlands, the Austrians received two provinces in northern Italy, Lombardy and Venetia. Through dynastic connections, Austria played a decisive role in the policies of the restored Grand Duchy of Tuscany and the Kingdom of the Two Sicilies. The strong Austrian presence just to the south of the Alps served as another barrier against French expansion. As for Italy itself, dominated by the Austrians and divided for the rest into a series of small kingdoms and duchies and the Papal States, it

Prince Metternich, the leading diplomat at the Congress of Vienna.

remained, as Metternich put it, "only a geographical expression."

To block France on the Rhine frontier, Prussia received a chunk of German territory on the river's left bank. Prussia's claim to all of Saxony, however, caused serious disagreement. The tsar agreed to back the Prussians on Saxony if they in turn would support his taking the lion's share of Poland. Both Castlereagh and Metternich objected to the enlargement and strengthening of two of their chief rivals. In consequence, Metternich, Castlereagh, and Talleyrand formed a secret pact, whereby the three powers would go to war rather than see the deal struck. In the end a compromise was worked out: Prussia took about half of Saxony, and Russia was given most of Poland.

Nowhere was the principle of legitimacy less observed than in Germany and central Europe. Napoleon's organization of the numerous states and kingdoms into 39 (37 states, Austria, and Prussia) was retained, and they were brought together into a larger unit called the German Confederation, which thus replaced the Holy Roman Empire. Although an appearance of German political unity was obtained, the confederation had little power, and in any case it was dominated by Austria.

The final agreement, as Metternich had intended, left no one the clear winner, and everyone with something. Britain, more interested in trade outside Europe, received territories in South Africa, South America, and the island of Ceylon. The mere descrip-

tion of the decisions of the Congress, which never once met in formal session, emphasizes the element of game playing. In the elegant drawing rooms of the Hapsburg capital, the fates of millions were decided by a handful of aristocratic diplomats. These men were profoundly unsympathetic to the dawning hopes of liberals and nationalists.

Yet the achievements of Metternich and his colleagues have more positive aspects. In the first place they negotiated rather than fought, itself a notable improvement after a generation of bloodshed. Secondly, the temptation to punish France for the excesses of Napoleon was avoided. Finally, the balance worked out at Vienna, for all its defects, provided a relative degree of stability in Europe for the next 100 years. This stability made possible precisely the revolutionary changes that Metternich so feared.

THE RESTORATION AND THE CONSERVATIVE ORDER

Metternich and his fellow conservatives were not merely trying to preserve the past for its own sake: their views reflected a coherent philosophical position, most cogently expressed in the writings of Edmund Burke (1729–1797). His *Reflections on the Revolution in France*

The British statesman, orator, and philosopher, Edmund Burke.

(1790), which appeared as early as the Revolution's second year, came to have a significant influence on conservative thought throughout Europe.

An outspoken opponent of the doctrines of the French Revolution, Burke believed that society should evolve slowly, in accordance with existing varieties of rank and status. Radical change, by its very unpredictability, was seen as dangerous. The intellectual movement from which the Revolution had sprung, the Enlightenment, emphasized the power of reason. Conservative thinkers argued just the opposite. Society was far too complex, and susceptible to human emotions and weaknesses, to be organized by any kind of rational scheme—a point of view that had much in common with the Romantic movement in the arts (see Part VII, Topic 7).

The conservative rulers of the restoration believed in preserving the existing institutions at all cost. If that required censorship, limits to free speech, the execution of dissenters, those were necessary prices. So rigid an attitude inevitably proved self-defeating. Even in Metternich's Austria, with its spies and police, its border controls and censorship of books and even music, the forces of change were irresistible. In 1848, a few weeks after the outbreak of revolution in France, public protests spread to Austria, and Metternich was forced to flee for his life.

Russia Under Alexander and Nicholas

The country whose rulers most thoroughly repressed attempts at reform was Russia. By comparison with western Europe Russia was still overwhelmingly an agricultural nation, made up of peasants and their aristocratic masters. There were few cities of any size, and thus no urban middle class had developed. The Orthodox church, far from defending the rights of its adherents, reinforced the policies of the tsar.

Once Alexander had recovered from his early bout of liberalism, he proved a formidable conservative, both at home and abroad. Censorship was strict, and the universities were carefully watched to crush the growth of any dangerous new ideas. Alexander ruled the Kingdom of Poland, given to Russia at the Congress of Vienna, with the same iron hand, even though in theory it had its own constitution with the tsar acting as king.

The only real challenge to authority came when Alexander died in 1825. A group of army officers inspired by Western ideas staged a revolt; they are known as the *Decembrists*, after the month of their attempt. The young liberals had little chance of success. Their uprising was poorly organized and soon crushed, but they gave Alexander's successor, Nicholas I (ruled 1825–1855), an excuse to tighten his grip even further; the 1820s and 1830s saw the introduction of many conspicuously reactionary measures. Nicholas put down a Polish revolt in 1831 with equal ruthlessness, and for the rest of his reign he maintained his rule unchallenged. He strengthened the army and police, and increased the power of the state bureaucracy. Little was done to improve the living and working conditions of Russia's vast peasant population, and all their attempts at rebellions were suppressed.

In spite of the lack of progress, however, with the slow spread of literacy Russians began to ask questions about their country's future. In the rarified intellectual circles of Moscow and St. Petersburg a debate developed between the westernizers and the Slavophiles. The former wanted their country to adopt Western European models, while the latter claimed that Russia's unique character should be preserved untouched by Western ideas and institutions, since it gave her a special destiny. The dispute was to play an important part in Russian cultural life later in the century.

The German Confederation and the Hapsburgs

The two rival major powers in central Europe, Austria and Prussia, shared a common fear: the rise of German nationalism. Charlemagne's original attempt to unite Germany, the Holy Roman Empire, had long since broken up into over 300 separate states. As a result, the idea of a united Germany had been impossible for centuries. With Napoleon, however, the separate states were consolidated under French rule in the Confederation of the Rhine, one of the consequences of which was a burst of German nationalism in protest.

Even the archconservative Metternich could hardly propose a return to the multitude of separate states. The creation in its place of the German Confederation was intended to prevent Germany from achieving any real political union by giving Austria, the confederation's permanent president, an edge over Prussia.

The Burschenschaften

Signs of nationalist and antiforeign stirrings began to occur in Germany during the war against Napoleon. Shortly after 1815, the nationalist mood intensified with the appearance of groups of student activists known as *Burschenschaften* (Brotherhoods) in university circles. In 1817, the 300th anniversary of Luther's publication of his 95 theses was celebrated by the Burschenschaften at the Wartburg Festival. The occasion was supposed to be a religious one, but the heady effects of speeches, song, and beer began to take over. To cheers from the crowd, a French officer's staff and a Prussian military text were symbolically burnt.

The Austrian and Prussian authorities anxiously waited for further confirmation of their fears. Two years

German students demonstrating for a liberal constitution at the Wartburg Festival, 1817.

later, when a fanatical student murdered a reactionary writer, Metternich seized his opportunity and summoned the rulers of the leading German states to a meeting at Carlsbad. The Carlsbad Decrees of 1819 abolished the Burschenschaften, tightened censorship, and had students and professors suspected of liberal tendencies put under careful watch. These measures revealed Metternich at his most reactionary.

Prussia and the Customs Union

The ruling family of Prussia, the Hohenzollern, shared Metternich's contempt for liberalism. The chief instrument of their power in Prussia was still the army which, together with the bureaucracy, was in the hands of the landed nobility, the Junkers. Any gesture toward nationalism would have been regarded by these warlords as a betrayal of Prussian virtue, yet ironically it was the Prussians who began to advance German economic unity.

Their motive was commercial self-interest. With the acquisition at the Congress of Vienna of the German territory on the left bank of the Rhine, Prussia consisted of two separate and unconnected parts. In 1819, to help facilitate the movement of trade, Prussia began to negotiate treaties with the neighboring German states, and encouraged them to adopt the Prussian system of unified tariffs. The leading advocate of removing tariff barriers was the German economist Georg Friedrich List (1789–1846), who later became a naturalized U.S. citizen and wrote on the American economy.

By 1834 almost all German governments were members of the Prussian *Zollverein* (customs union); the notable—and predictable—exception was Austria. The formation of the Zollverein proved to be a major step in the building of a united German nation, and helped Prussia emerge as its eventual leader.

Repression in the Hapsburg Empire

Prussia and the other German states were at least linked by a common language. The fear of nationalism which obsessed Metternich and his Hapsburg masters was based on the multilingual and multicultural nature of the Hapsburg state. With the acquisition in 1815 of Lombardy and Venetia, Italians were added to the Hungarians, Serbs, Croatians, Slovenians, Czechs, Slovaks, and others who chafed under Austrian rule.

The danger of a nationalist uprising took precedence over all other political considerations. Plans for internal reforms included the establishment of local councils of landholders and a decentralization of the bureaucracy, but they foundered on the necessity of maintaining a police state, albeit an extremely inefficient one. Censorship, surveillance by both police and spies, and the close supervision of universities and libraries combined to produce a regime second only to Russia for severity of repression.

THE CONCERT OF EUROPE

Not content with reinforcing their convictions in their own countries, Europe's conservative leaders felt the duty to go to the help of one another whenever a reactionary regime was challenged: the French Revolution had taught them that an uprising in one state could threaten another. Two of those present at the Congress of Vienna proposed schemes to present a united front against the forces of revolution. Tsar Alexander asked for support for his Holy Alliance, whose members would use Christian principles to govern their states and defend their interests in Christian brotherhood. Most European governments joined, although with little enthusiasm. The two states that refused to sign were Britain, unwilling to become involved in a continental enterprise, and the Papal States: the pope had no intention of surrendering his moral lead to an Eastern Orthodox ruler.

Metternich's Concert of Europe was a far more formidable affair: a military alliance among Austria, Britain, Prussia, and Russia, which guaranteed to maintain the Vienna agreement for 20 years. This international "force for order" was to meet at regular intervals to survey the situation and strengthen its resolve, as well as intervene to crush revolutions wherever they should occur. Metternich had called the tsar's Holy

Francisco Goya's horrific vision of *Saturn Devouring One of His Sons* (c. 1821).

Alliance a "sonorous nothing"; for all its initial success, in the long run the Concert of Europe had little more lasting influence than Alexander's scheme.

The allies' first congress, which took place at Aix-la-Chapelle in 1818 with Britain present as an observer, witnessed the successful resolution of postwar problems: foreign occupation troops were removed from French soil, and France, where Bourbon rule had been peacefully restored, was admitted to the alliance. The next meetings, however—at Troppau in 1820 and at Laibach in 1821—came in response to serious unrest in Italy and Spain.

The Conservative Order Challenged: Spain and Italy

The first signs of trouble appeared in Spain. With the expulsion of the French in 1814, the restoration of Ferdinand VII (ruled 1808, 1814–1833) seemed cause for celebration. It did not take him long, in true Bourbon style, to abandon the constitution and set up all the apparatus of state repression. Liberal leaders were arrested, the universities were closed down,

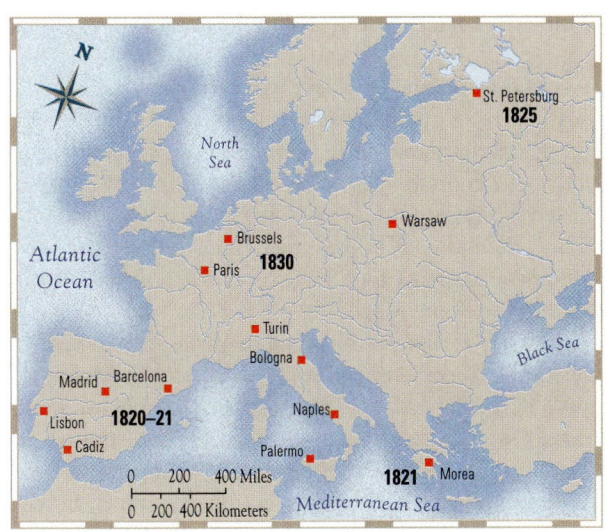

Map 5.1   European Revolutionary Movements, 1820–1830

censorship was revived, and even the Inquisition was restored.

Popular resentment came to a head in 1820, when an army which was formed to put down uprisings in the Spanish colonies in America turned on Madrid instead, and forced the king to accept a return to the Spanish Constitution of 1812, a liberal document adopted during the Napoleonic occupation and modeled after the French Constitution of 1791. The reforms did not last long, but news of the successful Spanish revolt had a galvanizing effect on revolutionaries in Italy.

For the Italian states, Napoleonic rule had meant more enlightened rule and fairer taxes. With virtually the whole of Italy now under the Bourbons, the Hapsburgs, or their supporters, the various states slid again into absolutism. Ruthless government repression put down all traces of public protest. In response, Italian nationalists soon began to form secret societies; their members, known as the *Carbonari* (the name means "charcoal burners," and may have been intended to emphasize support for the underprivileged), differed as to the degree of violence necessary to produce political change, but advocated free and independent Italian states governed by constitutional monarchies.

When word reached Naples of the events in Spain, a group of young army officers led a revolt against the hated Neapolitan Bourbon king, Ferdinand I (ruled 1759–1806, 1815–1825). As in the case of their Spanish military counterparts, at first the move succeeded, and the king of Naples was forced to introduce a liberal constitution based on the Spanish Constitution of 1812. Here was exactly the kind of situation that Metternich had envisaged. With the agreement of Prussia and Russia, an Austrian army was dispatched to Naples, and to Piedmont where a liberal revolt had also broken out in 1821. The young prince Charles Albert also adopted the Spanish Constitution. The rebels were crushed; those who did not manage to escape were either executed or thrown into prison. The Spanish liberals' turn was next. In 1822, the allies of the Concert of Europe met at Verona; this time it fell to the French to send troops, stamp out the revolt, suppress the constitution, and restore the Bourbon monarchy.

The interventions in Italy and Spain successfully fulfilled Metternich's scheme to oppose the forces of change, but they were the last effective antirevolutionary action taken by the great powers. The British observers at the Troppau congress in 1820, who had protested against interfering in other nations' affairs, objected to the dispatch of French forces. The Spanish king's violent and bloodthirsty treatment of his liberal opponents had a powerful impact on the horrified French soldiers, and France ceased to play an active part in the alliance. Austria's only remaining dependable allies were Russia and Prussia, and the Concert's next test was too severe even for them.

The Monroe Doctrine

The troops who started the Spanish uprising had been on their way to the Spanish New World colonies to put down rebellions led by, among others, Simón Bolívar (1783–1830). Replacing Ferdinand on his tottering throne did nothing to end the unrest in America, and Metternich decided that the principle of suppressing revolts in Europe should be extended to European possessions abroad. With his encouragement, therefore, Alexander prepared to launch a great fleet to bring the colonies to their senses, and return them to Spanish rule.

The British, quite apart from their opposition to interference in another nation's business, had every reason to wish the rebels well: they were causing trouble to Spain, Britain's chief trade rival in America, while at the same time providing new markets for the sale of British goods, the production of which had vastly increased since the industrial revolution. George Canning (1770–1827), who became foreign minister in 1822, therefore proposed to the United States that a joint British–United States declaration should condemn the involvement of the Holy Alliance—a name in itself offensive to American susceptibilities—in the affairs of the Western Hemisphere.

The Monroe Doctrine, announced by President James Monroe (served 1817–1825) to Congress in December 1823, consisted of a unilateral U.S. statement: any attempt by European nations to interfere in the Americas would be regarded by the United States as an "unfriendly act." With Britain, still Europe's supreme naval power, supporting the United States' position, Alexander chose to abandon any thought of sailing to restore Spanish rule in the colonies.

The Greek War of Independence

In the case of Spain's western colonies, at least the tsar was sympathetic to Metternich's urgings, if powerless to act. In a contemporary nationalist uprising on Europe's eastern frontiers, the Greeks' struggle to win independence from their Turkish rulers and found their own state, the Russians found themselves for the first time on the side of the rebels.

The Greeks' revolt began in 1821, only to be met by brutal Turkish reprisals. In 1824 the massacre of some 90 percent of the Greek population of the island of Chios shocked much of Europe, accustomed to thinking of Greece as the birthplace of European civilization; in addition, leaders of the Romantic movement such as Lord Byron did much to foster sympathy for the Greek cause. The Russians, furthermore, shared the Greeks' Christian Orthodox religion; indeed, Russia had been converted to Christianity by two Greek missionaries. To add a practical consideration to the demands of religious brotherhood, if Russia managed to defeat Turkey on behalf of the Greeks, her own position in the Mediterranean would be reinforced by winning control of the straits of the Bosphorus, an aim dating back to the reign of Peter the Great.

In such circumstances the founder of the Holy Alliance could hardly stand by idle. Britain, unwilling to see Russia use the Greeks' cause to gain a power base at the Turks' expense, surrendered its objections to involvement in other people's business; by joining the Russian forces, the British were able to keep a careful eye on their "allies." Against the agonized protests of Metternich, in 1827 Britain, Russia, and France intervened on the side of the Greeks. By 1829 the defeated Turks had no choice but to concede independence to a small mainland Greece, along with a measure of self-government to those Romanians and Serbs who lived in the Ottoman Empire.

Thus, by supreme irony one of the most reactionary members of the Concert of Europe joined with the two powers who had left the original alliance, in support of the very cause the allies had come together to combat in the first place: nationalism. Furthermore, the victory of the Greeks and their supporters violated

Eugène Delacroix's painting *The Massacre at Chios* (1824) helped rouse support for the Greeks in their struggle for independence.

Significant Dates

The Congress of Vienna and Its Aftermath

1814–1815	The Congress of Vienna meets
1818	First meeting of the Concert of Europe at Aix-la-Chapelle
1819	Peterloo Massacre
1820	Spanish Army revolts against Bourbons
1821	Revolt in Piedmont; Greeks begin struggle for independence
1823	Monroe Doctrine proclaimed
1824	Massacre of Chios; coronation of Charles X of France
1829	Greece becomes independent
1830	Revolution in France and Italy; Belgium becomes independent
1832	Reform Bill passed in Britain

the principle of legitimacy established at the Congress of Vienna. If the Greek War of Independence did not kill off Metternich's cherished notion entirely, it certainly dealt it a death blow. The concept of a united reactionary Europe, ready to crush the specter of revolution wherever it appeared, had no longer any relevance to a political and social world on the brink of revolutionary changes.

FRANCE AND THE POLITICS OF COMPROMISE

Louis XVIII, the Bourbon king restored to the throne of France, was by temperament a political moderate. His brother, Louis XVI, had died on the guillotine, and the so-called Louis XVII, Louis XVI's son and heir, died in prison without ever reigning. Any notion that his return to France might be the signal for popular demonstrations in favor of the Bourbons was soon scotched by the enthusiasm with which Napoleon's escape from Elba was greeted. In any case Louis himself, almost 60 and too fat and gouty to walk without help, had no wish to be deposed from what he called "the most comfortable of armchairs."

Shortly after occupying that chair, he issued a charter, which laid out the principles by which he intended to rule. Napoleon's legal system and centralized bureaucracy were to remain in force, along with the

Napoleonic tax structure. The country was to be governed by a parliament consisting of two chambers: the Chamber of Peers, made up of the aristocracy, and the Chamber of Deputies, elected by the votes of a tiny wealthy minority. The king could dissolve the Chamber of Deputies, appoint and dismiss his own ministers, and deal directly with foreign countries. Since he was also head of the army, the authority of either chamber of Parliament was, to say the least, limited.

The Ultraroyalists

Far from using his own concentration of power in the interests of the nobility, Louis fought to oppose the often reactionary demands of the "ultraroyalist" aristocrats who had trickled back into France. Eager to avenge the injuries inflicted on them by the Revolution, they returned to reclaim their lands and privileges.

If the aristocrats expected to see their property automatically restored to them by Louis' charter, they were bitterly disappointed. Peasants and middle-class citizens who had bought land from nobles or from the church were confirmed in possession of their holdings.

Furthermore, the retention of Napoleon's legal and bureaucratic systems meant that all citizens were equal in the eyes of the law, and that all had the chance of professional advancement.

While the aristocracy was enraged by the charter, middle-class liberal reformers were far from completely satisfied. It gave the middle classes little actual political power, for since political representation was based on land, rather than business wealth, most of them could neither vote for, nor take part in, the two chambers of Parliament. Nonetheless the presence of Louis himself, steering a moderate course between the "ultras" and the reformers, maintained a precarious peace.

Among the more autocratic leaders of the rebellious nobles was the king's younger brother and eventual successor, the count of Artois (ruled 1824–1830). While alive, Louis managed to keep his brother under control, and tried to persuade him of the need for moderation if the Bourbon family was to remain in power. In 1824 Louis died, and the new king, Charles X, did not take long to demonstrate the truth of the saying that "the Bourbons learnt nothing and forgot nothing" from the years following 1789. Charles' coronation at Rheims

Revolution breaks out at the Pont Neuf in Paris in 1830.

became the excuse for an ornate ceremony in Medieval style, to symbolize his intention to return to past glories.

Aristocratic landowners were given compensation for the loss of their estates; the money was raised from the interest on government bonds chiefly held by middle-class investors. A series of measures concerned with inheritance threatened to undermine the principle of equality before the law, alarming both middle classes and peasants. The church regained a strong role, with increased control of education, and the Jesuits were allowed to return to France and to their earlier influential position in the country's educational policies and political life.

The Revolution of 1830

Within a few years Charles had so alienated vast sections of public opinion that in the spring of 1830 even the chamber turned against him. The king dismissed it and called new elections. In spite of press censorship and official pressures, another liberal majority was returned. In July 1830 Charles again dissolved the chamber and produced an electoral system that would guarantee him a majority: only some 25,000 people—the richest men in France—could vote. All freedom of the press was suspended.

The result was revolution. In the July uprisings the workers and students of Paris blocked the streets with barricades. Among the first groups were workers in the printing trade. With the army unwilling to fire on the crowds, and in the absence of any firm political support, the last Bourbon king of France abdicated and took himself off to England, where he died, unmourned, in exile.

The revolutionaries had fought to bring back a republic, but France's political and business leaders were more cautious. Remembering the excesses of the Revolution of 1789, they decided to avoid the extremes of absolute monarchy and popular republic by creating a constitutional monarchy. In this way they hoped to achieve stability and at the same time maintain their own influence.

The same sense of compromise governed their choice for the new king. The duke of Orleans was an aristocrat, the descendant of a cousin of Louis XVI who had served on the convention and voted for Louis' execution in 1793. The duke thus had both noble and appropriately revolutionary family credentials, and had lived an unexceptionable middle-class life. After promising to honor the Constitution of 1814, he was duly crowned as Louis Philippe (ruled 1830–1848).

The Revolution of 1830, fought by workers, students, and artisans, served to abolish the absolute power of the king, but its chief beneficiaries were the middle-class property owners, who now controlled the legislature.

CONSERVATISM CHALLENGED: POLITICAL UNREST AND CONSTITUTIONALISM IN BRITAIN

The tumultuous events that swept continental Europe in the early 19th century reinforced the innate conservatism of British politicians. The Tory party, Britain's conservatives, had held virtually uninterrupted power since the 1780s, and guided their country to victory over Napoleon. Their parliamentary opponents, the Whigs, shared the Tories' aristocratic background. Whatever differences there might be on niceties of policy, neither party had any interest in a wider sharing of power or in a more equitable distribution of property.

The country was governed by two houses of Parliament, the Lords and the Commons. Members of both houses, virtually always landed aristocrats, were elected by a tiny minority of around 5 percent of the adult male population, themselves property owners. The counties and boroughs that these members represented were traditional aristocratic strongholds; the growing industrial centers of central and northern England sent no members to Parliament.

The Peterloo Massacre

In the aftermath of Waterloo and the economic depression that beset Britain, popular unrest began to mount. The misery of living and working conditions in northern cities such as Manchester, together with the fear of unemployment, inspired radical leaders to press for wider parliamentary representation, despite the economic character of their grievances. The very violence of government reaction proved its own undoing. In 1819 a crowd of some 60,000 gathered in St. Peter's Fields, in the center of Manchester, to attend a political demonstration in favor of reform. Troops of the Manchester and Cheshire Cavalry fired on the assembly, killing eleven people and wounding over 400. Radical leaders and critics in the press, in reference to the decisive Battle of Waterloo, dubbed the event the "Peterloo Massacre," and its victims became the first martyrs of the struggle for reform.

The Peterloo Massacre proved significant in another respect: over a quarter of those injured were women, demonstrating alongside men for political change. By the second decade of the 19th century, the development of industry had begun to change the part that gender played in the division of labor. Machines provided their own energy and required no special strength on the part of their users; they could be operated by women or men. The growing cities provided a greater range of employment for women, which often led to their exploitation by factory owners. At the same time women became increasingly aware of the domestic problems created by urban growth.

If the victims of Peterloo had chosen politics as a field for activism, other women turned to popular religion as a means of redressing injustices. A series of woman preachers began to address meetings of workers on the need for social justice. These preachers included Elizabeth Gorse Gaunt (b. 1777) and Ann Cutler (b. 1759), who was known as "Praying Nanny."

Pressure for Reform

In Parliament, however, the demand for social and political reform fell on deaf ears. Indeed, the Six Acts of 1819 passed in the same year as Peterloo—and the same year as the Carlsbad decrees—limited the right of public assembly, censored literature, and imposed a tax on newspapers.

So extreme a response alarmed many moderate Tories, whose general inclination was to aim for compromise. Some feared that government stubbornness could lead to revolution, while others were attracted by the new ideas of utilitarianism and genuinely interested in social reform. Under pressure from George Canning, Robert Peel, and other moderates, the criminal code was reformed, and workers were allowed to form unions, although not to strike. The tariffs on cheap imported grain, controlled by the Corn Laws—which had raised the tax after the Napoleonic Wars—were reduced; these taxes, which protected English landowners while keeping the price of bread high, had long been a source of popular resentment.

Reform of Parliament was a different matter. No Tory majority backed by the Anglican Church and the aristocracy would agree to revising the conditions of parliamentary representation. Many members of Parliament were either directly appointed by wealthy landowners or were elected by "rotten" or "pocket" boroughs—districts where electors were bullied and bribed to vote for the candidate of their landlord's choice; thus the election was in the "pocket" of the landowner. In the case of the "rotten" boroughs, members represented districts that were virtually unpopulated or had actually been abandoned.

It fell to the Whigs, with the support of the rising manufacturing and trading classes, to lead the cause of reform. They were inspired not by democratic principles but by the pragmatic belief that change would be "in the interests of the realm"; this characteristically British formula was bolstered in many cases by the ideas of utilitarian thinkers such as Jeremy Bentham (on the utilitarians, see Part VII, Topic 8). Furthermore, they hoped that middle-class members of Parliament would represent both middle- and working-class inter-

ests. In this way the workers would be satisfied and make no further protests, and a revolution could be avoided.

In 1830 an alliance of the Whigs and reform-minded liberals succeeded in defeating the Tories and forming a government. (Toward the end of the 19th century, the Whig party would change its name to the Liberal party.) The Whig prime minister, Earl Charles Grey (1764–1845), hastily drew up and forced through Parliament the Reform Bill of 1832.

Although the bill was to have momentous importance for British democratic life, it was intended to preserve the existing situation as far as possible. The vote was extended, but only on the basis of property; about 400,000 new electors were added to the voting rolls. Electoral districts were redistributed: the "rotten" boroughs were abolished and their seats given to the industrial cities of the north. No attempt was made, however, to create an equal balance between population size and political representation. As in France under Louis Philippe, the chief victors in 1830s Britain were the industrial middle classes, and their accession to a share in power served to promote a whole series of social reforms. Liberal legislation reorganized the church, reformed the divorce laws, and introduced the Poor Law of 1834. In 1833, on behalf of a reform society, a private member of Parliament successfully introduced a bill abolishing slavery throughout the British Empire.

In the years between then and 1847 the criminal code was further reformed, reducing the number of capital offenses to three; 20 years earlier there had been hundreds of crimes for which those found guilty had been executed. Working conditions for women and children were improved. Government grants were awarded to schools. In 1846, a Tory administration finally repealed the hated Corn Laws. The British had achieved the beginnings of revolutionary change without a revolution.

The years following Waterloo saw the apparent triumph of conservatism throughout most of Europe. The decisions of the Congress of Vienna and the subsequent formation of the Concert of Europe seemed to doom the liberal and nationalist causes to defeat right from the start. Effective power either remained in aristocratic hands, as in Prussia and Austria, or was returned there, as in France, Spain, and the kingdoms of Italy.

Yet, with the single exception of Russia, liberalism and nationalism were to have a profound effect on virtually every country in Europe, including Britain. Even where its manifestations were repressed, as in the Hapsburg empire, the demand for reform built to an irrepressible force. Further attempts to produce changes a generation after the Congress of Vienna led to violent action. In Britain, by contrast, political compromise led to a gradual process of reform that proved a continuous one.

In many cases one of the chief factors was economic. The growing demands of the rising industrial class in France proved fatal to the rule of Charles X, although his own misjudgments helped to hasten his fall. Prussia's plans for economic expansion led to the formation of a customs union that in turn prepared the way for a united Germany.

In some countries the very repression of nationalist uprisings served to inspire the forces of protest. The struggle to form a united Italy, know as the Risorgimento, had its roots in the Carbonari movement, born in opposition to Bourbon rule. The Greeks actually managed to achieve their freedom from the Turks, in large measure because the great powers—for selfish reasons of their own—decided to intervene.

Thus a battle that seemed definitively won in 1815 continued to rage at one level or another over the following decades. It says much for the persistence of the liberals and nationalists that so much progress was made so quickly. On the other hand the conservatives were determined and stubborn opponents: when the next round of protests came, in 1848, it led to violent revolution.

Questions for Further Discussion

1. How successful was the Concert of Europe in maintaining conservative policies in European affairs?

2. What role did Russia play in European politics following the Congress of Vienna? To what extent was this influenced by internal Russian developments?

3. What were the main stages of the Greek struggle for independence, and why was it successful?

Suggestions for Further Reading

Carr, R. *Spain, 1808–1939*. Oxford, 1982.

Church, C. *Europe in 1830: Revolution and Political Change*. London, 1983.

Dakin, D. *The Greek Struggle for Independence, 1821–1833*. Berkeley, CA, 1973.

Gildea, Robert. *Barricades and Borders, Europe 1800–1914*. Oxford, 1987.

Nicolson, Harold. *The Congress of Vienna: A Study in Allied Unity, 1812–1822*. New York, 1965.

Rude, G. *Debate on Europe*. New York, 1972.

de Sauvigny, G. *Metternich and His Times*. Atlantic Highlands, NJ, 1962.

Talmon, J. L. *Romanticism and Revolt*. New York, 1979.

Topic 6

THE NEW SOCIAL ORDER: WORKERS, WOMEN, AND THE MIDDLE CLASS

n the mid-18th century, Europe was still an overwhelmingly rural, agrarian society. Life for most people centered around traditional values associated with labor in the fields, family, and the church. The authority of the nobility on their lands and over the people who lived on them was largely unquestioned. The extended family, with several generations of relatives living and working together, prevailed. In agrarian families, women remained subservient to males, their roles limited to childbearing and rearing, to household duties, and to occasional participation in fieldwork and home-based textile making. Peasants, nobles, and clergy comprised the major social categories, while the merchant-capitalist class and those who lived in towns represented a small percentage of the population.

A hundred years later, much of that traditional way of life had changed. The development of technology and factory-based manufacturing pushed Europe increasingly toward an urban, industrial civilization. The structure of society grew more complex as two new groups—industrial workers and the middle class—joined the social order in ever larger numbers, giving rise to the modern class structure. As rural dwellers migrated to the cities in search of work, traditional values and family bonds began to break down, replaced by the urban nuclear family of parents and children. The status and role of women in this emerging industrial society also assumed new dimensions as tens of thousands of them left home for work in the factories.

By the middle of the 19th century, the general contours of European society as we know it today were formed. The years from 1789 to 1850 represented, then, a period of social transition, marked by great mobility and flux, and accompanied by growing political instability.

EUROPEAN SOCIETY IN TRANSITION

While advanced industrialization brought many changes to Europe, it also intensified some earlier social and demographic trends. The lure of the city for people living in the countryside, manifest even in the Middle Ages, accelerated, as did the growth pattern in Europe's population. The nascent industrial economy opened new opportunities for merchants and other longtime urban dwellers, while for others, such as artisans, it created problems and challenges. Moreover, as the French Revolution had shown, the political aspirations of different social groups could result in violence. Now, however, the new emerging social classes began to struggle over competing economic interests. The political struggles of the period after 1789 were to a great extent the result of growing class consciousness among both industrial workers and the middle class. Finally, while urban life had always presented governments with special challenges in public policy, the dramatic growth in the size and number of cities in the 19th century raised new dilemmas of planning and infrastructure and presented problems of enormous dimension in areas such as health, housing, transportation, and social control.

Population Patterns in the Age of Industrialization

As we have seen (see Part VII, Topic 2), in the first half of the 18th century Europe began to experience a tremendous growth in population. As industrialization spread, the numbers continued to increase, although not at a uniform or regular rate. The population of Europe grew by 40 percent between 1800 and 1850, from about 190 million to some 265 million. On the Continent (excluding Russia) the sharpest population rise occurred in the periods 1800–1820 (14 percent) and 1820–1830 (11 percent).

The agricultural revolution had enlarged the food supply in England, and during the 1820s and 1830s improved farming methods, including new machines and the cultivation of the potato, were gradually adopted on the Continent. Crop failures were less frequent but when they did occur, as in the Irish potato famine of the 1840s, they still caused widespread distress. A lower incidence of disease and improvements in diet slowly helped to raise the average life expectancy. Nevertheless, the basic staple of most diets, which for the majority of people were extremely limited and unbalanced, consisted of bread, grains, or potato. Milk, cheese, and green vegetables sometimes supplemented the staple foods, and meat or fish more rarely. In the town of Ghent, for example, an average of 2435 calories a day were consumed by each citizen, but 80 percent of that total—1479 from cereals and potatoes and 428 from beer—came from cereal carbohydrates.

Higher income levels also encouraged people to marry at a younger age and to have more children. The expanding cottage industry had the effect of improving the rural standard of living, while the relatively high factory wages increased the urban incomes.

Earlier marriage patterns and lower annual death rates slowly altered the general demographic profile of 19th-century Europe. Initially, younger age groups increased at a faster rate than the rest of the population, but during the second half of the century medical advances allowed older people to live longer. Moreover, the peasantry and working class tended to have more children than those higher up in the social hierarchy.

Population growth and higher living standards expanded the market for manufactured goods and provided a labor supply for the factories. Indeed, the combination of economic factors and political conditions in the 19th century produced massive shifts in Europe's population. Initially, factories in cities drew much of their labor from the urban poor, but increasingly after 1815 the cities attracted rural workers, especially the young. The volume of migration from villages to cities intensified as people flocked to the factories to take advantage of higher salaries and new opportunities. Typically the migrant was a male between the ages of 15 and 30, although women also moved. Many young girls left the countryside to take positions as domestic servants in the homes of the rising middle class, often returning to their villages to marry, while others sought employment in the textile mills after the decline of cottage spinning.

The numbers of people moving from country to city during the 19th century ran into the tens of millions. In addition to the permanent migration to urban areas, seasonal migration in agriculture was also common in many European countries, and it has been estimated that there were some 900,000 seasonal migrants in France alone in 1852. Migration between countries was more difficult, although in 19th-century Europe only Turkey and Russia had passport regulations. Nearly 400,000 foreign workers were employed in France at midcentury. Poverty and political repression also drove an estimated 50 million Europeans abroad during the 19th century, many of them emigrating to the United States and Latin America.

The Rise of the City

The most far-reaching population change in 19th-century Europe was the dramatic rise in the number and size of its cities. By 1850, many rural districts in England and the Continent were sparsely populated as millions moved to industrial towns and cities. Industrialization, together with the expansion of financial enterprises and government, spawned an urban revolution of unprecedented dimensions.

At the opening of the 19th century, London alone among European cities had a population over a million. Paris, the second largest, had half that number, while only five other cities could boast 200,000 or more. Within half a century, however, London had reached 2.6 million, Paris more than 1 million, and some 30 additional cities had in excess of 200,000 inhabitants. Most urban centers had at least doubled—and many trebled—in population. Glasgow, Leeds, Liverpool, and other British manufacturing cities experienced massive growth, while on the Continent Berlin, Brussels, Budapest, and Munich saw increases almost as startling.

Despite the rapid urbanization pattern, however, Europe remained a predominantly rural or small-town society throughout the 19th century. One estimate

Table 6.1

The Growth of European Cities, 1800–1850 (in 1000s)

	1800	1850
Barcelona	115	175
Belfast	37	103
Berlin	172	419
Birmingham	74	233
Bordeaux	91	131
Bristol	64	137
Brussels	66	251
Budapest	54	178
Cologne	50	97
Cracow	24	50
Dresden	60	97
Edinburgh	83	202
Glasgow	77	357
Kiev	23	50
Leeds	53	721
Leipzig	30	63
Liverpool	80	376
London	1,117	2,685
Lyon	110	177
Madrid	160	281
Manchester	90	303
Marseilles	111	194
Milan	135	242
Moscow	250	365
Munich	40	110
Naples	427	449
Paris	547	1,053
Rotterdam	53	90
Sheffield	31	135
St. Petersburg	220	485
Stuttgart	18	47
Vienna	247	444

classified 14.5 percent of Europe's population as urban in 1800 (counting cities of 5000 or more), a figure that rose to only 22.3 percent by 1850. England, Europe's industrial leader, had the most highly urbanized population: in 1850, 35 percent of its people lived in cities, whereas in that same year only 10 percent of the French and 7 percent of the German population fell into the urban category (counting cities of 20,000 or more). Even as late as 1910, only 43 percent of Europe's population was urban.

As Europeans increasingly lived in cities during the 19th century, a corresponding pattern of change took place, although at a slower pace, within the workforce. The percentage of the overall population earning its livelihood from agriculture dropped, while the percentage of those in industry and the service sector of the economy grew. England passed the halfway mark by 1850, when 51 percent of its working population were engaged in industry and only 22 percent in agriculture. The French were a distant second, after England, with 27 percent of their working population in industry and fully half still in farming.

Nevertheless, the industrial cities defined the flavor and character of European civilization and its new social hierarchy. The huge concentration of people in these burgeoning centers created unprecedented dilemmas for their inhabitants. Some of the new industrial cities had mushroomed rapidly and without planning from hardly more than small towns, while others had grown from already sizable foundations. In all cases, neither local nor national administrations were prepared to deal with the seemingly insurmountable array of problems that they now confronted. Public transportation was nonexistent during the first half of the century, so that workers had to live close to the factories. In older towns, workers crowded into inadequate housing in conditions of extreme congestion—in Paris, for instance, the number of people living in an average house rose from 21.9 in 1800 to 35.2 in 1851. Entire families lived in one or two tiny rooms, often in cellars or attics, most without heat, toilet facilities, or water. New working-class housing, thrown up in the form of cheaply constructed, densely packed tenements, was little better.

Sulfurous fumes from the burning of cheap coal and factories hung over the narrow alleys, while soot, garbage, and human excrement often filled the streets. Public water supplies were limited and generally unsafe. In the 1850s, only one out of five houses in Paris had its own water and most people in Berlin still used public fountains. Sewers, when they existed at all, were often merely open drains that emptied into the nearest river. In Britain, the first Public Health Act was passed only in 1875, while in France it was not until 1894 that sewage systems were required in all towns. The failure to separate the water supply from the sewage disposal was the cause for periodic outbreaks of epidemic. Ancient Rome of the 1st century A.D. had a cleaner water supply than most European cities in the 19th century.

Such conditions presented serious health hazards in the form of infectious diseases, especially for the urban poor. Cholera and typhoid, carried by polluted

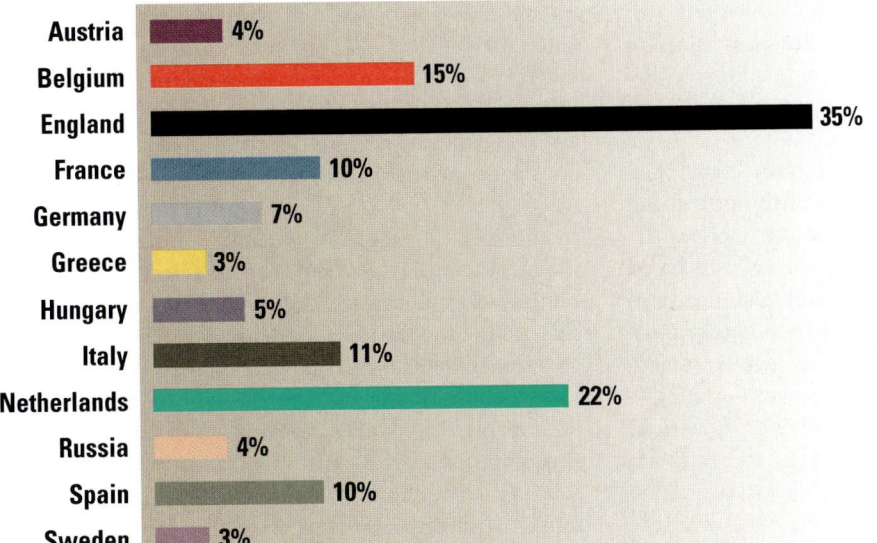

Graph 6.1   The Urban Population of Europe in 1850
(Percentage living in cities of 20,000 or more)

water, and typhus, spread by lice, were common. In Western Europe alone, tens of thousands of people were killed by a cholera epidemic in 1831–1832, and recurrences in 1846, 1848–1849, and 1866 continued to claim many lives. For the poor—the bulk of the population—the quality of urban life was generally worse than in the countryside during the first half of the century. The mortality rate was higher and the birthrate lower in the cities, and within large cities such as Paris or London death rates were higher in working-class areas than in fashionable districts. Reform movements to deal with issues such as health and urban welfare began in England in the 1830s (see Part VII, Topic 13), and efforts to improve the infrastructure of the cities spread through the Continent in the 1840s and 1850s. Not until the end of the 19th century, however, did conditions in most of Europe's cities begin to approach modern standards.

The Emergence of Class Structure

In 1844, the young German Friedrich Engels (1820–1895)—who later became a close friend and collaborator of Karl Marx—wrote a now classic book, *The Condition of the Working Class in England*. In this study of the laboring people, Engels explained how the industrial revolution had created both a "middle class" and

Mid-19th-century Manchester revealed the worst aspects of industrial pollution.

"an integral, permanent class," the "proletariat," or working class. The first he defined as the "possessing" or property-owning class (distinguishing, however, between them and the old landowning aristocracy) and the second as the "propertyless" class.

At the time Engels wrote, the term "class" had only recently come into use to describe the new social categories produced by industrialization. Before the Revolution of 1789, European society had been based on legally defined status groups known technically as "orders," membership in which was determined by birth and legal privilege. In prerevolutionary France society had been divided into three orders known as estates— the clergy, the nobility, and the rest of the population. The social hierarchy of the Old Regime had been seen as a pyramid, with a series of wide levels stretching from the poor and the peasantry at the bottom to the apex of princes and king at the top. Members of this social system were linked by relationships of authority and obligation.

By the beginning of the 19th century social classes were increasingly identified by income and occupation. Less tangible indicators, such as aspirations and values, were also important factors in determining one's class, but wealth or property, and how a person earned a living, became the chief measure of status.

Class identification along these lines was, however, neither absolute nor clear-cut, and the transition from the old hierarchy to the new structure evolved throughout the century. The distinctive male clothing of the privileged orders of the Old Regime—with its breeches, lace cuffs, and wigs—eventually disappeared for all except ceremonial occasions. Trousers and jack-ets which we associate today with "business" dress became the order of the day for both aristocrats and the middle class. Moreover, new manufacturing techniques reduced costs and enabled the working class to purchase inexpensive leisure clothing that was similar in appearance to middle-class dress.

In other ways, too, class distinctions were looser than in the prerevolutionary period. As liberal constitutional systems came to be adopted throughout most of Europe, the nobility and the middle classes increasingly shared the franchise as well as appointment to high government office. The richer segments of the upper middle class also bought or built luxurious residences in fashionable neighborhoods furnished in ways that made them indistinguishable from aristocratic palaces.

Titles of nobility, access to the royal court, and a sense of solidarity at first kept the old aristocracy at arm's length from the rising business magnates. Yet social relationships between the nobles and the upper middle class were not totally rigid. By the end of the 18th century, impoverished nobles and the wealthiest industrialists began to see mutual advantages in arranging marriages between their families, a trend that accelerated in the next century. Monarchs frequently bestowed titles on businessmen and received them at court, while some more enterprising nobles made the transition from living off land rents to capitalist agriculture and investment in industry. In the same way, successful artisans and skilled laborers began to accumulate sufficient resources and property, and move up into the ranks of the middle classes.

The new class structure revealed an unprecedented degree of mobility in which individuals often

The poverty of peasant life in rural Europe is depicted by Boisieu in *Peasants Begging.*

Robert Adam's design for the Marble Hall at Kedleston Hall, Derbyshire, suggests the opulence of life for the English aristocracy in the late 18th century.

moved from one level to another. This was especially true of Britain. Yet, although the pyramid of the Old Regime was no longer a valid representation of social structure, a different urban social hierarchy emerged in which the new distinctions of income and wealth between categories were at least as sharp.

THE CONDITION OF THE WORKING CLASS

As Engels himself recognized, the European working population was comprised not only of factory employees. Workers represented a much broader category that included artisans, domestic servants, cottage industry workers, and agricultural laborers. The complexities of social change brought on by the industrial revolution increased or further defined differences in status, income, and attitude within the worker hierarchy itself.

All working-class persons were linked by the factor of dependency—that is, they depended on others for employment, for the kind of work they did, and for the conditions under which they labored. Beyond this common denominator, the differences among them reflected the degree and nature of their skills. Industrialization not only created the new social category of the urban factory worker, but also affected existing categories. It had the effect of greatly extending the number of domestic servants by enlarging the middle classes; it also reduced the number of cottage workers, and it affected the status and income of artisans.

The Working-Class Hierarchy

As a whole, the working class comprised some 80 percent of Europe's urban population at midcentury (more than 90 percent if we include rural laborers and peasants). Industrial workers accounted for a small portion of that number, and only after 1850 did factory workers begin to dominate the production system. In France, at that point much less industrialized than England, 27 percent of the labor force was in industry, but factory workers were less than 5 percent. Moreover, industrial workers were unevenly distributed—they formed most

The Peterloo Massacre of 1819 revealed the class antagonisms of industrial England.

of the population of new industrial towns such as Manchester or Birmingham, but represented only a small portion of the inhabitants of older, large cities like London.

While the number of factory workers was relatively small in the first half of the 19th century, they were the fastest growing urban class. "The mightiest result," wrote Engels of the industrial revolution, "is the English proletariat."[1] In the early stages of industrialization, the majority of factory laborers came from rural areas. Most peasants went to the factories with great reluctance and kept their ties to the countryside. Among the first generation of industrial workers, as many as 25 percent went back to their rural areas in the summer for the harvesting of crops. Subsequent generations of workers, however, broke their ties with the countryside as they developed urban roots.

Skilled factory labor was generally scarce in the first half of the century, so that industrial pay was higher than rural wages. Even among industrial workers, however, differences were clearly delineated, most often according to the level of skill commanded. Unskilled workers, by far the largest group, earned too little to maintain the average working-class family of father, mother, and three children. This accounts for the presence of large numbers of women and children in the labor force, both in the factories and as servants.

Indeed, domestic servants made up an increasingly large portion of the working population. Among the unskilled were manual laborers such as ditch diggers and construction helpers, teamsters, dock workers, and factory employees who were assigned the simplest tasks.

Women and children were a strong presence in the lower ranks of the workforce, especially in the textile industry. Women constituted between 40 and 50 percent of all workers in cotton mills and children from 15 to 25 percent. In production requiring heavy operations, such as metal manufacturing, women and children were less seldom used, whereas in mechanical weaving they held virtually a monopoly of jobs. Perhaps as many as one-third of all teenage girls in England were domestic servants. Because employers knew that most—although by no means all—women and children worked to supplement family income, they were paid the lowest wages in the workforce. Women earned half as much as men in the same jobs, and children half as much as women.

Higher up in the social hierarchy were semiskilled workers, who earned an average of one and a half times the lowest rates. These included tradesmen such as carpenters (as opposed to cabinetmakers), plumbers, and brick masons. Moreover, as machinery came into wider use in the factories, the number of semiskilled industrial workers increased.

Skilled workers were the élite, representing only some 15 percent of the labor force. The pay of most skilled workers was at least twice that of the unskilled category, and some—such as expert machinists and

[1] Friedrich Engels, *The Condition of the Working Class in England,* ed. and trans. Victor Kiernan (Harmondsworth: Penguin, 1987), 61. First published in Germany in 1845.

iron puddlers—earned as much as five times the lowest rates. A few skilled workers eventually made their way into the lowest rung of management as foremen. Technological developments expanded the number of skilled workers as the need grew for machine toolmakers, railroad engineers, and other specialists.

Artisans Under Stress

The artisans engaged in highly skilled crafts—jewelers and goldsmiths, glassblowers, cabinet and instrument makers, bookbinders and printers—were the "aristocracy" of the skilled workers. Strong traditions of group identity and quality craftsmanship bound them together. Through their self-regulating guilds, hundreds of years old, artisans had established work standards, pay scales, and conditions of employment in small workshops. Under the guild system, years of experience were required for workers to pass from apprentice to journeyman, and only a few achieved the rank of master.

Industrialization adversely affected artisans, who outnumbered factory workers in the first half of the 19th century, even in countries such as Great Britain, France, and Prussia. They were, however, widely distributed in large European cities such as London, Paris, and Vienna, where the demand for high-quality luxury goods actually grew as middle-class wealth expanded.

Olaudah Equiano, a former slave from West Africa, gained his freedom in England and campaigned vigorously for abolition, while writing books and lecturing.

At first, factory production hurt specialty textile manufacturing, such as the finishing of wool cloth or lace making, and artisans in the cottage industry were most severely displaced by the new mechanical inventions in weaving. By midcentury mechanization and the factory system threatened to make the skills of artisans obsolete on a massive level. As a result, the guilds attempted to tighten their control over the craft trades and to make advancement more difficult, but new laws and capitalist economic policy often made this impossible. The revolutionary government in France had abolished the guilds in 1791, and in Britain the guilds disappeared gradually in the 1830s. By 1850, they had been eliminated in many of the German and Italian states as well as in the Low Countries and Spain.

As a group, artisans felt distinct from factory workers and the middle class. Industrial laborers increased three or four times as rapidly as artisans, but direct contact between the two categories was limited. Artisans inhabited long-established residential sections in cities, and their sense of dignity and higher status led them to regard ordinary workers as beneath them. Clinging resolutely to their traditional ways of life and work methods as the factory system spread, they tried to maintain tight family unity—artisan wives, for example, did not generally work in factories—and to limit the number of children they had in order to sustain their living standards. In addition, artisans tended to take great interest in education and self-improvement, and had disciplined savings habits.

Artisans clearly saw themselves under attack by the new forces of production. In the early stages of industrialization the artisans reacted to the introduction of new technology by smashing machines. As the crisis of the artisan class continued to unfold over the course of the 19th century, they became an element of increasing political instability in European society.

The Standard of Living

When he visited the English manufacturing towns in the 1840s, Engels came away with a devastating impression of the condition of the working class:

> Thus the working class of the great cities offers a graduated scale of conditions of life, in the best cases a temporarily endurable existence for hard work and good wages, good and endurable, that is, from the worker's standpoint; in the worst cases, bitter want, reaching even homelessness and death by starvation.[2]

Engels was not alone in calling attention to the miserable living conditions of the industrial workers, for some of the English Romantic poets (see Part VII, Topic 7) had also done so. These protests began an

[2] Engels, *The Condition of the Working Class.*

important and continuing debate over the impact of industrialization on working-class lives which centers on whether workers shared in the wealth created by the industrial revolution, or whether the new prosperity benefited only the middle class.

Throughout the 19th century, wages stayed ahead of the rise in the cost of living, except during periods of economic slump. This was especially true in England, where per capita real income doubled. Wages also rose on the Continent as industrialization spread after 1850. By comparison with the countryside, real wages in the cities were higher. Even Engels, who believed that working-class conditions would steadily deteriorate, admitted that the situation was complex and that his examples stressed the worst cases.

On the other hand, unskilled workers outside the factory system and cottage industry laborers suffered seriously from the dislocations. The housing conditions for factory workers that Engels described in the British cities were indeed miserable and the mortality rate rose among urban workers. Food consumption was hardly above subsistence for most urban workers, although they had better diets than peasants. The high consumption of alcohol among workers, regarded as a serious problem by contemporary social observers, reflected the stress of daily life and the limited opportunities for leisure time activities. In working-class families, wives and children worked more often than not in order to buy basic necessities rather than luxuries. Indeed, the poorest segment of Europe's population—a third of the whole, including the families of rural and urban workers—earned only about 10 percent of all income. Moreover, the uncertainty of employment was an ever-present source of demoralization, and a large percentage of male laborers were regularly without work in industrial towns. Chronic poverty remained widespread, affecting as much as 10 percent of the population of Great Britain, although it was, of course, by no means unknown before the industrial period.

Living standards among artisans were equally complex. Those with skills in demand earned high wages and increased their real income, while many less fortunate craftsmen who faced factory competition experienced declining pay and rising work hours. Wages for most artisans were higher than for most workers, and they generally enjoyed more material comfort. Yet the position of artisans was especially vulnerable in times of economic hardship, when the demand for their high quality products collapsed more quickly than for basic necessities.

On the whole, industrialization eventually raised the living standards of millions of Europeans, although the transformation was slow and took place against a backdrop of privation, dependency, and widespread suffering.

THE COMFORTABLE BOURGEOISIE

The middle class was as complex and varied as the other social groups, perhaps more so, and during the first half of the 19th century it underwent considerable growth and change. The category was so broad as to include at the top those whose wealth rivaled that of the old nobility, and at the bottom those whose income was scarcely higher than that of the best paid skilled worker. In fact, the wide range of economic status found within this social category suggests a range of middle classes rather than just one.

Certain general characteristics, however, help to define the middle classes as a social unit. By midcentury, they comprised perhaps 20 percent of the urban population of Europe, although the figure was lower in eastern and southern Europe, where industry and commerce were less advanced. Their numbers grew steadily along with industrial and economic development, as did their wealth. Elements of the middle classes were both the driving force behind industrialization and business expansion and its principal beneficiaries. Most, although not all, members of the middle classes owned some form of property. Their income afforded them a degree of comfort that was unattainable by the working classes.

The middle classes were the most mobile sector within the new urban social hierarchy. By midcentury, most members of the group had risen above their origins, and they regarded themselves as distinct from both the working classes and the titled nobility. Wealth and new status led the middle classes to demand participation in government alongside the aristocracy—indeed, the leaders of most political revolutions in Europe between 1789 and 1848 were from the middle classes. By 1870, the middle classes not only achieved a measure of political power almost everywhere, but also set the tone and values for most of society.

The Structure of the Middle Classes

During the first phase of the industrial revolution, most entrepreneurs came from relatively modest backgrounds: small businessmen, engineers, and artisans with their own shops. Three distinct segments are discernible among the middle classes. The upper level, consisting of large-scale industrialists, bankers, and merchants, was the smallest but wealthiest sector, making up less than 5 percent of the middle class. Together with the aristocracy, this group earned one-third of all income. As a result, the upper middle class was able to enjoy a sumptuous existence, with private mansions in exclusive areas of the city and villas in the country, a retinue of servants, and luxuries that imitated the lifestyle of the aristocracy.

The middle range of the bourgeoisie consisted of small manufacturers, moderate-sized merchants, and businessmen, as well as professionals. This group usually lived either in rented apartments in genteel urban neighborhoods, or owned their own homes in newer sections of the cities. The professionals included lawyers, physicians, and university professors, and a rapidly growing number of accountants, engineers, and chemists. While most lawyers and physicians had adequate but not spectacular incomes and little property, they had more advanced education than other middle-class groups. The professionals also stood apart from the business elements because they tended to be active in political and social reform. From this same segment also came most of Europe's intellectuals and creative artists, who often rebelled against the social conventions and material values of their class.

The largest and fastest growing element within the bourgeoisie was the lower middle class, consisting mainly of small shopkeepers and the relatively new white-collar workers, especially civil servants such as teachers, postal clerks, and secretaries. This group accounted for approximately half of the entire middle-class population. Their income was considerably less than the two higher bourgeois strata, and they owned little or no property. Nevertheless, they lived modestly but comfortably in decent apartments, managed to save money, and gave their children elementary educations.

As a whole, much of the wealth generated by industrial and economic growth—actually, almost one-half of all income—went to the middle classes. That wealth was unevenly distributed among the three levels of the bourgeois class. In England, for example, the savings of taxpayers in the highest income bracket increased fourfold between 1800 and 1850, while those of the lower middle class grew much more slowly. For manufacturers, the need for capital investment and rising pay scales for workers were offset by steadily falling production costs. For the shopkeepers, cheaper goods and the expanding purchasing power of all classes meant more customers. In the complex social environment of the cities, the lives of the middle classes contrasted vividly with those of the working class.

How the Middle Classes Lived

The bourgeoisie lived comfortably. The homes of the lower and middle classes, whether owned or rented, were furnished with solid, sensible furniture that conveyed a cozy, respectable well-being. In Austria and Germany before 1850, the popular style of middle-class furniture was known as *Biedermeier*, constructed of sturdy, light-colored woods with simple, clean lines. In England darker, carved pieces of what was later called "Victorian" furniture were to be found in bourgeois homes, while in France after midcentury the so-called

A French middle-class family at home.

"Empire" style—a heavier, less elegant variation of the neoclassical style favored during Napoleon's reign— prevailed. Success was partially measured by the number of servants a family had and by the elaborate, multicourse dinner parties that were provided for guests. The middle classes ate well, and in fact virtually half of all their income was spent on food and servants.

The lower ranks of the middle classes generally prized education, not as an end in itself but as a means of preparing children for adult responsibilities. Two standards of education, determined by gender, prevailed. Boys were taught practical subjects such as mathematics and accounting or technical skills, while training for girls was usually limited to music, poetry, sewing, and household management. This educational hierarchy, in turn, reflected the bourgeois separation of the outside male world of work from the protected sphere of domestic life that was thought to be the proper sphere of women. For most of the century, classical education in universities was largely the preserve of the sons of the wealthiest families and the aristocracy.

The middle classes centered their lives principally around work and the family. Hard work was thought to be the moral responsibility of every person, regardless of rank or status. The middle-class ethic held that those with the requisite energy and drive could succeed and prosper, while the poor had only themselves to blame for their plight. This attitude was in part a product of Enlightenment thought and the French Revolution, both of which had encouraged the notion that advancement depended on talent and ability rather than on birth or privilege. Habits of self-discipline and work were instilled in children from an early age because it was believed that these traits built character and would help to develop strong and responsible adults. Political economists and social theorists of the liberal persuasion incorporated this view into their analyses, which often offered contradictory approaches to the growing problem of urban poverty. While some argued that charity and aid to the poor would only serve to encourage laziness and dependency, others saw humanitarian assistance and charitable work as the responsibility of the more fortunate groups in society.

The work ethic reinforced the middle-class belief in *laissez-faire* economics and the spirit of free competition. Thrift, together with the importance and sanctity of private property, which all classes were encouraged to accumulate, were also central to the bourgeois worldview. Such attitudes contributed to the cult of material and spiritual progress that became a hallmark of middle-class thinking. Self-improvement would inevitably mean a better society for all, and modern technology and science would enable society to achieve unprecedented material advances and harness nature for human security and comfort.

In their efforts not only to order and control their own lives, but to imbue society at large with their values, the middle classes developed a moralizing ideology of respectability. This set of ideas particularly affected the way in which women could lead their lives and the structure of family life.

WOMEN IN A REVOLUTIONARY AGE

During the first half of the 19th century, the two major developments of the period—the French Revolution and the industrial revolution—deeply affected the status and role of women in European society. The Revolution of 1789 provoked the first serious public consideration of women's rights and gender relationships in a political and legal context, and stimulated women themselves to take up their own struggle for equality. Women entered the new industrial job market in a significant way, and the results changed not only how they worked and the nature of their dependency, but also their roles within the family.

Women, Law, and Government

The early revolutionary governments of France had legislated some basic legal rights for women in such matters as marriage, consensual age, divorce, and inheritance. These advances did not, however, survive the republican experience, for the Napoleonic Code of 1804 reestablished a patriarchal society, giving power to males in family matters. In this reversal of earlier reforms, a married woman had to assume her husband's nationality, could not take part in court proceedings or sue for paternity rights or support, and—unlike the husband—could be punished for adultery. These measures had the effect of removing women from a direct civil relationship with government. Women were denied not only legal identity as independent human beings but also those very "rights" of citizenship that the Revolution of 1789 had proclaimed so loudly.

Property laws further marginalized women in ways that were important to the new middle-class ideology of wealth. The Napoleonic Code allowed women to have virtually no control over their property, even when prenuptial contracts required that dowries be kept separate from other family resources. Wages earned by married working women passed to the husband, as did profits made by women who owned tiny shops or market stalls. Because the pattern of government in the 19th century was moving toward liberal institutions in which political rights hinged on property ownership, such measures were crucial to the status of women. As a consequence, nowhere in the Western world did women have equal civil status or political rights in the first half of the 19th century, although women soon began to organize themselves to achieve them (see Part VII, Topic 13).

The Napoleonic Code provided the basis for legal reform and precedent throughout much of Europe and the Americas. Implicit in its provisions regarding women were certain assumptions about gender differences—that women were "weaker" than men both

Mary Wollstonecraft, the prominent English writer and feminist.

physically and in character, and therefore required their protection. According to the jurists who wrote the code, women's place should remain within the one "natural" sphere of their competency, the home.

Women and the Industrial Revolution

The industrial transformation of Europe brought contradictory results for women as it affected patterns of work and home life. On the one hand, it widened the scope of activities for some women, and on the other it reinforced the separation of men's and women's roles endorsed by the Napoleonic Code. Women had, of course, always worked. In preindustrial Europe, rural wives often shared agricultural labor with their husbands, especially during harvesting, and were an important element in cottage industry. In urban centers, women had worked chiefly as domestic servants for the aristocracy or as sales clerks in family-run shops. Some women also sold food products in city markets and occasionally helped their husbands in artisan workshops. In almost all cases, however, these occupations were carried out as part of a family production unit, usually within the home, and their labor was viewed as a supplement to male labor rather than having any intrinsic value.

Industrialization changed female work patterns significantly. In the new textile factories women constituted a major portion of the labor force, and many also worked in tobacco and food processing. Women and children were often the largest number of workers in cotton mills. On the other hand, while an important element in the industrial working class, factory labor was not the typical work experience for women. At midcentury, for example, 40 percent of all British working women were servants and 20 percent textile workers, while 40 percent of Frenchwomen still worked in agriculture and only 10 percent in textiles.

Division of labor based on gender had existed in cottage industry and agriculture, and it continued in the factories, as men and women were separated by task and by area in the workplace. This was done not only because of differences in skill or physical strength, but because factory owners assumed that males and females working in close proximity to each other, often dressed in scanty clothing, would lead to immorality and thereby hamper productivity. Wherever women worked in the factories, they were almost always supervised by men.

Contrary to a once commonly held view, industrialization did not tear working families apart. In the early stages of the factory system, entire families—husbands, wives, and children—frequently worked together. Moreover, throughout the century most women in the factories were young and single. Some factory owners provided dormitories or boardinghouses where single women employees were able to live and eat at

low cost, and in England the Factory Acts of 1842 and 1844 limited the number of hours a day women could work. Some married working-class women earned extra income by sewing or doing laundry, but the growth of mass-produced consumer goods formerly made at home, such as ready-to-wear clothing, soap, and candles, limited domestic work in the cities.

For some women, a less respectable but profitable source of income was prostitution. Prostitutes in European cities numbered in the tens of thousands, and brothels were to be found in many neighborhoods. It has been estimated that by 1850 there were perhaps 80,000 prostitutes in London alone and 50,000 in Paris. Some women engaged in prostitution, which paid much better than most jobs open to them, only when they were unemployed or when their regular employment hit a slow season. Migrants from the countryside also turned to prostitution to support themselves when they first arrived in the city, as did women abandoned by their husbands or lovers. Most prostitutes, though, were single young women in desperate straits rather than women from very poor families.

Once working in this occupation, women often found that their income could be measurably improved over the meager factory wages they could earn. Some worked independently as streetwalkers, while others operated on a fee basis out of brothels. Beginning with the Napoleonic Code, many European governments regulated the prostitution business, requiring that prostitutes register with the police and submit to medical examinations. Despite periodic roundups and police raids, the 19th-century middle classes seem to have regarded prostitution as a "necessary evil"—the double standard of the period held that while women had no sexual drive, the "natural" sexual energy of men needed release.

Increasingly, married urban women, whether of the working or the middle classes, found themselves relegated to the role of homemaker, giving birth to and raising children, cooking, and caring for the family, while the new work discipline of the factories gave husbands little time to share in domestic duties. The growing distinction between the "paid" labor of males and the "unpaid" labor of females marginalized women further and contributed to the development of "separate spheres" defined according to gender.

MARRIAGE, FAMILY, AND SEX

The family remained the focus of life for the vast majority of women, including not only wives but also servants and unmarried female relatives. Nevertheless, the ways

DOCUMENTS ON HISTORY

The Rights of Women

Throughout most of the 18th century, the majority of women in middle-class and working families remained subservient to males, their roles limited to childbearing and rearing, to household duties, and to occasional participation in fieldwork and home-based textile making. But under the impact of industrialization, the status and role of women in the emerging industrial society began to assume new dimensions as tens of thousands of them left home for work in the factories. Moreover, as a result of the Enlightenment and the French Revolution, women increasingly struggled to achieve political and social rights, and in the half-century after 1789 developed theoretical and political arguments for those rights.

THE PETITION OF RIGHTS, 1790

Just as French citizens had petitioned the king with their grievances in preparation for the meeting of the Estates General, a group of working women appealed directly to Louis XVI for the opportunity for work and a better education.

Sire,

At a time when the different orders of the state are occupied with their interests; when everyone seeks to make the most of his titles and rights; when some anxiously recall the centuries of servitude and anarchy, while others make every effort to shake off the last links that still bind them to the imperious remains of feudalism; women—continual objects of the admiration and scorn of men—could they not also make their voices heard midst this general agitation?

Excluded from the national assemblies by laws so well consolidated that they allow no hope of infringement, they do not ask, Sire, for your permission to send their deputies to the Estates General; they know too well how much favor will play a part in the election, and how easy it would be for those elected to impede the freedom of voting.

We prefer, Sire, to place our cause at your feet; not wishing to obtain anything except from your heart, it is to it that we address our complaints and confide our miseries.

The women of the Third Estate are almost all born without wealth; their education is very neglected or very defective: it consists in their being sent to school with a teacher who himself does not know the first word of the language [Latin] he teaches. They continue to go there until they can read the service of the Mass in French and Vespers in Latin. Having fulfilled the first duties of religion, they are taught to work; having reached the age of fifteen or sixteen, they can earn five or six sous a day. If nature has refused them beauty they get married, without a dowry, to unfortunate artisans; lead aimless, difficult lives stuck in the provinces; and give birth to children they are incapable of raising. If, on the contrary, they are born pretty, without breeding, without principles, with no idea of morals, they become the prey of the first seducer, commit a first sin, come to Paris to bury their shame, end by losing it altogether, and die victims of dissolute ways. . . .

From *The French Revolution and Human Rights: A Brief Documentary History,* ed. and trans. Lynn Hunt (Boston and New York: Bedford Books of St. Martin's Press, 1996), 60–62.

THE DECLARATION OF THE RIGHTS OF WOMAN

*A*lthough self-educated, Olympe de Gouges (1748–1793) was a successful writer for the theater. In 1791, she wrote the "Declaration of the Rights of Woman and the French Citizen," modeled on the document issued by the National Assembly in 1789. In it, she argued that the framers of the original Declaration had ignored women and that equality between men and women conformed to the natural order. She urged women to take part in the struggle for liberty and sent her appeal to Marie Antoinette, "mother and wife."

In consequence, the sex that is superior in beauty as in courage, needed in maternal sufferings, recognizes and declares, in the presence and under the auspices of the Supreme Being, the following rights of woman and the citizens.

1. Woman is born free and remains equal to man in rights. Social distinctions may be based only on common utility.

2. The purpose of all political association is the preservation of the natural and imprescriptible rights of woman and man. These rights are liberty, property, security, and especially resistance to oppression.

3. The principle of all sovereignty rests essentially in the nation, which is but the reuniting of woman and man. No body and no individual may exercise authority which does not emanate expressly from the nation.

4. Liberty and justice consist in restoring all that belongs to another; hence the exercise of the natural rights of woman has no other limits than those that the perpetual tyranny of man opposes to them; these limits must be reformed according to the laws of nature and reason.

5. The laws of nature and reason prohibit all actions which are injurious to society. No hindrance should be put in the way of anything not prohibited by these wise and divine laws, nor may anyone be forced to do what they do not require.

6. The law should be the expression of the general will. All citizenesses and citizens should take part, in person or by their representatives, in its formation. It must be the same for everyone. All citizenesses and citizens, being equal in its eyes, should be equally admissible to all public dignities, offices, and employments, according to their ability, and with no other distinction than that of their virtues and talents.

7. No woman is exempted; she is indicted, arrested, and detained in the cases determined by the law. Women like men obey this rigorous law.

8. Only strictly and obviously necessary punishments should be established by the law, and no one may be punished except by virtue of a law established and promulgated

continued next page

before the time of the offense, and legally applied to women.

9. Any woman being declared guilty, all rigor is exercised by the law.

10. No one should be disturbed for his fundamental opinions; woman has the right to mount the scaffold, so she should have the right equally to mount the tribune, provided that these manifestations do not trouble public order as established by law.

11. The free communication of thoughts and opinions is one of the most precious of the rights of woman, since this liberty assures the recognition of children by their fathers. Every citizeness may therefore say freely, I am the mother of your child; a barbarous prejudice [against unmarried women having children] should not force her to hide the truth, so long as responsibility is accepted for any abuse of this liberty in cases determined by the law [women are not allowed to lie about the paternity of their children].

12. The safeguard of the rights of woman and citizeness requires public powers. These powers are instituted for the advantage of all and not for the private benefit of those to whom they are entrusted.

13. For maintenance of public authority and for expenses of administration, taxation of women and men is equal; she takes part in all forced labor service, in all painful tasks; she must therefore have the same proportion in the distribution of places, employments, offices, dignities, and in industry.

14. The citizenesses and citizens have the right, by themselves or through their representatives, to have demonstrated to them the necessity of public taxes. The citizenesses can only agree to them upon admission of an equal division, not only in wealth, but also in the public administration, and to determine the means of apportionment, assessment, and collection, and the duration of the taxes.

15. The mass of women, joining with men in paying taxes, have the right to hold accountable every public agent of the administration.

16. Any society in which the guarantee of rights is not assured or the separation of powers not settled has no constitution. The constitution is null and void if the majority of individuals composing the nation has not cooperated in its drafting.

17. Property belongs to both sexes whether united or separated; it is for each of them an inviolable and sacred right, and no one may be deprived of it as a true patrimony of nature, except when public necessity, certified by law, obviously requires it, and then on condition of a just compensation in advance.

From *The French Revolution and Human Rights: A Brief Documentary History*, ed. and trans. Lynn Hunt (Boston and New York: Bedford Books of St. Martin's Press, 1996), 125–126.

WOLLSTONECRAFT'S VINDICATION OF THE RIGHTS OF WOMEN

Mary Wollstonecraft (1759–1797), an English writer and the wife of anarchist philosopher William Godwin (see Part VII, Topic 7), was a woman of the Enlightenment. In her Vindication of the Rights of Women (1792), she based her argument on the belief in reason. Wollstonecraft chastised the framers of the French Constitution of 1791 for limiting the rights of citizenship to men and lectured them that women were equal to men as rational beings. She also replied in detail to Rousseau's position on female inferiority, stressing the need for educational equality.

Consider—I address you as a legislator—whether, when men contend for their freedom, and to be allowed to judge for themselves respecting their own happiness, it be not inconsistent and unjust to subjugate women, even though you firmly believe that you are acting in the manner best calculated to promote their happiness? Who made man the exclusive judge, if woman partake with him the gift of reason.

In this style, argue tyrants of every denomination, from the weak king to the weak father of a family; they are all eager to crush reason; yet always assert that they usurp its throne only to be useful. Do you not act a similar part, when you *force* all women, by denying them civil and political rights, to remain immured in their families groping in the dark? For surely, sir, you will not assert that a duty can be binding which is not founded on reason? If, indeed, this be their destination, arguments may be drawn from reason; and thus augustly supported, the more understanding women acquire, the more they will be attached to their duty—comprehending it—for unless they comprehend it, unless their morals be fixed on the same immutable principle as those of man, no authority can make them discharge it in a virtuous manner. They may be convenient slaves, but slavery will have its constant effect, degrading the master and the abject dependent.

But, if women are to be excluded, without having a voice, from a participation of the natural rights of mankind, prove first, to ward off the charge of injustice and inconsistency, that they want reason—else this flaw in your NEW CONSTITUTION will ever show that man must, in some shape, act like a tyrant; and tyranny, in whatever part of society it rears its brazen front, will ever undermine morality.

I have repeatedly asserted, and produced what appeared to me irrefragable arguments drawn from matters of fact, to prove my assertion, that women cannot, by force, be confined to domestic concerns; for they will, however ignorant, intermeddle with more weighty affairs, neglecting private duties only to disturb, by cunning tricks, the orderly plans of reason which rise above their comprehension. . . .

From Mary Wollstonecraft, *Vindication of the Rights of Women*.

WOMEN AND POVERTY

By the mid-19th century, the struggle for women's rights had extended well beyond Enlightenment ideals to more concrete economic issues. In 1841, the Belgian utopian socialist Zoe Gatti de Gamond argued that the abolition of poverty among women would be a major step toward social justice.

The most direct cause of women's misfortune is poverty; demanding their freedom means above all demanding reform in the economy of society which will eradicate poverty and give everyone education, a minimum standard of living, and the right to work. It is not only that class called "women of the people" for whom the major source of all their misfortunes is poverty, but rather women of all classes.

From that comes the subjection of women, their narrow dependence on men, and their reduction to a negative influence. Men have thus materialized love, perverted the angelic nature of women, and created a being who submits to their caprices, their desires—a domesticated animal shaped to their pleasures and to their needs. Using their powers, they have split women into the appearance of two classes; for the privileged group, marriage, the care of the household, and maternal love; for the other, the sad role of seduced woman and of the misfortunate one reduced to the last degree of misery and degradation. Everywhere oppression and nowhere liberty.

The question is not to decide whether it is fitting to give women political rights or to put

continued next page

them on an equal footing with men when it comes to admission to employment. Rather the question exists above all in the question of poverty; and to make women ready to fill political roles, it is poverty above all that must be effaced. Nor can the independence of women be reconciled with the isolation of households, which prevents even the working woman from being independent.

The system of Fourier, imperceptibly and smoothly introducing associations within society, resolves all the difficulties in the position of women; without changing legislation or proclaiming new rights, it will regenerate them, silence the sources of corruption and reform with one blow education and morals with the single fact that results naturally from the associational principles of his system: a common education and the independence of women assured by the right to work; independence rendered possible by the association of households, attractive and harmonious work, and the multiplication of wealth.

NATIONALISM AND FEMINISM

T*he Italian feminist and socialist Anna Maria Mozzoni (1837–1920) worked to secure basic rights for women in the context of the movement for Italian unification. In 1864, three years after the creation of the Kingdom of Italy, she wrote about the contributions that free women could make to national life and argued that the new national laws did not recognize women's rights.*

The revision of the Civil Code by the Italian Parliament has placed in my mind the following argument: woman, excluded by worn out customs from the councils of state, has always submitted to the law without participating in the making of it, has always contributed her resources and work to the public good and always without any reward.

For her, taxes but not an education; for her, sacrifices but not employment; for her, strict virtue but not honor; for her, the struggle to maintain the family but not even control of her own person; for her, the capacity to be punished but not the right to be independent; strong enough to be laden with an array of painful duties, but sufficiently weak not to be allowed to govern herself.

I begin with the principles that all rights and all duties have as their foundation and rationale to serve as the force which gives the conscience its ostensible legitimacy. This principle holds for each human being of whatever sex and I do not see for what reason this faculty should be in one case exercised freely and sometimes with force and in the other case buried and entirely suffocated. This occurs so much that in the miserable conditions in which society has cast her, woman, deprived of half her wealth, weakened because of the degrading work actually given her, finds herself dragged down to the fatal necessity to destroy herself through trade in her unhappy body.

Humanity and the nation, civilization and morality, need women on their side.

WOMEN AND WORK

I*n the 19th century many feminists began to address the question of work and women's relationship to it from a practical and a theoretical point of view. For some work was increasingly* *seen as both a right and a necessity for women who would be fulfilled and happy, while for others it was seen as a means toward liberation. In 1866 Jenny Heynrichs, a middle-class German woman and the coeditor of a journal entitled* Neue Bahnen (New Paths), *addressed the question in an article entitled* "What is Work?"

Work, liberating and liberated work, is the slogan of our association, the banner around which we gather. It may seem superfluous, therefore, to raise once more the question "What is work?" in the pages of our magazine; one should assume that no one could have any further doubt about the importance of our association with this word. . . .

Work, be it intellectual or physical, is always the lively and vigorous union of our intellectual and physical powers for a definite, clearly articulated purpose. Work is creativity accompanied by the comforting realization that one is bringing forth something really good and necessary, with the conviction that a sudden, arbitrary cessation would cause a sensitive void, produce a loss. The worker, wherever he may be employed, feels himself to be a link in a chain that holds society together, a link which, should it drop out, would have to be replaced at once by another. He knows that such a replacement could be found at once, that no man is irreplaceable. Yet there is something very inspiring in the knowledge that through his dropping out a replacement is required; that one does not disappear without vacating a place, as if one never had it. This knowledge makes one feel content, fit, strong; it ennobles the lowest kind of work. This knowledge is given to all men and if they lack it, they have only themselves to blame, not society. But thousands of women are lacking that knowledge because they are brought up for only one vocation — marriage. . . .

Most of our young women, not only those from the well-to-do and aristocratic families, but also those from families of modest and limited means, are taught a variety of things. They embroider and crochet, sing and play the piano, draw, read French and English, possibly lend a hand in the household while attending balls and going promenading, all this with the expectation of a suitor who is to provide them with a home and their own domain. But the years go by, the hoped-for savior does not arrive, and the home, the parental house that has sheltered them falls into ruin with the death of the father. They are left behind, uncared for as the sad saying goes. Thrown back on their own resources and taking stock of the many things they have learned, they discover with dismay that while keeping occupied they have whiled away their lives and are unable to do any kind of work.

Work is the practical application of that which one thoroughly understands, for which one has prepared oneself and has chosen as the business of one's life. And this kind of work is only open in a very few fields to our women and many among them have not grasped yet that this alone is what is meant by work. The goal of our endeavors is to open to women the blessings of the world. We do not want a break up of the social order, no political conquests, only a breakthrough for work. In this manner, we think we can deliver the world from the insufferable old maids, at odds with themselves and others, from the women who through poverty and misery have fallen victim to vice, from luxury which like a cancer erodes the happiness of family life. We think we can restore to marriage meaning and sanctity and the right to noble love. May God help us in this task.

in which women conducted their lives and defined their roles changed. The increasingly complex urban environment and the factory system also affected marriage patterns, sexual behavior, and family structures.

Marriage and the Family

Industrialization was one cause of a growing conflict for women between the private sphere and the workplace. The low pay scale for female workers meant that single women without family support experienced severe difficulties in maintaining themselves. Moreover, the spreading social ideology of the middle classes established norms of expected behavior for women that proscribed activity beyond that of wife and mother. For most women, marriage continued to be the only avenue for economic security.

European marriage patterns varied according to region and economic status. Among the urban working classes, poverty often prevented or delayed marriage. On average, working-class women married in their mid-twenties and men somewhat older, although the age for both began to reduce as living standards improved among low-income groups. Working couples usually married out of mutual attraction and love, so that when circumstances mitigated against a formal marriage, couples often lived together in common-law unions. City dwellers generally abandoned the tradition of long courtship common in the countryside, and parental consent ceased to be as important.

Middle-class customs differed from those of the working class in several ways. Among bourgeois families, marriages were to a large extent viewed as serious financial undertakings. Although arranged marriages were rapidly disappearing, parents were concerned about the economic prospects of possible sons-in-law or the dowries of daughters-in-law. The correct social environment, in which daughters could meet eligible men, was therefore vitally important. Longer courtships were also the rule for the middle classes and marriage plans frequently included prenuptial contracts and inheritance agreements. Because the middle classes valued financial security so much, their sons tended to wait until their incomes were sufficient to support a family. As a result, men were almost always older than their wives. Before marriage, parents carefully guarded the virginity of their daughters, while sons usually had considerable sexual experience by the time they became husbands.

Although ties among family members loosened as a result of the urban-industrial environment, family relationships remained vital, especially among the poor. In an age when government assistance was limited or nonexistent, family members were needed for financial help during periods of unemployment and for support during illness. Relatives also generally took in indigent widows and orphans.

Except among the wealthiest groups, the size of families began to shrink by midcentury. The marked decline in the birthrate in most Western European countries was due to a combination of factors. Efforts to sustain or improve an acceptable standard of living limited family size, especially among the middle classes, for whom educational expenses were a growing priority. Parents also restricted the number of children they had because declining infant mortality meant that more children survived into adulthood. Moreover, technological and medical advances in the 1840s made possible new and inexpensive birth control devices, although they were not yet widely available. Until then, *coitus interruptus* (withdrawal) and vinegar solutions had been the only widely practiced birth control methods, but thereafter condoms, vaginal sponges, and diaphragms were increasingly available as a result of the vulcanization of rubber. As early as the 1820s, birth control information was being distributed in England, although its proponents risked fines and imprisonment.

The typical early 19th-century family was a "patriarchal" unit in that the husband had legal authority over the wife and children. In actual practice, however, the influence of the wife within the family grew stronger as her role was confined to the home. Wives kept the family's budget and determined how a large portion of its income would be expended. Mothers controlled the rearing of children on a daily basis, including such matters as education and religious training. Affection between spouses and the nurturing care of children were the guideposts of the ideal bourgeois family, while the home was to be a tranquil haven from the harsh realities of the world outside. For wives, however, running a household was full-time work, often complicated and hectic.

Sex and the New Society

Sexuality is a difficult subject for social historians to write about because of the scarcity of accurate information about the intimate lives of past generations. Moreover, 19th-century middle-class morality made any discussion of sex a taboo. Nevertheless, government and church statistics on marriages, births, and family sizes, as well as private sources such as diaries and letters, provide some basis for generalizations.

The most basic statement we can make is that while men and women have always had sex, the circumstances in which it took place, attitudes toward it, and how people dealt with its consequences have changed over time. We know, for example, that premarital sex was widespread among working-class couples, for illegitimacy rates rose significantly in the early 19th century—in Austria, for example, as many as one in three peasant children was born out of wedlock. The migration of young men and women to the cities, away from the restraints of family and village community, made for freer sexual behavior. In the first decades of the 19th century, almost 40 percent of all births in Paris were illegitimate, while in Vienna illegitimate births outnumbered legitimate ones. By 1840, perhaps as many as one out of every three European babies was born out of wedlock.

Before 1850, celibacy among unmarried men and women seems to have been more prevalent in the middle than in the working classes, due in part to the greater bourgeois concern for financial security and moral conduct. Nevertheless, after midcentury the illegitimacy rate reversed itself. This was not, however, because premarital sex declined: it has been estimated that in the years after 1850, one out of every three working-class women was pregnant at the time of marriage. Rather, marriage itself had grown more popular among the working classes as their income grew and they absorbed notions of respectability.

Gender influenced attitudes about sex as well as sexual behavior. The middle class professed to adhere to a strict code of morality, particularly for women, who were conditioned to remain chaste and virtuous. Sex was supposed to be a distasteful obligation for women, necessary for purposes of procreation. The flavor of this 19th-century bourgeois convention is reflected in the premarital advice that Queen Victoria—the British sovereign who herself had nine children—is supposed to have given her daughter: during sexual intercourse, the royal mother suggested, "Close your eyes and think of England."

The anecdote about Victoria underscores the nature of the double standard that developed during this period. Not only were women not supposed to enjoy sex, but medical opinion of the time held that they did not have orgasms; men, on the other hand, were virile creatures who had to expend their natural urges in the sexual act. While fidelity in marriage was publicly expected of both men and women, law and custom imposed it only on wives. There are, of course, numerous contemporary accounts testifying to the fulfilling sexual relationships that many wives had with their husbands, but the prevailing ethos of conduct made it impossible for women to express their needs openly. The double standard served largely to reinforce the increasingly exclusive roles of mother and wife to which women were limited.

The transformations that took place in the half century following the French Revolution, with their attendant stresses and upheavals, shaped the character of European society. High-density population, large, rapidly growing cities, and a complex and changing social structure were the outward manifestations of this great transformation. The large and expanding working class received only a small portion of national wealth, while dependency and discipline in *the workplace, together with widespread urban poverty, marked the material lives of much of the new industrial labor force. For the new middle classes, however, increasing comfort and influence were the order of the day. Although women participated in both the political and the industrial revolutions of the period, their role in society was steadily circumscribed by an ideology that stressed family and home above all else. From these and related developments of the period from 1789 to 1850 came the political and social struggles of late-19th-century Europe.*

Questions for Further Study

1. What was the impact of the industrial revolution on European society?

2. How would you describe the way in which most workers lived? How did life change for most people in the period under discussion?

3. In what ways was middle-class life different from working-class life?

4. Was the role of women in society different after the French Revolution? If so, in what ways? If not, why not?

Suggestions for Further Reading

Applewhite, Harriet B., and D. G. Levy, eds. *Women and Politics in the Age of the Democratic Revolution.* Ann Arbor, MI, 1990.

Coleman, William. *Death Is a Social Disease: Public Health and Political Economy in Early Industrial France.* Madison, WI, 1982.

Corbin, Alain. *The Lure of the Sea: The Discovery of the Seaside in the Western World, 1750–1840,* trans. J. Phelps. Berkeley, CA, 1994.

Davidoff, Leonore, and C. Hall. *Family Fortunes: Men and Women of the English Middle Class, 1780–1850.* Chicago, 1987.

Harrison, F. *The Dark Angel: Aspects of Victorian Sexuality.* New York, 1977.

Himmelfarb, Gertrude. *The Idea of Poverty: England in the Early Industrial Age.* New York, 1984.

Landes, Joan. *Women and the Public Sphere in the Age of the French Revolution.* Ithaca, NY, 1988.

Lynch, Katherine A. *Family, Class, and Ideology in Early Industrial France: Social Policy and the Working Class Family, 1825–1848.* Madison, WI, 1988.

Marsden, G., ed. *Victorian Values: Personalities and Perspectives in 19th-Century Society.* New York, 1990.

O'Grada, Cormac. *The Great Irish Famine.* Houndmills, Ireland, 1989.

Sewell, William H. *Work and Revolution in France: The Language of Labor from the Old Regime to 1848.* New York, 1980.

Shapiro, Ann-Louise. *Housing the Poor of Paris, 1850–1902.* Madison, WI, 1985.

Sutcliffe, Anthony. *Towards the Planned City: Germany, Britain, and the United States, 1789–1914.* New York, 1981.

Topic 7

THE ROMANTIC VISION: ART AND CULTURE IN A REVOLUTIONARY WORLD

he comfortable and elegant world of the Rococo represented an essentially aris-
tocratic artistic style. As the shadow of revolution began to loom over European
political life, artists turned to new forms of expression.

In the latter part of the 18th century, the chief source of inspiration was
the world of Classical Antiquity, in particular that of Republican Rome, with its
emphasis on virtue and patriotism; painting and sculpture in this style are known
as "neoclassical." Architects also followed Classical models, while writers turned
to ancient sources for the plots of their plays and librettos or for historical accounts of the ancient world.

With the revolutionary changes which had swept over most of Europe by
the early 19th century, a new artistic vision was thrust forward: Romanticism.
Although Romantic artists produced works of a bewildering variety of types, they
shared certain characteristics. Instead of exalting the power of reason, they explored the irrational, probing the world of emotion. In contrast to earlier artists,
the Romantics were openly subjective, even autobiographical. Two aspects of life
made a special appeal: nature, with its mysterious unpredictability; and the exotic, in the form of remote times and faraway places.

One of the early centers of Romanticism was Germany, where the philosophy of Immanuel Kant sought to describe the nature of artistic experience. The
literary giant of the age was Goethe. Although many of his works were Classical,
they provided inspiration to the Romantic writers who followed him.

In England the Romantic poets gave expression to many of the concerns of
their times. William Wordsworth, often regarded as the founder of the English
Romantic movement, used a simple and direct style to explore the relationship
between humans and the natural world around them. George Gordon Byron,
who became the very symbol of Romantic melancholy, supported the liberal
causes of his day, including the Greek struggle for independence.

Romantic painters often used their art to protest against the violence of the
times. The Spanish painter Francisco José de Goya depicted the cruelty of the
French troops occupying Madrid. The leading French Romantic artist was
Eugène Delacroix, whose subjects ranged from political support for Greek independence to fantastic depictions of ancient Assyria.

Perhaps the supreme expression of Romanticism can be found in music, the
most intuitive and emotional of the arts. The towering figure of Ludwig van
Beethoven dominated the age. Firmly grounded in the Classical tradition, he

extended the range of his music to include the detailed depiction of emotion, the evocation of nature, and the striving for universal human peace.

By the mid-19th century Romanticism took a new turn, reflecting the preoccupations of the age; among its concerns were nationalism and a variety of social issues. The works produced in the century's first half, under the direct impact of revolution, are among the freshest and most vital in the Western artistic tradition.

NEOCLASSICISM AND THE REDISCOVERY OF ANTIQUITY

The art of the early 18th century reflected the lives of its aristocratic patrons. In reaction against the rhetoric and magnificence of the Baroque style, Rococo artists created a world of comfort and leisure to entertain the enlightened despots and their courts.

By the latter part of the century, with the growing interest in rational humanism, as evidenced in the work of the French Encyclopedists, and the increasing challenge to centuries-old social patterns, a new artistic style began to develop: *neoclassicism,* a revival of the art of ancient Greece and Rome. To some degree its inspiration was intellectual, even philosophical. The history of ancient Rome, in particular, contained many tales of stern patriotic virtue, and Greek and Roman Stoic philosophers put much emphasis on the notions of duty and lack of self-interest.

The Discovery of Herculaneum and Pompeii

An even more direct stimulus to the development of the neoclassical style, however, came from the chance discovery of the ancient cities of Campania, which lay just to the south of Naples. Buried by an eruption of the volcano Vesuvius in A.D. 79, they had virtually disappeared from history. A series of random events led to the discovery first of Herculaneum, in 1711, and then, in 1748, to that of Pompeii, the better preserved.

David's *The Oath of the Horatii* evokes the heroic spirit of Republican Rome.

The houses and villas of Pompeii, with their frescoes and fountains, public baths, theaters and shops, all provided an incomparably vivid picture of life almost two millennia earlier. Visitors from all over Europe traveled to the excavations, sketching the paintings and taking back copies of ancient objects. Among those most impressed was the greatest German writer of the age, Johann Wolfgang von Goethe, who commented that "There have been many disasters in this world, but few which have given so much delight to posterity."

Thus, at just the time that artists were searching for a language to express their new—if age-old—ideals, the discoveries at Pompeii and the other sites provided exactly what they were looking for. *The Oath of the Horatii*, painted by the French artist Jacques-Louis David (1748–1825) in 1784–1785, was a call to patriotic action. The subject, drawn from the early history of Rome, uses weapons, costumes, and even poses based on those in Pompeian frescoes. In 1791, Wolfgang Amadeus Mozart (1756–1791) composed his opera *The Clemency of Titus,* in which the Roman emperor Titus behaves with reason and moderation; the libretto was by the Italian poet Metastasio (1698–1782). One of the greatest literary achievements of the times, the vast and learned *Decline and Fall of the Roman Empire,* written by Edward Gibbon (1738–1794), provided a more general setting for this revival of interest in ancient Rome; the first volume was published in 1776.

Along with the writings of the *philosophes,* works such as these provided the intellectual background to the French Revolution. Gibbon believed that the decline of Rome was in large measure due to the rise of Christianity. His negative attitude to Christianity—and, indeed, to religion in general—was shared by the greatest philosophe of the day, Voltaire. In due course the Revolution's National Constituent Assembly secularized the church (see Part VII, Topic 3) and subordinated it to the state.

The neoclassical style forecast and underpinned the revolutionary changes which shook Europe at the end of the 18th century, but it could not express the immensely varied consequences of those events. In order to do justice to the new world they themselves were helping to construct, artists forged a new means of expressing themselves: Romanticism.

ROMANTICISM AND THE DISCOVERY OF SELF

The 18th century had exalted the power of human reason. The successes and, more significantly, the failures of the Revolution demonstrated the limits of human

A portrait of Beethoven by his contemporary, Waldmüller.

ability to construct a better world, and the uncertainties of history were reflected in the arts. Beethoven, one of the towering musical figures of the period, was inspired by Napoleon's early career to compose a symphony subtitled *Eroica*—"The Heroic"—dedicated to the Frenchman; Beethoven's own democratic convictions led him to see Napoleon as the champion of liberty. When his hero had himself crowned emperor in 1804, Beethoven in disgust struck out the dedication on the title page.

The Concerns of Romanticism

One of Beethoven's most quoted remarks provides us with a valuable insight into the perceptions of Romantic artists: "There will always be thousands of princes, but there is only one Beethoven." The chief concern of the Romantics was themselves: their emotions, their reactions to the world around them, their own individuality—all viewed in a context where freedom and social equality were the highest good. Artists used painting, music, and literature not to satisfy their patrons or to set forth generally accepted truths, but to express themselves.

In the quest for subjective emotional revelation, practitioners of all the arts turned to the irrational. Rejecting their 18th-century predecessors' emphasis on reason, they explored the power of dreams and the subconscious. This led in turn to a new vision of nature. The natural universe was no longer seen merely as a background for human activities, but as a mysterious world of its own, whose unpredictable workings corresponded to the fluctuations of human emotion. The desire to escape the constraints of their own objective situation produced another rich source for Romantic artists: remoteness of time or place. The Druids of ancient Britain and the Medieval world of knights in armor inspired operas and paintings. Writers and artists depicted the mysterious East and the wilderness of America.

The political enthusiasms of most Romantic artists were democratic and libertarian, and figures such as Byron and Delacroix publicly supported liberal causes. But the Romantic movement also had much in common with the other political philosophy of the day, conservatism. Both Romantics and conservatives distrusted the ability of human reason to create a better world. The conservative solution was to reconstruct the old political and social order, while Romantic artists tried to escape all confinements in the search for self-expression. Neither group had much sympathy for the chief proponents of liberalism, the middle classes.

THE ROMANTIC MOVEMENT IN GERMANY

Romanticism flourished throughout Europe, but nowhere did it affect as many aspects of culture as in Germany. Moral philosophy and theology, sociology and education, the natural sciences and chemistry were all influenced by the Romantic movement.

In addition to its cultural and intellectual interest, Romanticism presented an escape from the realities of German political life, together with the prospect of reform. At the time of the French Revolution, Germany was made up of hundreds of separate states, with no real chance of unification. Both the Revolution and the rise of Napoleon offered the possibility of decisive changes. Indeed, Napoleon's abolition of the Holy Roman Empire and merging of the smaller states into larger units seemed to presage the formation of a German nation-state.

The defeat and occupation of Prussia by the French armies served only to intensify the spirit of German patriotic fervor that had been created by the hectic course of events. In 1813 a coalition of German states, under Prussian leadership, defeated Napoleon at Leipzig.

Then came the realities of the Congress of Vienna, the Carlsbad Decrees of 1819 (see Part VII,

Topic 5), and the return to conservative censorship. In an age when the promise of political freedom had withered, thinkers and artists turned to the interior world of their own emotions in search of free expression. If hope had disappeared in the external universe, it could perhaps be regained in contemplating the ideal and the infinite.

The philosophical foundation of the German Romantic movement was provided by the writings of Immanuel Kant (1724–1804), who questioned the very nature of the real world. According to Kant, our impressions of external events are derived from our internal mental processes. Thus, what appears to be objective is, in fact, subjective. Kant's liberal religious views brought him into conflict with the Prussian government. A generation later, the German philosopher Friedrich Schleiermacher (1768–1834) laid the bases of modern Protestant theology (for a discussion of biblical higher criticism later in the 19th century, see Part VII, Topic 14). Kant himself was a rationalist, but his ideas, together with the high value he put on aesthetic pleasure, inspired a host of Romantic artists. In some cases his doctrines were pushed to extremes; the German dramatist Heinrich von Kleist (1777–1811) used Kant's theories on the limits of objective knowledge to prove that all knowledge is an illusion, and that the true will always be mistaken for the false. A stormy, even unstable personality, Kleist wrote both comedies and tragedies in which appearance and reality are constantly confused; only unqualified love and trust provide the hope of escape from disaster.

The Work of Goethe

Kleist's unrelieved pessimism is in strong contrast to the ethical and aesthetic worldview of the leading literary figure of the age, Johann Wolfgang von Goethe (1749–1832). Poet, critic, dramatist, novelist, Goethe also wrote on botany and zoology, and played an active role in politics. Many of his plays and poems are Classical in style, and throughout his long life he followed Classical principles of balance and order. Yet his works are touched by many of the characteristics of Romanticism; his early writings belong to a movement known as "Storm and Stress."

His first great success, the novel *The Sorrows of Young Werther*, is a largely autobiographical account of an unhappy love affair. Many of his lyric poems express emotional reactions to human experience and to the world of nature; and among the enormous range of influences he absorbed were the writings of Hafiz (?1326–1390), the Persian poet of love and wine. He was profoundly influenced by his travels in Italy, which he described in the *Italian Journey*; the journal provides an engrossing guide to the rich variety of his intellectual interests.

Etching of a dramatic scene in Goethe's novel, *The Sorrows of Young Werther.*

Goethe's most famous work, *Faust,* was published in two parts. The first, which appeared in 1808, deals with the nature of human experience and responsibility as seen in the relationship between Faust and Gretchen. In Part Two, published in 1832, at the end of his life, Goethe meditated on no less a subject than the nature and future of civilization. In spite of all the sufferings and faults that beset humanity, the divine spark which drives us in quest of knowledge—a search symbolized by Faust's pact with the devil—will guarantee our salvation.

The leading German Romantic painter was Caspar David Friedrich (1774–1840). Friedrich's mysterious landscapes seem to express the vastness and uncertainty of the world around us, in which isolated figures contemplate a dizzying emptiness or a remote seashore. In a sense Friedrich seems to deny the Romantic premise of the importance of the individual, yet in portraying the irrationality of human existence he illustrates one of the most important ways in which the Romantics broke with their predecessors.

"SPIRIT OF THE AGE": THE ENGLISH ROMANTIC POETS

Many of the chief poets of the early 19th century in England embodied an aspect of Romanticism in their

One of the key works of German Romanticism: Caspar David Friedrich's *Cloister Graveyard in the Snow.*

works. William Wordsworth (1770–1850), often held to be the founder of the English Romantic movement, personally witnessed the confusion of revolutionary France. He visited there in 1790, the year after the fall of the Bastille, and was inspired by the political idealism of the times—"Bliss was it," he wrote, "in that dawn to be alive." The later course of the Revolution, however, together with the ensuing war between England and France, undermined much of his enthusiasm for politics. He withdrew to the quiet of the English countryside, and by 1799 had settled in the Lake District in northwest England which his poetry was to make so famous.

The theme of his best works was the natural world and its relation to human experience. In language of deliberate simplicity, he aimed to express the calm remembrance of powerful emotions, and to draw from this contrast an understanding of human nature. He was strongly influenced by his sister Dorothy (1771–1855), whom he called "sister of my soul"; her *Grasmere Journal* contains vividly evocative descriptions of cloud and light, and of the local wildflowers.

Very different from Wordsworth's "emotion recollected in tranquility" were the stormy romances of George Gordon, Lord Byron (1788–1824). His mysterious and gloomy heroes and his own unconventional life provided the Romantic movement with one of its archetypal characters: the Byronic hero. Works like *Childe Harold's Pilgrimage*, set against exotic backgrounds, fed the public appetite for Romantic melodrama, while in *Don Juan* Byron struck a note of sophisticated irony. One of the most famous figures of his times, he shocked English public opinion by his relationship with his half-sister Augusta, and left London to resettle in Italy.

With his move to the Continent, Byron's fame and influence spread throughout Europe, where the writers inspired by his tormented heroes included the Russian Alexander Pushkin (1799–1837). The character who gives his name to Pushkin's novel *Eugene Onegin* is truly Byronic. Byron's support for libertarian causes led him to identify with the Greek fight for independence, and he died in 1824 while training soldiers in Greece.

By contrast with Byron's tempestuous career, the short life of John Keats (1795–1821) was outwardly uneventful. The influence of Romanticism on his work is superficially evident in *The Eve of Saint Agnes*, with its Medieval setting. A more profoundly Romantic vision of life and death infuses the *Ode to a Nightingale*, in which the poet's longing for extinction is set against the superhuman beauty of the song of a bird. The *Ode to Autumn* is also inspired by an identification with the splendors of nature, although in less tragic terms. Within a year of its composition Keats was dead, a victim of tuberculosis.

"THE HORRORS OF WAR": FROM GOYA TO DELACROIX

Neoclassical paintings such as David's *Oath of the Horatii* had set the stage for the heroics of the Revolution. Reality proved far less picturesque, and the early Romantic painters chronicled the brutality and suffering of war and violence.

The Art of Goya

In 1808 French troops imposed Napoleonic rule on Spain (see Part VII, Topic 4). When the French were finally driven out in 1814, the Spanish government commissioned the painter Francisco Goya (1746–1828) to commemorate the citizens of Madrid who had been executed for demonstrating against French occupation. The artist was also responsible for a series of etchings entitled *The Disasters of War*, begun a few years earlier. Goya's work achieves its terrible effect by throwing into relief the agonized emotions of the terror-struck victims, unforgettably illuminated by the light of torches, while their executioners, in shadow, turn towards us their hunched shoulders.

Goya had begun his career by painting Rococo scenes of aristocratic life, but his true interest lay in themes dear to the Romantic movement: dreams, the unconscious, the demonic. Toward the end of his life, cut off by deafness from the world around him, he decorated his own house with frescoes depicting an interior vision more hopeless than that of even the most melancholy Byronic hero.

Romantic Painting in France

Goya's despair drove him into seclusion. Other Romantic artists responded to cruelty and injustice in a more public manner. In 1816 the newly restored government of Louis XVIII was shaken by scandal. *The Medusa*, a French government ship, was wrecked off the coast of Africa. The vessel was ill-equipped with safety boats, and the captain and ship's officers were incompetent to deal with the emergency—it was later learned that they owed their appointments to political influence. A raft was thrown together, and passengers and crew spent days drifting under the tropical sun before the raft was spotted. Of the original 149 who were evacuated from the abandoned ship, 15 survived.

In *The Raft of the Medusa*, Théodore Géricault (1791–1824), a young French liberal, produced a dramatic rendering of the conditions of the last survivors at the moment of their sighting. The painting was put on public exhibition in 1819, and produced a sensation. Like Goya, Géricault used violent lighting

Théodore Géricault's *The Raft of the Medusa* (1818) illustrated one of the major scandals of the day.

contrasts to enhance the emotional effect of the scene. Other works of Géricault explore the Romantic obsession with madness and death, many of them painted directly from observation in mental institutions.

The greatest of all French Romantic artists, Eugène Delacroix (1798–1863), combined a virtuoso use of color with elaborate composition to create another masterpiece of Romantic political protest in *The Massacre at Chios*. The painting, which illustrates the Turkish slaughter of 20,000 of the Greek inhabitants of the island of Chios in 1824, was intended to rally support for the cause of Greek independence. Delacroix drew his inspiration from the writings of his distinguished English contemporary: "To set fire to yourself, remember certain passages from Byron," he recorded in his journal.

A work by Byron also inspired *The Death of Sardanapalus*. In this orgy of violence, the Assyrian king is seen seated atop his own funeral pyre. The Medes are at the gates of his capital, and he has chosen to destroy his possessions (including his wives) rather than let them fall into enemy hands. For all the brutality of the scene, the painting has a dreamlike quality, echoed in the brooding figure of Sardanapalus himself.

Delacroix's own sense of detachment is suggested by his nickname for the work: *Massacre No. 2*.

Although the Romantic style dominated French art in the early 19th century, one eminent painter of the period claimed to be a defender of Classicism. Jean-Auguste-Dominique Ingres (1780–1867) described the art of Delacroix as "the complete expression of an incomplete intelligence." Yet Ingres himself, brilliant academician that he was, did not remain untouched by the Romantic movement. Even in painting Classical themes, his treatment is often dreamy and sensual, and in his Turkish bath scenes the eroticism becomes explicit.

In any case, when in the mid-19th century Romanticism began to lose its appeal, it was replaced not by a return to Classicism but by a new movement called realism (see Part VII, Topic 14).

BEETHOVEN AND THE HEROIC IDEAL

The composer Ludwig van Beethoven (1770–1827) is the supreme example of an artist whose works passionately advocate liberty and universal peace. Deeply stirred by the lofty principles of the French Revolution, he was equally appalled by its degeneration into dictatorship. His one opera, *Fidelio*, is subtitled *Conjugal Love*: it describes how a devoted wife rescues her husband, a political prisoner, and sees just punishment meted out to his oppressor.

With his detailed depiction of nature in the *Pastoral* Symphony, daring use of harmony in the last string quartets, and introduction of words into the hitherto instrumental form of the symphony (Ninth Symphony), Beethoven served as the inspiration for generations of Romantic musicians. His own musical roots, however, were firmly imbedded in the Classical tradition.

Born in Bonn, Germany, he spent most of his creative life in Vienna, winning his first successes there as a virtuoso pianist. It was in writing for this instrument that he began to explore a freedom of form and a range of emotional content that were truly revolutionary. He himself subtitled the *Moonlight* Sonata "almost a fantasy."

The age of 32 marked a turning point in Beethoven's life: he realized that his increasing deafness was incurable. Driven to despair, he contemplated suicide. With the emotional crisis past, and determination renewed, his works took on a new heroic tone. One of the first fruits of this middle period was the Third Symphony, the *Eroica* (The Heroic), originally dedicated to Napoleon. In the Fifth Symphony the ominous sounds of "Fate knocking at the door," which open the work, give way to a triumphant conclusion in the final movement.

The music of his last years is in a deeper, more complex style, marked by emotional intensity and abrupt contrasts. At one end of the scale, the *Missa Solemnis* (Solemn Mass) and the Ninth Symphony, with its setting of Schiller's *Ode to Joy*, express the search for universal unity and peace. At the other extreme, the last string quartets lay bare the most intimate

Delacroix's *The Death of Sardanapalus* (1826): a typically Romantic blend of violence and eroticism.

PUBLIC FIGURES ● PRIVATE LIVES

MARY WOLLSTONECRAFT AND PERCY BYSSHE SHELLEY

It is hardly surprising that Mary Wollstonecraft's life (1797–1851) should have been an unconventional one, given the independent spirits of her parents. Her father was William Godwin (1756–1836), the political philosopher. Her mother, also named Mary, maintained herself by keeping a school and by writing and translating; her best-known work is *Vindication of the Rights of Women*, which appeared in 1792 during a crucial phase of the French Revolution (see Part VII, Topic 2). The following year she visited France and had an unhappy love affair there. On returning to England she attempted suicide.

Even before her trip to France she had formed part of a circle of radical thinkers, which included Thomas Paine, the Romantic painter John Henry Fuseli, and the anarchist philosopher William Godwin. Godwin now set up house with Mary. Four years later, in 1797, they married in order to protect the rights of the unborn child that she was by then carrying. A daughter was born to them that year, and named after her mother, who died shortly thereafter of puerperal fever.

The young Mary Wollstonecraft's early life was clouded by her mother's reputation. Her father had proudly published his late wife's posthumous works, which included *Maria, or The Rights and Wrongs of Women*, a novel which made a powerful case for sexual rights for women. He followed this up by writing her full and frank biography. Given the climate of the times, an outburst of public outrage was inevitable.

Brought up by her father and his second wife, Mary Wollstonecraft first met Percy Shelley when she was 16 and he 22—and already married for three years. Of all the English Romantics, none was more politically committed than Shelley (1792–1822). The son of a landed aristocrat, he was expelled from Oxford because of his publication of atheist beliefs. He had established something of a reputation for his unconventional ideas and behavior. This was reinforced when in 1814 Shelley and Wollstonecraft ran off together

continued next page

to Italy, and invited his wife to join them and live together.

A few months later Shelley's wife committed suicide, and shortly thereafter he and Wollstonecraft married. From 1818 to 1822 they were at the center of a group of English poets living in Italy that included Byron and Keats. Indeed, one of Shelley's greatest works, *Adonais*, was dedicated to Keats' memory. Shelley never developed a consistent and practical approach to social and political issues. He preferred instead to express large-scale visions of the human condition, and of ways of improving it. In the verse drama *Prometheus Unbound*, Shelley describes love as the only means of moral salvation. Elsewhere, particularly in lyric poems such as *Ode to the West Wind* and *The Cloud*, he uses ecstatic language to capture moments of high emotion.

While Shelley developed a series of warm if idealized relationships with women in his circle, he encouraged his wife to write fiction. Her first book was *Frankenstein*, one of the best of all horror stories.

This remarkable novel describes a character, Dr. Frankenstein, so arrogant and certain of himself that he circumvents the normal processes of procreation and makes a monster in his laboratory. A creature so abnormally produced is bound to act without love, and the monster—which at one point has been reading *The Sorrows of Young Werther*—ends by destroying its maker and mournfully seeking to obliterate its own vital spark. If the negative message of this is that a world without women is doomed to violence, the positive aspect is that maternal love is the key to happiness. The overriding theme of this complex work is the relationship between nature and science, especially when science is out of control—a growing issue for the 19th century.

Shelley himself was drowned in 1822 off the west coast of Italy, under circumstances that still remain mysterious. The following year Wollstonecraft returned to England, where she continued to write novels, two of which (*Lodore* and *Falkner*) include sympathetic portraits of Shelley.

Surviving her husband by almost 30 years, she wrote other romances; among them is *The Last Man*, set in the 21st century, in which humanity is destroyed by a plague which leaves only a single survivor.

and profound personal emotions; a section of one of them is explicitly described as a "song of thanksgiving for recovery from an illness."

Beethoven's visionary final works were far beyond the comprehension of his contemporaries, yet he was widely acclaimed as the greatest composer of his time. When he died in 1827, 10,000 people are said to have attended his funeral. The first musician to become a public figure, Beethoven played a vital part in creating the image of the artist as hero, voicing the feelings of all humans, not just a privileged few.

The Romantics After Beethoven

Beethoven's symphonies and sonatas, large-scale instrumental works, served as one model for Romantic musicians: the French composer Hector Berlioz (1803– 1869) wrote a *Fantastic Symphony*, which uses the orchestra to portray his own drug-induced hallucinations, and other major writers of symphonies included Felix Mendelssohn (1809–1847) and Robert Schumann (1810–1856).

Another form that appealed to Romantic composers was the small, intimate song or piano piece. The first great writer of *Lieder* (the German word for "songs") was Beethoven's younger contemporary Franz Schubert (1797–1828), who composed more than 600 songs to a wide variety of verse—some of it by Goethe. Schubert's lyric gifts also emerge in his chamber music, written for performance in the home. Like Schubert, Robert Schumann wrote songs on Romantic texts. Both composers produced superb piano miniatures, in Schumann's case often linked together into sets and inspired by literary characters and themes.

Beethoven had begun his career as a virtuoso performer, and the Romantic love of the spectacular encouraged the development of brilliant displays of instrumental skill. The most famous pianist-composers of the first half of the 19th century were Frédéric Chopin (1810–1849) and Franz Liszt (1811–1886), both of whom came to Paris from eastern Europe to make their careers. Chopin's music alternates between dreamy, often brooding, melancholy and fiery liveliness. Essentially retiring and introverted by temperament, his performances were generally given in the upper-class drawing rooms of Louis Philippe's Paris. Liszt was more robust, his music more rhetorical.

Portrait of the Romantic composer Chopin by the arch-Romantic Delacroix.

Among the sources of inspiration for this arch-Romantic were Dante's *Divine Comedy,* the Faust story, and poems by Byron.

The cult of the virtuoso reached its peak in the figure of Niccolò Paganini (1782–1840), perhaps the most astonishing violinist of all time. So impressive was his technical prowess that audiences whispered that, like Faust, he had sold his soul to the devil—a rumor that Paganini, enterprising showman that he was, did nothing to discourage. In his compositions he exploited every conceivable violin technique, producing solo pieces and concertos that, in his own time at least, only he had the skill to perform.

The French Revolution and the Napoleonic conquests opened up possibilities for social and political change that threatened the survival of the old aristocratic order throughout Europe. The process came to a halt at the Congress of Vienna, where Metternich and the other conservative statesmen endeavored to reconstruct the Old Regime and combat the cause of liberalism. The artistic and intellectual revolu- tion of the period could not be so easily checked. Many of those Romantic artists who had been inspired by the Revolution's original aims were disillusioned at its consequences, but that did not mean that painters, poets, and composers could go back to creating in prerevolutionary styles.

The Romantic movement was born of a desire for freedom, both personal and political. With liberty came a sense of a new status: Beethoven, Goethe, and Byron were among the most famous figures of their times, and the public exhibition of an important new painting was a major event. On occasions artists reacted against their privileges and responsibilities, for having to please a middle-class public could be just as frustrating as working for an aristocratic patron.

In response there began to develop a process of artistic alienation—the artist as rebel rather than as hero. Furthermore, creators who felt that they no longer needed to satisfy a specific audience were free to develop as they pleased. The notion of an "avant garde," whose ideas were always ahead of the public, grew throughout the 19th century, and with the rise and diffusion of popular culture, "high" art began to follow a course of its own.

But in the early decades of the 19th century this had not yet occurred. Artists were at the forefront of the campaign for reform, and their voices were still heard when political reformers could be—and were—silenced.

Questions for Further Study

1. Which characteristics of Romanticism are common to all the arts? What form do they take in the various artistic media?

2. What factors—cultural, social, historical—favored the development of the novel in the 19th century?

3. What role did nationalism play in the Romantic movement?

Suggestions for Further Reading

Canaday, J. *Mainstreams of Modern Art.* New York, 1981.

Chissell, J. *Clara Schumann: A Dedicated Spirit.* London, 1983.

Cooper, M. *Beethoven: The Last Decade.* New York, 1985.

Gage, J., ed. and trans. *Goethe on Art.* Berkeley, CA, 1980.

Paulson, R. *Literary Landscape: Turner and Constable.* New Haven, CT, 1982.

Talmon, J. L. *Romanticism and Revolt, 1815–1848.* New York, 1979.

Wolf, B. *Romantic Re-vision: Culture and Consciousness in Nineteenth-Century Painting and Literature.* Chicago, 1982.

Topic 8

THOUGHT AND ACTION: THE REVOLUTIONS OF 1848

In the 30 years following Waterloo, a number of important factors changed European life. The growth of industrialism revolutionized social and economic patterns. The old aristocratic order began to face an increasing challenge to its monopoly on political power from the middle classes, the champions of liberalism. The pressure of nationalism, generally with liberal support, offered the prospect of radical change in many parts of Europe, most notably in Italy, Germany, and Eastern Europe.

So widespread a reshaping of values and priorities depended on a series of intellectual and philosophical positions. In Britain the new industrial middle class found justification for their social and economic overturning of the old order in the writings of Thomas Malthus and Jeremy Bentham, both of whom advocated the primacy of the individual over society as a whole.

The most important systematic political philosophy to develop was socialism. Its general aims were an equitable distribution of wealth and social and political equality. Methods to achieve this, however, varied widely. "Utopian" socialists such as François Charles Fourier and Robert Owen put their faith in natural human goodness. By contrast, the more militant "scientific" socialists Marx and Engels advocated revolution: their *Communist Manifesto* appeared during the revolutions of 1848.

The 1830 revolution in France and the British electoral reforms of the 1830s (see Part VII, Topic 5) raised hopeful expectations for many elsewhere in Europe, but on the whole they were disappointed. The chief beneficiaries were the industrial middle class. The workers, who had erected the barricades in Paris, and demonstrated in the streets of Britain, won nothing. This lack of substantial change led to frustration not only in Britain and France, but throughout continental Europe. The growing discontent at the suppression of national freedom, and at the lack of representative government, led to a wave of revolutionary uprisings which swept over most of Europe in 1848.

As in 1830, France led the way. The frustrations of the industrial poor provoked savage street fighting in Paris. Within days Louis Philippe abdicated, and the Second French Republic was proclaimed. Others were quickly fired by the success of the French revolutionaries. Student liberals in Vienna, and nationalists in Hungary, Czechoslovakia, and Italy rebelled against Hapsburg rule and local monarchs. Metternich fled for his life, followed by his emperor, Ferdinand I. Tuscany, Naples, and Sicily all staged revolts against their rulers. Street riots in Berlin scared the Prussian king, Friedrich Wilhelm IV, into appointing a liberal government. The only countries not affected were Britain, where hasty compromise averted revolution, and Russia, still firmly under repressive tsarist rule.

Judged in terms of immediate success, the 1848 revolutions were a failure. Conservative forces returned to power throughout Europe. In France the middle and peasant classes, nervous at the rise of socialism, elected Louis Napoleon Bonaparte as president. Austrian troops restored Hapsburg rule to virtually all of the empire. Their success prompted the Prussian king to withdraw his liberal concessions, and the Prussian Army put down all protests. Only in Piedmont did a liberal constitution survive.

Yet the causes for which the rebels of 1830 had fought and lost the struggle—nationalism, liberalism, and socialism—were by no means doomed. A new realism replaced the idealism of much pre-1848 political thought. For the rest of the century both socialist and nationalist issues dominated the European political scene, with increasing success.

LIBERALS, NATIONALISTS, AND SOCIALISTS: REVOLUTIONARIES AND THEIR IDEALS

The conflicts that shook European society throughout the 19th century were in large part the result of a growing challenge to the conservative order. The three ideologies inspiring this opposition were liberalism, nationalism, and socialism. The first two played a part in the struggles immediately following the Congress of Vienna; the early development of modern socialism dates to the 1830s, and is best understood as a result of the gradual rise of the working classes.

Liberalism

Liberals could trace their ideas back to the Enlightenment and the moderate stages of the French Revolution, and both Romanticism and nationalism helped to shape their views of government. Political liberalism held that a representative system, generally in the form of constitutional monarchy, was the wisest form of government, for it allowed for stability, the participation of the middle classes, and the protection of basic freedoms such as equality before the law and freedom of speech. Liberalism itself was neither a systematic nor a static political philosophy. Rather, liberalism represented a set of attitudes that combined notions of social and political justice with a commitment to economic progress.

Liberalism varied greatly from country to country in the 19th century, but nowhere was it intended to be a democratic doctrine. As a political system of the middle classes, liberalism was based on a belief in the importance of private property, education, and the wisdom of the leisured classes. Liberals believed in change, but change that was the result of balanced, orderly growth as society in general underwent moral and material progress.

Liberal economic theory lay at the core of political liberalism. In the *Wealth of Nations* (1776) and other writings, the 18th-century thinker Adam Smith (1723–1790) had argued that prosperity would result from economic forces that were allowed to operate freely without government intervention. David Ricardo (1772–1823) expanded on Smith's theory, especially in his *Principles of Political Economy and Taxation* (1817). He expounded the "iron law of wages," which held that the price of labor, like commodities, depended on supply and demand. When the number of available workers is high, their pay will be low—around a mere subsistence level. Ricardo believed that labor, like land, is a commodity that should not be regulated but allowed to fluctuate with the marketplace.

Malthus and the Malthusians

The economic inequities of the industrial revolution that Ricardo found inevitable were reinforced by the pessimistic predictions of Thomas Robert Malthus (1766–1834). Malthus held that human suffering and poverty were unavoidable, a natural result of overpopulation; this in turn was due to the fact that people increased in number faster than food could be produced to feed them. Unless there was some conscious check on population growth, only famine or plague could restore the natural equilibrium. Even an increase in agricultural production would lead only to a rise in population and a repetition of the whole cycle.

In spite of his gloomy predictions, Malthus viewed himself as a humanitarian, believing that if society would only listen to his conclusions and take action to reduce population growth, it could reduce the quantity of human suffering. Nonetheless, in general he remained pessimistic, opposing any attempt by government or employers to alleviate the poverty and misery of the workers or the unemployed: charity, he believed, would make the situation worse by allowing more people to survive. Some economic liberals, however, tended to adopt a more positive attitude toward the Malthusian predictions. If human suffering was inevitable, middle-class manufacturers should not be surprised if their workers starved while they themselves grew rich, and liberals could reconcile themselves to manifest social injustice because it was unavoidable. Revolutionary concepts of equality were replaced by the realities of the marketplace, and the field of political economy became known as the "dismal science."

Although the harsh views of this "classical economics" were systematized into social theories later in the 19th century, other liberals rejected them. Original liberal notions of general freedom of thought and action crystallized into the concept of the "greatest good for the greatest number." The "utilitarianism" of political reform—its practical benefits as opposed to its theoretical desirability—was first clearly expounded in the writings of Jeremy Bentham (1748–1832).

According to Bentham, the criterion for judging a policy was not its natural appropriateness, but its utility. That which is good avoids pain and gives pleasure. Individuals can make their own estimates of what is to their advantage, while governments should aim for the same end result for their societies. The correct calculation of pleasure and pain would lead to a just society. Democratic government is useful because it satisfies the largest number of people, an argument that steps back from the doctrine of universal liberty. The broader implications of Bentham's ideas were explored in mid-century by John Stuart Mill (see Part VII, Topic 9).

The more immediate implications of Bentham's utilitarianism inspired a group of liberals known as the philosophic radicals. In their pursuit of "the greatest good for the greatest number," they pressed for widespread social reform. By 1832, the year of Bentham's death and passage of the Reform Bill, the philosophic radicals were leading campaigns to reform the legal system, education, prisons, and welfare.

Nationalism

The concerns of nationalism were of a different order. In its simplest form, nationalism is an awareness of cultural and territorial identity—the identity, that is, of people who share a common language, history, and traditions in a given region. The French Revolution and Napoleon's conquests were both major stimuli to the emergence of nationalism. Not only did the Revolution identify popular will with national sovereignty, but it also succeeded in mobilizing French citizens in defense of the revolutionary nation-state.

National consciousness in Germany, Italy, and eastern Europe was generated by French conquests in those regions. Under the impact of French invasion, two intellectuals, Johann Gottfried von Herder (1744–1803) and Johann Gottlieb Fichte (1762–1814) appealed to fellow Germans to seek for the common roots and culture of their *Volk* (people). With the growth of national awareness came a call for national self-determination, as peoples living under foreign rule began to demand political independence and unity.

Cultural campaigns were often as useful as political ones in instilling national consciousness. In Germany, Jakob and Wilhelm Grimm compiled Germanic folktales as well as German dictionaries and grammar books. In Hungary, Lajos Kossuth (1802–1894), future revolutionary leader, promoted the cause in articles appearing in the daily newspaper he edited from 1841 to 1844. He wrote these articles in Magyar, which had become the official government language in Hungary only in 1826. Frantisek Palacky (1798–1876), a Czech historian, fanned national consciousness with his five-volume *History of Bohemia*, which he began publishing in the 1830s.

The Polish poet Adam Mickiewicz (1798–1855) was deported to Russia for his political activities. On his release he settled in Paris, where in 1834 he published *Pan Tadeusz*, an epic poem set in the Polish Lithuanian villages where he grew up.

Giuseppe Mazzini

Like Mickiewicz, the Italian patriot Giuseppe Mazzini (1805–1872) spent most of his life in exile. The most important proponent of nationalism in the 19th century, Mazzini was a leading figure in the struggle to unify Italy, but his nationalist philosophy became a European as well as an Italian doctrine of liberty. A passionate, idealistic revolutionary, he believed in national self-determination as in a religion—indeed, he was sometimes called the "high priest" of Italian nationalism.

A member of the *Carbonari* in his youth, Mazzini took part in its conspiracies during the late 1820s. After a time in jail, he rallied the cause of Italian unity first from Switzerland and, when the Swiss government banished him, from France and later from London. In 1831 he created a revolutionary group of his own called *Giovine Italia* (Young Italy) with a tight organization and a specific program: popular insurrection led by youthful enthusiasts, Italian unity and independence, and—most subversive of all, from the point of view of the authorities—a republican government based on popular will and democratic principles. Mazzini, determined foe of the papacy as well as of kings, was a Romantic who hoped that a united Italy would establish its capital at Rome. From there, Italy would inspire a new "Europe of the Peoples," based on universal brotherhood, a sense of duty, and social justice.

Mazzini's very breadth of vision made him impatient with the necessities of practical politics, and his relations with other Italian leaders were generally stormy. In the 1830s and 1840s, Young Italy fomented countless ill-conceived conspiracies and uprisings, each of which failed, but in the process Mazzini had given a generation of idealistic Italians a strong sense of their common destiny. Throughout Europe, too, his example was followed as nationalist organizations modeled after Young Italy sprang up among other subject peoples. By the middle of the century, nationalism became a major force in European affairs, but after the achievement of national unity in Italy and Germany, nationalist idealism would be converted into a doctrine of national conflict and dominance: a state of mind rather than the fulfillment of national need.

The Rise of Socialism

At the same time as the industrial revolution was permanently changing European society, the first critics of industrialism began to appear. Their fundamental objection was that the growth of manufacturing did nothing to produce a more equitable distribution of wealth and, indeed, contributed to the exploitation of millions of workers.

The idea of a community in which the products of common labor are divided among all, according to their needs, was not a new one, although it had in general been limited to relatively simple societies. In modern Europe, this notion was first applied to industrial society in the 1820s, under the general name of "socialism." Socialists further advocated that economic equality should be accompanied by similar political and social reform.

The earliest socialist thinkers were derided by their more militant successors as "utopians," because their ideas were regarded as naive and impractical; later socialists tried to argue from objective, "scientific" principles, or, like Marx, from the notion of historical inevitability. Like many of the Utopians, Count Henri de Saint-Simon (1760–1825) was noble by birth. For all

the oversimplification of his beliefs—he proposed a massive plan of social reorganization based on the rule of technical experts and scientists—Saint-Simon coined what was to become one of the central teachings of the socialist creed: "From each according to his capacity, to each according to his work."

In Saint-Simon's ideal society, work had the highest value, and industrialists and technicians would replace theologians or philosophers as leaders. In the coming industrial age, he believed, the government of humans would give way to the administration of things. Religion also had a part to play, for it "should direct society toward the great aim of the most rapid amelioration of the lot of the poorest class."

After his death a cooperative farming and manufacturing community was organized in his name in Paris. In theory, women and men had equal status, and the community had a male and female leader. Before a suitable woman could be chosen, however, the community was closed down by the authorities, for it had extended equal rights to sexual as well as working relations. Women followers of Saint-Simon continued to meet, forming the most sophisticated women's movement of the times. They organized a women's newspaper and discussed the formation of a women's association, which would not imitate male organizations but take its own explicitly female form.

Another form of ideal community was proposed by Charles Fourier (1772–1837). Fourier believed that most of the ills of society were the result of the unsuitable physical and social conditions under which the vast majority of people lived. Thus the way to create a better society was to produce a more favorable environment. Fourier proposed to provide this in the shape of self-sufficient agricultural communities called "phalanxes," each with a limited population and economically self-sufficient, on pieces of land set aside for the purpose. Members of the community would receive wages according to their abilities and contributions.

Among Fourier's followers was Flora Tristan (1801–1844). In her speeches, letters, and diaries, Tristan proclaimed that at the root of industrial misery was the competition between women and men workers. The working class, she urged, should unite in the cause of women, and thereby help all workers.

In Britain, the chief proponent of utopian community life was Robert Owen (1771–1858). A prominent cotton manufacturer, in his own factories he cut the normal workday nearly in half, provided child care for working parents, and increased both productivity and profit. Owen believed that the price of manufactured products should be based on three factors: the cost of the raw material, the cost of labor, and an added amount to provide capital for future supplies.

Between the Revolutions of 1830 and 1848

1830 Belgium achieves independence; revolution in France makes Louis Philippe king

1831 Mazzini forms Giovine Italia

1834 Mickiewicz publishes *Pan Tadeusz*

1838 The Chartists circulate their "People's Charter"

1844 Marx and Engels found the Communist League

1846 Repeal of the Corn Laws

1848 *The Communist Manifesto* published

A TIME FOR CHANGE: THE ROOTS OF DISCONTENT

The revolutions of 1830 had signaled the advance of the liberal cause, but over the following years political reformers began to realize that the conservative order remained entrenched. Furthermore, those liberal concessions which had been won by popular demonstrations ended by benefiting the industrial middle class. The workers who erected the barricades in Paris or risked their lives at Peterloo gained little, if anything, from their actions.

The decade began with a nationalist victory. At the Congress of Vienna, Belgium (the former Austrian Netherlands) had been made part of the kingdom of Holland. Inspired by the French success in deposing the Bourbons, in August 1830 the Flemish citizens of Brussels staged a revolt in favor of Belgian independence. The Dutch held back, while Britain and France discouraged the threatened intervention of Russia and

Owen actually created a model community, to demonstrate that by minimizing profits and improving working conditions, he could still increase productivity; the community had its own housing and clubs, and a system of workers' benefits. Inspired by Owen, a number of crafts—weavers, glove makers, and others—set up unions and cooperative workshops, and working-class newspapers were founded. An industrial dispute put an end to the practical side of "Owenism," when tailors struck to protest at the hiring of women to work part-time in their own homes. Their successful action destroyed the ideal of solidarity which later socialists developed.

By the time of the 1848 revolutions, socialism had taken a new turn. In France and Germany, societies were formed calling for the abolition of all private property: communism. In 1844 two young Germans, Karl Marx (1818–1883) and Friedrich Engels (1820–1895), helped to found the Communist League, whose purpose was to overthrow the middle class (their term was the "bourgeoisie"); Marx used the term "Communist" to avoid confusion with the utopian socialists who, he believed, failed to see the historical laws that made revolution inevitable.

Engels, the son of a wealthy cotton manufacturer, met Marx in Paris, where they worked together on an analysis of the state of contemporary society, and a radical prescription for its reform. Their conclusions were outlined in *The Communist Manifesto*, published in 1848 for the gathering of Communists held in that year, in the midst of the revolutions. In the years after 1850, their ideas spread throughout Europe (see Part VII, Topic 13).

Engraving of 1832 showing Whig leaders united with the king to pass the Reform Bill.

Chartists at a protest meeting in London, April 1848.

Austria, and Belgium became an independent state guaranteed by international treaty.

Elsewhere, however, there were less encouraging signs of progress. A revolt in Poland was crushed by the Russians, and Mazzinian-inspired revolts in Italy were put down by Austrian troops. In a few German states minor upheavals did result in the granting of liberal constitutions, but Metternich was determined to prevent the rise of a nationalist movement which could benefit Prussia, and encouraged states to repress any uprisings. The Diet of the German Confederation duly followed Metternich's instructions.

As for the Hapsburg possessions in eastern Europe, the failure of revolt there is explained by the strength of the Austrians' control, and the ferocity of their reprisals at the first sign of rebellion. In addition, unlike Britain and France, and even Belgium, southern and eastern Europe had no industrialized middle class to organize and lead a revolution.

Britain: The Repeal of the Corn Laws

The first signs of popular discontent arose, ironically enough, in the one Western European nation which managed to avoid open revolutionary conflict: Britain. The Reform Bill of 1832 (see Part VII, Topic 5) had gone some way toward satisfying popular demands for increased parliamentary representation, but many were disappointed by it. In 1838 a group of radical reformers drew up a "People's Charter," which called for wholesale parliamentary reform; among the provisions were universal adult male suffrage, a secret ballot, and the abolition of property qualifications for members of Parliament. The Chartists, as supporters of the proposals were called, also campaigned against the revised Poor Laws (in theory, laws to protect the needy) which had been passed in 1834. As one of them wrote, "The new poor law is a law to punish poverty; making working men dislike the country of their birth, brood over their wrongs, and hate the rich of the land." The Chartists twice presented their Charter to Parliament, which rejected it out of hand both times.

The repeal of the hated Corn Laws in 1846 went some way to redressing the general sense of grievance, and its effects help to explain the sudden collapse of the Chartist movement. In 1848 a final petition demanding reform, accompanied by some 6 million signatures (many bogus), was carried to London by a mob so threatening that the government prepared to disperse it by force. In the end the crowd broke up peacefully, and so did the Chartist movement. Subsequent campaigns for reform were conducted by more orthodox means. Thereafter Britain remained untouched by events on the Continent, except for its function as refuge for political exiles. Among those who could have met one

Honoré Daumier, *Louis Philippe, the Last King of France.*

another in London in the 1850s were Marx and Metternich. There is no evidence that they did.

Revolution in France

By the early spring of 1848 the general frustration symbolized in Britain by the Chartist movement was spreading throughout Europe. Growing unemployment, and bad harvests in 1846 and 1847, increased tensions. As in 1830, the explosion originated in France, where on the surface the political scene seemed relatively calm. Both Louis Philippe and his chief minister,

François Guizot (who served as premier of France 1847–1848), followed a policy of order and prosperity at home and peace abroad.

Guizot, a self-proclaimed liberal, believed that the Constitution of 1830, which extended political power to the property-owning classes, provided a proper balance between liberty and order. Cautious and rigid, he opposed any further broadening of the franchise, hoping to combine industrial growth with political stability by preserving the status quo.

As elsewhere in Europe, however, industrialization had brought with it the rise of a large and underprivileged urban proletariat. The slum dwellers of Paris and France's northeastern industrial cities began to demand the right to form labor unions and to vote. When they received neither, workers protested at their living conditions and demanded reform; socialist ideas were increasingly circulated at political banquets.

A mass protest, in the form of a banquet, announced for February 22, 1848, was banned the day before by government decree. When a crowd in Paris gathered to protest against the restriction, street brawling broke out and workers began to build barricades. Louis Philippe tried to pacify the mob by dismissing Guizot,

Map 8.1   The Revolutions of 1848–1849

but in the rioting around the prime minister's residence a shot rang out. The troops guarding the house lost their nerve and fired on the crowd, killing a number of the demonstrators. The reverberations of their bullets echoed throughout Europe.

EUROPE AT THE BARRICADES: THE PATTERN OF REVOLT

For two days Paris was racked by street fighting. Workers erected some 1500 barricades. The troops of the National Guard either disappeared or joined the rioters. Louis Philippe had been brought to power by the 1830 revolution, and on February 25, 1848, he left it by the same route, abdicating like his predecessor and leaving for England. Always a moderate, he prevented a bloodbath by refusing to call out the army and by leaving so quickly.

The Second Republic

A provisional government assumed power and, to appease the demonstrators, proclaimed the Second Republic, its leaders chosen by acclamation from the crowds outside the Hotel de Ville (city hall). The poet Alphonse de Lamartine, an overnight convert to the republican cause, led the government, with a cabinet that included the socialist Louis Blanc, a token worker

named Albert Martin, and a radical republican, Alexandre Ledru-Rollin. The provisional government announced April elections for a new National Constituent Assembly.

The overthrow of the monarchy had temporarily united the competing political factions. Once the king was gone, the politicians took over and rival forces openly waged a struggle for power. The liberals favored a moderate extension of the vote. The republicans advocated permanent abolition of the monarchy and radical reform. Blanc, the only real socialist in the government, proposed a system of "national workshops" to pay the unemployed a small stipend and put them to work. The government set up a version of the scheme, but organized it so badly that the plan proved disastrous. Thousands of workers flocked to Paris to join the workshops, at immense cost to the taxpayers, while Blanc complained that the scheme had been deliberately set up in such a way as to guarantee its failure.

In spite of the political battles, the provisional government managed to make some positive steps. The new republic adopted universal male suffrage, abolished the death penalty, and rejected participation in any for-

A contemporary caricature by Andre Gill satirizing Louis Blanc.

Barrifade am Altfädter Brückenturm zu Prag am 16. Juni 1848.
Nach einer gleichzeitigen Darstellung der „Leipziger Illustrierten Zeitung".

Barricades at the Charles Bridge, in Prague, in June 1848.

eign wars. It also improved relations with the Catholic Church. The elections in April took place in relative calm, with around 85 percent of those eligible to vote actually doing so. The result was a triumph for the moderate and conservative republicans. Even the monarchists did better than the socialists, who won only a handful of seats.

Revolution in the Hapsburg Empire

While France began to rebuild some form of order, news of the cataclysmic events there reached Vienna. On March 12, workers and students finally threw off years of repression and rampaged through the city. The imperial palace was invaded. Under pressure from the emperor, Ferdinand I, Metternich resigned. The architect of conservative Europe hastily disguised himself and fled into exile in England, never returning to Austria. The emperor followed him, although only as far as Innsbruck, and a hastily convened liberal National Assembly drafted a constitution. Among other measures, peasant feudalism was abolished.

Elsewhere in the Hapsburg empire, Austrian rule faltered. Before the end of March, Milan and Venice rose up against their foreign rulers, while disturbances in Piedmont, Tuscany, Naples, and the Papal States forced the granting of constitutions. Taking advantage of these developments, Charles Albert (ruled 1831–1849), king of Piedmont-Sardinia, declared war on the Austrians with the aim of removing them from the affairs of the peninsula.

Charles Albert was an enigmatic and unstable man who, during the abortive Piedmontese revolt of 1821, had led an unsuccessful campaign against Austria. Now he planned to redeem himself and, once having driven out the hated foreigners, unite northern Italy under his rule. The constitution which he issued in February 1848 was a slightly modified version of the Spanish Constitution of 1812. Although it provided for representative government based on limited male suffrage, it also gave the monarch considerable powers and left the question of parliamentary authority vague. Thirteen years later, it would provide the basis for the constitution of a united Italy.

Units arrived from other Italian states, along with volunteers led by the dashing guerrilla fighter Giuseppe Garibaldi. Nevertheless, not all Italian patriots supported Charles Albert. Mazzini, from his exile in London, inveighed against the king of Piedmont and advocated a republic.

The election of Pope Pius IX (ruled 1846–1878) two years earlier had inspired liberal hopes and encouraged the Piedmontese moderate Vincenzo Gioberti (1801–1852), who had earlier proposed a "Neo-Guelph" program consisting of a federation of Italian princes under papal leadership (the Guelphs were the pro-papal forces in Medieval Italy who opposed the encroachments of the Holy Roman emperor). Pius had even sent a small detachment to assist Charles Albert, but by April he had concluded that he could not declare war against Austria. When Pius fled Rome in November, Mazzini rushed to the city with his followers, and in February 1849 became head of the Roman Republic. "The war of the kings is over," declared Mazzini, "the war of the people begins." Ideological

German troops storm a barricade in Frankfurt, September 18, 1848.

Significant Dates

The Revolutions of 1848

France:

February 22–24, 1848	Louis Philippe abdicates; Provisional Government formed
February 26	National Workshops begin
April	Constituent Assembly
June	Workers Revolt in Paris
November	Second Republic founded
December	Louis Napoleon elected president

Germany:

March 1848	Riots in Berlin; King Friedrich Wilhelm IV promises reforms
May	Frankfurt Assembly meets
December	Prussian constitution issued
March 1849	Friedrich Wilhelm refuses crown of Germany
June	Frankfurt Assembly dispersed

Italy:

January 1848	Uprising in Sicily
January–March	Constitutions issued in Naples, Piedmont, Tuscany, and Rome
July	Austrians defeat Charles Albert
November 1848– February 1849	Uprising in Rome, republic proclaimed
March	Charles Albert defeated and abdicates
March–August	Revolutions crushed in Italy

Austria:

March 1848	Revolt in Vienna, Metternich dismissed; Milan revolts
June	Revolt in Prague put down
October	Movement in Vienna crushed
April–August 1849	Hungarian independence proclaimed; crushed by Russians

divisions, together with considerations of religion, prevented a united front among the proindependence forces in Italy.

In Hungary, where Kossuth led the Magyar nationalist party, the Austrians agreed to the March Laws, guaranteeing a large measure of Hungarian self-rule. One of the new government's first acts, the reaffirmation of Magyar as the country's official language, alienated Hungary's ethnic minorities, in particular the Croats.

Such divisiveness did not augur well for the revolution's success. In Bohemia too there were ominous signs of the national rivalries that were to prove fatal to the cause of reform. The Czech majority and the German minority feuded over rival national conferences, a pan-Slavic one to be convened in Prague, and a pan-German one meeting in Frankfurt. By mid-1848, the Hapsburg empire may have seemed on the brink of collapse, but the revolutionary gains were precarious.

Riots in Berlin

In Berlin, the Prussian capital, Friedrich Wilhelm IV (ruled 1840–1861), the Hohenzollern king, had come to power supporting liberal reforms but had never carried them out. Now, in March, when he heard that Metternich had fled Vienna, the king issued a manifesto promising a constitution. Events took an unexpected turn, however. Crowds of demonstrators celebrating the news from abroad were provoked into bloody violence when government troops fired shots at them. Barricades went up in Berlin and the king eventually relented, appointing a liberal government and announcing a national assembly. This left both conservatives and radicals angry, the former because they wanted to see the demonstrations crushed, and the latter because they had already been fired on.

By May, liberals throughout the German states had sent delegates to an assembly at Frankfurt, where the Diet of the German Confederation had its seat. The Frankfurt Assembly was a well-meaning gathering of middle-class professionals—lawyers, professors, bureaucrats—convened to create a united German nation. The absence of any working-class representation, however, was a dangerous indication of the narrow base of the German revolutionary movement.

HOPES CRUSHED: THE REACTIONARIES TRIUMPHANT

Within less than a year the fires of revolution were spent. The revolutionaries were dead or in exile, and the reactionaries back in power. In France the return to order was self-imposed: in the April elections for the National Assembly, the middle class and the peasants, fearful of "socialist excesses," had voted for moderate candidates.

One of the new government's first acts was to abolish the national workshops, and to order the workers, who had collected in Paris, either to join the army or to go and look for jobs in the provinces. Rioting broke out in Paris, as desperate workers took once again to the barricades, with the slogan "better a death from bullets than from starvation." During four bloody "June Days," rebels fought troops in the streets until government forces under General Louis Cavaignac (1802–1857) brutally crushed the uprising at the cost of perhaps 5000 lives. The government victory, and the subsequent execution and deportation to the French colonies of rebel leaders, restored domestic peace. It also left wounds in French society that remained open for generations.

The assembly proceeded to draw up a constitution establishing the Second French Republic. Rule was divided between a one-chamber parliament, which retained legislative control, and a president, who had executive and administrative powers. Both instruments of government were to be elected by universal male suffrage; a bill for women's suffrage was defeated by 899 votes to 1.

The Election of Louis Napoleon

In December 1848 elections were held for president. Among the candidates to present themselves were Lamartine, Ledru-Rollin, Cavaignac, the conservative hero of the June Days, and Louis Napoleon Bonaparte (1808–1873), the late emperor's nephew, who claimed that he could restore the glory of France's imperial days.

A complex and eccentric figure, Louis Napoleon had acquired liberal ideas during his youth and something of a revolutionary pedigree. After living in exile in Germany and Switzerland with his mother, he had taken part in uprisings in Italy in 1830–1831. In 1840 he had been arrested for plotting a seizure of power in France, but escaped from prison and fled to England. A wily politician with a skillful instinct for creating popular poses, while in prison he had published a pamphlet entitled *The Extinction of Pauperism*, which won him support among the workers.

Amid utter confusion, the country prepared to vote. To the great surprise of many, Louis Napoleon swept the elections with 70 percent of the vote, becoming the republic's first president. A clever manipulator of opinion, he had played on the glamour of his name, promising to repeat his uncle's achievements—or at least some of them—and restore France to greatness. Moreover, he appealed to workers and revolutionaries as easily as he did to conservative peasants and monar-

chists. Less than four years later, in 1852, he overthrew the constitution, seized power, and crowned himself Napoleon III (the so-called Napoleon II, the dictator's son, died in 1832 without ever ruling). Thus France returned from the heady days of February 1848 to 20 years of authoritarian rule.

Revolution Crushed in Central and Southern Europe

The reassertion of Hapsburg rule was made possible by two factors: the innate strength of the Austrian Army and the continued destructive feuding amongst various ethnic groups. In Bohemia, divided by rivalry between the Czech majority and the German minority, the anti-German Czechs summoned a confederation of Slavs to gather in Prague, and refused to send a delegation to participate in the pan-German assembly meeting in Frankfurt. The German minority resented their government's refusal to allow them to participate in the Frankfurt discussions. Austrian forces took advantage of the mutual hostility between Slavs and Germans to reassert control in Prague. The troops were ordered in, moreover, not by the emperor, but by the new Austrian government, which, for all its liberalism had no intention of presiding over the breakup of the empire.

In northern Italy the excitement of freedom soon gave way to the only-too-familiar inability of the Italian states to cooperate. The troops of Piedmont, left to fight alone, were no match for General Radetzky and the Austrian forces, and in July concluded an armistice. In March 1849, under the urging of the Piedmontese radicals and his own desire for vindication, Charles Albert denounced the armistice and declared war on Austria for a second time.

Within a week the struggle ended in defeat. Abdicating in favor of his son, Victor Emmanuel II (ruled as king of Piedmont 1849–1861; and as king of Italy 1861–1878), from whom he had extracted a promise never to abrogate the constitution, he went into exile and died a few months later. To the south, the Roman Republic was soon surrounded and, although gallantly defended by Garibaldi, was finally defeated in 1849 by a force sent by none other than Louis Napoleon, the new president of France, anxious to impress his Catholic subjects by a show of support for the papacy.

Even before then, Hapsburg rule had been restored in Vienna. At the end of October 1848 forces loyal to the emperor occupied the city, and the government resigned. The new Austrian chief minister, Prince Felix von Schwarzenberg (1800–1852), proceeded to dissolve the National Assembly and impose his own authoritarian constitution throughout the empire.

Only Hungary remained independent for a short while longer. Early in 1849 the new emperor—

Ferdinand I had abdicated at Schwarzenberg's bidding—Franz Josef (ruled 1848–1916), accepted the assistance of Nicholas I of Russia in regaining Austrian control there. The tsar's motives were hardly altruistic. Quite apart from any loyalty to a fellow monarch, he feared the spread of revolt to Poland and Russia's western provinces. To make matters easier for the Austrians, they were joined by Hungary's own Croat population, who resented and feared the Magyars' success.

As for Prussia, where a middle-class National Assembly had been elected and was drafting a liberal constitution, as soon as Friedrich Wilhelm realized that the Hapsburgs were back in power, he dissolved the assembly and reasserted his authority. In the face of the Prussian Army, street demonstrations by radical workers were soon put down. The riots also confirmed middle-class distaste for the socialists, and scared them into accepting the king's rule. Later in 1849, the king surprised conservatives, however, by granting a constitution of his own (revised in 1850) that provided for a two-chamber *Landtag*, or legislature. The lower house of the Prussian *Landtag* was elected by a complicated voting system that gave control to the upper middle class.

The one continuing sign of liberal activity was the assembly in session at Frankfurt to discuss the future of a united Germany. One of the chief issues to divide the delegates was whether Austria should be included in the future German state. Those in favor comprised the *Grossdeutsch* ("Great Germany") faction; the others were called the *Kleindeutsch* ("Little Germany") party. After months of lofty debate, the matter was resolved in the end by the reactionaries' return to full control in Vienna: Hapsburg Austria could have no place in a liberal Germany.

In March 1849 the victorious "Little Germany" delegates offered the leadership of the German world to Friedrich Wilhelm. The Prussian king contemptuously refused it, proclaiming disdainfully that he had no need of a "crown from the gutter." The delegates despondently returned home. Just over a year after the first riots in Paris, the last sparks of reform were extinguished.

THE REVOLUTIONARY EXPERIENCE AND ITS MEANING

By midcentury even the most ardent revolutionaries had to admit that their prospects were not promising. For a few months the whole of Europe seemed on the

Satirical depiction by Daumier of the French Chamber of Deputies.

brink of irreversible change, only to slide back into reactionary hands. The reformers' failure was, of course, partly due to their opponents' superior strength. In the long run the Austrian Army and the Prussian Junkers had an advantage that not even the most fiery rebel could withstand.

Yet with hindsight it was clear that the revolutionaries themselves were in large measure responsible for the abruptness of their failure. In virtually all cases, leadership was indecisive and divided. Much of the actual fighting, with its consequent loss of life, involved the workers. With the battles over, and the time come for debating future moves, the middle class took over. The two factions never really shared a common interest, for the workers wanted to overturn existing society, while the others—who had not wanted a revolution in the first place—were concerned to reassert earlier gains. In addition the more extreme forms of socialism were used by conservatives to scare middle-class revolutionaries back into obedience. As a result of their experience in 1848, both parties learned to mistrust the other.

One of the principal goals of the revolutions, the promoting of national identity, turned out to be a two-edged sword. Divisions among ethnic minorities, which had often existed for centuries, allowed the Austrians to divide and rule. Broader national rivalries prevented the coordination of revolutionary movements across frontiers. Where, as in Germany or Italy, there was no actual difference of nationality, political disagreements and local rivalries stood in the way of united opposition to conservative regimes. Yet the experience of 1848 was not entirely in vain. At least some German and Italian nationalists drew the obvious conclusion that only united opposition could cause the collapse of a hated regime, and applied them with varying degrees of success in their struggles for unification later in the century.

Quite apart from political, social, or national differences, the events of 1848 demonstrated another gulf: the one between city dwellers and rural populations. For the most part the grievances that the revolutionaries sought most urgently to redress were those of city life—overcrowding, bad working conditions, unemployment. Issues such as these were of little interest to peasants and farmers, the wealthier of whom actually stood to lose by a wholesale restructuring of society. In France and Prussia self-interest, bolstered by a mortal fear of the "red peril" of socialism, led peasants to join the middle classes in putting down the revolution.

In the second half of the 19th century, as urban populations came to dominate most European countries, the balance of power shifted decisively to the cities; the working classes consolidated their power, and peasant farmers ceased to play a significant political role.

The 1848 revolutions were not totally without positive results for the liberal cause. A few measures enacted by liberal assemblies—the abolition of serfdom in Austria and Hungary, for example—remained in force. Some former conservative leaders remained in exile; Metternich was one who never returned to power. More intangibly, those who continued to press for reform learned to value realism, rather than idealism. Political theories and notions of human rights, or the rights of nations, could be put into practice only by organized and efficient leadership. The events of 1848 had demonstrated to even the most idealistic that utopianism was not enough.

The French Revolution anticipated the beginning of the modern world, but the revolutions of 1848 seemed to reinstate the old order. Yet although the conservatives were back in power, the society over which they ruled was undergoing a period of profound upheaval. Vast numbers of people were bitterly unhappy with the systems under which they lived. The causes of their dissatisfaction were only too clear. Most of them lived crowded together in cities, which increasingly became Europe's dominant social and economic units. Each country's wealth and political power remained in the hands of a tiny minority. The citizens of many parts of Europe remained under foreign domination.

For many of those who felt themselves oppressed, socialism offered the hope of escape. The rewards of liberalism seemed limited to one segment of society, while the triumph of nationalism still appeared distant. Under the influence of socialist ideas, working-class people began to take practical steps to organize themselves. Trade union and cooperative leaders forced industrialists to take them seriously. Many socialist theorists encouraged the feminist movement, which first developed in the 1850s in Britain.

Thus out of the ashes of 1848 arose the industrial world of the late 19th century. The conflicts which permeated it involved in increasing measure citizens who had hitherto played little part in shaping history: the industrial working class.

Questions for Further Study

1. What were the principal aims of liberalism and socialism, and how did they differ?

2. How did the political developments of the 1830s and 1840s in Britain differ from those in continental Europe?

3. What caused the rise of nationalism in the 19th century? How successful were its early leaders, and what were their methods?

Suggestions for Further Reading

Beecher, J. *Charles Fourier: The Visionary and His World.* Berkeley, CA, 1986.

Calhoun, C. *The Question of Class Struggle: Social Foundations of Popular Radicalism During the Industrial Revolution.* Chicago, 1982.

Church, C. *Europe in 1830: Revolution and Political Change.* London, 1983.

Droz, J. *Europe Between Revolutions, 1815–1848.* Ithaca, NY, 1980.

Seidman, S. *Liberalism and the Origins of European Social Theory.* Berkeley, CA, 1983.

Stearns, P. *1848: The Revolutionary Tide in Europe.* New York, 1974.

Thompson, D. *The Chartists: Popular Politics in the Industrial Revolution.* New York, 1984.

VII

Topic 9

THE LIBERAL STATE: DOMESTIC POLITICS IN BRITAIN AND FRANCE

vents in Britain and France in the years from 1850 to 1870 offer a contrast in the application of liberal doctrines at home and abroad. In both countries economic liberalism produced increasing domestic prosperity. Britain maintained its political liberalism, while avoiding involvement in European affairs. In the first part of his reign, Napoleon III restricted political freedom at home, and in foreign policy set aside the basic liberal ideal of international peace. During the 1860s, however, the French governmental system underwent a liberal transformation.

By mid-19th century, Britain embarked on a period of prosperity greater than at any earlier time in its history. Under a system of two-party parliamentary government, public opinion could play a part in producing peaceful political change. A policy of nonintervention in Europe (apart from the Crimean War) brought two decades of peace, further industrial growth, and a boom in free trade.

The chief political issue was parliamentary reform. The 1832 Reform Bill extended the franchise. In the 1850s and 1860s the Liberals (formerly the Whigs) sought to increase the number of eligible voters still further. The government of William Gladstone, the Liberal leader of the day, was defeated on the issue in 1866, but the following year his political rival Benjamin Disraeli, leader of the Conservatives (formerly the Tories), succeeded in passing a bill which doubled the number of eligible voters. He was subsequently defeated in the election of 1868.

In France in 1848 a cautious electorate chose, as the first president of the Second Republic, Prince Louis Napoleon, who had campaigned on a platform of "law and order" after the violence of the "June Days." During the Second Republic, Louis Napoleon did everything possible to enlarge his power base and popularity. In 1851 he became a virtual dictator, and the following year he assumed the title of Napoleon III, emperor of the French.

For a country long torn by political bloodshed, the Second Empire held out hopes of stability and peace. Napoleon's constitution, like that of his uncle a half-century earlier, offered the appearance of democracy while leaving all effective power in the emperor's hands. Political opposition was suppressed, newspapers censored, the universities strictly controlled. In economic terms, however, Napoleon encouraged private investment and free trade; he used social legislation to retain the support of the working class.

The merits of Napoleon's domestic program were undermined by his international involvements. In his quest for a French empire, he completed the

829

colonization of Algeria. French troops were sent as far afield as Indochina; a century later, the struggle for independence of the French colonies both in Indochina and Algeria proved disastrous. Napoleon's most grandiose scheme, the conquest of Mexico, was equally doomed.

Apart from the joint Franco-British force sent to the Crimea in 1854, the French were no more successful closer at hand. In 1859 the emperor first joined the Piedmontese and then abandoned them. His government's final miscalculation, the war with Prussia of 1870, proved his downfall.

SIR ROBERT PEEL AND THE RISE OF THE POLITICAL PARTY SYSTEM

British success in avoiding the outbreak of widespread public violence in 1848 was due in large part to the country's method of parliamentary government. Popular revolt had been forestalled in 1832, when a Whig majority, convinced that without some reform open class war would become inevitable, passed the Reform Bill (see Part VII, Topic 5). The British parliamentary system, with its two large parties, made possible the discussion of a change of policy and its carrying out, without the elimination of those upholding the minority position. Furthermore the parliamentary debates which led to the bill's passage inevitably reflected public opinion of the times.

Sir Robert Peel (1788–1850), the son of a wealthy manufacturer, was a major reformer in this tradition of realistic politicians. A member of Parliament from the age of 21 and a frequent cabinet minister, Peel evolved into an advocate for Catholic and Jewish rights, an equitable income tax, and penal reform. His best known innovation was his organization of a force of professional policemen for London, known popularly as "Peelers," or "Bobbies."

Repeal of the Corn Laws

Peel served briefly as prime minister in 1834–1835, and after resigning he set about forming a new coalition that would later become the Conservative party. During his second term as prime minister from 1841 to 1846, the repeal of the Corn Laws became the dominant issue in British politics. The Corn Laws, passed in 1815 to protect landowners by imposing a tariff on imported grains, not only caused hardship among the poor but offended liberal free traders. Furthermore, the rise in bread prices which they caused forced employers to pay higher wages to their workers.

Peel supported repeal in response to popular protest and the agitation of the Anti–Corn Law League established in 1839 by Richard Cobden (1804–1865). Peel hoped that increased trade and an income tax would offset the impact of repeal, and the misery caused by the potato famine in Ireland in 1845 convinced him to oppose the agricultural interests in his own party: in 1845, and again in 1846, a blight caused the potato crops in Ireland to fail. In the subsequent famine nearly a million Irish died and over a million emigrated, particularly to the United States. The repeal of the Corn Laws was passed in 1846 after bitter debates in the House of Commons.

The move split Peel's own Tory party and ended his political career. He can have had little doubt of his action's unpopularity with the Tories, many of them landowners with a vested interest in maintaining an artificially high price for domestic grain. He openly acknowledged, however, that his chief motive apart from his belief in free trade was to avoid a class war. The collapse of the Chartist movement two years later underlines the success of his achievement (see Part VII, Topic 8).

By 1850 there existed general public confidence in the ability of the parliamentary system to work out solutions to political problems based on compromises and practical considerations, rather than on theoretical dogmas. The controversy surrounding the Corn Laws contributed to the emergence of new political alignments and parties, but the ensuing battle over further reform was waged, for the most part, in the Houses of Parliament and not in the streets.

BRITAIN IN THE AGE OF VICTORIA AND ALBERT

The nominal head of that Parliament was, of course, the monarch, whose powers were limited but constitutionally significant. Queen Victoria (ruled 1837–1901)

Map 9.1 The Railway System in Britain, Mid-19th Century

brought a welcome stability to her role, both by the sheer length of her reign and by virtue of her public image. In place of the traditions of sovereigns who indulged their own selfish interests, taking lovers and squandering national resources, Victoria deliberately set an example of virtuous behavior.

The Victorian Example

Her own marriage—much of which was lived in the public eye—to Albert of Saxe-Coburg-Gotha (1819–1861), a minor German aristocrat, was tranquil and loving. Indeed, Albert's death in 1861 so devastated Victoria that for some time she hid herself from public life in Windsor Castle, earning the popular title of "the widow of Windsor." For years afterward she continued to have Albert's shaving kit put out each morning. Among the monuments to her late husband which she commissioned are the Albert Memorial in London's Hyde Park, and the nearby Royal Albert Hall.

As wife, mother, and widow, Victoria provided her subjects with an exemplary model for their behavior. She was clearly conscious of her public responsibilities. On ceremonial occasions she was always accompanied by one or two of her numerous children to emphasize the importance of the family (on "Victorian" values, see Part VII, Topic 13). In private, though, she confessed to disliking infants, their constantly waving arms and legs reminding her of frogs.

John Stuart Mill and the Feminist Cause

The placid, confident image that Victoria presented was only one aspect of her age. The rapid development of urban society and the political and economic issues it raised continued to perplex many liberal thinkers. In 1848 the greatest liberal philosopher of his times, John Stuart Mill (1806–1873), published *Principles of Political Economy,* in which he studied the effects of the growth in size and importance of the working class. Mill was also concerned with the theoretical principles of liberalism: *On Liberty,* published in 1859, is the most complete statement of his belief in the inherent value of individuals and their actions, while it also warns against the "tyranny of the majority." Mill took this conviction to its logical consequence both in his own lifestyle and in supporting the cause of women's suffrage.

The young Mill's interest in political philosophy had been first stimulated by his father, who subjected the child to a grueling training in the principles of Jeremy Bentham. After a period in which he became interested in the Romantic ideas of Coleridge, Saint-Simon, and other thinkers, Mill turned to politics, liberalism, and the philosophical thinking behind the French Revolution.

One of his least happy achievements was, in fact, the destruction of his friend Thomas Carlyle's book, *The French Revolution* (1837). Mill had borrowed the book in manuscript form to review and an overzealous maid found the untidy pages lying around in his house and burned them. Carlyle heroically rewrote the entire

Commemorative plate issued for Queen Victoria's Jubilee in 1887.

The British philosopher and economist, John Stuart Mill.

text, later grumbling that he had devoted so much effort to comforting the guilt-torn Mill that he was unable to think much about himself.

Among Mill's closest and most intimate friends was Harriet Taylor (1807–1858), whom he first met in 1829, and to whose influence and help he attributed many of his most important works. They labored together for the cause of women's rights, a movement which became organized in London in the mid-1850s. In contrast to Victorian attitudes toward gender, their partnership and subsequent marriage represented an early example of the feminist ideal of equality of status.

Mill's relationship with the smart and cultivated Taylor had the reluctant sanction of her husband, but caused much public gossip. Combined with his open support of the feminist movement, it made them favorite figures of fun for newspaper cartoonists. In 1833 Taylor and her husband separated, but neither she nor Mill would take the daring step of living together. Only in 1852, two years after her husband's death, did Taylor and Mill marry. Mill conceived of marriage as a voluntary business partnership between equals, one that was dissolvable, and he tried, perhaps excessively, to avoid the conventional relationship between husband and wife in which the power of the male predominated. Before their marriage, he even gave Taylor a kind of contract in which he renounced his rights, financially and sexually, as a husband.

After Taylor's death, Mill devoted considerable energy to the cause of women's rights. In *On the Subjection of Women* (1869), which incorporated many of Taylor's ideas, he stated many of the key doctrines of feminism: injustices in society were the result of the inequality of the sexes; if men were no longer tyrants and women slaves, happiness would increase both at home and in society. Two years before the book's publication, at the time of the great reform debate, Mill was one of the 73 members of Parliament who voted for a provision to introduce female suffrage; 193 voted against, and the measure failed to pass.

With the defeat of the bill, the feminist movement split over whether men should be allowed to continue to serve on its committees. Mill remained an active member of the campaign, however. *On the Subjection of Women* became one of feminism's classic texts, and his death in 1873 was seen as a major setback for the cause.

LIBERALS, CONSERVATIVES, AND THE POLITICS OF REFORM

The campaign for female suffrage waged by Mill and Taylor was part of a larger battle for electoral reform that dominated British political life for almost two decades. The issue of electoral reform brought together on the same side two groups: traditional middle-class liberals and workers. Many of those employed in the textile and manufacturing industries had achieved a measure of economic independence; now they felt unjustly excluded from the political system. The middle-class liberals, for their part, resented the hold that the landed gentry maintained on many institutions. The Anglican Church, for example, was dominated by the younger sons of aristocratic families and was supported by public taxes paid by all citizens, even those who were not members of the Church of England.

The Reform Bill of 1867

In general the Whigs were sympathetic to the cause of reform, but Lord Palmerston (1784–1865), the Whig prime minister for most of the period between 1855 and 1865, was more interested in rousing patriotic fervor at home and supporting nationalist movements abroad. The two rising politicians of the age, the Whig William E. Gladstone (1809–1898) and the Tory Benjamin Disraeli (1804–1881), were more responsive to public demands. In 1866, together with the Whig Prime Minister Lord John Russell, Gladstone introduced a reform bill to widen the suffrage. The measure was defeated and the government fell. The following year, however, a Tory government led by Disraeli introduced its own, more radical reform bill. Disraeli, a consummate politician, realized reform was inevitable and stepped in to claim the credit for it.

The Second Reform Bill of 1867 effectively doubled the number of the electors. All adult males paying ten pounds rent a year in the cities, or twelve pounds a year in the country, could now vote; in effect the measure enfranchised the upper working classes—the "skilled workers"—and the lower middle classes. Parliamentary seats were redistributed, with an increased number going to the populated and industrial north. The results of Disraeli's bill were a long way from universal suffrage: in addition to the poor, half of Britain's citizens—women—remained unenfranchised. The measure was sufficient, though, to satisfy most of the reformers.

Gladstone and Disraeli continued to lead their parties, by now known respectively as the Liberals and Conservatives, in a series of governments that promoted the liberal causes of representative government and free trade. Apart from joining other western European countries in the Crimean War against Russia (see Part VII, Topic 16), Britain avoided involvement

Significant Dates

Britain and France from 1846 to 1871

1846	Repeal of Corn Laws
1848	Louis Napoleon elected president
1852	Louis Napoleon becomes emperor
1856	Paris Peace Conference on Crimean War
1860	Chevalier-Cobden Treaty
1862–1867	French campaign in Mexico
1866	Gladstone's unsuccessful First Reform Bill
1867	Disraeli passes Second Reform Bill
1869	Mill publishes *On the Subjection of Women*
1870–1871	Franco-Prussian War

in European affairs. Closer to home, the question of whether to grant home rule to Ireland became increasingly controversial. The Irish nationalist leader Charles Stewart Parnell (1846–1891) led the battle from within Parliament in the years following 1877, finally convincing Gladstone to adopt a home rule policy (on the Irish question, see Part VII, Topic 15).

LOUIS NAPOLEON AND THE SECOND FRENCH REPUBLIC

With the election of Louis Napoleon as president in 1848, after decades of political in-fighting, ideological debate, and upheaval, the French were ready to unite behind a figure who seemed to promise peace, and provide conditions for the growth of prosperity. If their new leader was also able to become an international figure of consequence and place France back on the world stage, so much the better. Napoleon I had, after all, come close to conquering all of Europe. Who could tell what his nephew might accomplish?

Louis Napoleon and Public Opinion

Hopes like these, which Louis Napoleon adroitly fanned, persuaded the electors to trust him when, in the early months of his presidency, he imposed a series of repressive measures. Socialists were expelled from

A trade union membership certificate, 1851.

the assembly, press censorship was introduced, and public meetings were restricted. To distract attention, and to win the support of the majority, he appealed to the interests of large sections of the population. Thus the Catholics were pleased when the schools were returned to church control, and when a French military expedition overthrew Mazzini's Roman Republic to restore the pope to power (see Part VII, Topic 8). Other French patriots were also encouraged to see their country reasserting a role in international affairs.

For all his aristocratic origins, Louis Napoleon fully realized the need to establish a broad power base, and he set out to win over the middle class and the workers. The middle class was distracted from its loss of liberties by the enactment of laws encouraging business and trade. The introduction of state-supported old age insurance won him support among the poor. In 1851 he felt sufficiently sure of himself to dissolve the assembly and proclaim a temporary dictatorship; the alleged excuse was that of protecting the rights of the "masses."

Louis Napoleon's confidence was justified. In a plebiscite held in December 1851, an overwhelming majority awarded him unlimited power to create a new constitution. A year later another popular vote approved his assumption of the title Napoleon III, emperor of the French; more than 90 percent of the electors voted in favor. The Second Republic became the Second Empire.

A few lone voices of protest were heard, the most notable that of Victor Hugo (1802–1885), the leading writer of the day. Hugo at first supported Louis Napoleon, but when he realized the authoritarian direction in which the president was moving he changed his mind. In July 1851 he publicly denounced the intentions of the "Little Napoleon." After trying unsuccessfully to organize opposition, Hugo went into exile in the Channel Islands, from where he published works which bitterly attacked the emperor. He returned to France only on the fall of the empire.

Photograph of French Emperor Napoleon III and his wife, the Empress Eugénie.

NAPOLEON III AND THE SECOND EMPIRE

It is worth underlining the implacable hatred of Hugo and other French intellectuals for Napoleon III because it was far from generally shared. For the first half of his reign, the emperor maintained an iron grip on the state while remaining popular and admired. In the 1860s he permitted the transformation of his authoritarian regime into a more liberal rule, in a series of moves which served to pave the way for the Third Republic. With the relaxation of control, opposition to the emperor began to grow in Parliament, in part because it

was safer to oppose him and in part to urge him toward more liberal government, but he retained his general popularity. The empire was finally swept away only by the calamitous Franco-Prussian War, in which France was utterly routed.

Louis Napoleon himself remains a complex character. His rise to power shows him as devious. Fully aware of the havoc that his uncle had wreaked on most of Europe, he had no hesitation in playing on French thirst for glory and their highly selective memories. In personal dealings he impressed most of his contemporaries as gentle and charming, albeit a womanizer. Others found him a sensualist, sinister and insincere. Like Napoleon, he claimed to rule as tribune, rising above factions, and expressing the popular will. Yet he lacked his uncle's administrative brilliance, and his attempts to win an empire proved disastrous. Above all, it is difficult to see a consistent vision behind his rule—except that of retaining power by a constant series of manipulations. He was helped by the fact that a weary country seemed willing to be manipulated.

Politics in the Second Empire

The element of deception was present from the beginning of his reign, in the new constitution introduced in January 1852. Like Napoleon's constitution of 1799, it provided for a legislative body to be elected by universal male suffrage. This body had no real power or influence and could approve only measures which were drawn up by a Council of State, itself appointed by the emperor. In any case, elections were controlled, and candidates carefully selected. The emperor kept charge of the army, and of foreign and economic policy. When he desired to "consult" his subjects he could call a referendum, the result of which would be a foregone conclusion.

It is difficult to imagine a more complete rejection of liberal politics, yet this authoritarian regime was combined with a liberal economic policy that explains much of the widespread middle-class support for Napoleon III's rule. A number of successful credit institutions (see Part VII, Topic 12) were created to collect money available for investment; the funds were then used to increase the rate of industrial development and improve services such as the railroads. Private citizens were encouraged to invest by a law that limited their liability, if the company in which they had bought stock ran into debt. The fundamental liberal doctrine of free trade was honored in the signing of a pact with Britain in 1860—the Chevalier-Cobden Treaty—which reduced tariffs on both sides.

All these measures were intended to stimulate the economy and win the backing of the business classes. Meanwhile, other means were used to discourage any possible protests at government high-handedness. For the first decade of the Second Empire, no political opposition was tolerated, the press was censored, and the universities, traditional centers of rebellion, were kept under careful observation. In the years after 1860 there was a steady process of relaxation of these restrictions in an effort to cut off popular resentment before it had a chance to become dangerous. Open debate in the assembly was permitted, and the proceedings were made public.

While the middle classes were happily making money, and the intellectuals effectively silenced, the urban proletariat was provided with new social benefits. Medical facilities, public housing, and homes for the old were built, and in the process many jobs were created. A workers' insurance scheme offered security against loss of earnings in case of injury or ill-health, while a new law recognized workers' rights to certain limited strike action. As for the rural population, whose votes had helped to put Louis Napoleon in power in the first place, they were delighted with the general national prosperity and political stability.

The "Empire" Style

Napoleon III, like many another authoritarian ruler, set out to provide an appropriate setting for his reign. His most lasting legacy, the rebuilding of Paris, served a double purpose, in fact. The broad boulevards, elegant squares, and public parks, designed by Baron Georges Haussmann (1809–1891), give the city its special, personal character. At the same time the streets were intended to be too wide for any future revolutionaries to construct barricades, while the broad, direct routes facilitated the coordinated movement of troops if the need ever arose to put down demonstrations.

The plan was controversial at the time, and remains so still. The shady gardens continue to provide rest and refreshment in warm weather, but the formal squares, crossed by roads leading in several different directions, are apt to become jammed with traffic. The great monumental vistas—Place de la Concorde, Place de l'Étoile, with its Arch of Triumph—were conceived as ceremonial backdrops for imperial ceremonies, rather than as parts of a living city. Haussmann's ideas, which included such practical innovations as clean water supply and sewage systems, influenced designers of other 19th-century urban renewal projects such as those in Rome, Washington, and Mexico City.

Among the new buildings commissioned by the emperor was the Opéra, the Salle Garnier, named after its architect, Charles Garnier (1825–1898), a temple to the middle-class enthusiasm for public entertainment on a grand scale. The elaborate ornamentation visible on the façade of the Opéra is typical of the "Empire" style, with its blend of sober Classical elements and massive, swirling statues. The French use of the theater as political symbol was not limited to Napoleon III. The Bicentennial of the French Revolution in 1989 was marked by the inauguration of a new opera house on the site of the Bastille.

From clothes to furniture, clocks to table settings, the richly elaborate "Empire" style appeared in just about every aspect of daily life. One of its prime promoters was the emperor's Spanish wife, Eugénie (1826–1920). Her ornate silk gowns became famous—and much imitated—throughout Europe, and confirmed France's reputation as the center of high fashion. In contrast to Victoria and Albert, pillars of bourgeois respectability across the Channel, Napoleon and Eugénie set out to create an image of glamour and luxury, a picture which was only slightly marred in the

Boulevard de Sebastopol, Paris, in 1859.

public eye by Napoleon's philanderings. Eugénie's dignified behavior in the face of her husband's conduct won her the approval of many feminists, who applauded her encouragement of improved education for women. On the other hand, the empress was inclined to be narrow-minded, leading the unsuccessful fight to ban Gustave Flaubert's novel *Madame Bovary* (see Part VII, Topic 14).

The excitement generated by the Second Empire and its prosperity subdued early attempts at criticism, but over the long term Napoleon III had to deal with his liberal opponents. Throughout the 1860s, he continued to make concessions to them, which only fed the demands for more reforms. By 1869, opposition had crystallized in the form of a renewed republican party, which at one point actually named a premier. The government introduced an amended constitution, entrusting virtually complete power to Parliament, which was approved by a great margin—even including the opposition leaders, who supported the government. The sudden collapse overnight of the Second Empire was due not to

Napoleon III's political difficulties at home but to his failure to win success in France's overseas ventures.

FRANCE AND THE POLITICS OF EMPIRE

Louis Napoleon came to power with the claim that he could renew France's imperial glory. For all his domestic achievements, his mismanagement of foreign policy fatally undermined his popularity. He used the magic name "Bonaparte" to evoke memories of a French empire, but a string of French military losses was more likely to bring Waterloo to mind, and his disappointed subjects did not forgive him.

Matters began promisingly enough. The overthrow of the Roman Republic in 1849 was an early, if easy, victory. It was followed by France's leading role in the Crimean War, in which Russia was defeated. The ensuing peace conference met in Paris in 1856, expansively hosted by the emperor, who used it to demonstrate to his subjects his growing international prestige.

The French in Italy

Among the other European powers represented at the Paris Peace Conference was the small Italian state of Piedmont-Sardinia (see Part VII, Topic 11). Its prime minister, Camillo di Cavour, was trying to rally support in freeing the northern Italian provinces of Lombardy and Venetia from Austrian rule. In 1858, Napoleon III promised Cavour French aid in a war against Austria, in return for which France was to gain Nice and Savoy. More than territorial expansion, the emperor seems to have been motivated by a desire to enhance French prestige. When the war broke out the following year, Napoleon sent troops, and the combined French and Piedmontese forces did drive the Austrians out of Lombardy. At this point, to the general disgust of the supporters of Italian independence, Napoleon III suddenly signed an armistice with the Austrians, and withdrew his troops (see Part VII, Topic 11).

Whatever the consequences of French interventionism were for the Italians, its effect on morale in France was predictable. By opposing Catholic Austria, the emperor had offended Catholics back home. By deserting the Italian cause he confirmed the liberals' mistrust of him. Furthermore, the fighting, though brief, had been ferocious and the losses heavy. The only gains were Savoy and Nice, which France obtained from Piedmont in 1859–1860.

The expansion of French power outside Europe offered easier prospects. Charles X had begun the occupation of Algeria and Napoleon III completed it. French settlements were founded in West Africa and Indochina, although control of Indochina was not completed until the Third Republic. In the Pacific region, New Caledonia was occupied. The prestige that these conquests generated was not matched by any tangible benefits and Napoleon showed little interest in matching the commercial success of the British Empire. Indeed in the long run, the French colonies in Africa and Asia proved disastrous for many nations other than the French. The bloody history of Southeast Asia in the years following World War II, and the violence which ravaged New Caledonia in the late 1980s, are legacies of Napoleon III's attempts to build an empire.

The French in Mexico

His attempt to conquer Mexico was even more disastrous. Mexico had recently won its independence from Spain, and its government was ruled by the revolutionary leader, Benito Juárez. French forces were originally sent in 1862 as part of a joint expedition which also included British and Spanish troops; the motive was to compel the new regime to pay debts it allegedly owed to the countries involved. When it became clear that the French intended to annex the country, the British and Spanish troops returned home. Mexico City was captured; Juárez and his government retreated into the countryside, and the French installed as emperor a

A scene from the Franco-Prussian War: Leon Gambetta escaped by balloon from German-besieged Paris in October 1870.

Hapsburg prince, Maximilian (1832–1867), archduke of Austria and brother of the reigning Hapsburg emperor.

The United States invoked the Monroe Doctrine of 40 years earlier, prohibiting the Europeans from interfering in the affairs of their former colonies in the Western Hemisphere. In 1865, Union troops lately victorious in the American Civil War were despatched toward Mexico, and once again Napoleon III threw in his hand. In 1867 the last French soldiers set off back to France. The hapless Maximilian refused to leave, and remained in the hands of Juárez' men. They shot him. His young wife Carlota (1840–1927) had returned to Europe at her husband's request in a vain attempt to secure aid from Napoleon III and the pope. The news of Maximilian's failure and impending execution drove her hopelessly insane, and she spent the remaining 60 years of her life in seclusion near Brussels.

Napoleon III's final defeat was at the hands of Prussia, the culminating act in the German drive for national unification (see Part VII, Topic 11). From the French viewpoint, the Franco-Prussian War of 1870 was an unmitigated disaster. It ended France's role as the leading power of continental Europe. More immediately, France was invaded by the Prussian Army, Napoleon III was taken prisoner, and Paris was besieged for four terrible months in the winter of 1870. When news of the emperor's surrender of the army at Sedan reached Paris in September 1870, the Second Empire was declared dead, and liberal republicans formed a provisional government. Its first needs were to survive the starvation of the Prussian siege, and to begin the painful process of rebuilding the state.

Britain and France experienced the radical transformations of the years from 1850 to 1870 in very different ways. In one a constitutional monarchy and a parliamentary government presided over the peaceful extension of political power. In the other a charismatic leader offered high hopes but eventual calamity. Britain saw the victory of traditional liberalism and the triumph of compromise. In France, Napoleon III offered something to everyone, with a liberal economy and an authoritarian, aggressive state.

To judge with hindsight is notoriously easy, and the early years of the Second Empire seem to have had a genuine sense of exhilaration, especially when contrasted with the more stolid virtues of the Victorian age in Britain. The French desire for renewed self-esteem, fueled by the domestic successes of Napoleon III's early reign, led to their em-

peror's attempts to satisfy them abroad. Nor was he responsible for the tragedy of the Franco-Prussian War, which formed part of Bismarck's schemes for the birth of the new German nation. In any case, by 1870 the political balance of power in Europe was radically changed.

Yet the long-term consequences of Britain's success and France's defeat were to prove dire. The blow to French self-esteem left wounds which were reopened in 1914 and again in 1940, in the opening phases of the two world wars, when Anglo-French cooperation was vital. At the same time, pride in the achievements of Victorian Britain was easily converted into a belief in the divine right of the British Empire. The result was an aggressive, arrogant world power. A weakened France left Germany as Britain's chief rival on the European, and eventually world, scene. The German challenge to British superiority became increasingly strident. Eventual conflict between the two seemed inevitable, and in response militarism continued to grow during the last quarter of the 19th century.

Questions for Further Study

1. What are the main factors accounting for the differences in the political life of Britain and France from 1850 to 1870? How much were they the result of differing styles of leadership?

2. How did the Second Empire affect the social and cultural climate in France? What permanent changes, if any, did it leave?

3. What was Louis Napoleon's foreign policy, and what consequences did it have?

4. Why was Disraeli more successful than Gladstone in passing a reform bill, and what did his measure accomplish?

Suggestions for Further Reading

Guerard, A. *Napoleon III.* Westport, CT, 1979.

Joyce, P. *Visions of the People: Industrial England and the Question of Class, c. 1848–1914.* New York, 1991.

Mokyr, J. *Why Ireland Starved: A Quantitative and Analytical History of the Irish Economy, 1800–1850.* London, 1983.

Plessis, Alain. *The Rise and Fall of the Second Empire, 1852–1871.* Cambridge, MA, 1985.

Price, R. *A Social History of Nineteenth-Century France.* New York, 1988.

Seidman, S. *Liberalism and the Origins of European Social Theory.* Berkeley, CA, 1983.

Thompson, F. M. L. *The Rise of Respectable Society: A Social History of Victorian Britain, 1830–1900.* Cambridge, MA, 1988.

T o p i c   1 0

AUSTRIA AND RUSSIA:
CONSERVATISM ENTRENCHED

n the decades after 1848, most of Western Europe felt the growing effects of liberalism and nationalism. In Eastern Europe, however, the Hapsburg monarchy fought to limit the consequences of the revolutionary uprisings of 1848 by centralizing the empire. In Russia, virtually untouched by the ferment into which the rest of Europe was plunged, the first signs of a relaxation of autocratic rule appeared. Yet in spite of early reforms, political repression reemerged by the 1880s.

With the overthrow of Metternich in March 1848 and the abdication of Ferdinand I, the new emperor, Franz Josef, hoped that strong central government would provide the empire with greater authority. He believed that a single administration, with uniform laws and a consistent tax structure, would counterbalance the empire's ethnic and linguistic diversity.

Yet ethnic divisions ran too deep for bureaucratic solutions. The non-German-speaking peoples, including Magyars, Czechs, Slovaks, Croats, and Poles, were united in only one respect: their resistance to the German-speaking rulers who governed them from Vienna. In everything else, from territorial borders to school systems, they struggled for independence both from Hapsburg rule and from each other.

The chief opponents of Vienna's supremacy were the Magyars of Hungary. In order to meet some of their demands and still preserve the empire, in 1867 the Austrians—weakened by their defeat in the Austro-Prussian War of 1866 and plagued by economic problems—devised the *Ausgleich* ("Compromise"), which created the Dual Monarchy. Austria and Hungary became two separate nations. Franz Josef, while remaining emperor of Austria, was also king of Hungary.

The Dual Monarchy of the Austro-Hungarian empire was an uneasy attempt to provide an artificial bureaucratic solution to an impossibly complex dilemma. Predictably it provoked demands for similar treatment among other minorities, and required a careful balancing between large ethnic groups such as the Hungarians and smaller ones such as the Slovaks. The Austro-Hungarian empire survived for almost half a century, but its suppression of Slavic minorities fueled continuing resentments.

The Russians found themselves increasingly at odds with the Western European powers. The tough, authoritarian Nicholas I died during the Crimean War of 1853–1856. His successor, Alexander II, at first favored the liberalization of Russian society—if only to prevent spread of the "contagion" of revolution to

Russia. An additional strong motivation was the military ineptness of his army. In 1861 the land-bound serfs were emancipated, but the success of this long-awaited reform was limited. In the absence of a rigorous reshaping of the Russian economy, it merely transferred control over the serfs from their former noble masters to the village communities, or *mirs,* for which they now worked. At the same time, the Emancipation Edict created unrealistic hopes for real change that were further aroused by Alexander's reforms in education and local self-government.

A surge of socialist and intellectual enthusiasm produced by the mood of progress led to open advocacy of extreme radicalism and nihilism, aimed at the dismantling of the state. The official backlash was inevitable. When Alexander II was killed by a terrorist bomb in 1881, his son and successor Alexander III used harsh, autocratic methods to eradicate all liberalism in Russia.

THE AUSTRIAN EMPIRE: A MULTIETHNIC STATE IN THE AGE OF NATIONALISM

In the generation after 1848, in Western Europe, the spirit of nationalism inspired and brought to birth the new nations of Germany and Italy. During the same period, the unity of the Austrian empire was increasingly threatened by the ethnic minorities. They resented the rule of their German-speaking masters, who made up a minority of 23 percent of the population. Austrian domination was chiefly maintained by a careful manipulation of the divisions between the various nationalities. The national and cultural diversity of the territories under Hapsburg rule was, of course, one of the leading factors in the outbreak of revolt there in 1848. Even within each of the three principal geographical areas, Austria itself, Hungary, and Bohemia, there were ethnic tensions that the reassertion of Austrian control only exacerbated.

Pan-Slavism

The broadest of nationalist causes in Eastern Europe was Pan-Slavism, which involved peoples beyond the borders of the Austrian empire itself. Those who considered themselves Slavs included Czechs, Slovaks, Slovenes, Serbs, Croats, and Ruthenians, all of whom were under Austrian rule. The Poles, also Slavs, were divided. Some lived in territories governed by the Hapsburgs, while others were in that part of Poland which remained under Russian control (there were also Poles resident in Prussia). To complicate the situation

still further, a growing number of Russian intellectuals began to identify with the cause of Pan-Slavism, and to consider themselves not Russian but Slav.

All of these peoples spoke related languages, and could thereby distinguish themselves from the other groups in Eastern Europe and, more specifically, in the Hapsburg empire. These were the Magyars (Hungarian speakers whose ancestors had settled there in the 9th century), the Italians, and—above all—the German-

Conflict at the University of Vienna during the Revolution of 1848.

Map 10.1 Nationalities in Central and Eastern Europe, c. 1900

speaking ruling class. Yet for all their numbers and nationalist fervor, the various Slavic peoples never managed to forget their own differences and cooperate to throw off Hapsburg rule.

The Austrians, for their part, adroitly exploited national rivalries. Not the least of these was the traditional hostility between the Magyars and the Slavic peoples living in Hungary. In Hapsburg Poland, where Polish nationalist feeling was strong among the aristocracy, the authorities used tensions between the nobles and their serfs to create a class war and keep the country divided.

Yet the events of 1848 provided a warning: even conservative Austria could not maintain a monolithic indifference to the dissatisfactions of its subjects. The sense of a turn of direction was symbolized by the departure from the scene of the two figures who represented the old regime: the emperor Ferdinand I and his chief minister, the orchestrator of the Concert of Europe, Prince Metternich. The crown was assumed by Franz Josef (ruled 1848–1916), then barely 18 years old, while the government of the empire passed into the hands of the archconservative Prince Felix Schwarzenberg (1800–1852). Even Franz Josef's most fervent supporters could hardly have imagined that he would remain Austrian emperor for the better part of 70 years: he died in 1916, in the middle of World War I.

Schwarzenberg intended to forge the basis of unity throughout the empire in two ways: a single system of laws and taxes, and the administration of that system by an absolutist, centralized bureaucracy. His new constitution imposed political uniformity even on regions like Bohemia and Hungary that had won a measure of independence. The railway, which had already begun to revolutionize communications in western Europe, connected many of the chief urban centers under Hapsburg rule. Roads across the Alps, into the Austrian provinces of northern Italy, were improved.

Schwarzenberg died in 1852, before he was able to see his schemes fully implemented. In any case, any thoroughgoing change of government of the kind he contemplated would have required massive bureaucratic reorganization, together with the cooperation of the local officials whose job it was to carry out the reforms. In the end things reverted to their former state: German-speaking regional administrators, who were only nominally responsible to Vienna, continued to run the affairs of peoples whose cultures they looked down on, and whose languages they chose not to speak. Bureaucratic inefficiency, coupled with insensitivity to minority feelings, produced resentment and frustration among Austria's subject peoples.

Franz Josef and Constitutional Reform

In 1859 events in northern Italy brought about a crisis. French forces, with the help of Piedmont-Sardinia, defeated the Austrians and drove them out of Lombardy (see Part VII, Topic 11). Franz Josef, by now old enough to be his own master, and realizing the risk of further rebellions elsewhere in his empire, sought to forestall them by introducing a revised constitution. This document decentralized the government and gave considerable powers to regional assemblies. The reform drew a united burst of hostility from all sides. In the various regions, the nationalists could not agree on who should represent whom; the liberals in Vienna were appalled by the monarch's high-handedness; and bureaucrats throughout the empire protested at the confusion.

In the face of such opposition, within a few months the emperor reversed himself. In February 1861 yet another new constitution was introduced, which created a two-chamber parliament in Vienna: the *Reichsrat*. Having held up the promise of local independence, Franz Josef was now withdrawing it. To make matters worse, his electoral system guaranteed the German speakers a majority in the parliament's lower chamber. Anger among the ethnic minorities ran high, and Hungary's Magyars refused to send representatives.

By the fall of 1865 the emperor was forced to admit failure and suspend the constitution.

In the midst of political crisis, troubles abroad once again distracted attention. In his struggle to create a united German nation, Bismarck's plans required the elimination of the only other serious candidate for German leadership, Austria; he therefore sought a military confrontation, since Prussian supremacy was most easily established on the battlefield. By the end of the Austro-Prussian War of 1866 (see Part VII, Topic 11), Austria's defeat left its prestige in the German-speaking world considerably undermined. In addition, the new Kingdom of Italy, which supported Prussia in the war, was rewarded with Venetia, Austria's remaining province in northern Italy. If the emperor was to hold on to the rest of his possessions, a compromise was required.

THE AUSGLEICH: ILLUSION OF THE DUAL MONARCHY

The fiercest and most persistent opposition to Austrian rule was in Hungary, where the temporary successes of 1848 fueled an active Magyar independence movement. In 1867, Hungarian nationalist leaders seized on Austria's weakness and forced through a political compromise; the German word for "compromise," *Ausgleich*, is used to refer to the Austro-Hungarian agreement. Franz Josef's wife, Elizabeth, who had actively sympathized with the cause of Italian freedom, was a strong advocate of an independent Hungary.

Hungary and Compromise

In 1867, after Austria's defeat by Prussia, under the Ausgleich Hungary became an autonomous state with its own parliament, with Franz Josef as its king. This inaugurated the Dual Monarchy, whereby the emperor of Austria ruled simultaneously as king of Hungary. Theoretically, joint ministries of the two states, known as the "Delegations," decided questions of finance, foreign policy, and war. In practice, however, most of Hungary's domestic policies were now established internally. The Magyar business class and landowning nobility took control of the Hungarian economy. Foreign policy and defense remained under the control of the Delegations.

As part of the agreement the Romanian, Serbian, and Croatian minorities in Hungary were left to Magyar rule. Most of the other Slavic minorities in the empire, including the Slovenes, Slovaks, and Ruthenians, remained under the Austrians. The Czechs and Poles were given some privileges as a means of buying their collaboration. In this way the Austrians hoped to eliminate the risk of a Pan-Slavic union. The Hungarians were not a Slavic people, and their treatment of their Slavic minorities was notable for its harshness. A few years later, when the idea of a triple monarchy was voiced, in which the Slavs would have been represented, German speakers and Hungarians alike opposed it.

In Vienna the emperor played liberals and nationalists off against one another. The result was an impotent Austrian parliament, riven by ethnic divisions. Sessions were notorious for violent fighting, not always only verbal, between the delegates, and often paralyzed by noise makers. Effective power was held by the ethnic German bureaucrats, who continued to implement conservative policies. In combined numbers the minorities actually formed a majority in each half of the Dual Monarchy, but they remained as far as ever from self-government.

The Ausgleich was an attempt to buy off the Magyars at the expense of the other ethnic groups. In the long term so precarious a compromise was doomed to failure. The crisis finally came with World War I, when the collapse of the Austro-Hungarian empire, with its labyrinthine interweaving of alliances, brought with it conflict throughout Europe. Yet viewed as a desperate expedient, the Dual Monarchy achieved its limited objectives. For all their mutual mistrust, Austrians and Magyars shared a common interest in making the compromise work. The political stalemate in Austria and the dominance of the upper classes in Hungary reinforced and prolonged the strength of the empire, while at the same time bringing some economic advantages.

Nonetheless, the price of survival was a heavy one, and it was mainly paid by the nationalist minorities. The legacy of hatred and rivalry lasted late into the 20th century. Furthermore, the climate of growing frustration and resentment proved all too fertile for the growth of anti-Semitism. Peoples divided by so much shared in common their irrational discrimination against the Jews. Franz Josef's Vienna became at the same time a center for Jewish cultural life, and a breeding ground of anti-Semitism.

RUSSIA UNDER THE TSARS: THE EMANCIPATION OF THE SERFS

The only two major powers in Europe untouched by revolution in 1848 were Britain and Russia. Britain's way of dealing with the demand for political change was a policy of compromise. Russia's method was the precise reverse: repression. From the time of the Congress of Vienna in 1815, Tsar Alexander I maintained strict authoritarian control at home while generally assuming the role of defender of the conservative cause in Europe. His only significant departures from this, his initial support for Poland and for the Greeks in

A cartoon showing the hierarchical structure of the Russian state.

their war of independence, were sufficiently striking to worry Metternich. All domestic attempts at protest, such as the Decembrists' revolt in 1825, the Polish uprising of 1831, and periodic peasant rebellions, were ruthlessly repressed and served only to reinforce the hostility of Tsar Nicholas I (ruled 1825–1855) to any form of liberalism. Russia's only contributions to the events of 1848–1849 were to help the Austrians regain control in Hungary and to put pressure on Prussia to end the Frankfurt Assembly.

One consequence of so rigid a political stance was economic stagnation. While the rest of Europe underwent the transformation of industrialization, Russia remained primarily an agricultural country, dependent on the labor of the serfs, virtual slaves tied to the land of the great estate owners. A few factories were opened, but the technological progress that was reshaping western Europe made little impact in Russia.

The first impetus for change came as the result of Russia's defeat in a relatively limited conflict, the Crimean War, fought on the Crimean peninsula, which projects into the Black Sea. Formerly part of the crumbling Ottoman Empire, it had been conquered by Russia in 1783. In 1853, Nicholas I decided to use it as the base for further seizure of Ottoman territory in order to gain access to the Mediterranean and establish a presence in the Middle East. This drew the opposition of most of the Western European powers, and when the Turks declared war on Russia, Britain and France joined them in a triple alliance against Nicholas. Superior equipment and more efficient transport gave the Western allies an advantage that allowed them to cut short Russian ambitions. At the Paris Peace Conference of 1856, the terms negotiated underlined Russia's loss of military prestige.

Alexander II and the Serfs

A year before the conference, Nicholas I died, and was succeeded by the more moderate Alexander II (ruled 1855–1881). One of the first acts of the new tsar was to issue a manifesto promising reforms in working conditions, education, and the legal system. His motives were practical as much as humanitarian. Limited but controlled changes imposed from above were better than revolutionary uprisings from below. In any case, although a few aristocratic intellectuals already opposed serfdom on liberal grounds, most Russian nobles reluctantly accepted reform because they were con-

The allied fleet anchored at Balaclava in the Crimea, 1855.

vinced that the old system was making their country uncompetitive. Russia needed to develop urban manufacturing centers; even in farming the easy availability of serf labor had stood in the way of technological progress.

In a climate of hesitation and uncertainty, the tsar emancipated most of the serfs in 1861, a year before Lincoln's Emancipation Proclamation that freed slaves in areas in rebellion in the United States. (Alexander's emancipation of the serfs affected some 52 million, while the number of slaves freed by Lincoln was around 3 million.) Domestic serfs had to continue their service for two more years, and were then freed without any land. The others received most of the land they worked, but they had to redeem it by paying with interest for it over a long period of time, often at inflated prices. The most productive pastures, furthermore, generally remained in the hands of the aristocrats. Control of the land and farming was entrusted to the *mir*, or village commune, whose representatives assigned and redistributed holdings and decided what should be grown. The former serfs paid the landowners for their land, and paid taxes to the government; these "redemption dues" were collected by the mir and handed over to the state.

Far from satisfying liberal hopes, the Emancipation Decree's limited provisions increased resentment. The serfs had no economic independence and no political rights. Instead of working for an aristocratic landowner, they were now tied to their village commune, and spent most of their lives working to pay off their debts. (Freed serfs, on the other hand, could leave to go elsewhere, thus providing a potential labor force for the coming industrial revolution in Russia.) Peasant opposition continued to take the form of open rebellion, which was put down by official intervention.

REFORM AND REACTION UNDER ALEXANDER II

Alexander II's other reforms were more successful in addressing class grievances. In 1864 the *zemstvos* were introduced. These were local regional administrative councils, whose elected members were responsible for the roads, primary schools, and welfare institutions of their districts. Although the zemstvos had no influence on issues outside their immediate sphere of influence, and never led to the formation of a national assembly, they provided a forum for public debate and permitted middle-class professionals such as doctors and lawyers to take part in civic life. All effective power, however, remained in the hands of the tsar and his ministers.

The Russian mathematician, Sofia Kofalevskaya.

Educational reorganization ranged from a notable increase in the number of primary schools to the relaxation of controls in the universities. Alexander himself initiated secondary-level education for girls, and special university courses for women were introduced. Even though some of the changes were short-lasting, they broke down centuries of custom. In 1861, the Medical Surgical Academy in St. Petersburg admitted women for the first time, only to ban them again three years later. Thereafter, women who wanted a medical career left Russia to study in Western Europe. Zurich, one of their most popular refuges, developed a small Russian community which later became a center for political dissidents—among them Lenin.

Alexander II's reforms affected other aspects of Russian life. The legal code was revised. The new system introduced some Western liberal ideas by relaxing punishments for some crimes, although it never challenged the authority of the state. Modernization of the army led to greater efficiency. Most of the recruits were peasants, and the education they received while enrolled helped to increase the general spread of literacy. Beginning in the 1870s, planning and construction began on a vast railroad system, including the vital trans-Siberian line, intended to consolidate links within the vast spaces of Russia itself and to help in the delivery of exports to the West.

The results of Alexander II's reforms were to strengthen both extremes of the political spectrum. In response, police repression was used to control any protests that the apparent relaxation might encourage. A rebellion in the Polish territory under Russian rule was ferociously repressed in 1865. Ten years later the zemstvos were prohibited from even debating national political issues, and censorship was strengthened both in the press and in the universities.

The Radical Movement

The hopes encouraged by the new measures led at the same time to the growth of a radical socialist movement. The intellectual father of Russian socialism was Alexander Herzen (1812–1870), who became an early advocate of the "Westernization" of Russian society. Herzen spent 1848 in revolutionary Paris, and saw the failure there of socialism at the barricades. From exile in London, he wrote and published works in which he hailed the peasant commune as the best basis for socialism in Russia. By building on the communes, the Russians could avoid capitalism which, he believed, disfigured Western society, and move directly from an agricultural to a socialist society.

Herzen's writings and his journal, *The Bell*, inspired a number of intellectuals to live in peasant communities and try to sow the seeds of revolution. Those participating in this "back to the people" movement were called *Narodniki*. The innate conservatism of both the peasants and the authorities stood in the way of any success, however, and Herzen's followers were further inhibited by his strict advocacy of nonviolence.

By the 1870s Herzen's ideas were regarded as old-fashioned, and there developed in reaction a new radical socialism. Younger intellectuals called themselves "nihilists," or believers in nothing. Under the influence of the anarchist philosopher Michail Bakunin (1814–1876), they proposed to use violent means to overthrow the state and revolutionize society (on Bakunin and the anarchists, see Part VII, Topic 19). Although most limited themselves to talking about action, in 1877 Vera Zasulich (1849–1919), a young radical, killed the governor of St. Petersburg for mistreating prisoners. Two years later, some formed a secret society called "The Will of the People." The organization included a large number of young female activists—indeed, a third of its executive committee consisted of women. Its aim was to bring down the government by assassinating the state's leading figures. As socialist extremists moved further from their popular roots, the Pan-Slavic movement encouraged contempt for Western liberalism. The result was an increasing sense of isolation among Russia's intellectuals.

Alexander II's response to the restlessness and threats was at first to return to a policy of repression. By the end of his reign, however, he had reached the conclusion that he needed to give way to liberal sentiment.

The assassination of Alexander II, March 13, 1881.

The change came too late. In March 1881, the Will of the People assassinated the tsar in a bombing plot coordinated by Sophia Perovskaia (1853–1881) and others. Most of those involved in the plot were captured and hanged, and Perovskaia was the first woman executed in Russia for terrorism. On the dead tsar's desk was found legislation for providing Russia with a constitution, awaiting his signature.

The tsar's son and successor, Alexander III (ruled 1881–1894), blamed his father's death on excessive political reform. He had no intention of making the same mistake, and initiated a period of harsh, autocratic rule. Using the police, the army, and the Orthodox Church, he kept a careful watch on all levels of society. Most local control was taken away from the zemstvos, and given back to the landowning aristocrats. Local governors were appointed with wide powers. The persecution of Russia's Jewish population was encouraged. Almost a generation was to pass before socialist and liberal reformers had regained the strength to renew their protests.

At a time of widespread economic growth and rapid social change throughout Western Europe, Austria and Russia succeeded in maintaining conservative and authoritarian rule. In both cases liberal causes met with little success; even the emancipation of Russia's serfs created as many problems as it solved. In both countries nationalism, far from leading to reform, served the purposes of state repression. The Austrians, with Hungarian help, used nationalist divisiveness to keep the regime's opponents divided. In Russia, the strength of pan-Slavic sentiment presented a barrier to the introduction of Western-style reforms.

A number of common factors help to explain the ability of the conservatives to retain power. Russia and the Austro-Hungarian empire were, at least in comparison with the rest of Europe, economically underdeveloped. In conse-

quence, they lacked the great urban centers where a large working class was built up, and reform movements traditionally developed.

In vast countries, covering huge geographical areas, communications were poor. Intellectual life was limited to a handful of cities. Vienna was really the only Austro-Hungarian cultural center on the level of the capitals of western Europe, and Prague was the empire's other artistic center. In Russia, artists and thinkers were divided between Moscow and St. Petersburg. Many creative artists from Eastern Europe left their homelands to make their reputation abroad: the Hungarian Franz Liszt, the Pole Frédéric Chopin, the Russian Ivan Turgenev, all won their fame in Paris. Even as nationalist an author as Feodor Dostoevsky wrote most of his greatest works while living in Western Europe.

The result was an isolationism in political thinking as well as in culture that affected both the countries involved and also those parts of Europe from which they were isolated. To most observers in London, Brussels, or Rome, Russia was a remote and mysterious land, with its own version of Christianity, and a unique set of political institutions. As for the Austro-Hungarian empire, few in the West were likely to fight for the liberation of the Serbs or the Slovaks. The only genuine support for the independence of a people in Eastern Europe, the Greeks, was inspired by a kind of historical Romanticism. Vienna, it is true, played a key role in the formation of late 19th-century culture, but the Hapsburg capital always had an air of exoticism, and in any case showed the empire's multiethnic character at its best.

Yet, ironically enough, when these two conservative giants collapsed, they did so along with much of the rest of the world. It took World War I and its aftermath to depose the Austro-Hungarian emperor and tsar of Holy Mother Russia. The process and its consequences were cataclysmic.

Questions for Further Study

1. What political and economic factors created the differences between the speed of reform in Western Europe and in Austria and Russia?

2. What part did intellectual developments in Russia play in changing Russian society?

3. What was the impact of ethnic differences and the Pan-Slavic movement on the Hapsburg empire? What lasting effects, if any, was it to have in the 20th century?

4. In what ways did the Crimean War influence international European affairs in the mid-19th century?

Suggestions for Further Reading

Cahm, C. *Peter Kropotkin and the Rise of Revolutionary Anarchism.* New York, 1989.

Riasanovsky, N. V. *Russia and the West in the Teaching of the Slavophiles.* Boston, 1980.

Seton-Watson, H. *The Russian Empire, 1801–1917.* Oxford, 1967.

Schorske, Carl E. *Fin-de-Siècle Vienna: Politics and Culture.* New York, 1981.

Stites, R. *The Women's Liberation Movement in Russia: Feminism, Nihilism, and Bolshevism, 1860–1930.* Princeton, NJ, 1978.

Taylor, A. J. P. *The Habsburg Monarchy, 1809–1918.* Baltimore, MD, 1990.

Topic 11

Diplomacy and War: The Age of Nation Building

n the period from 1815 to 1849, those revolutions which had been influenced by a combination of Romanticism and nationalism produced little in the way of concrete political change. After midcentury, however, nationalism shed its Romantic idealism in favor of power politics and emerged as the most effective political ideology in Europe. The new nationalist movements achieved a measure of success denied to the previous generation only because they adopted the ideas and techniques of power politics. The ability of post-1850 leaders to forge national unity depended more on diplomacy and war than on cultural awareness or insurrection.

The amalgam of power politics and nationalism resulted in the creation of national states in Italy and Germany between 1850 and 1871. This was largely the work of two men—the Piedmontese prime minister Camillo Cavour and the Prussian minister-president Otto von Bismarck. Cavour and Bismarck were realists who wanted to achieve results and cared little about the morality of their means.

Cavour, the architect of Italian unification, enhanced Piedmont's prestige among the great powers by strengthening his country's economy and joining Britain and France in the Crimean War. In 1858–1859, Cavour and Napoleon III forged a military alliance and waged a successful war against Austria that allowed Piedmont to annex Lombardy and the smaller states of central Italy. In the following two years, Cavour seized the initiative again in the wake of Giuseppe Garibaldi's conquest of southern Italy and, using the Piedmontese army and the benevolent support of Great Britain, forged the Kingdom of Italy.

The territorial completion of the Italian state took place against the backdrop of German unification. Bismarck, who became minister-president of Prussia in 1862, strengthened the Prussian Army and the power of its king at the expense of constitutional liberalism. In 1866, he waged a brilliant war against Austria that excluded Austrian influence from German affairs and created a Prussian-dominated North German Confederation; the new Italian state, which had joined Prussia in the war, received Venetia as its prize. Finally, in 1870–1871, Bismarck eliminated French opposition to a unified Germany by defeating Napoleon III in another war and bringing all the states of Germany together in a single German empire; Italy, taking advantage of Napoleon's withdrawal of French troops from Rome, seized the Papal States and made Rome the new Italian capital.

While the peoples of Germany and Italy struggled to create new nation-states, the American people fought over the issue of national unity. In the Civil War of 1861–1865, regional loyalties combined with economic interests and moral issues to divide the young republic. As in Europe, the victory of the industrialized North under the leadership of Abraham Lincoln over the agrarian South reflected the triumph of power politics.

ITALY, GERMANY, AND THE UNITED STATES: PATHS TO UNIFICATION

At the opening of the 19th century, Europeans had begun to think increasingly about Italian and German unification. Nevertheless, Metternich's definition of Italy as a "geographical expression" accurately reflected the views of most delegates at the Congress of Vienna. A half-dozen sovereign states occupied the Italian peninsula, while the word "Germany" merely referred to a large area in central Europe made up of 38 independent kingdoms and smaller states. History had given each region a distinctive role which nationalists would later claim as the basis for national self-identity: for Italy, the heritage of the Roman Empire and the Renaissance, for Germany, the memory of the Holy Roman Empire. However, regional divisions and great power intrigue worked to prevent the development of centralized national states such as had emerged in England or France.

The wars of the French Revolution had first sparked nationalist sentiment in Italy and Germany. Napoleon Bonaparte reduced the number of states in the two territories and encouraged Italians and Germans to hope for unification, while the harsher aspects of his occupation elicited a nationalist reaction against French domination. The Congress of Vienna crushed these early nationalist aspirations by reestablishing most of the "legitimate" monarchies of the pre-Napoleonic period and sanctioning the principle of Austrian domination in both regions. Yet the failure of revolutionary movements to prevent the reactionary policies of the restoration of 1815 (see Part VII, Topic 5) did not hinder the growth of nationalist sentiment.

The revolutions of 1848–1849 represented the first major efforts to create national states in Italy and Germany, but the armies of Austria (and, in the case of Mazzini's Roman Republic, of France) proved triumphant. Yet the setbacks of 1849 were not without result. The ill-fated military campaigns of Charles Albert

(see Part VII, Topic 8) had at least positioned the Kingdom of Piedmont-Sardinia as the one Italian state committed to fighting for national independence. Similarly, Prussia emerged as the unquestioned leader of the German unification movement, especially because of its role in forging economic unity through the *Zollverein*, or customs union. Together and separately, Piedmont and Prussia would challenge the dominance of the Austrian empire in central Europe.

Significant Dates

Italian Unification

1820–1821	Revolutions in Naples and Piedmont
1831	Young Italy formed by Mazzini
1831–1848	Charles Albert reigns as king of Piedmont-Sardinia
1848–1849	Revolutions in Italy; Piedmontese *Statuto* decreed
1854–1856	Crimean War; 1856 Paris Peace Conference
1858	Treaty of Plombières
1859	Austro-Piedmontese War
1860	Garibaldi's expedition to Sicily
1849–1861	Victor Emmanuel II rules as king of Piedmont-Sardinia
1852–1861	Cavour prime minister of Piedmont-Sardinia
1861	Kingdom of Italy created
1861–1865	American Civil War; Lincoln serves as president
1866	Austro-Prussian War; Italians seize Venice
1870–1871	Franco-Prussian War; Italians seize Rome
1846–1878	Pius IX rules as pope
1861–1878	Victor Emmanuel II rules as king of Italy

Although Cavour and Bismarck revolutionized the European state system, their methods reflected the most conservative aspects of 19th-century liberal philosophy. They preferred monarchy to republicanism, had little faith in democratic principles, and manipulated both popular opinion and constitutional process to achieve their goals. Each believed that history was made from above, by political and economic élites, rather than from below, by "the people."

In the midst of this process of unification in Italy and Germany, the United States also faced its own serious crisis of national unity—the Civil War (1861–1865). In the 1840s and 1850s, American nationalism under the guise of "Manifest Destiny" expanded the boundaries of the United States west to the Pacific coast and south to Mexico. Like Cavour and Bismarck, the American president Abraham Lincoln struggled to impose centralized authority over regional and particularist forces that challenged the unity of this far-flung national state. Yet, although Lincoln also resorted to war and enhanced his executive power in order to preserve the American republic, his political faith derived from democratic principles.

PIEDMONT AND THE ITALIAN QUESTION

The regimes restored to power in Italy in 1815 fell into three geographical-historical categories. The first was northern Italy, which consisted of the provinces of Lombardy-Venetia, given to Austria by the Congress of Vienna, and the Kingdom of Piedmont-Sardinia. The Hapsburgs administered Lombardy-Venetia through a viceroy, and, because of the relative prosperity of the region, its citizens deeply resented Austrian domination. Piedmont, ruled by the House of Savoy, lay in the militarily vital northwest corner of the peninsula, along the French border. The Savoy kings, descended from an old and distinguished dynasty, had for centuries sought to extend their domain across northern Italy.

Map 11.1 The Risorgimento

The second, all of southern Italy, known as the Kingdom of the Two Sicilies, was ruled by the Bourbons of Naples. The kingdom stretched from Naples to Sicily, a vast region of poor peasantry who toiled on the estates of noble absentee landlords. Here, too, the Hapsburgs had considerable influence, as a result of dynastic connections. The Bourbon king, Ferdinand II (ruled 1830–1859), was scornfully dubbed "King Bomba" because he had ruthlessly bombed Sicilian cities in order to crush the 1848 insurrections.

The third, central Italy, included the Papal States and a group of small principalities, the most important of which was the Grand Duchy of Tuscany, also under the influence of Austria. The Papal States were territories of the Catholic Church. Their subjects experienced considerable political repression and widespread poverty, but the rule of the pope was supported by French troops stationed in Rome and the ever-vigilant Austrian Army of Italy.

The Debate over Unification

In addition to the opposition of the monarchs themselves, the movement for Italian unification—known as the *Risorgimento* ("resurgence")—was hampered by strong sectional loyalties. Moreover, Italian patriots were deeply divided over how to achieve the common goal of Italian unity and independence. Three major currents of thought proposed different solutions. The Young Italy organization founded by the nationalist leader Giuseppe Mazzini (see Part VII, Topic 8), called for a popular revolution and the establishment of a republic based on democratic principles and universal suffrage. Mazzini's radical ideas, which served to gain wide acceptance for unification among middle-class Italians, frightened many Italian nationalists who were more conservative in their politics. Mazzini's determination to make Rome the capital of a free Italy also pitted him against supporters of the papacy.

For those who saw the Catholic Church and monarchy as the twin pillars of a united Italy, the liberal priest Vincenzo Gioberti (see Part VII, Topic 8) organized a "Neo-Guelph" movement (during the Middle Ages, the popes and their allies called themselves Guelphs in the struggle with the Holy Roman emperors). Gioberti, a Piedmontese by birth, wanted a confederation of Italian states with the pope as its political head and the king of Piedmont-Sardinia as its military defender. Gioberti based the right of the Italian people to independence on their historical and cultural legacy, which he described in a book entitled *On the Civil and Moral Primacy of the Italians* (1842–1843). The Neo-Guelph movement received momentary encouragement with the election of Pius IX—born Giovanni Mastai-Ferretti (ruled 1846–1878)—as pope in 1846. Although at first Pius seemed to harbor nationalist sen-

Giuseppe Mazzini, Italian patriot and a leading theorist of European nationalism.

timents, his abandonment of Charles Albert in the war of 1848 doomed Gioberti's hopes. Moreover, most contemporaries believed it impossible to preserve the territories of the Catholic Church in the context of a united Italy, for not only did they cut the peninsula in half, but an ecclesiastical state could not easily coexist within a temporal state.

The third, and ultimately successful, solution for Italian unification was known simply as the "moderate" program. Led by Count Cesare Balbo (1789–1853) and other liberal aristocrats from Piedmont, the moderates rejected both the radical strategies of the Mazzinians and the pro-papal ideas of the Neo-Guelphs. Most of the moderates were Piedmontese patriots who had supported the reforms that Napoleon Bonaparte had brought to Italy. In 1843, Balbo published *The Hopes of Italy*, in which he argued that Piedmont's armies would drive out the Austrians and establish a constitutional monarchy ruled by the Savoy dynasty. Viewed from the perspective of these competing programs for unification, the Risorgimento was a struggle between conflicting political and social philosophies. The more practical and realistic approach was to succeed.

Cavour and the Triumph of the Moderates

The Austro-Piedmontese war of 1848–1849 greatly strengthened the position of the moderates. Although Charles Albert had been soundly defeated in 1849, Piedmont was the only Italian state to preserve its constitution in the wake of the revolutions. The new Piedmontese king, Victor Emmanuel II (ruled as king of Piedmont 1849–1861, as king of Italy 1861–1878), successfully maintained his father's constitution in the face of Austrian threats. It was, however, Camillo Cavour rather than the king who brought the moderate program to fruition.

Count Camillo Benso di Cavour (1810–1861) was born into the Piedmontese nobility, but like many liberal statesmen of his day he was more bourgeois than aristocratic in his values. Cavour was distinctly unim-

Camillo di Cavour, the Piedmontese statesman whose skillful diplomacy and manipulation of European opinion laid the basis for Italian unity.

pressive in appearance—he was round in girth and short in stature, and wore sober frock coats and wire-rim spectacles—and an uninspired public speaker. Moreover, he thought of himself first as a Piedmontese and only latterly as an Italian—in fact, he wrote more often in French than in Italian. Cavour possessed a razor-sharp intellect and proved to be one of the 19th century's most adept practitioners of the art of diplomacy. Calculating and single-minded, he never allowed moral principles to interfere with practical considerations. In his youth he had traveled widely, and in England had spent days on end watching the House of Commons from the visitors' gallery. His experience in industry, banking, and farming made him an advocate of economic liberalism.

Cavour won election to the Piedmontese Chamber of Deputies in 1848. Two years later Victor Emmanuel II appointed him minister of agriculture and trade, and his efficiency and experience gained him the prime ministership in 1852. In order to carry out an ambitious program of reform aimed at improving the country's economy, he forged an alliance of moderate forces in the Chamber of Deputies that served his purposes for the next decade. Cavour's domestic policies were tied to his Italian strategy, for he used them to enhance Piedmont's prestige in Italy and abroad. Realizing that by itself Piedmont was unable to oust the Austrians, he sought to gain the backing of Europe's great powers for Italian unification under Piedmontese leadership. Although he eventually created the Kingdom of Italy, Cavour had a more limited conception of unification than either Mazzini or Gioberti. At first, his goal was merely to expand Piedmontese territory throughout northern Italy, without involving either the Papal States or the Kingdom of the Two Sicilies.

In order to gain the favor of Britain and France, Cavour brought Piedmont into the Crimean War in 1854. Piedmont had no political stake in Near Eastern affairs, but its military alliance with the Western powers enabled Cavour to take part in the peace conference that convened in Paris in 1856. There Cavour convinced the British to condemn Austrian interference in Italian affairs, and established a friendship with the French emperor. As a young man Napoleon III had taken part in revolutionary uprisings in Italy. Cavour now convinced him to become an advocate of Italian independence.

In July 1858 the two ambitious politicians secretly concluded the Treaty of Plombières, which secured French assistance in fighting a war against Austria. They agreed that if the Franco-Piedmontese alliance proved victorious, Piedmont would annex Lombardy and Venetia and create a kingdom of northern Italy. The new kingdom would then join with the other Italian states in a federation under papal leadership. The Plombières agreement combined aspects of the moderate and the Neo-Guelph programs, the latter a concession to Napoleon's concern for Catholic opinion at home. Napoleon's reward would be the French annexation of Savoy and Nice, both Piedmontese territory. Because Napoleon was sensitive to European opinion, however, he insisted that Austria be made to appear the aggressor, and Cavour agreed to stage an incident designed for that purpose.

In April 1859, Cavour goaded the Austrians into making unacceptable demands against Piedmont. Napoleon immediately went to war against Austria and sent a large army to Italy to fight alongside the Piedmontese. The allies drove quickly through Lombardy, but before the invasion of Venetia could begin Napoleon—horrified at French losses, under pressure from domestic opponents, and nervous about Prussian military movements on the Rhine—unexpectedly concluded a separate armistice with the Austrians. The armistice of Villafranca, signed by Napoleon and the Austrian Emperor Franz Josef in July without Cavour's consent, violated the Plombières agreement—Austria agreed to cede Lombardy but not Venetia. Cavour, outraged at Napoleon's perfidy and Victor Emmanuel's acquiescence, submitted his resignation as prime minister.

Cavour himself had secretly made plans to go beyond the terms of the Plombières agreement. Even before Lombardy had been liberated, he had arranged uprisings to overthrow the monarchs of the central Italian duchies. After Villafranca, Cavour's agents aroused the inhabitants of the duchies to demand to be incorporated in the Kingdom of Piedmont. In January, Cavour—now back in office—put aside his grievance against Napoleon and secured French agreement to allow the Piedmontese annexation of the duchies. Cavour then manipulated local plebiscites to give the appearance of overwhelming public endorsement for his action.

CAVOUR V. GARIBALDI: UNIFICATION ACHIEVED

Cavour's machinations had largely determined the first phase of the Risorgimento. In 1860, however, he began to respond to events as leadership of the unification movement was unexpectedly grasped by Giuseppe Garibaldi (1807–1882). Unlike the unscrupulous and

Giuseppe Garibaldi conquered southern Italy and forced Cavour to include it in the united kingdom. This photo shows him wearing his South American poncho.

plotting Cavour, Garibaldi was an uncomplicated idealist—he had, noted the British poet Alfred Tennyson, "the divine stupidity of a hero." The son of a sea captain, from whom he inherited a love of adventure, Garibaldi had already become a popular figure who fought on behalf of Italy's common people. A populist in the Mazzinian mold, Garibaldi wanted a democratic republic, but his first goal was to secure Italian unification.

In the 1830s, after the failure of an uprising in which he participated, Garibaldi fled to South America, where he and his Brazilian wife Anita took part in a number of revolutions. While fighting in the jungles of Brazil and Uruguay, Garibaldi developed the tactics of guerrilla insurrection. With the outbreak of the 1848 revolutions he came back to Italy and raised a volunteer army in support of Charles Albert's war against Austria. When that campaign collapsed, he joined Mazzini in Rome and coordinated the defense of the republic. In 1859 Garibaldi led another volunteer force in the Austro-Piedmontese war.

The meeting of Garibaldi and Victor Emmanuel II in 1860, represented here in a contemporary engraving, was the culminating moment of Italian unification.

Garibaldi and the Red Shirts

Garibaldi was able to seize the initiative from Cavour because he conceived of Italian unity as embracing all existing regions, including the south. He planned an invasion of the Bourbon kingdom, starting from the island of Sicily and working his way northward. Cavour, who learned of the plans in the spring of 1860, worried about two things: Garibaldi's Mazzinian beliefs, and the possibility that Garibaldi would try to take Rome—a move that would certainly bring intervention by Napoleon III. Cavour decided, therefore, to make his own plans. While supplying weapons to Garibaldi and supporting his efforts to recruit an army of about 1000 "Red Shirts," he also secretly ordered the Piedmontese Navy to sink Garibaldi's ships if they turned toward Rome. (The term "Red Shirts" was derived from the fact that while in South America the only uniforms Garibaldi could afford to provide for his men were butcher's shirts, which were red in color; he dressed his men the same way.)

In May 1860, Garibaldi's expedition reached Sicily. The Bourbons had a considerable garrison stationed there, far outnumbering the Red Shirt forces, but Garibaldi managed to outflank them. With additional troop strength recruited from the local population, he conquered all of Sicily. He then landed on the mainland in September and seized the city of Naples, where he established a temporary government for the former Kingdom of the Two Sicilies.

As Garibaldi moved up the mainland, Cavour sent a Piedmontese army down into the Papal States—but while claiming that he wanted to secure the papacy against a possible attack from Garibaldi, he quickly occupied the Papal States, leaving Pope Pius IX only Rome itself and the territory immediately around the city.

The most dramatic moment in the Risorgimento took place in October, when the armies of Garibaldi and King Victor Emmanuel II met at Teano, north of Naples. The meeting between the leader of the radical movement and the king, the symbolic head of the moderates, could have resulted in a disastrous civil war. The day was saved, however, because Garibaldi, who placed the unity of Italy above all else, surrendered the lands he had conquered to Victor Emmanuel. Garibaldi himself remained a controversial figure in the Risorgimento, finally retiring to self-imposed exile on the island of Caprera. The Kingdom of Italy was established in March 1861, with Victor Emmanuel II as its sovereign and Cavour as its first prime minister. Charles Albert's *statuto* of 1848 became, with minor modifications, the Italian constitution.

As soon as the new nation had been proclaimed, it found itself overwhelmed with an array of serious domestic challenges. Italy lost its most adept political leader when Cavour died that May. Deeply rooted regional loyalties delayed the development of a sense of national identity, a fact poignantly underscored by the comment of one Piedmontese nobleman in 1861: "We have made Italy—now we must make Italians." Although a national economy had been created on paper, the differences between the northern and southern regions grew even sharper. In the North, capitalist farming was already widespread and a nascent industrial base emerging, while in the South agrarian poverty was chronic and disease and illiteracy were widespread. Suspicion and resentment of government compounded the fact that most Italians had no real political experience with parliamentary systems. Indeed, the bulk of the citizens were denied the right to vote, and the new parliament proved excruciatingly slow in coming to grips with such staggering problems. The challenges of nationhood would sorely test the new Italian leadership over the next half-century.

BISMARCK AND THE STRUGGLE FOR POWER IN PRUSSIA

The Vienna settlement of 1815 did not completely restore the prerevolutionary situation in Germany. The Holy Roman Empire, which Napoleon had dissolved, was too unwieldy to resurrect. Instead, a new German Confederation comprising 39 independent states was established. The members of the confederation varied greatly in status, from tiny states ruled by the Thuringian princes to the much larger and powerful kingdoms of Prussia and Bavaria. All members were represented in a parliament, known as the "Diet," which assembled periodically at Frankfurt to discuss common issues. Austria, technically a part of the confederation, dominated German affairs and its ambassador served as the confederation's permanent president. Religious differences reinforced Austrian control: since Prussia and the surrounding northern states were Protestant, Austria could present itself as the protector of the southern Catholic states. Austrian domination of the German Confederation was even more complete than its control of Italian affairs.

Prussian Ambitions and the German Confederation

On the surface, the parallels between the German and the Italian situations seemed obvious. Prussia's role was similar to that of Piedmont in Italy: Prussia was the only state capable of challenging Austrian preponderance in the German Confederation. The House of Hohenzollern, Prussia's autocratic dynasty, had greatly expanded its domains over the centuries, and King Friedrich Wilhelm IV (ruled 1840–1861) thought in terms of extending Hohenzollern authority through most of Germany. The major difference between the two ambitious states was one of scale and power, for while Piedmont had not been strong enough to best Austria by itself, Prussian industrial and military resources made it a formidable antagonist.

Dynastic ambition rather than the ideals of German nationalism put Prussia in the forefront of the German unification movement. The core of the kingdom's nobility, the conservative landowning *Junkers* from East Prussia, were narrowly insular in their outlook and hardly thought of themselves as "Germans." The middle classes, on the other hand, were vigorous advocates of both political liberalism and nationalism, as they were elsewhere in Europe. As far back as 1818, Prussian merchants had actively sponsored a free trade movement that was gradually extended into the *Zollverein*, or customs union, among neighboring states. The middle classes quickly came to see the economic possibilities of political unity. In deliberately keeping Austria out of the customs union, the Zollverein implemented on the economic level what political nationalists called the *Kleindeutsch*, or "Small Germany," approach to German unification (see Part VII, Topic 8).

During the revolutions of 1848–1849, the nobility and the military had blocked middle-class efforts to give Prussia a constitutional government and unify Germany. The reactionaries persuaded Friedrich Wilhelm to withdraw his support for a liberal constitution.

Later in 1849, with the revolution behind him, Friedrich Wilhelm issued a conservative constitution. This document established a parliament with two chambers, similar to that of the Piedmontese constitution of 1848: an upper house, the *Herrenhaus*, appointed by the king and an elected lower house known as the *Landtag*. Elections were in theory on the basis of universal male suffrage, but a complicated method of indirect voting kept poorer citizens greatly underrepresented and gave the advantage to the upper classes. Royal power remained far-reaching, and even in budget appropriations—a function that liberal constitutions generally reserved for the lower houses of parliament— the powers of the Landtag were unclear. Prussian liberals, resentful of the conservative nature of the constitution, worked to clarify budget procedures in order to assert parliamentary control over government spending.

Friedrich Wilhelm had turned down the Frankfurt Assembly's offer of the German crown in March 1849 (see Part VII, Topic 8) because he refused to accept the principle of popular sovereignty. He did not, however, reject the notion of German unification under Prussian

${S}$ignificant Dates

German Unification

1834	Zollverein created
1840–1861	Friedrich Wilhelm IV rules as king of Prussia
1848–1849	Revolutions in Germany; 1849 Prussian constitution issued
1861–1888	Wilhelm I rules as king of Prussia
1866	Austro-Prussian War; North German Confederation created
1862–1870	Bismarck serves as minister of Prussia
1870–1871	Franco-Prussian War; German empire created

The Risorgimento

The Italian movement for liberation and unification was in one sense an ideological struggle among a series of competing philosophies of government and society. From the time of the Congress of Vienna in 1815, Italian patriots argued about the methods that should be employed to achieve their goals and the kind of state that should govern a unified nation.

THE REVOLUTIONARY VISION

Santorre di Santarosa (1783–1825) was a young army officer in Piedmont-Sardinia and a liberal patriot. In 1821 he joined in a conspiracy that sought to force a constitution on his country and drive Austria from Italy. Here are his views on the Italian question after the failed revolution.

Italians must examine their country's situation and the weaknesses exposed by the revolt. Ours was the first revolution for centuries which was attempted in Italy without foreign help; it was the first in which two Italian peoples worked together at the two extremities of our peninsula. Its result, I know too well, has been to subject Italy entirely to Austria; but let the Austrians beware; Italy is conquered, but not subdued. Besides, what was Italy before July 1820? Had it not already been enslaved to the Austrian Emperor by the courts of Naples and Turin when they promised him to refuse to their people any beneficial political institutions? Our late misfortunes have only rendered our position clearer, our servitude more direct, our chains more obvious. . . .

The emancipation of Italy will occur in this present century; the signal has already been given. Our enemies may prepare at leisure their proscription lists, and docile Italian princes may continue to serve Austria, for they would sooner reign by her strength than by law. The Austrians may leave them to do so and thus begin to reap the fruits of their blindness. But all are deceived, because our passion for national independence feeds on the sacrifices which it imposes on us. Austria may retard the moment, but that will serve only to make the explosion more terrible. Our ancestors have given us great examples which will not be wasted; and when another European war shall arrive, when Austria then demands our children and money to support her cause, Italians will perhaps know better how to employ their resources.

Arbitrary royal rule is now confusing the great issue which confronts Europe. Italy is more involved in this than other nations. We have to conquer our national identity and win internal liberties, both at the same time.

YOUNG ITALY

he nationalist leader Giuseppe Mazzini founded the Young Italy society in 1831 as a vehicle for coordinating patriotic revolution throughout Italy. His goal was the creation of a unified republic.

It was during these months of imprisonment that I conceived the plan of the association of Young Italy (*La Giovine Italia*). I meditated deeply upon the principles upon which to base the organization of the party, the aim and purpose of its labors—which I intended should be publicly declared—the method of its formation, the individuals to be selected to aid me in its creation, and the possibility of linking its operations with those of the existing revolutionary elements of Europe.

We were few in number, young in years, and of limited means and influence; but I believed the whole problem to consist in appealing to the true instincts and tendencies of the Italian heart, mute at that time, but revealed to us both by history and our own previsions of the future. Our strength must lie in our right appreciation of what those instincts and tendencies really were.

All great national enterprises have ever been originated by men of the people, whose sole strength lay in that power of *faith* and of *will*, which neither counts obstacles nor measures time. Men of means and influence follow after, either to support and carry on the movement created by the first, or, as too often happens, to divert it from its original aim. . . .

At that time even the immature conception inspired me with a mighty hope that flashed before my spirit like a star. I saw regenerate Italy becoming at one bound the missionary of a religion of progress and fraternity, far grander and vaster than that she gave to humanity in the past. . . .

Why should not a new Rome, the Rome of the Italian people—portents of whose coming I deemed I saw—arise to create a third and still vaster Unity; to link together and harmonize earth and heaven, right [law] and duty; and utter, not to individuals but to peoples, the great word Association—to make known to free men and equal their mission here below?

GIOBERTI'S NEO-GUELPH IDEA

incenzo Gioberti's notion that only the pope could act as symbolic leader of a federated Italy of autonomous princes was widely accepted by Catholics and monarchists but its credibility collapsed in the wake of the 1848 revolution, when Pius IX abandoned the patriotic cause.

I propose to prove that Italy contains within herself, above all through religion, all the conditions required for her national and political resurrection or risorgimento, and that to bring this about she has no need of revolutions within and still less of foreign invasions or foreign exemplars. And to begin with I say that Italy must first and foremost regain her life as a nation; and that her life as a nation cannot come into being without some degree of union between her various members. This union can be interpreted and

continued next page

established in various ways, but, however it is achieved, it is a necessity, and if it fails our nation will be weakened and enfeebled beyond repair. . . .

Supposing we succeeded in putting an end to the present division in Italy by revolutionary means? Far from achieving the union we desire, we would be opening the door to fresh disorders. For political union cannot bring happiness to a people if it is confused and vacillating instead of tranquil and stable. The principle of public peace and security must be sought in the sovereign power, whatever form it may take; because without sovereignty there is no order, and without order there is neither peace nor security nor free living nor any other civil good. The sovereign power is based partly on moral force, that is to say on law, and partly on material force, that is to say on the army; and although, given human wickedness, arms are needed to protect public opinion, they cannot replace it, for it is impossible to restrain a few malcontents unless there is a general consensus among many men of good will. Only moral authority can justify a sovereign power, it being inconsistent that others should be expected to obey a system of rule that they think it morally legitimate to offend or annihilate. . . .

That the Pope is naturally, and should be effectively, the civil head of Italy is a truth forecast in the nature of things, confirmed by many centuries of history, recognized on past occasions by the peoples and princes of our land, and only thrown into doubt by those commentators who drank at foreign springs and diverted their poison to the motherland. Nor, to achieve this confederation, is there any need for the Pope to receive or take over any new power, but only to revive an ancient and inalienable right that has merely been interrupted. This selfsame right has been exercised in many ways, but always directed to one end, namely that of bringing the Italian states together in union. Thus, if Leo III provided for Italy's salvation by reviving the Empire and crowning Charlemagne (in which we should admire the intention rather than the outcome), at a later date Alexander III championed freedom by opposing that Emperor's degenerate successors. Alexander precisely obtained his intention by forming the Lombard cities into a League of which he was supreme head and military chief; and if this League was transitory and embraced only a part of Italy, the fault was certainly not that of the Pope.

The benefits Italy would gain from a political confederation under the moderating authority of the pontiff are beyond enumeration.

From Denis Mack Smith, ed., *The Making of Italy 1796–1870.* Harper & Row. Copyright © 1968. Reprinted with permission of Denis Mack Smith.

CAVOUR'S REALISM

Count Camillo di Cavour, prime minister of Piedmont and architect of Italian unity, was above all a realist with a practical sense of the possible. In this famous article, dealing ostensibly with railroads, he explained the idea of a gradual program of moderate development for unification under the leadership of the Piedmontese monarch.

If the future holds a happy fortune for Italy, if this fair country, so one may hope, is destined to regain her nationality, it can only be the consequence of a remodeling of Europe, or as a result of one of those great providential explosions in which the mere ability to move troops quickly by rail will be unimportant. The time of conspiracies has passed; the emancipation of peoples cannot result from mere plots or from a surprise attack. It has become the necessary consequence of the progress of Christian civilization and the spread of enlightenment. Once the hour of deliverance sounds, the material forces which governments possess will be powerless to keep conquered nations in bondage. Moral forces are growing daily which sooner or later, with the aid of providence, must cause a political upheaval in Europe; and governments will then have to yield. . . .

All history proves that no people can attain a high degree of intelligence and morality unless the feeling of its nationality is strongly developed. This remarkable fact is a necessary consequence of the laws which govern human nature. The intellectual life of the masses moves within a very limited range of ideas. Among the ideas which they are capable of acquiring, the noblest and most elevated are first those of religion, then those of country and nationality. . . .

[I]t seems likely that the precious triumph of our nationality cannot be realized except by the combined action of all the live forces in the country, that is to say, of the national rulers openly supported by every party. The history of the last thirty years, as well as an analysis of the various elements in Italian society, will prove that military or democratic revolutions can have little success in Italy. All true friends of the country must therefore reject such means as useless. They must recognize that they cannot truly help their fatherland except by gathering in support of legitimate monarchs who have their roots deep in the national soil. . . .

But more than by any other administrative reform, as much perhaps as by liberal political concessions, the building of the railways will help to consolidate the mutual confidence between governments and people, and this is the basis of our hopes for the future. These governments have the destiny of their peoples in trust, and railway building is therefore a powerful instrument of progress which testifies to the benevolent intentions of each government and the security they feel. On their side the people will be grateful for this and will come to hold their sovereigns in complete trust; docile, but full of enthusiasm, they will let themselves be guided by their rulers in the acquisition of national independence.

From Denis Mack Smith, ed., *The Making of Italy 1796–1870.* Harper & Row. Copyright © 1968. Reprinted with permission of Denis Mack Smith.

GARIBALDI AND VICTOR EMMANUEL

Giuseppe Garibaldi, the heroic guerrilla leader, had begun his career as a follower of Mazzini. After Garibaldi's troops wrested Sicily and southern Italy from the Bourbons in 1860, he made the fateful decision to turn his conquests over to King Victor Emmanuel of Piedmont in order to secure the unification of the country. The two men met at Teano on the Volturno River on October 26, 1860, as described here by British historian George Macaulay Trevelyan:

So the early morning wore on, while regiment after regiment of the Royal army marched past the Liberator. It was a damp autumn air, and Garibaldi was not only wearing his *poncho*, but had in homely fashion bound a coloured handkerchief over his head. His staff, in their war-stained red shirts, presented a curious contrast to the brilliant uniforms that were filing by them hour by hour. Suddenly the strains of the Royal march were heard, and the cry arose, "The King! The King is coming!" Garibaldi and his staff mounted their horses and rode forward to the edge of the road. Victor Emmanuel, on a prancing Arab, dashed up to meet them. The Dictator, sweeping his hat off his kerchiefed head, cried aloud—"*Saluto il primo Re d'Italia*"—"I hail the first King of Italy." The King stretched out his hand and the two men clasped and held hands for more than a minute.

"*Come state, caro Garibaldi?*" [How are you, dear Garibaldi?]

"*Bene, Maestà, e Lei?*" [Well, your Majesty, and yourself?]

"*Benone.*" [Very well.]

Then they rode on together, and the two staffs behind them, red shirts side by side with resplendent uniforms, crosses, and cordons of honour. It was an epitome of the union of

continued next page

conservative and revolutionary forces that had crushed the obscurantists and expelled the foreigners. The constrained conversation between the two groups betrayed the heart-burnings on either side and the grudging sacrifices that each was making to the other. But although there was cold politeness where there should have been enthusiasm, none the less that ride together was the making of Italy, and seen down history's lengthening vista, remains evermore a goodly sight.

After a while Garibaldi and his men turned off the road to the left and made their way back by country lanes to Calvi, while the King held on to Teano. "Garibaldi's countenance," writes Mario, "was full of melancholy sweetness. Never did I feel drawn to him with such tenderness." He said little that evening to his friends. Next morning they met Jessie Mario, who had crossed the Volturno to provide hospital arrangements north of the river. "My wounded," said Garibaldi to her somewhat sternly, "are all on the south of the Volturno." And then, relapsing into his gentlest mood, he added, "Jessie, they have sent us to the rear" (*"ci hanno messi alla coda"*). During their ride together Victor Emmanuel had told him in soft words the hard decree that the Royal army would take over all the operations of war and that the Garibaldini were no longer required.

From George Macaulay Trevelyan, *Garibaldi and the Making of Italy* (London: Longmans, Green and Co., 1911), 271–272.

leadership from above, although he preferred to achieve the goal in cooperation with Austria. In 1849, the Prussian chief minister, Josef von Radowitz (1797–1853), presented the king with a unification plan that called for the creation of a single German government based on the federal system, headed by Prussia but in permanent union with Austria. Foreign relations and military affairs would be conducted jointly by representatives of each state. Many of the smaller German states joined the union, but some of the larger ones, such as Bavaria, refused to adopt the plan. Austria rejected the Prussian proposal outright, and Friedrich Wilhelm backed down. In November he dismissed Radowitz and, in the face of an Austrian threat to go to war, humiliated himself by agreeing to a series of terms dictated at a meeting in Olmütz.

Bismarck: The Iron Chancellor

The "humiliation of Olmütz" weakened Prussia's self-appointed role as the leader of German unification. Not only did Friedrich Wilhelm's foreign policy fail to inspire confidence, but the unhappy monarch was afflicted with periodic bouts of insanity. In 1858 his brother Wilhelm was made regent, and in 1861 he succeeded his brother as king.

Wilhelm I (ruled 1861–1888 as king of Prussia, 1871–1888 as emperor of Germany), a soldier by training, was no less conservative and autocratic than his brother. In February 1860, he sent a controversial military reform bill to the Landtag. With the shadow of Olmütz still looming, he proposed a new budget meant to double the size of the Prussian Army and raise the terms of required military duty from two to three years. He also wanted to abolish the reserve militia, for he regarded its unprofessional civilian soldiers with disdain.

For the middle-class liberals who represented a majority in the Landtag, the reorganization bill presented a unique opportunity to assert the budgetary authority of parliament over the king, as well as to strike a blow against the influence of the military. Liberal opposition succeeded in forcing Friedrich Wilhelm to withdraw the measure, and in 1862 a similar measure was also defeated. Wilhelm dissolved the Landtag and called for new elections, but he was further embittered when an even larger liberal majority was returned. So frustrated was the king that he came close to renouncing the throne. Finally he decided to appoint Count Otto von Bismarck (1815–1898) as his new minister-president in an effort to resolve what had become a major constitutional crisis. Bismarck's own views on unification and his political philosophy seemed well suited to the moment. He envisioned a Prussian-dominated Germany from which Austria would have to be ejected by force, and he detested the liberals.

Bismarck's influence on the course of modern German history cannot be exaggerated. In appearance he was the exact opposite of Cavour: a towering and vigorous man, he seemed the embodiment of the patriarchal landowning class of Junkers from which he came. Yet, while more conservative than Cavour in his

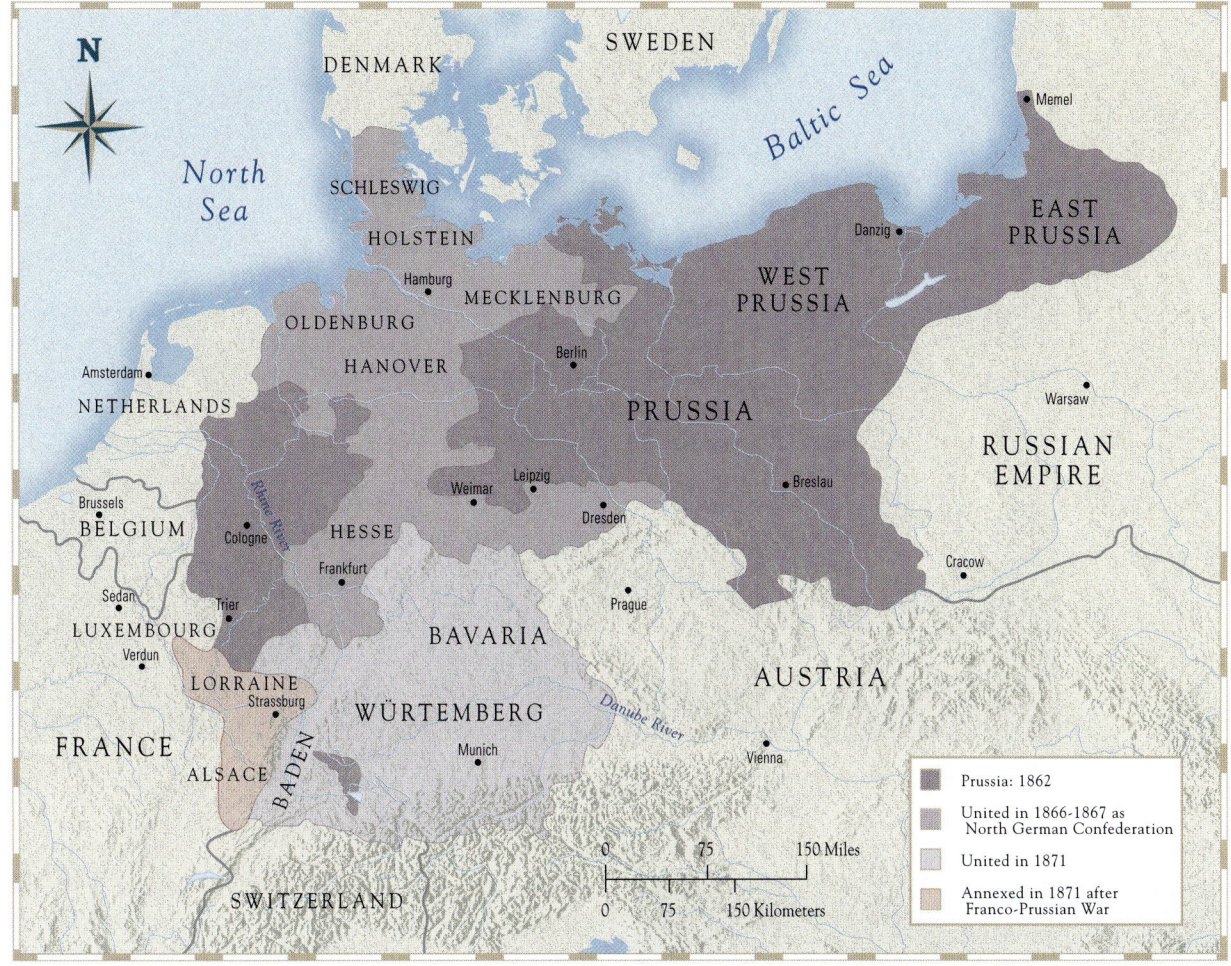

Map 11.2   Unification of Germany

politics, he had none of the narrowness of vision of the Prussian élite—his service in the Frankfurt Diet had given him a deep awareness of German affairs, while his experience as Prussian ambassador first to Russia and then to France had broadened his knowledge of European diplomacy. Flexible rather than rigid, he could nevertheless be unbending in the face of opposition. He cared little for constitutions and disdained liberals as impractical idealists. Like Cavour, Bismarck thrived on the intricacies and maneuverings of power politics.

Prussian liberals proved to be his bitterest enemies. He understood, however, that the industrial and financial expertise of the middle classes was essential to a strong Prussia, and that they themselves were the major advocates of national unification. At first Bismarck saw unification only in terms of Prussian dominance over the Protestant states of the north, and only gradually did his perspective widen to embrace all of Germany. He understood, too, that unification required the elimination of Austria from German affairs.

Bismarck saw the king's army reorganization bill as essential to the extension of Prussian power, for he was determined to give Prussia a military force capable of defeating the Austrian empire. Bismarck sidestepped the Landtag altogether not only by continuing to collect taxes but by raising funds for the army through the sale of bonds in government railroads and the sale of mines and iron works. The liberals attacked Bismarck's subversion of the constitutional process, but both he and the king ignored them. More difficult to ignore were the liberal views of Victoria, the princess of Hohenzollern (1840–1901), the English-born wife of Crown Prince Friedrich (1831–1888), the heir apparent, who ruled for only three months as German emperor before his death in 1888. This daughter of Britain's Queen Victoria was highly cultured and knowledgeable about politics and encouraged her husband to favor a unified German state free from military influence.

Bismarck viewed the liberal opposition as short-sighted obstructionists who failed to understand power

The proclamation of King Wilhelm I of Prussia as emperor of Germany in the Palace of Versailles.

Otto von Bismarck, minister-president of Prussia whose policies of diplomacy and war united Germany.

politics. He proclaimed unabashedly that only "iron and blood," not parliamentary speeches, would unify Germany. Constitutional theory, he told the Landtag, must give way to the necessities of military strength. Bismarck was certain that victory on the battlefield would convince the liberals that his budget manipulations were irrelevant.

The Seven Weeks' War

The war with Austria that Bismarck wanted began to take shape in the 1860s, and had its roots in the so-called "Schleswig-Holstein question." Years later, the British prime minister of the day, Lord Palmerston, remarked that the Schleswig-Holstein affair was so complicated that only three people had ever fully understood it: one of them was dead, a second had become insane, and the third—Palmerston himself—had forgotten the details.

The international status of these two duchies, both administered by the Danish king, was uncertain. Holstein, predominantly German-speaking, was a member of the German Confederation, but Schleswig, inhabited by Danes as well as Germans, was not. A crisis broke out in 1863, when Denmark annexed Schleswig. On Bismarck's suggestion, Prussia and Austria fought a joint war to reclaim the two provinces. After peace had been made, Austria and Prussia agreed to a joint administration of Schleswig-Holstein.

As Bismarck anticipated, disagreement over the future status of the provinces increased tensions between the two powers. Indeed, the Austrians soon demanded the union of Schleswig and Holstein as an independent state under a German monarch; Bismarck, however, wanted special economic privileges designed to integrate the region into the Prussian sphere. In 1865, the Convention of Gastein placed Holstein under Austrian administration and Schleswig under Prussian authority. Disputes between Austria and Prussia followed, and Bismarck soon found a suitable pretext for war with Austria.

Bismarck first cleared the way by ensuring that none of the other powers would intervene on Austria's side. Tsar Alexander II was likely to stay neutral, since Bismarck had assisted the Russians in crushing a revolt in their area of Poland in 1863. He was uncertain, however, of Napoleon III, and in 1865 he met secretly with Napoleon at Biarritz to discuss the situation. Napoleon assured Bismarck that he would remain neutral in a war between Prussia and Austria, and was made to believe that France would get land along the Rhine in return—a promise Bismarck had no intention of keeping. Napoleon expected, in any case, to secure Belgium no matter who won, for the Austrians had also promised the territory to France. In 1866 Bismarck, encouraged by Napoleon, offered Italy the province of Venetia in return for Italian help in the war he was preparing against Austria.

On June 1, 1866, Bismarck ordered the Prussian Army into Holstein after alleging that Austria had violated the Convention of Gastein. The Austrians responded by pushing the German Confederation into war against Prussia. Elated, Bismarck announced the end of the confederation and declared war against Austria.

Bismarck couched Prussian aggression in nationalist rhetoric, asserting that the future of Germany hung in the balance. Moving troops by rail, and employing the new breech-loading "needle" gun—Prussia was the first nation to do so—Count Helmuth von Moltke (1800–1891), chief of the Prussian general staff, stunned all of Europe by swiftly reducing one of the most powerful empires in Europe to total defeat. The effect of the Austro-Prussian War—known as the "Seven Weeks' War"—on subsequent European history cannot be overestimated, for it shifted the balance of power in central Europe.

Bismarck chose to deal reasonably with vanquished Austria. The Treaty of Prague, signed in August 1866, did not require Austria to pay reparations, and no part of its territory other than Venetia—ceded as promised to the Italians—was lost. On the other hand, Vienna had to agree to the dissolution of the German Confederation and to renounce its interest in Germany. Prussia annexed Schleswig-Holstein and some of the other states in northern Germany. The Catholic states in the south, which had supported Austria, were forced to enter into military alliances with Prussia.

Bismarck then forced all German states north of the river Main into a new North German Confederation, with the king of Prussia as its president and Bismarck as its chancellor. While its member states still controlled local affairs, military and foreign policy was in the hands of the central government. The confederation's parliament had two chambers, an upper house known as the *Bundesrat*, representing the states, and a lower house, the *Reichstag*, elected by universal male suffrage. The constitution granted extensive powers to the king of Prussia.

THE BIRTH OF THE SECOND REICH

Bismarck no doubt saw the North German Confederation as a temporary expedient, but he had not counted on the reaction of Napoleon III. The French emperor, who had not expected such a complete Prussian victory, was stunned by the rapid Austrian defeat, which left him no time to intervene. Moreover, Bismarck did not reward Napoleon for his neutrality with the territories hinted at in the Biarritz talks.

The Franco-Prussian War, 1870–1871

Coming on the heels of the failure of Napoleon's intervention in Mexico (see Part VII, Topic 9), the emperor's domestic opponents attacked him where he was most vulnerable—on the issue of French prestige. Napoleon saw belatedly that he would have to oppose the creation of a unified Germany on France's borders. Bismarck, on the other hand, believed that he could use a war with France to arouse nationalism and rally the other German states around Prussia's leadership in order to complete the unification process.

Relations between France and Prussia deteriorated as both sides fanned popular sentiment through press campaigns and formal protests. As in the case of the war with Austria, an obscure diplomatic issue provided the excuse for war—the question of whether a member of the Hohenzollern family would be made king of Spain. Much to Bismarck's dismay, Wilhelm I backed down in the face of French pressure. But the French, pressing their diplomatic victory too far, then demanded a formal guarantee that no Hohenzollern would ever again become a candidate for the Spanish throne. Wilhelm I met with the French ambassador at the resort town of Ems in July 1870, but politely refused the French demand for such a guarantee, and sent

Map 11.3   Europe in 1871

Bismarck a telegram recounting the details of the meeting. Bismarck, unwilling to see an excellent pretext for war disappear, carefully abbreviated the wording of the so-called "Ems Dispatch" so as to make it appear that the king had abruptly rejected the French proposal. Bismarck then made the telegram public. With the enthusiastic help of the popular press in both countries, the doctored telegram enraged public opinion and gave Napoleon III little choice—he announced hostilities on July 19, 1870. The Franco-Prussian War had begun.

Once again the devastating precision of Prussia's armies stunned Europe. Despite its defeat in 1866, Austria remained neutral, principally because Bismarck

had imposed such moderate peace terms on Vienna. Bismarck could also claim that the war was a "German," rather than a Prussian, struggle, since the other German states were bound to Prussia by military alliances.

The war was over in six months. On September 1, 1870, the Prussians struck a devastating blow against France at Sedan, capturing 100,000 French troops and taking Napoleon himself prisoner. In Paris, Napoleon was dethroned and a republic proclaimed on September 4. Although the outcome of the war was certain, for five months Republican France refused to give in and the Prussians laid siege to Paris. The French surrendered in January, and two months later Parisian radicals led the desperate population in a rebellion against the republican government and proclaimed the Commune (see Part VII, Topic 19).

Against the backdrop of the terrible siege of Paris, Bismarck staged the last act in the unification of Germany. On January 18, 1871, Wilhelm I was crowned German emperor in a ceremony held in the symbolic heart of former French glory—the Hall of Mirrors of the Palace of Versailles. The "Second Reich"—German nationalists counted the Holy Roman Empire as the "First" Reich—had been created.

Adolphe Thiers (1797–1877), the provisional head of the French government, negotiated with the German empire. The Treaty of Frankfurt was far different in spirit and intent from the generous terms Bismarck had given Austria five years earlier. Germany annexed most of the strategically vital province of Alsace and a large portion of Lorraine—areas in eastern France that held rich iron mines and flourishing textile mills. Although the inhabitants were mainly German-speaking, most preferred French rule. For the next five decades the loss of Alsace and Lorraine rankled deeply in the French psyche. The Prussians marched triumphantly through Paris and, to make matters worse, France was required to bear the humiliation of German occupation until it had paid a huge indemnity of 5 billion francs, a sum that amounted to more than twice the cost of the war for Prussia.

The Franco-Prussian War was one of the most far-reaching events of the 19th century. Bismarck had succeeded in unifying Germany under Prussian control, not through the spirit of liberal nationalism that had wanted it in 1848–1849 but in alliance with the conservative élites who had made Prussia into an autocratic, military state. The new Kingdom of Italy also took advantage of the Franco-Prussian War to complete its territorial unity: when Napoleon III was forced to recall the soldiers he had kept in Rome to protect the pope, the Italians marched into the city and made it their new capital. Bismarck's armies had defeated the two most powerful states on the Continent, and the German empire had emerged as the most powerful state in Europe. The European balance of power was irrevocably altered.

NATIONALISM, REGIONALISM, AND THE AMERICAN CIVIL WAR

The struggle for political unification that transformed Europe in the 19th century was also played out in the New World, where the recently created United States underwent a process of expansion and crisis (see Part VII, Topic 1).

European radicals, struggling against the Vienna settlement of 1815, were encouraged by the triumph of democratic principles in the United States, in particular by the adoption of the Bill of Rights. In 1828, while the Restoration was still firmly entrenched in Europe, Americans gave their democratic system a still broader popular base by sending Andrew Jackson (president 1828–1835) to the White House. In Italy, nationalists considered the American Revolution a model for the Risorgimento, and both Mazzini and Garibaldi identified with its struggle for independence.

Nationalism and the Civil War

American nationalism grew steadily in the first half of the 19th century, especially after the War of 1812 with Great Britain. Moreover, Americans not only believed that their national interests conflicted with those of Europe's great powers, but also thought of their political culture as fundamentally different from that of the Old World. A thirst for expansion further fueled nationalist sentiment as Americans pushed west and south from the original thirteen states, bringing enormous areas such as the Louisiana Purchase and the Northwest Territory under the control of the United States. America's "Manifest Destiny," claimed imperialists, was "to overspread the continent allotted by Providence for the free development of our multiplying millions." In this aggressive spirit, President James Polk (served 1845–1849) fought the Mexican War in 1846–1848 and, with the seizure of Texas and California, extended the boundaries of the United States to the Rio Grande and the Pacific coast.

This rapid expansion deeply divided Americans, for it raised the issue of the extension of slavery to the new territories. Tensions mounted between the southern states, where slavery was a key element in the plantation-based agriculture of the region, and those in the North, where industrialization was taking hold. Although slavery was only one element in a complex web of sectional disputes, it became the chief focus of the Civil War (1861–1865).

European nationalist leaders, particularly those in Italy, watched the Civil War closely. Because Abraham Lincoln (president 1861–1865) led the federal government in the struggle to maintain the American union, Italians regarded him as one of the most important statesmen of the century. Cavour and Garibaldi had been longtime admirers of the American political system, although for quite different reasons. Garibaldi had lived in New York in the early 1850s, and on several occasions Cavour seriously contemplated emigrating to the United States. While Cavour expressed dismay that the Civil War might set back the cause of national

A famous photograph of President Lincoln and the Union commanders during the American Civil War.

unification, Garibaldi was more interested in the moral urgency of suppressing slavery. In 1861 Lincoln actually offered Garibaldi command of an army corps, but the offer was never formalized: the American president was not prepared to accept Garibaldi's demands that he be given supreme command of the Union army and that slavery be abolished immediately. Cavour did not live to see the northern victory over the Confederacy, which eliminated slavery in the United States and successfully preserved the union. A half-century later, the amateur American historian William R. Thayer drew a deliberate comparison between the U.S. president and the Piedmontese prime minister.

In the two decades after the revolutions of 1848–1849, nationalism achieved its greatest successes. National unity in the United States was preserved, Italy and Germany were created, the Hungarians had forced the Hapsburgs to grant them a measure of autonomy within the Austrian state, and the inhabitants of the Balkans were beginning to stir against Turkish domination.

By the end of the 19th century, however, nationalism had taken on a new and significantly different meaning. The idealistic vision of Mazzini, who had seen nationalism as a liberating force that would give rise to an era of international cooperation among free nations, all but disappeared as a new brand of chauvinist patriotism gained sway. Cavour and Bismarck, who applied the methods of power politics to the task of national liberation, had forged domestic alliances with conservative élites—army officers, businessmen, and aristocrats—in order to achieve their goals. These conservative forces now controlled the destinies of the newly unified states and ushered in a period of intense national rivalry. After 1871, competition between nations for prestige and dominance increasingly shaped international relations.

Questions for Further Study

1. What were the principal programs for Italian unification? How did they differ?

2. What methods did Bismarck employ in his efforts to unify Germany? With which Italian leader would he be most readily compared?

3. What were the consequences of the way in which Italy and Germany were unified?

4. In what ways was the unification experience of the United States different from that of Italy and Germany?

Suggestions for Further Reading

Crankshaw, Edward. *Bismarck.* New York, 1981.
Di Scala, Spencer. *Italy from Revolution to Republic.* 2nd ed. Boulder, CO, 1998.
Hamerow, Theodore S. *The Social Foundations of German Unification, 1858–1871.* 2 vols. Princeton, NJ, 1969.
Kohn, Hans. *The Idea of Nationalism.* New York, 1944.
Mack Smith, Denis. *Cavour.* New York, 1985.
Mack Smith, Denis. *Garibaldi.* Englewood Cliffs, NJ, 1969.
Mack Smith, Denis. *Mazzini.* New Haven, CT, 1994.
Pflanze. Otto. *Bismarck and the Development of Germany.* 3 vols. Princeton, NJ, 1990.
Taylor, A. J. P. *Bismarck, the Man and the Statesman.* New York, 1955.
Woolf, Stuart. *A History of Italy, 1700–1860.* New York, 1986.

VII ....

T o p i c   1 2

TECHNOLOGY AND THE EUROPEAN ECONOMY

y 1850 Britain, long in the vanguard of the industrial revolution, had established its superiority over the rest of Europe in virtually all facets of economic life — technology, the factory system, energy production, commerce and trade. At mid-century a proud and self-satisfied Great Britain determined to show off its achievements to the rest of the world in the Great Exhibition of 1851.

The exhibition at the Crystal Palace was not, however, an exclusively British affair, but rather the first world's fair. Other European countries and the United States also displayed their machines and products. The international nature of the event underscored the fact that industrialization was spreading. The British economy maintained its lead until overtaken by Germany and the United States in the 1890s, but between 1850 and 1873, the rapid pace of its early growth slowed as continental Europe and the United States began to close the gap.

The two decades after 1850 were years of rapid industrialization on the Continent. Production levels in key sectors such as coal, iron, and textiles increased enormously. On the Continent, development took place as France, Germany, and other countries adopted — and sometimes improved — the new machines and factory organization already in place in Britain.

The railroad came into its own in this period. Indeed, Europe and America experienced something of a "railroad revolution," as country after country built dense networks of rail lines, creating national markets for the first time. The railroad boom became a major sphere of investment and banking activity and stimulated the further expansion of heavy industry.

Agriculture, having improved significantly since the late 18th century, also entered a phase of increased productivity. New farming regions were opened up in Eastern Europe, and increased mechanization went hand in hand with land reclamation and new fertilizers. The growth of urban centers also provided larger agricultural markets.

The accelerating growth of the continental economy in this period required significant change in the way in which Europeans conducted business. Old laws hampered modern financial operations, while huge amounts of capital were needed to buy machinery and to build factories and railroads. Industrial expansion encouraged the development of the modern corporation and banking systems, and contributed to the decline of trade barriers. Finance, business organization, and the nature of private property had been revolutionized.

By the 1870s, the industrial and financial world looked quite different from that of 1850. Europe was poised on the edge of the era of modern capitalism and global economy.

THE GREAT EXHIBITION OF 1851: THE PROMISE OF TECHNOLOGY

While visiting the Paris Exposition of 1849, Henry Cole (1808–1882), an English civil servant, conceived the idea of organizing an event in London that would reveal Britain's industrial superiority. With a population half the size of France, Britain produced two-thirds of the world's coal and more than half its iron and cotton cloth; its manufactured goods flooded markets everywhere and its ships carried the bulk of the world's trade. British per capita income was 50 percent higher than French and more than twice that of Germany.

The Crystal Palace

Prince Albert, Queen Victoria's husband, sponsored the exhibition through the Society of Arts, of which he was president. A competition was announced for the design for the exhibit pavilion, to be located in Hyde Park. After considering and rejecting some 245 projects, the organizers turned to Joseph Paxton (1803–1865). Paxton was a horticulturalist and self-trained landscape architect. He had achieved fame for the gardens and landscaping he supervised for the duke of Devonshire, including the construction of a glass-roofed conservatory supported by cast-iron columns.

Significant Dates

Technology and the Economy

1830	First successful steam railway opened in England
1843	End of British ban on exporting machinery
1844	Bank Charter Act in England; 1846, Bank of Prussia
1851	The Crystal Palace Exhibition
1852	Crédit Mobilier
1856	Incorporation with limited liability
1840–1860	Railroad boom
1865	Belgium, France, Italy, and Switzerland form the Latin Monetary Union
1871	Gold standard begins
1850–1900	Second industrial revolution

Paxton came up with an imaginative concept: a long, three-story building consisting of numerous round-headed bays in the neo-Gothic style then popular, each story stepped in from the one below. The roof was in the form of an enormous arc. In the interior, galleries for individual exhibits lined either side of the huge central space. Most daring of all, the pavilion would be built entirely of glass (a material never before used for major construction) and held together by wrought-iron framing supports—in effect, a "crystal palace."

The genius of Paxton's idea derived in part from the requirement that the entire building had to be erected in nine months. His design made it possible to accomplish this because the building could be put together from prefabricated, interchangeable parts assembled in modules. A triumph of civil engineering in the age of iron, the Crystal Palace covered an area of almost 20 acres and utilized 2224 wrought-iron girders, 3300 cast-iron columns, and 300,000 panes of glass—some being, at the time, the largest ever made. Sixteen huge semicircular arches of wood, reaching more than 100 feet high, provided additional support.

Londoners marveled as the structure went up, and Victoria and Albert made numerous visits to the construction site. Despite dire predictions of disaster from skeptics, the Crystal Palace did not collapse. The queen officially opened the exhibition on May 1, 1851, with some 500,000 people crowding Hyde Park for the occasion. "The sight," Victoria recorded in her diary, "was magical—so vast, so glorious, so touching."

Industrial Civilization on Display

Within Paxton's palace were displayed more than 100,000 industrial products from around the world, submitted by 7351 exhibitors from the British Empire and 6556 from other countries. The items were grouped into categories such as raw materials, machinery, textiles, metal and ceramic products, and the fine arts.

Not unexpectedly, the machine displays most interested the public. Visitors could see the full range of 19th-century industrial items, including many that were already dated, from railroad locomotives and steamship engines to machine tools of all sorts, from power looms to printing presses and envelope-making machines, from hydraulic turbines to fireplaces. The American exhibit attracted particular attention, for it was the most forward-looking and included such practical items as ice-making machines, a Cyrus McCormick reaper, a sewing machine, and Colt revolvers made from standardized parts. From California came a device for winnowing gold, and from Canada a hand-operated fire pump.

Engineering and architectural firms exhibited a variety of construction schemes, including lighthouses,

NORTH TRANSEPT, GREAT EXHIBITION.

Exterior view of the Crystal Palace, Hyde Park, London, 1851.

iron bridges, and a model for a canal across the Suez isthmus. Amid the products and inventions were also coal and iron ores, and the German firm of Krupp—described as "a manufacturer of Essen"—startled the public with a two-ton block of cast steel, the largest steel ingot ever seen. Weapons and scientific objects intermingled with telegraph machines, cameras, and cooking utensils. For the mid-19th-century consumer, the exhibition presented a feast of incredible items that delighted and awed spectators.

The Crystal Palace show was a major success. The queen came several times a week. The duke of Wellington was a frequent visitor, and was called upon for advice when a peculiar problem developed. The Palace had trees inside it, and the sparrows that nested in them constantly bespattered the visitors. Wellington's recommendation was "sparrow hawks"—trained birds that would kill the sparrows and then fly out of the building.

More than 6 million people, including streams of English schoolchildren, saw the exhibition (the Crystal Palace was dismantled after the exhibition and moved to another location, where it remained until a fire destroyed it in 1936). German princes and other dignitaries headed a long list of foreign notables and thousands of other pilgrims, all intent on seeing the wonders of the industrial age. Europeans had enjoyed a singular glimpse of the promise of technology.

CONTINENTAL INDUSTRY COMES OF AGE

Historians often speak of a "second industrial revolution" as having occurred between 1850 and 1900. Whereas the most important advances of the first industrial revolution were in textiles, iron, and the steam engine, this second phase of industrial and economic development focused on new industries—especially chemicals, steel, electricity, and, later, oil (on the latter phase of the second industrial revolution, see Part VII, Topic 17). Some scholars of technology have argued, however, that the years from 1850 to 1870 represented a distinct, preliminary stage of this second industrial revolution. In this period, an important convergence between technological adaptation and economic structure took place—that is, continental industry adopted British technology while also developing its economic institutions. Together, the two developments accounted for much of the growth experienced by the European economy.

The pace of industrialization in continental Europe between 1850 and 1873 was unprecedented. This expansion, best measured by production figures in coal, iron, textiles, and steam power, sometimes increased as much as 10 percent each year in the so-called industrial "inner zone" of France, Belgium, and Germany. Resources, government policies, political instability, and capital availability all affected the rate of growth.

Economic Growth: Wages, Prices, and Demand

The second industrial revolution took place in the context of a marked demographic change. The rapid and sustained growth in Europe's population that had accompanied the first industrial revolution slowed down considerably after 1850. The decline in births, especially in France, seems to have been due to a large degree to a conscious decision on the part of parents to limit the size of families in order to enjoy a better standard of living, as well as to a general effort to police the fertility of unmarried women more intensely. Population did continue to grow, since more and more children lived to maturity, but now at a reduced rate. Significantly, the lower birthrate did not have an adverse impact on the demand for consumer goods. On the contrary, the number of potential consumers had become less important than the volume of consumption, which rose on a per capita basis. Two factors account for this rising demand. As Europe's population aged, more emphasis was placed on industrial products than on food, and the general increase in prosperity produced rising sales. The opening of new markets overseas, especially in the United States, India, and East Asia, also stimulated demand.

Prices for both industrial goods and food generally went up between 1848 and 1873, when a long depression brought an end to this growth. Contributing to this pattern were the discovery of gold in California and Australia, which increased the money supply and investment; inflationary cycles during the Crimean War, the U.S. Civil War, and the wars of German unification; the high costs of capital investment required for

Table VII.12.1
Real Wages, 1848–1872 (1850 = 100)

YEAR	BRITAIN	FRANCE	UNITED STATES
1848	90	92	100
1850	100	100	100
1852	102	95	90
1854	96	84	88
1856	96	76	85
1858	102	100	83
1860	103	97	97
1862	105	103	86
1864	117	111	76
1866	116	111	83
1868	110	103	93
1870	118	113	120
1872	122	108	132

Adapted from Walt W. Rostow, *The World Economy: History & Prospect* (Austin and London: University of Texas Press, 1978), 157.

technological improvement and for the developing of new farmlands; and the overall rise in wages.

Despite the steady increase in prices, real wages—that is, actual purchasing power—grew in the more advanced countries. This increase in prosperity and wealth was an important spur to industrial development.

The Textile Industry

Industrialization affected the production of textiles after 1850 on the Continent as fully as it had in Britain at the opening of the century. Although heavy industry experienced more significant developments, the manufacture of textiles continued to be important because of the great demand and the huge number of workers employed in making them. Improved machinery was introduced into regions where preindustrial methods had prevailed, steam power became more widespread, and advances in chemistry were applied to the finishing of cloth, both cotton and wool.

By midcentury, Great Britain had completed its transformation to a fully mechanized textile industry. The self-acting mule—a steam-powered, fully mechanized spinning machine—had all but replaced hand-operated spinning jennies. Cotton remained the predominant fabric in terms of demand and quantity, a

position enhanced by the expanded supply of cheap raw material from the United States. The wool industry was mechanized later than cotton making, but in the 1850s it, too, changed as wool combing became a mechanical process. In the following decade improved power looms, capable of turning out a high quality fabric, had begun to be introduced almost everywhere, with the result that productivity rose sharply.

In 1843 Britain lifted the ban on the exporting of machinery. As a result, spinning machines were widely introduced in Alsace, the center of the French cotton industry, as well as in Switzerland, Germany, and even Russia. Those factories producing higher quality fabrics adopted the most technically advanced equipment. By 1870, France and Germany had made great progress in mechanization, although Britain still remained ahead: whereas the hand loom had virtually disappeared in Britain, France had only 80,000 power looms as opposed to 200,000 hand-operated looms, while Germany had 57,000 of the former type and 125,000 of the latter.

One of the most important aspects of textile manufacturing was the increase in output and the resulting decrease in production costs. Here again, Britain maintained its lead over continental regions. Compared to the best French and German factories, English mills used fewer workers—from a third to half

Women workers with a male overseer in an English mill—an idealized version of industrial labor far different from the harsher reality.

the number—to produce the same amount of spun yarn. By the 1860s, however, even on the Continent the hourly output per worker increased and the labor cost for each pound of yarn was drastically cut. One of the new wool-combing machines could turn out more than 45,000 pounds of combed wool a year, while even a good hand worker could produce less than 800 pounds.

The Expansion of Coal Production and Steam Power

Because coal was the major fuel source for 19th-century industries, the quantity produced helps to reveal the rate of industrial expansion. Between 1850 and 1870, the world's volume of coal increased almost threefold, from some 81 million tons to 213 million. Until the 1890s, when the United States began to take the lead, Britain remained the greatest coal-producing nation in the world.

Because many of France's coal deposits were of an inferior quality, one-third of its supply was imported. Many German states, however, possessed rich mineral resources, and after 1840 coal production rose rapidly. By the time of unification in 1871, Germany turned out two and a half times the amount of coal as France, and its output had reached almost a third of Britain's. The British consumption pattern, fairly typical of the period, revealed that iron makers and steam-driven factories used more than half of all British coal, while the rest went for heating, export, and as fuel in railroad engines and steamships.

For most countries, a critical problem in coal production was transportation. Many British coalfields were near the coast, so that the coal could be brought directly to ships, but in France transport costs increased the cost of coal tenfold. The exploitation of inland deposits required cheap transportation which canals and inland waterways only partially provided. It was the railroad that created a national market—that is, the condition which prevails when the price of a particular item is generally similar in all regions of a country. Once markets were easily accessible, new mines were developed in areas such as Pennsylvania, the Donets Basin, northern Britain, and the Ruhr. In the 1840s, French mining engineers discovered a major extension

of their northern coalfields, which brought production up from less than 5000 tons in 1851 to more than 2 million in 1870. In addition, a method for sinking shafts was developed in order to extract coal from deeper beds, and improvements were made in mine ventilation, water removal, and lighting.

The increase in coal supplies went hand in hand with the development of more efficient steam engines, which drove the new machinery. Great increases in horsepower were achieved by the introduction of high-pressure steam engines fitted with elaborate valve systems. The amount of steam energy generated in Europe followed the established pattern: Britain was in first place, with Germany second and France third. A French tariff on imported steam engines curtailed their adoption and French mills continued to rely on water-power years after British and German manufacturers had converted to steam. Even in Germany, only 62,000 horsepower was generated by 1855, although within 20 years it increased tenfold. World production of steam shot upward between 1850 and 1870, from some 4 million horsepower to more than 18 million.

Iron and Its Limitations

British breakthroughs in cheap iron making also moved across the channel in full force by midcentury. The Belgians were the first on the Continent to adopt British methods: instead of costly charcoal, coke was used in the blast furnace to smelt ore into cast iron. The "puddling" process, whereby the molten cast iron was constantly stirred in order to remove impurities, produced a cheap but tough wrought iron that would bend without breaking under tension (see Part VII, Topic 2). In addition, in the mid-1840s rolling mills had been designed that permitted large-scale production of iron "I" beams, which could be used in making rails for railroads.

In 1845, 90 percent of Belgian cast iron was made in coke blast furnaces. By contrast, in France, Germany, and the United States, where wood for charcoal was cheaper, the transition to coke took place much more slowly, primarily because of the shortage of good coal and the distance between the coal and iron deposits. In the 1850s, when railroads brought the two

Table VII.12.2
Coal Production (in millions of tons), 1850–1870

	BRITAIN	FRANCE	GERMANY	UNITED STATES
1850	50	4.4	6.9	2.5
1860	81	8.3	16.6	15.2
1870	112	13.3	34	42.5

A coke smelting operation in Upper Silesia in the 1840s.

materials together, France tripled its iron output within two decades. Coke smelting was introduced into Germany only in the 1840s, but the new technique took hold rapidly, and by 1862 Prussia—which accounted for most of the iron produced in the Zollverein states—was making almost 90 percent of its iron with coke.

The production of pig iron in major western areas between 1850 and 1870 increased about 70 percent each decade, with worldwide volume increasing threefold as the United States became a major producer.

Because cast iron made in coke blast furnaces was so brittle, it could be used only under compression for such items as columns, as in those of Paxton's Crystal Palace. Wrought iron was used for all purposes where tension bending was involved, such as the construction of suspension bridges. The demand for a stronger metal became intense after midcentury with the tremendous expansion of railroads throughout the Continent. The answer was steel, provided it could be made cheaply. Steel had been manufactured in limited quantities since the 18th century, but further technological breakthroughs were needed before the age of steel could be realized (see Part VII, Topic 17).

THE RAILROAD ERA

The world's first commercially successful steam railway opened in Great Britain in 1830, from Liverpool to Manchester. By 1835 the commercial benefits of the railroad had been proven, for in three hours goods could now travel the same distance that once required 36 hours on a canal. Within 20 years Britain had more than 8000 miles of rail lines that crisscrossed the country in all directions. Fifteen years later, the figure had almost doubled. Because of its small size and intense commercial activity, Britain had a traffic density on its rails greater than that of any other country.

The Railroad Boom

Britain had undergone its industrial revolution before the coming of the railroad, using waterways for moving coal and iron—the only country to have done so. On the Continent and in the United States, industrialization took place along with the development of railroads. Indeed, the two decades after 1850 saw the expansion of railroads on such a massive scale that one can speak of the "railroadization" of Western Europe.

Table VII.12.3
Pig Iron Production (in thousands of tons), 1850–1870

	BRITAIN	FRANCE	GERMANY	UNITED STATES
1850	2,285	406	210	560
1860	3,890	898	529	821
1870	6,059	1,180	1,260	1,690

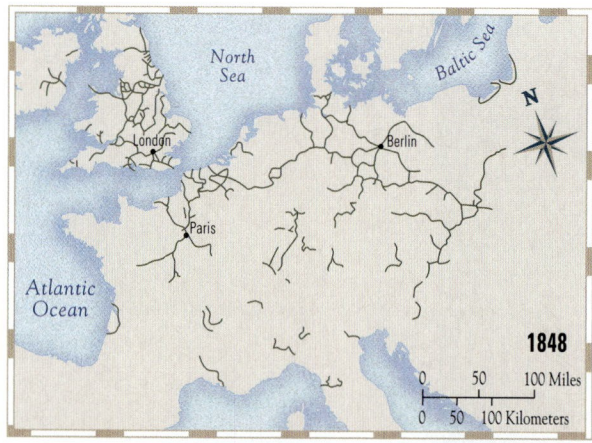

Map 12.1   The Railroad Explosion

By 1840, Belgium had essentially completed its main rail lines of more than 200 miles, whereas the much larger territories of France and Germany each had less than 400. By the end of the century, Belgium actually surpassed Britain in traffic density on its rails, in part because the Belgians built trunk lines to the German and French borders in order to attract freight headed for export to its port cities. The boom hit in the decades between 1840 and 1860, when a combination of political leadership and commercial factors pushed railroad building to the extreme. In France, an 1842 law called for close cooperation between government and private capital in realizing a national plan of trunk lines radiating from Paris. Napoleon III, a railroad enthusiast, encouraged rail construction with state support, and the Crédit Mobilier made large-scale financing possible. By 1870, France had almost 10,000 miles of rails. In Germany, after initial reluctance Prussia eventually took the lead in railroad building, and Berlin became the kingdom's rail hub. The Prussians, who paid particular attention to the military uses of the railroad, quickly outstripped France in total mileage—in 1850, German lines were already twice as long, while the main French line was completed only in 1860. On the other hand, on a per capita and area basis, the French railroad network was denser.

The Impact of the Railroad

Railroad lines were built and operated according to varying national policies. The British railroads were built with private capital, just as their turnpikes and canals had been private enterprises. Other governments either built the rail lines themselves, subsidized private enterprise, or combined these approaches. Belgium and Austria both decided on public ownership, whereas the French solution was a compromise. The state provided the land, planned the layout and prepared the roadbed, and then granted long-term leases to private companies that would run the lines.

Regardless of the particular national strategy, the impact of the railroad on economic and industrial development was enormous. It substantially lowered transportation costs and regional, national, and international markets. Railroads also stimulated the adoption of new technologies in the iron, coal, and machine engineering industries, and created a huge demand for these and other products. The need for more durable rails would act as a major inducement for the birth of the modern steel industry.

The enormous amounts of capital required to build railroads deeply affected systems of finance and business cycles in the second half of the 19th century. Railroads opened up vast new tracts of farmland, especially in the United States, where much European capital was invested. Investments in railroads, along with

Table VII.12.4
The Railroad Revolution (in miles), 1840–1870

	BRITAIN	FRANCE	GERMANY	UNITED STATES
1840	838	360	341	2,820
1850	6,620	1,890	3,640	9,020
1860	10,430	5,880	6,980	30,630
1870	15,540	9,770	11,730	53,400

This painting by Claude Monet, *Gare Saint-Lazare* (1877), was one of several treatments by the artist of the French railway station and the modern steam engine.

similar speculation in real estate, became a veritable craze at times, and widespread speculation was both the source of huge profits as well as the cause of financial panics. Investment banks were often started in order to raise capital, international loans were granted, and trading in rail bonds and stocks contributed to the rise of modern exchanges. Not less important was the fact that in many instances the capital accumulated in railroad speculation was then available for reinvestment in other industries.

The political and social consequences of railroad construction were equally far-reaching. Lines linking regions once isolated from one another contributed to the rise of national spirit and helped the process of domestic consolidation after unification. Generals rethought modern military strategy in the light of the rapid transportation of troops and war materiel now possible. Railroads encouraged the growth of cities, and changed their appearance as rail lines and stations dotted the urban landscape. Moreover, people—ordinary, working-class citizens—now had for the first time the possibility of traveling long distances at relatively modest cost, both for leisure and for work, and the railroads offered an opportunity for some to escape the inner cities and live in healthier, more pleasant suburbs.

MODERNIZING THE EUROPEAN ECONOMY: TRADE, FINANCE, AND THE CORPORATION

Two facts dominated the changing character of the European industrial economy in the period 1850–1873: technological modernization and the expansion of markets. These developments required money on a

The Great Eastern laying the transatlantic cable in 1866.

scale hitherto unknown—money to make the capital improvements dictated by the new technology, and money to operate the burgeoning industries in order to meet the production requirements of an increasingly international demand.

Barriers to European trade were generally lowered after midcentury. The formation of the Prussian-dominated Zollverein in the 1830s stimulated commercial relations in central Europe, and Great Britain moved toward free trade by the repeal of the Corn Laws in

The opening-day procession of ships through the Suez Canal, November 17, 1869.

1846. In the 1850s, international waterways such as the Danube, the Rhine, the Elbe, and the Baltic and North Seas were opened to free commerce by the elimination of levies and restrictions. But the most important move in this direction came in the following decade as a result of a series of commercial treaties between the leading industrial nations. The gradual adoption of the gold standard (see below) made international trade still easier in the latter part of the century, although the trend toward free trade was reversed after 1870.

The Rise of the Corporation

The pressures of expanding markets and industrialization meant that after 1850 business units had to be much larger than the old firms and partnerships. Joint-stock or corporate forms of business organization provided clear advantages. In joint-stock firms, a number of people pooled their capital in a common enterprise, usually with transferable shares. If incorporated, such enterprises are recognized by law as single units, or bodies (*corpora*), which can sue and be sued independently of their members. Thus, shareholders could have "limited liability" that protected their individual property.

Because unbridled speculation had resulted in a major financial crash in the early 18th century, Britain had passed the Bubble Act of 1720, which required special acts of Parliament to grant a joint-stock charter. This restriction was repealed in 1825, and further changes made it much easier to form such companies. In 1856, incorporation with limited liability became a simple matter of registration, and in the next decades France and Germany followed suit, while in the United States individual state governments chartered companies. The corporation soon became widely utilized by railroad companies in Europe and America, and by the end of the 19th century corporations took over most industries.

The Gold Standard and Banks

The rise of large corporations controlling huge assets and doing business across national boundaries created a need for new sources of money and a variety of banking institutions. In addition, the worldwide movement of capital was intensified and facilitated by the development of a new international monetary system based on gold.

As in the case of industrialization, Great Britain moved toward the gold standard before the rest of Europe. In 1821, the Bank of England made its notes convertible into gold, and the British pound sterling was guaranteed at a specific gold weight. In 1865, Belgium, France, Italy, and Switzerland formed the Latin Monetary Union, which sought to encourage a world currency system by adopting the franc as a common unit and minting coins of uniform weight in each country. Greece was the only other nation, however, to join the group, and in the 1870s the union gave up its efforts in favor of the gold standard, which the German empire had adopted in 1871. By the eve of World War I, all the other major powers had followed suit.

Despite the fact that most currencies eventually based their standard on gold, it was not the actual medium of exchange. Rather, gold became a form of reserve money, housed in banks, which in turn issued notes and bank certificates for circulation. Three kinds of banks evolved in the second half of the 19th century: central, commercial, and investment banks. Central banking came into being in Britain with the Bank Charter Act of 1844, which required that the Bank of England increase the quantity of its banknotes only if it increased its bullion reserves by the same amount. A new Issue Department received a monopoly on the printing of all future banknotes in England, while a Banking Department established a commercial checking system, which was also tied to reserves of cash and notes. Because the Banking Department maintained its reserves at from 30 to 50 percent, while smaller banks kept much smaller reserves, the Bank of England became the lender of last resort in times of emergency—in effect, a kind of bankers' bank.

The Bank of France, founded by Napoleon Bonaparte in 1800, received a monopoly on the issue of banknotes in 1848. Although the bank was privately owned, the government maintained close supervision of its activities, and it, too, kept high levels of reserves to support its notes. In Germany, central banking began when the Bank of Prussia, established in 1846, was converted into the Reichsbank in 1875. Both the Bank of France and the Reichsbank served an important business function by discounting bills of exchange (that is, exchanging them for cash), and established numerous branch banks for that purpose.

Unlike central banks, the chief function of commercial banks is to serve commerce and industry directly by providing short-term loans to businesses. Commercial banks became joint-stock companies in the 19th century, and tended toward a high degree of monopoly: the so-called "Big Five" (Barclays, Lloyds, Midland, National Provincial, and Westminister) dominated British commercial banking, while four firms—including Crédit Lyonnais and Société Générale—monopolized most of French commercial banking, and the Big Four "D" banks—such as the Deutsche Bank and the Dresdner Bank—controlled such operations in Germany.

Investment banks, on the other hand, were concerned principally with extending long-term credit in the form of stocks and bonds. Investment banks arose in order to provide capital for plants and equipment for railroads and large industrial firms. In the early 19th century the principal "investment" bank of Europe was really the House of Rothschild, which engaged mainly in financing government loans. Five brothers operated the firm, one in each of five major cities—Frankfurt, London, Paris, Vienna, and Naples. These and other international bankers facilitated the financing of railroads by marketing stocks and bonds.

Yet such investment banks tended to be cautious in underwriting new industries, and by the mid-19th century other avenues were needed. Napoleon III, unhappy over his dealings with the Rothschilds, promoted one of the most interesting experiments in investment banking—the Crédit Mobilier. Founded by the Pereire Brothers in 1852, it accumulated capital by selling its own stocks and bonds, and then lending the capital to make long-term loans to start new businesses; once the firms were established, the Crédit Mobilier would also sell the securities of the new enterprises to investors. It was highly successful for a time in promoting railroads, utilities, and industrial firms. Given the nature of its operations, the Crédit Mobilier was vulnerable in financial crises because it had little liquid assets. The company went bankrupt in 1867 and was liquidated in 1871. Similar institutions were established in Germany in the 1850s and in Britain in the following decade. Even the Rothschilds joined the trend, establishing the Credit-Anstalt in Austria. Later the American investment banks of J. P. Morgan and Kuhn, Loeb and Co. were to become giants on the international banking scene.

The national and international money markets established between 1850 and 1873 played a critical role in the industrialization of the Continent. The capital raised, invested, and circulated by these new banking institutions provided the financial basis for the remarkable growth of the European industrial economy, particularly in the decades after 1870, and in the creation of a global capitalist system.

The 20 years after 1850 represented an important phase of maturation for the European economy. The essentials of the industrialization process had reached the Continent. The growth rate maintained generally high levels as production in textiles, coal, and iron rose steadily—and sometimes dramatically.

The revolution in transportation, caused chiefly by the railroad, deeply affected every aspect of European civilization, from industrial and financial growth and market expansion to the shape of cities and the way in which millions of people led their daily lives. Along with the equally far-reaching revolution in banking and business organization, the railroads pointed the way toward an age of capitalist enterprise in which the links between technology, heavy industry, and the world of finance grew increasingly close.

As industrial and agricultural profits reached new heights in this era, the wealth of Europe was reflected in the improvement of real wages and living standards. Rather than a sign of crisis, the declining birthrate meant the emergence of new patterns of consumption and higher levels of comfort for many Europeans. The Great Exhibition of 1851, with which the period opened, symbolized the beginning of an age of enthusiastic and self-conscious materialism for European civilization.

Questions for Further Study

1. How did technology transform the European economy in the 19th century?

2. How did the development of railroads influence industrial and economic policy?

3. To what conditions did the rise of the corporations respond?

Suggestions for Further Reading

Ashworth, William. *An Economic History of England, 1870–1939.* London, 1960.

Cameron, Rondo. *A Concise Economic History of the World.* New York, 1989.

Carter, E. C., et al., eds. *Enterprise and Entrepreneurs in Nineteenth and Twentieth Century France.* Baltimore, MD, 1976.

Henderson, William O. *The Rise of German Industrial Power, 1834–1914.* Berkeley, CA, 1975.

Hobsbawm, Eric J. *The Age of Capital, 1848–1875.* New York, 1979.

Landes, David. *The Unbound Prometheus: Technological Change and Industrial Development in Western Europe from 1750 to the Present.* Cambridge, MA, 1969.

Milward, Alan S., and S. B. Saul. *The Development of the Economies of Continental Europe, 1850–1914.* Cambridge, MA, 1977.

Trebilcock, Clive. *The Industrialization of the Continent.* New York, 1981.

Topic 13

Middle-Class Values and Working-Class Realities

y the mid-19th century, the focus of European life had decisively shifted from the country to industrial cities. In this urban context the aristocracy slowly lost some of its traditional authority, while the middle classes, involved in trade and industry, grew in wealth and power. Bourgeois attitudes toward work and private life established a norm for all levels of society.

At the bottom of the social scale, the condition of the workers and urban poor seemed, if anything, even worse than that of agricultural laborers. Yet the sheer concentration of their numbers, and the manifest unfairness of their grim living conditions, led to pressure for reform. In some cases governments spontaneously tried to correct social and economic injustices; in others, public protest was needed to produce results. At any event, all classes of society were compelled to adjust to the new problems and pleasures offered by city life.

The moral tone of the midcentury was set by those who had gained most from the confrontations of earlier years: the middle classes. From the security of their financial independence, manufacturers, merchants, and professionals praised the virtues of hard work, honesty, and self-reliance. Material success, they claimed, could be achieved by combining these merits with a healthy dose of personal ambition. The high self-image sustained by the bourgeoisie was accompanied by a rigid code of behavior, laying out the duties of public and private conduct.

At the heart of the middle-class worldview lay the family. The house itself, with its furniture and decorations, provided the setting for domestic life and was defined as women's narrowly circumscribed sphere of influence. By contrast all other activities were largely restricted to men. Thus bourgeois women were enshrined at the center of a cult whose effects on all aspects of their lives were claustrophobic.

Such an idealizing vision did not, of course, apply to the whole range of 19th-century society. Even within the middle classes, there were rebels. The mid-1850s saw the formation of some of the earliest feminist groups. For many of the working-class poor, living in urban squalor, the bourgeois prescription for domestic happiness was meaningless. By the middle of the century, charity workers and social reformers had begun to attack some of the more basic problems. Public health, working conditions, education, and housing were all the subject of increasing government action. Progress was slow, in part because the continued rapid growth of the cities compounded the difficulties.

Pressure for reform began to come not only from middle-class humanitarians but also from the working classes themselves. Earlier worker protests had lacked a coherent sense of direction. In the mid-19th century the cause of the rights of the working class was given a philosophical basis and powerful expression in the writings of Karl Marx. His aggressive socialist vision of a newly ordered society, first published on the eve of the 1848 revolutions, prepared the way for the working-class parties which played a growing role in late-19th-century politics.

THE URBANIZATION OF EUROPE

The rapid transformation of European life from an agricultural to an urban society had begun in the early 19th century, spurred by industrialization and a quickly rising population (on urbanization between 1800 and 1850, see Part VII, Topic 6). In the two decades after 1850, the trend continued, but with some differences. Earlier the most dramatic urban growth had occurred in British towns, where industrial development had been concentrated. Although urban growth continued in Great Britain, after midcentury the pace of development there slowed down. It was on the Continent, and especially in German cities, that the most startling increase in urban populations took place along with the spread of industrialization. In Berlin, for example, the number of inhabitants doubled between 1850 and 1870 from some 400,000 to more than 800,000. In London during the same period, however, the population grew by little more than 40 percent, from 2,685,000 to 3,890,000.

The Social Impact of Cities

Despite its uneven character, urban growth, especially in western Europe, continued to produce revolutionary changes in social customs and patterns. By the 1870s, almost a third of all Europeans, regardless of class, gender, or income, lived in cities. Some of these were capitals that combined manufacturing and government offices, as in the cases of London and Berlin, while others were major industrial centers, such as Glasgow and Düsseldorf. In most cases the problems of urban life were the same.

The consequences of so vast and rapid a change in the lifestyles of millions of people were naturally complex and far-reaching. Viewed from the perspective of the late 20th century, with its fears of urban chaos and collapse, it is tempting to accentuate the drawbacks of city life at the expense of its very real benefits. Widespread application of new technologies and improved medical methods benefited increasing numbers of people. The continual growth of national prosperity helped to underwrite public welfare programs. Furthermore, the rise in the general level of education created a wider

Map 13.1 European Urbanization, 1860

Table VII.13.1
The Growth of European Cities (in thousands), 1850–1870

CITY	1850	1870
Berlin	419	826
Glasgow	345	522
Hamburg	132	240
London	2,685	3,890
Moscow	365	612
Paris	1,053	1,852
Rome	175	244
Sheffield	135	240
Vienna	444	834

citement of metropolitan existence. One visitor to Paris called it "a glass beehive, a treat to the student of humanity"—the essence of existence there was "the consciousness of being observed."

Yet inevitably behind the passing scene there lay the other side of city life: grinding poverty, overcrowding, squalor. Nor were such conditions limited to the northern industrial cities. When the novelist Charles Dickens (see Part VII, Topic 14) first arrived in the Italian city of Genoa in 1844, he was horrified at "the unusual smells, the unaccountable filth, the disorderly jumbling of dirty houses, one upon the roofs of another. I never, in my life, was so dismayed!" Conditions had little changed 20 years later. Many agricultural workers drawn from declining rural centers by the hope of making their fortunes in the cities found themselves drifting into marginal jobs: rag picking, scissor grinding, collecting human excrement. Others took to crime. More fortunate were those who found employment in domestic service, thanks to the growing demand of prosperous middle-class householders for servants. Nor did urban existence always prove fulfilling in social terms. One migrant to London described it as "a wilderness of human beings."

Dealing with the problems of expanding communities was complicated by a number of factors. Many provincial towns had drawn their prosperity from travelers on the old coaching routes, which had been busy for

audience for intellectual debate and cultural entertainment.

At a more mundane level, great cities like London, Paris, or Vienna provided public gardens, fireworks, and dance halls, pleasures that were easily accessible to the working class. The infinite variety of daily experience, street entertainments ranging from Moroccan dancers to mechanical men, the "busy idleness" of the throngs of people, all offered novelty to those who flocked from the provinces to enjoy the ex-

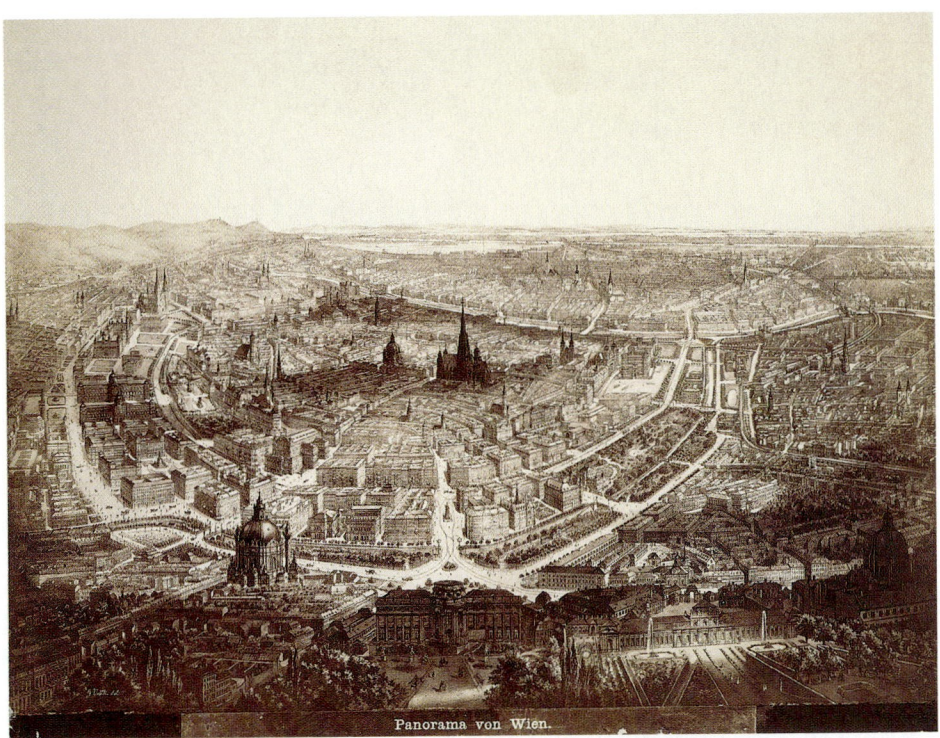

The expanding cities of late 19th-century Europe encompassed large areas beyond the historical core. Here is a bird's-eye view of Vienna.

a century or more. With the coming of the railroads, the economies of these centers collapsed overnight. Their populations abandoned them and poured into the big cities, providing yet another wave of homeless migrants.

The faster people crowded into the cities, the worse their conditions became. At the same time increasing industrial production created ever greater pollution, especially in the great mining and textile cities. "Muck means money," one Manchester cotton manufacturer is said to have observed. For his employees it also meant blackened windows, clothes, and lungs. The general replacement of wood by coal as a means of heating increased pollution further; it also meant that those who could not afford to buy coal lived in cold, damp conditions, with inevitable consequences for their health. In rural communities, on the other hand, firewood was collected routinely and at no expense as a natural resource.

Further difficulties were presented by the urgent need for urban planning. Some big industrial and commercial cities began to grow only in the late 18th century; they included the manufacturing centers of the Midlands and northern England, the Ruhr district of northern Germany, and Madrid. In these, at least, coherent planning was theoretically possible. Athens, one of the oldest cities in Europe, is the only European capital whose present center was laid out in the 19th century. After centuries of neglect under the Turks, the city was completely rebuilt by the German architects whom Otto (ruled 1832–1862), the first king of independent Greece, brought with him from Bavaria.

Most of the chief 19th-century cities, however, had been centers of population for centuries. Those of Medieval foundation frequently still had their city walls intact, adding to the complexity of organized expansion. Baron Haussmann's rebuilding of Paris during

Map 13.2 European Nationalities

In the countryside, poverty and primitive conditions still prevailed widely in many parts of Europe—here in a Russian village.

the Second Empire (see Part VII, Topic 9) had involved the demolition of Medieval quarters. Similarly, in 1865, in trying to adapt Florence to its new, although temporary, role as capital of united Italy, the architect Giuseppe Poggi chose the drastic solution of demolishing virtually the whole of the city's circuit of Medieval walls, and replacing them with broad avenues. Later generations severely criticized Poggi's decision, but its radical nature illustrates the seriousness of the problem he and other town planners faced. Haussmann's work in Paris inspired a similar project in Vienna, where walls were torn down to make way for the famous *Ringstrasse* in the 1870s.

Further difficulties lay in anticipating and providing for the new needs of urban life. The arrival of the railways required that cities be organized around station terminals and the various branch lines. Increased street traffic made it necessary to build wide avenues and to separate pedestrians and vehicles by constructing sidewalks. By the end of the 19th century, when it was clear that still more transport facilities were needed, subway systems were begun in London and Paris. Underground sewers and waterpipes had to be laid—the ancient Romans had both almost 2000 years earlier, but their use died out with the decline of the Roman Empire. Streets needed lighting, and garbage collection had to be organized.

With the increase in crime, city police forces were vastly expanded. Until the 19th century, order was generally maintained by the military. The police served principally as government spies, on the lookout for those regarded as opponents of the regime. As property holders came to demand protection, and the anonymous crowds of the big cities needed controlling, the police began to serve as maintainers of civic order. Sir Robert Peel, it will be recalled, established the first British police force in London in 1820 (see Part VII, Topic 9).

The teeming cities of 19th-century Europe provided the stage on which the political and social battles of the remainder of the century were fought: the struggle for the suffrage, women's rights, and social justice.

VICTORIAN VIRTUES: THE THEORY AND PRACTICE OF THE BOURGEOISIE

The attitudes to life developed by the prosperous middle classes in western Europe are often summed up under the general term "Victorian." "Victorian morality" is practically synonymous with a rigidly puritan lifestyle, involving pure women and upright men, whose duty was to produce children to serve the public good. Living in respectable homes, gathering daily for family prayers, spending their Sundays in decorous inactivity, Victorian families often seem to have lived in numbing respectability. The outward impression is of stern and decisive husbands and fathers, and women trapped as tightly in their domestic role as they were in the whalebone and steel corsets they wore.

Victorian Religion

The age was marked by a revival in religious observance, especially among women, who attended church services more regularly than men. What little opportunity middle-class wives, in particular, had for lives outside the home was often found in prayer societies and charitable organizations. In Catholic countries, including France and Italy, women who seemed unlikely to marry often entered convents; indeed, in the eyes of many, a cloistered life was the only respectable alternative to marriage. One of the most important aspects of child raising was religious education: the catechism, prayer, and regular church attendance.

The virtues which the devout hoped to encourage in their families were those that would maintain a tranquil home life. Children were taught to accept their destiny, forgive their enemies, and help those less fortunate than themselves. A home strengthened

Queen Victoria, Prince Albert, and their children (1846)—the idealized "Victorian" family.

by these would, in turn, serve as protection against the snares of the world outside: impiety, greed, and, most dangerous of all, sexual immorality. As for the poor, who clearly had little chance of enjoying the benefits of domestic bliss, they could best be helped by the distribution of hot soup and improving religious tracts.

So determined a program of self-denial and gloom did not make for an agreeable existence. Florence Nightingale (1820–1910), the "Lady with the Lamp" who revolutionized the care of the sick, wrote that "Life is a hard fight, a struggle, a wrestling with the Principle of Evil."

Yet the conventional version of bourgeois life provides a very one-sided impression of 19th-century society. The battle to maintain such exalted standards of virtue was probably won by only a few. Even at the time, the traditional picture of Victorian morality was recognized for what it was: a decorous façade behind which life remained as varied as it had always been. The young Queen Victoria grew up at a time when London's social life was dominated by luxurious whores and dissolute dandies, yet in the same years, Thomas Bowdler produced an edition of Shakespeare censored for family reading (the term *bowdlerized* derives from his name), and the Society for the Suppression of Vice was founded; the English wit Sydney Smith (1771–1845) suggested that this latter should have been called the Society for Suppressing the Vices of Persons Whose Income Does Not Exceed Five Hundred Pounds per Annum.

The "Necessary Evil"

Loose living and zealous puritanism continued to coexist throughout Victoria's reign. The spread of bourgeois propriety did nothing to decrease prostitution in the period after 1850. An English clergyman remarked in 1858 that England was "the most religious in pretension but in reality the most immoral and licentious under the sun." One source in 1857 claimed that the number of prostitutes in London was around 80,000, an estimate generally accepted by contemporary observers. If each prostitute received only 25 customers a week, the number of weekly male visits to a prostitute amounted to some 2 million—in a city whose total male population was about 1,300,000. Along with the British Museum and Buckingham Palace, the city's elegantly dressed courtesans were among its principal tourist attractions.

A phenomenon so widespread could hardly be ignored or concealed, and bourgeois society debated at length both prostitution and other social problems, including child abuse, alcoholism, infanticide, wife beating, and a thriving subculture of pornography. In the case of prostitution, some governments intervened. In 1860 Cavour introduced to the new nation of Italy a system of state control which he had worked out in Sardinia. Based on the assumption that prostitution was a "necessary evil," it regulated dress, living conditions, and the scale of payments. Cavour's system became popular with its clients, and by 1880 almost two-thirds of Italian prostitutes worked in officially regulated "closed houses," with the women having regular health controls. Legalized prostitution in Italy was abolished only in the 1950s.

Throughout the 1860s and 1870s, social reformers in France and Germany tried to construct brothels along the same humanitarian lines as hospitals or factories. The overwhelming majority of those employed in them were working-class women. Their purpose and justification were twofold: to free middle-class (and other) men from excessive passion, so that they could return purged to a tranquil domestic life, and to guarantee the virtue of pure women.

High society had its own share of courtesans. One of the most famous and admired was the French Marie Duplessis (1824–1847). Fragile and melancholy in appearance, she was described by one admirer as "a young woman of exquisite distinction, a pure and delicate type of beauty." Among her first conquests was the Prince de Bidache, who was to become Napoleon III's foreign minister. Her affair with the dramatist Alexandre Dumas *fils* (1824–1895), and her subsequent premature death of tuberculosis at the age of 23, inspired his play *The Lady of the Camellias*, which in turn formed the basis of the opera *La Traviata* by Giuseppe Verdi (see Part VII, Topic 14). In both play and opera, the heroine dies in poverty. The real-life character earned enough in her short career to leave quantities of jewelry, silver and porcelain, furniture, works of art, a horse and carriage, and a pony. The sale of her estate after her death took four days, and realized almost 100,000 francs.

The Bourgeoisie at Table

If state control and the laws of the marketplace took care of one basic human appetite, middle-class households became increasingly adept at satisfying another one. During the period from 1830 to 1865, the midday meal developed into the major social occasion of daily life, with children and governess taking their place at the parents' table. Preceded by a lavish breakfast and a glass of wine with a biscuit in the middle of the morning, lunch became a hot meal—it had previously consisted of a cold collation. Working-class men frequently could not return home at midday, and a hot supper was generally kept for them.

Outside the house, the middle classes sought to maintain the same practice of formal meals. Honoré de Balzac, the realistic novelist of French life (see Part VII, Topic 14), describes the menu of two young men of fortune in a Paris restaurant: six dozen oysters, six veal cutlets, a chicken, a lobster mayonnaise, peas, and a mushroom patty, washed down with three bottles of Bordeaux and three of Champagne. Even boarding schools provided lavish spreads. In September 1853, the French Ministry of Public Education circulated a list of standard meals to be served in state institutions,

organized by days of the week. On Tuesdays, lunch consisted of meat soup, boiled beef, veal or mutton stew, poultry or game in pastry, and cold pâtés, while at dinner—a lighter meal, as was customary by midcentury—roast mutton and stewed fruit were served.

Thus behind the theoretical austerity and self-sacrifice of the bourgeois ideal, the middle classes used their growing prosperity to live in as much comfort as possible. As the century progressed, furthermore, new discoveries made it possible to extend life's pleasures and conveniences to the less prosperous. Mechanized manufacturing processes made cheap shoes and clothing widely available. The wealthy had their clothes made for them, but their income was often based on the mass production and sale of ready-made garments, known as "reach-me-downs," stacked on the shelves of clothing stores. In the 1870s new processes of food preservation were developed, including canning and bottling. In 1870 margarine was invented and became a substitute for those who could not afford butter—twice the price—or fat drippings. A decade earlier, in 1860, the invention of the earth closet provided a more healthy sanitary system. The absence of drains meant that water closets did not become widespread, even in middle-class homes, until the turn of the century. The first water closets in Manchester appeared in 1898.

While preaching resignation and simplicity, the middle classes schemed and planned to lead lives of ever-increasing complexity. Yet the façade of Victorian virtue certainly had its effects, and claimed its victims. Its central tenet, the sanctity of the home and family, left women trapped in performing an increasingly burdensome role.

WOMEN AND THE CULT OF DOMESTICITY

Middle-class morality revolved around a basic principle. In the midst of social ferment and political revolution, the privacy of domestic family life, presided over by women, offered protection and tranquillity. Raising their children and looking after their homes, wives and mothers would fulfill their natural function. This simple belief served in practice to reinforce a whole series of prejudices, and to bolster the high self-esteem of the new bourgeoisie.

In the first place, the cult of domesticity drew immediate attention to the greatest strength of the middle classes: their strong financial position. The working class and the poor were automatically excluded from being home owners, while many of the aristocracy were forced to reduce their expenditures, in part because of

A photograph, around 1860, depicting women's place in the cult of domesticity.

their unwillingness to engage in commercial ventures. In any case, those great lords or princes who still maintained estates or palaces lived in splendor and opulence, but hardly in comfort. A middle-class home was intended to impress not by its frescoes or the grandeur of its salons, but by the convenience and ease of its appointments. Far more important than the possession of ancient treasures was the latest plumbing device or heating system. By comparison with the gilded elegance of the 18th century, 19th-century furniture was solid, and the chairs and couches stuffed—even overstuffed.

If their homes provided one way of defining their position, the difference between the lifestyles of middle-class and working-class women offered a second. The latter were compelled by necessity to seek labor, whether in factories or in the kitchens of bourgeois families, or in the brothels that served, paradoxically, to maintain middle-class respectability. They spent considerable time away from their own families, in the case of those in domestic service actually living in the houses of strangers. Working women often exchanged their freedom from the repression they had left behind at home for other forms of tyranny at the hands of their employers.

Bourgeois women, by contrast, were virtually forbidden to work, or to spend significant amounts of time away from home. Indeed, the more their status came to depend on their inactivity, the more the idea of an actively employed woman became discouraged. Thus the financial progress of the middle classes left bourgeois women theoretically superior, but in practice even less free than ever.

The exaltation of domesticity reinforced the controlling role of bourgeois husbands and fathers, for whose benefit the whole system operated. By entrusting the care of the home, although not the physical labor there, to their womenfolk, Victorian males assured themselves a monopoly on all other forms of activity: business, finance, higher education, politics, and public life. The only appropriate interests for women in public life, such as philanthropy and moral reform, evoked their maternal role. The cult of domesticity consisted of a means to occupy the time, or at least some of it, of urban middle-class women, and keep them safely trapped at home.

If women's sphere—or, as one writer described it, "kingdom"—was the home, they needed guidance in administering it. Handbooks on the new "domestic science" began to circulate widely. One of the most successful was the *Book of Household Management* (1861), by Isabella Beaton (1836–1865). Her advice on hiring and managing the servants, supervising the household accounts, and a host of bewildering social customs (the use of finger bowls, for example) was read, if not always followed, by more than one generation of Victorian housewives. She also provided information on hygiene and health, and on legal issues. Most important of all, she helped her readers to keep their husbands at home by maintaining an agreeable atmosphere and pleasing them with tasty, nourishing meals. The world of restaurants and clubs, a specifically male preserve, was seen as a potential threat to domestic peace.

The Feminist Movement

Not all 19th-century women accepted the role assigned to them. In some cases, however, the form their protest took was a tacit acknowledgement of the advantages in being a man. The French novelist George Sand (Aurore Dudevant) dressed as a man, and smoked cigars and a pipe. George Eliot (Mary Ann Evans), one of the leading literary figures of Victorian England, refused to marry the man with whom she lived, while her French contemporary, Daniel Stern (Marie d'Agoult), gave birth to several illegitimate children (whose father was the composer Franz Liszt). All three of these unconventional women wrote novels, which they published under male pseudonyms (on these authors and the novels they wrote, see Part VII, Topic 14).

A far greater threat to male supremacy was posed by the emergence, in midcentury England and America, of an organized feminist movement. In a general sense, feminism arose as a result of the social changes produced by industrialization, which had pushed countless women into the workforce. In a more immediate sense, however, middle-class women rebelled against the repressive limitations of the cult of domesticity. This was the theme of *A Doll's House* (1879), by the Norwegian playwright Henrik Ibsen (1828–1906): its heroine, a repressed housewife who leaves her husband for the challenges of the larger world outside marriage, shocked middle-class audiences of the day.

Like Ibsen's character, many bourgeois women resisted their exclusion from the world beyond the home, although in less dramatic ways. Women tried, for example, to find more meaningful lives by putting their time and energies into religious and charitable activities. Both American and British women joined the abolitionist cause, and after 1850 volunteered in ever-larger numbers to work in hospitals and working-class slums. By the end of the century, women were gravitating toward careers in nursing, teaching, and social work.

Participation in campaigns against slavery increased female consciousness of their own oppression. An important step in this direction came in 1840, when delegates to an international antislavery congress gathered in London. The American abolitionist Elizabeth Cady Stanton (1815–1902) and the other women present were outraged when they were required to observe the proceedings from an upstairs gallery, separated off from the male delegates. In 1848, Mrs. Lucretia Mott (1793–1880) joined Stanton in spearheading the first women's rights convention, which met in Seneca Falls, New York. The participants announced a "Declaration of Sentiments" that demanded equal rights to divorce, to own property, and to hold jobs, as well as to vote.

These demands were echoed by early British feminists, particularly Barbara Smith Bodichon (1827–1891), whose London address gave their organization its name: the Langdon Place Group. The *English Women's Journal*, which she helped to found, led to the creation of an employment agency in order to help women find jobs. By the 1860s, feminist groups had begun the long battle for the vote. Among their supporters was John Stuart Mill (see Part VII, Topic 9), who published his famous essay, *On the Subjection of Women*, in 1869, two years after Parliament had rejected a motion to extend the suffrage to women. Ironically, many of the leading opponents of the female franchise were Liberals, who feared that women would mainly vote for the Conservatives.

On the Continent, the cause of feminism advanced much more slowly. In France, Napoleon III was hostile to feminism, which he regarded as another form of revolution. The prominent working-class leader Pierre-Joseph Proudhon (see Part VII, Topic 19) actually opposed women's rights, asserting that women's physical, mental, and moral inferiority justified their being restricted to the home. Nor did the Society to Claim the Rights of Women, founded in France in the 1860s, advocate radical change, but rather continued in the broadly utopian traditions of Saint-Simon. Nevertheless, a real feminist movement under the leadership of Juliette Lamber and Jenny d'Hercourt did operate as a kind of underground political opposition to the repressive policies of the Second Empire. In the German states, Louise Otto-Peters (1819–1895) headed the All German Women's Union, formed in 1865, and founded the feminist newspaper *Neue Bahnen* (New Roads), which proclaimed that "Work, liberating and liberated work, is the motto of our organization."

Italian feminists were among many whose high hopes in unification were disappointed by subsequent events. Indeed, with the introduction of the Napoleonic Code, women lost many of the rights they had possessed under the previous Austrian administration. Nor was Cavour's official regulation of prostitution greeted with any enthusiasm by feminists who had fought in Garibaldi's army to liberate their people. Anna Maria Mozzoni (1837–1920), the best-known feminist in Italy, criticized the laws that regulated women's rights and family relations and attacked the Catholic Church. She also translated Mill's *On the Subjection of Women*. In 1868, Italian feminists began publishing *La Donna* (Woman), a newspaper that advocated Mazzini's notion of women as citizen-mothers.

Progress during the years from 1850 to 1870 was slow, yet the early feminists succeeded in establishing their cause as of fundamental importance in social and political reform. Together with that of universal suffrage, it became one of the central issues of public life in the late 19th and early 20th century (on feminism after 1870, see Part VII, Topic 19).

THE URBAN POOR AND SOCIAL REFORM

Unlike the middle classes, the working-class urban population seemed to have gained little from the industrial revolution. Many had given up the bare livelihood of a rural existence for the even grimmer task of scraping a living in overcrowded and polluted cities. Those engaged in work in middle-class homes were able to contrast their lot with that of their employers. Others could see the shops filled with luxury goods, and the

An urban working-class slum in Yorkshire, England.

An English classroom in the mid-19th century with working-class children of both sexes.

streets crowded with carriages. City life made class differences only too visible.

The struggle to improve the conditions of the poor was a long one, fraught with setbacks. In Great Britain, a system of poor relief administered by local counties added to wages that were below subsistence. The Poor Law of 1834, passed after much controversy, took a different approach. In order to make public assistance unappealing, paupers and unemployed were required to live in workhouses, where conditions were minimal and treatment harsh. As late as 1900 in Britain, then the most prosperous country in the world, one out of every five people received a pauper's funeral.

The problem lay partly, as we have seen, in the speed and complexity of urban growth. Another factor was the lack of sympathy on the part of artisans and the more successful workers, who saw the urban poor as a threat to their own upward mobility. Those who could see their way to social advancement eagerly accepted middle-class notions of property as the only real indication of status. As a result, they had little time for those with no hope of escape from the squalor of poverty, with its slums and chronic alcoholism. Middle-class attitudes blamed poverty on the poor themselves.

By the end of the century, working-class support for social reform at the bottom of the scale began to grow, in part due to the politicization of workers' movements. In the 1850s and 1860s, however, the poor were mainly dependent on government actions and the charity of middle-class benefactors.

Living Standards in Second Empire Paris

Even among the urban masses, there were wide divergences of income and lifestyles. In the Paris of Napoleon III, the average worker earned two francs 50 centimes a day, and a meal in a cheap, working-class tavern cost just over a franc. Those employed in the lower ranks of domestic service, such as footmen or maids, were paid 60 to 70 francs a month in addition to their board and lodging. A master chef or the chief butler could receive up to 200 francs a month.

Lower down in the scale were those who barely got by. Bernard D. was a laborer who had migrated to Paris from rural Lorraine. In 1859 he was supporting himself, his wife, and six of his fifteen children; two other children lived at home but worked, contributing part of their earnings to the family; the remaining seven children were independent. The family's total income for that year, including the earnings of the two working dependents, was 1612 francs, of which 200 went for rent. That left about 115 francs a month to support ten people. Their annual expenditure on meat was 70 francs, most of which was spent on two kilos of ox head a week; cooked in water, it provided soup and boiled meat.

At least the family was self-supporting. Many Parisian residents depended for their survival on charitable contributions. In December 1856 an appeal was circulated in the 1st *arrondissement* (district) of Paris: "More urgently than ever before, we solicit charitable offerings for the relief of many poor folk." The number of the destitute in this single district in danger of dying of starvation was listed as 4839.

Private Charity

The appeal described above was made by the city administration, but the most common form of relief was that provided by private organizations, whose numbers multiplied rapidly by midcentury. By the 1850s, over 450 charitable groups were operating in London. Many charities were inspired by religious motives. The Society of St. Vincent de Paul, founded in Paris in 1835, was active throughout France, Italy, Spain, and the Catholic parts of the Austrian empire. Its members, successful, educated men, were required to visit the poor and improve their lot both by financial help and by teaching them thrift. In addition to benefiting the needy, organizations such as this did much to inform the better-off of the terrible conditions of many of their fellow citizens.

The Society of St. Vincent de Paul was unusual in that its membership was restricted to men. The overwhelming majority of those engaged in practical charitable work were middle- and upper-class women. Often inspired by religious motives, they tried to establish direct personal contact with those from whom they were isolated both psychologically and physically—middle-class residential areas were kept at a distance from the poorer parts of cities. In addition to fulfilling Christian teachings of charity towards all, their work also became an extension of their domestic role, expressing "the flow of maternal love," applied to a broader notion of family.

In some cases the contribution was financial. The English philanthropist Angela Burdett-Coutts (1814–1906) donated over 3 million pounds for charitable purposes. In others the founding of an organization led to wide-ranging consequences. The Bible and Domestic Female Mission Society, created in London by Ellen Ranyard (1814–1879), sold Bibles and other religious works, and used the profits to help the needy. The Society grew rapidly, and became an important relief force. A similar organization was founded in Hamburg, the Female Association for the Care of the Poor and the Sick.

Others had more specific goals. In France, maternal societies provided help to mothers in need; during the Second Empire, the Empress Eugénie became actively involved in their work. Around 1850 the Italian reformer Laura Mantegazza established day care centers for the children of working mothers, and a few years later set up schools for the illiterate. In Spain, Concepción Arenal (1820–1893) campaigned for prison reform, and also wrote a guide for those engaged in charitable work, *The Visitor of the Poor* (1860).

The active participation of so many women in relief work made an enormous contribution to public welfare at a time when government aid was limited. It also caused many to question the bourgeois assumptions that lay behind the cult of domesticity. After seeing the conditions under which the poor lived, it was difficult to return unchanged to their material comforts, often enjoyed at the expense of others. Furthermore, women came to realize that, far from being helpless and best confined to the home, they could play a vital part in producing social reform. The growing sense of their own powers helped to inspire the movement for female suffrage later in the century.

KARL MARX AND THE VISION OF A NEW SOCIAL ORDER

One of the chief aims of 19th-century reformers was to redress social injustice. Those who had most to gain from reform—the workers and the needy—were in no doubt about their own plight, but for the first half of the century they were unable to articulate their case. When working-class protests were heard, they were often misdirected or unsustained. The Luddites' destruction of machinery (see Part VII, Topic 2) did nothing to hold back the industrial revolution. The Chartists mounted a more organized campaign but failed to carry it through.

What was lacking was an overarching vision of the radical social reordering needed to change the entrenched system. The middle class was too satisfied with its victories to theorize about the rights of others, and the establishment certainly had no interest in overturning an order of which they were the chief beneficiaries. When serious and sustained workers' protests did finally make themselves heard, toward the end of the century, they were based on a worldview derived in large measure from the writings of Karl Marx and his collaborator, Friedrich Engels (see Part VII, Topic 8).

Both men came from prosperous middle-class families, although Marx's financial position deteriorated with the death of his father. After studying at the universities of Bonn and Berlin, and obtaining a doctorate from the University of Jena, Marx—already a radical in his ideas—took up journalism. Hoping to be able to influence contemporary society, in 1842 he be-

Karl Marx and one of his three daughters. Note the cross hanging from her neck.

came editor of *The Rhineland Gazette*, a well-known liberal newspaper. Within a year his articles had won him the enmity of the Prussian government and of his own publishers, and he moved to Paris, the center in continental Europe of political exiles and radical debate.

There he renewed an earlier friendship with Engels, who had firsthand experience of the appalling conditions under which industrial workers lived. The Engels family owned a cotton mill near Manchester, and Engels wrote a searing account of his observations there, *The Condition of the Working Class in England* (see Part VII, Topic 6). Marx and Engels joined forces to diagnose the cause of society's ills, and to provide a prescription for their cure. On the eve of the revolutions of 1848 they published the *Communist Manifesto*. At the time the work made little impression, and with the end of the revolution in Paris, Marx made his way to London. He lived there in exile for the rest of his life, continuing his collaboration with Engels, who also provided him with financial support. The first volume of *Das Kapital* appeared in 1867; Engels edited the other two volumes (1885, 1894) after Marx's death.

The *Communist Manifesto*

Marx and Engels intended their work to accomplish two ends: to explain the nature of contemporary society by looking back to the pattern of European history, and to provide a practical means for correcting its faults. Thus the *Manifesto* is at the same time a broad philosophical statement and a handbook to revolution.

The Marxist theory of history takes its departure from the ideas of the German philosopher Georg Hegel (see Part VII, Topic 7). Hegel believed that "dialectic"—the clash of ideas in thesis and antithesis—would lead to a "synthesis," and that this resolution of conflict would mark a new stage in historical evolution. The clashing ideas were purely intellectual, however, and the resolution would always be a positive one. Rejecting Hegel's abstraction, Marx claimed that history was propelled forward by conflict not over ideas, but over economic interests, and that all aspects of society were determined by materialist factors, in particular by the means of production.

This "dialectical materialism" was responsible for changes in the past. The economy of the Middle Ages had been dependent upon the feudal system, whereby large numbers of serfs worked for a small, landowning, hereditary aristocracy. With the rise of commerce and trade, a new middle class began to develop. The "dialectic," or struggle, between aristocracy and middle class was resolved in the triumph of the bourgeoisie, first in England and the Netherlands in the 18th century, then in the American War of Independence and the French Revolution, and finally and decisively in the middle-class victories of the 19th century.

This Marxist analysis reveals his belief that historical change depends not only on economic factors, but also on an inherent and inevitable class struggle. Just as the middle class overcame the aristocracy, so in the next stage the workers—the proletariat—would overcome the middle class. In order to accomplish this and throw off their oppressors, the workers of the world needed to organize and unite, under the inspiration of their newly developed class consciousness. In the new order, the "dictatorship of the proletariat" would abolish existing political systems, make all production public, and bring about a classless society in which the state would "wither away."

The struggle would be made easier by the inherent defects in the middle-class economic system of capitalism. Since, Marx argued, capitalism by its nature required competition, those capitalists who succeeded would do so at the expense of others. Those who went out of business would join the proletariat. Since successful employers would be forced to cut wages and expenditures to remain competitive, the poor would continue to get poorer and the rich richer. In the end the capitalist system would collapse.

Marx and Marxism

The accuracy of Marx's historical and economic analyses has frequently been challenged. Furthemore, never did he or Engels really describe the precise nature of the society to be brought about under the dictatorship of the proletariat. Many developments that Marx did not live to see, such as mass communications, the spread of popular democracy, and expanding technologies, outdated some of his conclusions. The poor have not all continued to get poorer, and the capitalist system has not collapsed. Nor did Marx's rigorously economic determinism leave any place for the part played in history by individual human characteristics, or even pure random chance.

Yet after its early neglect, the *Manifesto*, along with Marx's other writings, went on to influence, directly or indirectly, countless millions of lives, and served as the inspiration for revolutionary movements throughout the world. The degree to which Marxist ideas have ever been applied in practice can be debated, as can the relationship between Marx's communism and the Communist party which came to power in Russia following the Bolshevik Revolution of 1917. Nevertheless, generations of political, social, and economic reformers turned to his writings.

Much of the appeal of Marxism lay in its positive view of the social role of workers and other underprivileged citizens, who had been accustomed to think of themselves as the dregs of society, beyond hope. Marx had less enthusiasm for them intellectually, believing them basically unable to discern their own interests, and thus in need of a "vanguard of intellectuals" to lead them. The socialist parties that were formed in the late 19th century drew much of their pride and energy from Marx's essentially optimistic view of their role in history and the inevitability of their eventual success, although by no means all of them were Marxists. Nor, like some other thinkers, did Marx seek to reverse the industrial revolution and return to a problem-free (and nonexistent) rural past. Indeed it was by means of greater productivity that the lot of most human beings was to be improved: Marx was the prophet of modernism, not its enemy. In addition, although he overstressed the role played by economics, his assertion of the need for radical economic change drove many to challenge the status quo. Finally, he made two claims for his analysis that were bound to appeal to many. It was, he said, scientific, and therefore intellectually sound. Furthermore, given his determinist view of history, sooner or later his long-term predictions were bound to come true; any setbacks or defeats would be only temporary.

Neither Marx nor Engels claimed that the dictatorship of the proletariat would be achieved quickly, but they and their followers believed that history was on their side. By the end of the 19th century, with the spread of socialism and the rise of the trade unions, many who were not Marxists began to share their conviction.

By 1870, the certainties of bourgeois existence were coming under increasing challenge. Just as Marx was undermining economic attitudes, so Darwin's work questioned the entire basis of traditional morality (see Part VII, Topic 14). Increasing numbers of middle-class women were becoming restless with the position assigned them in society. These developments took place at a time when governments in Western Europe were beginning to come under pressure to extend the franchise beyond the aristocracy and the prosperous middle class.

In Britain, Victoria continued her apparently everlasting reign, but the social situation was in a state of growing ferment. Elsewhere in Europe instabilities began to develop. The French Second Empire came abruptly to an end. Germany and Italy were faced with the new uncertainties of nationhood. The Austro-Hungarian empire lived on the brink of perpetual crisis. The only country where social conditions seemed likely to remain unchanged for centuries, as they had for centuries past, was Russia. By one of the ironies of history, amid the cataclysm of World War I Russian society was overturned and remade by self-proclaimed followers of the obscure German philosopher of the mid-19th century.

Questions for Further Study

1. What factors influenced the urbanization of Europe? How did urbanization affect social patterns?

2. Describe the principal values of the middle classes. How did they affect daily life?

3. What roles did "Victorian" values assign to women?

4. How did Marx explain the inevitability of the proletarian revolution? What would happen after the revolution?

Suggestions for Further Reading

Accampo, Elinor. *Industrialization, Family Life, and Class Relations: Saint Chamond, 1815–1914.* Berkeley, CA, 1989.

Berlanstein, Lenard R. *The Working People of Paris, 1871–1914.* Baltimore, MD, 1984.

Girouard, Mark. *Cities and People: A Social and Architectural History.* New Haven, CT, 1985.

Himmelfarb, Gertrude. *The Idea of Poverty: England in the Early Industrial Age.* New York, 1984.

Joyce, P. *Visions of the People: Industrial England and the Question of Class, c. 1848–1914.* New York, 1991.

Jones, Gareth. *Outcast London.* Oxford, 1984.

Marsden, G., ed. *Victorian Values: Personalities and Perspectives in 19th-Century Society.* New York, 1990.

Miller, Michael. *The Bon Marché: Bourgeois Culture and the Department Store, 1869–1920.* Princeton, NJ, 1981.

Pilbeam, Pamela M. *The Middle Classes in Europe, 1789–1914.* Chicago, 1990.

Ross, Ellen. *Love and Toil: Motherhood in Outcast London, 1870–1918.* New York, 1993.

Shapiro, Ann-Louise. *Housing the Poor of Paris, 1850–1902.* Madison, WI, 1985.

Stearns, Peter N. *European Society in Upheaval: Social History Since 1800.* New York, 1967.

Sutcliffe, Anthony. *Towards the Planned City: Germany, Britain, and the United States, 1789–1914.* New York, 1981.

Vicinus, Martha, ed. *Suffer and Be Still: Women in the Victorian Age.* Bloomington, IN, 1972.

Walkowitz, Judith. *City of Dreadful Delight.* Chicago, 1993.

Topic 14

Arts, Ideas, and Social Consciousness

y mid-19th century, European artists and thinkers were already beginning to take a critical look at the society produced by industrialization and political reform. The enormous speed with which the world was changing, not only politically but also as the result of developments in science and technology, encouraged analysis of the present and speculation about the future. At the same time, the rapidly rising literacy rate made new ideas circulate with ever-increasing speed.

The scientific study of human society—sociology—was enthusiastically advocated by Auguste Comte, whose optimistic belief in the power of human achievement inspired the rise of new fields of research: psychology, anthropology, and the social sciences in general. Charles Darwin's work on evolution presented a more serious challenge to conventional notions of the world. Plants and animals (humans included), he claimed, had not been created in their present form by divine plan, but had evolved over millions of years. Some of his successors sought to reconcile the principle of natural selection with Christian traditions, but the initial impact of his work produced widespread controversy.

The diffusion of worldviews which seriously questioned the teachings of Christianity increased debate by instilling tension between religion and scientific discovery. Furthermore, with the rise of the secular nation-state, Christian churches had to work out new ways of coexisting with civil powers.

In literature the most popular form of the day was the novel. No longer seeking merely to entertain, writers aimed to make public the chief issues of the times—social injustice, religious intolerance, evolving political patterns. Many of the leading novelists attracted a mass readership and succeeded in influencing substantial bodies of opinion.

Musicians also saw themselves as promoters of political causes, in particular that of nationalism. In Russia and among the peoples of Eastern Europe, traditional folk music was used as the basis for works that set out to reinforce ideas of national consciousness. The leading musician in Italy, Giuseppe Verdi, became the symbol of the unification of Italy under the House of Savoy. Many of his operas made indirect reference to political events, and served to ignite popular support for the *Risorgimento*.

In the visual arts, Romanticism gave way to a new movement, realism. Some painters produced realistic, unglamorized depictions of peasant and working-class life, while for others art was a means for revealing social injustice. Interest in realism was stimulated around midcentury by the invention and spread of photography.

In the arts, as in intellectual developments, the age was marked by an ever-widening popular audience for culture. Increasing ease of transport, the spread of literacy, and improvements in education meant that the ideas of Darwin and the novels of Dickens were widely distributed throughout Europe. They also made their way with increasing speed across the Atlantic, where American artists and thinkers were already forming their own rich tradition.

AUGUSTE COMTE AND THE PHILOSOPHY OF POSITIVISM

The chief artistic and intellectual movements of the early 19th century, Romanticism and utopian socialism, were inspired by the ferment of change that the revolutionary spirit of the times seemed to open up. Released from the bondage of traditional patterns of society, artists and thinkers explored possibilities for a new future. Even where, as in Germany, the old ways soon reestablished themselves, Romanticism continued to offer an escape from the realities of political power. Amid the hopes and delusions of postrevolutionary France, the utopian socialists tried to prescribe for a future ideal society (see Part VII, Topic 8).

By midcentury, Romanticism was giving way to realism, while new currents of thought examined humanity's place in the universe. Auguste Comte (1798–1857) arrived at an overarching view of civilization, which sought to rationalize the development of human understanding. Comte had spent many years as private secretary to the utopian Saint-Simon and inherited his predecessor's optimistic confidence in the progress of society. At the same time he constructed a philosophical system to explain the nature of historical change.

The Philosophy of Positivism

By the time of his death in 1857, Comte's philosophy of positivism was established as an international movement. His basic belief was that knowledge must be derived from experience or observation, and not from speculation. It was impossible to know why things happen, let alone what would happen in the future; the only certainties could be found by learning how things actually occur in the world. Study of this "positive" knowledge would eventually lead to an improved, "positive" society, based not on beliefs but on scientific facts.

Comte divided the history of civilization into a series of "progressive" stages. In the first, the "theological," people had tried to explain the world in terms of nature deities. This was followed by the "metaphysical" stage, in which religion was used to find hidden causes and understand abstract principles. By his day a new age was dawning, the "positive," in which society would achieve its highest form. Traditional religions such as Christianity played an important role in the development of civilization, but would in due course be replaced by a new "religion of humanity."

Reduced to its essence, Comte's positivism seems no more convincing than other optimistic philosophies—that of the 17th-century German Gottfried von Leibnitz, for example, parodied by Voltaire in *Candide*. Its appeal to his contemporaries lay in two factors. In the first place he warned that the progress from the "metaphysical" stage to "positivism" would involve struggle. The outward sign of this struggle was the upheaval of industrialization, with its social injustices and human misery. Thus his followers could accept the troubles of their times as the inevitable price to be paid for progress. The message was especially welcome to those members of the prosperous middle classes who felt pangs of guilt at the ignoble foundations on which their wealth seemed to rest.

Second, Comte's insistence on the scientific observation of human society created a new and intriguing way of looking at the world: sociology (Comte himself coined the term). During the second half of the 19th century, the scientific study of different forms taken by various societies led to widespread interest in the social sciences. Economics, psychology, anthropology, political science, sociology, history, all are ways of trying to satisfy Comte's requirement and provide objective, "positive" knowledge about society.

CHARLES DARWIN AND THE CASE FOR NATURAL SELECTION

Comte's positivism saw traditional religion as benign, although in the end to be superseded by humanism. The publication in 1859 of Charles Darwin's *On the Origin of Species* presented a far more severe challenge

Charles Darwin

of new habits, could transmit these changes to their off-spring. The theory was unsound. A man who develops strong muscles as a result of hauling sacks of flour will not pass on his physique to his sons and daughters. Nevertheless Lamarck's notion began to question the traditional religious teaching that life had been created according to a divine and unchanging scheme.

In his geological studies, Darwin was inspired by his contemporary Charles Lyell (1797–1875), whose *Principles of Geology* (1830) argued that all geological phenomena could be explained by natural causes. A general philosophical rationale was provided by the writings of Malthus (see Part VII, Topic 8), and the struggle for existence they describe. This struggle became, for Darwin, the basis of the process of natural selection.

Although all members of a species are generally similar, no two living creatures are identical. The random differences between individual members are transmitted to their offspring in a process that is, as we now know, genetic. Some variations are apparently irrelevant, while others—strength, speed, natural markings—are likely to improve the chances of survival. According to Darwin's theory of the survival of the fittest, the characteristics that are most likely to help in the struggle for life will, over millennia, be strengthened by the simple fact that the members of the species possessing them have a better chance of surviving.

When Darwin published his conclusions in 1859, encouraged by the independent formation of a similar theory by Alfred Wallace, he did not intend them as an open challenge to religion. He avoided speculation about the origins of life, or on why so many species have characteristics that cannot apparently be explained by this process. Nor did he emphasize natural selection as the most important of his ideas. Instead, the avowed tone of his publication was one of optimism at the notion of the "rising swell of the Great Chorus of Being."

The Impact of Darwinism

Inevitably, however, Darwin's work was seen as inextricably opposed to Christian teaching. The fittest survive, by implication, only because the overwhelming majority of living organisms are destroyed, a principle which Darwin clearly extended to the human species. This was impossible to reconcile with belief in an all-loving God—and one, at that, who created the world according to His own scheme and humans in His own image. Church leaders were horrified, and controversy raged. Darwin's publication of *The Descent of Man* (1871), which claimed that humans and anthropoid apes were both descended from a common apelike ancestor, was hardly likely to still the debate.

to established Christian beliefs; its implications still remain controversial.

As a young man, Darwin (1809–1882) began by studying medicine, his father's profession. He soon changed his mind, and decided to become a minister of religion, although without abandoning his interest in natural history. In 1831 the offer of an unpaid position as naturalist aboard H.M.S. *Beagle*, which was about to sail on an expedition to South America, tempted him away from his theological studies at Cambridge. The voyage lasted five years, and Darwin's work on South American fossils and bird and animal life gave him the basis for his theory of natural selection.

Like many important intellectual ideas, natural selection did not suddenly appear in a vacuum. Other scholars and scientists had begun to look for natural rather than divine explanations for the order of creation. The Scottish geologist James Hutton (1726–1797) published *Theory of the Earth* in 1795, which claimed that a continual process of geological evolution was responsible for the earth's natural features; his theory was called uniformitarianism. In 1809 the French biologist Jean Lamarck (1744–1829) proposed a hypothesis whereby animals that changed their characteristics due to the environment, or the acquisition

The theological implications of Darwinism remain unresolved. Many Christians, and others, managed to reconcile the idea of natural selection with the Bible's account of creation by taking the biblical description as poetic rather than literal. There continue to be those whose understanding of the Bible leads them to reject Darwin's theory of evolution by natural selection.

Darwinism also had widespread influence in social thinking and the arts, often in ways that went far beyond the intentions of its originator. For Darwin, survival was a fact that of itself was morally neutral. A species was neither "better" nor "worse" for having won the struggle. Self-styled "Social Darwinists," however, began to use the notion of the survival of the fittest to imply the survival of the best (see Part VII, Topic 20).

For contemporary poets and novelists, Darwin suggested new insights into the human condition. Romanticism drew attention to the uniqueness of the individual, but Darwin's work put existence into a very different perspective. The vision was not always a comforting one. In his famous poem, "In Memoriam," the eminent Victorian poet Alfred, Lord Tennyson (1809–1892) gloomily accepted the notion of a "Nature, red in tooth and claw," which proclaims: "A thousand types are gone; I care for nothing, all shall go." Under such conditions, life was "as futile, then, as frail!"

Writers began to emphasize the development of character and the external events that molded it. To do justice to their material, and the concept of change over time, they wrote novels that were longer and contained more naturalistic descriptions than those of their predecessors. Among the major writers influenced by the Darwinian worldview were Thomas Hardy and Émile Zola (see Part VII, Topic 21). Some students of literature collected information about conditions among the working class: the German essayist Bettina von Arnim (1785–1857), an important figure in the early-19th-century Romantic movement, now began to compile notebooks in which she documented working conditions in Berlin.

The immediate impact of Darwin gradually abated, and by the end of the century the new disciplines of psychology and sociology probably had a greater influence on European intellectual life than the religious implications of natural selection. Yet the theory of evolution remains an important and controversial topic, and not only for theologians. Modern scientists, using methods of genetic research and the study of the physico-chemical composition of DNA, are rapidly revising Darwin's conclusions. Darwin himself would surely not have been surprised: he himself predicted that future scientists would modify his theories as they explored the many unanswered questions concerning natural selection.

SCIENCE AND RELIGION IN A CHANGING WORLD

The theory of evolution was not the only idea to present problems for 19th-century organized religion. With the advance of science and the growth of the secular state, Christian leaders found themselves facing serious challenges. For centuries the various branches of Christianity had at least agreed on a central body of teaching, and they regarded themselves as uniquely qualified to expound it. Lutherans and Catholics alike agreed on the importance of the Scriptures. Biblical accounts had, it is true, been attacked since the 17th century by scientists like Galileo and philosophers such as Voltaire. Now, however, increasing numbers of laypeople exposed to the new ideas began to question truths that had been held immutable since the Middle Ages.

Some of the doubts came from biblical historians, who were trying, as they thought, to save Christianity from being too closely tied to the teachings of the Bible. The French scholar Ernest Renan (1832–1892) pointed out historical inconsistencies in the Scriptures, emphasizing that the human fallibility of its authors did not invalidate its general message. His most widely read book was *The Life of Jesus*, which appeared in 1863. It perfectly expresses the intellectual spirit of the times by substituting a heightened appreciation of the poetry and human achievements described in the Bible for blind faith. Renan's purpose was to emphasize the continuing relevance of the Christian story to modern life, and he described Jesus as "an incomparable man." However, the authorities of the Collège de France, under the influence of the Catholic party, forbade him to teach his version of Christianity.

A far more hostile opponent of Christianity was the English philosopher Thomas Henry Huxley (1825–1895). An energetic defender of Darwin, Huxley invented the term "agnosticism" to describe the belief that the existence and nature of God are unknowable. He was a pioneer in the field of popular scientific education, and a champion of free speech and investigation. Among the opponents of Darwin whom he lambasted in his newspaper articles was the British prime minister, William Gladstone, a deeply religious man who ranked among Darwin's most vocal opponents.

The German philosopher Ludwig Andreas Feuerbach (1804–1872) took an even more extreme position. The most fiery and uncompromising prophet of philosophical materialism, Feuerbach attacked belief in an afterlife and declared that all deities are merely personifications of human fears. Religion, he claimed, prevented the full understanding and enjoyment of physical and moral reality. Expressing one of

Louis Pasteur conducting an experiment.

the 19th century's most typical ideas, he wrote that "the characteristic of the modern age is that man sees himself as divine and infinite, and that the individual feels these qualities within himself in his individuality."

Meanwhile, science and technology did not so much challenge traditional religion as ignore it. Furthermore, by visibly improving the lives of countless people, advances in these areas were seen as a source of "progress" and material well-being. The work of Louis Pasteur (1822–1895) on bacteria revolutionized standards of public health and nutrition. Joseph Lister's (1827–1912) discovery of the value of carbolic acid as a disinfectant vastly improved surgical techniques. The development of the telegraph and the subsequent laying of a transatlantic cable from Europe to America between 1858 and 1866 produced miraculous changes in communication.

None of these innovations was hostile to Christianity, but to some puzzled believers they seemed to make religion increasingly irrelevant to modern life. The Catholic Church responded by taking the offensive, motivated by reasons of dogma, and also by its loss of temporal power in Italy as a consequence of Italian unification. In 1864 Pope Pius IX issued the *Syllabus of Errors*, in which he castigated materialism, freedom of thought, and the belief that all religions are equally valid. Five years later, in 1869, he summoned the first church council since the Counter-Reformation,

and proclaimed the doctrine of papal infallibility. According to this teaching, when the pope speaks "ex cathedra," from his position as head of the church, on any issue of faith or morals, he is infallible. Pius was speaking precisely from this position in condemning what he saw as dangerous modern tendencies.

The pope's assertion of authority met with a mixed reception, not least in Italy where tensions already existed between church and state. Protestants, lacking a central authority or a body of established dogma, were left with their consciences to guide them to an accommodation with new ways of thinking. Some turned to social commitment, and tried to contribute to progress by active work among the poor. They emphasized the ethical teachings of Jesus rather than faith in miracles and belief in original sin.

Christianity and the State

At the same time as the Catholic Church was fighting its moral battles, it was involved in a more temporal struggle. The papacy had never been sympathetic to the cause of Italian unification, which had sought to incorporate the Papal States into the new Italian nation. In 1871, the year after the seizure of Rome, the Italian parliament passed a law designed to define and guarantee the pope's status. Pius IX, who never accepted the loss of the Papal States, refused to accept the Italian government's stand. Instead, he withdrew into the Vatican, causing serious liabilities for the Italian government (see Part VII, Topic 15).

Elsewhere in Europe, political leaders and religious authorities found themselves in conflict. The governments of France and Spain, both predominantly Catholic countries, denounced the dogma of papal infallibility as proclaimed by the Vatican Council in 1870. In Germany, Bismarck's *Kulturkampf* (battle over culture) saw the introduction of a number of anti-Catholic laws between 1872 and 1875 which expelled the Jesuits and gave the state control over seminaries and the appointment of priests and bishops. Bismarck was concerned about a possible alliance of Catholic powers, and wanted to limit outside influence in Germany (see Part VII, Topic 15). The strength of the Catholic Center party forced the eventual repeal of the measures. Even the Church of England, whose official head was the monarch, found itself increasingly stripped by Parliament of the special privileges it had accumulated over the centuries.

By the end of the century the decades of controversy succeeded in producing a renewal of religious influence, as Christians of all denominations struggled to address theological and social problems with increasing flexibility. Yet in the end the real threat to organized religion came not from scientists or liberal governments, but from the rise of socialism.

THE WRITER AS CRITIC: SOCIAL REALISM AND THE NOVEL

With the spread of education and an increase in literacy throughout most of Europe, public demand for literature increased. The most popular form was the novel, and the most successful writers of the 19th century were those who managed both to entertain and to instruct their readers.

As industrialization and the growth of urban life intensified social discontent, authors turned from the self-centered images of Romanticism to deal with the practical problems of the day in a realistic style. Not content merely to describe society's injustices, in many cases they fought to correct them. In the process they criticized many of the mid-19th century's conventional beliefs.

The realities of social existence were memorably expressed by a number of women writers, many of whom took male names to reassure some readers who might not have otherwise taken them seriously. In England, George Eliot (1819–1880; her real name was Mary Ann Evans) dealt with questions of morality and philosophy, as well as creating, in *Middlemarch* (1871–1872), an unforgettable picture of provincial life. The French writer George Sand (1804–1876; in real life Aurore Dudevant) tackled just about every issue of the day, including women's rights. Her contemporary, the English poet Elizabeth Barrett Browning, called Sand "true genius but true woman."

Perhaps the most devastating attack on middle-class values and society is that found in *Madame Bovary*, the masterpiece of Sand's friend Gustave Flaubert (1821–1880). When the work first appeared in print in 1856–1857, its reception did much to confirm Flaubert's low opinion of his times: he was prosecuted for offenses against public morals, although in the end he was acquitted. The story's main character, Emma Bovary, has been brought up on a diet of romantic novels, which leave her unsatisfied by the dull reality of her respectable life in the provinces. Married to a boorish country doctor, she embarks on a shoddy affair and ends up fatally in debt. Flaubert's understated, impersonal recounting of the banal tragedy is filled with carefully observed details.

The most successful English novelist of the period was Charles Dickens (1812–1870), whose rich, many-layered books are filled with characters both realistic and bizarre—a far cry from the restraint of Flaubert or the measured tone of Eliot. Dickens' style is poetic, with an endlessly imaginative use of language.

An illustration for Dickens' *Oliver Twist*: "Please sir, May I have some more. . ."

His finest works combine insights into human behavior with searing indictments of the flaws and social inequities of his times. *Bleak House* (1853) attacked the British legal system, which was notorious for its interminable, inhumane delays and incomprehensible proceedings. The book played a part in the movement which led to legal reform in the 1860s. In *Hard Times* (1854), Dickens analyzed the ills of industrialized society, and powerfully underlined the fact that education without humanity can destroy those whom it seeks to help. Often unpopular with the establishment, Dickens won a huge and affectionate audience both in Europe and in America. The arrival in New York of a ship carrying the latest episode of one of his works attracted crowds to the docks.

Not all authors met with so appreciative a reception. The Russian novelist Nikolai Gogol (1809–1852) spent many years abroad, most of them in Rome, where he wrote his satirical masterpiece, *Dead Souls* (1842). Gogol's readers saw his satires of bureaucracy and serfdom as blows in the struggle for progress. He was, however, more concerned to castigate moral evil than social or political error.

Ivan Turgenev and Pauline Viardot

Gogol's contemporary, Ivan Turgenev (1818–1883), was a liberal and an advocate of the importation of Western ideas into his country. Among his early writings was a series of depictions of peasant life. His novels dealt with the great issues facing Russian society: the emancipation of the serfs in *On the Eve* (1860—a year before the emancipation became law); nihilism in *Fathers and Children* (1862); populist revolution in *Virgin Soil* (1877). The last of these was written in Paris, for discouraged by the lack of sympathy on the part of Russian readers and critics, Turgenev spent the last 21 years of his life in Germany and France. While in Paris he maintained a close relationship with Pauline Viardot, one of the most prominent opera singers of the 19th century.

Viardot and Turgenev provided a rare 19th-century example of two creative people who maintained a long relationship while preserving their personal and professional independence. Unlike traditional gender patterns of the period, the character of their interaction was one of equality. Each provided the other with a source of artistic inspiration. Furthermore, quite apart from their private lives, Turgenev and Viardot played an important role in introducing Russian artistic achievements to Western audiences. Viardot performed a great deal of Russian music written by Turgenev's friends, while her acquaintances, who numbered Flaubert and the young Henry James, acquired from their meetings with Turgenev a love of Russian literature.

Viardot and Turgenev met in Berlin in 1845, where he heard her sing, and they remained on close terms for the next 40 years. When Turgenev left Russia in 1862 to settle in Western Europe, he and the Viardots developed what their contemporaries thought was a "menage à trois." The three spent the first decade in Germany, since Louis Viardot was a vehement opponent of Napoleon III. When the Second Empire fell, all three moved back to Paris.

Many speculated on the exact nature of their relationship. Pauline Viardot no doubt avoided a breach with her husband in order to preserve her career. She saw advantages in maintaining her rapport with both men rather than choosing between them. While openly remaining her husband's wife, she and Turgenev—like John Stuart Mill and Harriet Taylor—traveled and visited friends as a couple. During a stay with George Sand, Viardot sang some of her songs and Turgenev told stories. "Last day of musical bliss," Sand noted in her diary as they prepared to leave: "Pauline sings bits of her operettas and Turgenev explains them. It's charming."

Viardot's attachment to Turgenev was a close one. Although she never had any children of her own, she brought up in her own household Turgenev's illegitimate daughter, born of a casual encounter between the writer and his mother's seamstress. Something of Turgenev's own ambiguous feelings about marriage can be gleaned from his play, *A Month in the Country*. Their relationship, certainly outside the gender norms pre-

scribed by society, reflected the unorthodox values of many European artists of the period, whose works and lives shocked the virtuous bourgeoisie.

MUSIC AND THE RISE OF NATIONAL CONSCIOUSNESS

Around the middle of the 19th century, composers in many parts of Europe became eager to write music that openly proclaimed their nationality. Some, such as the Czechs Bedřich Smetana and Antonín Dvořák, and the Italian Giuseppe Verdi, were inspired by their country's struggles to achieve nationhood. In other cases musicians of long-established countries began to turn from traditional musical forms and material, and incorporate folk tunes and popular melodies into their works.

In Bohemia, Bedřich Smetana (1824–1884) gave the Czech people a new sense of identity and self-confidence by the musical style he developed, and by his choice of nationalistic subjects for his operas and symphonic poems. In addition to *The Bartered Bride* (1866), his best-loved work, with its sparkling dances and lyrical songs, he wrote a set of six orchestral pieces called *Ma Vlast* (My Fatherland). The most popular, "Vltava," paints a musical picture of the river Vltava, flowing from its bubbling source through the Czech landscape, and finally rolling majestically into Prague.

His younger contemporary, Antonín Dvořák (1841–1904), became famous for his Slavonic dances and rhapsodies. Much of his music, including the symphonies and string quartets, uses traditional Czech folk rhythms like the polka. The famous *New World Symphony* (Ninth Symphony; 1893), composed during Dvořák's stay in America to commemorate the 500th anniversary of Christopher Columbus' landing in the Americas, is far more Czech in character than American, although his interest in folk music of all kinds led him to collect American spirituals and incorporate them in his later works.

The greatest Italian composer of the century, Giuseppe Verdi (1813–1901), became a symbol of his country's Risorgimento. He began his career at a time when Milan, the center of Italian operatic life, was under Austrian rule. Although forbidden by the Austrian censor from depicting politically suggestive subjects on stage, he found ways to allude to the nationalist cause. His opera *Nabucco* (1842) shows the captivity of the Jews under the Babylonians in the 6th century B.C. His Italian audience, under Austrian captivity, had no difficulty in identifying themselves with the plight of the suffering Jews, and the work was greeted with wild enthusiasm at its first performances.

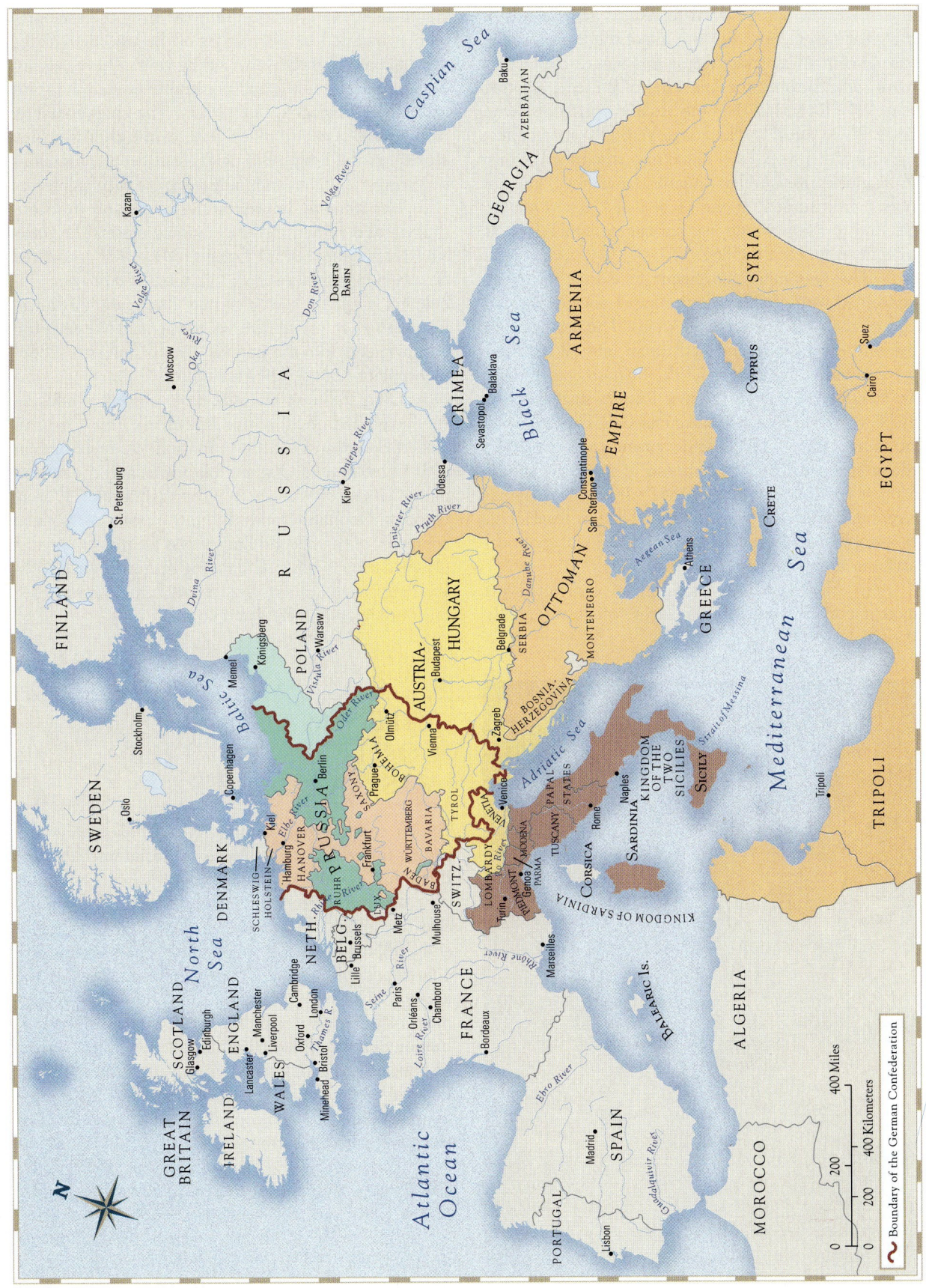

Map 14.1 Europe, Mid-19th Century

Even his name helped to remind the Italians of the great struggle in progress. One of the leaders of the Risorgimento was King Victor Emmanuel II of Piedmont, who became the first king of united Italy (see Part VII, Topic 11). For the excited spectators, who cried "Viva Verdi!"—"long live Verdi!"—after performances of his works, his name also stood for Vittorio Emmanuele, *Re d'Italia*—Victor Emmanuel, king of Italy. Verdi himself, at the request of Cavour, ran for election to the new national parliament, and served as a deputy from 1861 to 1865.

The nationalist movement in Russia was more concerned with establishing the importance of Russian culture than with political questions. The key figure in the birth of an independent Russian musical tradition was Mikhail Glinka (1804–1857), whose opera *A Life for the Tsar* (1836) was the first Russian stage work to make widespread use of folklike melodies. From an artistic point of view, Glinka's achievement was surpassed by the most original Russian composer of the 19th century, Modest Moussorgsky (1839–1881). Intensely imaginative, but tormented by a lifelong addiction to alcohol, Moussorgsky combined his musical career with political activism and family responsibilities.

In the late 1860s Moussorgsky completed his most important work, *Boris Godunov*, which was finally staged in 1874. The opera tells the story of Tsar Boris, who is haunted by his murder of the true heir to the throne and finally driven mad by guilt. The music incorporates folk motifs and powerfully evokes the spirit of Russian Orthodox Christianity. The chief character of the work is not so much Boris as the chorus, which represents the long-suffering Russian people, somehow surviving the crimes and indifference of their rulers.

On a more limited scale, musicians in Scandinavia also turned to their national musical heritage. The Norwegian Edvard Grieg (1843–1907) produced arrangements of Norwegian folk songs and provided incidental music for the Ibsen play *Peer Gynt*. Although his works were written within the general Western tradition, pieces like the popular Piano Concerto (1868) incorporate fresh, folklike melodies.

Even the most mainstream musicians of midcentury exploited their native resources. The Germans Robert Schumann (1810–1856) and Johannes Brahms (1833–1897) used German folk songs, and the mighty music dramas of Wagner (see Part VII, Topic 21) were based on German legends. In France, the most popular composer of the Second Empire was Jacques Offenbach (1819–1880), whose exhilarating operettas, such as *La Vie Parisienne* (Life in Paris; 1866), often commented on contemporary society and politics.

A scene from Act II of Verdi's opera, *La Traviata.*

THE IMAGE OF SOCIETY IN THE VISUAL ARTS

French painters and sculptors of the period showed a similar interest in the political and social world around them. Just as Offenbach made fun of the excesses of his contemporaries, Honoré Daumier (1808–1879) pilloried the follies of the times in paintings, lithographs, and sculpted statuettes. More bitter than his musical contemporary, Daumier often expressed anger at the abuse of power. He shared with Dickens a deep resentment of the injustices of the legal system and the corruption of those working in it. In a series of lithographs, he showed the indifference of lawyers to their clients' sufferings. Many of his small sculptures depict the leading politicians of Napoleon III's Paris, characterized by greed and self-satisfaction.

The paintings of Rosa Bonheur (1822–1899) and Gustave Courbet (1819–1877) also show realistic scenes, although they are less explicitly political in tone. Both of them rejected the full-blown Romanticism of Delacroix for naturalistic depictions of the world around them. Courbet preferred to paint peasants and workers, while Bonheur specialized in ani-

Honoré Daumier, *Third-Class Carriage* (c. 1862): the working class on public transportation.

Courbet's depiction of manual laborers, *The Stone Breakers*.

Thomas Eakins' *The Swimming Hole* shows the influence of photography.

mals. Her huge painting *The Horse Fair* was much admired by Napoleon III in 1853, and two years later she became the first woman to receive the Grand Cross of the Legion of Honor, France's highest official honor.

Courbet, who was a socialist, produced plain and unromantic scenes of village life. In *The Stone Breakers* (1849) his avoidance of the sentimental and underlining of realistic details are a visual parallel to the literary realism of his contemporary Flaubert.

The increasing tendency of artists to approach their subjects naturalistically was further stimulated by one of the most important inventions of the century: photography. In 1839, Louis Daguerre (1787–1851) gave the first public demonstration of a type of photographic process in Paris. The new technique was soon improved and hailed with excited enthusiasm by artists as different as Delacroix and Ingres, in part because, as Ingres observed, photographs provided "an exactitude that I shall like to achieve." The impact of photography on art and culture in general was vast and far-reaching. As the American painter Thomas Eakins perceptively realized, it represented no less a convention than traditional art. By stimulating painters to examine the actual process of literal observation, it inspired one of the most important artistic movements of the late 19th century, Impressionism (see Part VII, Topic 21).

In the early 19th century, artists and thinkers often saw themselves as leaders in the battle for social and political change. As time wore on they became commentators on the process, rather than participants. A number of factors were responsible for this gradual alienation from politics. In the first place, philosophical and intellectual developments such as the evolution controversy and the growing interest in psychology created a barrier between "advanced" intellectuals and the general public. The level of popular education was increasing, but not sufficiently to deal with these basic challenges to widespread beliefs.

Second, the increasing complexity of the industrialized world ruled out the broad, simple solutions of the early revolutionaries. Whatever the defects of urban life—and Dickens, Daumier, and others did not hesitate to point them out—nobody could seriously advocate that the process of modernization be suspended or reversed. Thus artists, whose ability to influence economic or technological developments was inevitably limited, began to describe rather than prescribe.

Furthermore, at least some of the goals of the early years of the century had been achieved. By the 1870s the new nations of Germany and Italy had been created, Hungary had obtained a measure of independence, political compromise had been relatively peacefully achieved in Britain, and even in Russia, bastion of conservatism, the serfs had been emancipated. All these developments brought their own problems with them. The rise of Germany entailed the humiliating defeat of France, and both the Austrians and their subjects were unhappy with the compromise of the Dual Monarchy. Yet many liberal aims had been fulfilled, few wept for Napoleon III, and the rapid rate of industrial transformation held out hope of further progress. Artists needed to absorb and reflect on the significance of their world, and reveal its true essence in their works, before they could move on.

Thus, in all the arts midcentury was a time for reacting to contemporary society and its problems, and relating it to an ever-wider public. The thirst for novels, opera performances, more easily affordable art objects in the form of prints and lithographs, and the immediate popularity of photography, were all signs that public enthusiasm for culture, far from diminishing, was in rapid increase. In part, the demand was due to the greater spread of affluence in western Europe. The middle classes of Victoria's Britain or the Second Empire in France were among the first worshipers at the shrine of conspicuous consumption, that cult which came to dominate Western society a century later. Yet in turning to the arts to seek explanations for their own lives and times, the public expressed a need that many artists fulfilled.

The spread of culture was not limited to Europe. In America the importation of European culture provided a stimulus to the growth of an indigenous artistic legacy. Paradoxically, the more the United States became exposed to European ideas and works of art, the more distinct was the voice with which American artists and intellectuals spoke. In response to the crisis of faith produced by Darwin, American thinkers developed the philosophy of Pragmatism: truth was whatever "worked." Painters like Winslow Homer and Thomas Eakins used the new realistic style to il-

lustrate their own landscape and people. Walt Whitman sang of himself and his country.

As the century neared its end, and the first ominous signs of future conflict began to appear, the arts themselves increasingly reflected contemporary uncertainties. In the generation after Turgenev, Verdi, and Daumier, the very language and structure of art were to be questioned and, in many cases rejected. The mood of growing political concern is perceptible in artistic developments between 1880 and 1914. In the 1870s, however, artists could still touch large numbers of people by revealing to them the nature of the world in which they lived.

Questions for Further Study

1. How did the role of artists change in the course of the 19th century? What effects did this have on the subjects and style of their works?

2. What were the philosophical and moral implications of Darwin's theories? How has reaction to them evolved since his time?

3. What was the impact of nationalism on the arts? Did it have a stronger influence on some art forms than on others?

Suggestions for Further Reading

Barzun, J. *Darwin, Marx and Wagner.* Chicago, 1981.

Bowler, P. J. *Evolution: The History of an Idea.* Berkeley, CA, 1989.

Chadwick, O. *The Secularization of the European Mind in the Nineteenth Century.* Cambridge, MA, 1977.

Dale, P. A. *In Pursuit of a Scientific Culture: Science, Art, and Society in the Victorian Age.* Madison, WI, 1990.

Kaplan, F. *Dickens: A Biography.* New York, 1989.

Longford, E. *Eminent Victorian Women.* New York, 1981.

Topic 15

POLITICS AND NATIONAL DEVELOPMENT IN EUROPE, 1870–1914

In the last decades of the 19th century a widening gulf separated the apparent condition of Western European society from its real state. For many liberal politicians, increased domestic prosperity and improved social conditions created a mood of optimism and encouraged a belief in uninterrupted progress. In fact, however, several factors combined to undermine stability, both in individual nations and in international relations.

In spite of a century's battles for broad-based political participation, huge numbers of Western Europeans still had no vote. The liberal reforms of midcentury gave political power to those with money or property, but left the majority of citizens disenfranchised. In another respect, political discrimination even transcended class, for no women could vote in national elections anywhere in Europe. Behind the apparent diffusion of political power, élite interests remained entrenched. A resurgent aristocracy continued to resist the spread of democracy, the rise of the workers, the women's movement, and ethnic nationalism, and thereby preserved domestic divisions within each country.

The successful struggle to build new nations left its own tensions and potential conflicts. In relations between countries, national pride encouraged rivalry and competition. Internally, it led to suspicion of minority groups and radicals, perceived as threatening to social stability and national interests.

With the rise of organized labor matched by the growing power of big business, widespread and at times violent industrial conflict developed, especially where workers failed to obtain from the state adequate social welfare legislation. All these factors gradually undermined confidence in liberal systems.

Instability in domestic politics was less manifest in Britain than elsewhere in Europe. Between 1867 and 1914, the extension of the suffrage was accompanied by social reform. Yet in the years immediately preceding World War I, British political life began to show signs of the turmoil already visible on the Continent. Strikes and industrial agitation led to clashes between workers and police. The suffragist campaign to obtain the vote for women became increasingly militant. In Ireland, the demand for national independence met with a combination of repression and reform.

Nowhere in Europe was there a greater contrast to the stability of Victorian England than in France. The bloodshed of the Paris Commune was followed by bitter political conflict between republicans and monarchists as the Third Republic was founded in 1875. For most of the rest of the century French politics were dominated by the moderate wing of the republicans. Periodic crises challenged government authority—first anarchists, then the threat of a coup led by the glamorous General Boulanger, labor unrest, and finally the Dreyfus affair.

The new national governments of Germany and Italy were both intent on crushing perceived internal enemies. In Germany, Bismarck first waged a campaign against the Catholics and then against the socialists. Bismarck undercut the socialists by introducing his own social welfare legislation. Kaiser Wilhelm II, who dismissed Bismarck in 1890, was determined to reassert the power of the monarchy. Nevertheless in 1912 the German Socialist party became the largest single party in Parliament.

In Italy, a very limited number of citizens could vote. Moreover, the similarity of the two chief parliamentary groupings reflected the dominance of upper-class élites. Under both parties, anarchists and socialists were crushed with equal severity. The lack of any significant difference between the two major political forces led to the phenomenon of *trasformismo*, whereby deputies elected from one group served in governments of the other and voted across party lines. The system did little to increase confidence in parliamentary government. After 1900, Prime Minister Giovanni Giolitti eased social and political tensions by the enactment of social welfare measures, increasing tolerance of the socialists, and a generally improving economy. Yet in 1914 Italy was still racked by political divisions.

Similar social conflicts unfolded in other parts of Europe. In the poorer regions of southern and eastern Europe, rural and working-class resentments led to revolts. Governments were brought down in Greece and Portugal, and mass protests erupted in Bulgaria and Spain. In the wealthier north, dissatisfaction focused on the demand for political and social reform. Sweden, Belgium, and the Netherlands all experienced strikes and demonstrations. Even the monolithic governments of Russia and the Austro-Hungarian empire were subject to serious challenges. In a climate of such massive disaffection, some political leaders welcomed the outbreak of war in 1914 as a distraction from domestic unrest.

POLITICAL REPRESSION AND PARLIAMENTARY RULE

By the 1870s many liberals in Western Europe looked with satisfaction at the world they had created. Revolutions earlier in the century had accomplished many of their goals: the property-owning middle classes had the right to vote; social welfare legislation was introduced by many governments; the nationalist cause triumphed in Germany and Italy; industrial development, together with scientific and technological advances, was almost daily improving the lives of thousands of people.

Yet only a few decades later, in the early years of the 20th century, the general mood of optimism was replaced with the fear that government and society were on the brink of collapse throughout Europe. When the Great War came in 1914, most of the participants were facing internal crises which seemed impossible to resolve without serious and wrenching changes. The issues varied from country to country, but the results were the same: mass demonstrations put down by police violence, the resurgence of deep class divisions, and economic dislocation.

The earlier optimism had been ill-founded. For all the achievements of the 19th century, serious problems remained in European society, many inherent in the very advances made. Thus nationalism led to dangerous rivalry for national superiority. The social welfare measures that had been passed were generally inadequate and only drew attention to the widespread poverty and misery still existing. Scientific and

Map 15.1   The Industrialization of Europe, c. 1860

technological progress created new problems and aggravated old ones, even as it solved others. By reducing infant mortality and prolonging life expectancy, and by constructing huge new cities with the means to travel around them, the advances led to overcrowded urban squalor.

The Right to Vote

For all the revolutions and reforms, effective political power remained in the hands of a restricted few. Most countries of Western and Central Europe were governed by constitutional monarchies, in which royal power was limited through a combination of constitutional guarantees and parliaments. These political systems had been the result of the triumph of bourgeois liberals in the revolutionary upheavals of the first half of the 19th century.

Parliaments consisted of two chambers, an upper and a lower. In Britain, members of the House of Lords either inherited their titles or were appointed by the monarch. The French Senate was elected by regional bodies. The German Bundesrat represented the con-

stituent states of the empire, while the Italian Senate was appointed by the king. The lower houses were generally elected through limited male suffrage, although France and Germany had universal male suffrage for their lower houses. The guiding principle of parliamentary liberalism was that through national elections the citizens of a country would choose representatives to formulate and enact national policies.

Parliamentary government distinguished countries such as Britain and Italy from autocratic monarchies such as Russia. Yet by 1900 only in France did more than a quarter of the citizens have the right to vote. In Britain, about one person in six was enfranchised, whereas of the Italians, new citizens of a new country, about one in fourteen could vote.

The right to vote depended on three criteria: gender, financial worth, and literacy. At the beginning of the 20th century, women had no vote in the election of any national assembly in any European country. The suffragist campaign (see Part VII, Topic 19) became increasingly active in the years before World War I, especially in Britain, but only in Finland (1906) and

Norway (1907) did women actually win the right to vote before World War I.

The other criteria, money and literacy, were deliberately applied in order to restrict the vote to the middle classes and the aristocracy, and to exclude the peasants and working classes from the political process. Even "enlightened" liberals did not advocate universal suffrage. Around midcentury the British historian and parliamentarian Thomas Macaulay (1800–1859) called it "utterly incompatible with the existence of civilization," and declared that if the people at large were given the vote, they would "plunder every man in the kingdom who had a good coat on his back and a good roof over his head." Restricting the suffrage to the wealthy was a way of protecting established interests.

Liberals and conservatives alike justified this limitation in several ways. In the first place, it was claimed that wealth was in itself a sign of intelligence, and that poverty indicated both stupidity and moral laxity. The rich saw themselves as being more involved in society, and thus having more at risk. Finally, in clear contradiction to this last argument, they asserted that their wealth provided them with the security to be able to make political decisions without consulting their own self-interest.

Throughout Europe complex electoral systems were devised that not only limited the vote to the prosperous, but gave additional votes according to the degree of prosperity. As late as 1911, British citizens who met property requirements in more than one constituency could vote in each of them—some cast as many as 20 votes. In other cases education was a criterion. In 1893 Belgium introduced a system whereby all males 25 or older received one vote, wealthy ones a second vote, and those with a higher education a third. By this means the effectiveness of universal male suffrage was virtually annulled, since the wealthy and educated could always outvote the rest.

So determined a grasp on power led in the end to widespread resentment on the part of the disenfranchised masses. Many who had fought for reform, or who had battled in the nationalist cause, found themselves still shut out from any political rights. The sense of frustration found release in the bitter and often bloody industrial disputes that shook most of western Europe in the years before World War I, and in the increasing militancy of the suffragist movement.

One other effect of frustrated nationalism was to drive some political extremists to terrorism and assassination as a means of undermining existing regimes. Indeed, the anarchists, generally associated in the public mind with political violence, advocated the overthrow of all governments (see Part VII, Topic 19). A rash of assassinations around the turn of the century, including the Empress Elizabeth of Austria (1898), King Umberto I of Italy (1900), and U.S. President William McKinley (1901), coincided with alleged terrorist activities in Spain, Ireland, and elsewhere.

GREAT BRITAIN: FROM VICTORIA TO EDWARD

In general, British political life remained relatively tranquil until around 1910, at least in part due to the sense of continuity and security provided by the monarchy. When Victoria died in 1901, the vast majority of her mourning citizens could not remember a time when she had not been queen. Although her son and successor, Edward VII (ruled 1901–1910), lacked his mother's immense prestige, his famous (for some, infamous) appetite for pleasure and self-indulgence gave its own character to his reign. Later, the Edwardian Era came to be looked on nostalgically as a last time of comfort and sunny confidence, before the darkness of war.

In 1867 the Conservative Prime Minister Benjamin Disraeli, with Liberal support, had passed the Second Reform Bill, widening the suffrage. William Gladstone, the Liberal leader, returned to power in

Striking matchworkers in England, 1888. They won this case and went on to organize a union.

Prime Ministers Benjamin Disraeli (left) and William Gladstone (right) alternated in introducing political reforms in Great Britain.

1880, and during the 1870s and 1880s both parties collaborated in approving a number of liberalizing measures (see Part VII, Topic 9). Secret balloting in elections was instituted, trade unions were legally recognized, elementary education was provided for virtually all children, and slum clearance projects were initiated.

In 1884, under Liberal leadership, Parliament accepted the principle of universal male suffrage. Yet once again theory and reality did not coincide, since only those males with an independent place of residence were qualified to vote. Given the living conditions of the time, around one out of five adult males was excluded. In another issue that arose at the same time, one group of voters managed for once to impose their wishes on Parliament. Charles Bradlaugh (1833–1891) was elected by the constituency of Northampton. On taking his seat in the House of Commons, he refused to swear the oath required of members on the grounds that he was an atheist. Bradlaugh was barred and reelected six times before finally being seated in 1886, and atheists were thereafter permitted to enter Parliament.

Ireland and Home Rule

For most of the period between 1870 and 1914, the most divisive issue in Britain was the Irish question. Irish farmers and laborers had long resented the fact

that about half the island belonged to absentee landlords, most of them Anglo-Protestants. Bad harvests in the late 1870s, and the subsequent eviction of many of the tenant farmers, led in 1879 to the formation of the Irish National Land League under the leadership of the fiery Irish parliamentarian, Charles Parnell (1846–1891). The League's slogan was: "The land of Ireland for the people of Ireland."

Gladstone tried to compromise. Those deemed agitators were arrested—Parnell himself was jailed in 1881—while tenant farmers were offered some measure of protection from eviction and excessive rent increases. An already tense situation became complicated the following year when the government's representative in Dublin was murdered by members of a secret society, although the group was not connected to the League. Public outrage forced Gladstone to impose three years of virtual martial law in Ireland.

In 1886, Gladstone's Liberals finally adopted Home Rule as party policy. The First Home Rule Bill, however, which was introduced in the same year, went down to defeat, precipitating a general election and a Conservative victory. The Conservatives subsequently maintained power almost uninterruptedly until 1906. The same tactics of combined repression and reform were adopted by the Conservative leader, Lord Salisbury (1830–1903). The government improved the terms of low-interest loans available to Irish tenant farmers for buying their own farms, instituted various public works, and introduced industrial and agricultural improvements. At the same time, however, harsh new laws clamped down on Irish nationalist activities. Salisbury's measures bought a brief period of calm, but resentment at the inequities remained. The issue flared up again in 1911, and a relatively long-lasting if uneasy compromise was not agreed on until 1922 (see Part VIII, Topic 5).

The Struggle for Reform
Successive Conservative governments introduced a number of moderate reforms in the structure of local government, the civil service, and education. Yet Conservative hostility to the trade unions led to a wave of strike protests, and in 1900 to the formation of a new political party, the Labour party. In the general elections of 1906, 29 Labour members were elected (see Part VII, Topic 19).

In that same election the Conservatives were overwhelmingly defeated, and the Liberals who swept back to power set out to redress working-class grievances by wholesale social reform. In 1909 the Liberal chancellor of the exchequer, David Lloyd George (1863–1945), prepared a budget that required extra revenue for social programs and for increased military

spending. He proposed to raise the funds with a system of progressive taxes according to which the more wealthy would pay a higher rate. His bill passed the House of Commons, but was rejected by an outraged House of Lords.

Seizing his opportunity, the Liberal prime minister, Herbert Henry Asquith (1852–1928), dissolved Parliament and fought an election on the two issues of the budget and the power of the House of Lords to block the government. In a famous speech during the election campaign, Lloyd George derided the noble members of the upper chamber, who inherited their seats from their fathers: "They need not be sound, either in body or in mind. They only require a certificate of birth, just to prove they are the first of the litter. You would not choose a spaniel on these principles."

Returned victorious to office, the Liberals carried their budget in both chambers. A bill to reform the House of Lords was passed by the Commons, but predictably rejected by the Lords themselves. At the end of 1910 Asquith repeated his move: he dissolved Parliament again, was voted back into office, and in August 1911 drove through a bill which effectively removed the Lords' power of veto.

The Liberal actions, far from satisfying the desire for thorough-going political reform, initiated a period

David Lloyd George in a photograph taken about 1904.

of widespread unrest. Between 1911 and 1914, strikes and demonstrations brought workers and troops into violent conflict. Labor leaders were jailed and strikers killed. During the same period the British suffragist movement pursued the cause of votes for women by increasingly militant means. Its members interrupted meetings, cut telephone wires, and smashed and burned public buildings. With violence erupting again in Ireland, Britain was plunged into a state of national disorder. The outbreak of war postponed the resolution of a crisis whose roots lay far back in the self-confidence of the Victorian Era.

FRANCE AND THE DILEMMAS OF THE THIRD REPUBLIC

If Britain's journey from the 1870s to the eve of war began in peace and prosperity, France began with a decade of social and political turbulence. After the Prussian victory over France at the Battle of Sedan in September 1870, the French republic had been proclaimed (see Part VII, Topic 11). The National Assembly chose as provisional president Adolphe Thiers (1797–1877), a liberal with monarchist sympathies.

In March 1871, the National Assembly angered the Parisians by moving the seat of government to Versailles, from where the monarchy had once ruled. This unpopular action was compounded by a cancellation of the moratorium on debts and a refusal to continue paying the National Guard, measures that had provided financial survival for many civilians during the siege of Paris. The final insult came when Thiers ordered the confiscation of some 200 cannon which the people of Paris had financed to fight the Prussians. In an outburst of popular fury, crowds rescued the cannon and killed two generals.

In the bloody civil war that ensued, Parisian radicals, inspired by the example of the 1792 revolutionary regime, proclaimed a Commune. The initial demands of its leaders were relatively moderate, but in May the republican government sent troops to crush the rebellion. The "Communards" defended the capital in bitter street fighting that lasted a week. The army shot hundreds of civilians. After the government had recaptured the city, some 20,000 Communards were executed and tens of thousands of others were sent to penal colonies. The brutal suppression of the Commune claimed more lives than any single event in the French Revolution.

In the aftermath of the Paris Commune, the Government of National Defense saw continued military rule in Paris and other large cities (see Part VII,

Topic 19). The press and public meetings remained under strict control, the International was banned, and suspected political agitators were arrested and transported to penal colonies in distant French Pacific territories.

The Third Republic

Meanwhile the politicians fought over the kind of political system that should govern France. Once again, as in 1849, the chief opponents were monarchists and republicans. In the elections of 1871 the voters returned a clear monarchist majority to the National Assembly. The main issue was that of war or peace, and the conservatives' support for the latter brought them victory.

Had it not been for a bitter split within the monarchist ranks into three factions—the two leading ones were the Bourbons who sought to establish a monarchy and the Orleanists who wanted a return to the empire—France would have seen the reestablishment of conservative rule. In any event, a prolonged standoff between the two royal clans led to an impasse and the creation of the Third Republic. The decision was passed in January 1875 by a majority of one vote, 353 to 352.

A two-chamber parliament was established, consisting of a Senate indirectly elected by local officials and a Chamber of Deputies chosen by universal male suffrage. Parliament was assigned the responsibility of electing a president to serve for seven years, who would appoint ministers, but much of whose power became ceremonial. Marshal Marie MacMahon (1808–1893), a monarchist, served as president until 1879. The stability of the Third Republic, which lasted until 1940, lay, paradoxically enough, in the lack of strong party rivalries and interests. Although ministries changed almost annually, most of them consisted of a reshuffling of the same politicians.

The only significant change of direction came in 1900, when the moderate republicans, the "Opportunists," were turned out of office by the repercussions of the Dreyfus affair, and were replaced by the so-called Radical republicans. In truth, the new government introduced few changes. One Radical faction fought for reform, but socialism was hardly influential in France until after World War I. For most of the period between the formation of the Third Republic and 1914, the government in office responded with varying success to the crisis of the day, while the ongoing task of running the country was left to an increasingly powerful civil service.

The Opportunists and the Dreyfus Affair

By 1879 both chambers of Parliament had a moderate republican majority. The Opportunists were so called because they believed in introducing reforms only when it was "opportune." Their leader, Leon Gambetta (1838–1882), once remarked, "There is no social question." Instead of social legislation, they concentrated on limiting the power of forces they thought dangerous: the church, the monarchists, and working-class radicals. The last of these, in the absence of serious government attempts at reform, began to develop an increasingly strong independent socialist party.

In the early 1880s a series of bomb attacks and attempted assassinations were attributed to anarchist plotters, and the authorities rounded up a number of well-known anarchists, including the Russian political theoretician Prince Peter Kropotkin (1842–1921). None of them could be linked to any of the incidents, but several, including Kropotkin, were sent to jail. The arrests aroused widespread protests in France and elsewhere in western Europe. When demonstrators took to the streets of Paris, the police made more arrests. Among those sentenced to jail was a woman named Louise Michel (1830–1905), known popularly as the "red virgin," one of the leading popular activists, who had played an important part in the Commune. By 1886 public opinion forced the release of all the jailed anarchists.

The anarchist scare was followed by a more serious potential threat to the government, in the shape of General Georges Boulanger (1837–1891). A dashing army officer, Boulanger appealed to the French weakness for glamorous authority figures, who promised to restore real or imagined past glories, and seemed to offer war and revenge against Germany. His danger lay in the fact that he managed to put together an informal coalition that included not only monarchists and nationalists, but also disgruntled urban poor. By the beginning of 1889, Boulanger-led forces seemed on the verge of power. At the news that the government was preparing to press false charges against him, however, the general suddenly took fright and fled to Belgium and the arms of his mistress. He subsequently committed suicide at her grave. His support abruptly melted away, but the very fact that such disparate elements backed him was a clear sign of serious discontent in French society.

At the turn of the century, French public life was rocked by the Dreyfus affair, a scandal which deeply divided the country and attracted attention throughout Europe. In 1894 Alfred Dreyfus (1859–1935), a Jewish member of the Army General Staff, was tried for espionage on behalf of the Germans; he was convicted, and transported to Devil's Island, France's notorious prison camp off the coast of South America. His brother Mathieu protested his innocence, avowing that his accusers, a group of monarchist army officers, were inspired by anti-Semitism. Both monarchists and nationalists became increasingly openly anti-Semitic in the

late 19th century. Another cause of discrimination was that Dreyfus came originally from Alsace, an eastern province annexed by Germany in the Franco-Prussian War; Alsatians who moved to central France after the war were never really regarded as fully French.

In 1897 evidence came to light which demonstrated conclusively that Dreyfus' conviction had been obtained by the use of forged documents. The government was asked to reopen the case. It refused, claiming that his supporters were trying to attack the honor of France in general, and the army in particular. With that, the entire country lined up as either pro-Dreyfus or anti-Dreyfus. On his side were liberals, socialists, and Radical republicans—the most famous of Dreyfus' defenders was the novelist Émile Zola (see Part VII, Topic 21). The distinguished general Georges Picquart also defended his military colleague, for which he was forcibly retired from the army and imprisoned. Arrayed against him were monarchists, nationalists, and reactionary Catholics, and also a substantial body of conservative working-class opinion.

Captain Alfred Dreyfus watches the breaking of his sword after his conviction for treason.

When one of the officers accused of forgery committed suicide, the government was forced to act. In 1899 a new court martial reached the absurd verdict that Dreyfus was guilty of espionage, but under "extenuating circumstances." In the face of widespread public protests, Dreyfus received a presidential pardon, and a further hearing in 1906 cleared him completely. His defender, General Picquart, was restored to active service, and served as minister of war from 1906 to 1909. Throughout the whole affair, in which strong opinions were often violently expressed and demonstrators frequently came to blows, the person who seemed least moved was Dreyfus himself. Unemotional, tight-lipped, as patriotic as the most fanatical of his accusers, he formed the still center of a storm that wrecked the Opportunists' grip on power.

The controversy left no doubt as to the continued strength of antirepublican sentiment in France, and Dreyfus' acquittal did nothing to lessen anti-Semitism. On the other hand justice was finally, if belatedly, done, and extended public debate ended with the monarchist forces largely discredited.

The Radicals in Power

The Opportunists' Radical successors did little to improve on the Opportunists' unimpressive record of social reform. French living and working conditions remained inferior to those in many other parts of western Europe. Government legislation concentrated on curbing the power of the church with sweeping anticlerical measures, provoked at least in part by the Catholic stand on the Dreyfus affair. Unauthorized schools and religious orders were prohibited, and in 1905 the union of church and state was dissolved. For the first time since Napoleon's reforms of 1801, all religions had equal status.

The industrial reforms of the 1870s, which included protective legislation for youths, women, and miners, went some way to reduce industrial unrest, and over the following decade, France had fewer strikes than most other western European countries. Around the turn of the century, however, the climate rapidly deteriorated. On several occasions between 1906 and 1910, militant strikers were ruthlessly beaten back, with deaths and injuries. Other demonstrators were arrested and jailed. France's prime minister, Georges Clemenceau (served 1906–1909, 1917–1920), openly described himself as his country's "number one policeman."

In 1910 and 1911 housewives across France staged massive protests at the steep rise in the price of basic commodities such as eggs and milk. In general French trade unions did not encourage women members. Now, however, in a mood of growing frustration, and impressed by the energy of the women's lobby,

union leaders organized them into consumer associations or enlisted them in the unions. Yet labor's struggle was an uphill one. When the railway strike of 1910 was crushed, most French socialists and political radicals came to believe that it was useless to look to the government to produce any serious reform in living and working conditions. Only direct action, they claimed, could bring about change. The fragile political stalemate between workers and management was barely maintained up to the outbreak of war in 1914.

GERMANY AND ITALY: THE PROBLEMS OF NATIONHOOD

For all the obstacles overcome, Europe's two new nations had yet more problems to solve in the task of achieving stable government and social justice. Political parties needed to be developed that could balance the existing social and economic forces against the requirements of nationhood—and this at a time of growing international tension. Both German and Italian leaders first tried to deal with groups they con-

Kaiser Wilhelm II put Germany on a collision course with France and England after the forced retirement of Bismarck.

sidered hostile to their regimes before addressing social and political reform, often failing to recognize the connection between the two issues. By 1914, neither country had reached a satisfactory resolution for its institutional problems.

The new German empire, created in January 1871, was in theory democratically based. Of the two chambers of Parliament, the lower house, or *Reichstag*, was elected by universal male suffrage, and the upper house, or *Bundesrat*, was made up of appointed representatives of the 25 states comprising the empire. In practice, however, Germany was among the least democratic nations in Western Europe. Prussia dominated all the other German states by means of its power of veto over constitutional changes, and by the authority of the Prussian king, who was also German emperor. He served as head of the army, and thus controlled foreign policy and the waging of war. Furthermore, German chancellors invariably came from Prussia. Bismarck served as minister-president of Prussia as well as chancellor of the Reich. Had there been a strong tradition of political parties represented in the Reichstag, the emperor's position might have been challenged. The failure of Prussian liberals to oppose Bismarck's manipulations of the constitutional system in the 1860s had sorely weakened German liberalism. As it was, even the most influential of his ministers served only at the monarch's pleasure, as Bismarck himself was to discover. Since the Prussian king continued to favor the interests of the Junker and business classes, the creation of Germany brought no real change in political policies. The consequence of reactionary government was the rise of an increasingly aggressive socialist movement.

Catholics and Socialists in Bismarck's Germany

Bismarck, who served as German chancellor from 1871 to 1890, was well aware of the threat posed to traditional interests by socialism. His first target, though, was the Catholic Church, and in particular the Jesuits, whom he believed to be the natural enemies of a Protestant Germany. In the early 1870s he began to wage the *Kulturkampf* (the "struggle for civilization") against the Catholic Church. His motives were by no means only religious. He was anxious to cement the new Germany, and resented the outside influence of the church; in addition, he feared a possible alliance of Catholic powers—Austria, France, Italy—against Germany.

The Jesuits were expelled from Germany, members of religious orders were not allowed to teach in Prussian schools, and political statements by members of the clergy were censored. Bismarck's reforms introduced civil marriage and divorce. The same program

was extended to Prussian Poland, which was predominantly Catholic. There, in addition to religious legislation, the elementary schools were required to teach their classes in German rather than Polish.

Discrimination against Poles continued, but in Prussia the German Catholics fought back. By 1878 Bismarck was forced by public support for the Catholic Center party to incorporate them in his alliance, and to withdraw most of the *Kulturkampf* legislation. Thereafter the church occupied the same position as elsewhere in continental Europe, one of support for conservative interests and opposition to socialism. In addition, Bismarck's questioning of Catholics' patriotism made them especially anxious to appear nationalistic.

Bismarck's battle with the socialists was a far more bitter and long-drawn-out affair. Indeed, government persecution of individual socialist workers' groups backfired. The separate organizations banded together in self-defense, and in 1875 laid the foundations of what was to become the Social Democratic party (SPD), Europe's first real socialist party. To Bismarck's horror, the new party soon had thousands of members, was publishing widely circulating newspapers, and won almost 10 percent of the votes in the elections of 1877.

The following year two unsuccessful attempts to assassinate the emperor gave Bismarck his chance to strike back. Even though the SPD had no connection with the attacks, in October 1878 the *Reichstag* passed an antisocialist law, banning any activity aimed at "the overthrow of the existing political or social order." The law remained in force until 1890. During the interim, thousands were arrested or driven into exile, and almost 1300 books, periodicals, and newspapers were banned.

The antisocialist law represented the negative side of Bismarck's campaign. His more positive effort consisted of a series of reforms that he hoped would eliminate working-class support for socialism. Beginning in 1883–1884, he introduced measures that made Germany a model of progressive social welfare. Workers were insured against incapacity due to illness, accidents, or old age. Maximum working hours were fixed for men, and limits were established for the employment of women and children. Official inspection of working conditions became mandatory. The aim of all this legislation was to wean workers from socialism.

Germany Under the Emperor

Whether the bizarre combination of repression and social benevolence would have enabled Bismarck to keep the socialists under control is impossible to say: in 1890 he was dismissed by the new emperor, Wilhelm II (ruled 1888–1918). Although Wilhelm's immediate pretext was his opposition to the renewal of Bismarck's antisocialist law, which lapsed in 1890, his real reason was that he was determined to rule in his own right. Wilhelm asserted Germany's role as a great power and would unravel Bismarck's cautious international policies.

Although the SPD could once again function openly, Wilhelm was a strong believer in the principle of divine right. After an initial period of tolerance in the "new course" of 1890 to 1894 that followed Bismarck's dismissal, he showed no greater sympathy with working-class problems than his Hohenzollern ancestors.

The emperor's chancellor from 1900 to 1909 was Bernhard Heinrich Martin von Bülow, who had previously held a wide variety of diplomatic posts. Bülow was anxious to achieve imperial glory for Germany, but his manipulation of foreign affairs led to the formation of an anti-German alliance of Britain, France, and Russia, and eventually to World War I. In 1909, in an argument over the budget, he lost the emperor's confidence and resigned.

Over the previous two decades an increasingly threatening gap had begun to appear between a rapidly swelling socialist party and a ruling class bent on preserving the privileges of the wealthy, the landowners, and the military. In the elections of 1912, the SPD became the largest party in the *Reichstag* and the strongest socialist party in Europe. When war came in 1914, the class divisions that had been endemic to German life throughout the 19th century were no nearer resolution.

Political Inequity in Italy

When, with the annexation of Rome in 1870, the patriots of the Italian Risorgimento finally achieved their goal, the high expectations aroused in the struggle for unity were far from matched by reality. The political system under which the new nation was governed between 1870 and 1922—the period of the so-called "Liberal State"—left much to be desired. As in Germany, the Italian constitution left significant powers to the king. The two-chamber parliament consisted of a Senate, appointed by the monarch, and an elected Chamber of Deputies. Formal political parties were not yet in existence, but in theory the two chief parliamentary groups stood for two opposing positions: the *Destra* (the Right), representing the conservative tradition inherited from Cavour, and the *Sinistra* (the Left), the forces that had opposed Cavour. Although the Sinistra began by championing the poor, especially those of southern Italy, in practice any real difference between the groups soon disappeared. Both proved to be equally repressive of those they saw as challenging their own élite interests. Before the end of the century, they had merged into a single "liberal" party.

In any case, the number of those qualified to vote was so limited that few Italians felt seriously involved in the political process. From 1870 to 1882, only about 2 percent of the population could vote; from 1882 to 1911 the average was around 8 percent. Virtually all voters were drawn from the traditional power bases: the upper and upper-middle classes. In consequence, the Destra and the Sinistra soon came to reflect the interests of the élite. As for the average Italian, frustration at being excluded from political life became expressed in the wry observation that "Things were better off when they were worse off."

Popular Protests and the Italian Socialist Movement

The Destra governments of 1869–1876 and the Sinistra administrations of the following decades followed the same policy of repressing radical movements. In 1877, the Italian branch of the International was banned outright, its leaders were arrested, and socialist newspapers were destroyed. Both were equally anticlerical and antirepublican. Repression reached its height during the premierships of Francesco Crispi (served as prime minister 1887–1891, 1893–1896), especially after the formation of the Italian Socialist party in 1892. In 1894 Crispi passed a series of harsh laws against those guilty of "incitement to class hatred." Crispi, once a radical hero of the Risorgimento, emerged as an ambitious prime minister with a bent for dictatorship.

Serious peasant uprisings in Sicily were followed in the fall of 1897 by a wave of strikes and demonstrations that swept through the country and was met with brutal government reaction; in some regions martial law was imposed. The worst violence was in Milan in 1898, where troops fired indiscriminately on unarmed demonstrators. General Fiorenzo Bava-Beccaris, who was decorated by the king for ordering the shootings, became popularly dubbed "the butcher of Milan." Even a Capuchin monastery was raided, and its monks charged with being revolutionaries in disguise. The government insisted that the various spontaneous riots formed a single socialist conspiracy to overthrow the regime. With the disorders under control, the government proceeded to round up thousands of "dissidents," ranging from Catholic priests to trade union leaders.

Trasformismo

The antigovernment riots were provoked by a variety of causes—rent increases, land seizures, rises in the price of bread. Beneath them all, however, lay deep popular resentment at the failure of Italy's parliamentary system to resolve the widespread poverty that afflicted the peasantry and the slowly developing working class. By the 1880s a phenomenon known as *trasformismo* developed, which lasted up to 1914. Under trasformismo, a politician of the left could hold office under the right by becoming "transformed." In practice this meant that the two chief parties divided up between themselves the advantages of power and handed them out to their respective members. This arrangement recognized that the labels left and right, used during the Risorgimento to describe differences of approach to the unification question, were no longer applicable. Patronage, coupled with the manipulation of election results, meant that the only politicians who had any chance of success were those who cooperated and joined the system.

Faced with such cynicism on the part of their rulers, many Italians lost any remaining faith in the possibility of serious social or political reform. The benefits of the few social welfare measures that were introduced, which included penal, educational, and public health reform, were outweighed by the bitter hostility between workers and government. By the end of the century the only major country in Europe with a more repressive regime was Russia.

Even the extension of the suffrage in 1882 had little effect, since on the urging of the pope, large numbers of Catholic voters abstained in protest at the government's anticlericalism. The Italian seizure of Rome in 1870 had driven a wedge between the new kingdom and the papacy that persisted for more than half a century. Pope Pius IX protested the Italian action by declaring himself a "prisoner of the Vatican," and refused to recognize the existence of the Italian state. In 1874 he issued the encyclical *Non Expedit*, by which he discouraged Italian Catholics from taking part in the political life of the kingdom, thereby preventing the formation of a Catholic-oriented political party.

Giolitti and the Politics of Compromise

In 1900, King Umberto I (ruled 1878–1900) was assassinated by an emigrant anarchist named Gaetano Bresci, who had returned to Italy from Paterson, New Jersey, to exact retribution for the bloodshed of 1898. The new king, Victor Emmanuel III (ruled 1900–1946), proved more sensitive to the need for a relaxation of social tensions. Under the leading Italian politician of the early 20th century, Giovanni Giolitti (1842–1928), a measure of confidence was restored. Far from abolishing trasformismo, Giolitti extended it to include those opposition elements that had previously been excluded: the Catholics, and, more crucially, the socialists. Thus the responsibility of power was shared over a wider political base as Giolitti attempted to coopt these new elements into the parliamentary system. Giolitti's motives were practical. He saw that the continual exclusion of Catholic and working-class interests from participation in government could lead only to crisis.

Prime Minister Giovanni Giolitti dominated Italian politics from the turn of the century until World War I.

The result of his policies was a notable lessening of social tension, although the compromise was often an uncomfortable one. Just as Giolitti accepted the necessity of collaborating with the socialists, so he also relied on the support of a substantial group of corrupt right-wing southern Italian and Sicilian politicians who were notorious for their manipulation of elections. To those reproaching him with double dealing, he replied that, "A tailor who has to cut a suit for a hunchback has no choice but to make a hunchback suit."

With the help of a major improvement in the Italian economy, and the reduction of class conflict, Giolitti's government introduced a program of social legislation. Life insurance and the railways were nationalized, with lower prices and better services made available on a broader basis, and the public health system was reformed. In 1911, to consolidate his support on the left, he passed a bill that introduced universal male suffrage; the Italian Socialist party did not yet officially endorse giving women the vote, although left-wing parties elsewhere in western Europe supported the suffragist cause (see Part VII, Topic 19). Not until after

World War I, however, did the full impact of the new suffrage law make itself felt.

In characteristically Giolittian style, at the same time he sought to mollify Italian nationalists by giving them what they wanted: a colonial war in Libya. Italy's desire to emulate her European neighbors and acquire an empire had already led to trouble at the end of the previous century, when Crispi had been forced to resign in 1896 by the disastrous failure of a colonial expedition he sent to Abyssinia (Ethiopia). In the Battle of Adowra, troops led by Menelik II (ruled 1889–1913) crushed the badly outnumbered Italian expedition, the first African army to defeat a European colonizing force. In the period of increasing international tension that preceded World War I, Giolitti saw a chance to move into North Africa. Libya officially belonged to the Ottoman Empire, but the Turks were in no condition in 1911 to defend their property. Italian forces occupied Tripoli, together with the group of Greek islands known as the Dodecanese (the largest is Rhodes), and the sultan conceded Libya and the islands to Italy. The general rejoicing this victory inspired underlined the Italian thirst for imperial status.

Yet, in the long run Giolitti's policy of trying to please all sides led to the return of political polarization. The nationalist right, fearing the consequences of the extension of the suffrage, created the Italian Nationalist Association and formed armed bands "for the defense of order." Radical socialists, opposed to the seizure of Libya, moved their party into a position of extreme opposition to the government. An economic decline in 1913 led to a resurgence of widespread strikes and industrial protests. In June 1914 a general strike led to violent demonstrations in many parts of the country. During "Red Week," rioters in central Italy cut telegraph lines and blocked train tracks, and managed to unfurl a red flag over the town hall of Bologna. By the late summer of 1914, with war being openly declared elsewhere in Europe, Italy was bitterly divided.

THE PACE OF DEVELOPMENT: NORTH AND SOUTH

Protest and repression were not limited to the major European powers. Industrialization and the gradual diffusion of socialist ideas affected the political climate throughout the continent. Even the absolutist regimes of Austria-Hungary and Russia were shaken by the spirit of the times (see Part VII, Topic 16). In general, protestors in the poorer countries of southern Europe continued to fight for political and economic reform right up to World War I. In northern Europe, where a measure of political and economic progress had been won by the 1890s, the remaining goals were social reforms: improvement of working and living conditions, the provision of insurance schemes, health care.

Political Oppression in Southern Europe

Spain, Portugal, and the Balkans remained the poorest, least developed parts of Europe right up to World War I. In 1868, Spain had been racked by a revolution that unseated its unpopular ruler, Queen Isabella II (ruled 1833–1868). A later revolt in 1873 forced the king to abdicate and created a short-lived republic. Thereafter, alternating conservative and liberal governments protected the interests of the ruling classes and exploited the advantages of power, while ruthlessly putting down workers' protests. The system of alternation was called *turno pacifico* ("taking turns peacefully"). In the 1880s the Spanish police used the alleged formation of a terrorist organization called the Black Hand to arrest and imprison thousands, although there is considerable doubt as to whether the Black Hand ever really existed. Worker response included massive demonstrations. In 1892–1893 some 20,000 Spaniards were jailed on the

Significant Dates

Western Europe 1870–1914

1875	France inaugurates Third Republic
1878	Bismarck withdraws *Kulturkampf* reform
1879	Parnell forms Irish National party
1880	Gladstone returns to power
1883–1884	Bismarck introduces social welfare legislation
1886	Gladstone's Home Rule Bill defeated
1892	Italian Socialist party formed
1894	Dreyfus convicted of treason
1900	Umberto I assassinated
1900	British Labour Party formed
1901	Death of Queen Victoria
1905	Finland first European country in which women can vote
1910–1911	Strikes across France
1912	German SPD becomes strongest socialist party in Europe
1901–1914	Giolittian era in Italy

accusation of having been involved in a series of violent incidents. In 1897 an anarchist assassinated Prime Minister Antonio Canovas del Castillo.

During the first decade of the 20th century, terrorist bombings and police reprisals continued to wreak havoc in Spain's public life. The coming of age of King Alfonso XIII (ruled 1886–1931) in 1902 did little to resolve national problems. A climax of sorts came in 1909, when in the *Semana Tragica* (Tragic Week), 30,000 demonstrators took over the city of Barcelona for several days. The police regained control by firing on the crowds. Among those arrested and executed afterwards was Francisco Ferrar, one of Spain's leading anarchist theoreticians. The day of Ferrar's execution was marked by massive demonstrations throughout Europe. The situation continued to degenerate, and by 1914 both political parties were torn by internal disputes. In the elections of that year the government failed to win a majority.

Portuguese public life was also controlled by two parties who protected one another's interests, the cynically named Regenerators and Progressives. The system that was devised to make sure they retained power, and thereby access to public funds—the equivalent of the Spanish turno pacifico—was called "rotavism." It led to widespread popular disgust at political corruption. In addition to worker protests, an increasingly strong middle-class republican movement began to form, which attributed Portugal's problems to its king, Carlos I (ruled 1889–1908).

In 1908 Carlos and the heir to the throne were both assassinated in Lisbon, and two years later, in October 1910, a republican uprising overthrew the regime and abolished the monarchy. The republicans were joined in the coup by left-wing forces, who shared their hatred of the Catholic Church and the crown, but the republicans soon alienated their allies. Republican Prime Minister Alfonso Costa (served 1913) enforced the violent repression of demonstrators. He also won the dubious distinction of being the only European government leader to secure passage of a bill actually reducing the suffrage. The electoral law of 1913 cut the number of voters in half.

At the other side of southern Europe, in the Balkans, economic conditions were even more wretched, and liberal government proved elusive. In the absence of an hereditary aristocracy, two forces, the ruling princes and kings, and professional city politicians, battled for power. The instruments used in the struggle were the army and the police, which were kept strong by the conscription and heavy taxes imposed on the peasants.

Bulgaria had been part of the Ottoman Empire from 1396 to 1878, when Turkish rule there was restricted by the Congress of Berlin. In 1894, the Bulgarian state spent less money on the combination of education, agriculture, justice, administration, and other public services than went to support the army. Thus living conditions which had been grim under the Turks deteriorated still further.

At the end of the century a series of disastrous harvests drove the Bulgarian peasants into open revolt. In 1900 thousands of demonstrators were dispersed only by wildly firing troops. In January 1907, a national railway strike led to widespread rioting. Among the leaders of the protests were students and professors from Sofia University. In retaliation the government closed the university and jailed many of the students. A few weeks later the prime minister was assassinated. By 1914 opposition to the regime was so strong that in the elections of that year only massive rigging, including the kidnapping of antigovernment candidates, kept the government in power.

Greece was the only country in southeastern Europe where some degree of liberal reform was introduced. In 1875 the young liberal politician Charilaos Tricoupis persuaded the king to call the first fair elections in his nation's history. In the absence of any democratic party tradition, the results were predictably confused. Between 1875 and 1882 Greece was governed by thirteen different ministries. Tricoupis managed to create somewhat more settled conditions for a few years, during which he encouraged economic development and tried to build a stable civil service.

On the death of Tricoupis in 1896, Greece's political life once again fragmented, with eight elections over the next twelve years. Finally, in 1909, army demands for reform were supported by mass popular demonstrations in Athens. The government fell, to be replaced by military rule. When that, too, proved unpopular, the Cretan politician Eleutherios Venizelos was chosen to lead a new national assembly, charged with rewriting the constitution. Venizelos' reforms were generally progressive, but they did little to change the basic character of Greek politics.

Social Protest in the North

In Scandinavia, political affairs were complicated at the turn of the century by hostility between Norway and Sweden, for Norway was ruled by the Swedish king, although it had its own parliament. After much diplomatic skirmishing, Norway was finally declared independent in 1905.

In all three of the principal Scandinavian countries—Norway, Sweden, and Denmark—the early years of the 20th century were marked by significant extensions of the suffrage. Socialist groups in Denmark and Sweden continued to lead protests, even though the International was banned in Denmark and socialists were harassed in Sweden during the 1880s. In 1893 and 1896 Swedish socialists organized two "People's Parliaments" in Stockholm to agitate for electoral reform. A reform bill was finally passed by the Swedish Parliament in 1907–1909, and followed by a flurry of social legislation. Old age pensions were introduced, the penal code was brought up to date, and working hours and conditions were made subject to control.

A similar process occurred in the Netherlands and Belgium: conservative governments unwillingly introduced electoral reform in response to widespread popular uprisings. The first serious riots broke out in 1886 in Belgium. Although they were violently quashed, they succeeded in making politicians aware of the degree of working-class discontent. Minor reforms were introduced, including restrictions on the employment of women and children. Demonstrations continued to rock Belgium almost annually, until in 1893 a form of universal male suffrage was introduced. Demands for the introduction of a more equitable system continued up to the war, including a socialist-led general strike in 1913, but universal and equal male suffrage became law only in 1919.

Although protests in the Netherlands were less violent, they proved in the long run more effective. A liberal government, in office from 1897 to 1901, passed a large number of social measures: it was dubbed the "Cabinet of Social Justice." Electoral reform proved more elusive. Large-scale demonstrations were held in 1910, 1911, and 1912, and hundreds of thousands of people signed petitions in favor of extending the suffrage. As elsewhere in Europe, however, it took World War I to effect the change: universal male suffrage was finally adopted in 1917.

By the outbreak of World War I, the optimistic confidence of the mid-19th century was long gone. Those countries which had tried to reconcile the interests of rulers and ruled had discovered it to be an agonizing process. Furthermore, there were still many areas on the fringes of Europe where conditions remained untouched by liberal reforms. However noble the ideal of a constitutional monarchy and parliamentary democracy might be, it proved almost impossible to implement to general satisfaction. The greater the pressure for change, the stiffer the resistance of those in power became. Since the rulers controlled the instruments of their rule—the police and the army—violent conflict was inevitable. When war came in 1914, the established order in most European countries was faced with serious challenges. Within the ruling classes, not a few regarded the war as an escape from the mounting threat to their authority. Events were to prove them wrong.

Questions for Further Study

1. What were the chief differences between the pace of political reform in Britain, France, Germany, and Italy?

2. What part did the development of socialist parties and trade unions play in the political crises of the early 20th century?

3. Why did the "Dreyfus affair" become so important at the turn of the century? What light does it throw on the nature of French society at the time?

4. To what extent were countries in northern and southern Europe faced with the same political problems as those in western Europe? To what extent—if at all—did they resolve them?

Suggestions for Further Reading

Avrich, P. *Anarchist Portraits*. Princeton, NJ, 1988.

Burns, M. *Rural Society and French Politics: Boulangism and the Dreyfus Affair*. Princeton, NJ, 1984.

Hause, S. C., and A. R. Kenney. *Women's Suffrage and Social Politics in the French Third Republic*. Princeton, NJ, 1984.

Lovett, Clara M. *The Democratic Movement in Italy*. Cambridge, MA, 1982.

Mommsen, W. J., and H.-G. Husung, eds. *The Development of Trade Unionism in Great Britain and Germany, 1880–1914*. Boston, 1985.

Sheehan, J. J. *German Liberalism in the Nineteenth Century*. Chicago, 1978.

Wehler, Hans-Ulrich. *The German Empire, 1871–1918*. Leamington Spa, England, 1985.

T o p i c   1 6

THE CRISIS OF EMPIRE IN EASTERN EUROPE

 he trend toward increased democracy in Western Europe was slow, but in most countries reformers made progress. In Eastern Europe, by contrast, liberal and worker demands were ever more rigorously and consistently repressed, with the result that opposition forces never managed to organize themselves. Where parliaments existed, they had little or no real power. In the absence of adequate social welfare legislation in countries that were inherently poor, living standards were far inferior to those in the West. Health care and education remained primitive, and the lack of widespread industrialization limited the development of organized labor. The one serious challenge to a regime, the Russian Revolution of 1905, was led by the only relatively industrialized working class in eastern Europe.

In the Austro-Hungarian empire, the Dual Monarchy became increasingly paralyzed by conflict between the empire's various nationalities. Power remained firmly in the hands of Emperor Franz Josef. Between 1870 and 1890 a socialist movement began to develop, but the government arrested its members and crushed any sign of rebellion. Civil liberties were repeatedly suspended. On the other hand, like Bismarck in Germany, the emperor tried to placate the workers with welfare legislation, to the disgust of conservatives. The years after 1890 saw the gradual extension of the vote, leading to universal male suffrage in 1906.

The Hungarians, like the Germans within the empire—a minority but a far more independent one—maintained their control by a blend of nationalist fervor and bureaucratic corruption in favor of the aristocratic landowners. Other ethnic minorities in Hungary were forcibly repressed. When the Magyars threatened to assert themselves even further by nationalizing their army regiments, Franz Josef suspended the constitution.

In Russia, Alexander III intensified the persecution of opponents and minorities. From 1881 until 1891, the government ruled with virtually unlimited powers of repression. Nonetheless, the gradual spread of education and the rise of an urban working class, coupled with a series of disastrous famines and cholera epidemics, produced growing public resentment. Under Alexander's successor, Nicholas II, agitation led to demonstrations and the revolution of 1905. Nicholas made concessions, but within a year he had withdrawn most of these reforms.

By the 1870s, the Ottoman Empire was in the last stages of disintegration. Turkish territories in the Balkans revolted continuously, and by 1878 the Turks had lost most of their European possessions. Within Turkey itself contempt for the sultan's corrupt and inefficient rule was compounded by the dawning of a new national pride. In 1908 a group known as the "Young Turks," supporting Western ideas, forced the sultan to introduce an elected parliament. A year later, they deposed him.

The effects of the Balkan conflicts went far beyond the Ottoman Empire, for they brought the European great powers into increasing tension. The period from 1870 to 1890 was dominated by Bismarck's elaborate but cautious diplomatic maneuverings. After 1890, however, international relations were marked by shifting alliances that ended with Europe split into two camps: Britain, France, and Russia versus Germany, Austria, and Italy. Repeated diplomatic crises after 1905 raised international tensions to a fever pitch. On July 28, 1914, a Serbian nationalist assassinated the Austrian Archduke Franz Ferdinand at Sarajevo, and the world was plunged into war.

THE SUNSET OF THE AUSTRO-HUNGARIAN EMPIRE

The formation of the Dual Monarchy (see Part VII, Topic 10) went some way to relieving tensions between Austria and Hungary, but the basic problem underlying the Hapsburg empire—the conflict between its numerous ethnic groups—remained unresolved. The few gestures in the direction of liberalization made things only worse, since as soon as minorities received a measure of political power they used it to protest their grievances. The only public figure in Austria who seemed to support liberal reform was Crown Prince Rudolf (1858–1889), who was found shot in the royal hunting lodge at Meyerling, together with the 17-year-old Baroness Mary Vetsera. The exact circumstances of their deaths have never been clarified, but it appears that the two may have taken part in a suicide pact.

The sheer number of parties and interest groups ensured that the Emperor Franz Josef remained firmly in control. Both the national parliament, the *Reichsrat*, and the regional parliaments served as little more than debating chambers, and were all dissolved by the time of the outbreak of war in 1914. The emperor and his governments ruled by decree. To maintain a sort of balance, Franz Josef shifted between liberal and conservative prime ministers, but the repression of left-wing opposition remained constant. The press was kept under strict control, and the authorities maintained a careful surveillance over the socialist and trade union movements that began to develop in Austria after 1870. By contrast to Vienna's reactionary political condition, cultural life there was astonishingly rich, varied, and creative (see Part VII, Topic 21).

The conservative Count Eduard von Taaffe (1833–1895) served as prime minister from 1879 to 1893. Following an outbreak of anarchist terrorism in the early 1880s, his government suspended civil rights in Vienna, broke up political associations, and made numerous arrests. Taking his example from Bismarck in Germany, Taaffe tried to head off workers' support for the socialists by offering a program of welfare legislation. One of the measures, the spread of education, exacerbated ethnic tensions, since the issue of which language should be used in the empire's various school districts became a major fighting point. His social reforms had already won him the opposition of his fellow conservatives, and the renewed bout of nationalist feuding brought down his ministry; the immediate cause was his attempt to introduce universal male suffrage.

Taaffe's successors drew the moral that to introduce even minor reform was dangerous, and later governments tried to maintain as inactive a position as possible. Public demonstrations compelled some degree of liberalization in 1896, when a form of suffrage was extended to virtually all adult males. In theory, some 20 percent of the population was thenceforth entitled to vote, but a complex class electoral system ensured that control over elections remained in the hands of the richest 2 percent. The Russian Revolution of 1905 encouraged a fresh outburst of popular resentment: in November of that year a quarter of a million people joined demonstrations in Vienna, and protests were also organized in other cities of the empire, including Prague and Trieste. In consequence, universal and equal male suffrage was introduced in 1906. Since parliament had such limited powers, however, this concession did little to change the political realities.

Emperor Franz Josef (center left) with dignitaries at a court ball in the Imperial Palace, Vienna, in 1913.

Ethnic Conflicts

Even if the Reichsrat had been given far more authority—and it was in any case disastrously divided into warring factions—there would have been scant possibility of its resolving the multiplying nationalist crises that bedeviled the last years of the empire. In Bohemia, Czechs and Germans remained locked in conflict, and Franz Josef's policy of favoring first one and then the other only compounded the mutual hostility. In the summer of 1893 the German-speaking authorities in Prague took advantage of a wave of violence directed against German and imperial signs and emblems to declare a state of emergency. Trials by jury and public meetings were suspended, stiff press censorship was renewed, and members of left-wing organizations were jailed. Schools were forbidden to fly Czech flags; when teachers protested, Count Franz Thun, the governor, told them: "If you do not do as you are told, I shall break your necks."

Several years later, in a characteristic attempt to balance both sides, the central government sought to win over the Czechs by requiring that all civil servants should speak both Czech and German. This time it was the turn of the German speakers to riot, both in Bohemia and Vienna. The dismissal of the prime minister responsible for the pro-Czech legislation led inevitably to another round of Czech protests and to the imposition of martial law.

The same pattern of worsening ethnic clashes occurred throughout the empire. In those parts of northern Italy still under Austrian rule, fighting broke out in 1904 between Italian and German speakers. In the former territory of Poland, now under Austrian rule, where there were very few resident Germans, the Austrians encouraged the Polish upper classes in their repression of the Polish and Ruthenian peasants, who lived as virtual serfs. Revolts against aristocratic landowners occurred in 1899 and 1902, and in 1908 a Ruthenian student assassinated the governor.

Nationalism in Hungary

The case of Hungary was rather different, at least in theory. Hungarian nationalists had already won many of the concessions for which other minorities in the empire were fighting: the Magyar language was used in schools, the courts, and public services, and the Hungarians, by the provisions of the *Ausgleich* (see Part VII, Topic 10), had their own government. These powers were used systematically to defend the interests of the landed aristocracy and to repress the other minorities resident in Hungary, in particular the Romanians. The result was further ethnic hostility. In one of the most notorious episodes, in 1892 a group of Romanians was jailed for having sent a petition of complaint to Franz Josef, who refused to read it and reported it to the local authorities.

In spite of the rights they had won, many Hungarians continued to demand further concessions from Vienna. In 1903 nationalist politicians began to agitate for the reorganization of the army, with the use of the Magyar language for Hungarian regiments. The scheme inevitably met with a blunt veto from Franz Josef, but the nationalists insisted, and parliamentary proceedings degenerated into uproar, with members overturning benches and tearing down paneling from the walls. In the political confusion that followed, socialist and trade union organizations, hitherto tightly controlled, staged strikes and protests.

Early in 1906, Franz Josef stepped in. Parliament was dissolved with the use of military force. The emperor appointed the new prime minister, and guaranteed him the grudging support of the Hungarians by threatening to introduce universal male suffrage if they did not cooperate: the extension of the vote to the lower classes and the other minorities would have meant the end of Hungarian aristocratic supremacy. The reality of the emperor's threat was brought home by repeated mass protests in favor of electoral reform in the years from 1906 to 1913. When parliament finally passed a reform bill, in March 1913, it raised the percentage of those eligible to vote from 6 to 8 percent of the population; on the eve of war, Hungary's electorate was the most restricted of any European country, including Russia.

By 1914 the Austro-Hungarian empire was irretrievably damaged by decades of bitter interethnic strife. Taaffe, the prime minister of the 1880s, had described his method of government as *fortwursteln* — "muddling through." Much the same could have been said of Franz Josef (who died in 1916), but with the coming of war the confusion was too great to resolve even by more systematic methods. To the astonishment and bewilderment of many of its citizens, who believed it, for better or worse, indestructible, in 1917, after three years of fighting, the Hapsburg empire simply collapsed in defeat.

THE RUSSIAN EMPIRE: INDUSTRIALIZATION AND POLITICAL CRISIS

When Tsar Alexander III (ruled 1881–1894) was brought to power in 1881 by the assassination of his father, Alexander II, one of his first acts was to order the public execution of those implicated in the attack. A crowd of over 100,000 attended. It set the tone for a reign marked by unrelieved reactionary repression. In August of the same year, a "provisional decree" gave the government almost unlimited powers of censorship, arrest, and deportation; the decree was regularly renewed, and remained in effect until the last tsar was deposed in 1917. The press and universities were placed under rigid control, and all student organizations were abolished.

By the time of Alexander's death in 1894, his policies had effectively suppressed all organized opposition throughout the Russian empire. His son and successor, Nicholas II (ruled 1894–1917), continued

Alexander's methods. All minority groups, especially Poles, Finns, and Jews, were subject to the process of "Russification." The Poles were forced to use the Russian language in their schools. In 1899 the Finnish Parliament was stripped of its powers and replaced by direct rule by the tsar. Protesting Finnish nationalists were roused by Jean Sibelius' stirring musical tone poem *Finlandia*.

Yet in 1905 massive public protests forced Nicholas to make major concessions. Several factors contributed to so remarkable a reversal. Nicholas himself, deceptively mild-mannered in appearance, was as committed to maintaining his autocratic rule as his father had been, but less aggressively single-minded in enforcing it. In addition, a series of terrible famines and epidemics of cholera in the 1890s led to widespread poverty and distress in the rural districts, and fueled anger among the peasants.

Perhaps even more significant was the rise of a working-class population, as industrialization began to concentrate large numbers of urban poor in the big centers of production. Although the pace of Russian industrial development lagged behind that in the West, by the end of the 19th century manufacturing and heavy industry plants existed in Moscow, St. Petersburg, Rostov-on-Don, and throughout southern Russia. In the 1890s, the tsar's minister of finances, Count Sergei Witte (1849–1915), adopted the gold standard in order to make the Russian currency easily convertible and instituted other fiscal reforms. Capital from France was used to finance Russian railway and telegraph construction, and the Franco-Russian understanding became ratified into a formal alliance in 1894. With the spread of the railways raw materials were transported to these new industrial centers, and the finished products distributed both in Russia and elsewhere in Europe.

The growth of manufacturing and trade, and improvements in transport, produced radical changes in Russian society, which had been stagnant for so long. At the bottom end of the ladder, the peasants were now joined by urban workers, who were congregated in the big cities. Unlike the rural poor, they could make their presence felt both by mass strike action and by demonstrations in the most important cities of the empire. At the same time a middle, business class began to appear, eager to speed the process of westernization in Russia, if necessary by the introduction of liberal principles of government.

The new classes sought to change Russia's monolithic regime by the formation of political parties. The Constitutional Democratic party represented the middle class and progressive landowners, while the Social Revolutionary and Social Democratic parties were led by radicals. The latter two had to operate for the most part underground, and many of their leaders either fled to exile in Western Europe, or had to face imprisonment, often in Siberia. The Social Democratic party was to play a crucial role in the later Russian Revolution of 1917. In 1903 it split into two groups, the more moderate Mensheviks, and the firmly revolutionary Bolsheviks, whose leader was Vladimir Ulianov (1870–1924), better known as Lenin.

The general mood of change also encouraged Russian feminists. The regime made considerable effort to prevent the Russian women's movement from forming links with international groups, and discouraged even the most harmless of feminist activities. Nicholas' wife, Alexandra, forbade the reproduction of her portrait on diplomas awarded for women's courses. Under the leadership of Anna Nikitichna Shabanova (1848–1932), however, Russian women began to combine philanthropic activities—the provision of housing and day care centers—with the demand for political rights. The Women's Progressive party was founded in the early years of the 20th century.

The Revolution of 1905

The time was ripe for major political protest, and would-be revolutionaries were unexpectedly given their opportunity by the outcome of the brief but bitter Russo-Japanese War of 1904, which occurred when the two countries tried to expand at the expense of the decaying Chinese empire. The Russians occupied Manchuria during the Boxer Rebellion (see Part VII, Topic 18), and seemed ready to take Korea. In February 1904, the Japanese attacked the Russian naval base of Port Arthur (now Lu-shun), and in May 1905 destroyed the Russian Baltic fleet in the Battle of Tsushima.

The humiliating defeat and the food shortages resulting from an inadequate transport system overworked by the war underlined the Russian government's failings, and protestors were quick to mount demonstrations. Their leader was a 35-year-old Russian Orthodox priest, Georgi Apollonovich Gapon, who persuaded them that their best hope lay in presenting a petition to the tsar in person, humbly begging him to set right the terrible injustices afflicting them.

On January 9, 1905 a crowd of some 200,000 people moved toward the Winter Palace in St. Petersburg. A few days earlier Gapon had written to Nicholas, telling him of the demonstration's peaceful intentions, and imploring him to accept the petition. The tsar's response was to depart at once for the country, leaving behind ranks of armed police and mounted Cossack soldiers. As the crowd collected in front of the palace, many holding up crosses and pictures of Nicholas and singing "God Save the Tsar," it was generally believed that their ruler would appear on the balcony and hear their pleas.

The palace guards ordered them to disband. As the throng stood in bewilderment, Cossacks and police

Theodore Roosevelt with the Russian and Japanese delegations to the peace conference ending the Russo-Japanese War.

Tsarist troops gun down protesters on "Bloody Sunday," Moscow, January 1905.

opened fire. They shot into the dense mass of people until the snow was stained red by the over 100 dead and hundreds of others wounded. Gapon escaped the massacre of what came to be called "Bloody Sunday" (according to some because as a police informer he was intentionally spared), and fled to Finland. In a letter to the tsar he wrote: "The blood of innocent workers, women, and children forever separates you and the people of Russia. May all the blood still to be shed, executioner, fall on thee and thine own kin!"

For once the regime had gone too far. The wave of strikes and agitations that followed forced even Nicholas to propose a compromise. First in March 1905, and then in August, he offered concessions. His limited reforms, which included the establishment of a *Duma*, or parliament, elected by a restricted franchise and with limited powers, were greeted with further riots. By the end of October, public anger was so widespread that Russia's economic life had ground to a halt. Finally, on October 30, 1905, the tsar gave way and is-

sued his October Manifesto. It guaranteed individual freedoms, broadened the electoral basis for the Duma, and gave it legislative power. Crowds danced in the streets.

Then the revolution petered out. In part the October Manifesto split the demonstrators. The moderates, who became known as the Octobrists, were satisfied, while the Social Revolutionaries and Social Democrats saw it as a trick. In part the mass of the population was simply exhausted by almost a year of chaos. A major factor, however, was the regime's use of massive repression to crush any remaining signs of protest. In the Baltic provinces alone over 2000 were executed. A last attempt at rebellion in Moscow in December, led by the Bolshevik wing of the Social Democrats, was ferociously put down by three days of heavy bombardment which left parts of the city in ruins.

Meanwhile Nicholas issued a series of decrees that withdrew almost all his concessions. An upper house was added to the Duma, with half its members appointed by the tsar, who also retained his power of veto and of appointing ministers; subsequently a new set of electoral laws gave the Duma itself a guaranteed conservative majority. At least Russia now had a parliament, and the aristocracy no longer possessed unlimited powers, but the tsar still controlled the army and Russia's foreign policy, and could dissolve the Duma.

The prime minister from 1906 to 1911, Peter Stolypin (1863–1911), sought to modernize the economy by introducing a land reform program. This redistributed the holdings of the communes and encouraged private ownership. At the same time increased foreign investment speeded the process of industrialization. Any chance that labor might organize itself sufficiently to challenge the regime once again was eliminated by Stolypin's ruthless repression of any sign of protest. By the time of his assassination in 1911 by a revolutionary who was also a police agent, all radical organizations

had been crushed; their leaders were dead, in jail, or in exile abroad.

Yet the 1905 Revolution proved not entirely in vain, although its long-term effects were psychological as much as practical. The mystical awe with which the tsar was regarded by his subjects was irretrievably damaged. Nicholas' public image was that of a shy, kindly man, most at ease with his family (on the influence of Nicholas' wife, Alexandra, and the role of Rasputin, see Part VIII, Topic 2). After Bloody Sunday and the subsequent extended campaigns of reprisal, even the most loyal of his citizens knew that behind the façade Nicholas was willing to unleash violence. Furthermore the growing pace of industrialization made further clashes inevitable, as a country in the course of rapid modernization remained ruled by an archaic and inflexible autocrat.

The first indications of new unrest began to appear in 1912, when half a million workers in Moscow and St. Petersburg went on strike. By the early part of 1914, three times that number struck. In July of that year, with war looming, a demonstration of St. Petersburg metal workers was fired on by the police. In their anger, fellow workers took to the streets and built barricades. The city was plunged into chaos.

Significant Dates

Central and Eastern Europe 1870–1914

1873	Bismarck negotiates League of Three Emperors
1878	Berlin Congress on the Balkans
1881	Alexander III encourages *pogroms*
1882	Triple alliance of Austria, Germany, and Italy
1893	State of emergency in Prague
1894	Franco-Russian Alliance
1896	Herzl publishes *The Jewish State*
1897	Lueger becomes mayor of Vienna
1903	Nationalist agitation in Hungary
1904	Russo-Japanese War; Entente Cordiale between Britain and France
1905	Revolution in Russia
1906	Franz Josef dissolves Hungarian Parliament
1907	Settlement of dispute between Britain and Russia
1908	Young Turks introduce liberal constitution; Bosnian crisis
1912–1913	Balkan wars

EUROPEAN JEWS AND ANTI-SEMITISM

In 1903 the Russian secret police faked and published a pamphlet entitled *The Protocols of the Elders of Zion*. The document, they claimed, proved the existence of a Jewish plot to take over the world. This notorious forgery represented a deliberate move to rekindle a long tradition of anti-Semitism in Russia. Nor was prejudice against the Jews limited to Russia, for in the late 19th century anti-Semitism became a factor in the national politics of many European countries.

Russian Jews and the Pogroms

Millions of Jews had become Russian subjects with the partition of Poland in the late 18th century. In 1791 Jews were confined to towns within a limited area in Russian-occupied Poland known as the Pale of Settlement. The repressive measures introduced by successive tsars in the course of the 19th century culminated in violent anti-Semitic outbreaks against Russia's approximately 5 million Jews.

Beginning in 1881, Alexander III encouraged "pogroms" (the Russian word for "devastation"), in which thousands of Jews were beaten or massacred and their property destroyed. In May 1882, the gov-

Map 16.1   The Jewish Population of Europe

Hitler drew many of his Nazi ideas from Chamberlain's book (see Part VIII, Topic 2).

Since the time of Napoleon, many Jews in central and western Europe had undergone a gradual process of assimilation into the societies in which they lived. Nonetheless, considerable social prejudice and religious discrimination continued to flourish. During the same period, discrimination began to take the form of political anti-Semitism. German Jews in the latter part of the 19th century had received increasing legal rights. In reaction, Adolf Stoecker (1835–1909), Protestant minister at the imperial court, founded the Christian Social Workers' party, which developed a comprehensive anti-Semitic program. In Austria-Hungary, Karl Lueger (1844–1910) took control of the anti-Semitic Christian Social Union in 1890 and became mayor of Vienna in 1897, having been triumphantly elected two years earlier but vetoed by Emperor Franz Josef. With his election, Vienna became the first major city in Europe to support a political party that included in its platform hatred for the Jews. Lueger was famous for his declaration: "I'll decide who is a Jew"—an attitude typical of his opportunistic anti-Semitism. As a student living in Vienna on the eve of World War I, Hitler admired Lueger but thought him too moderate.

In France, where Jews were prominent in politics and culture, public attitudes toward them became polarized by the notorious Dreyfus case. Catholic leaders, conservatives, and monarchists supported the government's treatment of the Jewish officer, while liberals, socialists, and intellectuals rallied to his support. In the process, anti-Semitism rather than the innocence or guilt of Dreyfus emerged as the real issue. Despite the victory of the Dreyfusards, anti-Semitism remained a potent force in French right-wing politics. Elsewhere in Europe, the path to Jewish emancipation was smoother. In Britain, the last restrictions against Jewish participation in public life were removed in 1858 when Jewish members of the House of Commons were able to take their seats. In Italy, Jews had taken their place as full citizens following the Risorgimento, and many played a prominent part in public and intellectual affairs. One Italian Jew became war minister—at a time when Jews in Germany could not even hold an army commission—and in 1910 Luigi Luzzatti (1841–1927) was appointed prime minister.

The Zionist Movement

By the late 19th century, many Jews felt themselves threatened from two separate directions: the continuing persecutions in eastern Europe and weakening of Jewish tradition through assimilation in the West. To meet these challenges, Jewish leaders organized the Zionist movement, the ultimate goal of which was the

ernment required all Jews living in the Pale to leave rural centers and move to already overcrowded cities. The pogrom of April 1903 was so savage that it shocked even enlightened public opinion in Russia as well as elsewhere in Europe. During the reigns of Alexander III and Nicholas II, countless Jews escaped the horrors of persecution by fleeing abroad. Some 2 million of them reached the United States.

During the 19th century, anti-Semitism flourished throughout Europe. Some extremists, largely from the radical right, began to develop theoretical justifications for age-old prejudices. Their pseudo-scientific theories of racial superiority inflamed extreme nationalist sentiments. The French diplomat Count Joseph de Gobineau (1816–1882) published *The Inequality of the Human Races* (1853–1855), which propounded the theory that the Nordic races were superior. Such notions reached an even more extreme expression in the works of the Anglo-German writer Houston Stewart Chamberlain (1855–1927), the son-in-law of Richard Wagner. His *Foundations of the Nineteenth Century* (1899) offered a racialist glorification of the Germanic past which depicted history as a struggle between "heroic" Aryans and the "destructive" Semitic peoples. Kaiser Wilhelm II himself read the book aloud to his children and urged its adoption by officer-training schools. A generation later, Adolf

The Zionist leader Theodor Herzl.

THE DISINTEGRATION OF THE OTTOMAN EMPIRE

To the southeast of Russia lay its long-term enemy, the Ottoman Empire. The sultan ruled some 40 million subjects, but his authority was seriously weakened by corruption and the pressures of nationalism. In Egypt, the sultan's strong-willed viceroy, Mohammed Ali (1769–1849), made the territory virtually independent, while elsewhere in North Africa the French seized Algiers. The first major loss of Ottoman territory in Europe occurred in 1829, when the Turks were forced to grant independence to Greece and autonomy to Serbia (see Part VII, Topic 5).

The Crimean War of 1853–1856, in which the Turks lost additional Balkan territory, was part of a larger international issue known as the "Eastern Question." The war stemmed in part from increasing competition between Austria and Russia over the Balkans, and in part from the longstanding Russian desire to gain control over the Dardanelles Straits so as to secure naval access to the Mediterranean. The latter issue especially concerned the British, who regarded the Middle East as a vital link to their empire in India, while the French vied with the Russians for the role of protector of the Christian holy places, an issue that masked more mundane political ambitions in the region.

The conflict, the first major breakdown of the Concert of Europe, broke out in 1853, when the Turks declared war following the Russian occupation of the provinces of Moldavia and Walachia. The following March, Britain and France allied with Turkey against Russia. Piedmont soon joined the allies as an active participant, and Austria became an allied nonbelligerent. At the peace conference that met in Paris in 1856, the powers stipulated the neutrality of the Black Sea and forced Russia to withdraw from Moldavia and Walachia (several years later the provinces were merged into the new Kingdom of Romania). The protection of the Christian holy places was left in the hands of the sultan.

The Paris conference preserved the Ottoman Empire only temporarily. By the 1870s Bosnia, Herzegovina, and Bulgaria were struggling against their Turkish rulers. The uprisings met with ferocious reprisals, and the Russians again took the opportunity to intervene. In the Russo-Turkish War of 1877–1878, the Russians proved so successful that they drove the Turks out of most of their European possessions. The Treaty of San Stefano would have made Russia the dominant force in the Balkans, but the other European powers had no intention of letting that happen. At the urging

creation of a separate Jewish state in Palestine, the home of their ancestors. Zionists believed that only in this way could Jews live in freedom.

The leading exponent of Zionism was Theodor Herzl (1860–1904). Herzl was born in Hungary and studied law in Vienna. While serving as foreign correspondent for an Austrian newspaper in Paris, Herzl covered the Dreyfus affair. The anti-Semitism associated with the case brought home to him his own sense of Jewishness (he had earlier advocated the mass conversion of Austrian Jews to Catholicism). In 1896, he published an influential pamphlet, *Der Judenstaat— The Jewish State: An Attempt at a Modern Solution of the Jewish Question*.

Herzl urged the formation of an international Jewish movement to secure a homeland in Palestine. In 1897, he presided over the first meeting of the World Zionist Organization, a movement which rapidly spread throughout the world. Encouraged by the enthusiasm of many Jews, Herzl sought the backing of government officials for the Zionist cause. Britain supported the idea with caution, and in 1903 he met with British officials to discuss plans for a Jewish settlement. After Herzl's death, these aims were advanced further by Chaim Weizmann (1874–1952), who succeeded him as head of the Zionist movement. Weizmann secured the cooperation of Arthur Balfour (1848–1930), British prime minister and later foreign secretary, in the creation of a Jewish state in Palestine. The return to Palestine after 2000 years was, however, to prove fraught with problems.

Map 16.2 Europe in 1878, after the Congress of Berlin

of Britain and Austria, Bismarck convened a congress in 1878 in Berlin, at which the captured land was divided. Russia, who felt cheated out of what it regarded as its just deserts, managed to hold on only to Bessarabia, while Greece was given Thessaly, Bulgaria became autonomous (a few years later it became an independent kingdom), and Bosnia and Herzegovina were placed under Austrian administration; this last decision proved to have ominous consequences 30 years later.

Internal Reform in Turkey

For many Turks the loss of their European empire was the final proof of the inefficiency and corruption of their rulers. Nationalist politicians began to claim that Turkey could make progress and enter the modern world only by adopting Western approaches to government and society. The movement for reform was led by a group of army officers and students calling themselves the Young Turks, who succeeded in 1908

in compelling the sultan, Abdul-Hamid II (ruled 1876–1909), to implement a liberal constitution; it had been drafted some 30 years earlier but completely ignored. The following year the sultan, who was known to his subjects as "Abdul the Damned," tried to reverse himself. The Young Turks seized their chance and deposed him.

Turkey's new nationalist rulers were liberal in their domestic politics, but continued to deal harshly with the ethnic and religious minorities living in the remnants of the empire. In 1908 Bulgaria was quick to assert itself as an independent kingdom. Crete, after suffering considerably under Turkish rule, became part of Greece, and the following year Albania finally won its freedom. Nor were Turkish losses limited to the eastern Mediterranean. In 1911 the Italians moved to fulfill a long-cherished ambition of founding their own North African empire by annexing Tripoli. By 1912 the Turks were forced to concede them Libya and the Greek islands of the Dodecanese.

Abdul-Hamid II, "Abdul the Damned."

GREAT POWER RIVALRY AND THE BALKANS

The political uncertainties hanging over all three of the empires described here produced an ominous instability in eastern Europe. The various national crises, furthermore, were compounded by increasing tensions between the great powers, whose relations were complicated by a series of fluctuating alliances. Rivalry between the leading European nations led eventually to global conflict, but the first skirmishes took place on the fringes of the Continent, in the Balkans.

The Bismarckian Alliance System

After the unification of Germany, Bismarck had determined to consolidate and develop the empire domestically. In his view, this effort required peace and security for Germany. Over the next 20 years, therefore, he devised a diplomatic system aimed chiefly at isolating France, Germany's acknowledged enemy. He sought to achieve this purpose by binding most of the great powers to Germany in a series of intricate, and sometimes conflicting, alliances.

The first step in building his system was to create a modern version of the old "Holy Alliance" (see Part VII, Topic 5). In 1873 Bismarck concluded the *Dreikaiserbund*, or League of the Three Emperors, with

Austria and Russia, which bound the three conservative powers to consult with each other in the event of international crisis, but the league collapsed as a result of Russia's anger over the outcome of the Congress of Berlin. In 1879, Bismarck, faced with choosing between Austria-Hungary or Russia as principal ally, chose the former; he sought to bolster German security through the Dual Alliance with Austria, which provided that each partner would assist the other in the event of a Russian attack. Bismarck then succeeded in resurrecting the Three Emperors' League in 1881, but now strengthened by a provision that, should one of the three partners go to war with a fourth nation, the others would stay neutral. The next year, Bismarck added still further to this web of agreements by negotiating the Triple Alliance, which pulled Italy—disgruntled over the French seizure of Tunis—into a defensive treaty with Germany and Austria.

Because of Russian suspicions concerning the Triple Alliance, Bismarck conceived the cornerstone of his diplomatic system, the Reinsurance Treaty of 1887 with Russia. This agreement provided for friendly neutrality should either partner be involved in a war with another power (a specific proviso, however, released the partners from this obligation should Russia attack Austria, or Germany attack France). Germany was therefore freed from what Bismarck called the "nightmare" possibility of a two-front war with France and Russia, while Russia was assured that Germany would not combine with Austria against her.

The relationship among these various alliances was dubious at best. There was even direct conflict between the Dual Alliance and the Reinsurance Treaty, since Bismarck promised both Austria and Russia that he would support them in the Balkans. Yet, despite the Iron Chancellor's having overstepped the thin line of diplomatic ethics, he had established German security. Moreover, while the delicate balance of his system depended largely on his own diplomatic skills, European peace was maintained for two decades.

Realignments and New Alliances

Bismarck's dismissal as German chancellor in 1890 brought about a diplomatic revolution. Kaiser Wilhelm II proceeded to reverse or cast overboard the basic tenets of Bismarck's foreign policy. In the first place, the emperor refused a Russian request to renew the Reinsurance Treaty, for he believed that Germany's proper ally was Austria and that a German-Russian alliance was counter to the spirit of Germany's obligations to the Austro-Hungarian empire. Naturally alarmed, the Russians approached France, which seized the opportunity to end its forced diplomatic isolation. The two nations concluded a defensive alliance in 1894, which was reinforced in 1904.

Although Britain was not tied to Germany by formal treaty, Bismarck had carefully avoided threatening British interests; he undertook no overseas ventures that might antagonize them, and refused to build up the German Navy. Wilhelm, however, was bent on achieving a "place in the sun" for Germany equal to England's empire. In addition to launching German expansion in Africa, he also began a massive naval buildup. The British saw both policies as serious threats to their world interests. Furthermore, Germany sought to play an important role in the Near East by proposing the construction of a railway from Berlin to Baghdad. The German threat to Britain eventually led to the conclusion in 1904 of the "friendly understanding," or *Entente Cordiale*, between Britain and France, resolving among other issues their longstanding colonial conflicts in North Africa.

The Entente Cordiale may have been informal, but it hardened in the face of Germany's new aggressive course. In 1905–1906, when Kaiser Wilhelm threatened French interests in Morocco, the British backed their new ally at an international conference at Algeciras, much to German chagrin. A second attempt to force a German presence in Morocco in 1911 was similarly prevented by Anglo-French cooperation.

The last step in the reshaping of European alliances occurred in 1907, when Britain settled its colonial differences with France's ally Russia (the British and Russians agreed to neutralize Tibet, to recognize British predominance in Afghanistan, and to divide Persia—modern Iran—into spheres of influence). The so-called *Triple Entente*, a loose series of agreements among the three powers, came into being. To the Germans' alarm their Triple Alliance was now matched by this potentially more dangerous alignment.

The Bosnian Crisis

The Russians, now able to rely on British and French backing, were in a far better position to interfere in the Balkans. When they did so, conflict with Austria was inevitable. In the past, Germany had tried to discourage Austrian aggressiveness in Eastern Europe, but now Austria was Germany's only important ally. As a result, Germany had little choice but to support Austria under all conditions. Any crisis breaking out in the Balkans was thus all too likely to lead to major international trouble.

The Austrians moved first. In 1908 they annexed Bosnia and Herzegovina, which had been placed under their administration at the Congress of Berlin 30 years earlier. Russia protested, and threatened action, encouraged to do so by the Serbians. Serbia, which had plans of its own to carve a great Slavic kingdom out of the southern parts of the Hapsburg empire, had wanted to include Bosnia in its territory. The Serbs looked to the Russians, fellow Slavs, for support. Russia, however, weakened by its defeat by Japan, racked by internal troubles, and pressured by the British, was in no condition to fight a war. When Germany announced its support for Austria, the Russians were forced to back down and to persuade the Serbians to reconcile themselves to the Austrian action.

Both Russia and Serbia were humiliated. As a consequence, the Russians stepped up their preparations

Bulgarian artillery during the First Balkan War, 1912.

for a war that seemed increasingly inevitable, while the Serbians continued to incite Austria's Slavic minorities to revolt against their imperial masters. The only comfort for Russia was that the Italians, feeling offended that their allies the Austrians had not even consulted them about annexing Bosnia and Herzegovina, signed a secret Italo-Russian pact promising mutual help: Russia would back Italy in North Africa in return for Italian support in the Balkans.

The Balkan Wars

In September 1911, Italy declared war on Turkey and seized Libya, which it annexed the following year. Encouraged by the weakening of the Ottoman Empire and goaded on by Russia, in 1912 an alliance of four Balkan states—Serbia, Bulgaria, Montenegro, and Greece—invaded the last Ottoman possession on European soil, the province of Macedonia. The Turks were in no condition to resist, beset as they were by an uprising in Albania. The revolt was just coming to an end when the First Balkan War began.

Austria then entered the struggle, however, in order to keep the Serbs from expanding to the Adriatic. Russian protests led in May 1913 to an international conference in London to settle the matter. As a result, the independent state of Albania was created on the Adriatic; Serbia received other land in compensation but remained deeply frustrated. That June, another war broke out in the Balkans. Serbia, together with Greece, Romania, and Turkey, relieved Bulgaria of much of Macedonia. In the process, Serbia doubled its territory.

The Balkan wars failed to resolve either Serbian ambitions or the growing tensions. In 1913, the Serbs had attempted to retake portions of Albania, but when Vienna demanded that they withdraw, Russia refused once again to support them. Moreover, the struggle for hegemony in the Balkans unsettled both Russia and Austria-Hungary, which began to question the loyalty of their own allies. The Austro-Hungarians harbored resentments over Germany's failure to support them more vigorously, blaming Serbia's aggressiveness on Berlin's timidity. For their part, the Russians were highly critical of their British allies, who had endorsed the creation of an independent Albania and thereby

checked Serbia's ac
Triple Entente an
seemed grim.

The battle
thus intensified
and Russia and
cator of the c
tension of
international level m
desperate state of relations u
Torn by rivalry in Europe, Asia, and
mestic crises which in the case of the ruling
Hapsburg and Russian empires proved fatal, the natio.
Europe plunged from the disaster of uncertainty to the all-too-certain catastrophe of world war.

Questions for Further Study

1. What caused the breakdown of the Hapsburg empire? What part did its collapse play in precipitating World War I?

2. How did resistance to authoritarian rule begin to develop in Russia? How did Russian rulers try to deal with their opponents, and how successful were they?

3. What were the main factors in the spread of anti-Semitism in Europe? What were the long-term consequences?

4. What were the main stages in the crisis in the Balkans of the decade before World War I?

Suggestions for Further Reading

Ascher, A. *The Revolution of 1905: Russia in Disarray.* Stanford, CA, 1988.

Evans, R. J. W., and H. P. von Strandmann, eds. *The Coming of the First World War.* New York, 1989.

Jelavich, C., and B. Jelavich. *The Establishment of the Balkan States, 1804–1920.* Seattle, WA, 1977.

Kennan, G. *The Decline of Bismarck's European Order: Franco-Russian Relations, 1875–1890.* Princeton, NJ, 1979.

McKean, R. B. *St. Petersburg Between the Revolutions: Workers and Revolutionaries, June 1907–February 1917.* New Haven, CT, 1990.

Sked, Alan. *The Decline and Fall of the Habsburg Empire, 1815–1918.* London, 1989.

T o p i c   1 7

EUROPE, THE UNITED STATES, AND THE WORLD ECONOMY

n the half-century after 1871, European social and economic conditions suggested contradictory trends. Most indices of social development, such as nutrition and health, education, mortality rates, housing and transportation, revealed a previously unknown degree of physical comfort. This achievement was due in large measure to the advances in science and technology. The economy, on the other hand, showed signs of considerable instability. After two decades of virtually uninterrupted growth and prosperity, in which industrial production, profits, and real wages rose to new levels, Europe entered a phase marked by recurrent cycles of alternating recession—in some sectors, of serious depression—and renewed economic vitality.

These economic setbacks were a result of the particular stage of Europe's industrial development and the structural nature of its economy. First of all, after 1870 Europe entered the later phase of the so-called "second industrial revolution" (on the two phases of the "second industrial revolution," see Part VII, Topic 12). Since midcentury, the Continent had been industrializing rapidly and the industrial zone was spreading. Moreover, new technologies—first in steel, then chemicals and electricity, and finally the internal combustion engine—began to give industrialization the main features that would distinguish it well into the 20th century. Germany, the United States, and even Japan eventually outstripped Great Britain both in the rate of growth as well as in the quantity of these and other goods produced. Even Russia experienced tremendous growth in this period. On the other hand, Britain remained unsurpassed in trade, banking, and insurance.

This was also the period in which business organization assumed the characteristics of what has been called "monopoly capitalism." The corporation had already emerged in preceding decades as the basic form of industrial and commercial structure (see Part VII, Topic 12). By the end of the 19th century, a few giant corporations dominated many industries. With huge resources at its disposal, "big business" formed monopolies within each industrial sector by gaining control of raw materials, transportation, production, and marketing, while consolidating many smaller concerns or driving them out of the field.

The emergence of the United States as a major industrial power not only had important economic repercussions in Europe, but reflected the development of a true global economy. Europe increasingly had to compete for worldwide customers as well as in its own domestic markets, and the international flow of investment capital linked the transatlantic economy. One of the first indicators of this growing interdependence was the so-called "Long Depression" that stretched off and on from 1873 to 1896, with effects in both America and Europe.

THE SECOND INDUSTRIAL REVOLUTION

The 18th-century industrial revolution had introduced machines and steam power as a substitute for human muscle and water power, principally in the making of textiles and iron. In the second industrial revolution, electricity and the internal combustion engine began to offer new sources and ways of producing energy, while two new industries—steel and chemicals—were born. Nonetheless, at the end of the 19th century, coal still provided some 90 percent of the world's energy.

The Age of Steel

Iron technology had made significant advances since the first industrial revolution, but the metal, whether wrought or cast, had basic disadvantages. Pig iron, which is hard and brittle, contains between 2.5 and 4 percent carbon. When cast, it cracked or snapped under tension. Wrought iron, on the other hand, which has a carbon content of less than 0.1 percent, is malleable, so that it wears easily and gives under pressure. Machines were made of both kinds of iron: cast iron for parts working under compression, and wrought iron for members working under tension. The early railroads had relied mainly on wrought iron for making rails, but the boom in railroad construction in midcentury, with heavier locomotives and increased traffic, created a serious financial problem: the iron rails wore out quickly and the expense of replacing them grew prohibitive.

Steel combines the characteristics of both forms of iron: with a carbon content within the range of 0.1 to 2.0 percent, it is simultaneously hard and elastic. It resists wear and abrasion and is exceedingly strong in relation to its weight and volume. For rail construction, and many other uses, steel appeared to be the answer, but in the mid-19th century it was not yet commercially available on a large-scale basis.

In the 18th century, a method had been developed whereby steel, far stronger than iron, could be made by melting iron in small crucibles (less than 12 inches high), skimming off the slag, and pouring it. It was an expensive, time-consuming process in which large pieces could be made only by the simultaneous pouring of many hundreds of crucibles.

The first technical breakthrough that made possible cheap steel was the work of the British technician Henry Bessemer (1813–1898), whose converter—patented in 1856—reduced the carbon content of pig iron cheaply and quickly. Bessemer's process forced air through molten pig iron in a converter (a brick-lined crucible housed in a wrought-iron casing) in order to reduce the carbon and produce steel, which could be made at about one-seventh of its former cost. This technique took about ten minutes instead of 24 hours to produce several tons of steel. The speed with which the operation took place, however, made it difficult to control the carbon content with any great precision. Moreover, because Bessemer's technique did not burn off phosphorus or sulfur, small quantities of which made the steel unworkable, only nonphosphoric iron ores could be used.

Significant Dates

The World Economy

1856	Bessemer process for steel making
1866	Underwater telegraph cables laid
1870s	German chemical industry develops
1873–1896	Long Depression
1876	Bell's telephone
1876	Internal combustion engine
1879–1892	European tariffs imposed
1881	Siemens electric power plant
1884	Steam turbine
1885	Daimler's automobile
1895	Marconi's wireless
1895	Principles of "Taylorism" developed
1909	Bakelite, the first synthetic resin

Improvements in the Bessemer method were made by several technicians. In the 1850s, the Siemens brothers in Germany developed a heat exchanger for blast furnaces that used waste gases from cheap grade coal to heat the air, thus achieving extremely high temperatures for melting and reducing the carbon content of the pig iron to make steel at a much lower cost. They then designed an open hearth version which was subsequently modified for steel making. In the 1860s, the Martins, a family of French metallurgists, succeeded in making steel by using the Siemens heat exchanger to fuse a mixture of scrap and pig iron. This "Siemens-Martin" process was slower than Bessemer's method, but allowed for careful control of the quality of steel by stopping the carbon reduction process at the desired point. In 1878, two British cousins, Sidney Thomas and Percy Gilchrist, made the final innovations by adding limestone into the molten iron and devising a crucible liner made of lime and magnesium, techniques which eliminated the phosphorus from iron ores and allowed for the use of more abundant, cheaper ores.

The production of inexpensive steel on a large-scale basis made possible by the combination of these

Table VII.17.1
Steel Production (thousands of tons), 1870–1913

	1870	1890	1913
Britain	240	3636	8500
Germany	126	2135	20,500
USA	69	4277	31,300
France	84	683	5100

technical advances did not really begin until the 1880s. When it occurred, however, it revolutionized industry and commerce. By 1885, the steel rail had taken the place of iron in railroads, and in the early 20th century steel became the fundamental material of industry, replacing iron not only in railroads but in ships, buildings, machines, engines, tools, armaments, and tens of thousands of consumer products.

The Chemical Industry

Before the age of steel, chemicals had already proven important to the development of the textile industry. Dyestuffs had long been obtained from vegetable and animal substances, but in midcentury British and French chemists had begun producing dyes from organic sources such as coal tar. Beginning in the 1870s, the Germans made significant advances in applying chemistry to industrial uses by developing synthetics.

In Germany, where the government placed a major emphasis on technical and scientific education, universities developed close ties with industry. Large sums of public money were made available for chemical research, and in 1872 British visitors in Germany discovered that the University of Munich alone had more chemistry students than all the English universities combined. By 1900, German firms produced 90 percent of the world's synthetic dyes.

The scientific principles on which the synthetic dye industry was based were also applied to a wide range of other products. From cellulose, for example, were derived explosives, lacquers, film, celluloid plastic, and artificial fibers. "Artificial silk," or rayon, was patented as early as 1889; bakelite, the first synthetic resin, in 1909; and cellophane was produced in 1912. Building on the research of Justus von Liebig (1803–1873) in the 1840s, German firms also pioneered in artificial fertilizers. Among the new products were pharmaceuticals such as aspirin and, much later, sulphur-based antiseptics and antibiotics.

The Energy Revolution

The turn of the century also saw a profound transformation in the forms of energy. Along with important

An 1876 print of steel manufacturing using the Bessemer process.

The gun shop at the Krupp factories in Essen, which provided Germany with much of its military hardware.

advances in steam power and steam-driven motors came the harnessing of electricity and the invention of the internal combustion engine—developments that would not only drive modern industry cheaply and more efficiently, but would eventually also transform the daily lives of millions of people.

The expansive working of steam at ever-higher pressures dramatically increased the efficiency and power of steam engines. By the 1890s, for example, big steamships had 30,000-horsepower engines as compared to the 60 horsepower of the first paddle wheel steamers. The steam turbine after 1884 made possible a breakthrough in power and economy. With the engine, the force of steam was first turned into reciprocating motion, and then converted into rotary motion; the turbine eliminated the middle step by receiving steam directly on to vanes mounted on a turning axis, much like a pinwheel, which could then turn a generator at much higher speeds.

The internal combustion engine dates to midcentury, when Étienne Lenoir devised the prototype of a motor fired by a mixture of air and coal gas. In 1876, Nikolaus A. Otto (1832–1891), making use of subse-

quent improvements, built the first practical engine. Otto's motor had marginal application in small industries. Within a few years some 35,000 were in use, but his system proved a dead end. Steam was finally replaced by electric motors. Labor costs were reduced and inexpensive gas was obtainable as a by-product of other industrial processes. Once liquid fuels were developed from petroleum, the internal combustion engine became even more practical because it could be moved from place to place without being tied to the source of the gas supply.

The cost of oil dropped significantly as new sources were exploited at the end of the century in Borneo, Mexico, Texas, and Persia. Ocean liners subsequently adopted oil in place of coal, followed soon after by naval ships. Although Gottlieb Daimler (1834–1900) built the earliest automobile in 1885, it was not until after World War I that gasoline-fueled automobiles gained significant ground. Eventually, France led in auto production in Europe, while the United States was the world's leading producer of cars. Airplanes, first flown successfully in 1903, were driven by internal combustion engines during World War I.

The telephone exchange in Paris, 1884.

Electrification

Electricity has two crucial characteristics—it can move energy across long distances without great power loss, and it can be easily converted into other forms of energy, such as light, heat, or motion. Electrification depended upon the development of the electric motor and generator. During the course of the 19th century, electrical experiments demonstrated its commercial potential, first applied in communications. The electromagnetic telegraph, using very little current, was first demonstrated in the 1830s in Britain and the United States, and by 1866 underwater telegraph cables had been laid across the English Channel and the Atlantic. Alexander Graham Bell's telephone (1876) and Guglielmo Marconi's wireless (1895) followed, both of which used feeble current.

By the end of the century, electric lighting, which had an important economic impact, came into use. Thomas A. Edison (1847–1931) perfected a high-resistance incandescent lamp, or lightbulb, which made electricity useful for the private home as well as for industry and commerce. Edison also understood that the illumination of hundreds of thousands of homes, as well as city streets, required a central power system. The generation and distribution of power in this broad sense were made possible by theoretical and practical advances achieved during the century.

The first public power station in Europe was built in England in 1881 by the German firm founded by Werner Siemens (1816–1892), who invented the dynamo and built the first electric railroad. By the mid-1890s a series of local stations had appeared throughout western and central Europe, but with no uniform equipment or standards. Here, too, the Germans took the lead, and in the years immediately before the war firms such as the General Electric Company (*Allgemeine Elektrizitäts-Gesellschaft*) had begun to adopt the principle of power distribution grids servicing commercial and home customers over large regions. By 1914, Germany led the world in the production of electrical equipment and products. The war itself created a tremendous demand for even more electrical energy, and after 1919 army engineers had plans for the building of huge centralized power grids crisscrossing entire countries.

In the less than 50 years between the Franco-Prussian War and the outbreak of World War I, the second industrial revolution transformed the material basis of much of European civilization. The practical applications of science and technology radically altered the relationship between human beings and their environment. The advent of steel not only made possible new, more precise and durable machines, but also enabled architects and builders to shift the growth of cities from a horizontal direction to a vertical profile—the Eiffel

Tower in Paris, built between 1887 and 1889, was the best-known symbol of this development. The chemical industry, for good or ill, reduced human reliance on the products of nature, and electrical power offered a seemingly unlimited source of energy and brightened the world for millions of ordinary people. Advances in transportation and communications "shortened" physical distances and changed the very conception of time itself.

THE AMERICAN CHALLENGE AND THE LONG DEPRESSION

By 1871, important shifts were beginning to take place in the industrial and economic development of Europe. For the long term, the two most crucial changes were Germany's steady encroachment on Britain's position as the prime industrial power, and the rise of the United States as a great industrial nation, soon to eclipse Europe's economic position.

The United States eventually surpassed Europe not only in the production of industrial products and manufactured goods, but in agriculture as well. The "invasion" of Europe by American—and Russian—wheat imports had serious repercussions on European agriculture and rural life.

American competition, both in industry and agriculture, contributed to economic setbacks in Europe. The transatlantic economy had become so closely intertwined that events on one continent directly affected conditions in the other. Uncontrolled speculation and bank panics, along with agricultural and industrial overproduction, combined to create a serious slump in the Western economy between 1873 and 1896.

The Growth of American Industry

The Civil War (1861–1865) stimulated American industry by sharply increasing demand for manufactured goods. Over the next several decades, the United States experienced unparalleled economic expansion as a variety of factors came together. Rich natural resources provided a basis for the technological applications in agriculture and industry that characterized the second industrial revolution. The railroad boom and westward expansion, together with a steady increase in population as a result of the flood of immigration from Europe, provided both employment and labor.

The increase in productivity was even more impressive than in Europe. The timber from America's forests provided an abundant supply of charcoal for making iron, but this advantage served to delay the transition to coke as fuel for iron smelting. America's localized and scattered iron industries were inadequate to meet its needs, and as late as 1850 some 60 percent of its iron for railroad tracks was imported from Great Britain. Once the British methods of iron production were adopted, however, the iron industry expanded rapidly. Production was concentrated near the coal mines of Pennsylvania. As in Europe, railroad construction provided a stimulus for iron manufacturing. Production of coal and iron rose in spectacular increments.

American coal and iron production virtually doubled every decade after 1860. By 1890, the United States was producing twice as much iron and coal as Germany. The most revealing figures, however, showed that by that date the United States had actually pulled ahead of Great Britain in iron, and at the turn of the century was producing twice as much iron and coal as the former leading industrial nation in the world. Moreover, American factories turned the world's steel production figures completely around. In 1870, both Britain and Germany each exceeded America's steel production, whereas in 1913 the United States made one-third of the world's steel, more than both European powers together. By World War I, the United States had become the world's leading industrial nation.

Table VII.17.2

Pig Iron and Coal Production (thousands of tons), 1870–1910

	PIG IRON			COAL		
	GB	USA	GERMANY	GB	USA	GERMANY
1870	5960	1690	1400	117,000	42,000	29,000
1880	7749	3835	2429	147,000	65,000	47,000
1890	7900	9200	4000	181,000	143,000	70,000
1900	8960	13,800	7429	225,000	244,000	109,000
1910	10,000	27,300	12,905	292,000	571,000	190,100

American Wheat and European Agriculture

The opening of the Great Plains to agricultural settlement in the years after 1865 coincided with two technological advances of great significance: the mechanization of farming and the westward expansion of the railroad. Among the important agricultural innovations were the polished steel plow, which enabled farmers to break the tough soil of the prairie; the mechanical, horse-drawn reaper designed by Cyrus McCormick; and the threshing machine. All three inventions had been first patented in the 1830s, but after the Civil War they came into wide use.

Once railroads had penetrated beyond the Ohio Valley and across the plains in the 1860s, the productivity of farms was linked to the rapidly increasing urban consumers of the east and American agriculture became market-based. During the decade before the Civil War, the United States had grown an average of some 137 million bushels of wheat a year. In the 1870s American farmers produced an average annual yield of 338 million bushels, and in the 1890s more than 1.3 billion bushels a year.

The abundance of wheat represented a huge surplus beyond the needs of the domestic market. Improvements in transatlantic transportation—the speed and cargo capacity of steamships and a significant drop in shipping rates—enabled American merchants to flood Europe with the surplus wheat at considerably reduced prices. Nor were American wheat exporters alone. In the 1880s, Canada, Australia, Argentina, and even India also began to send wheat to Europe, and at the turn of the century Russian wheat production surpassed that of the United States.

In the meantime, European agriculture had undergone its own transformations. There, too, railroads had linked urban markets to rural areas. In addition to higher productivity derived from mechanization and fertilization processes, new areas came under cultivation, especially in Russia (which tripled its wheat production between 1871 and 1914) and the Russian part of Poland, Hungary, and Romania. Markets that western European farmers once had almost completely to themselves suddenly closed with the influx of new wheat. The result was a severe drop in agricultural prices—by 1894, wheat could be bought in Britain for one-third of its price in 1867.

Individual countries weathered the crisis in different ways. In Britain, free trade policies had eliminated agricultural tariffs in the 1840s, and public opinion demanded continuing low food prices. The depression in agriculture caused by massive food imports hurt British landowners seriously. Many gave up farming and the total arable land under cultivation dropped by one-half in the two decades after 1875. France, on the other hand, protected its farmers by raising tariff walls against foreign grains starting in 1885. Although French wheat growers did not suffer like their British counterparts, wine makers in France experienced a serious depression because their vines were attacked by an insect pest, phylloxera. The Meline Tariff of 1892 placed almost all French agricultural products under tariff protection. In Germany, where a combination of Junker landowners, small farmers, and industrialists pushed for protection against foreign imports, Bismarck imposed a moderate tariff in 1879.

The crisis in agriculture had contradictory results. The lower wheat prices meant that basic food staples cost less, so that the urban working class did not suffer as it had during the famines of the 1840s; on the other hand, the drop in farming income created widespread hardship in the countryside, where peasants had generally experienced considerable prosperity in the preceding decades. In Britain, the hardest-hit country, the number of people involved in farm labor fell by 40 percent.

The Long Depression

The agricultural crisis caused by the flood of American wheat into Europe was one aspect of the overall slump that hit the transatlantic economy between 1873 and 1896. Although generally known as the "Long Depression," the period actually saw a series of separate economic setbacks and business cycle troughs punctuated by intermittent phases of recovery. The collective downturn of the economy appeared worse than it really was, because it came after two decades of sustained growth between 1850 and 1873.

The Long Depression encompassed three interrelated elements: agricultural depression, financial retrenchment, and industrial overproduction and contraction. The beginning of the agricultural depression coincided with a banking panic precipitated in 1873. The financial collapse occurred as a result of rampant speculation, especially in railroads, because the banks had made excessive loans based on securities issued by these firms. The first major bank failure occurred in Vienna, and panic spread from there to Berlin, Rome, London, and other European cities, and then to the United States, where Europeans had also invested heavily in railroads. One of the most catastrophic panics hit after the failure of Jay Cooke & Company, one of the leading American brokerage firms. Jay Cooke (1821–1905) had underwritten massive amounts of railroad stock, which he then resold. As banks failed and credit dried up, manufacturing slowed down. British iron production fell by almost 1 million tons in the 1870s and the wholesale price index dropped from 130 to 107. Unemployment soared from less than 1 percent to an all-time high of almost 12 percent, before declining again to around 2 percent.

Further recessions, less severe than the previous one, occurred in the 1880s. In 1890, however, another serious depression began with the failure (largely as a result of a revolution in Argentina) of the London banking house of Baring Brothers. Partly because of the gold standard, the financial panic spread to the United States. As British banks called in gold, the gold supply in the U.S. treasury began to move off to London and the stock market crashed in 1893. The gold drain became so severe that the investment banker John Pierpont Morgan (1837–1913) formed a private consortium which lent gold to the government, much to the anger of the public and Morgan's immense profit.

Prices, which had fallen irregularly since 1873, collapsed still further. Industrial overproduction was one factor that caused the deflation. The gold standard also contributed to lower prices because a shortage in the quantity of world gold had the effect of reducing the money supply, which in turn drove prices down. European industry experienced the same problem that had plagued agriculture—excessive supply in relation to demand. Indeed, the two factors were intertwined, since the decline in farming income as a result of the agricultural crisis meant that the rural population—some 60 percent of Europe's total—had less money to spend on consumer goods. Moreover, the techniques of mass production were so successful that the supply of manufactured items pushed ahead of the market. In an era when unregulated capitalism still held sway, overproduction led to cutthroat competition and destructive price wars.

The wholesale price index in most European countries reached its lowest level since midcentury—in Britain, it dropped from the 1873 high of 130 to 76 in 1896. International trade also declined. Industries cut back production and laid off workers. In 1892, Britain produced almost 2 million tons less of pig iron than it had a decade earlier, and unemployment jumped from 2.1 percent in 1890 to almost 7.5 percent in 1893.

Despite the recurrent cycles of economic slump, the Long Depression did not prove to be seriously destructive, and full-scale recovery began in late 1896. Although wages declined slightly during the worst years of the depression, they experienced an overall rise between 1873 and 1900. Moreover, low food and commodity prices offset some of the impact. By the end of the century, demand for consumer goods had risen again, especially in urban centers. Producers began to cultivate buyers and develop marketing strategies, including advertising, sale in large department stores, and mail-order firms such as Sears, Roebuck & Co. Prices recovered as a result of higher demand and protective tariffs. Governments also adopted new regulations to

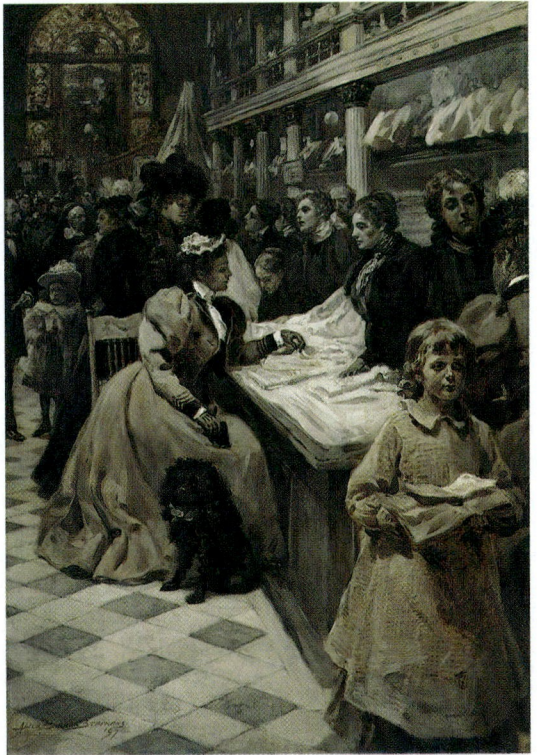

Alice Barber Stephens' painting *The Woman in Business* (1897), created as an illustration for *The Ladies Home Journal*, depicts women working as clerks in a large department store.

prevent speculative busts of the kind that had set off the panics of 1873 and 1890.

The followers of Karl Marx had predicted that in its final stage of development, capitalism would produce the seeds of its own destruction. The Long Depression, however, proved not to be the crisis of capitalism but rather a series of phases of readjustment that came after decades of extraordinary expansion. Moreover, the precarious nature of laissez-faire capitalism taught business leaders important lessons about the advantages of cooperation over unrestrained competition. Marx had also argued that wealth would tend to concentrate increasingly in the hands of fewer people as business moved toward the "monopoly" stage of its evolution. From the setbacks of the post-1873 period, industrial capitalism emerged altered but stronger than ever.

BIG BUSINESS IN THE AGE OF MASS PRODUCTION

The Long Depression encouraged the development of "big business" and the trend toward monopolies, thus bringing to an end the era of "heroic" capitalism that had prevailed since the first industrial revolution. By the turn of the century, a few huge companies dominated the field in most major industrial and commercial sectors, reversing the pattern of the early industrial period in which many small factories and firms had sprung up. The corporation, with its limited liability and large resources, made monopolistic-type agreements possible. Although business combinations took many forms, they all sought either to reduce costs or raise prices in order to accumulate capital to offset the huge capital costs of steel as opposed to iron production.

Cartels, Trusts, and Mergers

Business combinations generally fall into one of three types: (1) agreements known as *cartels*, in which firms remain separate and autonomous; (2) *trusts* or holding companies, in which financial control is exercised over several firms through a company created for that purpose; and (3) *mergers* or consolidations, in which individual firms are dissolved and their assets are put together into one new company.

Some of these business combinations were formed in order to achieve "horizontal" integration among firms within the same industry or stage of production, such as railroad companies or makers of steel girders. Other combinations sought to integrate companies "vertically," at separate stages of production or in different industries—such a combination, for example, might include coal mines, railroads, blast furnaces, and steel producers all in the same cartel or trust. Whatever the form, business combinations set prices and production quotas, reduced costs, delineated markets, and controlled or eliminated competition.

The legal traditions and economic attitudes of individual countries affected the way in which such combinations were formed. In Britain, Adam Smith's laissez-faire theories, together with business failures in the 18th century, reinforced hostility to monopolies and agreements that restrained trade. In Germany, however, where no such traditions existed, combinations were seen as desirable and even necessary. One of the earliest and strongest German combinations was the cartel of potash companies established in the 1870s. German coal producers also created loose agreements in the 1870s, and during the serious depression of 1893 they formed a famous cartel, the Rhenish–Westphalian Coal Syndicate, which fixed prices by limiting the output of coal for all its members. Steel manufacturers similarly created a number of cartels, and in 1904 these joined together in the German Steelwork Association, a huge combination that not only set prices by limiting production but also lobbied successfully for protective tariffs. By the turn of the century, two firms, Siemens and the AEG, dominated Germany's electrical industry and made agreements between them that fixed prices, defined areas of influence, and divided product specialization. By 1914, German industry boasted more than 600 cartels.

In Great Britain, the tendency toward monopoly manifested itself less intensely and by means of mergers (which the British called amalgamations) instead of cartels. British soap firms, for example, formed a cartel in 1906, but it was quickly replaced by the merging of almost a dozen companies into a giant amalgamation, Lever Brothers. The British-controlled Royal Dutch Shell Company, resulting from the merger of several petroleum firms, became one of the world's largest business combinations.

American businesses followed the European pattern. In the 1870s, the owners of the New York Central and the Erie Railroad created a "pool," or informal combination, to end a rate war that was wiping out profits. The pool divided rail traffic among them at fixed rates. One of the largest and most controversial combinations in the United States was the Standard Oil Trust, formed by John D. Rockefeller (1839–1937) in 1882. Even before the trust, however, Rockefeller had engineered a huge conspiracy to drive competitors out of business by controlling railroad transportation rates. He brought together more than 40 firms engaged in all phases of the oil business. The government saw such trends as a threat to consumer interests, however, and passed the Sherman Antitrust Act in 1890, which outlawed all trusts in restraint of trade, although the measure did not halt the trend toward monopoly. Between 1898 and 1900, monopoly combinations were established among makers of steel products. In 1900, Andrew Carnegie (1835–1919), owner of the largest steel company in America, sold out to John Pierpont Morgan for 500 million dollars. Morgan then formed a giant holding company known as the United States Steel Corporation, the world's first billion-dollar corporation, controlling three-fifths of the steel business in America.

At the turn of the century, big business came to be identified with the careers of business tycoons who amassed fabulous fortunes through ruthless business practices and preached a philosophy of "rugged individualism." Yet these "captains of industry"—Americans such as Rockefeller, Germans such as Alfred Krupp (1812–1887), or Britons such as William Armstrong (1810–1900)—were really products of a business system that had abandoned unrestrained free market capitalism under competitive pressure.

Mass Production and Scientific Management

Railroads and the rise in real wages created huge national markets, and the second industrial revolution met the consumer demand with a tremendous growth in productivity.

J. P. Morgan, American finance banker and "captain of industry."

Mass production resulted from a combination of two interrelated factors—technology and business management. The generation of electric power with the steam turbine permitted machines to run faster and more efficiently, while cheap steel and new machine tools made possible both standardized parts and more accurate machines. Machine tools—machines for precision cutting and finishing metals, such as planers, boring instruments, grinders, and lathes and other precision instruments—were a prerequisite for the making of interchangeable parts.

The American inventors Eli Whitney (1765–1825) and Samuel Colt (1814–1862) had used crude interchangeable parts to make small arms in what came to be called "the American system of manufacture," but neither adopted the principle of the moving assembly line, which began to come into use at about the time of the Civil War. It was Henry Ford (1863–1947) who combined interchangeable parts with moving assembly lines in his automobile plant in order to take advantage of economies of scale. By using several thousand standardized parts, with workers specializing in particular tasks, Ford was able to turn out a thousand Model "T" cars a day prior to World War I.

Along with the assembly line process, principles of management were devised in an effort to increase the rate of production and to raise the cost-effectiveness of labor in connection with the new factory equipment. Frederick Winslow Taylor (1856–1915), an American mechanical engineer, first proposed "scientific management." After developing high-speed machine tools, Taylor turned to a study of shop management. In 1895 he proposed two revolutionary principles: the establishment of performance standards and the creation of a permanent staff of "planners" who were not shop foremen. Basing his calculations on how long a job took, Taylor urged that workers be paid incentives for producing more than the minimum within the allotted time.

Taylor's theories were developed more fully in *The Principles of Scientific Management* (1911). His idea of task design was based on the notion that workers should be told "not only what is to be done but how to do it and the exact time allowed for doing it." He also advocated a total approach that included plant layout

The assembly line at the Ford Motor Company, 1913, which produced a thousand automobiles a day.

and tool design to maximize efficiency. By 1914, "Taylorism" had spread to Europe and Japan.

The consequences of the new "American" system of manufacture were many. Large-scale production met the growing demand of millions of working-class and middle-class buyers for inexpensive consumer goods. On the other hand, the quality and aesthetic appeal of industrial products generally declined. Corporate profit margins increased dramatically, but mass production eventually led to overproduction and business downturns. For those on the assembly lines, the new productivity standards and work pace depersonalized labor. The results were psychological as well as physical exhaustion, and increased worker hostility toward foremen and employers. The "management revolution" had an important social impact, for the growth of corporate organizations greatly expanded the white-collar group within the lower middle class.

EUROPE AND THE GLOBAL ECONOMY

Between 1870 and 1913, western Europe and the United States emerged as the focus of the modern industrial-capitalist world. Science, technology, and economic organization all combined to focus extraordinary wealth and power in the grasp of a half-dozen nations. Yet as the circle of industrializing nations slowly widened, important shifts in the international balance of power took place.

The World Dimensions of Competition

The most apparent change resulted from the fact that by the 1890s Britain had lost its industrial primacy as Germany and the United States raced ahead in the production of essential commodities, such as coal, iron, and steel, and seized greater shares of world trade and finance.

In the European context, Germany, united into a single state only in 1871, provided the most dramatic evidence of this transformation as it quickly became the new industrial colossus. By 1913, Germany produced more than twice the amount of steel as Britain, and also led all other countries in the chemical and electrical industries. Between 1870 and World War I, Britain's rate of growth slowed to 2.2 percent, while Germany achieved a 2.9 percent annual growth and the United States 4.3 percent. Although Britain

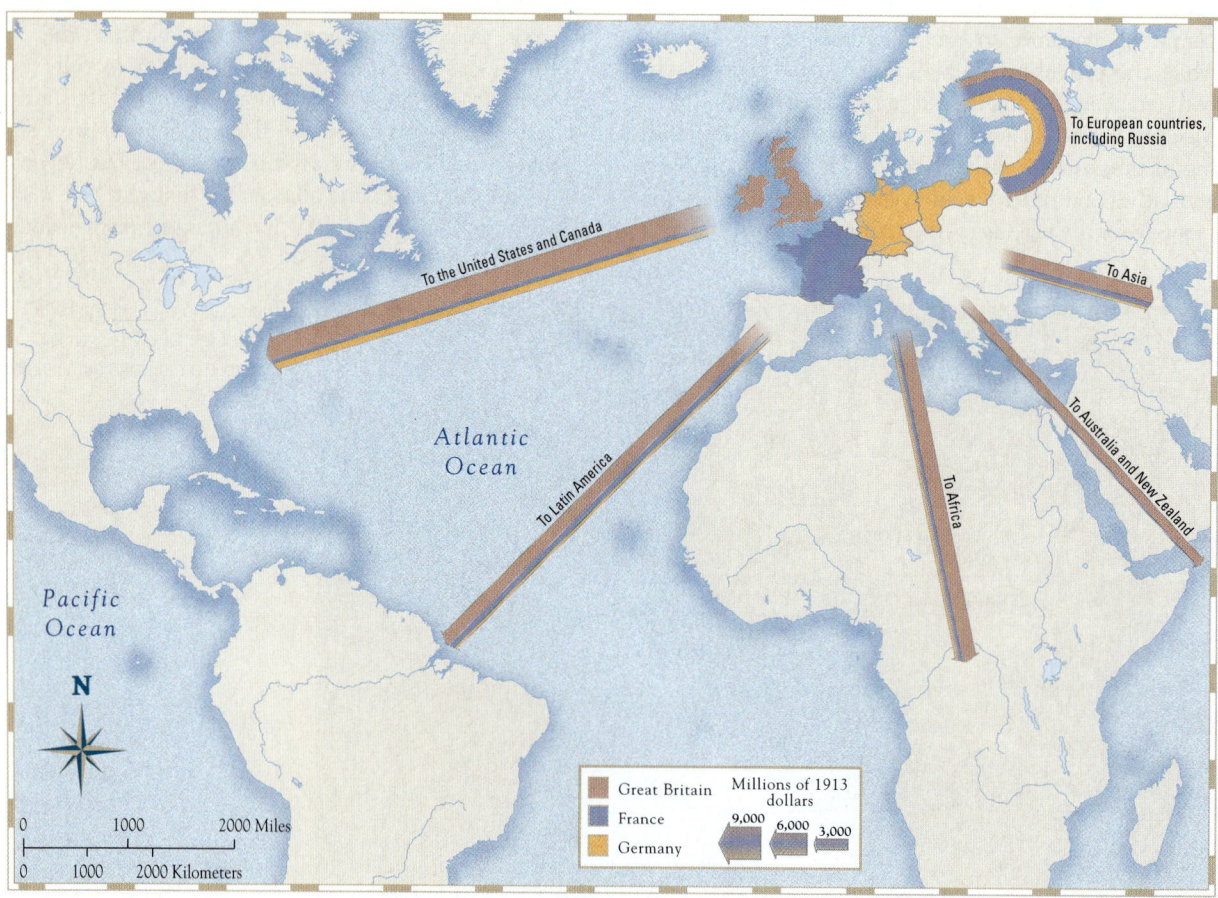

Map 17.1 European Foreign Investment, 1850–1914

remained immensely strong in trade, finance, and industry, statistically it had fallen to the world's third-ranking power.

Moreover, as Belgium and France slipped in terms of their share of industrial manufacturing, Russia, Italy, and Sweden entered the industrial ranks. Russia's industrial growth came late in the century, but it possessed more resources. Between 1860 and 1900, the number of cotton mills rose from less than 40 to more than 700, principally around St. Petersburg and Moscow. Private companies built railroads with government subsidies and foreign investment—by 1900 Russia had more than 35,000 miles of track and a Trans-Siberian line that connected Moscow to the Pacific coast at Vladivostok.

Russian coal production jumped from 1 million tons a year in 1873 to more than 36 million tons by 1913, yet it remained a small fraction of Germany's or Britain's output. Russia did produce iron, but by using fuels and methods long since abandoned in western Europe. By 1913, however, it boasted a steel output equal to two-thirds that of Britain. Russia stood out, furthermore, in the petroleum industry, for its rich fields near Baku and Grozny made it the world's leading oil producer until overtaken by the United States at the turn of the century. Moreover, damage to the Baku wells in the war with Japan in 1905 restricted production for years.

Although poor in natural resources, Italy began a phase of rapid industrialization in the 1890s, with heavy industry consuming enormous amounts of imported coal, which jumped from 300,000 tons a year in 1880 to 12 million by 1914. The silk industry had a world market, and railroads and shipping made considerable progress by the turn of the century, when the development of hydroelectricity enabled Italian industry to accelerate. On the other hand, Italian industrial development was concentrated within the northwestern triangle defined by Turin, Milan, and Genoa; most of southern Italy and Sicily remained untouched by industrialization. Sweden also began to industrialize, expanding its metalworking and silk industries and increasing exports in wood pulp, dressed lumber, paper, iron ore, and special varieties of coal.

The following table suggests the changing picture of world industrial production between 1870 and 1913.

International Trade and Investment

In the years after 1850, railroads had created not only national but international markets. Railroads, along with technical advances in steamship construction—steel hulls and fast, powerful steam engines—pushed the volume of world trade steadily upward. Although the British position in industrial production had slipped, it maintained an impressive lead in mercantile shipping. By 1914, Britain could claim 39 percent of the world's commercial tonnage, while Germany and the United States together possessed only 22 percent.

In the half-century after 1870, the volume of world imports and exports increased threefold, despite the slumps occasioned by the Long Depression. Overall trends revealed that Europe's share of this trade declined in that same period, while that of the United States and Japan grew accordingly. U.S. imports and exports were tied closely to Europe in the decades before 1914—60 percent of exports went to Europe, while half of American imports came from Europe. The position of Britain, which retained the largest single percentage of international commerce in 1913—61 percent—had fallen by more than 10 percent since 1870. Trade among European countries represented about two-fifths of all world commerce, although as the century drew to a close, European and American trade with Asia, Africa, and Latin America increased.

Europe's trade with the rest of the world consisted largely of an exchange of manufactured goods for raw materials. Most major countries imported more than they exported. With the exception of Britain, the industrializing nations ran up heavy balance of payments deficits with the suppliers of raw materials. The British, and other countries to a lesser extent, offset the payments imbalance with "invisible earnings," such as shipping and insurance charges and earnings on foreign investments.

International trade grew despite a general move toward protectionism after 1870, both on the part of the United States and of European nations. Trade treaties between individual nations helped to overcome tariff barriers, although, as we have seen, the exportation of American and Russian wheat to Europe in the 1870s led Germany, France, and other countries to

Table VII.17.3

Manufacturing (percent of total) by Nation

	GB	USA	GERMANY	FRANCE	RUSSIA	BELGIUM	ITALY	SWEDEN
1870	31.8	23.3	13.2	10.3	3.7	2.9	2.4	.4
1913	14.0	35.8	15.7	6.4	5.5	2.1	2.7	1.0

impose tariffs on agricultural goods. Some nations, such as Italy and France, engaged in tariff wars with one another. Industrialists joined the clamor for tariffs as the business slumps took hold, and nationalist rhetoric added to the impulse toward protectionism. Besides Britain, only Denmark, Finland, and the Netherlands retained free trade systems between 1880 and 1913. In addition to the tariff barriers, the existence of some 100 international cartels—in such industries as shipping, armaments, and aluminum—also restricted commercial competition. Nevertheless, neither tariffs nor cartels appear to have seriously hindered the growth of international trade.

During the second half of the 19th century, Europe "exported" huge portions of the capital that had been accumulated in industry and trade. Britain, France, and Germany took the lead in overseas investment, chiefly by buying foreign stocks and bonds or by extending loans to foreign banks and governments.

Britain remained the single most important source of foreign funds between 1870 and 1914, exporting between 4 percent and 9 percent of its national income each year. In 1914, British overseas investments accounted for 43 percent of all exported capital, with France coming in a distant second (20%) and Germany third (13%). Most revealing, perhaps, is the fact that almost half of these funds went to Latin America, Asia, and Africa.

On the eve of World War I, industrialization had ceased to be the preserve either of Great Britain or western Europe. Competition among nations, rather than the primacy of a single one, had become a principal feature of economic development. Moreover, patterns of trade, investments, and monetary policies revealed the formation of a global economy—one in which Europe played an important but no longer exclusive role.

The last three decades of the 19th century and the years immediately before World War I witnessed significant advancements in industrial technology and economic growth, both in Europe and the United States. The second industrial revolution, founded on steel, energy, and large-scale manufacturing, drew the two continents into a tightly knit transatlantic economy that became increasingly interdependent. The abundance of American wheat caused a sharp depression in European agriculture in the 1870s, and financial panic in Europe's capitals resounded in New York and Washington.

Changes of far-reaching consequence emerged from the economic slumps that beset Europe and America between 1873 and 1896. Corporations and industries adopted new forms of business organization designed to control economic fluctuations, limit price competition,

and stimulate consumer demand. From an era of overproduction—one cause of the Long Depression—came an age of mass production.

The transatlantic economy grew more complex as nations changed their industrial position in an absolute sense as well as their status vis-à-vis each other. The degree of economic competition intensified within Europe, while the industrializing countries expanded the parameters of their operations to Africa, Asia, and Latin America, creating a truly global economy.

It should be remembered, however, that the process by which Europe had achieved its economic ascendancy had not been entirely peaceful. Armed with scientific knowledge, technological skill, and great wealth, Europeans inaugurated an era of imperial expansion after 1870 that enabled them to subjugate and exploit vast portions of the globe (see Part VII, Topic 18).

From their position at the center of the world economy, Europeans—the great majority of whom enjoyed more physical comforts and a higher standard of living than any people in history—regarded the rest of the world with a sense of superiority. The exploitation of Asia and Africa, which accompanied the second industrial revolution, was intended to promote further European economic expansion. Some imperialists claimed that it also provided a means for extending the "advantages" of Western civilization to less developed regions of the globe.

Questions for Further Study

1. What was the second industrial revolution, and how was it different from the first?

2. How did the development of the American economy affect Europe?

3. To what extent is it accurate to use the term "Long Depression" to describe the European economy between 1870 and 1914?

4. What were the principles of "Taylorism," and why were they important to the modern world economy?

Suggestions for Further Reading

Ashworth, William. *A Short History of the International Economy Since 1850*, 4th ed. London, 1987.

Ashworth, William. *An Economic History of England, 1870–1939*. London, 1960.

Cameron, Rondo. *A Concise Economic History of the World*. New York, 1989.

Carter, E. C. et al., eds. *Enterprise and Entrepreneurs in Nineteenth and Twentieth Century France*. Baltimore, MD, 1976.

Davis, Lance E. et al. *American Economic Growth: An Economist's History of the United States*. New York, 1972.

Henderson, William O. *The Rise of German Industrial Power, 1834–1914*. Berkeley, CA, 1975.

Kenwood, A. G., and A. L. Lougheed, *The Growth of the International Economy, 1820–1960.* London, 1971.

Landes, David. *The Unbound Prometheus: Technological Change and Industrial Development in Western Europe from 1750 to the Present.* Cambridge, MA, 1969.

Milward, Alan S., and S. B. Saul. *The Development of the Economies of Continental Europe, 1850–1914.* Cambridge, MA, 1977.

Saul, S. B. *The Myth of the Great Depression, 1873–1896.* London, 1969.

Trebilcock, Clive. *The Industrialization of the Continent.* New York, 1981.

Topic 18

THE DRIVE FOR EMPIRE: EUROPEAN IMPERIALISM IN ASIA AND AFRICA

he latter half of the 19th century saw an increasingly frenzied drive on the part of many European powers for territorial conquest beyond Europe. Known as the "New Imperialism," to distinguish it from the earlier phase of European expansion beginning in the 15th century, this sudden surge of aggression resulted in the domination of virtually all of Asia and Africa by a handful of Western powers.

The most direct motivating force was economic, but other factors also encouraged the pursuit of empire. Pressure groups of business, military, and conservative interests promoted colonial expansion as a means of enhancing national prestige in the context of European power rivalries. The various Christian churches saw imperialist conquest as a means of spreading their faith, while some Europeans were genuinely interested in improving conditions in other parts of the world. Many Westerners believed that the exportation of their culture abroad fulfilled a mission to spread a superior culture and "civilize" the world.

The unification of India under British rule represented the crowning achievement of the age of imperialism. Nonetheless, as early as 1857 the "Indian Mutiny," as the British styled it, revealed Indian determination to resist foreign domination. After the unsuccessful rebellion, the British introduced limited political representation, educated Indians of the upper classes in schools under their supervision, and encouraged them to enter government service. This process of "westernization" speeded the development of national consciousness.

The Western powers had little need for direct rule over China, for they found it relatively easy to impose demands on the declining Chinese empire. Racked by internal disorder, China was forced to make continual concessions to Western nations. By 1900, the Chinese emperor allowed a combined European and American military expedition to restore order.

China's problems were compounded by Japan's highly successful adaptation to Western ways. In 1867 the Japanese, who had maintained their isolation from the outside world until as late as 1853, began a wholesale replacement of their feudal system of government and introduced Western-style reforms. They also emulated the Europeans by seeking their own imperialist conquests.

In Africa, the last quarter of the 19th century saw virtually all the western European nations fighting to win territory. In North Africa, the British and French took control of the tangled finances of Egypt, anxious as joint owners of the Suez Canal to protect their investment. In 1882, the British occupied the country, leading the French to find compensation in the Sudan, where the two powers came close to war at the end of the century.

With the fear growing that hostilities in Africa could lead to war in Europe as Belgium, Germany, and other states began to seize holdings in central Africa, a conference met in Berlin in 1885 to establish some rules for the dismemberment of Africa.

In South Africa, conflict was unavoidable. The British Cape Colony became increasingly at odds with two neighboring states settled by the Boers, colonial farmers of Dutch origin who had subdued or pushed out the Bantu. The Boer War broke out in 1899. It took over three years for the British to defeat their stubborn and determined opponents.

By the eve of World War I, Western nations—including the United States—dominated the economy and the political life of much of the globe. Yet competition outside Europe, far from resolving the tensions between the European states, only added to them. The result—global war—ended the age of European world influence with a speed that would have seemed inconceivable to the enthusiastic imperialists of the late 19th century.

THE IMPERIALISTS: EXPLORATION, COMMERCE, AND COMPETITION

Europeans had been in contact with other parts of the world for centuries, but with the new methods of transport, communication, and warfare available by midcentury, conquest and occupation of distant lands became a serious possibility for the first time.

The New Imperialism and Its Causes

The New Imperialism differed from earlier European expansion in a variety of ways. The first was the sheer speed—a mere 30 years—with which a handful of nations assumed control of vast portions of the globe. Britain took 4 million square miles, France 3.5 million, Russia 3 million, and Germany, Belgium, and Italy 1 million each. Second, instead of limiting contact to commercial exploitation, the European powers assumed direct administrative control over conquered territories. In the process, they made enormous capital investments which they sought to maintain by setting up colonial bureaucracies and military forces.

The advocates of imperialism claimed a variety of motives as their inspiration, including converting the "heathen," spreading Western civilization, advancing national glory, and exploration for its own sake—as in the daring exploits of Henry M. Stanley (1841–1904) or Sir Richard Burton (1821–1890), who charted much of the African interior. Moreover, the aggressive spirit of

capitalism, buoyed by the advances of science and technology, favored an outward drive for expansion.

Yet the deeper causes powering that drive were more prosaic. The pace of industrial growth had been so hectic that European economic interests needed a wider stage. With the vast increase in production and intense competition in European domestic markets, manufacturers had to find new customers. As businesses became more and more profitable, wealthy industrialists looked for ways to invest the capital they had accumulated. By 1870, with industrialization well under way throughout most of Europe, they were turning to other parts of the world where investment often brought quicker and higher profits than at home. Furthermore, mining and processing a country's natural resources—vital supplies for the investing nation—were in themselves forms of imperialism, as the Germans demonstrated by winning control of Chilean nitrates. Thus imperialism represented the domination of nonindustrialized areas of the world by industrialized or industrializing nations.

European prosperity also contributed to the imperialist impulse. With the transformation from an agricultural to an urban society, and the general rise in prosperity, the European demand was increasing not only for staple commodities such as beef and grain, but specialty goods not produced in Europe, such as coffee and sugar, as well as luxury items such as ivory and animal skins. Furthermore, manufacturers came to depend on a ready supply of materials not available in the West, including cocoa, rubber, and copper.

The ceremony, or *durbar,* investing Queen Victoria (in her absence) as empress of India, which took place at Delhi.

By the last third of the 19th century, a global economy had come into being that inextricably linked Western and non-Western interests (see Part VII, Topic 17). The two sides were not, however, equal partners, for modern technology gave the West an enormous power advantage. Moreover, the non-Western nations traded raw materials and food, while the West produced sophisticated and expensive manufactured goods, and transported the bulk of the world's trade. As European economic prosperity became increasingly dependent on maintaining its dominance, the European powers looked for ways to control those regions that were necessary for their prosperity. Given their military and technological superiority, the most direct means was outright conquest. The superiority of European weapons reinforced the notion of racial superiority. In Nigeria in 1897, 32 Europeans and 500 African mercenaries defeated an army of 31,000 with the use of machine guns; the following year the British killed some 10,000 Muslims with machine guns at Omdurman in the Sudan.

Yet a generation that had seen the abolition of the European slave trade (it ended in 1834), and upheld the importance of "morality," could hardly acknowledge so calculating a motive for acquiring foreign territory. The notion that it was "the white man's burden" to civilize the world—that is, to westernize it—provided a moral justification for taking over and governing other people. Other important factors could be adduced. From the time of the Crusades, there had been a strong belief in the superiority and eventual triumph of Christianity. With the growth of Western power throughout the world, European missionaries, both Protestant and Catholic, could spread their faith, while improving local health care and bringing Western education to local populations. Some religious leaders saw imperial conquest as not only justifiable but as an obligation, particularly at a time of growing religious doubt at home.

For many European governments, imperialistic projects helped to distract attention from domestic dissatisfactions. A successful campaign or a heroic victory, appropriately celebrated by the press, could serve to deflect, at least temporarily, demands for broader political participation and for increased social justice. Some classes and individuals for whom urban, industrial life had little appeal were naturally drawn to colonial existence. Aristocrats, by becoming imperial administrators, could take up positions of authority and superiority. Those for whom the cities of 19th-century Europe were anonymous, and for whom industrial employment represented monotonous drudgery, had the prospect of excitement, and maybe financial profit, in the colonies. In Germany, colonial expansion was a safe outlet for German nationalism.

Imperialism and National Rivalries

One motive for imperialism that no government ever tried to conceal was *patriotism*—the enhancement of national interests, especially when in conflict with those of a rival nation. France's imperial ambitions increased after 1871 in order to compensate abroad for her defeat by Germany at home. Britain sought to maintain a dominant position in Egypt after 1882 in order to protect the Suez Canal and offset the risk of the crumbling Ottoman Empire falling under Russian control. Even those smaller countries without the public resources to launch a campaign entered the race. In 1876, the king of Belgium, Leopold II (ruled 1865–

1909) joined with a group of financiers to found the International Association for the Exploration and Civilization of Central Africa. Intended in theory to underwrite the explorations of Henry M. Stanley, the association helped Leopold to claim "trusteeship" of large tracts of the Congo as possessions of the crown.

With tension between nations rising in Europe, and the pace of imperialism increasing, particularly in Africa, the danger of outright war was clear. In 1884–1885, a conference met in Berlin to lay some ground rules for the acquisition of empire, and thereby avoid clashing interests. The participants agreed that possession of coastal territory brought with it the right to the interior, provided, however, that the claimant was actually occupying the land with military or administrative forces. This arbitrary drawing of borders, with no regard for indigenous African cultures, produced a set of artificial "countries" that satisfied the colonizers, but proved disastrous in the years of decolonization after World War II (see Part VIII, Topic 10).

By the early years of the 20th century, India and virtually the whole of Africa were under European rule, China was at the mercy of Western demands, and Japan had adapted itself to Western political ideas, including that of territorial conquest. For many Europeans, it seemed that imperialism had triumphed and that Western civilization was destined to become the dominant world culture. Yet the European grip on the world was soon shaken by three factors. Growing hostility among the European powers themselves reached its peak in World War I, while the United States played an increasingly prominent role in international affairs. Within the colonial territories, the rise of national consciousness eventually combined with the weakening position of the Western powers to bring an end to imperialism.

THE BRITISH IN INDIA: FROM MUTINY TO NATIONAL CONSCIOUSNESS

Through the East India Company, the British had maintained commercial links with India since the 18th century, and by the middle of the 19th century, with virtually the whole subcontinent informally "ruled" by the Company, British domination was producing considerable resentment.

The Sepoy Rebellion

The first signs of trouble developed in May 1857, among *Sepoys* (the Hindi word for "troops") in the Company's Bengal Army, stationed near Delhi. A new type of rifle, lately introduced, employed greased bullets. A false rumor spread that the fat used for the cartridges came from cows and pigs—the former sacred to Hindus, the latter regarded by Muslims as unclean. In the ensuing revolt, which the British contemptuously

Lord Curzon, viceroy of India, and his wife with the raja of Chamba and staff.

DOCUMENTS ON HISTORY

The Drive for Empire

Even at the time, imperialism was the subject of great debate in Europe and the United States among social critics, political and business leaders, and writers. Arguments for and against imperialism disagreed not only about its causes but about its impact and its future.

THE ARROGANCE OF EUROPEAN IMPERIALISTS

The British journalist and explorer Henry M. Stanley (1841–1904) embodied the arrogant attitudes toward non-Westerners that typified many of his generation. In his memoirs, he explained the "necessity" of his harsh manner in dealing with Africans.

The natives rapidly learned that though everything was to be gained by friendship with me, wars brought nothing but ruin.

When a young white officer quits England for the first time, to lead blacks, he has got to learn to unlearn a great deal. We *must* have white men in Africa; but the raw white is a great nuisance there during the first year. In the second year, he begins to mend; during the third year, if his nature permits it, he has developed into a superior man, whose intelligence may be of transcendent utility for directing masses of inferior men.

My officers were possessed with the notion that my manner was "hard," because I had not many compliments for them. That is the kind of pap which we may offer women and boys. Besides, I thought they were superior natures, and required none of that encouragement, which the more childish blacks almost daily received.

From Henry M. Stanley, *Autobiography,* ed. Dorothy Stanley. Houghton Mifflin. Copyright © 1909.

THE ECONOMIC IMPULSE

In 1898 the American financial expert Charles A. Conant wrote an important article on the economic necessity for American participation in imperial expansion.

This new movement [imperialism] is not a matter of sentiment. It is the result of a natural law of economic and race development. The great civilized peoples have to-day at their command the means of developing the decadent nations of the world. What this means, in its material aspects, is the great excess of saved capital which is the result of machine production. . . . There must always be savings in a progressive industrial society to repair the wear of existing equipment and to meet new demands, but under the present social order it is becoming impossible to find at home in the great capitalistic countries employment for all the capital saved which is at once safe and remunerative. . . .

For the means of finding new productive employments for capital, it is necessary that the great industrial countries should turn to countries which have not felt the pulse of modern progress. Such countries have yet to be equipped with the mechanism of production and of luxury, which has been created in the progressive countries by the savings of recent generations. They have not only to obtain buildings and machinery—the necessary elements in producing machine-made goods—but they have to build their roads, drain their marshes, dam their rivers, build aqueducts for their water supplies and sewers for their towns and cities. Asia and Africa are the most promising of these countries. Japan has already made her entry, almost like Athene full-armed from the brain of Zeus, into the modern industrial world. . . .

The United States cannot afford to adhere to a policy of isolation while other nations are reaching out for the command of these new markets. The United States are still large users of foreign capital, but American investors are not willing to see the return upon their investments reduced to the European level. Interest rates have already declined here within the last five years. New markets and new opportunities for investment must be found if surplus capital is to be profitably employed. . . .

From Charles A. Conant, "The Economic Basis of 'Imperialism'," *North American Review* (September 1898).

IMPERIALISM AS SOCIAL ATAVISM

Austrian economist Joseph Schumpeter (1883–1950) rejected the view that imperialism was driven by capital economics. Instead, in 1919 he argued that imperialism was actually a precapitalist phenomenon, a social throwback to an earlier stage of human development in which expansionism was undertaken for its own sake.

Wherever capitalism penetrated, peace parties of such strength arose that virtually every war meant a political struggle in the domestic scene. The exceptions are rare—Germany in the Franco-Prussian war of 1870–1871, both belligerents in the Russo-Turkish war of 1877–1878. That is why every war is carefully justified as a defensive war by the governments involved, and by all the political parties, in their official utterances—indicating a realization that a war of a different nature would scarcely be tenable in a political sense. . . . In the distant past, imperialism had needed no disguise whatever, and in the absolute autocracies only a very transparent one; but today imperialism is carefully hidden from public view—even though there may still be an unofficial appeal to warlike instincts. . . . Every expansionist urge must be carefully related to a concrete goal. All this is primarily a matter of political phraseology, to be sure. But the necessity of this phraseology is a symptom of the popular attitude. And that

continued next page

attitude makes a policy of imperialism more and more difficult—indeed, the very word imperialism is applied only to the enemy, in a reproachful sense, being carefully avoided with reference to the speaker's own policies. . . .

Among all capitalist economies, that of the United States is least burdened with precapitalist elements, survivals, reminiscences, and power factors. Certainly we cannot expect to find imperialist tendencies altogether lacking even in the United States, for the immigrants came from Europe with their convictions fully formed, and the environment certainly favored the revival of instincts of pugnacity. But we can conjecture that among all countries the United States is likely to exhibit the weakest imperialist trend. This turns out to be the truth. . . . The United States was the first advocate of disarmament and arbitration. . . . Even in the United States, of course, politicians need slogans—especially slogans calculated to divert attention from domestic issues. Theodore Roosevelt and certain magnates of the press actually resorted to imperialism—and the result, in that world of high capitalism, was utter defeat, a defeat that would have been even more abject, if other slogans, notably those appealing to anti-trust sentiment, had not met with better success. . . .

These facts are scarcely in dispute. . . .

It follows that *it is a basic fallacy to describe imperialism as a necessary phase of capitalism, or even to speak of the development of capitalism into imperialism.*

From Joseph A. Schumpeter, *Imperialism and Social Classes*, trans. Heinz Norden. Copyright © 1951.

A CRITIQUE OF IMPERIALISM

One of the most important analyses of imperialism was the critique of British economist John A. Hobson (1850–1940), who in 1902 argued that the scramble for colonies served the interests of unregulated capitalism. Hobson asserted that colonization impeded social reform at home and maintained the gap between rich and poor.

In view of the part which the non-economic factors of patriotism, adventure, military enterprise, political ambition, and philanthropy play in imperial expansion, it may appear that to impute to financiers so much power is to take a too narrow view of history. And it is true that the motor-power of Imperialism is not chiefly financial: finance is rather the governor of the imperial engine, directing the energy and determining its work: it does not constitute the fuel of the engine, nor does it directly generate the power. Finance manipulates the patriotic forces which politicians, soldiers, philanthropists, and traders generate; the enthusiasm for expansion which issues from these sources, though strong and genuine, is irregular and blind; the financial interest has those qualities of concentration and clear-sighted calculation which are needed to set Imperialism to work. An ambitious statesman, a frontier soldier, an overzealous missionary, a pushing trader, may suggest or even initiate a step of imperial expansion, may assist in educating public opinion to the urgent need for some fresh advance, but the final determination rests with the financial power. The direct influence exercised by great financial houses in "high politics" is supported by the control which they exercise over the body of public opinion through the Press, which, in every "civilised" country, is becoming more and more their obedient instrument. . . . Add to this the natural sympathy with a sensational policy which a cheap Press always manifests, and it becomes evident that the Press has been strongly biased towards Imperialism, and has lent itself with great facility to the suggestion of financial or political Imperialists who have desired to work up patriotism for some new piece of expansion.

Such is the array of distinctively economic forces making for Imperialism, a large loose group of trades and professions seeking profitable business and lucrative employment from the expansion of military and civil services, and from the expenditure on military operations, the opening up of new tracts of territory and trade with the same, and the provision of new capital which these operations require, all these finding their central guiding and directing force in the power of the general financier.

From John A. Hobson, *Imperialism: A Study*. Copyright © 1938.

THE MARXIST INTERPRETATION

Russian radical activist V. I. Ulianov (1870–1924), better known by his pseudonym Lenin, was leader of the Bolshevik (Communist) party. He wrote the most sophisticated early Marxist interpretation of imperialism. Influenced by the ideas of Hobson, Lenin claimed that imperialist economic competition abroad represented the last phase of a dying capitalism.

If it were necessary to give the briefest possible definition of imperialism, it would be defined as the monopoly stage of capitalism. Such a definition would include the essential feature; for, on the one hand, finance-capital is the banking capital of the few biggest monopolist banks, fused with the capital of the monopolist groups of manufacturers; and, on the other, the division of the world is a transition from a colonial policy, ceaselessly extended without encountering opposition in regions not as yet appropriated by any capitalist power, to a colonial policy of monopolized territorial possession—the sharing out of the world being completed. . . .

Imperialism is capitalism in that phase of its development in which the domination of monopolies and finance-capital has established itself; in which the export of capital has acquired very great importance; in which the division of the world among the big, international trusts has begun; in which the partition of all the territories of the earth amongst the great capitalist powers has been completed. . . .

Monopoly has grown out of colonial policy. To the numerous "old" motives of colonial policy the capitalist financier has added the struggle for the sources of raw materials, for the exportation of capital, for "spheres of influence," *i.e.*, for spheres of good business, concessions, monopolist profits, and so on; in fine, for economic territory in general. When the European powers did not as yet occupy with their colonies a tenth part of Africa (as was the case in 1876), colonial policy was able to develop otherwise than by the methods of monopoly—by "free grabbing" of territories, so to speak. But when nine-tenths of Africa had been seized (towards 1900), when the whole world had been shared out, the period of colonial monopoly opened and as a result the period of bitterest struggle for the partition and the repartition of the world. . . .

From all that has been said on the economic nature of imperialism, it follows that we must define it as capitalism in transition, or, more precisely, as dying capitalism. It is very instructive in this respect to note that the bourgeois economists, describing modern capitalism, employ with great fluency such terms as "interlacing," "absence of isolation," etc.; the banks are "enterprises which by their objective and their course of development have a character not purely economic, but are departing more and more from the sphere of private economic management." And the same Reisser, to whom these last words belong, declares with the greatest seriousness that the "prophecy" of the Marxists concerning "socialization" has not been realized!

From V. I. Lenin, *Imperialism: The Highest Stage of Capitalism*. Vanguard Press. Copyright © 1926.

continued next page

THE HUBRIS OF WORLD POWER

British Nobel prize–winning poet Rudyard Kipling (1865–1936) was thought of as the official poet of the empire. His famous poem "The White Man's Burden," which appeared in 1899, was an appeal to the United States to help the British and other powers in assuming the "burden" of imperial rule. But in this poem, written two years earlier on the occasion of Queen Victoria's diamond jubilee, he pointed out that all things pass, including world empire.

God of our fathers, known of old—
Lord of our far-flung battle line—
Beneath whose awful hand we hold
Dominion over palm and pine—
Lord God of Hosts, be with us yet,
Lest we forget—lest we forget!

The tumult and the shouting die—
The Captains and the Kings depart—

Still stands thine ancient sacrifice,
An humble and a contrite heart. . . .

Far-called, our navies melt away—
On dune and headland sinks the fire—
Lo, all our pomp of yesterday
Is one with Nineveh and Tyre!
Judge of the Nations, spare us yet,
Lest we forget . . .

If, drunk with sight of power, we loose
Wild tongues that have not Thee in awe—
Such boasting as the Gentiles use
Or lesser breeds without the Law—. . . .

For heathen heart that puts her trust
In reeking tube and iron shard—
All valiant dust that builds on dust,
And guarding calls not Thee to guard,
For frantic boast and foolish word,
Thy Mercy on Thy People, Lord!

From Rudyard Kipling, "Recessional," *Barrack Room Ballads: Recessional and Other Verses.* Robert McBride. Copyright © 1910.

labeled the "Indian Mutiny," the rebels seized Delhi, where they killed many of the British inhabitants, together with large sections of north-central India.

In March 1858, with the aid of considerable reinforcements, British troops finally broke the rebellion, and the British government took over direct control of India, ruled by a viceroy. In 1876, Queen Victoria was crowned empress of India. It was clear that, whatever the immediate cause, the "Mutiny" had reflected widespread discontent, and a few measures were taken to redress grievances. Indians received limited political representation at a local government level. Social reforms included the abolition of slavery.

The British made a thoroughgoing attempt to replace traditional cultural patterns with Western values. The government discouraged the rigid barriers of the caste system, whereby members of different castes could not mix in public places or on trains, and put limitations on child marriages. Hindus who became Christians were eligible for government jobs. Although regional varia-

tion was unavoidable in so vast a country, a British-type legal system operated nationally, and taxes were collected by the government, rather than by regional princes.

Schools and universities were run along British lines. Instruction was generally in English, which thus became the common language of the educated, who in due course were to lead the battle for Indian independence. Science and technology replaced traditional Hindu and Muslim learning. The products of this educational system were eligible for posts in the Indian Civil Service. After 1864, Indians in theory could be appointed to the highest ranks; in practice, appointees (generally Hindus) were restricted to lower positions, where many became familiar with Western notions of bureaucracy.

Improved communications assured effective control of the colony. The authorities constructed a telegraph system during the 1850s, and laid thousands of miles of rail tracks. By 1900, the Indian rail network

Sir Chamrajendra Wadiyar, maharaja of Mysore, and his children, 1890.

extended for over 26,000 miles. These modernizations, together with the introduction of Western agricultural methods, also served to increase prosperity for colonial entrepreneurs and the limited but growing number of local business interests.

For the majority of Indians, illiterate and living at a bare subsistence level as their ancestors had for centuries, the effects of British rule were mixed. Among those better off, there continued to be considerable resentment. Upper-caste Hindus disliked seeing the caste system challenged. Muslims, who had been accustomed to forming the ruling class, now found themselves discriminated against. Both groups resented the Christian missionary work that often formed part of the school program.

Another challenge to the British came from a number of educated Indians who combined a sense of national identity with a belief in Western ideals of freedom. The Indian National Congress party first met in 1885 to advocate greater Indian participation in the Civil Service. Over the next few decades, it campaigned with increasing vigor for Indian independence, both political and economic. Yet, ironically, the very fact that Congress party leaders represented progressive ideas cut them off from most of their fellow Indians, traditionalists who saw no essential difference between British governors and upper-caste intellectuals. India did not achieve independence until 1947.

THE OPENING OF CHINA AND THE BOXER REBELLION

For the first centuries of European exploration in Asia, the Chinese empire succeeded in maintaining its isolation from Western culture. By the early decades of the 19th century, however, internal administrative and financial problems hampered Chinese resistance to the presence of foreign merchants and traders. As the imperial government found itself under increasing challenge from peasant rebels, it turned to outside help in the struggle to retain control.

Chinese helplessness in the face of European military force became manifest in the Opium War of 1839–1842. British merchants in India had developed the custom of exchanging opium for Chinese tea, porcelain, and other goods. The Chinese wanted silver and gold in return, but the British feared problems with their balance of payments, and traded opium instead. Use of the drug, the harmful effects of which were well-known, was not traditional in China, and the government attempted to prevent its importation. The Chinese emperor even addressed a personal appeal to Queen Victoria, but she turned a deaf ear, feeling that it would be inopportune to give up such a major source of revenue.

The result of the Chinese attempts to ban opium was open war and a British blockade of the Chinese coast. China, with no real sea power, was forced to give way and accept humiliating terms of settlement. Several ports, including Shanghai and Canton, were opened to the British, who also received the island of Hong Kong. Hong Kong's mainland territory was added in 1898, when China gave the British a 99-year lease, which expired in 1997. British merchants continued to trade in ever-increasing quantities of opium: 6,000 cases were shipped to China in 1820, 100,000 in 1880.

Chinese suspicion of Western influences received further reinforcement when peasants led by Christian converts staged a major uprising to demand tax and land reform. The Tai Ping Rebellion lasted from 1851 to 1864, and was finally crushed only with the help of Western forces, including a British contingent led by General Charles "Chinese" Gordon (1833–1885). During its course, a number of other nations, including France and the United States, took advantage of the government's weakness to force further trade and territorial concessions. In 1860 a Franco-British force occupied Peking (now spelled Beijing), drove out the emperor, and burned the Summer Palace.

Whereas in India a colonial power had taken the responsibility of direct rule, in China competition among Western imperialists led European powers to seek financial control without taking the country over. As long as a weak central government was dependent on European troops and advisers, the Chinese were at the mercy of Western demands. Nor, given the Chinese reverence for tradition, was there any move to modernize. With the Tai Ping Rebellion crushed, the government tried to revive traditional principles of Confucianism. Among its tenets was the saying, "Acknowledgement of limits leads to happiness," a dangerous attitude with which to face driving capitalist Europeans.

Before the century was over, China lost territory to its neighbor Japan. The Japanese had followed the opposite tactic of adopting Western ways wholesale, and used them to wrest control of Korea from China in 1894–1895. The shock of defeat by its much smaller rival finally induced the Chinese emperor to initiate a campaign of reforms.

The Boxer Rebellion

The attempt at domestic reform came too late. In 1898, Tz'u-Hsi (1835–1908), the previous emperor's formidable widow who had earlier ruled as regent, seized power. Bitterly anti-Western, she maintained control through a small clique of conservative ministers. To reinforce her rejection of outside influences, she also encouraged the activities of a secret society,

Dead bodies of Boxer rebels executed by Chinese officials.

the "Harmonious Fists," called by Europeans the "Boxers." In the Boxer Rebellion of 1900–1901, members of the society killed missionaries and Chinese converts to Christianity, murdered the German minister in Peking, and besieged the foreign embassies there.

The uprising was suppressed by a joint European and United States military force, which in turn demanded yet further concessions. By the terms of the Boxer Protocol, China paid a huge indemnity to the United States and the European powers involved. New treaties gave Britain, France, Germany, and Russia long-term leases on ports, from which they could expand inland. With effective power and no responsibility, the European nations constructed railroads and developed river transport to open up the interior. The dowager empress grimly held on to what authority she could, finally westernizing the army and imperial bureaucracy, but by now the internal pressure for change was too great. Within three years of her death in 1908, open revolution ended imperial rule and replaced it with the Chinese Republic.

JAPAN AND THE WEST

Like China, Japan came under heavy pressure from Americans and Europeans to end its isolation and open itself to international trade. In contrast to their neighbors, however, the Japanese quickly reformed their country along Western lines and adopted Western technologies. So swift was the transformation that by the end of the century Japan, too, had become an imperialist power.

Japan's exposure to international pressure was both later and more violent than that of China. In 1853, the American Commodore Matthew Perry (1794–1858) sailed four vessels into Tokyo Harbor, threatening bombardment and refusing to leave until a Japanese envoy agreed to accept a United States demand for a diplomatic and trade treaty. The next year he returned to conclude the agreement. Britain, the Netherlands, and Russia were quick to follow, claiming their rights to fish in Japanese waters and to trade. With little in the way of naval power, the Japanese had little choice but to concede.

Both progressives and conservatives in Japan began to urge reform, the former inspired by Western models, the latter in the belief that their nation's independence could be assured only by radical change. In 1867 they found a leader in the new young emperor, Meiji (ruled 1867–1912)—a word meaning "the enlightened one," chosen in place of his real name, Mutsuhito. In place of the old feudal system of regional lords known as shoguns, the emperor himself assumed

Japanese portrait of Commodore Matthew Perry.

symbolic leadership, and the country was governed by his advisers, a small group of elder statesmen. Responsible to the emperor rather than to the Diet (parliament), they provided the authoritarian leadership that made possible rapid change.

In looking for a model for their institutions, the Japanese turned to Europe and the United States. Western experts were brought in to help build up a navy, while the new Japanese army adopted German systems of conscription and training. A new constitution, introduced in 1890, was also based on that of Germany. State investment and the rise of a business class encouraged industrialization along Western lines. On the other hand a new system of universal education, while it included scientific and technical subjects, also laid strong emphasis on patriotism and loyalty to the emperor.

During the last three decades of the 19th century, Japan adopted a variety of aspects of Western culture, including the metric system and the calendar. Christianity made little impact, however. Nor did the Japanese have any interest in taking up the cause of feminism, which was beginning to advance in western Europe, and Japanese women retained their traditionally inferior status, confined to the home.

Japan's first major adventure abroad, the war with China over Korea (1894–1895), was almost too successful. By its end, the Japanese had taken not only Korea itself, but the island of Taiwan (Formosa) and a piece of the Chinese mainland. This was too much for Russia, which found support in France and Germany. The European powers had no intention of sharing China with another Asian nation and insisted that the Japanese withdraw from the mainland. Yet the acceptance of Japan as an imperialist country was underscored in 1902, when Britain, the leading colonial power, and Japan signed an alliance. Further success came in the Russo-Japanese War of 1904–1905, when superior Japanese naval power helped them to victory.

By the early 20th century, Japan had achieved many of the goals of Western society, including industrialization, prosperity, and imperial conquest, without the upheaval or revolution that marked the modernization of most European countries. The methods—the encouragement of obedience and unquestioning patrio-

tism, and firm repression of any dissent—helped to shape the character of modern Japan.

NORTH AFRICA: THE BRITISH AND FRENCH IN CONFLICT

The fiercest competition of all for imperialist conquest occurred in the "scramble for Africa." In 1870, a European presence in Africa was limited to the northern regions above the Sahara and a few coastal ports. By the end of the century virtually the entire continent was under European rule.

In the north, a new era began with the completion of the Suez Canal in 1869. The construction of the canal was jointly financed by the khedive (viceroy) of Egypt, ruling on behalf of the Ottoman Empire, and French investors. The original inventor of the scheme,

Map 18.1   Africa on the Eve of World War I.

Scottish troops relaxing in front of the Sphinx.

and the director of the company involved in the canal's construction between 1859 and 1869, was Ferdinand-Marie de Lesseps (1805–1894), who later worked on the Panama Canal project. The immense engineering project was intended to facilitate French commercial expansion to the east, since ships bound for India and East Asia would be able to sail directly from the Mediterranean to the Indian Ocean, without having to circumnavigate Africa.

Egypt's participation had resulted in heavy debts to British banks, and by as early as 1875 its financial state was so calamitous that the khedive was forced to sell his shares. The British prime minister, Benjamin Disraeli, jumped at the chance to buy into France's engineering achievement and challenge French influence in North Africa. The two great rivals thus found themselves in joint control of Egypt.

When in 1882 a nationalist revolt by the Egyptian Army tried to drive out the foreigners, the French and British planned a joint intervention. The French cabinet fell and France backed off, whereupon the British went ahead on their own, taking the oppor-

tunity to reinforce their position. Ships of the Royal Navy bombarded Alexandria, and British troops moved in to take control of the country, leaving the khedive as a mere figurehead. The British protectorate over Egypt lasted until well after World War II.

With the British established in Egypt, the French were anxious to strengthen their bases elsewhere in North Africa. They had begun their conquest of Algeria, also Ottoman territory, in 1830. In 1881 they took Tunisia, another possession of the crumbling Ottoman Empire. Shortly after 1900, a French military force also entered Morocco, where their control was unsuccessfully challenged by Germany in the years leading up to World War I (see Part VII, Topic 16). A subsequent Franco-British agreement of 1904 recognized French control of Morocco in return for British rule in Egypt. With the Italian capture of Libya in 1912, by the eve of World War I the whole of Muslim North Africa was in European hands.

The direct confrontation between two imperialist powers, which the British and French avoided in Egypt, reached a crisis point in the Sudan. In 1898, a French military expedition under commander Jean-Baptiste Marchand (1863–1934) making its way toward the Red Sea from West Africa arrived at the Nile settlement of Fashoda, just as British troops led by General Herbert Kitchener (1850–1916) were occupying the southern Sudan. In the steamy swamplands, two grand imperialist schemes came face to face: the French plan for a territory stretching across the continent from the Atlantic to the Indian Ocean, and the British idea of an equally vast empire running north to south, from Cairo to the Cape of Good Hope. After several weeks of tension, the French troops withdrew on government orders. The French government realized the error of risking war with Britain when their real enemy was Germany; as the radical republican leader, Georges Clemenceau (1841–1929), said, "war with Britain is not worth a few marshes on the upper Nile."

The British had begun the subjugation of the Sudan in the 1880s but they were opposed by Sunni Muslim forces led by Muhammad Ahmad (1844–1885), the self-styled *Mahdi* (the Mahdi were a series of self-proclaimed saviors in the Sunni Muslim tradition).

In 1885, the Mahdi's army attacked a British garrison in the city of Khartoum, killing General Gordon and massacring its inhabitants. The death of Gordon, who had won popularity in Britain for his role in the suppression of the Tai Ping Rebellion in China and for ending the slave trade in the Sudan, provoked British anger and the collapse of William Gladstone's government. Ten years later, in 1898, Kitchener decisively defeated the Mahdi forces at Omdurman, where British soldiers mowed the Muslims down with machine guns.

THE DISMEMBERMENT OF CENTRAL AFRICA

European involvement in the affairs of North Africa went back to the days of ancient Rome. Africa south of the Sahara, however, was little known to Europeans before the mid-19th century. Coastal cities such as Lagos and Dakar served as trading centers, principally for slaves, but the interior remained unvisited except by Arab traders and the most intrepid explorers. With the decline and eventual end of the slave trade, two states on the West African coast were settled by freed slaves. Liberia, the oldest black African republic, became independent in 1847, although it remained under informal American influence. Sierra Leone, which became a British colony in 1808, combined an indigenous population with freed slaves from the West Indies and prisoners liberated from slave ships intercepted by the British Navy.

With the burst of imperialism after 1870, the Europeans forced their way into the African interior, drawing artificial boundaries, and inventing new countries. By 1900, the British controlled Nigeria in West Africa and a string of territories running south from Egypt, consisting of Kenya, Uganda, and Rhodesia (the territory comprising Rhodesia now forms the two countries of Zambia and Zimbabwe). The French held most of the rest of West Africa, with Dakar, the largest city in Senegal, as their administrative center. They constructed roads, railways, and harbor facilities there, and opened a university. Senegal had sent a deputy to the French parliament as early as 1848, although the first black deputy was elected only in 1914.

The heart of the continent fell to the Belgians, whose ruthless exploitation of the Belgian Congo soon became notorious. In the Horn of Africa on the Red Sea and the Indian Ocean, the Italians seized part of Somaliland (modern Somalia), other portions of which were occupied by the British and French, and Eritrea (now part of Ethiopia). They tried to conquer Ethiopia itself in 1896 but were driven back by the Ethiopian army at the Battle of Adowra, the first European colonizers to be defeated by indigenous African forces.

Leaders of the German forces in East Africa (1889) with local officers.

Portugal increased its hold on Angola and Mozambique, both of which it had used as trading bases for slaves as early as the 16th century. Unlike other colonizing powers, Portugal was not rich enough to invest in building infrastructure for its colonies (Belgium was in the same position). Work was done by a system of forced labor—virtually a form of slavery—and contracts were farmed out to foreign companies, which had even less interest than the government in the welfare of the indigenous populations.

The Germans were slow in developing a serious colonial drive. Bismarck was one of the few statesmen of the times who remained doubtful of the benefits of imperialism, and realized that the quest for German colonies would serve only to antagonize Britain. Nevertheless he began the German colonization of South-West Africa and the Cameroons in 1884, more as an outlet for German nationalism than for economic motives. After Bismarck's dismissal by Kaiser Wilhelm II in 1890 (see Part VII, Topic 15), Germany embarked on a vigorous imperialist policy. Its only possessions of any size were South-West Africa (now Namibia), a barren area of little economic value, German East Africa (now Tanzania), gained in 1891, and some important Pacific islands.

THE BOER WAR AND THE UNION OF SOUTH AFRICA

Although the southern part of Africa is farthest from Europe, the history of European involvement there goes back to the end of the 15th century, when Portuguese mariners sailed past the Cape of Good Hope into the Indian Ocean. In 1652, the Dutch East India Company founded a settlement at the Cape, to serve as a supply base for ships, and to search the interior for slaves and precious metals. Over the next century and a half the Dutch expanded eastward, taking land from the indigenous Bantu, Bush people, and Hottentots, who were either killed off, enslaved, or pushed out of the region. Other slaves were imported from West Africa and Mozambique. The present "colored" people of South Africa are the descendants of children born to unions between Dutch settlers and indigenous people, and Dutch and imported slaves. South Africa's "Indians" are descended from Indian and Malayan workers and merchants imported during the 19th century.

The Dutch colonists, who called themselves the *Boers* (the Dutch word for "farmers"), spoke a Dutch dialect which came to be known as Afrikaans. As they continued to take over good farming land wherever they found it, the only native people to put up any serious resistance were the Bantu. The first Bantu War of the 1770s was only the beginning of a series of bitter conflicts in which the Europeans gradually gained possession of Bantu lands. In the process, the Boers developed their notion of "apartheid," which claimed that the two cultures were separate and irreconcilable. Opposition to any form of multi-racialism was thus embedded in Boer political life from the beginning of their destruction of indigenous culture.

The Cape of Good Hope was annexed by the British in 1815. Relations between newly arrived British settlers and the Boers, unfriendly at best, were exacerbated further when in 1834 the British authorities banned slavery. From 1835 to 1845, in a migration known as the Great Trek, Boer farmers moved northeastward out of the British Cape Colony in search of new land. They founded two independent republics, the Orange Free State and the Transvaal. The indigenous Zulu warriors who opposed them, armed with shields and spears, were shot down in large numbers,

and in the 1870s the British crushed the remaining Zulu forces in spite of fierce resistance.

A few years later, first diamonds (in 1867) and then gold (in 1886) were discovered in the Transvaal. The conquered peoples provided cheap labor for the mines, but the Boers urgently needed capital to exploit their resources. The British were only too willing to step in. The Cape Colony's aggressive prime minister, Cecil Rhodes (1853–1902), went further. He had first come to Africa as a sickly young man, and quickly made a fabulous fortune in diamonds. Driven by ambition to unite Africa from the Cape to Cairo under British rule, Rhodes set out to subvert the Boer republics. In 1895, having first encouraged a rebellion among white, non-Boer mineworkers, he sent a force of volunteers to raid the Transvaal. The illegal and disastrous Jameson Raid, named after its leader, Leander Starr Jameson (1853–1917), was supposed to spark an uprising of foreigners in the Transvaal and provoke the Boers into outright war. The Boers located the arms caches the British had hidden, and the scheme failed. International outrage at the unprovoked attack on fellow westerners drove Rhodes from office.

Boer resentment at growing British interference was bound to lead to conflict sooner or later. The Boer War broke out in 1899, and bitter fighting went on until 1902. After taking the offensive, well equipped with arms by Germany, the Boers soon began to give way as British reinforcements were poured into South Africa. For the last two years Boer efforts were confined to guerrilla fighting, in a struggle that was grim and determined on both sides. The British, for their part, spared no means to discourage the guerrilla combatants, burning their farms and imprisoning their families in detention centers—the first modern concentration camps.

The British finally prevailed, and in 1910 the various territories were incorporated into the Union of South Africa. The legacy of resentment continued to influence relations between the British and the Afrikaaners for decades, while the true losers in the "white man's war" were the native populations. At the same time, the spectacle of two European, "civilized" peoples fighting over land and natural resources to which neither had any right underlined the true nature of imperialism, and the lengths to which Europeans were prepared to go to achieve conquest.

By the first decade of the 20th century, the history of Africa had been irrevocably changed. A few regional kingdoms remained, and Ethiopia retained its independence; the rest of the continent was divided up into a series of colonies, which often fragmented single tribal groups or combined rival peoples.

Cecil Rhodes, colonial administrator and financier.

The impact of westernization varied according to the policies of the colonizing power. The British tried to introduce educational and health systems on a fairly broad scale, but did not encourage local peoples to become involved in administrative positions. The French, by contrast, aimed to produce an African élite, versed in Western culture; it is no coincidence that many of the leading African writers of the first half of the 20th century came from French colonies. Other imperialist powers, notably Belgium and Portugal, were almost exclusively concerned with making profits from their colonies.

The overall phenomenon of Western imperialism in Africa and Asia was so vast, affecting so many millions of lives, that generalization about its effects is difficult. For many of the conquering powers the benefits of empire were dubious. With the exception of the British Empire, most of the colonies cost vast sums of money to maintain, and few Europeans actually wanted to live in them. Yet one recurring pattern can be seen: the growth of nationalism. The pursuit of national identity, one of the most powerful forces in the late 20th century, first developed in many parts of the world as a way of resisting the imperialists of the late 19th century and their successors.

Questions for Further Study

1. How did motives for colonization vary among the European powers? How did these differences affect their approach to establishing and governing their colonies?

2. To what extent were economic interests significant in the drive for colonization? How far were economic expectations fulfilled?

3. What effect did European colonization have on the creation of nationalist identities in the colonized territories? What were the long-term effects?

Suggestions for Further Reading

Baumgart, W. *Imperialism: The Idea of British and French Colonial Expansion, 1880–1914.* New York, 1982.

Christopher, A. J. *Colonial Africa.* Totowa, NJ, 1984.

Doyle, M. W. *Empires.* Ithaca, NY, 1986.

Hobshawm, E. J. *The Age of Empire, 1875–1914.* New York, 1987.

Lewis, D. L. *The Race to Fashoda: European Colonialism and African Resistance in the Scramble for Africa.* London, 1988.

Moon, P. *The British Conquest and Domination of India.* Bloomington, IN, 1989.

Pakenham, T. *The Scramble for Africa.* New York, 1991.

VII

Topic 19

The Social Order Challenged

he triumph of modern capitalism in the half-century before World War I did not go unchallenged. Opponents of laissez-faire economics attacked big business for exploiting the working class in the quest for ever-increasing profits. Social critics insisted that while prosperity enhanced the already privileged existence of the bourgeoisie, grinding poverty oppressed the daily lives of millions. Radical political leaders charged that parliamentary liberalism served the interests of the upper classes through repressive domestic policies designed to maintain the status quo.

Critics of the established order claimed to speak for two distinct but overlapping groups that represented most of Europe's population: the working classes and women. Governments everywhere saw the demands of these groups as dangerous to political stability and social peace, and used the coercive apparatus of the state—the police and the armed forces—against the forces of change. Neither working-class nor women's organizations, however, were united in their leadership, methods, or aims, and often there was little cooperation between them.

The divisions within the working-class and women's movements centered on a fundamental disagreement over long-range goals. Moderates wanted to improve conditions by reforming the existing political and social systems. This was essentially the aim of reformist socialists, trade unionists, and middle-class feminists, all of whom sought to extend the suffrage, elect representatives to parliaments or achieve other forms of representation, and pressure governments or business into granting concessions. Radicals, on the other hand, wanted to destroy the existing order completely and replace it with a new society in which the underlying causes of inequality and exploitation would be eliminated—this was the intention of anarchists, revolutionary socialists, and socialist feminists.

By 1914, moderates and radicals found themselves no closer to resolving their differences. Some significant reforms had been achieved, including the right to strike and to unionize, and the adoption of universal male suffrage in almost all countries. Yet capitalism was still fully entrenched, and almost nowhere did women even gain the vote, let alone more deeply rooted personal and legal rights. It took the trauma of the Great War and the subsequent Russian Revolution to shake the liberal-capitalist order to its foundations.

THE FIRST INTERNATIONAL: ANARCHISTS V. SOCIALISTS

In the mid-19th century, the working-class movement found two major theories—among a host of other possibilities—on which to base its revolutionary struggle against industrial capitalism: anarchism and Marxism. Among the early anarchists were the "Mutualists," who followed the ideas of the Frenchman Pierre Proudhon (1809–1865). In *What Is Property?* (1840), Proudhon declared that "Property is Theft!" and asserted that small-scale private ownership of property in a federation of communes was the best guarantee of individual freedom.

The Russian exile Mikhail Bakunin (1814–1876) advocated a different direction: the elimination of the state and all private property, to be achieved by revolutionary violence. By the 1860s, anarchism emerged as the principal rival to Marxism. The worker movement itself began to divide between anarchist principles and the "scientific" socialism advocated by Karl Marx and Friedrich Engels (see Part VII, Topic 13). Anarchists and Marxist socialists agreed, at least theoretically, that revolutionary violence was the only means of destroying capitalism. Marxists and most anarchists also accepted the idea that private property was the root cause of inequality and exploitation and had to be eliminated.

Where anarchists and Marxists clashed was in their view of the nature and the purpose of the state. Marx declared that the immediate aim of the revolution was for the workers to wrest power from the bourgeoisie by conquering the state and creating a working-class government—the "dictatorship of the proletariat." The anarchists, on the other hand, saw the state as the principal source of oppression, regardless of its nature, and insisted on eliminating it completely, along with other forms of authority. "All exercise of power perverts," wrote Bakunin, "and all submission to authority humiliates."

Mikhail Bakunin, Russian revolutionary exile and leader of the anarchist opposition to Marx in the First International.

Cover of the original edition of *The Communist Manifesto* (1848), by Karl Marx and Friedrich Engels. The slogan "Workers of the world, unite" appears on the page.

sis of the Commune, *The Civil War in France* (1871), Marx described it as the first example of the dictatorship of the proletariat. But although communists, socialists, and anarchists had fought against the government, many more thousands of French citizens with no ideological agenda sustained the Commune, which could not be described as a Marxist phenomenon. Nevertheless, the uprising struck terror among European governments, most of which clamped down on their own radicals and workers.

Marx, Bakunin, and the First International

The International Workingmen's Association—commonly known as the First International—was founded in London in 1864 by a disparate group of radicals that included German Marxists, anarchists, British and Belgian trade unionists, French supporters of Proudhon, and Italian followers of Mazzini. The International sought to act as a clearing house for radicalism and to focus revolutionary strategy. Instead, it became the stage for an ongoing debate between Marx and Bakunin, whose personalities and ideas represented the extreme alternatives of revolutionary leadership.

From the outset, Marx tried to run the International, but Bakunin opposed him. In September 1871, after the repression of the Commune, its representatives met at a congress in London, where Marx pushed for the adoption of a platform calling for the seizure of political power by the workers through the creation of socialist parties in all countries. Moreover, he insisted that the International's executive committee be given the power to impose centralized control and ideological uniformity over the International's local sections and federations. Bakunin's anarchist followers and other "antiauthoritarian" radicals lined up against Marx, whose rigid program was supported chiefly by German communists. A year later, at the Hague Congress, the struggle between Marxists and antiauthoritarians further polarized the International, but Marx triumphed by securing the expulsion of Bakunin and the anarchists.

Regrouping after the Hague meeting, Bakunin and the antiauthoritarians held their own meeting at Saint-Imier, Switzerland, where they rejected the principle that central committees or congresses could dictate policy to members. Instead of the seizure of political power that Marx demanded, the Saint-Imier delegates called for the destruction of power.

The First International, by then consisting only of Marxists, was officially dissolved in 1876. Over the next 20 years, while the Marxists forged ahead with the creation of socialist parties, militant action remained largely in the hands of the anarchists. Bakunin and a

Another theoretical point of disagreement lay in identifying the revolutionary class that would lead the struggle. Marx pinned his hopes on the modern industrial proletariat of advanced nations such as Britain and Germany, which he identified as the only true revolutionary class. Bakunin, on the other hand, argued that the industrial proletariat was already in the process of being indoctrinated by bourgeois values and had lost its revolutionary potential. Instead, Bakunin focused on what he called the "proletariat in rags," those desperately poor elements at the bottom of society—workers in small shops and landless peasants—in preindustrial countries such as Spain, Italy, and Russia.

These and other ideological currents derived inspiration from the uprising of the Paris Commune, a crucial moment in the development of European radicalism (see Part VII, Topic 15).

European radicals saw the Commune as a class war between workers and the bourgeoisie. In his analy-

The Paris Commune, a radical republican government in opposition to the National Assembly. This photograph is a portrayal, probably used as anti-Communard propaganda, of the killing of 62 hostages. The massacre actually occurred at night at the hands of a mob the Commune leaders could not control.

new generation of libertarian leaders worked to arouse the masses. Peter Kropotkin, a Russian prince living in London, called for working-class solidarity, while the Italian Errico Malatesta (1850–1932) shifted his anarchist doctrine away from the collectivist formula of "from each according to his abilities to each according to his labor" to that of anarchist communism, which replaced the word "labor" with "need."

Most anarchists maintained the antiauthoritarian tradition, while some individuals, not all of whom were anarchists, adopted terrorist tactics. In the 1870s German anarchists made two attempts to kill Kaiser Wilhelm I, and in the 1890s a cycle of retaliation against state repression induced a few practitioners of "propaganda of the deed" to assassinate political leaders and monarchs—among them, French President François Sadi-Carnot in 1894, Prime Minister Antonio Canovas del Castillo of Spain in 1897, the Empress Elizabeth of Austria-Hungary in 1898, and King Umberto I of Italy in 1900. Most anarchist theorists did not believe that such terrorist acts would bring the revolution into being, but saw them as the inevitable result of government oppression. Governments reacted sharply to the assassinations, convening an antianarchist conference in Rome in 1898 to coordinate police efforts on an international level.

THE SECOND INTERNATIONAL: IDEOLOGY AND SOCIALIST POLITICS

Socialism emerged as a major force in Europe between 1870 and 1914. Mass-based political parties inspired by Marxist principles grew rapidly, and by the 1890s one existed in almost every country, together with a vast network of subsidiary organizations, unions, newspapers, and clubs. Their leaders were optimistic that they were on the verge of attaining a socialist society.

The Rise of Socialist Parties

The first and most important socialist party in Europe developed in Germany. From the beginning, however, German socialists were divided into two camps— Marxists and those who followed the ideas of Ferdinand Lassalle (1825–1864). Flamboyant and brilliant, Lassalle had taken part in the 1848 revolutions before studying political philosophy and socialist theory. Unlike Marx, who wanted to "smash" the bourgeois state, Lassalle sought to democratize it for the working class. Lassalle had taken from the British economist David Ricardo (see Part VI, Topic 11) the notion of the "iron law of wages." According to this theory, wage increases resulted in the growth in the number of workers, which in turn created labor competition that drove down wages to the subsistence level. To overcome this tendency, Lassalle urged the formation of worker cooperatives, in which the workers would be the owners and thus control their own earnings. In his view, strikes and unions were futile. In 1863, a year before his death in a duel, he established the General Association of German Workers, which advocated universal suffrage and a program of peaceful, legal means to achieve socialism.

In opposition to Lassalle, Wilhelm Liebknecht (1826–1900) and August Bebel (1840–1913) founded the Social Democratic Labor party in 1869. Although not officially a Marxist party, the group was closer to the ideas of Marx and Engels than those of Lassalle. In 1875, they agreed to issue a joint platform, the "Gotha Program," in alliance with Lassalle's moderate supporters. This policy, which merged aspects of Marxist dogma with the reform strategy of Lassalle, formed the basis of the German Social Democratic party (SPD). Three years later, Bismarck passed the Anti-Socialist Laws designed to stamp out socialism, but the repression actually served to give a focus to the party's identity and it struggled underground for years before Kaiser Wilhelm II repealed the laws (see Part VII, Topic 15).

Marx criticized such blending of his revolutionary ideas with the reformist approach of the Lassallians, but the latter seemed appropriate to the many German socialists who felt that working-class power could be attained peacefully. This was the view of Eduard Bernstein (1850–1932), whose book *Evolutionary Socialism* (1899) was the first major work to "revise" Marxist theory in the light of changing circumstances. Bernstein, an old friend of Engels who had absorbed the views of British moderates known as the Fabians, argued on the basis of the German experience that Marx was wrong in predicting that the status of the working class would inevitably deteriorate. Marxist socialists, he contended, should eschew revolutionary violence and work through the political process to achieve bread-and-butter benefits for workers. He therefore believed that socialist deputies in the Reichstag should collaborate with bourgeois political parties to reform German society. Orthodox Marxists in the SPD attacked Bernstein's revisionism and virtually drummed him out of the party.

The success of German "social democracy" and the trade unions in winning worker support acted as a model for socialists throughout continental Europe. Despite efforts to create a Marxist party in Great Britain, socialism there was generally moderate and a socialist party developed after the trade unions. The most important socialist group was the Fabian Society (1884), named after Quintus Fabius Maximus, a Roman general of the 2nd century B.C. who used evasive tactics instead of direct battles in the Punic Wars. Its founders were middle-class intellectuals such as the writer H. G. Wells (1866–1946) and the dramatist George Bernard Shaw (1856–1950), and among its most important members were Sidney and Beatrice Webb (see Part VIII, Topic 5). In 1900 the Fabians, who favored peaceful political change rather than revolution, combined with the growing trade union movement and other socialist organizations to found the Labour party, in which Marxist elements were a distinct minority.

Belgians, Russians, Austrians, and Italians established their own parties in the two decades after 1870. The first Marxist party in France was formed by Jules Guesde (1845–1922), but several other groups vied for the loyalty of French workers, including the "Possibilists," so-called because they rejected Marx's all-or-nothing doctrines, and a group of "Independent" socialist intellectuals. Only in 1905 did French socialists unite under the leadership of Jean Jaures (1859–1914) with a largely Marxist party program.

The Second International

In 1889, on the centenary of the French Revolution, a large assembly of socialist societies gathered in Paris and founded the Second International. Unlike the First International, whose members were a disparate group of individuals, the Second—known as the "Socialist International"—was based on party affiliation. Marxist revolutionary as well as reformist parties were included, but from the beginning the anarchists were kept out. Through propaganda activities such as "May Day" parades and periodic congresses, the International coordinated socialist activity on a worldwide level in order to raise the consciousness of workers. International congresses were held in 1891, 1893, 1896, 1900, 1904, 1907, 1910, and 1912.

Just as Marx had dominated the First International, the SPD was able to exercise considerable hegemony over the Second, largely because of its more than 1 million members and the large number of deputies it had in the *Reichstag*. Yet the ideological divisions between Marxist orthodoxy and reformism continued to mark the International's deliberations.

Within the International, the German socialist August Bebel and his French rival Jean Jaures epitomized the cleavage between revolutionaries and reformists. The main controversy that divided them revolved around whether socialists should accept ministerial positions in nonsocialist governments. Bebel and Jaures debated these questions constantly at International congresses.

Bebel led the German Social Democrats with an iron hand for almost 50 years, and achieved a series of electoral gains that by 1912 made the SPD the largest party in the *Reichstag*. His orthodox Marxism maintained that socialist parties should be formed to seize power, not to work within parliamentary systems or cooperate with bourgeois parties. As a result, he bitterly criticized his French comrades when one of them agreed to serve in a republican cabinet in 1899. Yet, despite its revolutionary rhetoric, in practice the SPD's parliamentary behavior was moderate.

Jaures, an energetic and courageous politician, had helped to galvanize the coalition that defended Captain Dreyfus in the wrenching scandal dividing turn-of-the-century France. He advocated collaboration between socialists and bourgeois parties in order to obtain reforms. In his polemics with Bebel, Jaures argued that the strength of French parliamentary democracy made it possible for socialists to transform capitalist society peacefully, whereas in Germany that was not possible because the *Reichstag* had no real power. He attacked the SPD for seeking to impose its doctrines on the socialists of all other countries. Later, after the Second International came out in opposition to what it called the "opportunism" of the reformists, Jaures agreed to adhere to a truer Marxist position in the interests of socialist solidarity.

A trade union and socialist protest in London.

LABOR ON THE OFFENSIVE: TRADE UNIONS, STRIKES, AND REVOLUTIONARY SYNDICALISM

As Bernstein pointed out, events eventually demonstrated the inaccuracy of Marx's conclusion that the material lives of workers would deteriorate. In the decades after 1850, working-class living standards tended to rise as prosperity spread throughout European society. Better conditions, together with the widening of the franchise, in turn made labor leaders less radical and inhibited the appeal of unions for many workers. Labor unionists agreed to operate within the context of capitalist society—hence, the role of unions was not to foment revolution but rather to improve working conditions, raise wages, and secure benefits for their members.

The Rise of Trade Unions

In many European countries restrictions on trade unions predated the French Revolution. In 1791, the revolutionary government of France passed the Le Chapelier Law, which prohibited labor gatherings as detrimental to "the free exercise of industry and work."

In 1810 Napoleon's penal code outlawed strikes for changes in salaries and contracts. In Britain similar measures had been enacted, and although unions were given partial recognition in 1824, they were too weak to sustain lengthy strikes. The utopian reformer Robert Owen tried to create a single Grand National Union in 1834, but it too collapsed in the face of opposition from the Whig government. Unions and strikes were similarly banned at midcentury in Prussia, Russia, Austria, Spain, and most of the Italian states. Only later in the 19th century did unions win the legal right to exist and to strike, although many countries retained limitations on union activity and prohibited strikes until well toward the end of the century.

After 1870, the development of large-scale unions coincided with economic expansion and the rise of big business. In 1871, when William Gladstone's Liberal government granted full recognition to unions and legalized strikes, British trade unionists demonstrated their moderation by disassociating themselves from the violence of the Paris Commune. On the Continent, effective trade unions emerged in the years between the economic depression of the 1870s and the end of the century. Napoleon III, who had once used the army to put down strikes, allowed the formation of French unions in 1864. The French republican government curtailed union activity after the Commune, but the Third Republic finally extended legal status to them in 1884. Although unions were theoretically legal in the Second Reich, Bismarck used the antisocialist laws to suppress them between 1878 and 1890. In 1891 the German Imperial Industrial Code did legalize strikes, but imposed severe penalties on worker violence.

The end to the prohibition of strikes led to a large increase in the number of industrial work stoppages. Between 1880 and 1914, strikes—especially during periods of economic crisis—were a common aspect of industrial life, with hundreds of thousands of workers participating every year. By the late 1880s a "new unionism," different in character and dimension, was emerging. The early efforts at labor organization had involved craft unions, embracing only skilled workers and artisans. Now, however, industrial unions of unskilled workers began to form as a result of long and often bitter strike activity, involving many thousands of workers: they included the strike of Belgian miners and glass workers in 1886, the British match girl strike of 1888, and those of London dock workers and Ruhr coal miners in 1889.

As mass-based unions were established, labor leaders sought to create unified national organizations embracing workers in different industries. French unions formed a national federation in 1895, the *Confédération Générale du Travail* (CGT), while in England the British Trades Union Congress, established in 1868, merged with socialist groups and created the Labour Representation Committee. In 1906 Italian so-cialist unions set up the *Confederazione Generale del Lavoro* (CGL). By the eve of World War I European labor unions had a total membership of more than 9 million, including 4 million in Britain, 3 million in Germany, 1 million in France, some 700,000 in Italy, and 250,000 in Russia.

Revolutionary Syndicalism

In the 1870s, elements of the anarchist tradition merged with an aspect of trade union strategy to produce a unique current of radical thought known as *revolutionary syndicalism* (the term is derived from the French word for "union," *syndicat*). Fernand Pelloutier (1867–1901), its principal theorist, propounded the view that the seed of the future stateless society lay in the concept of the union. Syndicalists proposed direct action by the working class to bring about the revolution, with the general strike as their principal weapon. Pelloutier rejected all forms of the state. Instead, he advocated a social organization "limited exclusively to the needs of production and consumption."

Many syndicalists were influenced by the theories of the French intellectual Georges Sorel (1847–1922). A civil engineer by profession, Sorel argued that it was through the union rather than through political parties that socialism would be achieved. He believed that governments would repress general strikes with violence, and that the workers would respond with revolution. Sorel's major theoretical work was *Reflections on Violence* (1908), in which he posited the "myth of violence" as a force in history. Such all-encompassing strikes were attempted on a number of occasions—in 1893 in Belgium, in 1902 in Belgium, Sweden, and Spain, in 1903 in the Netherlands, in 1904 in Italy, and in 1909 in France and Sweden—but had little success. Nevertheless, socialist and syndicalist theorists continued to believe in the efficacy of the strike.

Significant Dates

The Suffrage Movement

1868	British women given the right to vote in local elections
1869	National American Women's Suffrage Association
1879	Bebel's *Women in the Past, Present and Future*
1884	Engels' *The Origins of the Family, Private Property, and the State*
1903	Emmeline Pankhurst founds Women's Social and Political Union
1904	International Women's Suffrage Alliance
1906	Finland gives women right to vote

WOMEN AND THE VOTE

The rise of socialism after midcentury coincided with the development of feminism, a term just then coming into use. By the 1870s European women interested in liberation strategies had the option of joining a variety of organizations. Women not inclined to direct political activism had worked in an array of reform movements, from the older temperance societies and private charities to settlement houses and educational groups. For those more urgently committed to improving women's rights and gender relations through political action, the choices were challenging. They could opt for Marxist-based movements associated with political parties striving to create socialist societies, or "bourgeois" movements that sought rights for women within the framework of capitalist society.

Politics and the Women's Movement

Like their male counterparts in liberal or socialist politics, feminist leaders debated aims and strategies. What united them was a commitment to break down the institutional and cultural legacies of a patriarchal society in which women's identities and rights had been long submerged under a system of male dominance. Laws in every country still limited the equality of women in such basic social institutions as marriage and divorce, or property ownership and inheritance. Yet the issue around which women of all social classes and nationalities rallied in the last decades of the 19th century was suffrage.

The right to vote was central to the privileges and responsibilities of citizenship in parliamentary systems of government. Some women viewed the right to vote as their reward for having served as coparticipants with men in the development of modern society, while others saw the vote as a means to improve conditions for themselves as well as for the working classes. By the eve of World War I, the suffrage issue had become the foundation for the first mass-based women's political movement, in the United States as well as in Europe.

Hundreds of thousands of women joined suffrage groups in France, Britain, Italy, Russia, and other countries.

British women were given the right to vote in local elections in 1868. The following year American activists Susan B. Anthony (1820–1906) and Elizabeth Cady Stanton (see Part VII, Topic 13) founded an organization that later became the larger National American Women's Suffrage Association, with a membership of over 2 million. By the 1870s, local governments in Finland and Sweden granted some women the vote, as did some American states in the 1890s, but in these cases suffrage was limited to single women who owned property. In no European country—Finland was the exception—did women have the franchise in national elections before World War I.

Most nonsocialist women's movements included suffrage in their platforms. French women had a popular if controversial hero in Louise Michel, a former schoolteacher turned political activist who had suffered years in prison at hard labor for her role in the Paris Commune (see Part VII, Topic 15). Under the Third Republic, the French feminists Maria Deraismes (1828–1894) and Hubertine Auclert (1848–1914) began to organize French women around the suffrage issue, despite strong resistance from republican leaders.

When Emmeline Pankhurst (second from left) issued a manifesto urging people to storm the House of Parliament in 1908, she was arrested. Here an officer reads the arrest warrant.

PUBLIC FIGURES *and* PRIVATE LIVES

ANNA KULISCIOFF AND FILIPPO TURATI

The lives of Anna Kuliscioff (1854–1925) and Filippo Turati (1857–1932) exemplified the trials and achievements of the many European men and women who challenged the established order at the turn of the century. Turati and Kuliscioff combined a lifelong commitment to the welfare of both the working class and women. Their own relationship was one of mutual respect, but the conventional gender patterns of the day compelled them to adopt distinct roles: Turati was able to build an active career both in socialist politics and as a member of the Italian Parliament. Kuliscioff, on the other hand, exerted her indirect influence chiefly through the intellectual discourse of her salon, one of the few ways in which women could traditionally affect politics.

Kuliscioff was born Anna Rosenstein in Simferopol, a small town in the Crimea. At 17, the precocious and strong-willed Kuliscioff went to Zurich to study medicine, since Russian women were not permitted advanced technical educations at home. In Switzerland, the center of radical exiles from all over Europe, she joined a group of Russian revolutionaries, and in 1872 married a young anarchist, Peter Makarevic. A year later the couple returned to Russia to work in the underground with a terrorist group. Makarevic was arrested in 1877 and renounced anarchism while in prison. Kuliscioff fled Russia, never to see her husband again.

In Paris, she impressed the radicals who met her by her commitment to revolution as well as by her beauty. The blonde, blue-eyed Kuliscioff had a brilliant intellect. One of the men attracted to her was Andrea Costa, a handsome young Italian anarchist. They fell in love, and collaborated in the anarchist cause. It was then that she took the alias of Kuliscioff: many exiled radicals lived under false names as a security measure. Both she and Costa were arrested. Kuliscioff was freed after the Russian novelist Ivan Turgenev intervened on her behalf, and she was expelled from France. When she attended a radical meeting in Florence in 1878, the Italian authorities arrested her and sent her to jail for two years.

The harsh prison experiences, together with the inability of the anarchist movement to achieve results, prompted Kuliscioff and Costa to move toward socialism and the creation of a working-class political party. They helped to establish *Avanti!*, which became the official newspaper of Italian socialists, and Costa soon became the first socialist elected to the Italian parliament.

In 1881 Kuliscioff gave birth to a daughter, named Andreina, but the relationship with Costa had cooled. Kuliscioff spent several unhappy years alone in Naples, where she went for her health—her long stays in cold prison cells had brought on a pulmonary disorder and severe arthritis.

In 1885, while resuming her medical studies in Naples, Kuliscioff met Filippo Turati. A young man of middle-class background ridden with psychological neuroses, Turati studied law but was drawn to literary and social issues. His interest in politics and in socialism was recent, but Kuliscioff sensed in him a quiet courage and deep humanitarian instincts.

Turati went to Milan to help organize the socialists. After completing her medical degree despite great prejudice against her in the Italian universities, she joined him there. They spent the next 35 years together. Their Milan apartment became the headquarters for *Critica Sociale*, an important journal of socialist theory which they edited. As their fame and stature grew, their home also became a well-known political salon. Young and idealistic socialists, as well as more seasoned radicals of European fame, called on them and debated the issues of the day.

Turati is generally considered the principal strategist of the Italian Socialist party (PSI), which he and Kuliscioff helped to found in 1892. Yet Turati evolved his political ideology under Kuliscioff's influence and, after his election as a deputy in 1896, was guided in much of his political dealings by her advice. Kuliscioff no doubt had the superior intellect. She was more decisive and, as outsider to parliamentary politics, less plagued by doubts, whereas he often ag-

onized over decisions and lived in a world of political compromise. One frequent visitor to their salon perceived the gender distinction that marked the couple's relationship when she described Kuliscioff as "the grey eminence behind the red cardinal."

Kuliscioff introduced Turati to the study of Marxism, and under her influence his socialist philosophy acquired a "scientific" basis—the belief that in order to understand society, it was necessary to understand the nature and causes of economic change. As a "positivist" who emphasized factual data, he came to the conclusion that day-to-day changes in the material condition of society should guide political strategy, as Bernstein's revisionist ideas had suggested.

Kuliscioff's interest in women's issues was long-standing and committed. Her lecture on "The Monopoly of Men" (1890) was a point of departure for Italian women—like Zetkin in Germany, Kuliscioff argued that women were oppressed both as workers and as women. At the PSI congress in 1897 she proposed a law regulating female labor, and Turati pushed for such legislation in Parliament. In 1912 she and other Italian women started a newspaper for women, *La difesa delle lavoratrici* (Defense of Women Workers).

The same divisions between reformists and revolutionaries that disturbed party unity elsewhere in Europe also caused a major rift in the PSI, and the Turati–Kuliscioff reformist wing of the party was alternately in and out of power. At the congress of 1912, however, the revolutionaries seized control of the party, and Turati never again exercised an equal degree of influence.

Their last years were clouded by the trauma of World War I and the rise of Fascism. Kuliscioff's death in December 1925 devastated Turati. He escaped from the Fascists the following year and fled to Paris, where he died in 1932. Together, they had inspired and led the left-wing struggle for freedom for more than a generation.

Auclert gained notoriety for her symbolic acts of protest, which included refusing to pay taxes and overturning voting urns. In 1909 a French Union for Women's Suffrage was founded.

As early as the 1880s American leaders had proposed the creation of an international organization to advance women's suffrage, but only in 1904 did an organizing conference meet. It gave rise to the International Women's Suffrage Alliance (IWSA). Like the Second International of socialist parties, the IWSA sponsored several world congresses in the years before World War I.

The Suffrage War in Britain

British women created a number of suffrage organizations in the late 19th century. The first group of prominence was the National Union of Women's Suffrage Societies (NUWSS), led by Millicent Garrett Fawcett (1847–1929). Working-class women in the textile mills set up associations of their own that underscored the middle-class interests of the NUWSS. The best-known suffrage movement, however, was the Women's Social and Political Union (WSPU), founded by Emmeline Pankhurst (1858–1928) in 1903.

Pankhurst's uncompromising militancy made the suffrage issue a cause célèbre in the early years of the 20th century. While a student in Paris she had been impressed by French feminists. Later she and her husband campaigned in England on behalf of women's rights to control their own property.

Pankhurst, who had joined women in the London match girl strike, believed that Fawcett's NUWSS was too timid. She concluded that only direct, violent action would secure women the vote. The WSPU campaigned against political candidates who refused to endorse female suffrage. With the help of her daughters Sylvia and Cristabel, Pankhurst declared war on the British government, organizing suffragist marches against Parliament and rallies before the royal palace.

When Prime Minister Herbert Asquith (served 1908–1916) refused to endorse women's suffrage in 1911, Pankhurst led a systematic assault on London's most exclusive shops, breaking windows to draw attention to the suffrage cause. Yet, despite a nine-month prison sentence, her activities became still more dramatic. One of her followers slashed a famous painting that feminists found offensive, while another assaulted Winston Churchill (1875–1965), then a young antifeminist politician serving as home secretary. A WSPU member chained herself to the gate outside the official home of the prime minister, shouting at passersby, and a few militants even started fires. As a result of a bomb plot against David Lloyd George, chancellor of the exchequer in Asquith's cabinet, Pankhurst was given a three-year prison term. Even prison, however, did not dampen her enthusiasm for the cause—to the dismay of government authorities, she and her daughters repeatedly declared hunger strikes.

Enemies of women's rights criticized such tactics, but the suffragists succeeded in making the vote for women a public issue that would not go away. The final victory in the suffragist war was not won until after World War I, but Pankhurst's struggles symbolized the determination of countless other women in all countries to secure their rights.

THE SOCIALIST PATH TO FEMINISM

Most socialist parties and labor unions recognized the importance of gaining the adherence of women, who in some countries accounted for almost half the industrial workforce. In Germany, Eleanor Marx, the daughter of Karl Marx, was among those who recruited women into separate organizations affiliated with the SPD. By 1914, the party had some 175,000 women involved in its activities.

Socialism and Feminism

Socialist parties generally supported women's suffrage, along with civil—as opposed to religious—marriage and the right to divorce. Birth control was a more problematic issue, since socialists long viewed birth control as associated with the ideas of Thomas Malthus and the notion that workers were to blame for their own poverty. Nevertheless, many socialists did not see gender issues as separate or distinct from working-class concerns and notions of masculinity often excluded women from socialist or union activism. While some women won positions of prominence within labor or socialist movements, few actually held important executive posts—exceptions to the rule were the Russian exile Angelica Balabanoff (1869–1965), who served on the executive committee of the Italian Socialist party and later was secretary of the Third (Communist) International, and Ottilie Baader (1847–1925), a long-time member of the SPD's executive committee.

The SPD produced two important theoretical works on the women's question: Bebel's *Women in the Past, Present and Future* (1879) and Engels' *The Origins of the Family, Private Property, and the State* (1884). Each traced the suppression of women to the development of the principle of private property—men, they argued, oppressed women so as to guarantee the legitimacy of children, which they deemed necessary in order to transfer property to their sons. Bebel saw in the relationship of wives to their husbands a parallel with the worker's relationship to employers, concluding that women were oppressed both as workers and as women.

The most important proponent of feminism within the SPD was Clara Zetkin (1857–1933), an incisive thinker and the editor of *Die Gleichheit* (Equality), a women's paper. A committed revolutionary socialist, Zetkin strongly disliked revisionism and denounced reformists as bitterly as Bebel and others did. She decried collaboration between the socialist women's movement and bourgeois feminism as loudly as they condemned cooperation between socialist and bourgeois parties.

Zetkin had two related concerns: to keep working-class men and women united in the socialist movement, and to prevent bourgeois feminists from drawing working women into their movement. She paid close attention to the economic status of women, stressing that they were not paid for their work as homemakers and mothers. She agreed with the arguments of Engels and Bebel that under capitalism women had become simply a form of male property. She was convinced, therefore, that the liberation of women could be achieved only within the larger socialist effort to eliminate private property. On the other hand, Zetkin joined other socialists in aiming to avoid a division of the working class along gender lines, and stressed the need to focus on women as workers rather than as wives.

In the half-century between 1870 and 1914, Europe witnessed the emergence of two major but unequal forces—socialism and feminism. Each stood in stark opposition to the prevailing values and power structure of the age. Anarchism and socialism posited drastic solutions to the problems of capitalist society, and the alternatives appealed to an increasing number of Europeans. The Marxists eventually gained command of the socialist movement, but their ranks were also split as revisionists challenged the assumptions of Marx's strategies. The creation of huge political parties and labor unions nevertheless gained the adherence of millions of workers, while syndicalists proposed to bring down the capitalist system with the general strike.

To the élites governing society, the women's movement appeared to be almost as dangerous. Many women rallied around the issue of the suffrage, creating national groups and an international organization devoted to gaining the vote. Other, more radical feminists emphasized broader questions of gender relations and political revolution. Some women combined feminism and socialism in their militancy, creating further disputes over strategy and theory within their ranks.

While there was little unity of position within either movement, both fought with great determination to eliminate economic and social injustice in European society, providing a rich legacy that was inherited by later generations of men and women.

Questions for Further Study

1. What theoretical and practical differences separated anarchism from socialism?

2. What issues were of most importance to socialist parties?

3. Why did the idea of the strike assume political importance?

4. Why were many women drawn to radical movements? What was the difference between the goals of suffragettes and those of women socialists?

Suggestions for Further Reading

Adams, Carole. *Women Clerks in Wilhelmine Germany: Issues of Class and Gender.* New York, 1988.

Berlanstein, Lenard R. *The Working People of Paris, 1871–1914.* Baltimore, MD, 1984.

Cahm, Caroline. *Peter Kropotkin and the Rise of Revolutionary Anarchism.* New York, 1989.

Franzoi, Barbara. *At the Very Least She Pays the Rent: Women and German Industrialization.* Westport, CT, 1985.

Joll, James. *The Second International, 1889–1914.* New York, 1966.

McClellan, David. *Karl Marx: His Life and Thought.* New York, 1978.

Ross, Ellen. *Love and Toil: Motherhood in Outcast London, 1870–1918.* New York, 1993.

Taylor, Barbara. *Eve and the New Jerusalem: Socialism and Feminism in the Nineteenth Century.* New York, 1983.

Thoennessen, W. *The Emancipation of Women: The Rise and Decline of the Women's Movement in German Social Democracy.* London, 1973.

Tickner, Lisa. *The Spectacle of Women: Imagery of the Suffrage Campaign, 1907–1914.* Chicago, 1988.

T o p i c   2 0

SOCIETY IN TRANSITION:
THE MODERNIZATION OF EUROPE

ith the coming of the second industrial revolution, European society underwent major changes, developing a structure that in the course of the 20th century spread throughout much of the world. The concentration of large numbers of people in ever-growing cities, many of them living at an adequate economic level and possessing the right to vote, produced a new element—the proletarian masses.

The rise of an urban proletariat had an important effect on the role of the middle classes. For much of the 19th century, middle-class liberalism was the chief spur to political and social change. By the end of the century, however, many businessmen saw working-class advancement as a threat to their own interests. As a result, the wealthiest and best educated—the upper middle class—developed alliances with the old aristocracy. The formation of this upper-class élite left the remaining members of the middle classes with considerably reduced influence. Society became increasingly polarized into élites and the masses.

The continued growth of big business underlined the division by enlarging the gulf between the vast incomes of the new industrial barons and the modest wages of the workers. Earlier industrialists, many of them traditional liberals, had at least made some attempt to use their prosperity to enhance the lot of their employees. The upper classes of the turn of the century proudly and ostentatiously flaunted their wealth as a sign of their superior power and status.

Behind the changes in social structure and within classes lay vast changes in population patterns. Improved medical care reduced the rate of infant mortality and extended life expectancy. At the same time, all over Western Europe birthrates were dropping by the end of the 19th century. This was due in part to the introduction of contraceptive methods, which helped parents to plan their families. On the whole, there seemed to be a general resolve to limit the size of families. In Eastern Europe, where social change was slower, the population continued to increase, and by 1910, population growth was higher there than in Western Europe. This represented a reversal of the situation 50 years earlier.

The political and social battles of the 19th century, along with the general rise of prosperity, had enlarged the numbers of people able to vote. Both liberals and the new conservative élite concurred in the need for the education of these new electors, in order to prepare them for the duties of citizenship. As a result, state-run systems of mass education were introduced, with important political consequences. Increasing popular literacy played some part in strengthening trade union activities and protest movements. The principal thrust of school curricula, however, was to encourage nationalism, in order to encourage loyalty to the state and its ruling classes. The spread of mass peacetime military conscription also increased the sense of national consciousness. The growing mood of strident nationalism in Europe provided an appropriately belligerent setting for the events leading to World War I.

THE CHANGING SOCIAL STRUCTURE

As in earlier periods of the 19th century, industrialization continued to affect social patterns in important ways in the decades after 1871. By the eve of World War I, factories had swelled cities with many more workers and middle-class inhabitants, so that much of Europe reached the halfway mark in the transition from a rural to an urban society.

Population Growth and Urbanization

Between 1870 and 1910, Europe's population (excluding Russia) rose by 44 percent, from approximately 230 million to 330 million. This growth was not, however, constant everywhere, since the size of families in western Europe tended to diminish. Throughout the latter part of the 19th century, in fact, the birthrate declined rapidly, and only a reduction in the mortality rate allowed for population increase.

The pace of urbanization intensified toward the end of the 19th century because of three factors: the continuing shift of people away from the countryside, the increase in the number and size of cities, and their growing population density. In Britain, the most highly urbanized nation, city dwellers in 1914 comprised almost 80 percent of the population, as compared to about 60 percent 50 years earlier, while France similarly increased its urban population from 33 to almost 45

Table VII.20.2
Population Growth (in thousands) for Major European Cities

CITY	1870	1900	1910
Amsterdam	264	511	574
Belfast	174	349	387
Berlin	826	1889	2071
St. Petersburg	667	1267	1962
London	3890	6586	7256
Milan	262	493	579
Paris	1852	2714	2888
Rome	244	463	542
Stockholm	136	301	342
Vienna	834	1675	2031

percent. Because Germany underwent a dramatic rate of industrialization in this period, the proportion of people living in cities there virtually doubled to 55 percent, while 90 percent of the country's overall population increase was in urban areas.

In the years between 1870 and 1900, most large European cities, including the older capitals, doubled their populations and continued to increase sharply over the following decade.

The railroad contributed greatly to urbanization. Many large cities, especially capitals, formed concentrations of rail systems. Urban facilities such as water supply, sidewalks, and sewers, or fire and police forces, expanded by the end of the 19th century, and the physical appearance of cities began to change as the construction industry was revolutionized by developments in civil engineering and building materials. The use of steel and reinforced concrete made it possible for architects to design skyscrapers: the first of these tall buildings, New York's 130-foot-high Equitable Life Assurance Society Building, was built in 1870. By combining steel and wrought iron with glass, European city planners created new forms of public space, such as the enclosed galleries built in London, Paris, Milan, and Naples.

Table VII.20.1
Population (in thousands) of Selected European Countries

COUNTRY	1870	1900	1910
Britain	22,712	32,528	36,070
France	36,103	38,451	39,192
Germany	41,059	56,367	64,926
Hungary	15,512	19,255	20,886
Spain	16,622	18,594	19,927
Sweden	4169	5137	5522

The Growth of the Urban Proletariat

Most of the political and social progress made in the first part of the 19th century was due to the informal alliance of middle-class liberalism and working-class protest. The combination of the two forces succeeded in challenging established values and reducing the power of the old aristocracy. By the end of the century, however, conditions were changing. The cooperation between the two classes had depended upon the tacit understanding that middle-class reformers would decide what was in the best interests of the workers. With the gradual improvement in conditions of urban life and the extension of the franchise, the urban masses were becoming a political force in themselves.

The emergence of an urban proletariat in western European society profoundly affected old alliances. Trade unions and socialist parties were no longer dependent on the good will of the middle class for reforms, for an increasingly active membership provided them with new bargaining power. The wealthier members of the middle class, in turn, began to see the various protest movements as a challenge to their business interests. In their search for allies, they turned to their former opponents, the aristocracy. The combination of rich industrialists and aristocrats who were prepared to compromise formed a new upper-class élite.

Although the influence of the aristocratic ruling classes had declined, they still retained considerable prestige. Marriages between the daughters of wealthy businessmen and impoverished heirs to noble titles provided both sides with gains. Although money was beginning to replace birth as the ultimate social status symbol, the combination of both was the most desirable aim of all. In some cases European aristocrats turned to America in search of rich brides. In 1874, Lord Randolph Churchill (1849–1895) married Jennie Jerome, a member of a prosperous New York family. Their elder son was Winston S. Churchill.

Contact between the two classes was not limited to family affairs. Aristocrats who became involved in public life, whether in politics, government bureaucracy, or the army, often found themselves working with colleagues of business origins. Relations became even more closely cemented as the richest industrialists began to send their sons to schools hitherto attended only by the nobility.

With an increasingly militant working class at one end of the social spectrum, and a new alliance of upper-class élites at the other, the median segment of the middle classes lost influence. Growing religious skepticism undermined bourgeois Victorian morality. Social élites developed ever more elaborate and glamorized forms of traditional "high" culture such as opera houses and art galleries. New York's Metropolitan

Map 20.1 Europe's Population, c. 1890

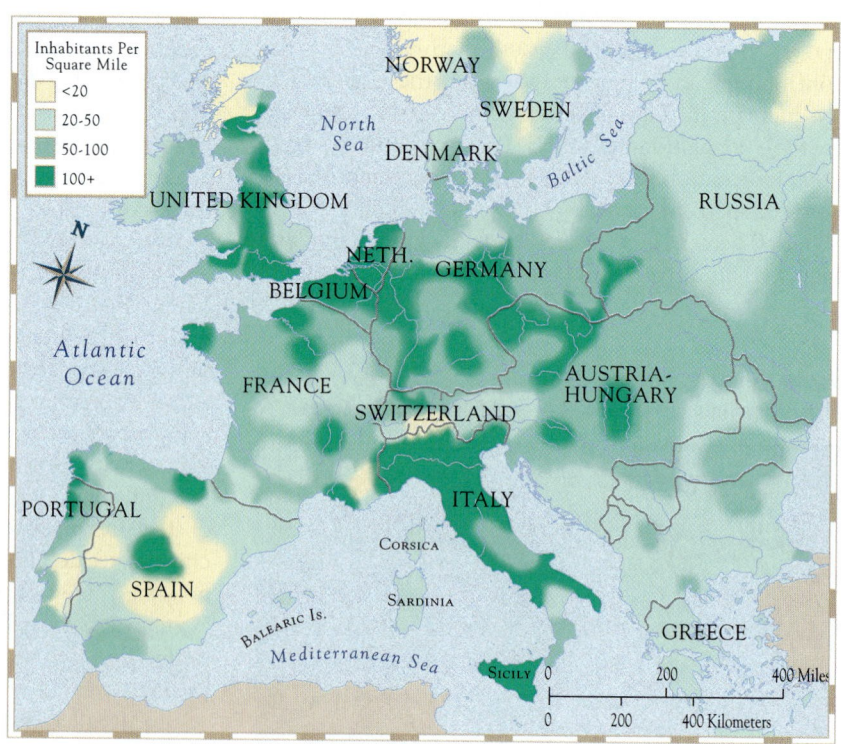

Paul-Emile Chabas, *A Corner of the Table* (1907) captures a moment in the rarified lives of the wealthy classes.

Museum of Art was founded in 1870, and the Paris Opera opened in 1875. At the same time, the working classes began to enjoy their own forms of popular culture. London's first music hall, a place for popular shows, was built in 1849, and held 100 people. By 1890 London had some 500 music halls; the largest offered continuous performances to a changing audience of as many as 45,000 in a single evening.

The class structure of European society became increasingly polarized between two extremes. The rise of the masses created vast new commercial possibilities that business entrepreneurs were quick to exploit. At the same time it posed a potential threat to governments, which they sought to defuse by developing ways to manipulate and control mass responses. Meanwhile, as conditions for most citizens continued slowly but perceptibly to improve, the very rich became even richer.

WEALTH, POVERTY, AND SOCIAL DARWINISM

For those living in Europe at the turn of the century, the age seemed, and for the privileged few was, one of unprecedented luxury and extravagance. In Paris, the *Belle Époque* (Beautiful Age) brought lavish banquets and balls. The city's cabarets and night life, vividly depicted in the art of Impressionist painters such as Auguste Renoir (1841–1919), were as famous as its parade of elegant courtesans, described by Parisian wits as

"les grandes horizontales" (the great recliners). No less a figure than the eldest son of Queen Victoria, the future Edward VII, entertained his mistress at Maxim's, a glamorous Parisian restaurant.

When Edward became king in 1901, his reign introduced a similar mood of opulence to Britain. The Edwardian Era was marked by extravagant "house parties," weekends in the country at which the nobility and eminent industrialists ate, drank, and shot together. On December 18, 1913, at Hall Barn in Buckinghamshire, seven marksmen killed 3937 pheasants, still a record for a single shoot. The Austrian Archduke Franz Ferdinand, whose assassination in 1914 finally precipitated the outbreak of war, was also an enthusiastic shot. Shortly before his death he expressed satisfaction at having killed his 3000th stag.

The English well-to-do, like American travelers of later days, were famous in continental Europe for their demand for hygiene and efficient plumbing. Individual water closets with flushing toilets, rare in England before 1900, became increasingly common in the larger towns, although only the largest establishments were equipped with more than one. Even a big upper-class English house, scene of weekend parties, generally had only one bathroom, which was usually reserved for the family. Fixed baths were first made of porcelain, but by 1910 cast-iron tubs were becoming popular. Bathroom fixtures included showers, either in the bath itself or independent, and heated towel rails. As overnight guests took their morning tea and biscuits, a maid would draw the curtains, light the fire, and set out a portable bath in front of the hearth, to be filled from a hot water can. The comfort of the upper

A street scene of working-class children in London's East End.

classes required the existence of a household of servants, although the growing introduction of inventions such as vacuum cleaners and washing machines began to reduce the size of domestic staffs.

The Urban Poor

The lives of most of the population were in stark contrast to those of the rich. In the London district of Bermondsey at the turn of the century, an observer noted that one water pipe served for 25 houses, with the water turned on for only two hours a day and not at all on Sundays. The same 25 families had one water closet between them, outside which queues of people lined up every morning before going to work.

Despite the material progress of the 19th century, large sectors of the populations of all European countries continued to live in poverty. A survey conducted around the turn of the century in London, the capital of the richest country in the world, found the proportion of paupers to be 30.7 percent. In eastern and southern Europe, conditions were even worse. In 1900, the average life expectancy in Spain or the Balkans was under 35 years.

Even those whose earnings allowed them to live above the level of bare subsistence were subject to the constant threat of insecurity. The loss of a job through illness or age brought inevitable ruin to a family. The first country to introduce health insurance and pensions was Germany, where Bismarck enacted legislation in 1883 to combat the appeal of socialism among workers. In Britain, early voluntary insurance programs had been run by some of the trade unions, and the government introduced national policies only in 1911. Even these measures, however, did not cover large categories of workers, including the domestic servants, upon whom the upper classes depended, and the self-employed. The uncertainties of illness, accident, or premature death hung over most working homes.

Yet the lives of urban workers did undergo some improvements. Between 1880 and 1914, wages rose considerably, and purchasing power almost doubled in England, Germany, and France. Mass production and marketing, combined with fast transport, reduced the price of many goods. The production and sale of food continued to increase and its price to decline (see Part VII, Topic 17). By 1891, nearly 600,000 in England were employed in the food trades. At the same time, there were 40 percent more grocers and fishmongers than ten years earlier, and 82 percent more jam and preserve makers. Most workers' families ate vegetables and some form of meat (often a poor one) on a regular basis. One student of working-class conditions noted that "puddings and tarts are not uncommon, and bread ceases to be the staff of life. In this class no-one goes short of food."

One of the results of the gradual improvement in material conditions was increased leisure time. The increased pace of production meant that most factory workers no longer needed to put in 12- or 14-hour days to maintain output. Workers and trade unions themselves fought for less hours, to devote more time to their families and leisure activities. In the earlier years of the industrial revolution, factory employees had time for little but working and sleeping. By 1900, many urban workers still put in ten-hour days or more, with Sunday free. In Britain some had Saturday afternoon free as well, in what became called the "English weekend."

Leisure pursuits increased as fast as people had the chance to enjoy them. Technical advances in paper making and printing made possible mass circulation newspapers and magazines, which higher literacy made available to a growing readership. They stirred patriotic fervor and popular enthusiasm for imperialism by running dramatic stories of adventure and conquest in exotic places. Popular writers of the day reached mass audiences with science fiction tales and detective stories. The Frenchman Jules Verne (1828–1905) incorporated the latest scientific developments in fantasies such as *Twenty Thousand Leagues Under the Sea* (1870), while the British writer Sir Arthur Conan Doyle (1859–1930) created Sherlock Holmes, the most memorable fictional detective in Western literature. Amusement parks and dance halls offered the chance for relaxed entertainment. Cycling led to a new exercise craze and had a special appeal to middle-class women. Competitive team sports became popular. In Britain in the 1880s, associations were founded to organize athletics, boxing, lawn tennis, rowing, swimming, hockey, and football events. In 1896, the first modern Olympiad took place in Athens, reviving the Olympic Games of ancient Greece.

The increased use of leisure time for simple relaxation and fun was accompanied by a decline in religious observance. Sunday became a day to spend in the country or at the seaside, rather than at church. Virtually the only country in Europe where church attendance actually increased was Ireland, where the Catholic Church symbolized opposition to the hated Protestant British rulers. During the reign of Pope Leo XIII (ruled 1878–1903), official Catholic teaching sought to reconcile church dogma with science and liberalism. Leo's famous encyclical, *Rerum Novarum* (1891), on the condition of the working classes, tried to counter anticlericalism by linking the church to the

working class. Churches began to organize their own leisure activities, including youth groups, for the urban masses. On the whole, however, the trend away from organized religion continued.

Social Darwinism

Those who were struck by the increasing gulf between the modest improvements in the living conditions of the workers and the extravagance of the wealthy found a handy explanation in the philosophy of Social Darwinism. Charles Darwin's *Origin of Species* (1859) (see Part VII, Topic 14) taught that life is a fierce and constant struggle, in which only the fittest survive. Darwin had been concerned with the natural process of evolution, but a rising business class was all too ready to apply his arguments to commercial progress. The bitter strife of competitive industry, they claimed, would lead slowly but inevitably to the upward movement of civilization. Thus, Social Darwinists asserted that those who were emerging at the top were evidently the fittest and thus qualified to survive and continue the process.

The philosophical underpinning of this worldview was to be found in the writings of the British philosopher Herbert Spencer (1820–1903). His version of evolution argued that species develop from simple to complex forms, in a process of automatic improvement, and that any attempt to interfere with change (including economic change) would stand in the way of progress. Spencer's most enthusiastic followers were to be found in the United States, where a Rockefeller remarked that "the growth of a large business is merely the survival of the fittest."

In contrast to the Social Darwinists, increasing numbers of people found new ways of alleviating the plight of the urban poor. Beatrice Potter Webb (1858–1943), a British social reformer, investigated conditions in London's slums to demonstrate their misery. Social workers, both government employees and private individuals, developed organizations to provide practical assistance and training to the needy. The most famous such institution was the Salvation Army, which was formed in 1878 by William Booth (1829–1912). The organization grew out of a mission he founded in 1865.

PATTERNS OF GENDER AND SEXUALITY

As society as a whole underwent profound change, many women and some men began to question traditional attitudes to family and gender roles. In the late 19th century, increasing numbers of women had jobs outside the home. Most women worked in textile and clothing factories, or in domestic service, the most common field of female employment. The number of

By the beginning of the 20th century, women were entering the workforce in even larger numbers in areas once filled by men, including secretarial work in corporations.

single female employees rose steadily. By the eve of World War I, more than 90 percent of working women were unmarried.

Traditional attitudes toward the division of labor within the family, however, remained unchanged. Working-class men played no role in domestic life, apart from providing their wives at intervals with a sum of money to cover expenses. Some men even left their wives to pay for household needs, requiring them to earn money by working themselves or by taking in boarders. Working women remained wholly responsible for all domestic duties.

Domestic violence was common, frequently the result of heavy drinking. The center of working-class life was generally the café or pub, where friends could meet. Alcohol offered an escape from grinding poverty and the rigors of overwork and a temporary warmth for those whose houses were unheated. Returning drunk to a cold home, many men took out their frustrations on their family, beating their wives and children.

In other cases, the violence was sexual. Within the confines of her home, a woman ran the risk of assault by relatives or boarders. With increased numbers of women at work, the phenomenon of sexual harassment on the job developed, whereby a woman was threatened with the loss of her work if she did not submit to sexual advances. Some women gave in under pressure, but as more acquired their working independence, women employees sometimes stood up and de-

fended their rights. Single women living and working in large cities were subject to rape and other forms of sexual violence.

Violence against women in late 19th-century cities riveted the lurid fascination of a mass public. In London, poor working-class women were the victims of a notorious killer nicknamed Jack the Ripper, a man

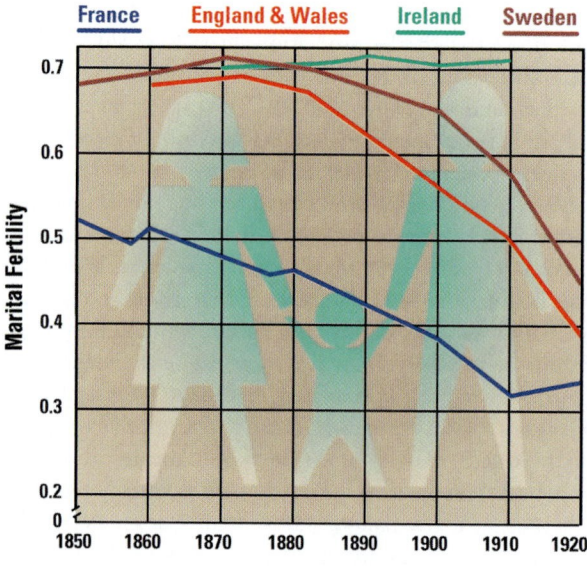

Graph 20.1

whose real identity has still not been definitively established. In the months from August to November of 1888, he perpetrated a series of gruesome murders, all of them involving single women. Similar, if less spectacular, killings, occurred in Paris and the main German cities. For many contemporary observers, the moral to be drawn from the violence was not that single women needed better protection, but that women who did not follow traditional patterns of behavior were likely to suffer for their daring.

Sexual Rights and the Middle Classes

The work of the Austrian psychoanalyst Sigmund Freud (see Part VIII, Topic 7) made sexual behavior a subject for explicit discussion among the educated. In the flood of investigation and imaginative writing that followed, some longstanding attitudes came into question. Homosexuality and lesbianism were studied more sympathetically. The German psychiatrist Magnus Hirschfeld (1868–1935) wrote of homosexuality as a "third sex," and under his influence the Scientific Humanitarian Committee was formed in Berlin for the study of homosexual culture. In Paris, the salon of Natalie Barney (1876–1972) became a center for women

Oscar Wilde (left) and Lord Alfred Douglas, c. 1893. Their affair was the cause of great scandal in the 1890s.

whose rebellion against conventions took the form of lesbianism.

Nevertheless, society as a whole still condemned sexual minorities, and laws were passed that made sexual relations between men illegal. In 1885 the British Parliament enacted the Criminal Law Amendment Act, which for the first time prohibited "indecent" sexual relations between adult consenting males and prescribed a sentence of up to two years in prison with hard labor. One of the most prominent public figures to be punished under this law was the Irish writer Oscar Wilde (1854–1900), who was prosecuted for his relationship with Lord Alfred Douglas (1870–1945). The middle-class refusal to see women as sexual beings was reflected in the fact that the law was restricted to men. When this omission was pointed out to Queen Victoria, she is reported to have replied, "No women would do that."

Freud's theories promoted a new openness toward sexual behavior. This led in turn to new attitudes to the relationship between the sexes. No longer regarded as either untouchably pure or mere reproductive machines, women began to change their self-perceptions. Many played an increasingly aggressive role in the feminist movement (see Part VII, Topic 19). Among those campaigning for a change of attitudes was the German Helene Stocker (1869–1943), who believed that a new way of talking and thinking about sex would make sexual relations more ennobling. Other women took the opposite extreme, claiming that traditional relations between the sexes were the curse of civilization and should be completely overthrown. In her book *The Great Scourge* (1913), Cristabel Pankhurst (1880–1958) described marriage as a dangerous institution, and men as the scourge of society.

Birth Control

The growing use of methods of contraception in the late 19th century was another vital factor in changing society and the nature of family life. With the reduced rate of infant mortality, parents no longer needed to produce more children than they could support, under the assumption that some would die early. Furthermore, with the spread of education and the ability of more families to accumulate savings, parents preferred to have fewer children, better educated, to whom to leave their property.

Methods of contraception varied, and knowledge of them spread both by word of mouth and by active campaigning. British laws forbade the publication of birth control material, but in 1878 the Fabian reformer Annie Besant (1847–1933) joined Charles Bradlaugh (1833–1891) in challenging the law. After 1880 they circulated tens of thousands of birth control leaflets. On the Continent, one of the early promoters of birth control was Arletta Jacobs (1851?–1929), the first woman awarded a medical degree in the Netherlands. In her work among the poor in Amsterdam, she encouraged the use of the "Dutch cap," a form of individual cervical covering first invented in Germany. One of the most common methods for dealing with unwanted pregnancies was abortion.

Inspired by the writings of the early-19th-century economic philosopher Thomas Malthus (see Part VII, Topic 2), Neo-Malthusian leagues were formed in many countries. They advocated population control as a means to improving marital relations and promoting social harmony. Although the Neo-Malthusians encouraged working-class support, the movement was basically a middle-class one.

The effect of contraception on population growth was dramatic. Around 1870, the average English family contained 6.6 children; 50 years later, the number had fallen to just over two. The most extreme declines occurred in the countries of western Europe, where by 1910 the birthrate had fallen by 30 percent or more; the only exception was Ireland, where it actually rose slightly. In southern and eastern Europe, birthrates did not begin to decline until after World War I, with the result that on the eve of war Western Europe was actually surpassed in population growth.

Although contraception was used by working-class couples, the predominantly middle-class advocacy and adoption of birth control were reflected in birth patterns. In the period from 1879 to 1893, the number of children born to families in Rotterdam varied according to social class: for every three children whose parents were professionals, there were six whose fathers were laborers or artisans. In London at the turn of the century, the birthrate in the working-class East End was a third higher than in more fashionable districts.

Yet as the use of contraception spread, it had far-reaching consequences for all levels of society. Free of the necessity of continual childbearing, growing numbers of women strove to take their place alongside men in the workplace and in public life.

THE INTEGRATION OF SOCIETY: LITERACY AND MILITARY SERVICE

Between 1870 and 1914, most European governments deliberately indoctrinated large groups of citizens with a sense of national consciousness, especially the work-

Compulsory elementary education was being adopted by most Western nations in the last quarter of the 19th century. Jennie Brownscombe's *The New Scholar* (1878) reveals growing consciousness among women of the importance of education.

Universal military service was a major element in forging national identity. Here this is seen in a photograph of British recruiting in 1915.

ers and peasants who had traditionally been marginalized. Universal elementary education and compulsory military service provided two important instruments for national integration.

Public Education

Beginning after 1880, most Western governments took the first steps to introduce mass education. In France, the government of Jules-François-Camille Ferry (served as prime minister 1880–1881, 1883–1885) established free compulsory secular education as part of anticlerical legislation. By 1890, primary education for males and females up to the age of twelve was compulsory in many countries. In Austria, for example, the number of children attending primary schools rose from 1.9 million in 1870 to 4.2 million in 1914, while in Britain during the same period enrollment increased from 1.4 million to 6.2 million. The possibilities of secondary education for women began to increase, but universities were still mainly reserved for men. At the first lecture of the Greek scientist Angeliki Panajiotatou (1875–1954), students shouted at her: "Back to the kitchen!" In 1881, Spain's first female medical students were stoned.

Although both liberals and conservatives agreed on the need for the spread of education, their motives differed. For those who encouraged upward social mobility, education—in particular the basic ability to read, write, and perform simple calculations—was an essential key to advancement. In some countries, notably France and Italy, secular leaders also encouraged state-run education as a means of offsetting the influence of the Catholic Church.

Conservative governments, on the other hand, saw public education as a way of maintaining control over the masses. As growing numbers of citizens acquired the right to vote, they needed to be directed toward using their powers in a way acceptable to the authorities. General literacy played some part, it is true, in helping protest groups to circulate written campaign material and win new members. On the whole, however, compulsory education served to promote carefully devised state programs.

The chief goal of these was to instill strong feelings of national pride. Official textbooks presented the view of national history and development that favored each state's image, often by denigrating other nations. On many occasions the very language used, or not used, for lessons became a nationalist issue, as in parts of the Austro-Hungarian empire. After leaving school, former students would read similar nationalistic messages in popular newspapers, which celebrated their country's achievements and vigorously bemoaned any perceived slight to national honor.

Military Service

Although obligatory military service dates back to the ancient world, it first began to evolve in modern

Albert Morrow's poster (c. 1896), *The New Woman*, depicted the modern woman who flouted convention and assumed new roles in society.

less fervor for national interests than their rulers. As a result, there developed a popular demand for diplomatic and military victories that played a significant part in the buildup to war. When World War I came, furthermore, even the socialist parties which had condemned nationalism rallied to the national cause.

By 1914, European society was beginning to shed some of its traditional characteristics. Class patterns created by 19th-century reforms were shifting, as social groups changed alliances. Rich tradesmen and impecunious aristocrats, former enemies, joined forces. The ranks of the lower middle class swelled with the growth of government and corporate bureaucracies. With the coming of universal male suffrage, the working classes, whose condition slowly improved, began to emerge as a potentially powerful political force.

Radical changes in birthrates modified ways of family life that had been constant for centuries. The hitherto universally accepted notion of male dominance was under increasing attack. The taboo on open discussion of sexual matters had begun to be challenged. Traditional habits of religious observance were yielding to secular pressures. Popular literacy made it possible for large numbers of people to follow debate on the great issues of the times.

Questions for Further Study

1. How was the condition of the aristocracy and the middle class changing after 1870?

2. In what ways was science applied to social analysis?

3. To what degree did sexual practices conform to social expectations?

4. What is meant by the "modernization" of society? What factors were most important to that process?

Suggestions for Further Reading

Accampo, Elinor. *Industrialization, Family Life, and Class Relations: Saint Chamond, 1815–1914.* Berkeley, CA, 1989.

Duberman, Martin, M. Vicinus, and G. Chauncey. *Hidden from History: Reclaiming the Gay and Lesbian Past.* New York, 1989.

Girouard, Mark. *Cities and People: A Social and Architectural History.* New Haven, CT, 1985.

Hayes, Carlton J. H. *The Generation of Materialism, 1871–1900.* New York, 1941.

Joyce, P. *Visions of the People: Industrial England and the Question of Class, c. 1848–1914.* New York, 1991.

McLaren, Angus. *Birth Control in Nineteenth-Century England.* New York, 1978.

Miller, Michael. *The Bon Marché: Bourgeois Culture and the Department Store, 1869–1920.* Princeton, NJ, 1981.

Moch, Leslie P. *Moving Europeans: Migration in Western Europe Since 1650.* Bloomington, IN, 1993.

Pilbeam, Pamela M. *The Middle Classes in Europe, 1789–1914.* Chicago, 1990.

Europe in the late 18th century; it was introduced by the radicals in France in the fall of 1792, and took the form of mass conscription. Prussia's successes in the 1860s were due in large measure to its custom of maintaining a large body of trained soldiers, even in peacetime. After the Prussian victory over the French in 1870, France took a lesson from its enemy and introduced the military draft. Austria followed suit, as did many other continental nations. Britain did not introduce peacetime conscription until just before World War II, although military service was required during World War I.

The effects of conscription reinforced those of compulsory education. Recruits were generally sent away from their home district in order to break their local loyalties. In their place, military training encouraged recruits to develop a broader sense of identification with the military itself, and, ultimately, with the nation-state.

The increasing appetite for nationalist victories, nourished by imperialist conquests, distracted attention from discontent at home. It also succeeded in uniting large masses of each country's population in a common enthusiasm. Socialist leaders opposed nationalism and called for class solidarity to transcend frontiers, but in general members of the urban proletariat showed no

Shapiro, Ann-Louise. *Housing the Poor of Paris, 1850–1902.* Madison, WI, 1985.

Stearns, Peter N. *European Society in Upheaval: Social History Since 1800.* New York, 1967.

Sutcliffe, Anthony. *Towards the Planned City: Germany, Britain, and the United States, 1789–1914.* New York, 1981.

Wiener, Joel H., ed. *Papers for the Millions: The New Journalism in Britain, 1850s to 1914.* New York, 1988.

Topic   21

ART AND SCIENCE:
THE MODERNIST REVOLUTION

he decisive break with the past which World War I was to foreshadowed in the artistic and intellectual developments of the preceding decades. Beginning in the last quarter of the 19th century, changes began to occur that revolutionized Western culture, although to some extent these had their roots in earlier artistic movements: Richard Wagner, the prophet of the "art work of the future," was also the high priest of Romanticism. In many cases the new ideas made return to former ways impossible. The philosophy of Henri Bergson, and the psychoanalytical theories of Sigmund Freud conditioned vast areas of 20th-century behavior, while the writings of Friedrich Nietzsche anticipated the darker aspects of 20th-century political life.

In literature, Freud's ideas stimulated writers to explore the human subconscious, probing neuroses and repressions. Sympathy for the growing tide of political protest in western Europe led some writers, including Émile Zola, to adopt an increasingly realistic style. By contrast, others sought refuge from the harsh realities of the times in devising complex, symbolic language. By the early 20th century, in the works of Marcel Proust and James Joyce, the very use of language itself represented a revolutionary break with the past.

Painters, too, explored new attitudes to their art, increasingly rejecting traditional pictorial values in favor of abstract qualities. The Impressionists emphasized how things appeared to their eyes rather than how they really were. Their abstract treatment of form reached a point of no return around the turn of the century in the works of Paul Cézanne. It was only a step from here to the total breakdown of formal realism that Cubism and Futurism represented.

Just as Cubism opened a new chapter in painting by rejecting centuries of traditions, so the revolutionary musical style of atonality broke with 400 years of Western musical history. Devised by Arnold Schoenberg, it abandoned traditional harmony (or "tonality") in search of a new musical language. Not all composers accepted Schoenberg's method, but many agreed that the times required a break with the past. Igor Stravinsky, in his revolutionary masterpiece *The Rite of Spring*, experimented with new approaches to rhythm.

At the same time as artists were forging the ideas of Modernism, science was making its own contribution to the changing world. Einstein's "special theory" of relativity, first formulated in 1905, not only conditioned developments in modern physics but also opened the way to the nuclear age.

Thus the intellectual and cultural life of the generation before World War I reflected forces of disruption that were also operating on a much larger scale. At a time when traditional philosophies or religious belief seemed inadequate for the restless spirit of the age, artists sought refuge for their own disturbed visions in reshaping the world of their art.

TOWARD A NEW CULTURE: THE ART OF RICHARD WAGNER

The revolutionary artistic and intellectual movements of the late 19th century abruptly thrust Western culture into the Modernist era. Even so, they did not represent a complete novelty which appeared overnight. Few, if any, developments in the history of human thought occur without a process of transition. In the case of Modernism, the transformation of Western culture was symbolized to a remarkable degree by the life and art of Richard Wagner (1813–1883).

Wagner is best known today for his huge music dramas, the name he coined for his operatic works. In his time, he was also involved in many of the political issues that shook the second half of the 19th century, from the revolutions of 1848—he fought on the barricades in Dresden, later fleeing to Switzerland—to Prussia's nationalist war against France in 1870. A tireless campaigner on behalf of a bewildering array of causes from vicious anti-Semitism to wholehearted vegetarianism, he also wrote extensively on the arts. Among his early writings of significance was *The Artwork of the Future*, which appeared in 1849.

Many features of his operas are firmly within the German Romantic tradition. He often based them on his own versions of traditional Teutonic myths, or used them to recreate an ideal world of Medieval chivalry. Like many Romantic artists, Wagner incorporated elements of the natural world in his works, such as the surge of a great river or the radiant beauty of spring sunshine. Furthermore, his music often

Painting by Wilhelm Beckmann of Wagner at home in Bayreuth (1880).

reflects the characteristic Romantic preoccupation with death.

Yet this supremely Romantic creator was, at the same time, the most revolutionary artistic figure of his day, in many ways a true Modern. His musical style pushed the harmonic language of the mid-19th century to its limits, paving the way for the atonality of the early 20th century. His use of a short theme (*Leitmotiv*) to represent an individual, object, or concept allowed him to explore depths of psychological penetration. The use of these often reveals a character's subconscious thoughts or motivations. In the opera *Tristan und Isolde* (1865), he depicted virtually every shade of sexual love with a frankness generally unknown in works for public performance until our own time. His last stage work, *Parsifal* (1882), portrays the renunciation of sex with insights that can only be called Freudian. His advocacy of the *Gesamtkunstwerk* (Total Work of Art), a creative work that connects music, the visual arts, words, and movement into one experience, foreshadowed the achievement of Sergei Eisenstein (1898–1948) and other important filmmakers.

The Cycle of *The Ring*

Most remarkably of all, his most complex work, *Der Ring des Nibelungen* (The Ring of the Nibelung, 1851–1874), can be seen as a diagnosis of the flaw at the heart of industrial society: the corrupting influence of power and money. This tetralogy (made up of four separate operas) is in many respects the climax of Romanticism, with its gods, giants, and magic dragon. Yet, as productions in the late 20th century continue to reveal, by drawing on the world of myth supplemented by acute psychological insight, it also makes a powerful commentary on the development, and eventual crisis in 1914, of European civilization.

Even in his own lifetime, Wagner aroused enormous controversy. Today his music continues to divide opinion between those for whom a performance of his greatest works provides a supreme aesthetic experience, and those who find them long and bombastic. Yet there can be little debate over his influence on Western culture, for better or worse. Many subsequent composers followed him, many reacted against him, but few ignored him. His work was an inspiration to the French poet Charles Baudelaire (1821–1867) and the Symbolist poetic movement which arose from Baudelaire's writings at the turn of the century. More generally, by raising the importance of the arts to a level where they acquired an almost "sacred" function, he revolutionized aesthetic attitudes. The theater he had built at Bayreuth, in Germany, for the staging of his works soon became known to friends and foes alike as the "Temple on the Green Hill." Finally, in showing the power of mythic symbols to express universals, he anticipated much important 20th-century thought.

PHILOSOPHERS OF INSTINCT AND LIFE: NIETZSCHE, BERGSON, AND FREUD

Among Wagner's most passionate admirers in the 1860s was the German philosopher Friedrich Nietzsche (1844–1900). A brilliant Classical scholar, he heralded the Wagnerian works as the first since the time of the Greeks to develop a philosophy of culture based on tragedy. Beginning in 1876, however, he abruptly reversed his opinion and rejected Wagner and the idea of aesthetic redemption. The romantic illusions of art, Wagner's in particular, were contributing to a mood of human weakness and self-deception, which would lead to a crisis in European civilization. Only strong, free

Edvard Munch, who also painted *The Scream* (see p. 996), executed this portrait of Friedrich Nietzsche in 1906–1907.

spirits would survive the inevitable collapse, with its basic message that "God is dead."

Nietzsche expanded on his vision of a new world order in the remaining years of his active life. Civilization, he claimed, is nothing more than a collective fantasy. Religion, morality, the arts, even science, are all ways of distracting attention from reality, which lies in the "will to power." Only those who reject all moral restraints, and use their unbridled energy in their "will to power," can win independence. An individual who rejects all illusions in a free assertion of the will is capable of establishing a new order of nobility and goodness. Such a person would be an *Übermensch* (Superman). The most poetic description of these new humans appears in *Also sprach Zarathustra* (Thus Spoke Zarathustra, 1883–1892). In the process of the emergence of a new race of Supermen, all the weak and helpless should be cast aside, together with Judaism and Christianity, which traditionally protected the downtrodden.

Nietzsche's profound and original analysis of the crisis in Western culture proved increasingly influential as his ominous predictions seemed to be coming true. Indeed, the rise of Fascism and Nazism in the 1920s was explained by some as the realization of his ideas. It is true that Nietzsche despised militarism and nationalism as much as he did democracy or equality. In any case, his concept of the new world in which his Supermen would live seems poetic at best, and often shadowy. Yet the anger he expressed toward contemporary society, and the ruthlessness with which he contemplated the tearing down of all barriers, provided a dangerously heady brew. Nietzsche may be more prophet than instigator of 20th-century dictatorships and racial persecution, but a distorted version of his concepts served to fuel them.

Henri Bergson

No less original are the writings of Henri Bergson (1859–1941), one of the most influential intellectual forces in the early 20th century. Bergson urged a move from reason and abstraction to the subjective, and to a kind of inner reflection he called "intuition." This attitude required, in turn, a new attitude to time, which was not merely quantifiable in terms of physics, but became "experienced duration." Unlike Nietzsche, Bergson esteemed the creative process highly. In *Creative Evolution* (1907), he describes it as the expression of an *élan vital* (vital impulse). Nor did he reject the value of religion and morality, although he distinguished between "closed," or formal, elements and "open," or spiritual, ones.

Bergson's overall contribution to the intellectual life of his time was to free it of an excessive dependence on intellectualism and rationalism. Furthermore,

the Existentialist philosophers of the later 20th century (see Part VII, Topic 13) built their notions of the self providing its own sense (and justification) on Bergson's emphasis of the dynamic power of the subconscious. Contemporary authors were also quick to exploit the literary device of recording the stream-of-consciousness thought processes of their characters. Among the most successful were Marcel Proust (1871–1922), James Joyce (1882–1941), and Virginia Woolf (1882–1941).

Freud and Psychoanalysis

Nietzsche addressed himself to the political ills of European culture, and Bergson was concerned with providing the means of intellectual renewal. The Viennese physician Sigmund Freud (1856–1939) sought to understand nothing less than the human subconscious and unconscious. In the process he developed ideas that have revolutionized the way humans see themselves and their relationships with others. His theories remain controversial, and some of his successors challenged specific points of interpretation while accepting the general direction of his research. Nonetheless, Freud probably played a larger part in the formation of the characteristically 20th-century Western view of human existence than any other single individual.

Regardless of the accuracy of his analyses, Freud was one of the first figures to write frankly and explicitly about human sexual behavior, discussing it in clinical and not moral terms. At a time when society in general preferred to ignore open discussion of sex, Freud openly claimed that all individuals were born with a strong sexual identity, with genital, anal, and oral drives. These components, however, had no inherent gender identity. The quality of masculinity or femininity was acquired during childhood, as a result of specific experiences, in particular those involving the relationship with parents. Freud described the most powerful of these in terms of the Greek myth of Oedipus. Children are aware of parental power to block their sexual functioning; in the act of rejecting this, they achieve a "normal" gender identity.

In a society where the family was conventionally regarded as a bastion against worldly vice, Freud taught that family relationships based on incest were at the root of the human psyche and were often the cause of emotional disturbance. Nor was sex simply an anatomical function, for it was strongly affected by psychological and cultural factors. The challenge to traditional middle-class attitudes could hardly have been stronger.

Yet even more shocking for many of his contemporaries was Freud's claim that society's repression of women's sexual drives was responsible for many cases of female "hysteria." Far from being a sign of weakness or sickness, the symptoms of women prone to fits or fainting attacks were due to abnormal sexual development. Whatever the accuracy of his diagnosis, in making this claim Freud broke new ground. He demonstrated that women's sexual drive is equally as powerful—and potentially as fulfilling or destructive—as that of men.

Freud himself was cautious in exploring some of the implications of his insights. Although he portrayed women as trapped by the conventions of society, he approved of their maintaining a passive domestic role to offset the more aggressive male function. As for homosexuality, he believed that although all children pass through a homoerotic phase, "normal" children emerge from it. His contemporary, Havelock Ellis (1859–1939), by contrast saw homosexuality as merely another form of human sexual behavior. Freud's subsequent work continued his research into the nature of the human subconscious by studying various forms of neurosis, and the significance of dreams. In doing so, he established methods of psychoanalysis that subsequently led to the foundation of a variety of analytical techniques. At the end of his career he wrote *The Future of an Illusion* (1927) and *Civilization and Its Discontents* (1930), two magisterial works which offered a broad analysis of modern culture.

The achievement of founding the new and important discipline of psychoanalysis was in itself out-

Sigmund Freud.

standing enough, but Freud's contribution to the modern world goes much further. Ever since his time, it has been impossible to ignore those aspects of human behavior which cannot be explained by reason. Furthermore, his demonstration of the existence of deeply buried forces in the human personality, capable of both dynamic and destructive acts, was confirmed by the carnage of two world wars.

VARIETIES OF LITERARY EXPERIENCE: REALISM AND SYMBOLISM

Writers throughout Europe continued to produce realistic novels in the tradition firmly established earlier in the 19th century by Flaubert and Dickens (see Part VII, Topic 14). With increasing social and political tensions, however, the treatment of the issues of the day became more polemical.

The French writer Émile Zola (1840–1902) set out to dissect society in order to understand its workings, comparing the novelist's "enquiries" with the experiments of a scientist. Zola believed that individual lives were principally shaped by heredity and environment. As a result, many of his characters are destroyed by forces of nature that they are seemingly powerless to control, and Zola's work is often called, in fact, naturalistic rather than realistic.

His best novels deal with specific social ills: alcoholism in *The Dram Shop* (1877), prostitution in *Nana* (1880), and industrial exploitation in *Germinal* (1885). The brutal, often lurid evocation of life at its grimmest horrified many of his readers, and led to accusations of distortion and pornography. Zola made his own accusations when, in 1898, he became one of the antigovernment forces in the Dreyfus affair, wading into the fray at considerable risk to himself (see Part VII, Topic 15). In a short but powerfully worded pamphlet, *J'accuse!* (I Accuse, 1898), he attacked the army's handling of the case and rallied liberal and intellectual support on Dreyfus's side.

Whereas Zola's bleak world contains shafts of hope, the novels of Thomas Hardy (1840–1928) offer a picture of unrelieved despair, in which one character after another is broken on the wheel of an unrelenting fate. The background of most of his stories is English country life. He actually invented a county, "Wessex," (bearing a close resemblance to the English West Country county of Dorset) to provide their realistic setting.

Hardy wrote at a time when industrial progress had wrecked traditional agricultural life, and he saw modern efficiency as a profoundly destructive force. Yet for all his nostalgia at the passing of a way of life, he showed the confining conventions of rural existence to be no less devastating. The heroine of *Tess of the D'Urbervilles* (1891) is destroyed by a rigid code of social behavior that ends with her execution (by hanging) at the hands of a self-righteous society. In his last novel, *Jude the Obscure* (1896), the chief character sees every one of his attempts to emerge from obscurity relentlessly frustrated by the workings of destiny. Hardy has sometimes been criticized for his uncompromising pessimism, an angry man shaking his fist at an indifferent Creator. Yet the hopeless tone of his works is tempered by their passionate and sensitive concern for the sufferings of humanity.

The novels of Mrs. Humphry Ward (1851–1920; her real name was Mary Augusta Arnold) present a much more optimistic view of contemporary society, albeit one that reflected her own comfortable background. Coming from a well-to-do family, she actively campaigned against the feminist movement. Like Hardy's, her books contain realistic and well drawn accounts of agricultural life, as well as urban settings. One of their recurring themes is the nature of religion, reflecting contemporary doubts about the meaning of Christianity. In *Robert Elsmere* (1888), a young clergyman loses his faith in the divinity of Jesus, leaves the church, and devotes himself to helping the poor in the slums of London's East End. In addition to producing a stream of highly successful books, Mrs. Ward devoted considerable time to her own charitable activities.

The primitive, brooding world of Grazia Deledda (1871–1936) is a far cry from the intellectual doubts of cultivated Londoners. Deledda was born and grew up in Sardinia, and most of her books and stories are set in the island's wild landscape. They describe the struggles of inarticulate peasant folk to surmount the obstacles provided by nature and by destiny. In her best books, which include *Ceneri* (Ashes, 1904), she offers a lyrical picture of the gaunt beauty of her island, while at the same time conveying the harsh lives of its inhabitants.

The Symbolists

At the opposite extreme from these realistic writers, the Symbolists aimed to use poetry as a means of escaping from reality. In often difficult and obscure verse, they endowed words with a rich, magic quality that transcends their mundane significance.

The Symbolist movement was born in France in the early 1870s. Among the small group of writers groping for new forms of expression was Arthur Rimbaud (1854–1891), who claimed that a poet should sharpen his perceptions by undergoing every kind of experience, and then transmit what he perceived without any conscious control. In poetic terms this meant abandoning

traditional notions of rhyme and meter. Rimbaud called his collection of passages entitled *Les Illuminations* (Illuminations; written 1872–1873, published 1886) "prose poems."

Rimbaud's own life was equally unconventional. Rebellious and violently anti-Christian, he set out to shock the bourgeois world of the Third Republic. At the time of writing *Les Illuminations*, he was in a relationship with a fellow poet, Paul Verlaine (1844–1896). After a bitter quarrel, in the course of which Verlaine shot Rimbaud in the wrist, the younger poet abandoned writing altogether. At the age of 19 he set off on a series of wanderings through Europe and the East, exploring, trading, and gunrunning.

The leading German Symbolist poet, Stefan George (1868–1933), was associated for a while with Baudelaire, Verlaine, and other writers in Paris, and with the Pre-Raphaelite group in London. In 1890, claiming to despise the decadence of his age, he withdrew to Munich, where he lived among a circle of admiring disciples, self-consciously dedicated to a life of the spirit. His attacks on materialism and naturalism dominated German intellectual debate, while in his lyric poems he sought to revitalize German poetry by the use of classicism.

The Belgian Maurice Maeterlinck (1862–1949) was one of the few dramatists to write successful Symbolist plays. They involve legend, allegory, and fairy tale to create a sense of mystery and brooding; their characters are passive victims of nameless, unseen forces. The best known, *Pelleas et Melisande* (1892), which was turned into an opera by Debussy, takes place in a kind of dreamworld, filled with mysterious silences and symbolic events, in which even the characters themselves do not know what is real. In one scene, a flock of sheep being led unknowingly to the slaughter symbolizes the helplessness of the human condition in the face of fate.

IMPRESSIONISM, POSTIMPRESSIONISM, AND EXPRESSIONISM

The restless search for new forms of expression in the visual arts produced a flurry of styles in rapid succession: Impressionism, Postimpressionism, Fauvism, and Expressionism. The burst of "isms" culminated in the birth of Cubism and Futurism just before World War I, and the complete overturning of traditional ways of looking at the world. All these styles rejected realism, and emphasized abstract qualities of color, shape, and line. In doing so, they broke with an approach to art that was initiated by Giotto at the dawn of the Renaissance.

Mother and Child (c. 1899) by the American painter Mary Cassatt, one of her many works on this subject.

Just as Rimbaud tried to communicate experience directly, without shaping it, the Impressionists (the name was derisively applied to them by an unenthusiastic critic) sought to give a literal impression of light and color. Avoiding any kind of organized form, and hoping to paint without interpreting their subject, they tried to reproduce the overall visual impact of what they saw. Thus, when Claude Monet (1840–1926) painted a pool with water lilies, he was concerned to record glowing colors and reflecting lights, rather than an actual pond with real flowers.

A number of the leading Impressionist painters were women. Berthe Morisot (1841–1895) gave up a career as a successful society painter to join the radical new movement. Her landscapes and scenes of Paris show a fascination with light, conveyed by free brush strokes and subtle colors. The American Mary Cassatt (1844–1926) settled in Paris to study with the Impressionists. Like her close friend Edgar Degas (1834–1917), she preferred to paint spontaneous scenes from daily life. Her unsentimental depictions of mothers and children, like Degas' scenes of women bathing, show their subjects caught unawares, in a moment of intimacy.

Postimpressionism

Although many artists continued to work in the Impressionist style—Monet used it right up to his death—the restless spirit of the times drove other painters to find new approaches. The Postimpressionists are so called because they all rejected Impressionism, but have little else in common. Georges Seurat (1859–1891) used thousands of tiny dots of color to build up simple geometrical forms. By contrast, the exotic scenes of Paul Gauguin (1848–1903) consist of broad washes of paint.

The range of Postimpressionist artists emerges most vividly in the work of the two greatest, Paul Cézanne (1839–1906) and Vincent van Gogh (1853–1890). Cézanne's monumental landscapes and ordered still lifes achieve an abstract sense of balance that derives from their use of geometric forms. He advised his fellow-painters to "treat Nature in terms of its geometrical shapes, the sphere, the cylinder, and the cone." At the opposite emotional extreme, van Gogh depicted the "terrible passions of humanity," in works filled with swirling lines and violent color contrasts.

Fauvism and Expressionism

Although the emotional intensity typical of van Gogh's work was partly due to his own tragic life, it also reflected the uneasy climate of the times. Two other schools of painting developed in the first decade of the 20th century which pushed the sense of explosiveness even further. In France the *Fauves*—the word

The Scream (1893), a painting by the Norwegian Expressionist artist Edvard Munch.

Vincent van Gogh's ecstatic painting, *The Starry Night* (1899).

means "wild beasts"—painted canvasses that broke with all traditions of form and color. The movement was so destructive, in fact, that it soon fell apart. One of its members, however, went on to become a major influence in 20th-century art. Henri Matisse (1869–1954), unlike most of his contemporaries, painted luminous, festive scenes and glowing still lifes. One of his first important works was actually called *The Joy of Life*.

The Expressionists, who were mainly German, used their art to express strong emotions. The tone of the Expressionist movement had been set at the end of the 19th century by the Norwegian Edvard Munch (1863–1944). Munch said of his famous and horrifying painting *The Scream*, "I hear the scream in nature." His German successors used similarly bold images to capture the expression of extreme states of mind, frequently those of loneliness and alienation. The alarming, even hysterical mood of their paintings reflects all too clearly the mood of the age.

THE MODERNIST REVOLT: CUBISM, FUTURISM, AND ATONALITY

During the years from 1908 to 1914, the hectic speed of cultural change reached a breakneck pace. A mere catalogue of some of the main events conveys the sense of upheaval. In 1908, the Cubist paintings of Pablo Picasso and Georges Braque challenged centuries of pictorial conventions, and Schoenberg was the first composer for 300 years to write music with no tonal center. In 1910, the Futurist works of Umberto Boccioni attempted to combine time and space, and Wassily Kandinsky produced the first purely abstract work of art. In 1913, the first volume of Marcel Proust's stream-of-consciousness novel appeared, and a year later Joyce, who revolutionized the use of language in his later books, published his first prose work.

Cubism

If Cézanne had laid the foundations for a new way of painting, two young artists working in Paris between 1908 and 1914 built on them to create Cubism. The French Georges Braque (1882–1963) and his Spanish fellow-artist Pablo Picasso (1881–1973) challenged the idea, universal since the Renaissance, that works painted on a two-dimensional surface should try to show three dimensions. They abandoned traditional

Violin and Palette (1909–1910), an early Cubist painting by Georges Braque.

perspective, and in a series of experimental canvasses tried to find new ways of seeing their subjects geometrically. In some of Picasso's early Cubist works, he used the entire surface of the painting as a geometric grid. The image to be depicted was then broken up into separate squares and located in various places. Braque developed the technique of showing simultaneously aspects of an object that could in reality be perceived only separately. In one well-known picture, he showed the front, back, and sides of a violin on a single plane.

In the years following World War I, Picasso, Braque, and a host of other artists moved from a strictly analytical style to develop a wide range of variations on Cubism. Guillaume Apollinaire (1880–1918), a leading writer in Modernist circles in Paris, was one of the first champions of the new style. The important contribution of the early works was to release painters definitively from the bonds of realism, and encourage them to produce abstract art, in which the most important ingredients were color, line, and geometrical composition.

Braque and Picasso had at least based their early Cubist works on real subjects, such as portraits or violins. At exactly the time of analytical Cubism, another artist was producing purely abstract art. Wassily Kandinsky (1866–1944) began his career as an Expressionist painter. His interest in expressing mystical emotions through color led him to increasing abstraction, however. In 1910 he painted the first pure abstraction in the Western tradition, *First Abstract Watercolor*. In the period between the wars, Kandinsky continued to produce works inspired by his belief in the infinite nature of the cosmos. He also wrote a pioneering treatise on the theory of abstract art, *Concerning the Spiritual in Art* (1922).

The Futurist Movement

In Italy, the Modernist revolt in the arts took a dramatic form with the appearance of the Futurist movement. In their first manifesto (1909), the Futurists boldly rejected all traditional forms of culture. They turned instead to the cult of the machine and the technological future. Filippo T. Marinetti (1876–1944), its founder, proclaimed that "a roaring automobile, which runs like a machine-gun, is more beautiful than the Winged Victory of Samothrace. . . . We wish to glorify war."

Umberto Boccioni (1882–1916), the greatest of Futurist artists, developed an aesthetic theory called Dynamism that sought to express energy in terms of motion and light. His *Unique Forms of Continuity in Space* (1913) seeks to convey a sense of accelerating movement in sculpture. Boccioni and his fellow Futurists glorified violence and war as means of overthrowing established values, and they greeted the coming of World War I with great nationalist enthusiasm.

The most original phase of Futurism ended with the death of many of its leading exponents in the course of fighting.

Atonality in Music

Many composers of the turn of the century followed Wagner's example in their increasingly free attitude to conventional rules of harmony. The Frenchman Claude Debussy (1862–1918) wrote music that drifts from key to key, with frequent dissonances. His abandonment of traditional forms for shifting sound pictures led his contemporaries to compare his works to Impressionist paintings, while his opera *Pelleas et Melisande* (1902), based on Maeterlinck's play, allied him for a while with the Symbolists.

Yet even Debussy's shimmering, evanescent works do not represent a dramatic break with the past. The decisive move came in 1908, when the Austrian Arnold Schoenberg (1874–1951) wrote his *Three Piano Pieces*, Op. 11. Schoenberg was convinced that the traditional system of harmony, which had been used in Western music for 300 years, had lost its value. Pursuing Wagner's experiments to their ultimate conclusion, he wrote piano pieces that were "atonal"— that avoided any sense of a fixed tonal center, or key.

In the period immediately preceding World War I, Schoenberg's free atonal works eerily echo the instability and morbidity of the times. His musical composition, *Pierrot Lunaire* (1912), employing texts of symbolist poems, uses a cross between song and speech to create an Expressionist mood of macabre fantasy. Schoenberg also produced a number of Expressionist paintings. In the 1920s, Schoenberg and his followers developed new ways of organizing their musical material to replace those that they had rejected. The most important was the famous twelve-tone system, or serialism.

Critics reviled Schoenberg's atonality as a "perversion." His great contemporary Igor Stravinsky (1882–1971) met with even less sympathy. When in 1913 Stravinsky's ballet *Le Sacre du Printemps* (The Rite of Spring) was first performed in Paris, the composer was accused of "the destruction of music as an art." Throughout his long career, Stravinsky continued to write in an astonishing variety of styles, many of which used a version of traditional harmony; years later he finally adopted serialism. His revolutionary contribution to music lay in his new approach to rhythm. In *Le Sacre*, Stravinsky replaced the more or less regular beat of conventional music with a combination of constantly fluctuating rhythmical patterns. The sense of barbaric energy, whipped up by a vast orchestra, drove its first hearers, sophisticated Parisians though many of them were, to unprecedented scenes of shouting and stamping.

Developments in Literature

The Modernist movement in literature was to emerge at the end of World War I, but its character was already established. In 1913, the French novelist Marcel Proust (1871–1922) published the first volume of his seven-part work *À la recherche du temps perdu* (Remembrance of Things Past; the work was written between 1907 and 1919, and published between 1913 and 1927). Semiautobiographical, Proust's work explores the nature of time and memory, and the role of the subconscious. Its narrator sets out to recreate his past life. In the process, he realizes that all past experiences remain within us but can be called up again either by the perceptions of our senses or by the agency of art. Thus, for all the futility of individual human effort, art can recreate the past and transcend death.

The Irish writer James Joyce (1882–1941) took the stream-of-consciousness style used by Proust's narrator to even greater lengths. His first work of fiction, *Dubliners*, appeared in 1914. It sets out many of the themes that were to dominate his later books: the need to escape one's environment (in this case Dublin), the loss of illusions, or the acknowledgement of failure. Although *Dubliners* includes realistic treatments of the lower-middle-class setting, it also foreshadows the subtlety of Joyce's later work. In *Ulysses*, begun at the beginning of the war and finished in 1922, he used a stream-of-consciousness technique to describe a single day in the lives of two Dublin men. The resultant blend of fantasy, surrealism, and pastiche, filled with complex wordplay, proved to be one of the 20th century's most influential novels.

SCIENCE FROM CERTAINTY TO RELATIVITY

The astonishing technological advances of the late 19th century were accompanied by new discoveries in all branches of science, especially in physics. These developments, which profoundly altered human perceptions of the nature of the physical world, may have seemed theoretical and of little relevance to everyday life. Yet discoveries made shortly after 1900 eventually ushered in the atomic age.

Virtually all scientists working at the end of the 19th century accepted the view that matter consisted of indivisible atoms that responded to fixed natural laws observed by Sir Isaac Newton (1642–1727) in the 17th century. According to Newton, absolute time passed uniformly, and absolute space was immovable— both "were unrelated to any outward circumstances."

Yet classical physics failed to account for certain observations. In 1895 the German physicist Wilhelm

Albert Einstein outside his laboratory in Berlin, 1920.

in the early years of the 20th century his quantum theory. According to this, energy is not infinitely subdivisible, but exists as a series of discrete bundles, or quanta. In light of this, Newton's laws of motion as graduated and continuous could not be correct.

Einstein and Relativity

The most shattering theoretical advances in physics were made by the German physicist Albert Einstein (1879–1955). His theory of relativity, which was first formulated in 1905, was to have far more general consequences and represented an even more decisive break with past ideas of stability. Since everything in our universe is in motion, any observation will be affected by the observer's relative position. Thus space and time, far from being uniform, are relative. The change of relative position governs the measurement of space; the duration of movement, in the space crossed in that spatial change, governs the measurement of time. All energy and matter are related in this space-time continuum.

The notion that it is not possible to distinguish between space and time, or between matter and energy, was startling enough. Einstein's famous equation, $E = mc^2$, went on to prove the relationship between mass (m), energy (E), and the speed of light (c). This played a vital part in the development of nuclear physics, since it explained the nature of nuclear energy.

Einstein's demonstration of the relativity of forces that had always been regarded as unchanging was a major blow to the idea of a stable universe. Intensifying challenge to the established political order, struggles for wide-ranging social reform, the shattering of centuries of artistic traditions—all these were now joined by a view of the material world based on perpetual change. By 1914, European society and culture were on the brink of the most complete and wrenching shift of all.

Questions for Further Study

1. In what ways did art and literature at the turn of the century reflect the changing role of women?

2. How did the ideas of Freud and Einstein revolutionize Western culture?

3. What similarities are there in developments in music, painting, and literature in the early years of the 20th century? How are they linked with parallel historical events?

Suggestions for Further Reading

Calder, N. *Einstein's Universe*. New York, 1980.
Clark, T. J. *The Painting of Modern Life: Paris in the Art of Manet and His Followers*. New York, 1984.

Roentgen (1845–1923) discovered X-rays when he observed the highly energetic, invisible electromagnetic radiation emitted by certain wavelengths. These rays produced a form of energy capable of penetrating opaque materials. Other scientists discovered similar rays produced by uranium. The British physicist Ernest Rutherford (1871–1937) built on this work to develop a theory of radioactivity. He argued that radiation was caused when atoms of radioactive substances disintegrated. In 1911, Rutherford proposed his nuclear theory of the atom and the potential energy within it.

To explain the phenomenon of radioactivity, the German physicist Max Planck (1858–1947) developed

Gay, P. *Freud: A Life for Our Times*. New York, 1988.

Golding, J. *Cubism: A History and an Analysis*. Cambridge, MA, 1988.

Herbert, R. L. *Impressionism: Art, Leisure, and Parisian Society*. New Haven, CT, 1988.

Kern, S. *The Culture of Time and Space*. Cambridge, MA, 1983.

Lipton, E. *Looking into Degas: Uneasy Images of Women and Modern Life*. Berkeley, CA, 1986.

Watson, D. *Richard Wagner: A Biography*. New York, 1981.

PART VIII

THE CONTEMPORARY ERA

Conflict, doubt, and pessimism have dominated the mood of much of the 20th century. The century began with the basic values of European civilization under attack by cultural and intellectual revolution. From the philosophical "revolt against positivism" to the iconoclastic Postimpressionist artists and the belligerent Futurists of the years before the Great War, the assumptions of rationality and order were steadily undermined. Einstein's theories of the universe and Freud's revelations about the subconscious reinforced the sense that humans were unable to grasp, let alone control their destinies.

The political and diplomatic crises of the early 20th century reinforced the collapse of the old moral order—the first half of the 20th century was dominated by two gigantic military conflicts. The Great War of 1914–1918 wreaked unimag-

ined destruction and death on the European world, shattering permanently the notion of Western superiority and dominance. In its wake, as Europeans experimented with new forms of social and cultural energy, they also invented new forms of political control that in their worst manifestations produced totalitarian regimes in the Soviet Union as well as in Fascist Italy and Nazi Germany. The economic chaos of the Great Depression not only helped to bring the new totalitarian movements to power, but threw Western society in general into deep crisis.

The ultimate consequence of the totalitarian nightmare was World War II (1939–1945), in which the struggle for mastery assumed more horrific proportions than in the Great War, reaching its nadir in the racial policies of the Nazi dictatorship and the Holocaust. This second conflict was a truly global one, and its implications for the future were enormous.

The last half of the 20th century in Europe has seen the passage from the grim certainties of the Cold War to the increasing unpredictability of its final decade. The fall of the Berlin Wall in 1989 brought to an end a period in which Europe was firmly divided into two blocs. Western Europe, much of which emerged shattered from World War II, rebuilt its cities and the institutions of its sovereign states with help from the Marshall Plan organized by the United

States. The western European nations based their transatlantic alliances on NATO. At the same time, they sought a closer form of unity among themselves by forming the European Economic Community (EEC), intended to provide an economic union which might eventually lead to forms of political cooperation.

Meanwhile, in eastern Europe, the Soviet Union led the postwar recovery, in the process imposing client regimes. The defensive organization uniting the Soviet Union and the countries of eastern Europe was the Warsaw Pact. Yugoslavia, the only significant East European country to defy Stalin and leave the Soviet bloc, subsequently became one of the leading members of a third bloc—that of the "nonaligned" nations, many of which were Asian.

Relations between East and West were ultimately conditioned by each side's capability to wreak destruction on the other by use of atomic weapons. A series of crises, beginning with the Berlin Blockade of 1948, and continuing with Soviet invasions of Hungary and Czechoslovakia, saw the two blocs develop the art of "brinkmanship," with neither side finally willing to push the dispute to outright confrontation. Meanwhile, the United States was embroiled in a series of conflicts outside Europe. They included the Korean and Vietnam wars, and—in a clash that seemed to bring the world to the edge of nuclear war—the Cuban missile crisis.

By the end of the 20th century, in a world where technology and culture were ever more global, European history was inextricably linked with that of the rest of the globe. The original EEC membership of six had grown to fifteen by 1997, with the possibility of adding eastern European members by 2000. Its founders' hopes that a European Union might some day provide the basis of a United States of Europe still seemed optimistic, however. Individual nations preferred to find their own solutions to the problems dominating the end of the century: unemployment, increasingly aging populations, terrorism, and the threat of ecological disasters, among others. The collapse of the Soviet Union, and the future of its former members—most importantly Russia itself—raised new questions about the role Europe will play in the next century.

Topic 1

THE GREAT WAR

oday, historians refer to the events of 1914–1918 as "World War I," but those who experienced the conflagration called it "the Great War."

At the time, there was nothing to compare with the Great War. The last conflict that had engulfed all of Europe—the wars of Napoleon—had ended a century earlier. Thereafter, wars were localized or of short duration. In the Great War, the European battles were fought as far west as France, as far east as Russia, and as far south as Italy and the Balkans. Fighting also took place in Africa, the Middle East, and East Asia.

Few generals or political leaders expected the war to last more than a few months. Nevertheless, in all the belligerent countries many idealistic young men enlisted with enthusiasm. "It's all great fun," the English poet Rupert Brooke (1885–1915) wrote to his family in the first winter of the war.

As the realities of the catastrophe into which Europe stumbled were driven home, participants came to regard it with a bitter sense of irony. "Great" hardly described the horrors of the battlefield, the destruction of life and property, and the social and political upheavals caused by the fighting. The war burned itself deep into the human psyche, with consequences that made themselves felt for much of the rest of the 20th century.

The immediate cause of the Great War was a murder in a province of the Austro-Hungarian empire in June 1914. Monarchs and their ministers mismanaged the resulting diplomatic crisis, and in August the guns began firing. In another sense, however, the war was the culmination of historical developments, including nationalism, militarism, and imperialism. Decades of international tensions, aggressive national policies, and diplomatic suspicions had fed the roots of the 1914 crisis.

Europe's great powers aligned themselves into two military blocs: Britain, France, and Russia—the "Allies"—on one side, Germany and Austria-Hungary—the "Central Powers"—on the other. As the war unfolded, each side drew other states into its camp. Because of their geographical position, the Central Powers fought a two-front war. On the Eastern front, they effectively cut Russia off from vital supplies, and under the pressure of great losses and internal opposition, the tsarist autocracy finally collapsed in 1917. On the Western front, where the military character of the war was defined almost immediately, both sides became locked in the terrible stalemate of trench warfare. The entrance of the United States on the side of the Allies in 1917, coupled with the exhaustion of Germany, brought about the collapse of the Central Powers and the end of the war.

The signing of the armistice in November 1918 ended the fighting, but the impact of the war continued to reverberate throughout the rest of the 20th century. Tens of millions of human beings had died. The effects on society of "total war," in which civilians played as vital a role as soldiers in the outcome, were first seen on the home front. Governments mobilized entire populations—men, women, and children—behind the war effort, reorganized national economies, and bolstered civilian morale as a vital military operation. Gender and class lines were blurred, family life reshaped, social values altered, and liberal ideals suspended.

THE ORIGINS OF THE FIRST WORLD WAR

Since the mid-19th century, technological developments had changed the way in which modern wars were fought, while the likelihood of war was enhanced by the growing political influence of military officers. Arms manufacturers, who derived economic benefits from hostilities, also influenced government policy.

Modern Weapons and Military Competition

During the last third of the 19th century, several factors contributed to a huge increase in armaments: the intense competition among the great powers for colonial territories, the rise of nationalist tensions in the Balkans, the hardening alliance systems, and repeated diplomatic crises. The major powers were engaged in a dangerous race to strengthen their military postures.

Each major country had its own armaments manufacturers, most of which also sold weapons on the international market to all parties. Krupp, the German firm, and Armstrong-Whitworth, the British company, poured large sums into research and development and made large profits. Other industries often combined with armaments makers to influence defense programs. They backed nationalist and imperialist organizations that supported the arms race and, together with antiforeign propaganda and the popular press, pressured politicians to vote for larger military budgets. By 1914, per capita military expenditures had increased to six times their 1871 level in Germany and had more than doubled in France.

Military strategy continued to be based on the infantry soldier. By the 1870s, Britain was the only great power that had not enacted a peacetime draft. When war broke out in August 1914, Russia's 1 million-man army was the largest, followed by Germany with about 850,000, France with 700,000, and Austria-Hungary

with 450,000; Britain, which relied on its naval superiority for defense, had only 250,000 men under arms. Strategists believed that reserve training would allow each of the great powers to mobilize a force more than five times the size of its standing army. During the war itself, the number of men actually brought under arms more than doubled these estimates—Russia eventually mobilized 12 million, Germany 11 million, France 8 million, and Britain and the British Dominions 9.5 million.

Sheer numbers themselves were not decisive, for the quality of training and weaponry, military planning, transportation facilities, and industrial productivity all affected a country's ability to wage war. Most governments adopted the German practice of maintaining a permanent general staff, which was responsible for military strategy, training, and weapons development.

Hand-held infantry weapons were greatly improved during the 19th century. By the 1870s most armies had substituted the breech-loading rifle for the muzzle-loading musket. In the 1880s, the introduction of the magazine rifle permitted more rapid firing. But the most significant change came with the development of the machine gun, which fired several hundred rounds a minute. Its considerable weight—about 100 pounds—made it effective only when fixed in position, but the machine gun greatly enhanced defensive operations and, during World War I, caused enormous casualties.

Special alloys of hardened steel and the use of ferroconcrete enabled countries to build huge fortresses as protection against invasion, and even the most sophisticated technological advances in heavy weapons systems failed to undermine the effectiveness of such defenses. Siege howitzers could pound enemy positions and reduce cities to rubble from long distances, but after months of the heaviest artillery bombardment in history, fortresses such as Verdun did not fall to the enemy.

Other developments took place at sea, where Britain and Germany engaged in a feverish "naval race"

Map 1.1 The European Alliances, 1914

that heightened tensions between them. With the passage of the Naval Defense Act in 1889, Britain aimed to make its fleet twice as large as the combined size of the two next biggest navies. The competition began when Admiral Alfred von Tirpitz (1849–1930) became German naval secretary in 1897. Tirpitz was an Anglophobe and under his direction Germany passed a series of naval bills between 1898 and 1912 designed to build a battle fleet two-thirds the size of Britain's. Tirpitz's "risk theory" held that such a fleet would be so powerful that in the event of war Britain would not risk attempts to destroy it.

Britain responded to Germany with a massive naval buildup and the creation of a North Sea Fleet. In 1906, the British revolutionized naval warfare with the *Dreadnought*, a large, heavily armored, and highly maneuverable battleship. Driven by powerful oil-fueled turbine engines, it carried 12-inch guns that could strike targets many miles away. Despite these advantages, *Dreadnought*-class ships were by no means invincible—other countries copied the technology, and both torpedo boats and destroyers could sink even the *Dreadnought*. By 1914, heavy-oil engines and storage batteries made possible the building of submarine fleets that would challenge conventional naval warfare.

The Germans did copy the *Dreadnought* idea, and by the eve of World War I had 18 such ships to Britain's 29. Germany's naval strength rose from seventh to sec-

ond place. Berlin brushed aside proposals to limit naval construction, and British fears of German ambitions grew accordingly. Secretary of War Richard Haldane (1856–1928) went to Berlin in 1912 to seek an accommodation with Germany, but the mission proved unsuccessful. As a result, Britain and France then reached an important agreement: Britain concentrated its naval forces in the North Sea, France in the Mediterranean. Although no formal alliance was made, self-interest now bound the two nations as never before.

Military Strategy and the Schlieffen Plan

Despite the new weapons, military planners continued to employ strategies inspired by the theories of the Prussian General Karl von Clausewitz (1780–1831), who advocated offensive operations designed to achieve victory with speed, mobility, and surprise. Moreover, most general staffs worked out military plans for fighting wars with anticipated enemies.

Based on accurate maps, railroad transportation, and precise timetables, such plans aimed at moving huge numbers of troops rapidly over large areas. The so-called Schlieffen Plan, developed by General Alfred von Schlieffen (1833–1913), chief of the German General Staff, was the most famous. Although his strategy anticipated that Germany would be at war with both Russia and France at the same time, Schlieffen thought principally in terms of how to defeat the French in the West. He devised his plan in 1905, while Russia was still reeling from its defeat by the Japanese and from domestic uprisings. He argued that since Russia, weak and disorganized, would require at least a month to mobilize its armies, Germany should concentrate on a quick victory against France, after which it could deal easily with Russia.

Schlieffen held that because French fortifications such as those at Verdun were too formidable, Germany's only alternative was to launch a surprise attack against France through the level terrain of the Low Countries. Keeping the Russians at bay in the East, two separate German armies would form a large pincer in the West, with one larger arm closing around the French from behind. Schlieffen planned for a powerful right wing to drive through the Netherlands, Luxembourg, and Belgium while a much weaker left wing would move toward Alsace-Lorraine. When the French counterattacked in the South, as he believed they would, two German army corps would be shifted from there in order to reinforce the right flank—the weakened left wing would then retreat on to German soil in order to draw the enemy away from the real arena of decision in the North.

Schlieffen's plan held several strategic risks—he had banked on the assumption that Russia would not attack until its mobilization had been completed, that the Belgians would offer no serious resistance, and that the timing would go according to schedule. Furthermore, the German authorities believed that military needs would outweigh the political repercussions of violating Belgian neutrality. In 1906, von Schlieffen was succeeded by Count Helmuth Johannes von Moltke (1848–1916), the plodding and insecure nephew of the brilliant strategist who had executed Prussia's victories during the struggle for German unification. The younger Moltke so changed Schlieffen's original plan as to enhance the risks of disaster. He increased the strength of the left wing significantly, partly by weakening the Russian Front, and thereby changed the fundamental thrust of the assault.

The French, who had gained a sense of the Schlieffen Plan, developed their own "Plan XVII," which called for a holding action against the German armies in Belgium while attacking Germany with a superior force through Lorraine. The logic of "military necessity" made both the German and French generals overconfident. Strategies such as the Schlieffen Plan increased the chances of war, for their success hinged on the ability of the general staffs to deploy millions of soldiers and a huge quantity of equipment on a war footing *before* the outbreak of hostilities—hence, while civilian authorities attempted to resolve diplomatic crises through negotiation, the military de-

manded immediate mobilization so as to be able to strike first.

FROM CONFRONTATION TO CRISIS: THE COMING OF WAR

Between 1882 and 1914, countries chose membership in one of the two great alliance systems in order to gain a measure of security against their enemies. Thus Great Britain, France, and Russia were aligned in the Triple Entente, and Germany, Austria-Hungary, and Italy were grouped in the Triple Alliance. Yet the increasingly tense character of diplomatic relations, especially after 1905, produced the opposite effect. Based on the assumption that powerful alliances supported them, countries tended to be less cautious during international disputes. Such disputes restricted the maneuverability of the blocs as allies strove to demonstrate their support for each other. Thus, the alternatives available to the great powers narrowed dangerously during international confrontations.

Assassination at Sarajevo
Relations between the Triple Alliance and the Entente deteriorated as one international face-off followed another. The Balkans, the scene of considerable turmoil as a result of the Bosnian crisis of 1908 and the wars of 1912–1913, proved to be the seedbed of the Great

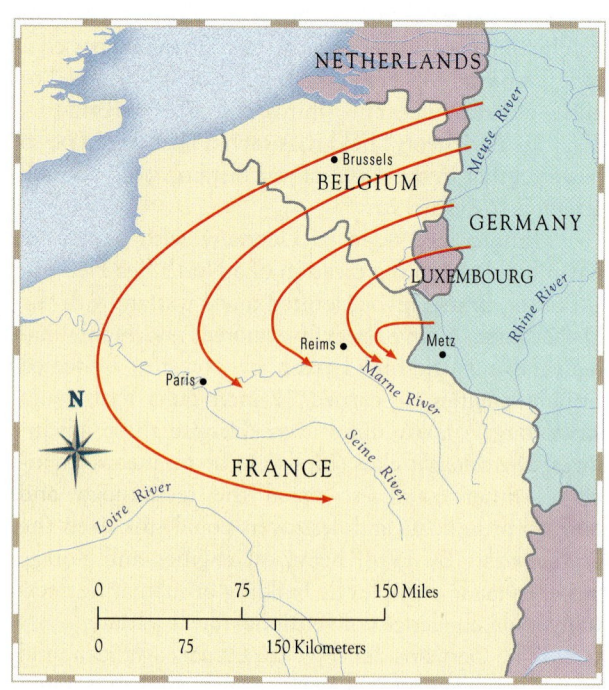

Map 1.2   The Schlieffen Plan

Map 1.3   The Balkans, c. 1914

to back them. Austria-Hungary was intent on blocking Serb ambitions, which could undermine the multiethnic Dual Monarchy.

These forces clashed head-on at Sarajevo, the capital of the Austrian possession of Bosnia, in the summer of 1914. On the morning of June 28, the Archduke Franz Ferdinand (1863–1914), heir to the Austro-Hungarian throne and nephew of Emperor Franz Josef, was shot and killed while riding through the streets of Sarajevo in an open car. His wife, the former Countess Sophie Chotek (1868–1914), was also killed. The royal couple was on an official tour of Bosnia and at the moment of their death had been returning from a reception at the town hall.

Seven young men—five teenagers and two in their twenties—took part in the assassination conspiracy. A student named Gavrilo Princip (1895–1918) fired the fatal shots. All were members of a nationalist organization called "Young Bosnia." They had made Franz Ferdinand their target because he was known to favor autonomy for the Slavs of the empire, much as the Magyars enjoyed. Were Franz Ferdinand to come to the throne and implement this policy, Serbian ambitions would be crushed.

Serbia bore indirect responsibility for the murder. Officers in the Serbian Army had provided the assassins with rudimentary training and weapons. Princip and his friends had been in contact with a Serbian terrorist group known as the "Black Hand," which had been supported by the Ministry of War. Perhaps most damning, although members of the Serb cabinet had known

War, for the clashes between Russia and Austria-Hungary destabilized the region (see Part VII, Topic 16). Serbian nationalists, who wanted their country to form the core of a large Slavic empire, expected Russia

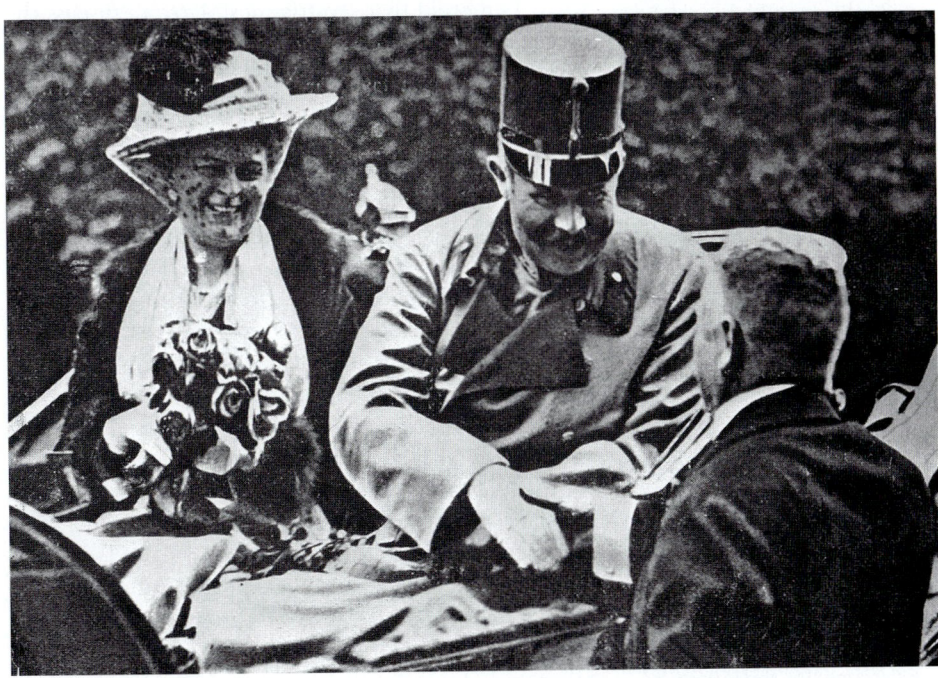

Archduke Franz Ferdinand and his wife Sophie in Sarajevo, the fateful day, June 28, 1914.

Gavrilo Princip, the gunman responsible for the assassination of Franz Ferdinand and his wife Sophie.

that an attempt on Ferdinand's life would be made, they did almost nothing to stop it.

Austrian officials were not unduly upset at the murder, for many thought Ferdinand's political ideas dangerous. Moreover, his marriage to a minor aristocrat had angered the emperor and the royal court, who felt that the archduke had married beneath his station. Despite these private misgivings, Austria-Hungary decided to use the event as a pretext for extracting retribution from Serbia. Count Leopold von Berchtold (1863–1942), the wealthy aristocrat who served as Austrian foreign minister, advocated a march on Belgrade. But the army chief of staff urged caution, for an attack against Serbia could mean war with Russia. Berchtold then turned to Berlin, hoping to secure assurances that Germany would back Austria-Hungary if war broke out.

How Europe Stumbled into War

On July 5, Wilhelm II gave Count Berchtold what he wanted: the infamous "blank check," by which Germany pledged military assistance in the event of war between Austria-Hungary and Russia. The German

chancellor, Theobald von Bethmann-Hollweg (served 1909 to 1917), confidently predicted that Russia would not intervene if Austria acted quickly. Unknown to him, however, on July 21 French President Raymond Poincaré, who was visiting St. Petersburg, encouraged Russia to be firm. On both sides, the inevitable logic of the alliance systems took hold.

Over the weeks that followed the German assurance of support, Berchtold deliberately kept Berlin ill-informed of Austrian plans. Finally, on July 23, Vienna issued an ultimatum that clearly threatened to violate Serbian sovereignty. The Austrians insisted that the Serb government suppress all anti-Austrian activities and that Austrian officials be permitted to investigate the assassination in Serbia. At 5:55 P.M. on July 25, Belgrade—which had already ordered mobilization—responded with some concessions, but refused to accept all of Vienna's demands. At 9:23 P.M., the Emperor Franz Josef ordered Austro-Hungarian mobilization.

The two mobilizations shocked Europe's diplomats into action. The German ambassador in St. Petersburg persuaded the Russians to suggest talks with Berchtold to end the crisis. British Foreign Secretary Sir Edward Grey (1862–1933) appealed to the kaiser to hold the Austrians in check and called for mediation talks. Bethmann-Hollweg, who misunderstood the gravity of events because of Berchtold's deceptions, failed to forward Grey's proposals to Vienna, and when Wilhelm returned from a cruise on July 27, he angrily asked his chancellor, "How did it all happen?"

That night, the chastened German minister wired Berchtold that Austria must agree to discuss the Serbian concessions. But in Vienna, a declaration of war had been drafted and Berchtold got the aged Emperor Franz Josef to sign it by falsely claiming that the Serbians had already begun to attack. On the morning of July 28, Austria delivered its declaration of war to Serbia, while in Berlin the kaiser decided that he would attempt to mediate the dispute between Austria-Hungary and Serbia. The next day, Bethmann-Hollweg telegraphed sternly to Berchtold that "We [Germany] must refuse to let ourselves be drawn . . . by Vienna into any general conflagration because she has ignored our advice." Had such a message been delivered on July 5 instead of the "blank check," events might have taken a different course.

On July 28, the French ambassador assured the Russians that France would stand by its ally. Tsar Nicholas II, who had been persuaded to order partial mobilization, telegraphed to Kaiser Wilhelm: "Very soon I shall be forced to take extreme measures that will lead to war." The royal cousins exchanged telegrams, signed "Willy" and "Nicky," which were so friendly that Nicholas countermanded the mobilization order. But when Wilhelm learned that Russian mobilization had been under way, he exploded in anger and ended the discussions. The tsar signed a full mobilization decree on July 29.

Although Germany had not been a direct party to the events in the Balkans, General Helmuth von Moltke, bearing in mind the time constraints of the Schlieffen Plan, now urged immediate mobilization.

Events rushed forward. On July 31, Austria-Hungary mobilized against Russia; Germany issued two ultimatums—one demanding that Russia call off its mobilization, the other giving France 18 hours to decide whether it would remain neutral if Germany and Russia fought; France ordered mobilization. On August 1, Sir Edward Grey promised that Britain would keep France neutral if Germany would not act, but the German ambassador misinterpreted the comment. The kaiser concluded that he would be free to attack Russia if he left France alone, although von Moltke insisted that the Schlieffen Plan could not be changed. Nevertheless, Wilhelm ordered German troops already moving toward Luxembourg to stop, but von Moltke deliberately held the order back. The same day, the German ambassador in St. Petersburg asked the Russian foreign minister whether his country would cancel the mobilization. Having received a negative answer, the ambassador then presented a declaration of war.

Throughout the crisis, France had pressed Britain for a clear statement of support, but without result. Instead, Sir Edward Grey had asked for assurances from both France and Germany that the international treaty guaranteeing Belgian neutrality would not be violated. France agreed but the Germans avoided a clear answer. On August 2, Germany demanded free passage for its troops through Belgium, but King Albert I (reigned 1909–1934) refused, declaring that "Belgium is a country and not a road." The next day, Grey got an endorsement from the House of Commons to defend Belgian neutrality if it were violated. In the meantime, Germany had declared war on France and its armies were marching. Using an unhappy choice of words to describe the treaty on Belgian neutrality, on August 4 Bethmann-Hollweg expressed his chagrin that Britain would go to war over "a scrap of paper." War between Britain and Germany began at midnight.

For two tension-ridden months, Europe's statesmen had stumbled their way through a mounting crisis. With the failure of the diplomats, the generals now took command. In a mood of deep despondency, Grey gazed out of the window of his London office at the street lights. "The lamps are going out all over Europe," an aide heard him say; "we shall not see them lit again in our lifetime." It is a measure of the bitter irony surrounding these events that Grey did not remember having made that remark.

FIGHTING THE WAR

From the first, the Schlieffen Plan broke down. Belgian resistance slowed the German advance, a British force of 100,000 quickly joined the French Army, and the Russians moved against East Prussia sooner than expected. Surprised by these developments, von Moltke made further changes—instead of retreating on the left flank so as to draw the French away from the real battle zone, German reinforcements were sent to Lorraine. More crucial still, von Moltke weakened the assault against France by withdrawing troops from the West to halt the Russian attack.

As the Germans advanced to within 30 miles of Paris, General Joseph Joffre (1852–1931), the French commander-in-chief, retreated in orderly fashion. In September, Joffre counterattacked along the Marne River, pushing the Germans back. Once the Germans halted, however, the front line stabilized. Following the Battle of the Marne, each side tried unsuccessfully to outflank the other by moving northward around the enemy in what has been called the "race to the sea"—when that tactic failed, the combatants moved southward, so that the front soon consisted of a 400-mile line stretching from the North Sea to Switzerland. For

Significant Dates

The Great War

August 1914	Outbreak of war
September 1914	Failure of Schlieffen Plan
November 1914	Turkey joins Central Powers
April 1915	Chlorine gas used at Ypres
May 1915	Italy joins Allies; *Lusitania* sunk
1916	Battles of Verdun and the Somme
March 1917	Russian Revolution; November, Bolshevik coup
1917–1918	Offenses on Western front
April 1917	U.S. joins Allies
November 11, 1918	Armistice
January 1919	Paris Peace Conference opens
June 28, 1919	Treaty of Versailles

DOCUMENTS ON HISTORY

World War I: Who Was Responsible?

Ever since the outbreak of World War I in August 1914, diplomats, politicians, and scholars have debated the question of responsibility: did the blame for the war rest on one country, as the Allies claimed for Germany, or did some or all of the European powers share responsibility collectively? Were the causes of the war systemic—that is, was it the result of the kind of diplomatic system that prevailed in Europe, with its secret military alliances? Did the clash of imperial interests globally contribute to the war, or did the arms race and the influence of military industrialists bring about the disaster? At the time, each of the major states involved in the war issued its own diplomatic documents, and later statesmen and generals published their memoirs, all in an effort to explain the causes of the war in a way that would be advantageous to their own nations or to their personal interests. The selection of documents that follows may shed some light on the vexing question and on the difficulties of sifting historical truth out of official records.

WAR GUILT AND THE VERSAILLES TREATY

Although diplomats were aware of the importance of responsibility while the events were unfolding, it was with the formulation of Article 231 of the Treaty of Versailles—the famous "war guilt" clause—that the entire blame for the war was forced on Germany and its wartime allies:

The Allied and Associated Governments affirm and Germany accepts the responsibility of Germany and her allies for causing all the loss and damage to which the Allied and Associated Governments and their nationals have been subjected as a consequence of the war imposed upon them by the aggression of Germany and her allies.

From Alexander Baltzly and A. William Salomone, eds., *Readings in Twentieth-Century European History,* Appleton-Century-Crofts, Copyright © 1950.

After the outbreak of the war, the major powers published collections of official documents designed to prove their innocence in bringing about the conflict. The following selection of documents is designed to suggest the complexity of the "war guilt" question.

THE GERMAN RESPONSE

On July 5, 1914, Count A. Hoyos of the Austrian Foreign Ministry and Ambassador Count L. de Szogyény saw Kaiser Wilhelm in Berlin, where they asked whether they could count on German support if Austria took strong action against Serbia. The next day, Theobald von Bethmann-Hollweg, German foreign minister, described the kaiser's response to his ambassador, Heinrich von Tschirschky, in Vienna:

Finally, as regards Serbia, His Majesty, of course, cannot take any position in regard to the questions pending between that country and Austria-Hungary, as they are outside his authority. But Emperor Francis Joseph can rely on His Majesty's taking his stand loyally at the side of Austria-Hungary in accordance with his duties as an ally and his old friendship.

Quoted in Luigi Albertini, *The Origins of the War of 1914,* trans. I. M. Massey, II. Oxford University Press. Copyright © 1952.

AUSTRIA-HUNGARY'S ULTIMATUM TO SERBIA

During conversations in Vienna as to the nature of the Austro-Hungarian response to Serbia, Austrian Foreign Minister Count Leopold Berchtold told German Ambassador Heinrich von Tschirschky that he would advise Emperor Franz Josef "so to formulate these demands that their acceptance appears impossible." When Russian Foreign Minister Sergei Sazonov heard the text of the ultimatum (technically the Austrians called it a "timed note" rather than an ultimatum), he exclaimed, "This means a European war." The following terms were presented to Serbia on July 23:

The Royal Servian Government further undertakes:

1. To suppress any publication which incites to hatred and contempt of the Austro-Hungarian Monarchy and the general tendency of which is directed against its territorial integrity;

2. To dissolve immediately the society called Narodna Odbrana [The People's Defense], to confiscate all its means of propaganda, and to proceed in the same manner against all other secret societies and their branches in Servia which engage in propa-

ganda against the Austro-Hungarian Monarchy. . . .

3. To eliminate without delay from public instruction in Servia, both as regards the teaching body and the methods of instruction, everything that serves, or might serve, to foment the propaganda against Austria-Hungary;

4. To remove from the military service, and from the administration in general, all officers and functionaries guilty of propaganda against the Austro-Hungarian Monarchy whose names and deeds the Austro-Hungarian Government reserves the right of communicating to the Royal Government;

5. To accept the cooperation in Servia of representatives of the Austro-Hungarian Government in the suppression of the subversive movement directed against the territorial integrity of the Monarchy;

6. To take judicial proceedings against accomplices in the plot of the 28th of June who are on Servian territory. Delegates of the Austro-Hungarian Government will take part in the investigation relating thereto;

7. To proceed without delay to the arrest of Major Voja Tankositch and of the individual named Milan Ciganovitch, a Servian State employee, who have been compromised by the results of the preliminary investigation at Sarajevo;

8. To prevent by effective measures the participation of the Servian authorities in the illicit traffic in arms and explosives across the frontier; to dismiss and punish severely the officials of the frontier service at Schabatz and Loznica who have been guilty of having assisted the perpetrators of the Sarajevo

continued next page

crime by facilitating their passage across the frontier;

9. To furnish the Imperial and Royal Government with explanations regarding the unjustifiable utterances of high Servian officials, both in Servia and abroad, who, notwithstanding their official positions, did not hesitate after the crime of the 28th of June to give utterance, in published interviews, to expressions of hostility to the Austro-Hungarian Government; and finally

10. To notify the Imperial and Royal Government without delay of the execution of the measures comprised under the preceding heads.

The Austro-Hungarian Government awaits the reply of the Royal Government at the latest by 6 o'clock on Saturday evening, the 25th of July.

James Brown Scott, ed., *Diplomatic Documents Relating to the Outbreak of the European War*, Part I. Oxford University Press. Copyright © 1916.

THE FRENCH RESPONSE

French President Raymond Poincaré and Foreign Minister René Viviani had been in St. Petersburg on an official visit in late July, and the Austrians had deliberately waited until after their departure before submitting the ultimatum to Serbia. On July 24, Maurice Paléologue, French ambassador in St. Petersburg, gave a luncheon for the English ambassador and Sazonov, and later wrote in his memoirs that he had said the following to his guests:

. . . I had no hesitation in advocating a policy of firmness.

'But suppose that policy is bound to lead to war?' said Sazonov.

'It will only lead to war if the Germanic powers have already made up their minds to resort to force to secure the hegemony of the East. Firmness does not exclude conciliation. But it is essential for the other side to be prepared to negotiate and compromise. You know my own views as to Germany's designs. The Austrian ultimatum seems to me to provoke the dangerous crisis I have anticipated for a long time. Henceforth we must recognize that war may break out at any moment. That prospect must govern all our diplomatic action.'

The English ambassador, Sir George Buchanan, reported to London the following:

The French Ambassador gave me to understand that France would not only give Russia strong diplomatic support but would, if necessary, fulfil all the obligations imposed on her by the alliance.

Paléologue, *An Ambassador's Memoirs*, 3 vols.

BRITISH RESPONSE TO THE CRISIS

Sir Edward Grey, British foreign secretary, consistently took a rather detached and almost fatalistic attitude toward the unfolding diplomatic crisis. On July 24—a day on which the cabinet spent almost all its time discussing the Irish problem rather than the diplomatic crisis—he told German Ambassador Lichnowsky that Britain was in no position to rein in its Russian ally following the Austro-Hungarian ultimatum:

I said that if the Austrian ultimatum to Servia did not lead to trouble between Austria and Russia I had no concern with it; . . . I was very apprehensive of the view Russia would take of the situation. I reminded the German Ambassador that some days ago he had expressed a personal hope that if need arose I would endeavor to exercise moderating influence at St. Petersburg, but now I said that, in view of the extraordinarily stiff character of the

Austrian note, the shortness of the time allowed, and the wide scope of the demands upon Servia, I felt quite helpless as far as Russia was concerned, and I did not believe any Power could exercise influence alone.

The only chance I could see of mediating or moderating influence being effective, was that the four Powers, Germany, Italy, France and ourselves, should work together simultaneously at Vienna and St. Petersburg. . . .

The immediate danger was that in a few hours Austria might march into Servia and Russian Slav opinion demand that Russia should march to help Servia; it would be very desirable to get Austria not to precipitate military action and so to gain more time. But none of us could influence Austria in this direction unless Germany would propose and participate in such action at Vienna.

The Serbs rejected outright only the sixth clause of the ultimatum, and the kaiser thought that their carefully worded response made war avoidable—"every reason for war drops away. . . . On the strength of this, I should never have ordered mobilization." Nevertheless, on July 26 General Helmuth von Moltke, chief of the German General Staff, drafted for his files an ultimatum demanding free passage for German troops through Belgian territory. When Austria-Hungary declared war against Serbia on July 28, Moltke wrote a memorandum to the German chancellor on the military necessity for swift action, and the next day he sent the Belgian ultimatum, sealed inside two envelopes, to the German Embassy in Brussels with orders to be opened only upon instructions from Berlin. Here is Moltke's memorandum:

Austria, if she enters Serbia, will be faced not only with the Serbian Army but with strong Russian superiority; she will thus not be able to wage war with Serbia without making Russian

intervention certain. That means she will be forced to mobilize the other half of her army, for she cannot possibly put herself at the mercy of a Russia ready for war. The instant Austria mobilizes her whole army, the clash between her and Russia will become inevitable. Now that is for Germany the *causus foederis.* Unless Germany means to break her word and allow her ally to succumb to Russian superior strength, she must also mobilize. That will lead to the mobilization of the remaining Russian military districts. Russia will then be able to say, "I am being attacked by Germany" and that will make her sure of the support of France who is bound by treaty to go to war if her ally Russia is attacked. The Franco-Russian agreement, so often praised as a purely defensive alliance brought about only to meet German plans of aggression, comes thereby into operation and the civilized states of Europe will begin to tear one another to pieces. . . .

THE RUSSIAN DECISION TO MOBILIZE

The Russians, who responded to the Austrian declaration of war with alarm, had two military contingencies. They could declare partial mobilization for operations along the Austro-Hungarian frontier, or general mobilization along both the Austro-Hungarian and the German borders. Tsar Nicholas II signed both edicts and on July 29–30 shifted back and forth twice between ordering general and then partial mobilization. But Russian military commanders put increasing pressure on Foreign Minister Sazonov and the tsar, pointing out that partial mobilization would jeopardize Russia's ability to carry out general mobilization in the event of an enemy declaration of war. The following account of the fateful meeting with

continued next page

Nicholas on July 30 is from the memoirs of Baron von Schilling, head of the Chancery of the Russian Ministry of Foreign Affairs:

During the course of nearly an hour the Minister [Sazonov] proceeded to show that war was becoming inevitable, as it was clear to everybody that Germany had decided to bring about a collision, as otherwise she would not have rejected all the pacificatory proposals that had been made. . . . Therefore it was necessary to put away any fears that our warlike preparations would bring about a war and to continue these preparations carefully, rather than by reason of such fears to be taken unawares by war.

The firm desire of the Tsar to avoid war at all costs, the horrors of which filled him with repulsion, led His Majesty . . . to explore every possible means for averting the approaching danger. Consequently he refused during a long time to agree to the adoption of measures which, however indispensable from a military point of view, were calculated, as he clearly saw, to hasten a decision in an undesirable sense. . . .

Finally the Tsar agreed that in the existing circumstances it would be very dangerous not to make timely preparations for what was apparently an inevitable war, and therefore gave his decision in favour of an immediate general mobilization.

From Baron M. F. Schilling, *How the War Began In 1914*, translated by William C. Bridge. Allen and Unwin. Copyright © 1925.

On Friday, July 31, Germany presented two ultimatums: one to Russia that it would mobilize unless the tsar suspended all military operations within twelve hours; and one to France asking whether Paris would remain neutral in the event of a German-Russian war and, if so, to permit German occupation of French frontier fortresses. At five P.M. on Saturday, having received no answer from either the Russians or the French, the Germans began mobilization. An hour later, the German ambassador in St. Petersburg handed the Russians the text of their declaration of war.

the remainder of the war, the Western front hardly moved more than a few miles in either direction.

Stalemate in the West

The Battle of the Marne shattered German hopes for a quick victory. General Erich von Falkenhayn (1861–1922) replaced von Moltke as chief of staff. For the next four years, each side slaughtered the other repeatedly in futile attempts to wear the enemy down and achieve a breakthrough. Despite some differences in military and industrial capability, the Allies and the Central Powers were each sufficiently strong to prevent victory or defeat.

The assumptions behind modern military strategy collapsed as armies constructed a web of trenches that eventually measured a combined length of 25,000 miles. These trench systems were cordoned by miles of barbed wire, with a fearful "no man's land" dividing them. Behind the trenches, a vast transportation network moved millions of soldiers and hundreds of millions of tons of equipment in preparation for assaults. To all except the generals who commanded the front, the principal tactic adopted by both sides was horrific in its simplicity: long-range artillery pounded the enemy for days. Then, at a prearranged moment, officers led the infantry soldiers out of the trenches to attack. Machine guns cut them down as they scrambled through exploding shells that blasted craters in the earth and filled the air with dirt and smoke. Eighty percent of all casualties were caused in this manner—between August and November 1914 alone, more than 1,640,000.

The Great War produced few "heroes" in the traditional sense of the word. Each assault caused tens of thousands to die anonymously on the battlefields, while millions more huddled in the trenches amid mud, slime, and the stench of rotting corpses. New weapons, such as poison gas and tanks, were employed—the

British soldiers leaving the trenches for a night attack.

Germans first used chlorine gas at Ypres in April 1915, and the Allies responded in kind—but it failed to prove decisive and only introduced a fiendish element into the conflict. Yet the generals refused to see the futility of their tactics, instead waging a war of attrition.

This war attained grotesque dimensions in 1916. The Germans deliberately sought to bleed the French into defeat by unleashing a major assault on Verdun. They correctly expected the French to defend the fortress at any price. More than 1 million German artillery shells fell on Verdun on February 21, the open-ing day of the attack. In August, daily German casual-ties began to exceed French losses and the kaiser replaced von Falkenhayn with General Paul von Hindenburg (1847–1934), who had been called out of retirement to command the Eastern front. When the siege was finally lifted in December, 700,000 had died—600,000 French soldiers and 100,000 Germans.

The most fearsome battle of the Great War, which began while Verdun was still under siege, took place along the Somme River. General Douglas Haig (1861–1928), the British commander, had for some

A French soldier shot while advancing from the trenches.

Map 1.4   The Great War, 1914–1918

time planned a "big push" at the Somme, and the bloodletting at Verdun failed to dissuade him. The British first pounded the Germans with an immense artillery attack that began on June 24, sublimely confident that the three-quarters of a million soldiers they had amassed would then be able to occupy the enemy trenches. But when the offensive opened on July 1, the damage to German installations proved to be superficial: 20,000 British were killed and 40,000 wounded.

Haig refused to call off the battle, which raged on throughout the summer. In September, for the first time, he used tanks, which the British had been developing, but they proved unreliable. A snowstorm ended the Somme offensive in November, but not before the

blood of more than 1 million had soaked the battlefields: Haig's "big push" had cost the British and French 600,000 casualties, and the Germans 500,000. When David Lloyd George (1863–1945) became prime minister in 1916, he tried to end these costly offenses but gave in when Sir William Robertson (1860–1933), chief of the Imperial General Staff and a man with powerful political and newspaper connections, insisted that they continue.

Crisis in the East

In the East, the imbalance between the combatants and the huge space over which supplies and armies had to move prevented the kind of stalemate that had bogged down the fighting on the Western front. When the war broke out, the Russians had moved against Germany before completing mobilization and achieved a surprise advantage in East Prussia. It was at that point that von Moltke had shifted four divisions from the Western theater to stop the Russians.

Rather than fighting the numerically larger Russian forces along all points, Hindenburg, who had taken command of the Eastern front with General Erich Ludendorff (1865–1937) as his deputy, chose to take on sections of the Russian armies individually. In this way, they won an important engagement at the Battle of Tannenberg, where the Germans took over 100,000 prisoners, and another at the Masurian Lakes. By the time the Battle of the Marne had been determined in the West, the Russian "steam roller" had been stopped. Farther to the south, along the Austro-Hungarian front, Germany's principal ally was less successful, for the Russians drove through Galicia and invaded Hungary. In the Balkans, the Austrians also experienced reverses as the Serbs repulsed their armies and retook Belgrade. By the end of 1914, the results of the fighting on the Eastern front were therefore equally inconclusive.

Turkey's declaration of war against the Allies in November 1914 seriously weakened Russia's position. Tensions between the two countries, already sharp, were exacerbated by the presence of the Armenians, a Christian people living on both sides of the Russo-Turkish border. The Armenians had suffered centuries of persecution by both the Russians and the Turks. In 1915, after failing to secure their support against Russia in the war effort, the Turks forcibly relocated the Armenians in the Anatolian interior. In the process, more than a million Armenians died of disease, starvation, and slaughter.

Upon entering the war, the Turks closed the Dardanelles Straits in order to stop vital supplies from reaching Russia. In March 1915, British and French naval forces attempted to open the straits, but the plan failed. In April, the Allies landed along the Gallipoli peninsula, which juts out from the southern coast of European Turkey and guards the straits, but the Turks were able to trap the invading forces below from their higher ground. After suffering great losses, the expedition was recalled.

In the spring of 1915, von Falkenhayn launched a major offensive against the Russians. The Germans pierced the Russian line and moved forward, taking Warsaw and pushing east from the foothills of the Carpathian Mountains. Because the Russians lacked machine guns and heavy artillery, the offensive cost them some 2,500,000 men killed, wounded, or taken prisoner.

The Allied position was strengthened in May 1915 by Italy's declaration of war against Austria-Hungary. The previous month, Italy had concluded a secret agreement with the Allies that ended months of bitter domestic debate over the war. In return for its intervention, the Treaty of London pledged to give Italy the Trentino, the southern Tyrol, Istria, and the city of Trieste, as well as territory along the Dalmatian coast—all territories under Austrian rule. The new front thus opened along the Italian-Austrian border relieved some German pressure against Russia. That October, Bulgaria threw in its lot with the Central Powers, and the following August Romania joined the Allies.

The year 1917 brought major crises to the Allies. In March, revolution broke out in the Russian capital and forced the abdication of Tsar Nicholas (see Part

French troops pass through the ruins of Verdun, 1916.

VIII, Topic 2). A provisional government dominated by Alexander Kerensky (1881–1970) proclaimed a continuation of the war, but the Russian people demanded peace. Convinced that the imminent collapse of Russia would soon end the two-front war, the Germans erected a fortified defense system on the Western front known as the Hindenburg Line. While the German armies waited, the French flung themselves at the Hindenburg Line in April in a wasted effort that cost 250,000 casualties. Between July and November, Haig led another huge assault at Ypres, but the fighting in the muddy fields of Flanders resulted in an additional 300,000 British casualties.

THE HOME FRONT

The Great War placed tremendous stress on society. Europeans found it difficult to absorb the psychological impact of the carnage. As each side suffered millions of casualties, the excitement that had greeted the outbreak of war in 1914 turned to horror. At home, morale began to waver under the joint pressures of the fighting and the demands increasingly placed on civilian populations.

Domestic Opposition

The war aroused opposition from pacifists, women's groups, churches, and the left. Almost all the socialist parties, however, had voted for war credits in 1914—only in Italy did they adopt the neutral position of "neither sabotage nor support"—and leaders of churches in belligerent countries rallied to national interests. Governments of national unity brought all major parties into coalitions, including socialists. In August 1917 Pope Benedict XV (ruled 1914–1922) issued an appeal for peace.

As the terrible toll of dead and wounded mounted, opposition took more direct forms. In May 1917, after the failure of a bloody offensive, some French regiments that had suffered heavy casualties ignored orders to attack and revolts broke out in other units. A total of between 30,000 and 40,000 soldiers may have been involved in such incidents, and the French command issued some 400 death sentences against mutineers. One British camp in France experienced a riot, and even the Germans had to deal with individual cases of desertion. During the summer, the crew of one German ship staged a hunger strike to protest the better food rations of their officers. In the Russian Army, chronically short of weapons, uniforms, and food, mutiny and desertion were widespread.

Incidents of civilian revolt were deeply troubling to wartime governments. The British faced a critical problem in Ireland, where support for the war effort clashed with anti-British sentiment. During Easter of 1916, Irish nationalists tried to capitalize on the war to stage a rebellion against British rule. The Irish politician Sir Roger Casement (1864–1918) arranged for the Germans to supply arms to the rebels from a U-boat, but British destroyers intercepted the vessel and Casement was captured. After a week of street fighting, the rebellion was crushed and 15 nationalist leaders, including Casement, were hanged.

The March 1917 revolution in Russia, provoked in part by conditions at the front, sent shock waves throughout Europe. In July, Matthias Erzberger (1875–1921) of the German Center party introduced a peace resolution in the Reichstag. The resolution, which called for a peace based on understanding, and rejected territorial acquisitions achieved by force, passed by a margin of almost two to one. The following month, revolutionary socialists staged an antiwar uprising in the Italian industrial city of Turin. Some 50 workers were killed and 200 wounded when the government used army units to restore order.

Morale on the home front was as vital to victory as the willingness of soldiers to fight. The war made tremendous demands on national economies and the workforce. In order to deal with continued shortages of food and clothing, most nations imposed rationing as well as limited wages and prices, and most labor unions adopted voluntary restraints. Industrial commissions, composed of business and labor leaders, government officials, and experts, directed national production. Every country was caught off guard by the "technical surprise" of the war—that is, the insatiable demand for raw materials and weapons that increased beyond all expectations every day of the fighting. Stock piles of artillery shells, for example, that prewar estimates assumed would last for six months were consumed in a single day at the front.

Women and the War

The wartime economy created an artificial prosperity that greatly affected women. At first, many female workers found themselves unemployed because the demand for consumer goods traditionally made by women, such as dresses and textiles, declined. But the drafting of millions of young men created a labor shortage. By the second year of the war, women were working in heavy industry and munitions plants, and by 1918, perhaps one out of three industrial workers was a woman. Women appeared on streetcars and subways as drivers, ticket takers, and conductors. In addition to the home front, they served in combat zones as ambulance drivers and military nurses, and were active in assisting civilian refugees.

Governments proclaimed female labor essential to the war effort, although they were not always wel-

German women working in a shell factory.

comed by male workers and were paid lower wages. Nor were women taught technical skills beyond those required for their immediate work, for industry and labor unions considered female labor a temporary measure. Many munitions factories provided day care centers for working mothers, but after ten- or twelve-hour shifts, they still had to care for their families.

Yet the war made a great difference in the lives of many women and on how men perceived them. Not only did a great number earn wages for the first time, but they often experienced a degree of social independence that they were unwilling to give up when peace came. Single women appeared in public, attended theaters and ate in restaurants alone, dated more freely, and dressed with fewer constraints. The criticism and ridicule that some working women experienced resulted in part from sexual tensions that accompanied changing female roles. The unprecedented requirements of "total war" made it impossible to maintain a traditional gender separation between the male warrior and the female wife or mother. "Girls are doing things," wrote the poet Nina Macdonald, "They've never done before . . . All the world is topsy-turvy/Since the War began."

Official propaganda attempted to mitigate the impact of the war on gender roles, as in the case of the British nurse Edith Cavell (1865–1915). Volunteer nurses were in high demand because of the terrible casualty rate of trench warfare. These women faced daily the searing psychological experience of dealing with bloodshed, mutilation, and death. Working near the front lines, they, like the soldiers they assisted, con-

fronted serious physical dangers. Although a professional nurse, Cavell was a British patriot who used her position at a Red Cross facility in Belgium to aid captured Allied soldiers. The Germans tried Cavell for espionage and executed her. In Britain, France, and Italy, she provided a powerful symbol of the virtuous, brave woman murdered by an uncivilized enemy. In the wake of Cavell's death, posters were printed portraying monstrous German soldiers raping women and mutilating children. Such propaganda themes played on patriarchal notions of gender roles—by portraying themselves as fighting for the honor of women, the Allies not only presented the enemy in the worst possible light, but reconfirmed the manhood of soldiers at the front. A famous Red Cross poster of 1918, entitled "The Greatest Mother in the World," portrayed a huge nurse, holding a wounded soldier on a stretcher, in the pose of a *pietà*.

Vera Brittain (1893–1970), on the other hand, demonstrated how the wartime experience actually helped her to achieve personal independence. Brittain, who had been studying at Oxford, became a volunteer nurse in London and then in France. Devastated when both her brother and her fiancé were killed at the front, she found herself at first "without confidence or security." Eventually, however, she came to realize that, contrary to what women had been brought up to believe, a man was not essential to personal fulfillment. Instead, she resumed her studies at Oxford after the war, where she developed a deep friendship with Winifred Holtby (1898–1935). Brittain and Holtby inspired each other and both eventually became noted writers.

A propaganda cartoon portraying the German execution of English nurse Edith Cavell.

Civilian Populations and Total War

Inevitably, society became regimented under the pressures of the war. Governments demanded complete loyalty and dedication from all citizens in order to wage total war. Civilians were subjected to military requirements, which took precedence over matters not essential to the war effort. Fundamental legal rights, such as freedom of the press and habeas corpus, were set aside. Generals wielded more authority than civilians in government deliberations. In Germany, General Ludendorff practically dictated domestic policy until 1918. Political leaders asked their populations for more and more sacrifices, and to justify the steadily mounting cost in lives and money, governments developed war aims that stressed lofty ideals such as democracy, justice, and permanent peace.

Domestic propaganda created the impression that class differences diminished as all social groups pulled together for the general good. Working-class women rolled bandages together with duchesses; businessmen and labor leaders served together on production committees; and in the trenches peasants died along with intellectuals and shopkeepers. Peasants comprised the

majority of all draftees, whereas officers came from the upper classes. Because lieutenants and captains were the first out of the trenches in assaults against the enemy, the casualty rate among social élites was disproportionately high. In most armies, lower-rank officers and drafted soldiers tended to work together in the face of common peril.

In the war of attrition, great stress was put on efforts to undermine enemy civilian resistance. Cities of no military significance were bombed by long-range artillery and Zeppelins, and blockades attempted to keep food, medicines, and other vital supplies from reaching the enemy. Turkey's control of the Dardanelles Straits severely restricted Russia's access to Allied supplies, and Britain's dominance of the sea was effective in cutting off Germany and Austria-Hungary from much maritime trade. France and Britain, on the other hand, had access to American and other overseas sources of food and matériel, even during the height of submarine warfare. Germany was the first to adopt a ration system, and most of the other belligerents followed suit. In the so-called "Turnip Winter" of 1916–1917, when frigid temperatures and the naval blockade created extreme food shortages, many Germans lived at the edge of starvation.

THE WORLD CONFLICT

The conflict widened steadily as more nations intervened and, alongside the main theater of operations in Europe, a peripheral war was fought in the Middle East, Africa, and the Pacific. In 1917, the balance of power among the belligerents finally shifted as the United States abandoned its neutrality and joined the Allied cause.

The Global Dimensions of War

The military outcome of the Great War was to be determined in Europe, but both sides were concerned about global strategic issues. Britain was especially interested in the Middle East because of the importance of the Suez Canal to its Indian realm, and tried to wrest control of the region from the Turks.

After their failure to seize Baghdad in November 1915, the British sought to foment a revolt against the Turks by openly encouraging Arab independence. They supported Hussein ibn-Ali (1856–1931), of the Holy City of Mecca, who declared himself ruler of an Arab kingdom embracing the region between the Red Sea and the Persian Gulf. Hussein raised an army in 1916 and declared a holy war against the Ottoman Empire. At the same time, however, the French and the British planned to divide the Middle East between themselves. The Sykes-Picot Agreement, named after British diplomat Mark Sykes and French diplomat Georges Picot, stipulated that Lebanon and Syria would come under French authority, and that Palestine and Iraq would fall within the British sphere. In 1917, the archeologist T. E. Lawrence (1888–1935), then a British officer, worked with Hussein's son, Prince Faisal (1885–1933), in organizing an Arab Army. Together, Hussein and "Lawrence of Arabia" succeeded in taking Jerusalem and Damascus. Despite Britain's pro-Arab stance, however, in November 1917 Foreign Secretary Arthur Balfour angered Arab leaders when he announced support for the Zionist goal of establishing a Jewish state in Palestine.

The British also occupied the German colonies of South-West Africa (Namibia) and Togoland (Togo). The Germans managed, however, to keep the Allies busy in German East Africa (Tanzania) until 1918, using local African recruits to wage a guerrilla campaign. In Asia, the British believed their interests were endangered by their Japanese allies, who immediately occupied the German islands in the north Pacific. To prevent further Japanese expansion, troops from New Zealand and Australia seized Samoa and New Guinea. In 1917 the Chinese government also joined the Allied cause, yet when Japan ousted the Germans from the port of Tsingtao, it refused to return the stronghold to China.

The United States
and the European War

Public opinion in the United States was divided over the war, but President Woodrow Wilson's (served 1913–1921) own sentiments leaned toward Britain, although publicly he argued for strict neutrality. In the end, it was Germany's reliance on the submarine that acted as the catalyst for American intervention.

International law proscribed attacking neutral ships not carrying war contraband. In 1915, however, each side attempted illegally to keep all goods from reaching the other, although only the British blockade proved to be effective. Germany's U-boat fleet was a powerful weapon in this campaign, but submarines sank enemy ships by underwater torpedo, not by surface battle, and could not lose the advantage of surprise in order to determine whether a vessel's cargo contained war matériel. As a result, unarmed merchant ships as well as citizens of neutral countries fell victim to U-boat attacks, which caused significant shipping losses.

The United States reacted sharply against the U-boat campaign, especially after more than a hundred Americans were among the almost 1200 passengers killed when the Germans sank the British passenger liner *Lusitania* in May 1915. The crisis caused a debate inside the German government, with Chancellor Bethmann-Hollweg arguing for a cessation of submarine warfare and Admiral von Tirpitz insisting that it was Germany's only chance for victory.

In September 1915, the kaiser limited submarine operations, but he was finally convinced that the military advantage of submarine warfare outweighed the danger of antagonizing American opinion. In late January 1917, Wilhelm therefore ordered unrestricted U-boat attacks to be resumed. During February, the U-boats destroyed 781,500 tons of Allied shipping.

In protest, President Wilson severed formal ties with Germany on February 3, 1917. Toward the end of that month, the British passed on to American authorities an intercepted coded telegram from a German Foreign Ministry official, Arthur Zimmermann (1864–1940), to the German minister in Mexico. The Zimmermann telegram proposed an alliance between Mexico and Germany in the event of American belligerency, with Mexico receiving Texas, New Mexico, and Arizona as its compensation. Wilson's outrage reached the breaking point in March 1917, when the Germans torpedoed two American ships. By the end of the month, an additional 500,000 tons of Allied shipping had been lost. On April 2, he asked for a declaration of war against Germany, which Congress passed overwhelmingly four days later.

General John J. Pershing (1860–1948), commanding the American Expeditionary Force (AEF), brought the first U.S. troops to France in July. The contribution of the United States to the Allied cause came in the form of industrial supplies as well as soldiers. American intervention also struck an important blow for morale at a critical moment. In March, Russia had been shaken by revolution; that October, Italy was almost overrun by the Central Powers during the disastrous rout of Caporetto, and lost a half-million soldiers in their efforts to halt the enemy at the Piave River; in November, the Bolshevik coup augured the eventual withdrawal of Russia from the war.

At the beginning of 1918, President Wilson declared the famous "Fourteen Points," which he believed would provide the basis for a permanent peace—hence, the slogan, "the war to end all wars." Wilson's goals included elimination of the arms race and secret diplomacy, adherence to the principle of self-determination for all peoples, and freedom of the seas. One legacy he left to the future would be the idea of a world organization, known later as the League of Nations, designed to preserve peace.

PEACE AND ITS CONSEQUENCES

While Wilson issued the Fourteen Points, Germany still planned for a decisive breakthrough on the battlefield. Teenagers were being called up as its manpower was depleted, and the supply of food and equipment

Map 1.5   The Peace Settlements

grew critically short. Moreover, on January 28, 400,000 Berlin workers stopped working to demand peace and democracy, and the strike spread to other industrial cities. On the other hand, Russia finally withdrew from the war in March 1918 after Germany and the Bolshevik regime concluded the Treaty of Brest-Litovsk (see Part VIII, Topic 2).

Germany Sues for Peace

The end of the fighting on the Eastern front allowed General Ludendorff to strengthen German forces in the West and to attempt a large offensive against the Allies. The last-ditch attack, initiated on March 21, succeeded at first in pushing the enemy back to the Marne. By June, however, the Allies, now reinforced by large numbers of American soldiers, broke the advance and shattered all hopes for a German victory. In mid-July, the Allies counterattacked.

In September 1918, General Ludendorff reluctantly told the Crown Council that German forces had

to go on the defensive, and by the end of the following month they were in retreat along most of the Western front.

A new, more liberal German government was formed in late September under Prince Max of Baden (served as chancellor October–November 1918), who then asked Wilson for armistice terms derived from the Fourteen Points. The American president, however, insisted that Kaiser Wilhelm abdicate before an armistice was concluded. During the weeks that followed, Germany's allies withdrew from the war and a full-scale mutiny among German sailors at Kiel sparked revolutions in Berlin and elsewhere. Still the kaiser vacillated, until on November 9, Prince Max forced the issue by publicly announcing the abdication. Wilhelm II left secretly the next day for the Netherlands, where he spent the rest of his days in exile. In Berlin, a republic was declared and Social Democratic leader Friedrich Ebert (1871–1925) took the reins of government (see Part VIII, Topic 2). The armistice agreement, concluded in a railway car at Compiègne, went into effect at 11 A.M. on November 11, 1918. The Great War was over.

The Politics of Peace Making

The armistice ended the fighting, but technically the great powers still remained at war until peace treaties were signed. The making of peace proved to be difficult because the price of war had been so high. Almost three dozen nations had fought in the Great War. Some 11 million people—soldiers and civilians—had been killed as a direct result of the fighting, and 20 million were wounded or disabled; countless others died of disease, starvation, and forced relocation. The monetary costs of the conflict forced Europe to reverse its former position as a capital exporter: henceforth, the United States was Europe's creditor. The economic transition to peace was made more difficult by the fact that widespread physical destruction had weakened Europe's capacity to produce food and industrial goods.

Wartime propaganda raised public expectations that both domestic governments and the peacemakers were unable to fulfill. National interests and broad Wilsonian principles clashed at the conference table, despite the fact that both sides had agreed to make peace on the basis of the Fourteen Points. Moreover, the generally conservative mood of the victorious nations stood in sharp contrast to the radical revolution unfolding in Russia.

The international conference called to make peace gathered in Paris in January 1919. It included delegates from some three dozen states as well as leaders hoping to gain recognition from the great powers, such as Prince Faisal and his Arab delegation. The immediate purpose of the Paris Peace Conference was, of course, to arrange peace treaties with the defeated Central Powers and their allies.

Not since the Congress of Vienna of 1814–1815 had so many heads of state and their ministers assembled in one place to discuss common problems. In a dramatic departure from America's isolationist past, Woodrow Wilson crossed the Atlantic to argue for the ideals he had publicly declared. His erstwhile colleagues were experienced and shrewd statesmen— French Premier Georges Clemenceau (1841–1929), British Prime Minister David Lloyd George (1863–1945), and Italian Prime Minister Vittorio E. Orlando (1860–1952). Each leader was accompanied by a staff of advisers and experts in matters ranging from economics and international law to linguistics and cartography.

Despite the rhetoric of democracy that marked Allied propaganda, decision making at the Paris Peace Conference operated according to traditional

The Big Four at the Paris Peace Conference—V. E. Orlando, Lloyd George, Georges Clemenceau, and Woodrow Wilson.

principles of power politics. An informal executive group of the "Big Five"—the United States, Britain, France, Italy, and Japan—was supposed to settle basic positions, but in reality both Italy and Japan were excluded from the inner core of the "Big Three," consisting of Clemenceau, Lloyd George, and Wilson. Their ideological antipathy to Communism led them to exclude the new Bolshevik regime in Russia from the conference, and public opinion among their political constituencies at home demanded that the Germans not be accorded equal status with the other participants. The new German republican government was invited, therefore, merely to send observers. Peace would be dictated to the defeated enemy, not negotiated.

The Peace Treaties and the League of Nations

Discussions surrounding the German question divided the Allies from the outset, and the final settlement with Germany—the Treaty of Versailles—represented an unhappy compromise. The French, painfully aware of the experiences of both 1870 and 1914, wanted to carve an independent state out of German territory in the Rhineland that would protect France's eastern border against attack. Clemenceau and Wilson clashed head-on over this issue, the American president insisting that the French proposal ran counter to the spirit of self-determination. They finally reached a compromise, one that the French accepted reluctantly and that proved in the long run to be unworkable. In return for an American commitment to sign a military alliance with France, Clemenceau agreed that Germany would be forbidden to keep a military force in the Rhineland and in an area 50 kilometers east of the Rhine River.

The Allies would occupy this "demilitarized" region for a period of 15 years. The coal mines and factories of the Rhineland's Saar district formed part of the arrangement, for Britain and France wanted to use these economic resources to offset the huge debt they had incurred to the United States. The Allies agreed that during their occupation, the newly founded League of Nations would administer the Saarland in order to ensure the delivery of fixed amounts of goods and raw materials to them.

Although Germany did not permanently lose the Rhineland, it did lose other territories. In the west, France received the provinces of Alsace and part of Lorraine, which Germany had taken from it in 1871, and Belgium obtained several strategic towns and fortresses. In eastern Europe, where the Allies created a series of new independent states, Germany lost additional territory: Poland received portions of East Prussia and Upper Silesia, and the port city of Danzig (now Gdansk, Poland) was made a free city under League of Nations authority. From territory formerly in the Austro-Hungarian empire, Czechoslovakia was given the German-speaking area of Bohemia known as the Sudetenland. Because the new state of Austria consisted chiefly of the German-speaking portion of the old Hapsburg empire, there was considerable sentiment both in Germany and Austria for a union (known in German as *Anschluss*) between the two countries. In November, the provisional Austrian assembly declared itself to be a part of Germany, but the Allies expressly prohibited *Anschluss*.

These territorial losses clearly implied that the Allies held Germany responsible for the war, as did the economic provisions of the settlement, which required Germany to pay reparations for costs inflicted on Allied

The signing of the Treaty of Versailles.

civilians. The concept of responsibility was directly incorporated into the peace treaty with Germany in the form of Article 231. This "war guilt" clause made Germany liable for all financial losses suffered by the Allies "as a consequence of the war imposed upon them by the aggression of Germany and her allies." Reparations were eventually set at 35 billion dollars.

The Versailles Treaty also imposed rigid military restrictions on Germany. The army was limited to 100,000 volunteer officers and soldiers, and the General Staff and all officer-training schools were eliminated. The navy was permitted a few ships under 10,000 tons and no submarines. Offensive weapons, such as tanks, long-range artillery, military airplanes, and chemical weapons, were similarly forbidden.

The Treaty of Versailles was both unconventional and unusually harsh. Contrary to any precedent in international affairs, the Allies charged Kaiser Wilhelm with war crimes and demanded a trial, although the Dutch government granted him political asylum. Then, too, the unstated purpose of the peace settlement was clearly to destroy Germany's status as a first-rank world power, but the statesmen at Paris failed to consider the human suffering it would cause or its long-range political impact. In 1919 one prominent British expert at the conference, John Maynard Keynes (1883–1946), denounced the Versailles Treaty in a book entitled *The Economic Consequences of the Peace*. Keynes warned that the economic provisions of the treaty would make Germany unstable and endanger the peace, arguing that the reparations payments were unreasonable because of the loss of coal and iron deposits as well as other vital assets that Germany was forced to sustain (on Keynesian economic theory see Part VIII, Topic 3).

The text of the Versailles Treaty was made known just as the infant German republic was struggling to establish itself against serious odds. When the Germans balked at the terms, the Allies said they would continue to fight. On June 28, 1919, two German political leaders, Hermann Muller of the Majority Socialists and Johannes Bell of the Center party, signed the document in the Hall of Mirrors of the Versailles Palace.

The Paris Peace Conference completely recast Eastern Europe, including the Balkan region where the Great War had begun. The Dual Monarchy was dismantled in conformity with the notion of self-determination (see Part VIII, Topic 5). In addition to Poland, created from former German, Austro-Hungarian, and Russian territory, Austria and Hungary—both considerably reduced in size—became separate states, as did Czechoslovakia. The new nation of Yugoslavia was created out of the former states of Serbia and Montenegro and the provinces of Bosnia, Herzegovina, Slovenia, and Croatia. Greece was enlarged at the expense of Bulgaria and Turkey, the latter retaining a small area around Istanbul and Asia Minor itself. Although Turkey kept control of the Dardanelles, they were henceforth open to the peacetime commerce of all nations.

When Woodrow Wilson first suggested the idea for a League of Nations, the other Allied statesmen had not given it an enthusiastic reception. Wilson persisted, however, and the League's charter (known as the Covenant) was included as an integral part of the individual treaties. The League sought to preserve peace through collective security, largely by providing a forum for discussion and arbitration. The League had limited authority in administering international agreements, as in the case of the free city of Danzig and the Saarland. Through the mandate system, it also supervised the administration of Germany's former colonies by France and Britain, which were to prepare the mandates for independence.

Serious weaknesses doomed the League from the start. It could fight aggression only with the moral force of its decisions, for it could not enforce even its economic sanctions against sovereign nations. Germany and Russia were not invited to join the international body, and despite Wilson's key role in its conception, the U.S. Congress rejected the Treaty of Versailles and membership in the League.

The Great War vastly changed the nature and focus of international power. Europe's economy never fully recovered from the physical destruction to farmland and factories, the dislocation of trade, and the draining of its resources. Nor did the European psyche, deeply wounded by the trauma of a war of attrition, regain its equilibrium. In politics, the impact of the war was equally devastating. Even before peace was restored, three historic empires—Russia, Austria-Hungary, and Germany—had collapsed. Within a few years, the world's first socialist government had been established by Lenin in Russia and the first fascist state in Italy by Mussolini. Britain and France, once the dominant Western powers, never regained their former positions of world influence, for their hold on their imperial domains steadily weakened and the United States began to emerge as the arbiter of world affairs. The Great War was truly the great divide in European history.

Questions for Further Study

1. Is the question of "responsibility" for the war a useful one for historians?

2. How would you describe the causes of the war?

3. In what ways was the fighting in World War I different from that of previous wars?

4. How did the war affect social conditions behind the lines?

5. Was the Paris Peace Conference a success or a failure?

Suggestions for Further Reading

Evans, R. J. W., and H. P. von Strandmann, eds. *The Coming of the First World War*. New York, 1989.

Fussell, Paul. *The Great War and Modern Memory*. New York, 1975.

Higgonet, Margaret R., J. Jenson, S. Michel, and M. C. Weitz, eds. *Behind the Lines: Gender and the Two World Wars*. New Haven, CT, 1987.

Hynes, Samuel. *A War Imagined: The First World War and English Culture*. New York, 1991.

Joll, James. *The Origins of the First World War*. London, 1984.

Kocka, Jurgen. *Facing Total War: German Society, 1914–1918*. Cambridge, MA, 1984.

Leed, Eric J. *No Man's Land: Combat and Identity in World War I*. New York, 1979.

Schmitt, Bernadotte E., and H. C. Vederler. *The World in the Crucible, 1914–1919*. New York, 1984.

Travers, Tim. *The Killing Ground: The British Army, the Western Front, and the Emergence of Modern Warfare, 1900–1918*. Boston, 1978.

Williams, John. *The Other Battleground: The Home Fronts*. Chicago, 1972.

Winter, J. M., and R. M. Wall. *The Upheaval of War: Family, Work, and Welfare in Europe, 1914–1918*. New York, 1988.

Wohl, Robert. *The Generation of 1914*. Cambridge, MA, 1979.

VIII

Topic 2

RADICAL EXTREMES: THE RUSSIAN REVOLUTION AND THE RISE OF FASCISM

etween 1917 and 1919, Europe experienced a series of events that would shape the course of the 20th century. To the east, imperial Russia was struck by two successive revolutionary upheavals in the spring and fall of 1917 that toppled the centuries-old tsarist autocracy and set in its place the first self-proclaimed socialist state in history. Two years later, in central and southern Europe, events took place that would eventually bear no less far-reaching significance: Italy gave birth to Europe's first Fascist movement, while Germany followed six months later with the founding of the Nazi party.

Russia had been ill-prepared to fight the Great War. After three years of social and economic strain that brought the Russian war effort near to collapse, riots and demonstrations at home forced Tsar Nicholas II to abdicate in March. A provisional government led by liberals took power, first under Prince Georgi Lvov and then under the moderate Alexander Kerensky. Their refusal to take Russia out of the war proved their undoing. In November, V. I. Lenin led his radical Marxists, known as Bolsheviks, in a successful coup against the provisional government.

Lenin proclaimed the founding of the Communist state, eventually called the Union of Soviet Socialist Republics (U.S.S.R.). Over the next three years, after withdrawing Russia from the war, the Bolsheviks struggled to secure their power through a bloody civil war with political opponents and a military campaign against foreign intervention. Upon Lenin's death in 1924, a power struggle ended with the victory of Joseph Stalin, who ruled the Soviet Union as a dictator for 25 years.

In Italy in March 1919, a former socialist and war veteran named Benito Mussolini, once hailed as "Italy's Lenin," created a radical movement of another kind, known as Fascism. Its program combined left-wing and right-wing elements, and it took advantage of the postwar atmosphere of nationalist frustration and the fear of Bolshevik revolution that pervaded Italian political life. Mussolini came to power in 1922 on a wave of systematic violence carried out by his paramilitary "Black Shirt" squads. Three years later, after a major political crisis, Mussolini proclaimed a dictatorship.

In Germany, the fascist seizure of power took longer. There, in September 1919, Adolf Hitler, would-be artist and himself a war veteran, joined and soon dominated the National Socialist German Workers' party. The Nazis, as its members came to be called, capitalized on the political weakness of the new

German state, known as the Weimar Republic, as well as on the economic and social dislocation following Germany's defeat in World War I.

Hitler's propaganda stressed a combination of extreme nationalism, working-class rhetoric, and middle-class values, but the core of his new ideology was a rabid racism that took the form of virulent anti-Semitism. Hitler, too, created a paramilitary organization of "Brown Shirts," which he used against his political enemies. After a failed coup in 1923, it took another decade of political maneuvering, violence, and propaganda, combined with the disaster of the Great Depression, before Hitler came to power in 1933.

REVOLUTION, LEFT AND RIGHT

The upheaval in Russia in 1917 was a revolution on the extreme left, inspired by the theories of Karl Marx and Lenin's Bolshevik political strategies. The fascist revolutions in Italy and Germany began with a blend of socialist and nationalist principles, but by the 1920s, fascism became symbolic of extreme right-wing political values.

Both Bolshevism and fascism entailed revolutionary change. The existing governments fell in a context of social upheaval and civil war. In the aftermath of the revolutionary seizure of power in the countries involved, new political and economic structures were created. Lenin, Mussolini, and Hitler were revolutionary leaders who came from segments of society with hitherto little influence, and who rose to power on a wave of mass support. Each, whether of the left or the right, was a masterful manipulator of public opinion who sought to evoke blind obedience and ideological fervor from his followers. These men represented a new kind of political power, claiming authority from popular will or historical inevitability and maintaining it in part by modern technology and new systems of mass communications. The political movements they brought to power established a new form of government known as totalitarianism. It was characterized by the use of terror and repression to stamp out political opposition and minorities, backed up by educational programs and massive propaganda campaigns designed to impose conformity of thought.

Although inspired by opposite political ideologies, both left-wing and right-wing revolutionaries wanted to create economic systems dominated by state planning and control. Under the Bolsheviks, private property rights were abolished and the state dictated production levels in accordance with socialist principles. In the fascist regimes of Italy and Germany, however, capitalism and private property continued to

exist, although they were subject to government regulation.

Between the two world wars, European political life was dominated in large part by the struggle between the ideologies of communism and fascism. Supporters of both camps battled one another in bloody confrontations while simultaneously threatening estab-

Significant Dates

The Russian Revolution

March 8, 1917	Women's march in Petrograd
March 10, 1917	General Strike
March 12, 1917	Provisional government
March 15, 1917	Nicholas II abdicates
March 1917	Petrograd Soviet formed
April 20, 1917	Lenin's "April Theses"
May 16, 1917	Kerensky heads provisional government
July 1917	Coup against provisional government fails
November 6–7, 1917	Bolshevik coup
January 1918	Lenin closes Constituent Assembly and establishes dictatorship
March 15, 1918	Treaty of Brest-Litovsk
1918–1922	Russian civil war
March 1921	New Economic Policy introduced
December 1922	Union of Soviet Socialist Republics established
1924	Lenin dies
1929	Trotsky exiled

lished governments almost everywhere in Europe. By the early 1930s, traditional liberal democratic notions were under siege from both right and left.

THE MARCH REVOLUTION AND THE BOLSHEVIK SEIZURE OF POWER

The Russian Revolution of 1917 consisted of two separate upheavals—the first in March, the second in November—which occurred against the background of the enormous strains caused by World War I. The first stage saw the overthrow of the centuries-old monarchy of the tsars, and the establishment of a provisional government. In November, the Bolsheviks staged a coup d'état and seized power in their own right, laying the basis for a communist state. In their determination to demonstrate the irreversible break with the past, Bolshevik leaders ordered the execution of Tsar Nicholas II and his family.

The Crisis of Tsarist Russia

The first serious threat to the autocratic rule of the tsars had come in 1905, when working-class protestors managed to extract limited political concessions from Nicholas (see Part VII, Topic 16). The tsar had permitted the formation of the Duma, or parliament, and promised a measure of individual freedom. Two years

later, however, the electoral law had been changed and the tsar resumed autocratic rule. The result was growing alienation among wider segments of Russian society.

The problems of the imperial government were compounded by the character and personality of the tsar and his wife, Alexandra (1872–1918). Nicholas lacked sufficient strength of will or keenness of intellect to be an effective ruler. He believed in absolutism and divine guidance, but was too easily influenced by those around him. Nor was Nicholas comfortable with change. The Tsarina Alexandra, a German princess by birth, was even more of an absolutist than her husband, and she counseled Nicholas not to give in to pressures for reform. Deeply religious, to the point of superstition, Alexandra's views were reinforced by Gregori Yefimovich Rasputin (1871?–1916), a bizarre holy man of peasant origins. As a young man he gained such an unsavory reputation that he was given the nickname of "Rasputin," meaning a debauchee. When he arrived in St. Petersburg in 1905, he came to the attention of the tsarina for his mystical powers and his supposed ability to improve the hemophiliac condition of her young son. Soon he exerted enormous influence over the royal family and in political affairs. Rumors of corruption and sexual license within the court helped to erode public confidence in the imperial government.

Although Nicholas had no military experience, he assumed personal charge of Russia's armies in 1915. He also changed the name of the capital from its German form, St. Petersburg, to the Russian Petrograd, so as to stress Russian nationalism. These efforts had

The Bolsheviks storm the Winter Palace in Petrograd (formerly St. Petersburg), November 6, 1917.

little impact, for when military defeats took place he then had to bear personal responsibility for them. Russian soldiers lacked food and equipment, and were often sent into the field without even a rifle. With each military defeat, the troops grew more discontented.

The Tsarina Alexandra actually ran the day-to-day operations of the government while her husband was at the front. Food shortages and the lack of basic necessities aroused civilian restlessness in the cities, and advisers and court officials urged reforms in order to bolster morale. But at Rasputin's insistence, Alexandra refused any concessions and temporarily closed the Duma (legislative assembly). In a desperate effort to end his pernicious control of government policy, three noblemen killed Rasputin in December 1916. His death was as strange as his life. At a private party arranged for the purpose, he was fed a cake containing an enormous amount of poison, but he remained alive; in the end, the assassins had finally to shoot him and fling his body into a river. When the corpse was recovered, the authorities determined that he had died of drowning.

Such desperate actions came too late to prevent the revolution. When the Duma reopened, the conservative deputies joined the radicals in calling for the end of the monarchy.

The First Revolution

By 1917, some 7 million soldiers were dead, wounded, or missing. In early March, workers joined housewives in protests against the lack of food. When the socialists staged a massive Woman's Day demonstration, thousands of workers moved into the city avenues and squares. Nicholas demanded that the demonstrations be crushed, and on March 11 soldiers fired at the demonstrators. Soon, however, the troops went over to the side of the rioters. As the tsar became the target of popular outrage, the Duma formed a provisional government led by Prince Georgi Lvov (1861–1925). Nicholas was persuaded to abdicate when it became clear that the army's loyalty could not be guaranteed.

Lvov announced plans to hold elections for a constituent assembly and for the introduction of universal suffrage for males, and enacted basic civil liberties. To gain popular support, the provisional government promised to distribute land to the peasants, mandated an eight-hour day for workers, freed the tsar's political prisoners, and proclaimed that Jews would no longer be persecuted.

Although the provisional government gained the support of a wide stratum of Russians, its leadership was undermined by the Soviet (Council) of Workers' and Soldiers' Deputies, a radical organization consisting of worker representatives. The Petrograd Soviet quickly came to direct the activities of hundreds of similar councils that were created in industrial factories, the armed forces, and in rural villages across Russia.

The Soviets were formed mainly by socialists, who were divided amongst themselves, however, into Social Revolutionaries and members of the Marxist-inspired Social Democratic Workers party. The Social Revolutionaries were agrarian radicals who believed that Russian society could best be changed by the peasants through established village councils. Members of the Social Democratic Workers party had split into two groups, the Mensheviks and the Bolsheviks. *Menshevik* means "minority" and *Bolshevik* "majority." The terms had nothing to do, however, with their size but rather were derived from a vote that had been taken in 1903 on matters of party organization, in which the Mensheviks had gotten a minority of the vote. Both shared an adherence to Marxist principles, but they disagreed over fundamental questions of strategy. The reformist Mensheviks wanted to create a mass-based party in the way that socialists had done in Western Europe. The Mensheviks expected to bring about a socialist society by peaceful reform, but not until industrial capitalism had spread more fully and had created a large urban working class.

The Bolsheviks disagreed with both principles. Their leader, Vladimir Ilyich Lenin (born Vladimir Ilyich Ulianov, 1870–1924), fought against the reformist ideas of the Mensheviks. He believed that such peaceful tactics were not possible under tsarist absolutism and insisted that revolutionary violence alone could achieve socialism. Lenin also disagreed with Marx's notion that revolution was not feasible in an agrarian society like Russia's that had only an infant industrial working class. Moreover, Lenin saw the party not as a mass movement but as a small élite of professional revolutionaries. Such a vanguard would not only provide the party with discipline and leadership, but would be able to seize power when circumstances were favorable. Although the Soviets lacked a uniform ideological position, they competed with the provisional government by backing the demands of the urban workers and rural peasants. The Duma, on the other hand, which supported the government, was dominated by liberal elements who favored a constitutional monarchy. Because the Bolsheviks were not in the government, they could distance themselves from the Lvov regime.

The provisional government and the Duma stubbornly refused to make a separate peace with the Germans, declaring it their duty to fight alongside the Allies. In May, after the government announced once again its determination to pursue the war effort, popular pressure persuaded some members of the government to resign. This crisis was compounded by the government's inability to meet the demands of the workers or the peasants' cry for land.

The Bolshevik Seizure of Power

Under the skillful leadership of Lenin, the Bolsheviks took full advantage of the government's failure to secure popular support. Despite his unassuming appearance, Lenin had an immense appeal, not only to party militants but to workers. Possessed of a brilliant mind, he had become an opponent of the tsarist regime at the age of 17, when his brother was executed for attempting to kill Tsar Alexander III. He later became a militant in the Social Democratic Workers party and spent years in prison and in Siberian exile because of his antigovernment activism. In 1900 he escaped to Western Europe, from where he directed the Bolshevik faction of the party and led the split with the Mensheviks over tactics for achieving a socialist state.

Lenin was in Switzerland at the time of the March revolution, but the Germans, hoping that the Bolsheviks would disrupt the Russian war effort, allowed him to cross their country by railway to reach Russia. Not until April did Lenin arrive in Petrograd, but he immediately went on the offensive. Instead of supporting the provisional government, he ordered his fellow Bolsheviks to plan for another revolution. The seizure of power in Russia, he said, would be the first step toward upheaval in the industrialized societies of Western Europe.

The collapse of the government's offensive against the Central Powers in July 1917 sparked a large-scale military insurrection in Petrograd. Lvov, who quelled the mutiny, accused the Bolsheviks of treachery and arrested some of their leaders. Lenin escaped in disguise to Finland. Yet the uprising suggested the need for the provisional government to broaden its support. Alexander Kerensky (1881–1970), a moderate Social Revolutionary, therefore became head of government. Like Lvov, however, Kerensky quickly lost credibility by refusing to make immediate peace with the Germans. In September, Kerensky followed this mistake with another—permitting a reactionary officer, Lavr Kornilov, to strike at the Soviets. Kerensky panicked, however, when he thought that Kornilov intended to seize the government and he provided arms for the Soviet's Red Guards. Kornilov's attempt was forestalled.

By now, Kerensky's ability to govern rested on the Soviets, which Lenin sought to take over. Bolshevik support grew rapidly as he launched a campaign for "peace, land, and bread" that contrasted sharply with the government's inability to achieve any of the three. Lenin then demanded "all power to the Soviets." When the Bolsheviks won control of the Soviets of both Petrograd and Moscow, Lenin made his way back to Russia in October.

Lenin prepared to take power with the help of Leon Trotsky (real name Lev Bronstein, 1879–1940), whose keen mind and organizational genius made him the mastermind of the Bolshevik victory. Trotsky, who headed the Petrograd Soviet, first gained crucial advantage by securing appointment as the council's military commander of the capital. He then persuaded government soldiers to join with the Soviets. Together, on the night of November 6, Trotsky's forces quickly took control of the railroads, power stations, telephone building, bridges, and important government departments. At the same time, Soviet sailors moved the ship *Aurora* along the Neva River and trained its guns on the Winter Palace, Kerensky's headquarters. Kerensky fled. While these events transpired, the Bolsheviks announced that the Soviets had taken power and had made Lenin the new head of government. In one sudden blow, the Bolsheviks had won.

THE SOVIET UNION IN THE MAKING

A stable Bolshevik government would not emerge for more than three years, during which the country was racked by civil war, famine, and foreign invasion.

The Leninist Dictatorship

The first goal of Lenin's regime was to satisfy the people's demands for an end to war and hunger. Lenin nationalized the land, and the Soviets were to convert the large estates into collective farms. In fact, however, many peasants had already taken plots of land and were allowed to keep them. These measures did not, however, address the burning problem of hunger, since the small landowners refused to send their crops to the cities. The civil war, combined with successive harvest failures, exacerbated the problem and contributed to mass starvation.

Lenin also found the restoration of peace difficult. Germany demanded severe terms from the Soviets, and some Bolsheviks even suggested continuing the war as a revolutionary struggle against the West. But Lenin was determined to make peace. The Treaty of Brest-Litovsk, negotiated by Trotsky and concluded on March 15, 1918, gave to Germany all the land it had conquered from Russia during the war, including the Baltic regions of Finland, Estonia, Latvia, and Lithuania, as well as the Ukraine and eastern Poland. Despite the heavy price, the return of peace was greeted with deep satisfaction by millions of Russians.

Russia had no experience with democracy, either on the national level or among the local peasant councils. Only the Soviets practiced a form of democracy,

Map 2.1 Russia, 1918–1919

and in factories and army units workers and soldiers elected officials and exercised some authority. The lack of democratic tradition conformed to Lenin's purposes, for his idea of a centralized, highly disciplined party would prevail in the aftermath of the November revolution. The Bolsheviks never claimed to admire Western-style democracy. Lenin's dictatorial views were made clear when elections for a constituent assembly were held in November: the Social Revolutionaries won nearly twice as many delegates as the Bolsheviks, and Lenin closed the assembly down after only one meeting. In its place he created a "dictatorship of the proletariat." The Communist party—the new name assumed by the Bolsheviks—now ruled Russia.

The Bolsheviks began to put their political and economic policies into practice in 1918. The capital of the country was moved from Petrograd to Moscow, deep in the interior. There, a centralized state bureaucracy controlled by the Communist party was established. All peasants were now forced to surrender their crops to urban markets. When it was clear that the factory committees were failing to meet the government's demand for higher industrial production, party trade unions replaced the worker committees. Every branch of industry was nationalized and placed under centralized state control. Dozens of state trusts were created within several years, and each was placed under the authority of a Supreme Council of National Economy that coordinated economic planning and production.

The Civil War

Lenin argued that these measures—he called them "war communism"—were needed because the new Communist government had to fight for its existence against foreign and internal opponents. Reactionaries, moderates, and Social Revolutionaries formed legions known as the "White Army" to bring down the regime. Then, too, a host of ethnic minorities and nationalities sought independence from Russia. In 1918, some 100,000 soldiers from the United States, France, Great Britain, Japan, and other nations invaded Russia in an effort to topple the Communists from power. Finally, peasants launched a counterrevolutionary war against the Red Army that was confiscating their crops.

The Treaty of Brest-Litovsk hurt the Allied military position, for the Germans were now able to move their troops from the Eastern to the Western front. The German Army pierced Allied lines and advanced against Paris. Although the Germans were turned back, Allied governments worried that Communist revolution might affect their own war-torn societies. On July 16, 1918, after the British and French sent some 20,000 troops to Archangel and Murmansk on the Arctic Sea, the Bolsheviks killed the imperial family lest the White Army or the Czechs try to rescue them.

The United States intervened ostensibly in response to the plight of thousands of Czech prisoners of war in Siberia who broke out of their prison camps and seized the railroad in order to get home, where they hoped to fight for Czech independence. To support the Czechs, the United States agreed to a combined landing of American and Japanese soldiers at Vladivostok, on the Pacific coast. That winter British troops captured the railroads between the Caspian and the Black seas, and a French-Greek operation seized Odessa.

After the armistice was concluded in November, Allied troops stayed in Russia. Yet Lenin's immense prestige, together with the Communist party's internal discipline, kept the Red Army intact, while the White Army was deeply divided by ideological differences. The Bolsheviks dominated the center of Russia and fought along interior lines, while the enemy forces were stretched out along an immense border.

Trotsky, who had been the architect of the Bolshevik coup in 1917, now directed the government's military operations with masterful efficiency. He raised, equipped, and trained the Red Army, traveling incessantly across the huge theater of operations in a railroad headquarters. Special political commissars attached to each army unit were responsible for soldier morale.

By late 1920, the Red Army victory was so complete that the Allies withdrew their forces from Russia. The Bolsheviks succeeded in recovering much of the territory they had lost to the Germans. The Soviet state now began to take shape. Some ethnic minorities and border nationalities had achieved a measure of self-determination during the civil war, but the Soviets now reestablished command of Russian Armenia, Azerbaijan, and Georgia. In December 1922, Lenin created a centralized Russian-dominated federal system of "autonomous" states united into the Union of Soviet Socialist Republics.

The New Economic Policy

The civil war, together with disease and starvation, killed millions of Russians. Farms and urban centers had been destroyed and the transportation network was in shambles. Engineers, doctors, and other professionals were desperately needed, and the shortage of raw materials was critical. Industrial production fell to less than a fifth of its pre-1914 level. Crop failures and hoarding contributed to persistent starvation. The Bolsheviks, who now had responsibility for government policies, lost more popular backing.

In the wake of worker and peasant unrest, a military uprising at Kronstadt broke out in March 1921. Lenin moved to regain control of the situation. He introduced a "New Economic Policy" (NEP), which represented a compromise with socialist theory. The NEP allowed a measure of private ownership in retail shops and small industries. In the countryside, it stopped crop confiscation and permitted peasants to sell their goods competitively. Communists debated the NEP hotly, for it created a new category of middle-class peasants

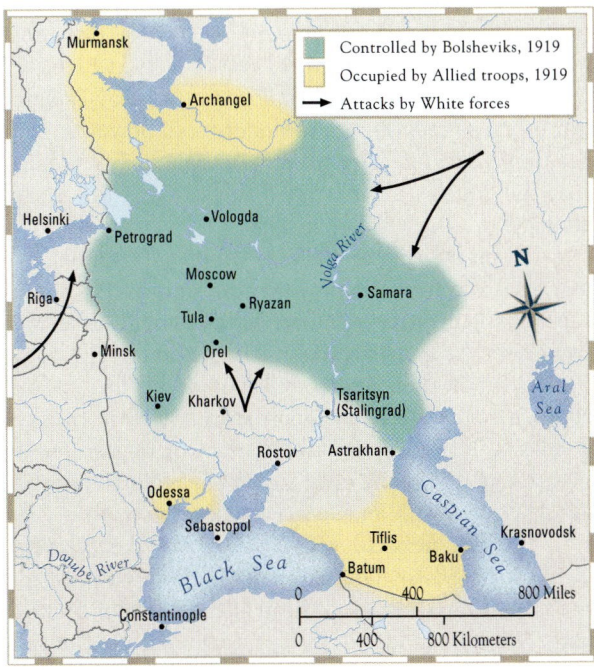

Map 2.2 The Russian Civil War

Lenin (left) and Stalin: Stalin had his own image added to this photograph of Lenin to show how closely they had worked together.

known as *kulaks* ("big peasants"), in contradiction to the socialist ideal of a society with no class distinctions. Viewed as a temporary expedient, the NEP did not end state ownership and management of banking, large industries, and transportation. The program had limited success, and only by 1928 did industry and farming return to prewar production levels.

The Soviet constitution provided for an All-Union Congress of Soviets, a representative body that in theory wielded supreme authority. The Congress elected a Council of People's Commissars, an Executive Committee, and a Presidium that presided when the Congress was not in session. In 1936 the name of the Congress was changed to the Supreme Soviet, and that of the People's Commissars was altered in 1946 to the Council of Ministers. It was the party, however, that actually governed the Soviet Union. The party's Central Committee, with some 50 members, gathered only occasionally and chose a ten-member Politburo. Executive power rested in a Secretariat of from one to three members, selected by the Politburo.

The Rise of Stalin

Lenin had two strokes in 1922 that prevented him from exercising leadership on a regular basis. Many thought that Trotsky, his closest collaborator, would be his successor, but Trotsky's ambitions led important party officials to oppose him. Late that year the party leaders created a *troika*—a three-person executive—that included the general secretary of the party, Joseph Stalin (real name Joseph Djugashvili, 1879–1953).

While most of the Old Bolsheviks—those who had led the 1917 Revolution—were from the middle class, Stalin was a man of the people, born in the region of Georgia. Stalin's father had been a shoemaker and his grandfather a serf. He became a Bolshevik when he was about 20, when he adopted the underground name of Stalin ("man of steel"). Like Lenin, he spent years in prison and in Siberia, but Stalin never lived abroad. As a result, he was more provincial in outlook and lacked perspective. His thirst for power was limitless, and he was shrewd and ruthless. He used his position as general secretary of the party to create a cadre of bureaucrats who owed allegiance to him.

In December 1922, after his second stroke, Lenin began to think about his successor, but was anxious about Stalin just as others were becoming concerned about Trotsky. He dictated to his wife and confidant, Nadezhda Krupskaya (1869–1939), a political testament in which he analyzed the strengths and weaknesses of Stalin and Trotsky as possible successors. He was uncertain as to whether Stalin was capable of exercising power prudently and when he learned that Stalin had used brutal methods in subduing the anticommunist opposition in Georgia, Lenin added a codicil to his testament rejecting Stalin and advising his comrades to select another leader.

After Lenin's death in 1924, Krupskaya tried unsuccessfully to have his testament and the codicil read to a party congress. Instead, Stalin presented to the congress his theory of "Socialism in One Country." He wanted the Soviet Union to build an industrial economy that would preserve socialism inside the country and eschew the export of revolution elsewhere. Trotsky countered Stalin's position with the more orthodox Marxist idea of "Permanent Revolution," in which the Soviets would struggle continuously to destroy capitalism in every country. Stalin understood, however, that the Russian people were tired of struggle and crisis, and that the country did not have the strength for armed conflict with the Western powers.

In his power struggle with Trotsky, Stalin outmaneuvered the hero of the civil war, and in 1925 won the backing of party members in removing him as war commissar. In 1929, Trotsky was forced into exile. One by one, Stalin then disposed of the Old Bolsheviks, including those who had supported him against Trotsky. For years Trotsky stood as a symbol of opposition to Stalin's brutal regime, until in 1940 a Stalinist assassin murdered him with an axe in Mexico City.

For the next 20 years, Stalin was the absolute ruler of the Soviet Union, wielding more power than the tsars. Krupskaya lived through the terror of Stalin's purges and held a position on the party's Central Committee until her death in 1939, but the fact that Lenin had rejected Stalin remained secret. Under

Stalin, Lenin's goal of creating a workers' democracy disappeared, replaced by a program of forced modernization aimed at making Russia a world power. For that goal, the Russian people paid a heavy price.

"MUTILATED VICTORY": ITALY FROM WAR TO FASCISM

Italy entered World War I a year later than the other European powers. From the summer of 1914 to May 1915—the period known as the "interventionist crisis"—the country remained neutral while negotiating with both sides the highest price for its support. By the Treaty of London, which promised her extensive territorial gains in the event of an Allied victory, Italy joined the war in 1915 alongside Britain, France, and Russia (see Part VIII, Topic 1).

At war's end, however, Italy found itself in a difficult position. Politicians and intellectuals had agonized over the question of intervention. Millions of men, mainly peasants, had been drafted, and many of them

Significant Dates

The Rise of Fascism

1883–1945	Life of Benito Mussolini
1902–1904	Mussolini in Switzerland
1912	Mussolini becomes editor of *Avanti!*
November–August 1914	Mussolini breaks with PSI; founds *Popolo d'Italia*
April–May 1915	Pact of London; Italy's entrance into war
1916	Mussolini serves at front and is wounded
November 1918	Armistice
March 1919	*Fascio di Combattimento* formed
September 1919	D'Annunzio invades Fiume
1920–1922	Fascist violence
October 29, 1922	Mussolini becomes prime minister
1924	Fascist electoral victory; Matteotti crisis
1924–1926	Fascist dictatorship created

had been killed or wounded. The fighting had drained the national treasury, and the government had made generous promises to the lower classes in order to maintain morale. By late 1919, inflation had struck, and angry veterans wanted jobs at a time when some 2 million Italians were out of work.

At the Paris Peace Conference, the Italians were denied most of the territory that had been promised them—the south Tyrol and the Trentino, the Istrian peninsula and the city of Trieste, the Dodecanese Islands, and the entire Dalmatian coast. Instead, Dalmatia was given to the new nation of Yugoslavia. When Italy demanded the port of Fiume (now Rijeka) as compensation, the Allies refused. This blow to Italian national prestige was especially hard for the veterans. Irate nationalists fanned the flames of patriotism, blaming government for having accepted a "mutilated victory."

Mussolini the Revolutionary

One of the most outspoken critics of the government was Benito Mussolini (1883–1945), who had become an ardent interventionist during the war. Mussolini was a native of the Romagna region in northeastern Italy, where his father had been a blacksmith and a socialist agitator. Prone to violence even as a child, he had been expelled from several schools before becoming a schoolteacher. By 1901, he too had joined the Socialist party. He spent the years 1902–1904 in Switzerland as a draft dodger, and it was there that he completed his political education. Neutral Switzerland was refuge for hundreds of revolutionary exiles from all over Europe, especially Russian radicals such as Lenin who had escaped the tsar's police. There Mussolini helped organize workers and gave speeches on behalf of the Italian Socialist party (PSI).

Back in Italy again in 1904, Mussolini began to make a name for himself among revolutionary socialists. He proved to be a powerful orator and writer. When Italy and Turkey fought over Libya in 1911–1912 (see Part VII, Topic 16), he joined other pacifist socialists in condemning imperialism, spending several months in prison for his antiwar activities. In 1912 he took part in a revolutionary socialist coup against the reformist leaders of the PSI, and became editor of *Avanti!*, the official Socialist party newspaper.

During the interventionist crisis, Mussolini did an about-face. Arguing that the war would spark revolution, he pressed for Italian intervention on the Allied side, for which the PSI expelled him. He then began publishing an interventionist newspaper, *Il Popolo d'Italia*, and volunteered for military service, serving at the front and being promoted to sergeant. In 1916 he was wounded and mustered out of the army, returning to politics. During the last years of the war, Mussolini's

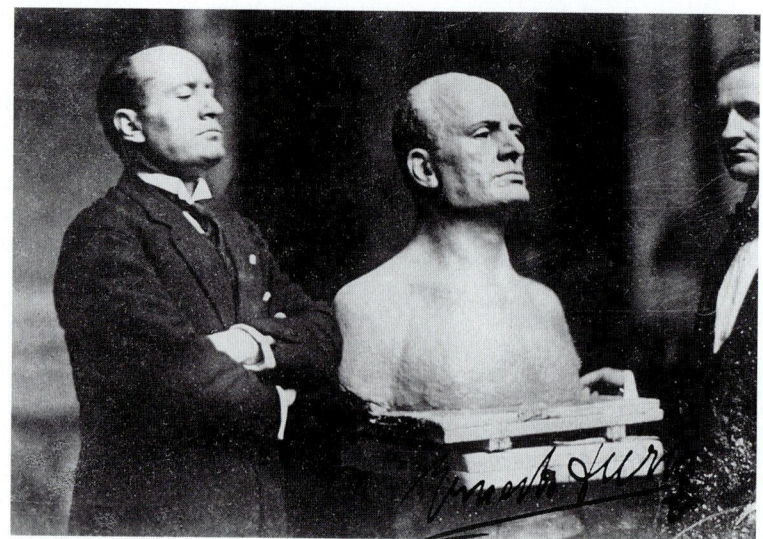

The day after becoming prime minister, Mussolini posed for a sculptor.

thinking underwent a further evolution as he replaced the Marxist doctrine of class struggle with the principle of nationalism.

The Birth of Fascism

Mussolini soon emerged as spokesman for the war veterans, repeatedly condemning Italy's lost peace. Some of his thunder was stolen in September 1919 by the flamboyant nationalist poet Gabriele D'Annunzio (1863–1938), who led war veterans in the seizure of Fiume. When the Italian government refused to accept Fiume from his hands, D'Annunzio proclaimed it an independent state. Italy expelled him from the city a year later, but the expedition had inflamed nationalist feeling and suggested the ease of staging a military takeover. From D'Annunzio, Mussolini learned something about the choreography of political propaganda, and eventually took as his own D'Annunzio's Roman salute, with its outstretched arm and cry of *"Viva il Duce!"*—*Duce*, from the Latin *dux*, is the Italian word meaning "leader."

Meanwhile, the liberal government had become the target of popular resentment. In November 1919, national elections based on universal manhood suffrage were held, and the liberals lost the majority they had held in Parliament since 1861. Instead, the PSI and a new Catholic party became, respectively, the two largest parties. But with the socialists and Catholics refusing to form a coalition government, King Victor Emmanuel III felt free to choose liberal prime ministers.

This political crisis unfolded in a context of massive social unrest—almost 2000 industrial and agrarian strikes took place in 1919. Poor peasants seized land in the South, and others organized huge associations in the northern Po Valley, while in September 1920 some

500,000 workers, supported by socialist leaders such as Antonio Gramsci (1891–1937), occupied factories in the major industrial cities of the North. Such labor tensions, together with the electoral success of the PSI, frightened many middle-class Italians into thinking that Bolshevik revolution was imminent.

Fascism was born in these unstable conditions. Mussolini founded the movement in Milan on March 23, 1919, at an unimpressive rally of little more than 100 followers who were later called the "Fascists of the

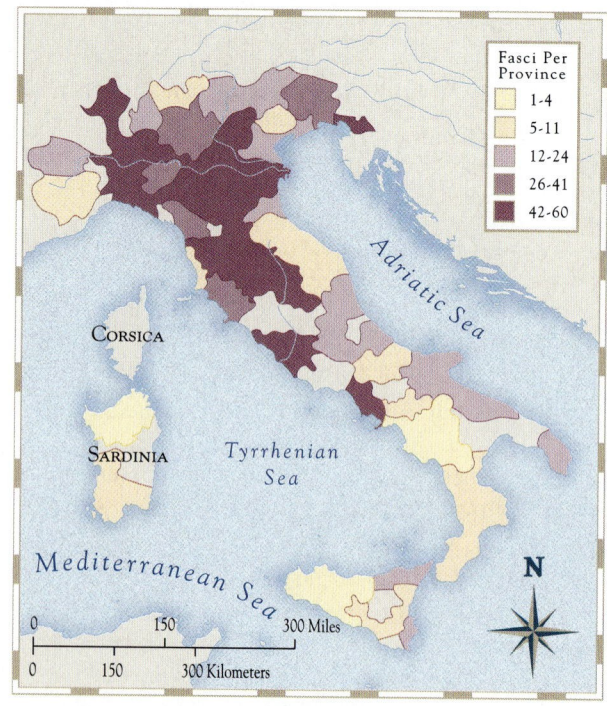

Map 2.3 Fascism in Italy (May 1922)

first hour." The members of this *Fascio di Combattimento* ("combat group") were war veterans, nationalist intellectuals, Futurists (see Part VII, Topic 21), and former interventionist socialists and syndicalists like Mussolini. He took the movement's name from the Latin *fasces* (sticks bound around an axe handle and used in ancient Rome as a symbol of unity), a common term for left-wing radical movements at the time.

A program issued later that year combined left-wing ingredients such as the eight-hour workday, worker participation in management, a republican constitution, and the vote for women and 18-year-olds, with right-wing demands for an aggressive foreign policy and strong secular, nationalist education. Later, under pressure from conservative supporters, the program underwent a pronounced shift to the right.

The Struggle for Power

Most active members of the Fascist movement were from the lower middle class, especially young veterans inspired by the spirit of bravery and comradeship they had experienced in the war, and bound by loyalty and discipline. These men generally stood against the established order, resentful of privilege and wealth, and committed to avenging the "mutilated victory" of 1919. They made up the rank and file of the armed Fascist squads, whose bludgeons and daggers, blackshirted uniforms, and skull and crossbones insignia represented a new, dangerous element in European politics.

Organized in military fashion and led by powerful regional chieftains, these so-called *squadristi*, many of whom were simply brutish thugs, plunged Italy into a bloody nightmare of violence aimed not only against Fascism's political enemies, but against those perceived as defeatists and pacifists. Armed with military weapons, they went on "punitive expeditions" against socialists and labor union activists, terrorized peasant groups, and broke up strikes.

THE FASCIST VICTORY AND MUSSOLINI'S DICTATORSHIP

Because of the "Red Scare" that swept over Italy in 1920–1921, the war against the socialists enabled Mussolini to secure financial support from landowners and industrialists. The liberal government, secretly anxious to see the weakening of the PSI, failed to stop the Black Shirt violence. In 1921, the Fascists began attacking the state, raiding municipal halls, provincial councils, and railroad and telegraph stations. Soon they threatened to take over the central government itself.

Fascism had grown rapidly—the number of recruits, which had numbered not quite 1000 in the summer of 1919, jumped to 250,000 by 1922. Fascist violence, combined with official inaction, gave the appearance that the movement was the only viable force capable of governing the nation.

From Duce to Prime Minister

Mussolini himself played a shrewd game, preserving the public fiction that he was an ordinary, respectable political leader while goading on his Black Shirt followers. In 1921 he changed the Fascist movement into the Fascist National party (PNF). In the elections that year Mussolini and 34 other Fascists won seats in the Chamber of Deputies. Giovanni Giolitti, the liberal prime minister (see Part VII, Topic 15), failed, however, to understand that Fascism was no ordinary political party. He tried unsuccessfully to entice Mussolini into the government as part of a moderate-conservative front called the National Bloc. But the Fascists would not be drawn into traditional establishment politics—they wanted nothing less than full power.

In late 1922, Mussolini's hardline Fascists convinced him to attempt the seizure of power. They planned a "March on Rome" to force King Victor Emmanuel III into appointing a Fascist government. At the end of October, while Mussolini remained in his office in Milan, the Black Shirt chieftains launched a three-pronged drive toward Rome with some 50,000 men. The regular army could have mustered much stronger forces to protect the capital, but the king, afraid that the country would be thrown into civil war or that the military would go over to the Fascists, failed to declare a state of emergency. The prime minister, Luigi Facta (served February to October 1922), resigned, and the king then collapsed in the face of the Fascist threat. On October 29, Victor Emmanuel offered Mussolini the prime ministership. Traveling to Rome by train, Mussolini, having discarded his Fascist uniform, took the oath of office as the youngest prime minister in Italian history.

The March on Rome never really happened. Mussolini became prime minister in accordance with the provisions of the Italian constitution. Nor was he yet a dictator, for only half of his cabinet members were Fascists, and of the more than 500 deputies in Parliament, the party could still count only 35. As a result, Mussolini worked to solidify his position.

Mussolini asked for and received special powers to rule by decree and to censor the press, and in 1923 convinced the liberals to enact legislation aimed at giving the Fascist party control of Parliament. The so-called "Acerbo Law" provided that the party that made the strongest showing in a national election would, provided it received at least 25 percent of all votes cast,

After the March on Rome, October 1922, Mussolini
and his Black Shirts celebrate the Fascist victory.

receive two-thirds of all seats in the Chamber of
Deputies. In the 1924 elections, the Fascists won the
required number of votes by renewed violence and poll
fixing. With the party now dominant in Parliament,
Mussolini felt more secure, but relations with the
Italian Army remained unresolved. He secured the
backing of the military only after agreeing to turn the
Black Shirt squads into a Fascist militia, controlled by
the regular army.

Still, Mussolini hesitated to move toward full
dictatorship. An unexpected political crisis later in

1924 changed the situation. Giacomo Matteotti
(1885–1924), a bold and popular Socialist deputy, began to expose the illegal manner in which the Fascists
had stolen the recent election. That summer Fascist
agents murdered him, possibly on orders from
Mussolini. A wave of public indignation exploded, and
the non-Fascist press turned against the prime minister. Even the king wavered in his support of Mussolini,
and some liberal statesmen urged that he be dismissed.
Leaders of the anti-Fascist opposition withdrew en
masse from Parliament and called themselves the

After he moved his office to Palazzo Venezia,
Mussolini used the piazza under his balcony for
mass demonstrations.

"Aventine Secession," in memory of the secession of the Roman people in the years of the ancient Roman Republic, some two and a half millennia earlier. While Mussolini wavered, the more intransigent Fascist chieftains confronted him and forced him to abandon all pretense of democratic rule. Going before a special session of Parliament on January 3, 1925, Mussolini delivered the most important speech of his life, in which he took total responsibility for everything that had happened and announced that he would restore order to Italy. In the following weeks, the "second wave" of Black Shirt terror was unleashed against the anti-Fascists. In this way, Mussolini silenced the opposition and either arrested or forced into exile its most prominent leaders. Between 1925 and 1929, he began to build the Fascist state.

THE GERMAN REVOLUTION AND THE WEIMAR REPUBLIC

Nazism is the German variety of generic fascism—indeed, scholars refer to Italian Fascism with a capital "F," and to the generic phenomenon with a lowercase "f."

Significant Dates

The Rise of Nazism

1889–1945	Life of Adolf Hitler
1909–1913	Hitler in Vienna
1914–1918	Hitler serves in army and is wounded
November 9, 1918	Kaiser Wilhelm II abdicates; German Republic established under provisional government
November 11, 1918	Armistice
January 6–15, 1919	Spartacist Week
June 1919	Treaty of Versailles
September 1919	Hitler joins the DAP
1920	DAP becomes the NSDAP, or Nazi party
March 1920	Kapp Putsch
1923	French occupation of Ruhr
November 1923	Munich Putsch

To contemporaries, the two seemed virtually the same. Each was, after all, a radical movement with utopian ideologies that mixed nationalism with socialist and syndicalist ideas, each worshiped an all-powerful *Duce* or *Führer*, and in both instances the average militant was a lower-middle-class veteran. Moreover, Fascism and Nazism boasted paramilitary armed squads and both exalted violence, which they used against Marxists and their other political enemies, including liberal democracy.

There were, however, differences. Nazism was based on a theory of racism, whereas a more conventional form of extreme nationalism lay at the heart of Fascist philosophy—a fact that has something to do with the more pervasive and systematic violence that marked the Nazi regime. Hitler's Nazi government is also considered a more efficient example of totalitarianism than Mussolini's Fascist state, and this difference may be partially explained by Germany's more advanced levels of technical education and industrialization.

The Weimar Republic

At the end of 1918, Germany seemed poised at the edge of a revolution as far-reaching as that in Russia. Defeated on the battlefield, Germany's society and economy were exhausted. Moreover, its political system—based on the old Prussian constitution and an all but absolute emperor—had lost its credibility. As a result, left-wing agitation erupted and soldiers and workers set up groups that resembled the Russian Soviets. Sailors at the northern ports, inspired by revolutionary ideas, staged mutinies in late October. The most dramatic event took place on November 8, when the Independent Socialist Kurt Eisner (1867–1919) formed a Bavarian Republic in Munich. Eisner himself was assassinated and the radical experiment crushed in the wake of bitter street fighting with right-wing reactionaries.

In Berlin, events took a similar turn. Kaiser Wilhelm II abdicated on November 9, 1918, following pressure from the Allies, and Prince Max, the imperial chancellor, resigned. Philipp Scheidemann (1865–1939) and Friedrich Ebert (1871–1925), leaders of the Social Democratic party, formed a provisional government. Then, in order to forestall the more radical Revolutionary Marxists, otherwise known as Spartacists (from Spartacus, a gladiator who led a rebellion of slaves against Rome in the first century B.C.), Scheidemann announced the birth of the German Republic. Scheidemann became president and Ebert his chancellor.

The republic quickly became the target of Marxist and right-wing radicals, each of which tried to take power from it. In order to protect the republic, Ebert struck a deal with the German officer corps: in return

Karl Liebknecht and Rosa Luxemburg, leaders of the radical German socialists known as the Spartacists, were both killed while in government custody.

for protecting the republic against its enemies, the government would pledge to maintain the army intact. The agreement worked only too well. Between January 6 and 15, 1919, the Spartacists, led by Rosa Luxemburg (1870–1919) and Karl Liebknecht (1871–1919), attempted a coup in Berlin known as "Spartacist Week." Government troops, assisted by illegal paramilitary organizations known as the *Freikorps*, put down the revolution with considerable bloodshed. Luxemburg and Liebknecht were arrested, but they were both mysteriously killed on the way to jail. The Freikorps, composed of veterans, were to provide Nazism with some of its first members.

In the midst of this instability, delegates to a National Assembly gathered in the city of Weimar to create a permanent government for Germany. The delegates represented a large number of political parties, including the Social Democrats, the Catholic Center party, and the liberal Democratic party—together these three parties constituted the moderate "Weimar Coalition" that was to govern the nation throughout the 1920s. In July 1919 they approved a constitution that created the German Republic, one of the most progressive European governments in interwar Europe. Because of its association with the liberal city of Weimar, the republic came to be known as the Weimar Republic.

The constitution, inspired in part by the example of the United States, embodied modern notions of social justice and popular democracy. "Political authority," read its first article, "derives from the people." The head of state was a president, elected for a seven-year term by universal suffrage, and a British-style cabinet government over which a chancellor, appointed by the president, presided. Legislative power resided in a parliament, consisting of a lower house called the *Reichstag*, and an upper chamber, the *Reichrat*, that represented the various German states. A bill of rights protected civil liberties. As a safeguard, Article 48 permitted the president to enact special powers in the event of national emergency.

In retrospect, it seems as if the Weimar Republic was a compromise that no one wanted. It attracted enemies on the left and the right. A series of coups tried to overthrow the government, the most serious of which was the March 1920 *Putsch*, or coup, led by Wolfgang Kapp (1858–1922), who wanted to restore the monarchy. A general strike organized by the socialists put an end to Kapp's revolt.

In the summer of 1920, elections for the *Reichstag* were held. Ominously, the Weimar Coalition lost significant popular support, its share of the vote falling in subsequent elections from more than 75 to less than 50 percent. Instead, the smaller, extremist parties gained considerable strength. Because the centrist parties were unable to secure a majority thereafter, the republic experienced 20 governments between 1920 and 1933.

At best, most Germans regarded the Weimar Republic with skepticism. The very circumstances of its birth were the cause of considerable concern. The kaiser had, after all, abdicated because the Allies wanted him to, not because the German people had expressed their will. The Allies had also pronounced Germany "guilty" of having caused war, but many Germans did not believe that their weakness had really lost it. Reactionary elements, especially monarchists and the military, invented the "stab in the back" myth, according to which internal traitors had destroyed Germany's war effort. Hitler would tell the people that these traitors were Jews and Marxists. Finally, of course, the Allies had forced Germany to accept the Treaty of Versailles.

The army pledged its support to the government, but senior officers never fully accepted the republic, and senior civil servants, such as judges and police officials, favored the right. When extremists murdered two cabinet ministers—Matthias Erzberger (1875–1921) and Walther Rathenau (1867–1922)—the courts gave those responsible light sentences.

The serious economic difficulties that plagued Germany after 1919 further undermined public confidence in the republic. The economic provisions of the Versailles Treaty had deprived Germany of vital resources and income, and unemployment was widespread. Lacking the resources to deal effectively with the crisis, the government printed millions of dollars worth of paper money, which made the *mark* worthless and sparked rampant inflation. When the French occupied the Ruhr Valley in 1923 in order to extract late reparations payments from Germany, the economy declined further. The cost-of-living index rose on a daily basis, wiping out the value of salaries and pensions. Millions of working- and middle-class Germans were ruined by the inflation, and life in the Weimar Republic took on a real sense of desperation.

HITLER AND NATIONAL SOCIALISM

Like Fascism in Italy, Nazism was a product of the post-war crisis. Yet to an even greater degree than was the case with Mussolini and his movement, Adolf Hitler shaped and dominated the Nazi party.

Adolf Hitler

The most infamous man in German history actually began life as a subject of the Austro-Hungarian empire. Hitler (1889–1945) was born in Braunau, Austria, the son of an unimportant customs bureaucrat. As a youth, Hitler was estranged from his father, who tried to discourage him from studying art. The boy was bright but was not a good student. He failed to graduate from high school, and remained intent on becoming an artist.

Hitler moved to Vienna in 1909, and remained there until the eve of World War I. It was there that he first sought to develop his aesthetic inclinations by study at the Vienna School of Architecture. Despite limited talent as an architectural draftsman, however, Hitler was twice disappointed when his application to school was rejected. Thereafter, he led a squalid, frustrated life trying to earn a living by painting street scenes and working at menial jobs.

Vienna served for Hitler the same purpose that Switzerland had for Mussolini: it provided an opportunity for study and practical experience, during which he

An enthusiastic crowd in Munich welcomes news of the war, August 1, 1914, among them a young Adolf Hitler.

PERSPECTIVES ON HISTORY

The Nature of Fascism

Stanley G. Payne
University of Wisconsin–Madison

Fascism was the only completely new force among the major radical movements active in European affairs after World War I. Though ingredients that made up fascism were not themselves new, they had never coalesced into a specific form prior to 1919. Moreover, fascism was also difficult to understand or to categorize. Though fascists strongly opposed the movements of the left, such as communism and socialism, they denied that fascists themselves were of the right. Fascists claimed to represent a synthesis of both the left and right, and some fascist movements even called themselves "national socialists," as distinct from Marxist or international socialists. Communists, in turn, usually denounced fascism as the instrument of the "most reactionary and violent" sector of the bourgeoisie, but fascists always claimed to be a popular force that united people of diverse social and class backgrounds in the service of the nation.

Fascism was even more confusing because fascist leaders boasted of being activists and pragmatists, relatively indifferent to doctrines or ideology. Later, after World War II, the understanding of fascism even sparked controversy among professional historians. Some would complain that the term "fascist" was applied too loosely and vaguely as a mere political epithet, or used to encompass a wide variety of political movements that were mutually contradictory. Others sought to explain the nature or historical meaning of fascism according to social, economic, philosophical, or even psychological factors.

The term "fascism" was derived from the Italian *fascio*, meaning a union or league, and commonly adopted by new Italian political forces in the later 19th and early 20th centuries. Thus a new group of radical Italian nationalists led by Benito Mussolini found it natural to call themselves the "Fasci Italiani" in 1919 and later transformed the term into an adjective when they organized the "Italian National Fascist Party" two years later, giving rise to "fascist" and "fascism." The movement soon developed a mass membership, enabling its leader to become prime minister in October 1922 and to convert Italy's government into a one-party dictatorship in January 1925.

Its nearest major counterpart, the National Socialist German Workers' party (known to their enemies as "Nazis") sprang from a small group organized in Munich in 1917, then reorganized under Adolf Hitler three years later. Whereas Mussolini came to power relatively rapidly, the same process took Hitler much longer, though he built an even larger and more potent political movement along the way. By the time that Hitler took power in 1933, other new radical nationalist parties had appeared in most other European countries. They became strong mass movements, in one form or another, in only four other countries: Hungary (the Arrow Cross), Romania (the Iron Guard), Austria (the Austrian Nazis), and Spain (Spanish Phalanx).

Though these individual fascist-type movements sometimes differed a good deal among themselves, they also shared certain fundamental characteristics and goals which as a whole tended to set them off from other kinds of political forces. The fascists were first of all unique because they were opposed to nearly all the existing political sectors. They were antiliberal, anticommunist (as well as antisocialist in the social democratic sense), and also anticonservative, though sometimes willing to undertake temporary alliances with rightist groups.

Fascist movements represented the most intense and radical form of nationalism known to modern Europe. They intended to create new nationalist authoritarian states not based on traditional models. They all planned to develop some new kind of regulated, multiclass national economic structure, diversely called national corporatist, national socialist, or national syndicalist. In foreign affairs, all the fascist movements aimed at national imperial expansion or at least at a radical change in the nation's relationship with other powers to enhance its strength and prestige. Though fascist movements did not have a formalized ideology such as Marxism, they had distinctive mentalities, based on a philosophical orientation of idealism as opposed to materialism, and voluntarism or willpower as opposed to rationalism.

Fascist uniqueness was expressed through style and organization. Fascist leaders placed great emphasis on the aesthetic structure of meetings, symbols, and political "choreography," relying especially on romantic and mystical aspects. The fascist movements all attempted to achieve a mass mobilization, with the specific intent of militarizing political relations and creating a mass party militia. Fascists not merely practiced violence (like some other radical groups) but also espoused violence philosophically as a desired end in itself, as a positive value that made nations stronger, more serious, and more unified. They strongly stressed the masculine principle and male dominance, while championing a new élitism and exalting youth over other phases of life. They also cherished the cult of the authoritarian leader—a special figure endowed with charismatic powers, which German Nazis called the *Führerprinzip*, or "leadership principle."

What differentiated fascists from the right was their rejection of philosophical as well as economic conservatism, and their determination to replace the established social élites of the right. They differed profoundly from the left in their rejection of internationalism and egalitarianism or equal rights, as well as in their antipathy to socialized materialism. They sought to remake Europe in the form of a nationalist/imperialist "New Order," profoundly different from the liberal 19th century or the new Marxist-Leninist system of the Soviet Union.

Fascist movements drew support from highly diverse social sectors. In their earliest phase, followers came from former military personnel and small sectors of the radical intelligentsia, sometimes university students. Though some fascist movements enjoyed a degree of backing from the upper bourgeoisie, the broadest sector of support was often provided by the lower middle class. In Germany and Hungary, considerable support also came from workers, while university students were especially important in Italy, Germany, Spain, and Romania, and poor farmers were often recruited in Romania.

A bewildering variety of theories and interpretations have been advanced since 1923 to explain fascism. Among them are (1) theories of socioeconomic causation, primarily of Marxist inspiration; (2) the application of modernization theory, which posits fascism as a phase in modern development; and (3) the theory of totalitarianism, which interprets fascism as one aspect of the broader phenomenon of 20th-century totalitarianism. None of these theories is entirely convincing. The diversity of the basis of social recruitment and political backing makes any simple theory of social determinism implausible, while the fact that numerous societies have undergone modernization without succumbing to fascism seriously weakens any theory drawn primarily from modernization. The theory of "totalitarianism" is of little help because it tends to ignore the differences between fascism and communism, as well as the differences in historical milieu between the countries in which these two diverse movements triumphed.

Probably the only way to account for fascism is by a "historic" approach that isolates the five key variables in the historical situation of countries in which the main fascist movements emerged. The main *national* variable was one of military defeat, frustration, disunity, and status deprivation. The main *political* variable had to do with countries that were just beginning, or had only recently begun, the transition to direct political democracy. (Conversely, stable and satisfied countries, and those in which political democracy had already existed for a generation or more, were not susceptible.) The key *cultural* variable was the influence of currents of new philosophical idealism and vitalism (propitious to fascism) in a nation's cultural life, as contrasted with materialism and rationalism. The key *economic* variable was either depression or underdevelopment in a context where problems seemed both national in scope and to some

continued next page

extent international in origin. The key *social* variable involved widespread discontent not merely among the young and sectors of the lower classes, but among the lower middle class as well. No one or two or even three of these variables by themselves sufficed to produce a significant fascist movement. Only in those few countries where all five variables were present at approximately the same time were conditions propitious for the emergence of major fascist movements.

Even comparatively large fascist movements were rarely successful. The only independent regimes established by fascist leaders were those of Mussolini in Italy (1922–1943) and Hitler in Germany (1933–1945), and only in the German case did the movement's leader achieve complete power over the state. In nearly all countries an-

tifascists were much more numerous than fascists and profascists. The fascists' own calls to violence and extremism tended to limit their appeal, as did the nonrationalist, voluntarist character of their doctrines. The broader influence of fascism during the decade 1935–1945 was due above all to the great expansion of military power of Nazi Germany, not to the individual political victories of the various national fascist movements, which were in fact few. Similarly, the complete military defeat of Italy and Germany shattered the hopes of all the fascist movements, and in the great majority of cases resulted in their physical obliteration as well.

Does fascism have a future? Worried foes sometimes fear so, but it is doubtful that the specific forms of early 20th-century European fascism can be revived. Broad cultural, psychological, edu-

developed his political ideas and his notions about race. Reading widely but without purpose, he was exposed to the kinds of extremist, irrational prejudices that proved to be the foundation of his Nazi philosophy.

Vienna was a microcosm of the ethnic diversity of the Austro-Hungarian empire, and it was in that environment that Hitler discovered racism. At the turn of the century, Vienna bred a number of political leaders who tried to capitalize on racial fears and on Austrian anti-Semitism. Such men were among Hitler's first political heroes. Karl Lueger (1844–1910), the leader of the reactionary Christian Social party, won election as mayor of Vienna—"the greatest German mayor of all times," Hitler wrote of him years later—on an anti-Semitic platform. Lueger's example taught Hitler how a radical movement could achieve power by making a campaign against the Jews the basis of mass-based urban politics. Another contemporary, Georg von Schoenerer, was a parliamentary deputy who preached Pan-Germanism and described the Germans as a higher race who deserved to dominate the other peoples of Europe. From such views he derived his belief that all Germans everywhere had to be united into a "greater Germany." Racial theories soon dominated Hitler's mind, and by the time he left Vienna, he had become convinced that Jews and Marxists were the cause of Western cultural and political corruption and the cause of Europe's degeneracy.

At the start of World War I, Hitler immediately joined the German Army. He saw frontline combat, for which he earned a corporal's rank, and was injured in a poison gas attack at the end of the war. It was while undergoing recovery that he was approached by Captain Ernst Roehm (1887–1934), later a major Nazi leader, and recruited to work for the army in Munich as a civilian investigator.

The Nazi Party

In September 1919, while engaged in gathering information on extremist politics for Roehm, Hitler joined the German Worker's party (DAP). The tiny organization was founded by an anti-Marxist, anti-Semitic worker who wanted the working classes to become fervid nationalists.

Hitler soon dominated the party and emerged as a brilliant public speaker and a powerfully inspiring leader, despite a somewhat comical appearance. He was able to conjure up a unique intensity of emotion in his audiences that eventually captured the loyalty of millions of Germans. In 1920 the party was rebaptized as the National Socialist German Workers' party (NS-DAP), soon known popularly as the "Nazi" party— "Nazi" is derived from the German pronunciation of the first two syllables of the German word for "National." He gave talks at rallies all over Munich, increasing the party's membership and shouting his political and racial ideas to all who would listen. His appeal

cational, and economic changes have made the reemergence of something so murderous as Nazism in a modern industrial nation almost impossible, just as international interdependence seems to rule out war among the major European and industrial countries. The prevailing culture of materialism and consumerism militates against extreme positions, and any appeal to mass vitalist and irrationalist politics.

Movements and regimes most similar to fascism during the second half of the century have been more important in certain "Third World" countries than in the West. There, nationalist one-party dictatorships have not been uncommon. More than a few governments in Africa, Asia, and the Middle East have preached their own versions of national socialism (for example, "Arab socialism") and have propagated doctrines

based on violence, and grounded in mysticism, idealism, and willpower. There too the "cult of personality" and charismatic dictatorship have sometimes been popular. Nonetheless, it is not possible to refer to more than specific features and tendencies. The nationalist movements and dictatorships of the Third World have also developed unique identities and profiles of their own, and in no instance have literally copied or revived European fascist movements. The exact characteristics of interwar Europe, like those of any particular historical epoch, cannot be precisely repeated or reproduced. New authoritarian movements of the 1990s would have to develop qualities appropriate to their own times to achieve support, for a literal revival of the past—particularly of a past so discredited as that of fascism—is doomed to sterility.

grew as he made the "stab in the back" legend and the Treaty of Versailles the cornerstones of his platform. His devoted followers called him the *Führer* (leader), and within five years his tiny party had become a large and vocal force in Weimar politics.

The Nazi party soon had a daily newspaper, the *Völkischer Beobachter* (The People's Observer). Its official platform contained 25 points, chief among them being the creation of a "Greater Germany," an end to the hated *Diktat*—the Treaty of Versailles—and the creation of a prosperous and loyal working and middle class. The platform also aimed to remove the rights of citizenship from Jews. Hitler never believed in the importance of the socialist rhetoric in which the Nazis couched their appeals to the workers. "Left-wing" Nazis like Gregor Strasser (1892–1934) were important in spreading Nazism among the industrial workers of the North, but once they had served their purposes Hitler purged them from the party.

In 1921, Roehm created and took charge of the SA (*Sturmabteilung*), a paramilitary unit that wore brown-shirted uniforms with the swastika as its symbol. The swastika symbol was used in a variety of ancient cultures, from Egypt to China, and it appeared later in Estonia, where the Freikorps saw it during the fighting in 1918–1919. The Ehrhardt Brigade used it on their steel helmets in Berlin during the Kapp Putsch, and Hitler no doubt saw it when the brigade came to Munich in 1920. Soon the swastika appeared on arm

bands, flag, and uniforms, for Hitler saw it as the symbol of "the mission of the struggle for the victory of the Aryan man."

The SA's rank and file came from the lower middle class, especially war veterans and Freikorps members, many of whom were little more than hooligans. Roehm told his followers that only through violence would the Nazis achieve power. Later, in 1925, Heinrich Himmler (1900–1945) organized the elite guard unit called the SS (*Schutzstaffel*), whose black uniforms and lightning bolt symbols became dreaded symbols of Nazi brutality. Like Mussolini, Hitler used torch-lit parades, impressive ceremonies, and other techniques that Joseph Goebbels (1897–1945) eventually made into the most effective propaganda machine in history.

In 1923, a year after Mussolini's March on Rome, Hitler tried to take power, but only on a local level. The French occupation of the Ruhr and the severe inflationary cycle that erupted that year had been psychologically and economically devastating to most Germans (see Part VIII, Topic 3). In Munich Hitler sought to exploit these conditions by plotting a Putsch that he thought would be supported by municipal authorities. He also enlisted the retired General Erich von Ludendorff to bring a measure of national prestige to the attempt. The abortive coup took place on November 8, but it ended less than 24 hours later when the police intervened. Hitler and several others were

Adolf Hitler in a characteristic pose while speaking.

arrested, and although he was sentenced to five years in prison, he spent only nine months in jail. While serving his time, Hitler dictated *Mein Kampf* (My Struggle), a long and discursive book in which he laid out his political and racial theories and explained how he intended to conquer. The Munich fiasco also taught him that he had to adopt a legal strategy for achieving power that would go hand in hand with Nazi violence.

In 1924, Hitler and Roehm vied with each other for control of the Nazi party, whose membership now reached some 25,000. Roehm tried to make the SA the focus of the party's power, whereas Hitler sought to make the SA the party's tool. Hitler proved the more skillful of the two, driving Roehm into exile and restoring his own authority over the party.

Hitler's new strategy had only limited success, electing some twelve deputies in 1928. Economic conditions in Germany improved after 1924 and the political unrest that had weakened the Weimar Republic quietened down. Although Hitler succeeded in raising Nazi membership to more than 175,000, his prospects for obtaining power legally seemed dim. It would require another five years and the impact of the Great Depression before Hitler came to power (see Part VIII, Topic 4).

Between 1917 and 1933, three new political regimes came to power in Europe—the Soviets in Russia, the Fascists in Italy, and the Nazis in Germany. Together they posed a major challenge to the Western notion of parliamentary democracy. Indeed, in all three cases absolute dictators now controlled the destinies of their countries. Each proclaimed that he would completely reorganize society according to a utopian ideology that stressed community, discipline, *and sacrifice for the general good. While the communists in Russia rejected capitalism, the fascists claimed to represent an alternative to both capitalism and communism. As the Great Depression imposed suffering and misery on millions of Europeans, many lost hope with traditional governments and turned in desperation to these radical extremes.*

Questions for Further Study

1. What is meant by "Leninism"? How does it differ from conventional socialism?

2. Why did revolution come to Russia instead of to England or France?

3. What were the origins of fascism? How did fascism differ from Bolshevism? How did Italian Fascism differ from German Nazism?

4. Is it useful to speak of a generic "fascism" that combines the Italian and the German varieties?

Suggestions for Further Reading

Bullock, Alan. *Hitler, A Study in Tyranny.* New York, 1964.

Carr, Edward H. *The Russian Revolution: From Lenin to Stalin.* New York, 1979.

Daniels, Roger V. *Red October: The Bolshevik Revolution of 1917.* New York, 1967.

De Felice, Renzo. *Interpretations of Fascism.* Cambridge, MA, 1977.

De Grand, Alexander. *Italian Fascism: Origins and Development,* 2nd ed. Lincoln, NE, 1989.

Fest, Joachim. *Hitler.* New York, 1974.

Fitzpatrick, Sheila. *The Russian Revolution.* New York, 1982.

Lyttelton, Adrian. *The Seizure of Power: Fascism in Italy, 1919–1929.* London, 1973.

Mack Smith, Denis. *Mussolini.* New York, 1982.

Payne, Stanley. *A History of Fascism.* Madison, WI, 1995.

Ulam, Adam. *The Bolsheviks.* New York, 1965.

T o p i c   3

THE EUROPEAN ECONOMY: BOOM AND BUST

he impact of the Great War was felt for decades to come, not only within Europe but on its position in world affairs. As we have seen in the preceding two topics, the political upheavals wrought as a consequence of the war changed Europe's map, altered relationships among the great powers, and gave rise to new kinds of political systems. No less dramatic, however, were the effects of the war on Europe's—and the world's—economy.

Wartime government controls, together with the demands made by the military, had created an essentially artificial economic situation in every belligerent country. Once peace came, the domestic and international economies had to readjust suddenly to peacetime production as well as to free market conditions. The European economy responded with a brief but intense postwar boom, followed in turn by collapse. Thereafter, despite periodic adjustments in economic conditions, the 1920s saw considerable prosperity and growth. The new prosperity greatly affected social developments as millions took part in the unprecedented economic expansion and the spread of mass-produced consumer products (on the social conditions of the interwar period, see Part VIII, Topic 6).

Not that the 1920s were without economic difficulties. Two long-range financial legacies of the war, reparations and war debts, made recovery more difficult and fueled international tensions. A series of agreements—the Dawes Plan in 1924 and the Young Plan in 1929—attempted unsuccessfully to settle these touchy questions, but only the Great Depression put an end to both issues in any real sense. Moreover, the wartime economic dislocations, together with the peace settlements and inflationary cycles, destabilized Europe's major currencies, causing them to drop in value in international exchange. Governments attempted with varying degrees of success to deal with this problem by instituting deflationary policies and balanced budgets at home. This was combined with a return to the gold standard.

In the 1920s, the United States and Great Britain made extensive foreign loans, generally to countries with weak economies, thus adding an element of instability to the world financial markets, while at the same time the unchecked speculative boom in the American stock market only added to the stresses on the economic system. Nor was the boom of the 1920s universal: chronic agricultural depression marked most regions, while some countries, such as Germany, Great Britain, Italy, and Japan, hardly shared in the prosperity of the period.

When the New York stock market crashed in October 1929, the first major crack in the world economic system appeared. By 1930, the Great Depression had begun, shattering industrial productivity and making conditions in the already depressed agricultural sector worse. The following year, the financial markets collapsed in Europe. The Great Depression proved to be the most serious, deep-seated economic crisis in modern history, causing enormous human misery and putting huge pressures on political and social stability. Lasting well into the decade, governments—both democratic and authoritarian, both of the left and the right—adopted strategies of public spending and public works projects to cope with the massive unemployment. In addition, the widespread suffering attendant on the Depression led governments to expand public assistance programs and the passage of legislation that gave rise to the modern welfare state.

THE ECONOMIC CONSEQUENCES OF THE WAR

The economic impact of the war took a variety of forms, from the direct physical destruction of factories, railroads, and farms to the disruption of trade and the financial drain on national budgets. The peace settlements, responsive as they were to nationalist pressures, made the economic terms of the peace treaties political issues of great importance that were to hound international relations throughout the decade.

Significant Dates

The European Economy

1919	Keynes' *The Economic Consequences of the Peace*
April 1921	Reparations Commission announces $33 billion debt for Germany
1923	French occupation of the Ruhr
1924	Inflation in Germany
January 1925	Gold Standard Act in England
1929	Young Plan
October 1929	Wall Street crash; onset of Great Depression
May 1931	*Creditanstalt* fails
June 1931	Moratorium on war debts
1933	Franklin D. Roosevelt elected U.S. president

Readjustment and Boom

In 1919, Europeans found it necessary to deal with two industrial issues: the need to change over from the production of war matériel to peacetime consumer goods, and the task of raising production back up to prewar levels. In the period from 1914 to 1920, industrial output had declined by 39 percent in Germany, 34 percent in France, 26 percent in Italy, and 12 percent in Britain. These production drops were the result of a combination of circumstances, especially lower demand caused by the closing of foreign markets and the lack of raw materials. In countries overrun by armies, the physical destruction was an equally important factor. Belgium, for example, lost half of its steel mills and the bulk of its railroad lines.

Four years of fighting had undermined Europe's industrial supremacy. The productive capacities of the United States, Canada, and Japan expanded as each country took a larger share of the world's exports, and new home industries had begun to spring up in Latin America, India, and most of the British Dominions.

Table VIII.3.1

Share of Selected Countries in World Exports (in percent)

	1913	1925
Great Britain	13.9	12.4
Germany	13.1	7.0
France	7.2	7.2
Italy	2.6	2.4
Russia	4.2	1.0
USA	13.3	16.0
Canada	2.4	4.4
Japan	1.7	3.0

The resulting change in the pattern of world trade reflected the fact that Europe's economic status had been significantly altered.

The wartime naval blockades, the shortage of commercial carriers, and the loss by European nations of overseas markets all contributed to this changed trade pattern, although in the case of Russia the Bolshevik Revolution, the civil war, and the loss of territory to newly created nations explained the drastic drop of that country's exports.

Another important change in Europe's economic posture was in its role in international finance. The belligerent nations had borrowed huge amounts of money to finance the war. As a consequence, Germany's national debt rose from roughly 5 billion to more than 100 billion marks. In Germany's case, this money had been raised entirely by floating domestic war bonds. Although the British and French were equally burdened (the British and French debts, when measured in real purchasing power, were about the same size), about 25 percent of their increased debts came from American loans—by doing so, the two Western powers, once the world's greatest creditor states, had become debtor nations, even though they continued to lend money to the other Allies during the war. Countries on both sides had also resorted to the increased printing of paper money, thus fueling inflation.

Despite these problems, the years 1919–1920 saw an economic boom in Europe and the United States, characterized by high profits and low unemployment. The sudden prosperity was due to the fact that because the stock of consumer goods had been depleted during the war, with peace the demand for these goods rose sharply. As a result, prices—and profits—grew, and producers borrowed heavily at increasing rates of interest to expand their operations. A speculative boom followed as businesses recapitalized and expanded. Official British figures put unemployment at only 2.4 percent, or about half the prewar levels. The boom was short, for by the summer of 1920 the supply of consumer goods caught up to the demand, especially as prices rose so high as to discourage some buying. To encourage sales, prices were lowered. This did not work. As the price index fell precipitously, production slackened off, unemployment increased, and numerous bankruptcies were declared. By the end of 1921, British unemployment stood at 17 percent.

The postwar depression was temporary, and was followed in a few years by a longer period of increasing prosperity. For Europe, however, the significant fact was that although the world's productive capacity grew in the 1920s, a greater proportion of that capacity lay elsewhere.

REPARATIONS, INFLATION, AND WAR DEBTS

In the century before the Great War, Europe had created and maintained perhaps the highest standard of living in history. In a sense, this material well-being had been achieved in large measure because it had been able to import more than it exported. The difference had been paid for by two sources of income: interest earned from loans and investments made abroad, and profits from shipping charges. All this changed, however, once European nations became debtor states, a condition made worse by the huge costs of reconstruction, which required even more foreign loans.

The Allies hoped to meet their war debt obligations by reparations from Germany, which had been forced by the Treaty of Versailles to make such payments. Yet the onerous economic terms imposed on Germany by the peace treaty made it virtually impossible for Germany to make its reparations payments.

Problems of German Recovery

The payment of reparations was a political issue as well as an economic problem. Public opinion in the Allied countries demanded a punitive peace with Germany. To complicate matters, the French regarded reparations as a means of keeping Germany in a weakened state. Article 231 of the Treaty of Versailles had stipulated that Germany would pay reparations because it was responsible for having caused the war, a position that the German people strongly resented. Moreover, the Allies could not agree on a specific sum in 1919, and created a Reparations Commission that would eventually determine the amount and collect the payments. At the time they signed the treaty, therefore, the Germans did not know how much they would be required to pay.

In April 1921, the Reparations Commission settled on a figure equivalent to $33 billion, a staggering sum in view of the fact that Germany had lost some 15 percent of its total productive capacity, 36 percent of its coal supply, 72 percent of its iron ore, more than 90 percent of its merchant shipping, and almost all of its foreign investments. In a brilliant book entitled *The Economic Consequences of the Peace*, the British economist John Maynard Keynes (1883–1946) argued that the harsh economic terms of the Versailles settlement would make it impossible for Germany to meet its obligations and would have an adverse effect on the European economy as a whole.

Germany paid its first installment late, and only after a loan from British bankers. By 1923, the Germans had made additional payments only in kind

Inflation in Germany was so severe that it was cheaper to light stoves with currency than to buy kindling wood with it.

rency into real goods. The most serious result of this hyperinflation was to ruin the entire German middle class, whose savings and pensions were wiped out, thus making the soil in which the Nazi party grew more fertile—indeed, it was in the midst of the inflation crisis that Hitler attempted his Munich *Putsch* (see Part VIII, Topic 2).

Reparations and War Debt Settlements

The German economy was stabilized beginning in late 1923, when the government issued new currency tied to the gold standard in the context of an international settlement of the reparations problem. A committee of financial experts headed by the American Charles G. Dawes (1865–1951) agreed to a two-year moratorium on reparations, the return of the Ruhr to Germany, and a $200 million loan to the beleaguered Germans. Germany committed itself to making regular payments on an increasing scale.

A large part of the international loan was sold in the United States, where it was underwritten by the House of Morgan. The success of this loan stimulated a frenzy of foreign loans, not only to European countries but to South America as well. Moreover, as confidence was restored in the economy, the Germans borrowed lavishly from abroad for public works projects and to rebuild their industrial base.

In 1929, another committee, also chaired by an American, Owen D. Young (1874–1962), devised a revised reparations arrangement. The Young Plan also involved an international loan, this time for $300 million, and the creation of a Bank for International Settlements, through which Germany would pay its reparations over a period of 59 years.

War debts similarly plagued international relations. By 1919, European nations owed the United

and then announced that they could not continue payments at all. It was then that the French and Belgians occupied the Ruhr Valley, sparking passive resistance in the mines and factories of the region and prompting the German government to begin printing paper currency recklessly. The mark, 100,000 to the dollar in June, reached a low of 6.30 trillion by November. Wages could not keep up with prices, and every day saw a stampede to convert the almost worthless cur-

France sent troops, including these colonial soldiers, to occupy Germany's Ruhr district in 1923 to force reparation payments.

States almost $10 billion in war debts, including some $4.7 billion from France, $4.2 billion from Great Britain, and $1.6 billion from Italy. In addition, however, significant debts existed among the smaller Allies—France and Italy, for example, were in debt to Britain, and Belgium and Yugoslavia to France. Russia owed $2.5 billion to Britain and $900 million to France, but these loans were repudiated by the new Soviet government.

Some economists had suggested that all war debts be canceled, and British leaders repeated the idea formally to the United States in the early 1920s. American authorities, however, refused, insisting that they were willing to negotiate the debts owed to them, but with each individual nation. The European Allies had hoped that the combination of war debts and reparations would create a three-tiered financial relationship: German reparations payments would be made to countries such as Belgium and France, which would use that income to pay their war debts to Great Britain, which would in turn repay the wartime American loans. The United States insisted on keeping the reparations and war debt issues separate. Beginning in 1923, the United States began to settle the debt question with some 13 countries, beginning with Great Britain, which agreed to pay its obligation with interest over a period of 62 years.

RECOVERY AND PROSPERITY

After the collapse of 1921–1922, the European economy underwent a period of recovery, centered principally around the stabilization of Europe's major currencies. The end of runaway inflation and the issuance of the new currency in Germany, capped by the settlement of reparations in the Dawes Plan, marked the beginning of this process.

Currency Stabilization

The 19th century had been a period of relative monetary stability, with major paper currencies retaining their relative values and readily convertible into silver or gold. The war changed all this, lowering the buying power of Europe's major currencies, and doing so unequally. Wartime inflation had struck every belligerent country, and in the first postwar boom of 1919–1920, price inflation rose higher, although nowhere so drastically as in Germany. Moreover, the gold standard, adopted in the late 19th century (see Part VII, Topic 17), collapsed during the war and currencies fell still further in value. By the end of the war, the monetary systems of Germany, Austria, Hungary, and Russia were virtually destroyed. International monetary conferences

attempted to restore some stability in the 1920s, and the German rescue operation was the most dramatic of these efforts.

In Britain, where the commitment to restoring the prewar parity of the pound to the dollar—$4.86—was a moral as well as a financial question, recovery was slow in coming and never fully realized. The British had lost important markets to the Americans and Japanese, and by 1921 were exporting half the value of goods traded in 1913. To get its huge national debt under control, Britain imposed heavy taxation at home and reduced government expenditures. Although the pound fluctuated, in the second half of 1923 it recovered to about $4.30, and when it almost reached parity in January 1925, the government passed the Gold Standard Act that pegged the pound at $4.79. In retrospect, it is clear that the pound was overvalued, and this had the effect of making British exports even more difficult to sell abroad. By then, unemployment was down to around 11 percent, where it hovered for most of the decade after its high point of 17 percent in 1921. Britain never fully regained its prewar prosperity.

In 1919, the French franc stood at only half its prewar value of 19¢, and by 1926 depreciated to 2¢. French leaders insisted on the importance of reconstruction, even at the price of ever larger deficits and more foreign loans, especially after the fiasco of the Ruhr occupation. In less than two years, ten finance ministers tried unsuccessfully to resolve the chaos of French finances. When Premier Raymond Poincaré (see Part VIII, Topic 5) came to office in July 1926, he finally took stern measures to stabilize the franc at 25 to the dollar, or one-quarter of its prewar value. This cheap franc helped to sell French goods abroad. That same year France also settled its debt with the United States.

The Era of Prosperity

After the stabilization of inflated currencies and the settlement of war debts, the pace of economic development picked up. New industries developed or expanded, with industrial growth taking place mainly in the production of consumer goods that were designed to make life easier or more enjoyable. A host of new appliances invaded the middle-class home, from vacuum cleaners and electric mixers to refrigerators and radios. In Britain alone, there were perhaps 36,000 radio sets in 1922, but by the end of 1929 that number had jumped to almost 3 million. The output in rayon, plastics, chemicals, and aluminum also rose substantially—in the case of aluminum, for example, from 64,000 tons in 1913 to more than 580,000 in 1938. The production of electrical energy doubled in the 1920s, and by the end of the next decade had doubled again in the major industrial countries.

Map 3.1   Industrialized Zones of Europe, c. 1930

The automobile was by far the most important product of the period, both from the economic viewpoint as well as in terms of its social impact. Automobiles had been appearing on European roads since the early 20th century—France alone produced some 16,500 in 1902—but they had not come into mass use before the Great War. The war itself, however, greatly increased the demand for automobiles and trucks. Henry Ford's ability to produce the Model T inexpensively and in great quantity made the automobile the biggest selling wholesale product in the United States by 1928. European manufacturers copied Ford's methods, lowering production costs by using standardized parts on the assembly line and concentrating production in fewer companies. High protective tariffs shielded European producers from American cars in the 1920s. The table below shows the remarkable expansion in the ownership of automobiles.

Table VIII.3.2
Registered Motor Vehicles, 1913–1938 (in 1000s)

	BRITAIN	GERMANY	FRANCE	U.S.
1913	208	93	125	1258
1921	464	91	236	10,494
1926	1042	319	891	22,053
1930	1524	67	1460	26,532
1938	2422	1816	2251	29,443

The automobile industry acted as an important stimulus to other industries and raw materials, including metals, rubber, gasoline, and lubricants—the world's production of crude petroleum increased from 400 million barrels in 1914 to 1.5 billion in 1938. Road construction came into its own in the 1920s as a result of the spreading use of the automobile.

In the late 1920s, industrialization began to spread to less developed nations, especially to the Soviet Union and the countries of Eastern Europe. In addition, industry everywhere underwent a process of rationalization, whereby less economical plants with older equipment and production methods were closed down and production either shifted to new factories or concentrated in more efficient ones. Rationalization was further enhanced by the introduction of new labor-saving machinery, the standardization of parts, and the adoption of mass production assembly line techniques. In the postwar period, this process was easier in those countries, such as France and Belgium, where physical destruction required that new factories be built, or in planned economies such as the Soviet Union and Fascist Italy.

Britain did not participate fully in the era of prosperity. Unemployment never fell below 1 million and the British share in world trade never returned to prewar levels. Moreover, while the United States outproduced Britain in the new industries, the former "workshop of the world" faced serious handicaps in traditional industries such as coal mining, steel, and textiles. Production declines were registered in all three industries during the two decades following the war. That British industries could no longer compete as they had once done was fully revealed by the steady abandonment of the free trade that had been followed since the 19th century.

France was troubled less by trade patterns than by the need for industrial reconstruction. Reparations, together with the recovery of Alsace-Lorraine and the new, modernized factories that were built in the north-

Unemployed British workers march on London, 1930.

ern portions of the country, stimulated French industrialization. As a result, France emerged in the interwar era with a greatly expanded industrial sector. Germany relied on massive foreign loans to rebuild and modernize its industry. The Germans also experienced a boom in construction, especially by public funds, after 1924. On the other hand, in the entire period from 1923 to 1936 unemployment fell below 7 percent only once, in 1925, when it registered 6.9 percent, and it actually soared to 18 percent in the following year. In 1929, with the boom in full swing, some 2 million German workers were without jobs. For Europe as a whole, figures show that the number of unemployed rose from a low estimate of 3.5 million in the first half of the decade to perhaps as high as 5.5 million during the era of prosperity.

Hence, although the second postwar economic boom stretched across the second half of the 1920s, it was by no means general and all-pervasive. European production as a whole regained the 1913 level only in 1925, whereas in the same period it had increased by 25 percent in North America and 20 percent in Asia. Textiles, once the most important product of Europe's industrial revolution, stagnated in the face of cheaper Japanese production. Moreover, Europe's share of world industrial production shrunk steadily, from 57.6 percent in 1913 to 47.1 percent in 1928, while that of the United States rose from 32 to 39.3 percent. In the same period, Europe's share of world trade declined

from 54.5 to about 49.2 percent. From 1913 to 1939, per capita real income actually grew in Western Europe, but the growth was slower than it had been during the Long Depression of the late 19th century (see Part VII, Topic 17).

THE CRASH: WALL STREET AND THE FINANCIAL COLLAPSE

There is no agreement among economists or economic historians as to the underlying causes of the Great Depression, nor is there consensus as to where it began or why it was so widespread. On several other points, however, experts do agree. In view of the crucial role played by the United States in world affairs after 1917, its economic policies, both internally and externally, had much to do with the coming of the Depression as well as its longevity. Unlike the pre-1914 era, the new international financial system had shown itself to be unstable, and the United States would not play the role that Britain had once played as watchdog of the system. Then, too, postwar recovery had proved to be less than universal, and much of the newly generated wealth was poorly distributed. Moreover, there were signs that the economy was far from in perfect order well before the stock market crash of 1929.

America in the Twenties

In the United States the age of postwar prosperity was known as the "Roaring Twenties," a term that captured the sense of modern, fast-paced life in a society marked by uncontrolled speculative investment, soaring profits, and the thirst for material well-being. Two Republican presidents, Warren G. Harding (served 1921–1923) and Calvin Coolidge (served 1923–1929), identified the nation's welfare with that of private business and followed a policy of noninterference in the workings of the economy. "This is a business country," proclaimed Coolidge, "and wants a business government." Federal spending was slashed, as were taxes for the highest income levels. Laws regulating business monopoly were eased, and the stock market was permitted to soar upward virtually without regulation.

The United States was not immune from the kind of flaws that marred European prosperity. A boom in Florida land speculation had burst in 1925, and in 1927 the industrial production index fell as a result of Ford's decision to close down his automobile plants in order to change over from the Model T to the Model A. Nevertheless, between 1923 and 1929, corporate profits increased by 62 percent, while real income for the average worker rose only 11 percent. One-third of all personal income went to the richest 5 percent of the population, and workers were unable to share adequately in the prosperity or to buy the huge quantity of industrial goods being produced. Overexpansion and large inventories of unsold goods led to job layoffs and business slowdowns even before the crash.

The economic growth of the 1920s had been financed largely by credit—business, personal, and international. Those who extended credit for business expansion assumed that borrowers could repay their loans with their profits while continuing to purchase capital goods. Similarly, stock investors bought heavily on a credit system known as "margin trading," which permitted them to pay out only a small part of the cost of their securities by borrowing most of the price from the brokers, who were themselves operating on bank credit. These practices fueled the unchecked financial speculation that led to the 1929 crash. Consumer credit was widely available in the form of installment plans. The ease of obtaining credit encouraged overspending for major purchases such as automobiles, appliances, and even houses. High sales expectations induced retailers and wholesalers to pay their suppliers with borrowed money. The danger, of course, lay in the fact that a call for repayment by any creditor would require everyone in the system to pay their debts in cash. Because most investors borrowed more than they could repay, the system was fraught with potential disaster.

America, Europe, and the Crash

On the international level, the credit system of the 1920s was equally precarious. Lavish loans were extended to many small nations, especially in Latin America and eastern Europe, despite their inability to repay the obligations. The decision of one creditor state to withdraw funds from a foreign bank or call in its loans threatened at any moment to upset international finances.

In the six years from 1924, the United States loaned 6.4 billion dollars abroad, mainly in short-term loans liable to sudden recall. Then, starting in June 1928, the American loans suddenly began to dry up. This shift in foreign lending was due primarily to the fact that as profits soared on the stock market, investors removed their resources from loans and put them into securities. (High interest rates in the United States also attracted foreign capital.) The problem, of course, was that the market value of securities was being inflated far beyond their actual worth. In 1928–1929, the average price of stocks on the New York Stock Exchange rose by 60 percent. The halt to U.S. lending placed a severe financial strain on a number of debtor countries, where economic activity began to decline.

The crash itself was precipitated when the Bank of England raised its interest rates at the end of September 1929, largely in order to attract capital back to London—the same day that the New York Stock Exchange reached its peak. Prices began to slip on October 3, and gave way to panic on October 24, known as "Black Thursday," as orders to sell exceeded orders to buy. A frenzy of selling swept the floor of the exchange, and panicked brokers demanded payment of margin payments that triggered bankruptcies among thousands of small investors. Confidence was partially restored when a group of powerful bankers pooled resources to buy securities. The next week, on "Black Tuesday," October 29, the market fell even more precipitously. Many who had bought cheaply the previous week were now forced to sell at great losses. As the collapse continued into November, increasingly larger investors went under. The spiral of ever-rising prices reversed itself as the market collapsed.

Given the fragile nature of the international financial system, the impact of the crash was bound to be felt abroad. American creditors called in their overseas loans. In May 1931 the *Creditanstalt*, which held two-thirds of all Austrian assets, failed, despite a loan from the Bank of England. The panic spread across Europe. Investors withdrew their capital from Germany, the largest recipient of foreign loans, and banks also began to fail there. In June 1931, U.S. President Herbert Hoover (served 1929–1933) declared a moratorium on all international debt payments. By July, British banks began to suffer, and in

October 1929 outside the New York Stock Exchange.

September the government there took the country off the gold standard.

THE GREAT DEPRESSION

The stock market crash did not cause the Great Depression, for the economy was already in deep trouble, but the panic brought a sudden halt to the years of economic optimism and led to a scramble for liquidity. Banks that had themselves invested heavily in securities failed, businesses cut back as sales and orders declined, both at home and abroad. Unemployment figures shot up throughout the world as the financial panic gave way to general economic depression.

Industry and Agriculture

As the financial crisis spread to business, large corporations slowed down or stopped production, for markets for industrial goods and raw materials soon disappeared. Compared to 1929, world industrial production dropped by 38 percent and global trade by two-thirds. The human impact of the Great Depression was devastating, giving rise to unprecedented misery. The ranks of the unemployed had grown so large that the very fabric of society was on the verge of being torn apart. As early as 1931, one-third of the entire German labor force—more than 6 million people—was jobless. The next year, when the Depression was at its worst, the number of unemployed in the United States reached 13 million. The following table gives an idea of the dimensions of the problem.

Table VIII.3.3

Percentage of the Labor Force Unemployed
(selected countries, 1929–1936)

	BRITAIN	GERMANY	SWEDEN	U.S.
1929	10.4	13.1	10.7	3.2
1930	16.1	22.2	12.2	8.7
1931	21.3	33.7	17.2	15.8
1932	22.1	43.7	22.8	23.6
1933	19.9	26.3	23.7	24.9
1934	16.7	14.9	18.9	26.7
1935	15.5	11.6	16.1	20.1
1936	13.1	8.3	13.6	16.9

The Depression caused widespread demoralization, both on the individual level and throughout society in general. In many instances, desperation grew into anger against existing governments and often expressed itself in radical political movements.

Throughout the 1920s, agriculture had been suffering from a chronic state of depression. One-fifth of Europe's wheat fields had been taken out of cultivation by the war, and the resulting rise in prices had encouraged farmers in North America to increase their output and to buy more land at relatively high prices. European output increased substantially for a variety of reasons. Improvements in mechanization now permitted a farmer to reap and bind five times more grain than was possible before the war. Political changes also

Parisians stood in long lines to collect free food during the Depression.

affected agriculture. In the new countries of Eastern Europe, the bulk of the population was still agrarian: three-quarters of the population of Yugoslavia, Romania, and Bulgaria, and two-thirds of all Poles, lived by farming. Between 1913 and 1939, cultivated areas increased by more than 17 million acres. Many of the large landed estates that had once dominated the

economic life of the region were broken up and small plots distributed to peasants.

Despite these reforms, however, the fall in agricultural prices—some 30 percent between 1925 and 1929—resulting from overproduction and competition from abroad hurt farmers everywhere. European governments tried to protect their farmers by raising agri-

Graph 3.1   Industrial Production in the Great Depression

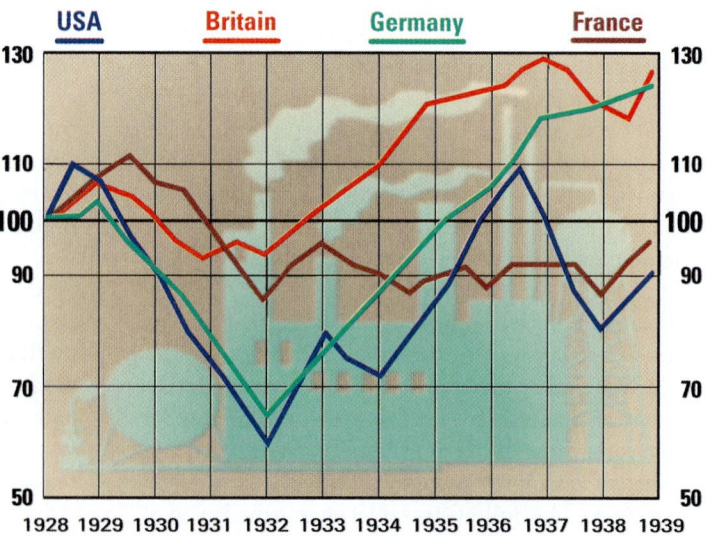

(Figures are shown for June of each year.)

cultural tariffs, a move that damaged producers elsewhere. With the coming of the Great Depression, prices fell even more sharply, making a bad situation worse. In general, agricultural interests suffered heavier losses than industrial interests during the Depression.

The New Economics and the New Deal

For many contemporaries, the Great Depression represented a crisis that confirmed long-held beliefs about the evils and weaknesses of capitalism. Karl Marx had asserted the inevitability of class conflict, and during World War I, Lenin had foreseen the collapse of capitalism as Western nations competed with each other over colonies and markets. Now, Marxists and others seemed about to be proven correct. Prime Minister Ramsay MacDonald of Great Britain (see Part VIII, Topic 5), himself a socialist, announced in 1930 that capitalism had to be blamed for the Depression: "We are not on trial," he said, "it is the system under which we live. It has broken down . . . everywhere, as it was bound to break down."

Government reaction to the Great Depression differed from country to country. In would-be totalitarian regimes such as Fascist Italy and the Soviet Union, governments created jobs for the unemployed and already provided a range of social services, including health care and other benefits (see Part VIII, Topic 4). In democratic states, however, where the principles of laissez-faire economics and limited government intervention prevailed, the policy adjustments caused by the economic collapse were more wrenching to tradition (see Part VIII, Topic 5).

First reactions, even under MacDonald's Labour government, included government spending cuts and tight fiscal policies, but when it was clear that such deflationary approaches only worsened conditions, the democracies turned increasingly to methods already in place elsewhere, including public works projects and extensive social insurance programs. Public officials took a more active role in shaping the economic and social affairs as the Depression forced governments to deal with the devastating impact of the collapse on millions of their citizens.

Even before the Depression had struck, the British economist John Maynard Keynes had begun to evolve theories about the economic responsibilities of government. A brilliant and eclectic thinker, Keynes was a member of the Bloomsbury Circle of intellectuals and artists (see Part VIII, Topic 7), a high-ranking civil servant, and taught at Cambridge University. He served as chief economist with the British delegation to the Paris Peace Conference in 1919.

As Keynes observed the already depressed conditions under which the British working class suffered in the second half of the 1920s, he began to rethink the entire basis of prevailing economic principles, and in the process offered a powerful critique of both laissez-faire capitalism and socialism. Keynes published his ideas in a variety of articles and books, including *The End of Laissez-Faire* (1926), and brought his arguments together in *The General Theory of Employment, Interest and Money* (1936). The classical theory of capitalist economic policy had long been that the laws of supply and demand would, if left to operate without interference, establish a healthy equilibrium of prices, wages, and production. But the chronic state of unemployment that dogged the British economy, together with his analysis of the Depression, led Keynes to conclude that the economics of free enterprise was imperfect and misguided. Instead, he argued that government should intervene actively in the economy, manipulating such controls as the interest rate, monetary expansion, and public works programs, to correct the weaknesses of capitalism. According to his theory, in times of economic dislocation governments could stimulate demand by priming the economic pump through public spending, which would in turn spark production and create jobs. Whether consciously or not, as bad times dragged on, most governments eventually adopted Keynesian principles in dealing with the Depression, and his ideas came to dominate economic thinking for generations to come.

It was in the United States, rather than in Europe, that Keynesian theories found their first widespread application among the democratic states of the West. As we have seen, nowhere had the principles of the free enterprise market economy been more freely or completely practiced than in the American economy of the 1920s, and nowhere was the collapse more extreme. The Hoover administration had initiated a number of programs to deal with the financial crisis as well as with the effects of the Depression. It was, however, with the election of Franklin D. Roosevelt (served 1933–1945) as president that American society underwent a major transformation.

Roosevelt's "New Deal" policies were aimed at bringing America out of the Depression by reforming the capitalist system so as to save it from destruction. His economic advisers, familiar with Keynesian ideas, pushed for massive government intervention in the economy. Roosevelt introduced far-reaching laws to regulate banking and investment, and created a host of government programs to stimulate business recovery, help the devastated farmers, strengthen labor organization, and create jobs. He also introduced several basic social welfare programs into American national life, including Social Security and unemployment compensation. The New Deal programs did stimulate recovery and cushioned the impact of the Depression for millions of citizens, although by the eve of World War II employment had not returned to pre-1929 levels. Nevertheless, the improvement in economic conditions was so successful that American voters eventually endorsed the New Deal reforms by reelecting Roosevelt to an unprecedented third term.

As soon as he was elected, Roosevelt had sent a special envoy to Fascist Italy to study how Mussolini's corporate state was coping with the Depression. The president's political opponents on the right charged that he was replacing capitalism with socialism, while those on the left accused him of fascism. It was, however, the ideas of Keynes that provided both the inspiration and the theoretical justification for the most radical transformation in modern Western economic thought. Reformers in Great Britain, France, and other democratic states eventually adopted similar programs, although not always with such enthusiasm as the New Dealers in the United States.

Despite the optimism that had greeted the end of the First World War, and the flashes of fast living and prosperity that marked the postwar era, the economic life of the interwar years was also characterized by partial recovery, instability, and uneven development. The momentary boom of 1919–1920 was followed by a longer period of recession and readjustment, after which some countries enjoyed a wave of prosperity while others went through a variety of economic experiences that ranged from the doldrums to real crisis. The legacies of reparations and war debts were in themselves partially responsible for the difficulties of recovery and for making the international financial system uncertain. The crisis of the Great Depression, when it came in 1929, should not have been totally unexpected.

The Depression was responsible in many instances for major change: in politics, for a radicalization of popular opinion that resulted in the rise of extremist movements and, in the case of Germany, contributed to the Nazi seizure of power; in social and economic policy, for an abandonment of the principles of laissez-faire economics by most Western nations and the inauguration of an era of government activism. The economic crisis weakened democracy and made other, totalitarian alternatives attractive to many millions of people who experienced the trauma of a world turned upside down.

Questions for Further Study

1. What effect did World War I have on the European economy?

2. What caused the Great Depression?

3. How did governments respond to the Great Depression?

Suggestions for Further Reading

Cameron, Rondo. *A Concise Economic History of the World.* New York, 1989.

Evans, Richard J., and D. Geary. *The German Unemployed: Experiences and Consequences of Mass Unemployment from the Weimar Republic to the Third Reich.* New York, 1987.

Galbraith, John K. *The Great Crash, 1929,* rev. ed. Boston, 1962.

Holtfrerich, Carl-Ludwig. *The German Inflation, 1914–1923.* Berlin, 1986.

Jackson, Julian. *The Politics of Depression in France, 1932–1936.* New York, 1985.

James, Harold. *The German Slump: Politics and Economics, 1924–1936.* Oxford, 1986.

Keynes, John M. *The Economic Consequences of the Peace.* London, 1919.

Kindleberger, Charles P. *The World in Depression, 1929–1939.* Berkeley, 1973.

Kuromiya, Hiroaki. *Stalin's Industrial Revolution: Politics and Workers, 1928–1932.* New York, 1988.

Maier, Charles S. *Recasting Bourgeois Europe: Stabilization in France, Germany, and Italy.* Princeton, NJ, 1975.

Topic 4

Mussolini, Hitler, Stalin: The Totalitarian Nightmare

he years between the two world wars saw the development of a new kind of anti-democratic political system known as totalitarianism. Europe had, of course, known powerful, centralized government in past centuries, and many of its monarchs had wanted to incorporate all power in their own hands, invoking the notion of divine right to legitimize their authority. The totalitarian state was a unique development in political theory, although in practice it is doubtful that a true totalitarian society was achieved in any of the three nations—Fascist Italy, Nazi Germany, and the Soviet Union—in which leaders aspired to create one.

Mussolini had become a dictator of Italy by 1925, and over the next 20 years he sought to make his government the first totalitarian regime in history, although it fell short of such expectations. Alongside the preexisting constitutional structure that had governed the country since unification, he created new Fascist institutions which he empowered with theoretically supreme authority.

After coming to terms with the Catholic Church, which exercised a powerful influence over Italian loyalties, he set about regimenting Italian society in an unparalleled fashion: revamping the educational system and dragooning all Italian youth into special organizations designed to indoctrinate and train them according to Fascist ideology. Mussolini's bureaucrats brought all aspects of intellectual and cultural life under government authority.

In order to mold popular consensus and extract obedience, the Fascist state combined positive image making with an atmosphere of terror. Mussolini did this by twin policies: by building a vast propaganda machine that shaped the values, ideas, and information received by the entire population; and by creating an elaborate police state that rounded up anti-Fascists and employed paid informants, torture, and internment programs.

Hitler built his totalitarian state in much the same manner. In Germany, where official theory was more clearly articulated, the degree of control exercised by the government was more effective and the party permeated the government bureaucracy and daily life more completely. Moreover, whereas Mussolini was largely uninterested in art and viewed it as propaganda, Hitler had clear and definite views about the kind of style and image he wanted German art to project.

There had been no real tradition of anti-Semitism in Italian Fascism, and Fascist racial policies were not as drastic as Nazi programs, nor were they implemented with any degree of enthusiasm. Most Italians greeted them with revulsion. Hitler's anti-Semitic policies, on the other hand, were at the core of Nazi belief. They began by stripping Jews of their rights as citizens, and ended with the horrors of the Holocaust. The Nazis' racism, together with the efficiency they were able to achieve in German society, made the regime there infinitely more brutal than that of Italy.

The totalitarian state in Stalin's Russia also reflected differences that derived from ideology and national circumstances. In his obsession to modernize Russia's economy, Stalin pushed his country into a vast experiment in social regimentation that aimed at maximizing agricultural and industrial productivity. Stalin was so driven to accumulate all power in his own hands, that he destroyed an entire generation of Soviet leaders to safeguard it. To combat the resistance against his development plans, and in a blind effort to wipe out his enemies, Stalin resorted to mass exterminations, labor camps, and purges that were unparalleled in their scope.

THE NATURE OF TOTALITARIANISM

The historical examples of Fascist Italy and Nazi Germany on the one hand and of the Soviet Union on the other suggest that totalitarianism is a politically neutral concept, linked neither to the left nor

Significant Dates

Fascist Italy and Nazi Germany

October 1922	Mussolini becomes prime minister of Italy
1926	Ministry of Corporations created
1929	Lateran Pacts
1930s	Fascistization of Italian society and culture
1930	Nazi electoral victories
January 1933	Hitler becomes chancellor
1930s	Regimentation of German life
1933	Mussolini sets up Institute for Industrial Reconstruction
June 30, 1934	Night of the Long Knives
1935	Nuremberg Laws
1938	Night of the Broken Glass
1938	Mussolini creates Chamber of Fasci and Corporations
October–November 1938	Anti-Semitic laws passed in Italy

the right. Totalitarianism is a type of government that seeks to exercise total control over the citizens of a given country, and to put into practice a set of beliefs designed to alter human society radically.

A set of common characteristics is usually found in all totalitarian regimes. Totalitarian states are dictatorships in which the ruler claims to exercise authority in the name of a political ideology. Mussolini, Hitler, and Stalin were radicals, each bent on forcing millions of citizens to conform to his values and each with a vision of an ideal future society. In the name of ideology, the most extreme crimes and horrors were committed and rationalized. In each case, the dictator was made the object of secular worship in order to justify his unlimited power.

Totalitarian governments are dominated by one political party and by the suspension of the most basic civil liberties. So intertwined are the dominant political party and the state bureaucracy that lines of authority are blurred. Totalitarian regimes are police states, in which force, violence, and terror are used against their own citizens. Such governments normally control the educational systems and mass media, and create an array of social institutions to indoctrinate and mobilize the population. Regardless of whether a particular regime rests on a socialist or capitalist footing, all totalitarian governments aim to centralize and shape economic policy.

ITALY UNDER MUSSOLINI: REGIMENTATION IN THE FASCIST STATE

Mussolini's totalitarian state continued to evolve over the entire two decades that he was in power. Yet within less than three years he had established the basic struc-

Map 4.1   Interwar Europe

ture of the regime: the one-party state, a secret police to arrest and a military tribunal to try anti-Fascists, press censorship, and loyalty oaths for government employees.

The Fascist State

Mussolini's regime grafted Fascist institutions on to already established government. Technically, the Italian constitution was the fundamental legal document of the realm and King Victor Emmanuel III still ruled, with the right to appoint and dismiss the prime minister (see Part VII, Topic 15). Mussolini allowed traditional forms to persist alongside his own, partially in order to preserve the fiction of legitimacy. He created, however, a Fascist Grand Council that included party and state officials and was to be the supreme organ of state. Mussolini personally selected the members of the Grand Council as well as candidates for Chamber of Deputies elections. The Grand Council was to abolish Parliament altogether in 1938 and put in its place the Chamber of Fasci and Corporations, whose members were elected not from political parties but job categories.

Ever since Italy had seized Rome from the papacy in 1870, the Vatican had refused to recognize the existence of the Italian state. One of Mussolini's most popular decisions was to make peace with the Catholic Church. There were two chief reasons for this. Millions of Italians were devout Catholics and were loath to divide their loyalties between church and state; and the church was perceived as acting as a stable, conservative influence in modern society. In 1929, therefore, he and Pope Pius XI (ruled 1922–1939) concluded the Lateran Pacts, according to which the Vatican City became an independent state ruled by the pope inside the confines of Rome. The government also repealed the anticlerical legislation passed since 1870. Mussolini further agreed to pay the Vatican a large sum of money in compensation for the lost papal territory around Rome. Perhaps more important, however, the church's popular

Official "Fascist" architecture under Mussolini evolved into a modernized classicism, as in this "Palace of Civilization" built for the 1942 world's fair in Rome.

youth organizations were now permitted to operate without harassment, and the Vatican was to have its own newspaper and radio station. Mussolini also implemented compulsory religious instruction in public schools. This "concordat" was an important success for Mussolini, who not only guaranteed himself the public support of the church, but instantly won the admiration of Catholics everywhere.

The Making of Consensus

Mussolini enjoyed considerable popular support, at least until his foreign adventures in the mid-1930s. Such consensus was the result of a dual policy of coer-

cion and socialization. The Fascist police system was a complicated affair, consisting of several traditional Italian police units as well as a special division of "political police" and a network of paid informants operated by an agency known as OVRA. In addition, tens of thousands of anti-Fascists were rounded up and placed under surveillance or sent to domestic exile in remote and barren parts of Italy. As effective as this structure was, it proved less gruesome than the mass killings in Hitler's or Stalin's police states.

The Fascists devised numerous methods for forging consensus among intellectuals and artists. Some were appointed to a new Royal Academy, others were given secret government subsidies or government employment, and others were simply ignored as long as they did not openly oppose the regime. In the 1930s Mussolini created a Ministry of Popular Culture that controlled newspapers, radio, theater, film production, and book publishing. Mussolini's longtime mistress and confidant, the art critic Margherita Sarfatti (1880–1961), presided over a famous salon and attracted many talented artists and writers to the regime. She even started an art movement of her favorite painters that stressed a return to classical values couched in a modern style. While the regime did not officially endorse this or any other artistic movement, it also did not condemn artists for their style or theories. Within limits, intellectuals and artists were allowed a surprisingly wide margin of freedom.

The Fascist party played a crucial role in regimentation. A host of organizations provided Italian youth with political indoctrination and physical training. Although many parents refused to send their children to party groups, by the mid-1930s they had enrolled more than 3 million boys and girls. Popular

Regimentation programs in Fascist Italy included Fascist party organizations that trained and indoctrinated children and youths from the age of six. Here "Sons of the Wolf" are on parade in Rome.

leisure time programs, including cultural events, vacations, and light entertainment, were provided by the "after work" organization, known as the *Dopolavoro*. Millions of Italians joined the party in the 1930s, for job opportunities if not out of conviction.

Under the fanatical direction of party secretary Achille Starace (1889–1945), the regime even tried to change the way in which Italians behaved in their daily lives. Starace, who became something of a joke among many Italians, ordered civilians not to use words of foreign origin, to salute each other instead of shaking hands, and to wear black shirts instead of dresses and business suits.

The party propaganda machine exalted Mussolini as the *Duce* of Fascism, the wise, strong, and all-powerful leader who would make Italy great again. Absurd slogans, plastered on public buildings and taught to schoolchildren, were intended as secular chants to the myth of the Duce: "Better one day as a lion than a hundred years as a sheep," or "Believe! Obey! Fight!" Partly under Sarfatti's influence, the regime merged Fascist themes with ancient Roman images, and Mussolini—portrayed in official sculpture and painting as the new Caesar—promised to restore the glories of the imperial age.

The other side of life in Mussolini's Italy was represented by the many ordinary Italians who opposed Fascism. When Mussolini declared his dictatorship, many anti-Fascists were beaten or arrested, but a remarkable number of prominent political leaders managed to escape abroad, where they regrouped and established resistance organizations. Inside the country, many others engaged in minor acts of opposition or were involved in underground networks. Not all such people were active anti-Fascists, but during World War II, hundreds of thousands of Italians participated in the armed resistance.

HITLER'S GERMANY: RACE AND REPRESSION IN THE NAZI REGIME

The coming of the Great Depression in 1930 gave the Nazis the huge popular following that Hitler needed. In 1925, Field Marshal Paul von Hindenburg, the hero of World War I, was elected president of the Republic. Hindenburg, already in his late seventies, was an upright, stolid patriarchal figure who gave Germany an aura of stability. Yet not even Hindenburg's prestige could stave off the terrible economic plight that struck Germany, which experienced a more severe setback than any other European state in 1930. With industrial production at 39 percent of its former level and some 6 million out of work, the economic crisis devastated the German working class and wiped out the incomes and savings of much of the middle class.

The National Socialist Victory

Such extreme conditions undermined popular consensus for the centrist parties that had stabilized the Weimar Republic since its birth, and created the conditions under which the Nazis could come to power. In their desperation, the German electorate turned to extremist forces on the right and the left. The Nazis increased their seats in the Reichstag dramatically, first to 107 in September 1930 and then to a startling 230 in July 1932, making it the largest single party in Parliament. The Communists jumped from 54 to 89. Hitler stood at the edge of power.

In 1932 Germany experienced a three-way race for the office of president. The aged Hindenburg was persuaded to run again, and against him were arrayed the Communist candidate Ernst Thaelmann and Hitler. Hitler won enough votes to enter a runoff election with Hindenburg, who won. Nevertheless, Hitler had attracted some 13 million voters, many of them from the working class. In the November parliamentary elections that same year, the Nazis dropped down to 196 seats while the Communists increased their strength to 100. In Germany, as in postwar Italy, the specter of the radical left frightened many middle-class citizens into the arms of the right. Conservative forces grew more comfortable with the notion of a Hitler-led government and began to provide the Nazis with money and support, thinking that once in office Hitler would become tame. Hindenburg was finally persuaded to ask Hitler to form a cabinet.

Hitler took office as chancellor on January 30, 1933. He immediately dissolved Parliament and prepared for elections. At that moment, the Reichstag building itself burned down in a mysterious fire, and Hitler accused the Communists of responsibility. The German people went to the polls in an angry mood, while the Nazis unleashed another round of violence on their enemies. The Nazis won 44 percent of the seats in the Reichstag, enabling them to form a coalition with the Nationalists, who held 8 percent.

Armed with a majority, Hitler then invoked Article 48 of the constitution and proclaimed a state of emergency. He ejected the Communists from Parliament and had the rump Reichstag grant him extraordinary powers. All political parties except the Nazis were outlawed, and when Hindenburg died in August 1934, Hitler merged the offices of president and chancellor into his own hands. Adolf Hitler had become dictator of Germany.

Hitler's totalitarian state took shape more rapidly than Mussolini's. Within a year of coming to power in 1933, he had established most of the institutions that would characterize Nazi Germany. The Nazi restructuring of German life was in many respects more radical, and the impact on Europe more profound. Hitler, who liked to think in sweeping historical clichés, called his creation the "Third Reich" (the first *Reich* was the Holy Roman Empire, from 800 to 1806, and the second was imperial Germany, from 1871 to 1918) and predicted that it would remain for a thousand years.

The Third Reich

Hitler made himself the supreme leader (*Führer*) of the German state. So powerful was he that the very concept of sovereignty—the legitimate right to rule—emanated not from the people or a deity, but from himself. The German legal system was completely Nazified. Thenceforth, the higher interests of the state provided the basis for all laws. Nazi "justice" was meted out by People's Courts in the name of the Führer.

The German Republic, like the Second Reich before it, had been a federal arrangement composed of a variety of state governments, such as Prussia and Bavaria. Hitler did away with these states, substituting in their place a highly centralized government. In keeping with the Nazi theory of the "conquest of the state," appropriate party leaders assumed command of equivalent positions in the government administration. Hitler retained the Reichstag, but removed all real authority from it.

Hitler could neither remain in power very long nor carry out his strategy for world hegemony without the support of the German Army. But most of the German officer corps, with a long tradition of status and aristocratic privilege behind it, considered Hitler and his Nazi entourage low-class thugs. From their perspective, the generals saw Hitler as a temporary expedient who would serve a useful purpose in destroying the Republic and restoring the army to its former position of strength. Like Mussolini, Hitler had to compromise with the generals, and like Mussolini he did so by sacrificing his own storm troops, the SA.

Ernst Roehm, the deposed leader of the SA, had come back to Germany on Hitler's urging in 1930 and had been instrumental in the seizure of power (see Part VIII, Topic 2). But Roehm had always resented the power and pretensions of the generals, and after 1933 he demanded that Hitler replace the German Army with the SA. For Hitler, the choice between the SA and the army was clear, and he secured a pledge of loyalty from the generals in return for the destruction of Roehm's forces. The agreement was executed on the night of June 30 in a series of surprise raids of SA camps throughout Germany. The purge, known as the "Night of the Long Knives," ended with the cold-blooded murder of Roehm and his followers.

The Nazi police state was as complex as Mussolini's structure. The secret police (*Gestapo*) sought out anti-Nazis and other internal political enemies. Information and confessions were extracted by torture and blackmail, but the victims of Nazi terror were often summarily executed or incarcerated without

Nazi propagandists organized carefully choreographed public ceremonies and party rallies. Here Hitler addresses a huge 1936 event.

formal charges. As early as 1933, Hitler opened the first concentration camp at Dachau, where political prisoners were kept. Almost a dozen more were subsequently constructed. Heinrich Himmler, who served both as head of the Gestapo and the SS, ran the camps, where prisoners were either used as slave labor, were allowed to die of hunger, or were otherwise brutalized. During World War II, the death camps became the most horrible manifestation of Nazism.

Hitler, Mussolini, and Racial Policy

Hitler's own twisted contempt for Jews, Slavs, gypsies, and other ethnic groups that he considered "inferior" became the basis of Nazi ideology. Yet, in making racism a part of his political program, he called upon an extensive European tradition of prejudice and hatred. The Nazis mixed these traditions with 19th-century Pan-German sentiment, believing with Hitler that the German "Master Race" would inevitably rule the world. Hitler's obsessive hatred for the Jews was the focus of a huge and systematic effort by the Nazi state of unparalleled evil—their mass extermination.

Anti-Semitism became official policy almost immediately. Jews were purged from government employment in April 1933. Two years later, in 1935, the so-called Nuremberg Laws stripped Jews of their rights as citizens, and made it a crime for them to marry "pure" Germans. Jews were forbidden to practice medicine or law and could no longer attend or teach in universities (see Part VIII, Topic 9). The regime then launched a moral and physical assault against the Jewish communities of Germany.

SA commander Ernst Roehm (right) and SS leader Heinrich Himmler (center) confer with police officer Kurt Daluege, 1933.

In November 1938, Goebbels orchestrated an assault on Jewish businesses and synagogues known as *Kristallnacht.*

Those Jews who recognized the danger tried to leave Germany, but too many found it impossible. In 1938, a Polish Jew killed a German diplomat in Paris, and the crime became the excuse for the unleashing of a premeditated attack against German Jewish synagogues, homes, and businesses. Many Jews lost their lives in the carnage, and the government then levied heavy taxes on the victims. After this destruction—known as *Kristallnacht* (Night of the Broken Glass)—it was increasingly difficult for Jews to flee the country, and those who managed to get away found in many cases that the Western powers were not disposed to take them in. While some Western leaders criticized German policy, their warnings fell on deaf ears.

In November 1938, Mussolini reversed himself on the question of the Jews. Before that, he had claimed repeatedly that Fascism was not anti-Semitic. Indeed, his mistress, Margherita Sarfatti, was Jewish. The decision to introduce anti-Semitic legislation was a purely political one—his desire to align Italy in a united front with Germany. The measures that Mussolini enacted, although thoroughly reprehensible, were not nearly as severe as those in Germany. Italy's 50,000 Jews had to abandon most professions and universities, but Italian-born Jews retained their citizenship. Mixed marriages were forbidden and Jews were not allowed to own land. On the other hand, unlike Nazism's immutable "scientific" racism, Fascist laws enabled some Jews—such as early members of the Fascist movement, war veterans, and children of mixed marriages who did not profess Judaism—to escape their provisions.

The Regimentation of German Life

To Nazi ideologues, the German churches, whether Catholic or Protestant, competed with the state for control over the minds of the German people. Parents were pressured not to send their children to religious schools and the authorities deliberately encouraged anti-Christian cults based on old Teutonic deities. Hitler, therefore, persecuted the churches, confiscated their newspapers, and even arrested their priests and bishops. The state tried without success to impose a "German Christian" church on Protestants. A group of clergy under the leadership of Pastor Martin Niemoeller (1892–1984) and others was the center of Protestant resistance. Niemoeller himself was an outspoken critic of Hitler and was interned in a concentration camp in 1937. Many Catholic priests were similarly engaged in anti-Nazi activities and offered refuge to Jews and other victims of Nazi persecution. In 1937, Pope Pius XI issued the encyclical *Mit Brennender Sorge* (With Burning Sorrow) to reject Nazi racism.

Nazism presented itself as a revolutionary force in German society, promising prosperity and equality. Its propaganda was most successful among the middle classes, who saw the regime as having saved them from the despair of the Great Depression. The Nazi party instituted the same array of social and leisure organizations as Mussolini had created in Italy, including "Strength Through Joy," similar to Mussolini's *Dopolavoro*. The *Hitler Jugend* (Hitler Youth) indoctrinated young Germans with Nazi ideas and the virtues of discipline and obedience. The educational system, from elementary schools to universities, was reorganized and the faculties purged. Hitler did actually break down some of the social distinctions that had existed, especially for middle-class German men, and both the government and the party bureaucracies offered opportunities to many for rapid advancement.

Joseph Goebbels (1897–1945), one of Hitler's closest associates, a brilliant manipulator of public opinion, was minister of Propaganda and Enlightenment. Goebbels imposed rigid controls on all aspects of intellectual and artistic life, including the mass media, literature, publishing, music, and art. Books that were banned by the government were burned in dramatic public bonfires.

Hitler was, for obvious reasons, especially concerned with art and architecture. Modernism and abstraction were anathema to him, examples of what he called "decadence." He purged the art academies and the museum staffs and in 1937 opened an "Exhibition of Degenerate Art," in which were displayed the works of the Cubists, Expressionists, and other modern movements. He insisted that art inspire German values. Official painting presented versions of Nazi mythology: Germanic knights, idealized peasant families, nudes in classical poses, and beautiful youths enraptured by the Nazi ideal. In architecture, Hitler closed down the Bauhaus, which had been the center of Europe's functional international style (see Part VIII, Topic 7), and worked closely with Albert Speer (1905–1981), the government's official architect, in designing monumental structures in the neo-Greek revival style.

THE DICTATORS AND THE DEPRESSION: LABOR, BUSINESS, AND ECONOMIC POLICY

Mussolini and Hitler pursued similar economic policies, designed to make their countries self-sufficient and capable of waging modern war. Although neither dictator wanted to end private property, both imposed state intervention in the economy that went far beyond the measures taken by the Western powers during the Great Depression. The fascist regimes devised new methods for government control and participation in private industry, and set production goals for key sectors vital to national security. Public works programs and rearmament did much to alleviate unemployment caused by the Depression, and public monies funded state welfare agencies and unemployment insurance, and pensions. Each pursued strong currency policies and inflation control.

Mussolini's Corporate State

The Fascists, who came to power in part because they opposed Marxism, appeased the business interests by outlawing strikes and traditional labor unions. They also permitted manufacturing associations to bargain with Fascist unions and the government.

Such measures did not sit well with Fascist syndicalists, and in 1926 Mussolini created the Ministry of Corporations. Corporativism was to be a system of institutional arrangements in which capital and labor were integrated into units. In this arrangement, each unit, or corporation, was supposed to regulate a particular sector of industry or the economy, supervised by the disinterested power of the state. The theory behind this unique concept was that class conflict, which Marx had said was inevitable, would be overcome.

Between 1929 and 1932, the minister of Corporations was the Fascist intellectual Giuseppe Bottai (1895–1959), who tried unsuccessfully to use state authority to dictate to both management and labor. Mussolini insisted the "corporate state" remain a fiction, for the private sector had grown too powerful. The corporate system, which was advertised to the world as a "third way" between capitalism and communism, served only as a propaganda device.

The effects of the Depression were not as severe in Italy as they were in Germany. Nevertheless, it did wipe out many of the gains that the boom of the 1920s had created. Unemployment stood at 1 million in 1933, stock prices fell by 39 percent, and the previously balanced budget went into deficit. The policy of "autarchy," designed to make Italy self-sufficient in agriculture and some industries, tended to force workers into unprofitable areas of production and to drive up prices. Although wheat production went up, other kinds of crops went down. Higher tariffs, used to protect Italian manufacturers, pushed the cost of living up and created shortages.

Another novel aspect of Fascist economic policy was the Institute for Industrial Reconstruction (IRI), established in 1933. The IRI bought up the large stock holdings of big banks and companies on the edge of bankruptcy, thus making the government a major stockholder. By 1939, the government owned 70 percent of pig iron production and 45 percent of steel manufacturing, and could control both.

Spending on public works projects, used by most governments in Europe and America to alleviate effects of the Depression in the 1930s, doubled. Mussolini drained swamps and marshes to produce more farmland, roads and rail lines were constructed, and thousands of government buildings and subsidized housing projects sprang up the length of the peninsula. Nevertheless, the Depression, combined with Mussolini's economic policies, meant a decline in the standard of living for most Italians.

The Nazi Economy

Hitler's efforts to fight the Great Depression with public works projects were even more extensive. Here, too, swamps were drained and forests replanted, public housing was built and highways extended across the country. Agriculture was important to the Nazis, not only because of their back to the soil movement, but to make Germany self-reliant in the event of war. Government subsidies were extended to farmers along with long-term loans. The regime also encouraged scientists working in private industry to develop synthetic products such as plastics and alternative food stuffs.

As in Italy, German workers lost most of their economic rights, although unemployment virtually disappeared and the standard of living improved. In 1936 Hitler launched a Four-Year Plan that regulated all sectors of the economy, from prices to wages and from factory regulations to production levels. A National Labor Front took the place of labor unions and strikes were forbidden, while industrial associations were recognized as part of the state structure. Private industry remained intact, although government regulations were more stringent. Although most workers had more stable jobs, they generally worked longer hours and earned lower wages.

In the case of both fascist regimes, economic policies were not based on long-term development, and whatever stability existed was achieved at the price of the destruction of working-class freedoms.

STALINIST RUSSIA: STATE PLANNING, COLLECTIVIZATION, AND THE POLICE STATE

Stalin's totalitarian dictatorship differed in several respects from those in the West. In the first place, according to Marxist theory, the state itself was supposed to be temporary. Then, too, instead of having to create a new revolutionary regime, when Stalin came to power in the late 1920s the communist state was already in place. Politically, his aim was simple—to consolidate

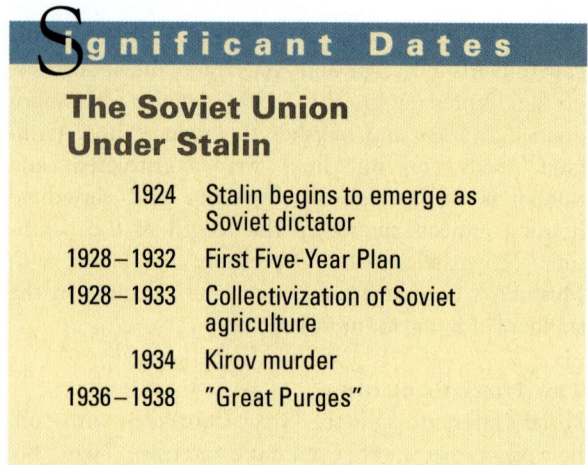

and strengthen his personal power (on Stalin's rise to power, see Part VIII, Topic 2).

Stalin was, of course, committed to Communism, and had always considered Lenin's NEP program a temporary makeshift. His ambition was to make the Soviet Union a great industrial giant and to socialize agriculture as well as industry. To achieve these goals, Stalin would remake the country's society.

The fundamental techniques employed by Stalin in his drive to industrialize and modernize the Soviet economy were similar to those employed in Italy and Germany: state intervention and centralized planning. Here, however, the degree of regimentation and coercion of the working class was even greater.

The Planned Economy

Stalin devised the idea of a Five-Year Plan, the first of which unfolded between 1928 and 1932. Under this plan, every national resource was to be mobilized in order to achieve a fundamental transformation. Stalin eliminated all vestiges of private property and instituted industrial quotas that were determined by an agency of the Communist party. The emphasis was placed on heavy industry and transportation, which received the greatest resources, so that the production and availability of consumer goods suffered and rationing was imposed.

The quotas established for every individual worker and production unit were almost always too high. Stalin's plan anticipated more than doubling industrial manufacturing and tripling steel making. While workers and plant managers who reached their goals were rewarded, those who failed to meet the quotas were penalized. Most Russian workers were unskilled and not accustomed to the pace and discipline imposed by the Five-Year Plan, and managers had to learn on the job.

The first Plan achieved only part of its goals, largely because of the unreasonably high quotas.

Equipment was overused and often of poor quality, so that mechanical breakdowns were not unusual, and parts were difficult to obtain. The same could be said for the products themselves, since quantity was stressed at the expense of quality. Much of the machinery and many technical advisers were brought to the Soviet Union from Western countries.

Despite these setbacks, Stalin, who had learned some lessons, announced the second Five-Year Plan in 1932, which moved at a more reasonable rate (the Second Plan covered the years 1933–1937, and the Third 1938–1942). By 1938, iron and steel production had increased four times and coal three and one-half times. On the eve of World War II, the Soviet Union was the third nation in the world in industrial output, being surpassed only by the United States and Germany, and was ahead of Great Britain in steel and iron.

In the agricultural sector, Stalin sought to place the entire Soviet harvest under government control. Surpluses could be sold abroad to buy the sophisticated machinery needed at home. To achieve these goals, Stalin decided on the destruction of the entire class of landowning peasants known as the *kulaks*, who had prospered under the NEP. The kulaks—a term of derision used to describe greedy money lenders—were sufficiently prosperous to hire farm laborers and to extend loans to the local villagers. The elimination of the kulaks would enable the government to consolidate the numerous small farms into huge agricultural collectives, where modern equipment and farming techniques could be used efficiently.

Collectivization and the Peasantry

The collectivization program required that all peasants turn their land and livestock over to the state, keeping only their houses and personal property. As in industry, every collective received production quotas. Peasants shared the work as well as the profits or losses the cooperative earned.

The peasants staunchly resisted collectivization, and fought back against the state by hiding or burning their crops and killing their animals. The resulting shortages of food caused deep concern in Moscow. In the Russian countryside, a massive rebellion soon consumed an untold number of lives—Stalin himself admitted later to 10 million.

Collectivization wreaked havoc on Soviet agriculture. The kulaks, generally the best farmers, were either killed or deported to Siberia, and half of all farm animals destroyed. Grain production hardly increased in the decade after 1928. Collectivization also produced a terrible famine in 1932–1933, and it killed an estimated 3 million persons. The heavy price paid by Russian peasants brought Stalin a political success, for he could now claim that socialism had reached the

In the 1930s, Stalin sought to collectivize Soviet agriculture. Here farm workers engage in a meeting to discuss production.

countryside. By 1933, more than half of all farming families had joined collectives, and five years later the figure had passed 90 percent.

Soviet Society Under Stalin

The ambitious plans that Stalin set transformed the Soviet Union. Thousands of factories were built in the 1930s, and the industrial expansion swelled the size of older cities and gave rise to new urban centers in isolated regions of Siberia and Asiatic Russia. Millions of people were moved en masse from rural regions to the new cities to supply the workforce.

Life everywhere was difficult for the average Soviet citizen. Housing was primitive and in short supply and the steady rise in prices produced a serious drop in the standard of living. In the decade following the start of the Five-Year Plans, for example, the purchasing power of an industrial worker declined by some 40 percent. The constraints of political indoctrination were oppressive. Adults and children alike became captive audiences for party lecturers, and the government-operated mass media were filled with official information. Mass organizations for the young, women, and workers assisted in the indoctrination process. In addition to selling the virtues of Communism, Soviet propaganda stressed a theme that was crucial to the dictatorship: the creation of the cult of Stalin. Stalin's face became familiar to all Russians as his photograph and portrait appeared everywhere.

Some important positive advances were made in Soviet life during Stalin's dictatorship. Nearly every able-bodied citizen found a job, although most involved unskilled heavy labor. The government provided free education and medical care, cheap housing, and pensions. In education the progress was more impressive. Stalin sought to wipe out illiteracy and brought free elementary schooling to the far reaches of the country. For those with superior skills, higher education was available. Education, especially of a technical nature, could lead to higher salaries, privileges, and status. A managerial class eventually joined the political and intellectual élites, giving the lie to the notion of a "classless society."

The Stalinist Terror

Although the police state was a pervasive feature of life in the fascist dictatorships, neither Hitler nor Mussolini used it in quite the same way as Stalin, who unleashed a reign of terror on a vast scale against the Soviet population at large.

The suppression of the peasants during the collectivization and the Five-Year Plans had caused considerable unrest, not only among ordinary Soviet citizens but in the inner circles of the Communist party and the state administration as well. Stalin decided in the mid-1930s to use his domestic security forces to crush any signs of discontent and eliminate possible opposition to his rule. The so-called "Great Purges" were so indiscriminate that even high-ranking military officers suffered the fate of dissidents. For two years, between 1936 and 1938, millions of Soviets suffered imprisonment, forced labor, and death at the hands of a ruthless dictator.

Stalin first struck in late 1934, when one of his most trusted followers, Sergei Kirov (1888–1934), was murdered. Stalin himself no doubt had Kirov killed, and then used the murder as a pretext for wide-scale purges. Announcing a plot against him by Trotsky's followers, he held a number of infamous show trials in Moscow. In 1936, the court accused 16 prominent Old Bolsheviks of conspiracy and ordered their execution. The next year, a number of less important party leaders were similarly eliminated, followed by the court martial of General Mikhail Tukhachevsky (1893–1937) and other high-ranking officers. Soon, vast numbers of innocent people, including government and party bureaucrats and intellectuals, workers and factory foremen, fell victim to the ever-expanding purge. In the end, Stalin completed the process by having officials of the NKVD—the internal security unit—themselves eliminated. The statistics of Stalin's terror can only be estimated, but perhaps as many as 8 million people were held in prisons or work camps, 90 percent of whom eventually died, and the total number of deaths may have exceeded 10 million.

When the Great Purges were over, Stalin had succeeded in clearing out entire categories of the Soviet leadership. The officials whom he appointed to the vacant positions represented a new breed of bureaucrat, not tied to the Old Bolsheviks or to the Revolution of 1917, but bound only by loyalty and fear to Stalin himself. Stalin's power was now virtually without limits.

WOMEN AND TOTALITARIANISM

The interwar totalitarian dictatorships were the first national governments to implement clear policies regarding the position of women. These programs responded in part to the ideologies of each movement, and in part to the economic and social priorities of the regimes. Fascism was a philosophy of conquest, in which women were to be subsumed to men's desires, whereas the earliest Soviet laws had accepted the notion of women's equality. Yet both forms of totalitarianism allowed only limited scope for women to develop their potential in society or to share in the exercise of power.

Fascism and Women

Among the "Fascists of the First Hour" in 1919 were to be found a number of Italian women, including the female Black Shirt leader Regina Teruzzi and Mussolini's lover, Sarfatti. Nevertheless, Fascists in general held most women in contempt, regarding them primarily as wives, mistresses, and mothers. Mussolini himself was never loyal to the many women in his life, and yet his public reputation as a womanizer inflated his popular image.

Fascists considered it the natural duty of men to possess women sexually. In official lore, Fascists were by definition young and virile warriors, and all Italian males were to be "new men," ruthless, hard, and heroic. Women, on the other hand, were to be pure and subservient keepers of the hearth. The regime's propaganda machine reinforced a stable and traditional patriarchal social order of the kind that was familiar to most Italians. The Fascist party ran separate youth organizations for all males and females ages six through seventeen.

Because Mussolini wanted to increase Italy's population, the regime encouraged large families. Adolescent females were given instruction in caring for a home and children, and the state gave mothers free birthing and medical assistance, hygiene care, and prizes to the families with the largest number of children.

For a brief period before coming to power, Mussolini had demanded women's suffrage, but he later changed his mind. During the 1920s and 1930s, fewer and fewer women were active in the industrial workforce, a trend accelerated by the large unemployment figures of the Great Depression. Some specialized fields, such as nursing and teaching, were regarded as suitable for women, but by and large females were discouraged from entering the professions. By law, husbands retained superior rights over children and property, and divorce went unrecognized.

Women and the Nazi State

Like Mussolini, Hitler found little room for women in his Nazi movement or in his government. He did not marry until just before his suicide in 1945, and although for a number of years he had maintained a liaison with Eva Braun, the relationship may have been purely platonic. The Führer demanded that women provide Germany with children who would become workers and soldiers. Government policies and party programs encouraged larger families and modern medical care for mothers and children.

The Nazi party deliberately recruited women, and in the early 1920s about one in five members of the NSDAP was women. After the seizure of power, women never achieved important positions in the regime. Nazi women, on the other hand, supported Hitler's goal of restoring family values, and were active in community work designed to foster such attitudes. At first, women were not encouraged to work in factories or agriculture, but when Hitler began to rearm Germany, they moved into the labor force in larger numbers.

Women were an important part of the Soviet workforce in industry as well as agriculture.

There was in Nazi aesthetics an element of repressed sexuality, whether in painting, sculpture, or film. Hitler had always railed against cultural decadence and pornography, but prized the nude in art. Women were portrayed as the embodiment of the ideal German female, virtuous and pure, while male bodies were presented as athletes and warriors. In the propaganda films of the great director Leni Riefenstahl (see Part VIII, Topic 7), there is, among the thousands of semi-clothed young Germans whom she idolized, an underlying if unacknowledged sexual tension. Riefenstahl subsumed that tension in images of perfect beauty, choreographing them in dances of dominance and power.

Soviet Women

Marx and Engels had both seen the repression of women as a function of the suppression of the working class, arguing that in capitalist societies women were a form of property. Lenin agreed, and as early as 1918, the party had set up a special Women's Bureau to mobilize women into the party. Alexandra Kollontai (1872–1952), an early Bolshevik leader, pushed for sexual freedom and laws that would make her feminist ideals a reality. The Soviet constitution embodied full rights and equality for women, yet although Russian women did gain the right to divorce and abortion in the 1920s, reality never matched the official rhetoric.

Under Stalin, the position of Soviet women changed. He played down talk of gender equality, but his drive to industrialize and increase production brought women into the workforce in large numbers, just as the collectivization of agriculture did for rural women. Low salaries encouraged women to seek employment in even the heaviest kind of work. The acute shortage of trained professionals and technicians also led Stalin to make education available to Soviet women. Although women had greater access to employment and education in the Soviet Union than in the West, they did not receive equal pay for equal work. Nor were they relieved of the burdens of child rearing and housekeeping.

The totalitarian experience in interwar Europe had profound repercussions. In their effort to control the minds and the values as well as the loyalties of their subjects, these regimes succeeded in mobilizing millions of people in an unprecedented fashion. Programs of indoctrination and socialization drew formerly isolated sectors of Europe's population into the mainstream of national life, and politicized them for the first time. Never before were the lives and deaths of such vast numbers of citizens so directly affected by government actions.

Mussolini, Hitler, and Stalin were major figures of the period, whose personalities and policies dominated public events for years. Their revolutions were designed to destroy ordinary politics of the kind familiar to most westerners, and each of their regimes was built with the intention of implementing a particular worldview and a philosophy of life. That philosophy preached the attainment of utopia through dominance, power, and control. The human suffering that resulted has perhaps never been equaled in modern history.

Questions for Further Study

1. Is the concept of "totalitarianism" useful for historians? Why? Why not?

2. What similarities and differences existed between the Fascist state and the Nazi state?

3. What was the nature of totalitarian economic policy? How did the fascist dictators respond to the Great Depression?

4. What factors explain Stalinist terror?

5. What role did women have in totalitarian societies? Was it different from their role in democratic societies?

Suggestions for Further Reading

Bracher, Karl D. *The German Dictatorship*. New York, 1970.

Cannistraro, Philip V., and B. R. Sullivan. *Il Duce's Other Woman*. New York, 1993.

Conquest, Robert. *The Great Terror: A Reassessment*. New York, 1989.

De Grand, Alexander. *Fascist Italy and Nazi Germany: The Fascist Style of Rule*. London, 1995.

Kerhsaw, Ian. *The Hitler Myth: Image and Reality in the Third Reich*. New York, 1987.

Koonz, Claudia. *Mothers in the Fatherland: Women, the Family, and Nazi Politics*. New York, 1987.

Mack Smith, Denis. *Mussolini*. New York, 1982.

Peukert, Detlev J. K. *Inside Nazi Germany*. New Haven, CT, 1987.

Tannenbaum, Edward R. *The Fascist Experience: Italian Society and Culture, 1922–1945*. New York, 1972.

Tucker, Robert C. *Stalin in Power*. New York, 1990.

Ulam, Adam. *Stalin: The Man and His Era*. New York, 1973.

Topic 5

THE WESTERN DEMOCRACIES AND EASTERN EUROPE

n the 20 years between the two world wars, the viability of European democracy was put to the test by a variety of destructive forces. The rise of fascism, and particularly the success of the movements in Italy and Germany, combined with the triumph of communism in Russia, appeared to forecast the wave of the future. With the 1929 crash and the resultant Great Depression, the social and economic systems of the two great Western democracies, Britain and France, came under tremendous stress.

In the 1920s, the prevalent trend in domestic politics was the search for stability, a goal that proved impossible in the context of postwar conditions. Readjustment to peacetime economies had been difficult, and alternating cycles of unemployment, inflation, and depression jarred Britain and France. Working-class discontent grew markedly, and even the formation of Britain's first socialist government—that of Ramsay MacDonald in 1924—failed to quell the unrest or its causes. The Conservatives returned quickly to power in an atmosphere of fear over communism, and despite their unsympathetic handling of the 1926 general strike, they remained in power until 1929. MacDonald formed another government that year but quickly abandoned full responsibility for dealing with the Depression by forming a coalition cabinet that persisted for five years. Nevertheless, drift rather than decisive action remained the order of the day.

In France, where the Depression hit later than elsewhere, the right and the left also alternated in power and produced equally unimpressive results. As in Britain, the first postwar elections returned a conservative majority, but its strident nationalism over the Ruhr invasion in 1923 frightened many Frenchmen into voting for the left. The Socialists formed a coalition with the Radicals, but the financial irresponsibility of Édouard Herriot's ministry saw serious inflation and the collapse of the franc. Confidence was restored for a time by the temperate administration of Raymond Poincaré. When the Depression finally did arrive in France in 1932, retrenchment and the lack of clear policies made matters worse. The outbreak of serious riots in 1934 and the growing polarization of French politics created a crisis of confidence unequaled since the Dreyfus affair (see Part VII, Topic 15).

Despite the unimpressive record of government in responding to the Depression, the economic collapse did cause liberal democratic governments to readjust their thinking about the obligations of the state to its citizens. As a result, they inaugurated an era of social intervention and economic activism that has marked Western society ever since. The United States, with the election of

Franklin D. Roosevelt and the implementation of his vigorous New Deal programs, went further than either Britain or France in restructuring the government-citizen relationship. By the end of the 1930s, the institutional basis of the modern welfare state had been built.

In Eastern Europe, the prospects for democracy were equally uncertain. There, upon the ruins of the old Austro-Hungarian, German, and Russian empires, a series of newly created, independent states arose after World War I. From the start, these new countries were burdened with serious, sometimes insurmountable, problems: illiteracy and the lack of social modernization, and economies that rested primarily on agriculture and that suffered from a small and underdeveloped middle class. Moreover, the myriad of nationalities that comprised the region meant that every nation had ethnic minorities within its borders to cause unrest and tension, as well as constant friction with neighbors over borders and nationality issues. Finally, the lack of liberal parliamentary traditions in Eastern Europe put the new democratic regimes on shaky ground, and the area experienced a decisive trend toward authoritarian and fascist regimes.

GREAT BRITAIN AND THE IRISH QUESTION

It is difficult to speak of a British "recovery" from the trauma of World War I, for in the domestic arena the country experienced the next 20 years as one long, continual series of trials and failures. If government—whether of the left or the right—was unable to cope adequately with the economic dislocations of the postwar period and the accompanying labor unrest, it could hardly have been expected to deal successfully with the Great Depression. And while the British did succeed, at long last, in coming to terms with Ireland's future as an independent state, the agonizing ordeal of the Irish people continued in a devastating civil war.

The Postwar Drift

The British electorate, like that in France, was in a decidedly conservative mood as World War I drew to an end. Wanting a harsh settlement with defeated Germany, the 1918 "khaki election"—so-called because of the large number of veterans who participated—returned a strong Conservative majority to the House of Commons. The Conservatives permitted Liberal Prime Minister David Lloyd George to continue in office at the head of a coalition government, but they held the real power. In the autumn of 1922, however, the Conservatives pushed Lloyd George out, chiefly over his Irish policies, and formed a cabinet under the elderly Scotsman, Andrew Bonar Law (served 1922–1923).

Significant Dates

European Democracy

1916	Easter Rebellion in Ireland
1918	"Khaki election" in England
1921	Irish Free State (Catholic) and Northern Ireland (Protestant) created
1923–1930	Dictatorship of Primo de Rivera in Spain
1923	Labour government in England
1924–1926	Cartel of the Left in France
1925–1929	Conservatives return to power in England
1926	Dictatorship of Pilsudski in Poland
1926–1929	Poincaré premier of France
1926	General strike in England
1929	Royal dictatorship under Alexander I in Yugoslavia
1929–1931	Labour government in England
1931	Spanish Republic founded
1932	Gombos prime minister of Hungary
1936	Dictatorship under Metaxas in Greece
1936	Popular Front in France

In the elections of 1922, the working class was in an especially aggressive mood, for the Labour party doubled its strength, making it the second party in Parliament. Nevertheless, the Conservatives gained even more ground and elected Stanley Baldwin (served 1923–1924, 1924–1929, 1935–1937). The following year, further elections increased the strength of the Liberals, now in a position to form a coalition with the Conservatives or Labour. Instead, Herbert Asquith (1852–1928), the Liberal leader, declared that Labour should have an opportunity to form a government. The decision was an important one for two reasons: the liberals would never again head the government, and Ramsay MacDonald, who led the new Labour ministry, became the first socialist prime minister in Western Europe.

Ramsay MacDonald (served 1924, 1929–1931, 1931–1935), the man who held that distinction, was a Scotsman of working-class origin. Although good-looking and eloquent, MacDonald possessed little leadership ability or firmness of character. Not only did he prove indecisive, but once in office he felt it necessary to convince everyone that the country had little to fear from the Labour party. His recognition of the Soviet Union did not, however, endear him to those on the political right.

MacDonald fell as a result of scare tactics. The opposition accused the government of not prosecuting a communist editor who advocated sedition, and during the election itself a letter was circulated, allegedly from Grigori Zinoviev, head of the Comintern (the communist international organization), suggesting connections with the Labour party. The letter was a fake, but it was sufficient to give the Conservatives a huge majority.

Baldwin came back to 10 Downing Street, heading the British government for the next five years. During that time, he offered the country what he described as "sane, commonsense government," and his manner inspired public confidence. In reality, however, this meant an almost total failure to come to grips with the problems of inflation, industrial slump, and unemployment that were plaguing British society. The most progressive steps taken between 1924 and 1929 were the measures instituted by Baldwin's health minister, Neville Chamberlain (1869–1940), who established pensions for widows and retired people and reformed local government.

The low point of Baldwin's second ministry was the general strike of 1926, during which he succeeded in exasperating class tensions and antagonizing the workers. In 1925 a royal commission was appointed to investigate conditions in the coal industry, which had been suffering badly as a result of the general economic slump. Neither the miners nor the owners were satisfied by the commission's report, and in the face of a

London in the 1926 General Strike—machine-gun-armed vehicles patrol the city.

threatened general strike, the mine owners shut down operations. For nine days in May 1926, some 2,500,000 workers in all fields of endeavor struck, while the government organized middle-class volunteers to run basic services. Some local violence and considerable anger marked the strike, and when negotiations collapsed, Baldwin forced the unions into a settlement that virtually gave up the miners' demands. When the general strike ended, the miners stayed out on their own for another six months, embittered at the government for having engineered their defeat. To make matters worse, in 1927, the government passed the Trade Disputes Act, which prohibited sympathy strikes and otherwise weakened labor's position.

The National Government

In the wake of the 1926 strike, working-class sentiment against Baldwin intensified, and when he called elections in 1929, he was swept out of office. Labourites campaigned on the unemployment issue and blamed the Conservatives for Britain's economic troubles. Although Labour won more seats than the Tories, it lacked a majority and had to form a coalition government with the Liberals. In addition, Labour was still burdened with Ramsay MacDonald as its leader.

The second MacDonald government faced a deteriorating economic situation. During 1930 alone, unemployment jumped from 1 million to 2.5 million. The government's response was simply to increase government financial support for the unemployed (known as the "dole"). This caused a huge increase in the deficit. The next year, experts advised MacDonald that only a cut in expenditures—that is, a reduction in the dole—would prevent bankruptcy. An atmosphere of crisis spread, causing heavy withdrawals from banks and the virtual depletion of the country's gold reserves. American financiers refused to extend further credits to Britain without cutbacks. In August 1931, MacDonald told his cabinet that unemployment benefits would have to be cut; when they balked, he asked them to resign.

Instead of submitting his own resignation, however, King George V (ruled 1910–1936) persuaded him to form a new, broad-based coalition with himself as prime minister and Stanley Baldwin as second in command. In fact, the Conservatives dominated this so-called National Government and MacDonald was their pawn. Labour, stunned by what they considered MacDonald's betrayal, expelled him from the party.

From 1931 to 1935, MacDonald and Baldwin ran the government. Together, they added Britain to the growing number of countries that were abandoning the gold standard. The international value of the pound did drop from $4.86, but held at $3.40, thus defying the

warnings of conventional economists. Parliament also approved a 10 percent reduction in unemployment benefits. The financial crisis began to ease, and the government called for new elections for a vote of confidence. Despite a coalition effort, the Conservatives took the lion's share of votes—out of 556 seats in Parliament, they won 472 while Labour lost some 85 percent of its seats.

MacDonald continued to serve as prime minister until 1935. With the National Government ratified, it pushed through Parliament a program of tariff protection, thus ending Britain's long-standing tradition of free trade. When failing health led to MacDonald's retirement, Baldwin moved to Downing Street, where he remained until 1937.

Britain came through the Depression with minimal damage to its political traditions, despite the rather lame policies of the Labour and Conservative ministries. Conditions in some parts of England, as well as those in Wales and Scotland, remained depressed, but something of an economic revival began to take hold by the end of the decade. The coming of World War II interrupted that process, and in its aftermath Britain seemed to pick up where it had left off.

Britain, Europe's most advanced industrial society, was the perfect microcosm for studying the shortcomings of industrial capitalism. In the 19th century, social and economic conditions there had attracted incisive critics, from the German Friedrich Engels to England's own John Stuart Mill. No one, however, was more knowledgeable about or more committed to the improvement of the working class than Beatrice and Sidney Webb, Britain's greatest social reformers.

Beatrice Potter (1858–1943) was born into a well-to-do provincial family. She educated herself, principally by reading extensively and by discussions with the numerous visitors whom her father entertained. In London she immersed herself in social work among the poor. She now questioned the assumptions of her father's world and found charitable organizations ill-equipped to deal with the overwhelming poverty she saw. In *The Cooperative Movement in Great Britain* (1891), she examined working-class organizations. One of the people she had been advised to consult while doing her research was Sidney Webb (1859–1947).

Webb was a native of London, born into a lower-middle-class family. He left school at 16 and obtained a civil service job by studying at night, and eventually passed the bar examinations. In 1885, Webb was persuaded by his close friend George Bernard Shaw (1856–1950) to join a newly founded socialist organization called the Fabian Society (see Part VII, Topic 19).

Potter and Webb met in 1890, and he immediately fell in love with the good-looking and intellectual young woman. For her part, Potter had been greatly impressed by Webb's socialist ideas, although she was not immediately attracted to this unkempt, rather ugly little man. They were married in 1892 and set up house in London. For the next 50 years, the couple devoted themselves to pioneering social research and political reform, turning out important books such as *The History of Trade Unionism* (1894) and *Industrial Democracy* (1897).

Webb and Potter also collaborated in bringing about significant social reforms and the creation of important new institutions. Webb, who served on the London County Council, introduced the basis for the system of public secondary education and helped to establish technical schools. Together, they founded the London School of Economics, which became part of the University of London. The Webbs believed that the government must provide a minimum education for all citizens, just as it had to provide minimum standards of health and sanitation. Webb also provided the basic content for the Education Acts of 1902 and 1903, which became the basis for English public education for generations.

Like their fellow Fabians, Beatrice and Sidney Webb combined a belief in socialism and scientific principles with a moral "righteousness." In 1905 Potter, as a member of the Royal Commission on the Poor Laws, produced her important *Minority Report*, which advocated social security and provided a detailed outline for what later became the welfare state.

In 1913 they founded the left-wing journal *The New Statesman*, and the next year, after the ranks of the Fabian Society split, the Webbs joined the Labour party. In 1918 Webb drafted the party's policy statement on "Labour and the New Social Order," and was chosen by the miners' union to serve as their representative on a commission to investigate mining conditions. He so won the loyalty of the miners that in 1922 they elected him to Parliament. In 1924, Prime Minister Ramsay MacDonald appointed him to the Labour cabinet as president of the Board of Trade.

When MacDonald formed the National Government in 1931, the Webbs became disheartened with Labour's prospects and left England for the Soviet Union. They "fell in love" with what they saw in Stalin's Russia and seem to have lost their confidence in the idea of gradual social reform.

The Quest for Irish Independence

The Irish question remained one of the most vexing and agonizing issues in modern British history. Since the 17th century, Ireland had been virtually a British colony, ruled by a small Protestant gentry which insisted on maintaining ties with England. The Protestant minority comprised the six counties of Ulster in the northeastern portion of Ireland. The

Map 5.1   Ireland

larger section of the island, in the south and west, was comprised of Catholics who increasingly demanded Home Rule—that is, Irish control over domestic affairs. The Liberal party under William Gladstone had incorporated Home Rule in its platform, but the Conservatives opposed it.

In the late 19th century, two efforts to get Home Rule approved in Parliament failed. The extension of the suffrage to Irish males, however, resulted in the election of a growing Irish Catholic delegation to Parliament. A third Home Rule bill passed in 1914 but was then postponed because of the war. Among Irish nationalists, extremists grew impatient and sparked the 1916 Easter Rebellion (see Part VIII, Topic 1), which intensified feeling on both sides.

In the 1918 elections, Irish nationalist sentiment triumphed when some 70 candidates were sent to Parliament by a new party, Sinn Fein (Gaelic for "We Ourselves"). Its members abandoned Home Rule in favor of complete freedom and, instead of taking their seats in Parliament, proclaimed themselves an Irish Parliament called Dail Eireann. That January, they declared Ireland independent.

The government of Lloyd George responded slowly to the Sinn Fein's actions, but by the end of the year was lending the "Black and Tans," a special army of volunteers in Ireland that distinguished itself by its exceptional brutality, official support. As this cruel war escalated and casualties grew, public opinion in Britain began to turn against the repression. Finally, in the summer of 1921 Lloyd George agreed to meet with Irish leaders, and the result was the signing of a formal treaty in December that created the Irish Free State out of the Catholic regions as a self-governing nation with

The ruins of Dublin following the British bombardment during the Easter Rising, 1916.

Dominion status. Protestant Ulster became an autonomous region within the United Kingdom, under the name of Northern Ireland.

The Irish Free State did not satisfy a radical minority of Irish nationalists who united under the leadership of Eamon De Valera (1882–1975). Born in New York City, De Valera was raised in Ireland and became an ardent republican who played an active role in the Easter Rebellion. Refusing to recognize the treaty, his followers organized the clandestine Irish Republican Army (IRA) and carried on a terrorist civil war to prevent the separation of Northern Ireland. The bombings, raids, and deaths escalated on both sides of the border. In 1923, De Valera's forces were overwhelmed and he was imprisoned. The next year, however, he started a new party, Fianna Fáil, continued the struggle, and won power in 1932. De Valera was elected prime minister five years later, and declared the country independent, renaming it Eire. During World War II, Eire remained neutral, and in 1949 it left the British Commonwealth and became the Republic of Ireland. The 1921 Irish settlement remains unchanged and the tragic civil war goes on, as does the agony of the Irish people.

FRANCE: THE QUEST FOR STABILITY

The somber mood of British public life in the 1920s contrasted sharply with the more exuberant tone of life in France. In the aftermath of World War I, Paris re-

gained its position as the capital of the European avant-garde (see Part VIII, Topic 6). But if France led the way in cultural life, its politics left much to be desired. The relative stability of Britain's governmental experience contrasted sharply with the tense, unstable French political arena. One reason for this difference was the extensive damage the country suffered in the war, and the considerable resources needed to rebuild. The French had not managed their war financing well, and between 1914 and 1919 the circulation of banknotes had increased sixfold. War debts to Britain and the United States added to the pressure, and politicians wavered in their determination to raise taxes both to meet the deficit and to reconstruct the economy. Once the Depression hit in 1932, the strain on financial resources increased still further.

The Era of Stability

Because the electoral system was based on proportional representation, a myriad of political parties competed for power. Pressure on the republic was particularly strong from the right, which formed a coalition known as the Bloc National to compete in the postwar elections. In 1919, the French people chose a solidly conservative, highly nationalist Chamber of Deputies—the "Blue Horizon Chamber," so named after the large number of veterans in blue uniforms represented in it.

In 1923, however, Premier Raymond Poincaré (served 1912, 1922–1924, 1926–1929) occupied the Ruhr Valley in order to force payment of German reparations. The resulting war scare, combined with high inflation, led voters to turn to the left. The radical socialist Édouard Herriot (served 1924–1925, 1932), supported by the *Cartel des Gauches* (Cartel of the Left), succeeded Poincaré but lasted only one year. Herriot, ignorant of financial matters, did nothing to deal with the country's enormous war debts, nor could he control the rising inflation that seriously hurt the working and middle classes. The ineffective Herriot stepped down, but his two immediate successors did not improve the situation. By 1926 the French franc, once among the most stable currencies in the world, had lost 90 percent of its value on the international market. More serious still was the fact that the middle classes lost three-quarters of their savings.

Poincaré came back into office in 1926 and established a "National Union" ministry that included six former premiers. Aloof, sober, and unimaginative, yet with a strict sense of duty, he was the right man for the moment. Poincaré did nothing dramatic to deal with the economic crisis. Rather, he moved carefully and precisely to improve specific aspects of the larger problem, collecting taxes more effectively, making administrative savings, ending overspending in government programs, and generally presenting an air of confidence and stability that had been lacking in the body politic. Gradually, the franc was stabilized and the sense of relief that resulted helped to soothe national tensions. Poincaré remained in office for three years, longer than any other interwar premier, and retired in 1929.

Depression Politics

Between 1929 and 1932, a large number of premiers held office, but none of them had Poincaré's stature or his commitment to the republican tradition. When the Depression struck France in 1932, unemployment in France was not as severe as in other countries, but it did have a destabilizing effect on political life. Herriot returned to the premiership for six months, and was

quickly followed by four others. Once again the government failed to deal effectively with the crisis, and when the restored prosperity of the late 1920s dissolved, social tensions reemerged.

The most dramatic proof of the instability of French political life was the upheaval following the mysterious Stavisky scandal. Serge Stavisky (1886?–1934) was a master financial swindler who had sold millions of worthless bonds. His trial in December 1933 and his subsequent suicide caused a sensation. The radical right exploited the scandal, spreading accusations that high government officials had been implicated with him in the affair and that the government had then covered up their involvement. The findings of the official investigation supported these charges. On February 6, 1934, huge crowds organized by right-wing forces filled the streets of Paris demanding the ouster of Premier Édouard Daladier (served 1933, 1934, 1938–1940). When they attempted to break into the Chamber of Deputies, police fired on the crowd, killing eleven people. The Daladier government collapsed in a storm of indignation.

Not since the Dreyfus affair at the turn of the century (see Part VII, Topic 15) had the people of France been so violently divided, nor the republic so completely called into question. Nor did subsequent governments have any more success than their predecessors in dealing with the effects of the Depression. France was the only country to remain stubbornly on the gold standard. Moreover, social unrest increased as a result of the government retrenchment and the lowering of salary levels.

The danger from the right grew so threatening that the French communists—taking their cue from the Comintern, which the year before had endorsed alliances with other leftist parties—formed a "Popular Front" with the socialists and Radicals, and presented a

Socialist Léon Blum (left with glasses) and communist Maurice Thorez with other members of the French Popular Front, July 1937.

joint platform in the 1936 elections. The Front won a huge victory, and formed a government under socialist Léon Blum (served 1936–1937). A cultured and sensitive man, Blum brought union officials and employers together and produced an agreement that laid the basis for the welfare state, including minimum wages, the 40-hour week, and collective bargaining.

Blum's reforms reduced social stress, but he was the target of attack from enemies to his right and his left. Bigots pointed to the fact that he was Jewish as evidence of the decline of France, while conservatives gathered strength from business interests and eventually slowed down his programs. Meanwhile, the communists attacked him for not going far enough. The Blum government resigned in June 1937. By the eve of World War II, the French people were deeply divided over the future of the republic. For many, the widening appeal of the radical right, and especially the coming to power of Adolf Hitler in Germany, was deeply troublesome.

THE SPREAD OF FASCISM

Blum's dilemma was repeated elsewhere in Europe. By the mid-1930s, European political life was polarized between the extremes of communism and fascism. Every country experienced, to one degree or another, an increasingly bitter ideological war, and the danger was especially fierce from the right. From the British Isles to the shores of the Black Sea, fascism—which had already come to power in Italy and Germany—appeared to be on the ascendancy.

Great Britain and France spawned their own native varieties of fascism, although they neither created a mass following nor seriously challenged the power base of those democratic societies. In Great Britain, a number of small groups inspired by Mussolini's Black Shirts were started in the 1920s, but never amounted to very much. In the early 1930s the rich and well-educated Sir Oswald Mosley (1896–1980) founded the British Union of Fascists. A great fan of Mussolini, Mosley based his organization on the Italian model. Like Mussolini, he had been a prominent member of the British socialist movement, having served as a Labour minister. Mosley became increasingly interested in Hitler's regime after 1933. He spoke of a "Greater Britain" in which all citizens were regimented to achieve broad national goals. The British Union attracted many disreputable thugs, and Mosley himself extolled the use of violence, a fact that led the government to try to limit the movement by placing a ban on the wearing of political uniforms. It did not, however, represent a serious threat to British political stability.

In France, conservative and reactionary movements drawing inspiration from the country's monarchist past were established as early as the turn of the century. In 1898, the poet and journalist Charles Maurras (1868–1952) started the *Action Française* (French Action), a group that stressed extreme nationalism and advocated anti-Semitism. Maurras wanted a restoration of the monarchy and a return to a corporative society based on hierarchy and aristocracy. The government banned the movement in 1936.

In the interwar period, an array of proto-fascist political groups, some directly modeled on Mussolini's

Oswald Mosley, leader of the British Union of Fascists, marches in a rally.

Fascism or Hitler's Nazism, appeared in France. The most notorious of these were the *Jeunesses Patriotes* (Young Patriots) and the infamous *Capoulards* (Hooded Men). At the height of the Depression the *Parti Populaire Française* (French Popular Party) attracted some 500,000 followers. The sheer number of such radical movements, each with its own ideology and platform, mitigated against the creation of a united right.

The Spanish monarchy, incapable of guiding the country's transformation into the 20th century, proved no barrier to the formation of a fascist movement. By the early 1920s, a dictatorship was created by General Miguel Primo de Rivera (1870–1930). The dictator's son, José Antonio Primo de Rivera, organized a real fascist movement, the *Falange*, in 1931. When the Spanish Civil War erupted, the movement was taken over by General Francisco Franco (1892–1975) and eventually merged into his own party (see Part VIII, Topic 8).

The Austrian case is a good example of how fascist movements competed against each other. The situation there was complicated by the fact that two paramilitary groups, the Social Democratic *Schutzbund* (Alliance for Defense) and the Christian Socialist *Heimwehr* (Home Guard), not only espoused conflicting ideologies, but opposed the Austrian Nazis. The Heimwehr, headed by Prince Ernst Rudiger von Starhemberg (1899–1956), fought to undermine the country's republican government but wanted to preserve Austrian independence. Chancellor Engelbert Dollfuss (1892–1934) tried to play the Heimwehr off against the Nazis and the Social Democrats, inviting it to join the "Fatherland Front" that worked against the *Anschluss* (union) of Austria and Germany.

As fascist movements spread across Europe in the 1930s, the prospects for democracy looked grim indeed.

THE NEW SHAPE OF EASTERN EUROPE

At the Paris Peace Conference, the Allied statesmen had made a deliberate decision to create a group of new states in Eastern Europe from the ruins of four empires—Austria-Hungary, Germany, Russia, and Ottoman Turkey. Eastern Europe provided a test case for the principle of self-determination that President Wilson advocated so strenuously. Yet there were other reasons that had to do more with power politics than justice which compelled the creation of these new nations: they would serve a useful purpose for the Allies in acting as a buffer along the western border of the Bolshevik Russia, and along the eastern frontiers of Germany.

These newly created nations—Austria, Hungary, Poland, Czechoslovakia, Yugoslavia, and the Baltic republics of Latvia, Estonia, and Lithuania—are known as "successor states," because they took the place of the older empires. With the inclusion of Greece, Romania, Bulgaria, and Albania, Eastern Europe consisted of a dozen independent states.

The States of Eastern Europe

The governments of the successor states began as models of the parliamentary system. Each was either a Western-style republic or a constitutional monarchy. Yet, by the eve of World War II, most of these nations had yielded to authoritarianism. They found that the combination of domestic and foreign policy problems

Map 5.2 Ethnic Groups in Central and Eastern Europe

was so demanding that parliamentary government was not adequate to their needs.

Because of history and geography, the new states of Eastern Europe had remarkably mixed populations. Along with the dominant ethnic and religious group in each country, one or more minority nationalities coexisted in uneasy rapport. In Czechoslovakia, Poland, Hungary, Yugoslavia, and Romania, these minorities were themselves large groups. The minorities posed serious problems for the governments, most of which wanted to forge cohesive social and political units out of their populations. The minorities, on the other hand, sought to maintain their distinctiveness and to protect their separate identities. In some instances, such as the case of Nazi Germany and the German minority in Czechoslovakia, a foreign power deliberately appealed to these minorities over the heads of their governments. On the whole, most states in the area treated their minority populations unfairly. The exception was Finland, where the Swedish minority enjoyed constitutionally assured rights. The result was continuing tension that kept domestic tranquillity off balance.

After the euphoria of independence had subsided, the successor states found themselves burdened with the legacy of the past. For one thing, their efforts to develop their economies were blocked by a wide range of liabilities. Before World War I, Eastern Europe had been by and large a semicolonial region in which the great powers made investments and sold manufactured goods, while the area itself supplied raw materials and agricultural goods. With the coming of independence, however, these new states lost what had been guaranteed markets for their products. Hence, while they lacked sufficient revenue, the resources they now needed in order to undertake industrialization were expensive. The entire infrastructure and financial structure of the region mitigated against rapid development: local capital was virtually nonexistent; trading and business practices were antiquated; and roads, railways, and communication systems required building from the ground up. Moreover, in an area that was overwhelmingly agricultural, farming techniques and mechanization were outdated.

In Austria and Czechoslovakia, a small but thriving middle class, mainly of German and Jewish origin, had existed for some time, but the other states lacked managers and experts. Wealth and status were concentrated in the hands of a relatively small but powerful landowning aristocracy, as well as in the ranks of the church hierarchy. The workforce in such traditional agricultural societies—that is, the bulk of the population—consisted of millions of poor peasants whose lives were not much better than their serf ancestors. As a result, poor health care and nutrition, high birth and death rates, and illiteracy made the task

of national development still more difficult and in the long run weakened the strength of the new parliamentary governments.

The Failure of Democracy

Under these circumstances, the prospects for democratic government in Eastern Europe were bleak. The fact that most of these societies lacked formal experience with parliamentary government undermined the opportunities for stable political progress. To make matters worse, while authoritarian traditions were strong in many states, the new parliamentary systems generally spawned numerous political parties, a fact that made for instability and a poor legislative record.

Nationalism represented by far the most serious political problem facing the East European states. Nationalist sentiment in the region was fierce, especially in Poland, Bohemia, and Hungary, each of which had an old nationalist heritage. World War I had intensified the nationalist animosities between the states of the region. Austria, Hungary, and Bulgaria were "revisionist" states which were unhappy with the peace settlements and wanted to regain lost territories. The older independent nations of Greece, Albania, and Romania, on the other hand, wanted to keep what they had gained from the war. Finally, the new countries of Poland, Czechoslovakia, Estonia, Latvia, and Lithuania indoctrinated their citizens with patriotic fervor in an

Marshal Pilsudski, authoritarian leader of the new Poland.

effort to create a loyal population willing to fight to preserve independence. The result was an intricately intense web of national fears and animosities that made regional cooperation difficult and kept international relations tense.

Liberal democracy did not fare well in these circumstances, and in virtually all cases eventually collapsed in the face of authoritarianism. The Hungarian case was one of the saddest. In 1919, the communists set up a socialist dictatorship in Hungary under Béla Kun (1885–1937), which was put down by a Romanian army sanctioned by the Allies. Admiral Miklós Horthy (1858–1957) was made regent of the country, remaining as a figurehead until the Nazis deposed him in 1944. Horthy appointed Count Stephen Bethlen prime minister (served 1921–1931), and he ran the government with only a pretense of parliamentary responsibility for a decade. Then followed General Julius Gombos (prime minister 1932–1936), the head of the anti-Semitic Race Defense party who made a farce of Hungary's representative system and worked closely with Mussolini and Hitler in foreign affairs.

In the 1920s, dictators or authoritarian leaders took power in Albania, Lithuania, Yugoslavia, and Poland. In the latter country, Marshal Jozef Pilsudski served as president from 1918 to 1922. When internal divisions paralyzed the state, Pilsudski staged a "march on Warsaw" in 1926 and seized the government, making himself dictator. In the following decade, a combined leadership emerged under army officers and a fascist-like organization.

In Eastern Europe, unlike Britain and France, parliamentary government could not withstand the strains of the Depression. In 1930 the controversial Romanian monarch, King Carol II (1893–1953) returned to his country after having deserted his throne and family to live in Paris with a mistress. Carol deposed his son Michael and ruled as a dictator, being deposed by Hitler in 1940. Over the next several years, dictators also took power in Austria, Estonia, Latvia, Bulgaria, and Greece.

The one successor state in central Europe able to prevent its democratic system from succumbing to dictatorship was Czechoslovakia. The Czech state was relatively prosperous, and the government had implemented important reforms, including the breakup of the large estates. Its founder and first president was Thomas Masaryk (1850–1937), a former professor of philosophy and a humane man of principle. He served

as president for 17 years. His successor, Edouard Benes (1884–1948), was a close associate of Masaryk. Together, such upright leaders might have resolved the country's serious domestic problems had it not become the target of Hitler's aggression.

The record of European democracy in the interwar period was mixed. In Western Europe, Great Britain and France, along with most of the smaller states, maintained their political systems intact. After World War I, most of them had instituted universal suffrage and had begun to develop social programs designed to integrate their citizens into a uniform national experience. During the Great Depression, this trend accelerated as the governments created the basic institutions of the welfare state, designed to insulate their citizens from the worst aspects of the crisis.

The Western democracies successfully resisted the lure of fascism, although such movements appeared in virtually every country. Only in Italy and Germany did fascism seize power before World War II, although in Spain a rightwing dictator came to power in the 1930s after a tragic civil war. The experiment with democracy in Eastern Europe, however, proved a dismal failure, as the enthusiastic hopes of the Allied statesmen of 1919 were dashed by the rise of authoritarian dictatorship.

Questions for Further Study

1. What were the chief political concerns in postwar England and France?

2. What were the origins of the Irish question?

3. To what conditions did fascism appeal?

4. Why was democracy so tenuous in postwar eastern Europe?

Suggestions for Further Reading

Cassels, Alan. *Fascism.* New York, 1975.

Greene, Nathanael. *From Versailles to Vichy.* New York, 1970.

Hughes, Judith M. *To the Maginot Line: The Politics of French Military Preparations in the 1920s.* Cambridge, MA, 1971.

Jackson, Julian. *The Popular Front in France: Defending Democracy, 1934–1938.* New York, 1988.

Jelavich, Barbara. *History of the Balkans: Twentieth Century.* New York, 1983.

Kitchen, Martin. *Europe Between the Wars: A Political History.* London, 1988.

Roberts, Mary L. *Civilization Without Sexes: Reconstructing Gender in Postwar France.* Chicago, 1994.

Seton-Watson, Hugh. *Eastern Europe Between the Wars, 1918–1941.* Cambridge, MA, 1962.

Taylor, A. J. P. *English History, 1914–1945.* New York, 1965.

Topic 6

SOCIAL VALUES AND
THE LOST GENERATION

n 1914, European social conditions still reflected the manners and mores of the Victorian Age. Life both within and beyond the family was bound by tradition, patriarchy, and class, and the prevailing sexual code insisted on virtuous behavior but in reality condoned dual standards for men and women. Moreover, European civilization was still predominantly rural and the majority of people lived by farming.

The Great War began a process of social transformation that profoundly changed the way in which most Europeans lived. Daily life became more open to change and more democratic, social and sexual codes relaxed, and people felt less tied to tradition. The new yearning for personal freedom and modern life was reflected in the public behavior of the so-called "Jazz Age," in which fast-paced, expressive dancing and music became the rage as high society flocked in large numbers to the new nightclubs. The postwar era also saw the rise of a new mass culture in which millions of citizens with greater leisure time enjoyed the automobile, radio, motion pictures, and sports as part of everyday experience.

The new social values reflected the shift to an urban-based, industrial, nonagrarian society. In the 1920s and 1930s, the most important social factor was the expansion of the white-collar class, a social category composed of people who worked for a living and did not own significant property, but who thought and behaved like the middle class. At the same time, the upper ranks of the bourgeoisie and the old aristocracy increasingly joined together in support of social stability and authoritarian government in the face of the new political and organizational power of the industrial working classes, whose cause was now championed by the Soviet Union and the growing strength of socialist parties.

The year 1929 marked a phase in social development that was different in tone and spirit from the 1920s. Social stress increased markedly in the 1930s, as the effects of the Great Depression made themselves felt. The spirit of class conflict, already noticeable in the previous decade, became more intense, especially among the middle classes, whose security and savings were decimated by the economic collapse, and among the working classes, who experienced widespread misery. As optimism and opportunity gave way to fear and insecurity, Europe underwent a loss of social momentum. The birthrate declined because young people delayed marriage and the rearing of families. Along with the economic difficulties of the decade, Europe's political future seemed dark as totalitarian dictatorships held millions in their grip and the threat of war loomed.

MOBILITY AND STATUS: SOCIAL CLASS UNDER STRESS

Since the first industrial revolution in the 18th century, two broad trends had characterized European development: the rise of cities in what had been a predominantly rural society, and the diversification of a once overwhelmingly agrarian economy with the growth of the industrial and service sectors. In the 20th century, these trends matured. As a result, class structure became more complicated as wealth and status shifted and tensions among the classes increased.

Trends in European Society

Industrialization had drawn millions of Europeans from the countryside to the cities. During the 19th century urban dwellers steadily increased in proportion to the total population, and this process of urbanization transformed society. By 1910, Great Britain was the most urban European nation, with some 65 percent of its population living in cities, while Belgium, Germany, and the Netherlands each counted slightly less than half their populations in the urban category. France was still only around 38 percent urban, and in Italy, Denmark, Austria, and Hungary about a third of the people lived in cities with 20,000 or more inhabitants. In the agrarian countries of southern and eastern Europe, much smaller proportions of the populations were urban—Bulgaria, for example, was only 9 percent urban.

On the Continent, only the Netherlands reached the 50 percent mark before World War II, but everywhere the trend was apparent. The position of cities with more than 100,000 inhabitants was strengthened in some countries: between 1910 and 1930, the proportion of Germans living in such large cities rose from 21 to 37 percent, while for Italians the increase was from 11 to 17 percent. In 1910 there were seven European cities with populations over 1 million, while in 1940 the number had more than doubled. The table (at top right) shows the population growth of some of Europe's largest cities in the interwar period.

Another indicator of a society's development is the distribution of the working population among the three "sectors" of agriculture, industry, and services (the latter including such work categories as trade, banking, public administration, and education). All European countries have followed the same general pattern, although at different rates of development. The percentage of people employed in agriculture has fallen steadily, that of industry first rose and then fell, while the service sector has increased constantly. In 1910, 41 percent of the European workforce was in agriculture, 34 percent in industry, and 25 percent in the service sector. By 1930,

Table VIII.6.1
Major Cities of Interwar Europe (in 1000s)

	1920	1940
Berlin	3801	4332
Brussels	685	913
Budapest	1185	1163
Glasgow	1052	1132
Hamburg	986	1682
London	7488	8700
Madrid	751	1089
Milan	836	1116
Moscow	1050	4137
Paris	2907	2830
Prague	677	928
Rome	692	1156
Vienna	1866	1918
Warsaw	931	1266

agriculture remained at 41 percent, but industry had declined to 30 percent, and services had grown to 29 percent. This trend continued through the rest of the century; by 1950 the services represented 31 percent of the workforce and in the 1980s Europe entered the "postindustrial" era when the service sector reached 50 percent.

As in the case of urbanization, this pattern differed widely, depending on the region of Europe and the country. In Eastern Europe, for example, the agricultural sector stood at 75 percent in 1910 and by 1930 had fallen only to 64 percent. The following table illustrates the developmental variation among countries:

Table VIII.6.2
The Working Population of Selected Countries by Sector, 1910/1930 (in percent)

	1910			1930		
	A	I	S	A	I	S
Britain	9	51	40	6	46	48
Germany	37	41	22	29	40	31
France	41	33	26	36	33	31
Italy	55	27	18	47	31	22
Hungary	58	20	22	53	24	23
Poland	77	9	14	66	17	17

Source: Adapted from Gerold Ambrosius and William H. Hubbard, *A Social and Economic History of Twentieth-Century Europe* (Cambridge, MA: Harvard University Press, 1989), 58. A, I, and S stand for agricultural, industrial, and service.

The same general pattern could also be discerned for a variety of other social indicators, including rates of literacy, mortality, industrial production, and income. In the case of literacy, important gains had been made since the last decade of the 19th century, when systems of universal primary education were widely introduced. By 1900, 95 percent of the British and French people could read and write, whereas in Italy almost half the population could not. After 1918, a wave of democratization swept school systems in many countries. Between 1920 and 1940, the proportion of secondary school students doubled in countries such as Britain, Germany, Italy, Sweden, and Austria. By 1921, the number of illiterates in Italy had been almost halved, and a decade later the illiteracy rate there had fallen to 21 percent. By the 1930s one-third of all secondary school students in western Europe were girls. With the exception of the Soviet Union, however, higher education remained a class prerogative, and in the more developed nations of Europe only 2 percent of the college-age population attended university. In the 1930s, women comprised 25 percent of university students in Britain, but the percentage was much less in other countries.

Class Boundaries, Wealth, and Status

Class distinctions are determined by a variety of factors, ranging from legal differences in the case of the aristocracy to manner of dress, and they generally involve lifestyles and attitudes. Income and wealth are, however, among the most crucial factors, not only of class but of the broader question of social equality. Measured by gains in per capita national product and real wages, a process of leveling has characterized European development during the 20th century, although the greatest gains in a more equal income distribution have been made since World War II.

One important change was that the economic significance of the very wealthy declined. In 1913, British society was still marked by an immense gulf between rich and poor: the richest 1 percent of the population controlled 70 percent of all personal wealth. By 1930, that proportion had declined to about 60 percent, and by 1945 to some 50 percent. In France, similar changes took place. Real wages followed the broad economic trends of the postwar period (see Part VIII, Topic 3). In Western Europe they dropped sharply after the bust of 1921, rose until the Great Depression, and then rose again beginning in the mid to late 1930s, depending on the particular country. After 1950, they jumped significantly. Nevertheless, living standards continued to differ considerably between classes. For workers and the lower middle classes, the bulk of all income—as much as 80

percent—still went for basic necessities such as food, clothing, and shelter, as well as taxes. Moreover, poverty grew significantly during the Great Depression, when mass unemployment affected millions in all but the highest social classes.

Contrary to the trend begun in the 19th century, the post-1919 period did not see the continuing growth of the working class. Instead, the fastest growing group was the white-collar worker, whose ranks swelled with the expansion of government and private sector bureaucracies. Self-defining attitudes put most of these employees in the lowest levels of the middle classes, but in fact many earned salaries that were the same or even lower than factory workers. In Germany, one out of four white-collar workers had come from a working-class family. In this respect, the Depression stimulated considerable social instability, for unemployment forced many white-collar workers to go back to the factories.

Generally, upward mobility within the middle classes declined in the interwar period. A few speculators made huge fortunes, but most of the bourgeoisie experienced slow gains, if any, in income and status, and for many living standards actually declined as inflation and then depression wiped out their savings. In Germany, where they were hardest hit, inflation destroyed more than half of the capital of the lower middle class. The professional classes were in oversupply in some countries, and many college graduates were unemployable.

Because the condition of the middle classes declined in the 1930s, the gap between them and the upper classes widened. Despite the decline in the position of the wealthiest portion of the population, most of this group weathered the Depression relatively unscathed. The aristocracy, which maintained its status and power most fully in eastern and southern Europe, experienced some difficulties. This was especially true of those who derived their income from landed estates, for the agricultural depression and land reform both weakened the landed nobility. Political reforms, particularly in the new nations of Eastern Europe, also weakened aristocratic power. Only in the Soviet Union, however, was the aristocracy actually wiped out, and in countries such as Britain and France it retained significant influence.

In those countries in which the nobility was weakened, the status of the peasantry generally improved. In agrarian countries where parliamentary democracy was introduced, peasant political parties developed and reforms gave many peasants their first opportunity to own their own land. In Czechoslovakia, slightly more than 10 percent of the land was divided, and in Romania significant progress was made, whereas much less land distribution took place in Poland and Hungary. Such changes did not always mean a real improvement in peasant lives, for they tended to use antiquated farming methods and generally were forced into debt to meet the costs of their own production. By the late 1920s, peasants everywhere faced increasing economic hardships.

Millions of workers were without jobs for most of the Depression years, having to subsist on limited public assistance. For them, the 1930s were demoralizing and without hope. Most countries saw considerable labor agitation. A minority of workers supported the communists, but most gravitated either to socialist parties or trade unions, using the strike as their principal instrument of protest. Radical political movements such as Italian Fascism were in part a response to worker demands and in part a reaction against them. As the Great Depression descended, the middle and upper classes grew more agitated and insecure, not only about their own condition but about working-class demands. The result everywhere was heightened social tension and class conflict. The Depression, like the Great War, proved to be a profoundly unsettling experience for European society.

NEW YORK, PARIS, AND BERLIN: THE AGE OF CABARET

The postwar years were filled with contradictions. While government leaders spoke of a return to "normalcy" after the deprivations and sacrifices of wartime, popular opinion clamored for a new era of expressive freedom and self-indulgence unlike anything known before the war. In the United States, the era of Prohibition was simultaneously the era of the "speakeasy." Indeed, one reflection of the relaxed social conditions that prevailed in the postwar period was the popularity of the nightclub. Although not an entirely new social institution, the modern nightclub offered an ideal backdrop for the culture of the "Jazz Age."

Prohibition and the Jazz Age

In the United States, where a sense of Protestant moralism remained strong, the Eighteenth Amendment, passed in January 1919, prohibited the consumption or sale of "intoxicating beverages," and later that year the Volstead Act made traffic in such beverages illegal. The

Photographer Lewis Hine captured the soaring spirit of New York City in this image, entitled *Skyboy,* of a young worker during the construction of the Empire State Building (1931).

Actress Louise Brooks embodied the modern Jazz-Age look of postwar American women.

anti-alcohol campaign reflected the more conservative values of rural America, but in the big cities life assumed a frenetic and modern pace despite—and in part because of—Prohibition.

The Eighteenth Amendment was widely ignored by average Americans, and some used the demand for whisky and beer to reap huge profits from bootlegging. Illegal clubs, known as "speakeasies," served these beverages to private customers—in New York City alone there were some 5000 of them by 1922. Gangsters such as Al "Scarface" Capone (1899–1947) in Chicago and Arthur "Dutch Schultz" Flegenheimer (1902–1935) in New York built powerful criminal organizations on the profits from bootlegging. With their machine guns, big automobiles, and flashy lives, these hoodlums became folk heroes to some Americans, especially when Hollywood immortalized them in the new talking films. In the literary imagination, the hero of "Roaring Twenties" America was the protagonist of the novel *The Great Gatsby* (1925), by F. Scott Fitzgerald (1896–1940). A wealthy young man of mysterious origins who made a fortune in bootlegging, Jay Gatsby grew famous by giving fabulous parties at his elaborate Long Island estate. Fitzgerald himself lived a dissolute life not dissimilar to Gatsby, and his female characters were "flappers," young women with men's hair styles and short, slinky dresses who used lipstick and smoked and drank in public.

The nightclub became the quintessential entertainment spot of the era, and New York City was the nightclub capital. The first nightclub opened in New York in 1921, and they spread rapidly. High society frequented the clubs, especially those in Harlem, then the scene of a major black cultural movement known as the Harlem Renaissance.

One of the most famous of Harlem's nightclubs was the Cotton Club, owned by a mobster. Duke Ellington and Fats Waller (1904–1943) performed there, as well as singers such as Ethel Waters (1896–1977) and the dancer Josephine Baker (1906–1975).

The Cotton Club, the Harlem nightclub that was all the rage in the 1920s.

But although the best black entertainers could be seen at the Cotton Club, black patrons were prohibited. "Everyone rushed up to Harlem at night," remembered one socialite, "to sit around places thick with smoke and the smell of bad gin, where Negroes danced about with each other until the small hours of the morning." While wealthy white audiences packed the Harlem clubs night after night, the black writer Langston Hughes (1902–1967) underscored the exploitation and racism involved in this experience with his cynical comment, "the Negro was in vogue."

The 1929 crash brought the flashy era of the Harlem night spots to an end, for the clubs there had been driven largely by white money. The end to Prohibition in 1933 destroyed the speakeasies, which had attracted many of their high-society customers by the very allure of illegality. As the grim realities of the Depression set in, the "Gatsby" set's fascination with Harlem dissipated and blacks there were left to the miseries of ghetto impoverishment.

Europe and the Image of America

In the 1920s, America and its popular culture became the rage in Europe. European travelers to the United States brought back images of a super-modern society of skyscrapers and machines that looked to the future. In Fascist Italy, young Italians of anti-Fascist sentiment gravitated toward American culture as an escape from the conformity of the reactionary regime, and Mussolini eventually prohibited jazz as a "corrupting" influence.

Europeans became especially fascinated with black American culture. Foremost among the cultural imports was jazz (see Part VIII, Topic 7), whose chief admirers were the French. Indeed, in this respect, Europe's counterpart to New York was Paris, the city that since the second half of the 19th century had been the premier European center of the cultural avant-garde.

In the 1920s, many Americans made Paris their home, attracted by the Bohemian atmosphere and liberal attitudes that the city extended to even the most unconventional behavior. Paris drew a large number of expatriate American intellectuals. The writer Gertrude Stein (1874–1946) had been there since 1904 and, together with her lover Alice B. Toklas (1877–1967), held court at one of the most famous cultural salons of the century. Stein was one of the first to appreciate the genius of the painter Pablo Picasso and other artists, and her apartment became a mecca for young American writers—Stein called them the "lost generation"—searching for their own cultural identity. F. Scott Fitzgerald lived in Paris much of the time, as did the writer Ernest Hemingway (1899–1961). Black American entertainers flocked to Paris, where they performed in a host of cabarets famous

Pablo Picasso painted this portrait of American writer Gertrude Stein in 1905–1906, when they both were relatively unknown émigrés in Paris.

since the 1880s, foremost among them the Moulin Rouge, immortalized by the artist Toulouse-Lautrec. Parisians found black Americans, especially women, exotically sensuous. In 1925, an all-black musical called *La Revue Nègre*, which ran first in New York, was booked to play in Paris at the Théâtre des Champs-Elysées. When Josephine Baker arrived in Paris as the lead in the review, she joined a group of black musicians who played the blues in the bohemian quarters of the city. The singer Bricktop was already there, and owned a popular night spot. Baker became an overnight hit and remained in Paris for the next 50 years, opening her own cabaret, the Chez Joséphine, and marrying an Italian count. Duke Ellington made his first European tour in the late 1920s and was wildly acclaimed.

If Paris had long been a major cultural center of Europe, Berlin had no such heritage. Rather, the city of almost 4 million inhabitants had been the capital of the former German empire and its economic life. Yet in the 1920s, Berlin transformed itself into the center of an extraordinary flowering of modern culture, and also earned a reputation as one of Europe's most notorious fleshpots. "Sex," said the actress Louise Brooks, "was the business of the town."

The atmosphere in postwar Berlin was iconoclastic and innovative, and the city drew creative young

African-American entertainer Josephine Baker was a sensation at the Folies-Bergère in Paris.

Germans attracted by the counterculture of modernity. Bars, restaurants, prostitution houses, and music halls sprang up, offering free-wheeling entertainment. The city became especially known for its hundreds of bars frequented by lesbians and gays, whose experiences were chronicled in a series of short stories by British-born author Christopher Isherwood (1904–1986). American jazz became the rage here, too, and cabarets, originally imported from France, flourished. In Berlin, however, the cabarets assumed an original aspect, for in many of them light music and comedy were used to convey serious political and social satire. The cabarets also inspired the artist George Grosz (1893–1959), a communist supporter. His brilliant talent created political drawings that savagely assaulted reactionary forces, especially the Nazis, whom he passionately hated.

As in America, in Europe, too, conditions in the 1930s altered the social atmosphere. The Great Depression, the rise of Hitler, and the looming threat of war combined to bring an end to the era of rampant pleasure seeking and the spirit of the age of cabaret.

GENDER, SEXUALITY, AND THE FAMILY

The great popularity of the nightclub among the middle and upper classes reflected the greatly changed attitudes about women, gender, and sexuality. Women not only attended the cabarets, but acted in public places generally much as men did, for they drank, smoked, danced, and enjoyed themselves, often without male companions. Women's fashions, revealing portions of the body that had been kept hidden during the Victorian era, paralleled the emergence of a "new woman"—independent, accomplished, and interested in self-fulfillment. Such attitudes and behavior would have been inconceivable for most women 20 years earlier. The changing status of women in society was part of a broader social transformation that included major shifts in sexual standards and behavior, in marriage and birth patterns, and in the way in which the household was organized.

The New Woman: Opportunities and Limitations

World War I had begun the process of altering gender roles, for hundreds of thousands of women had moved into the factories to replace the men who served in the armies (see Part VIII, Topic 1). In the aftermath, women gained new freedoms and privileges. The contribution of women to the war effort was in part responsible for the passage of female suffrage laws in the immediate postwar period. Denmark and Iceland, both neutral during the war, actually gave women the vote in 1915, and the Netherlands followed in 1917. In 1918, Britain was the first major European state to enact female suffrage, although it was limited to women over 30. The first women candidates who ran in the elections that year were all defeated. The Weimar Republic gave German women the vote in 1919, while Belgium did so for war widows only. In the new states of Eastern Europe, women also achieved the vote, while in France and Italy voting remained a male preserve until after World War II.

Despite the politically conservative mood of most Western European countries in the postwar era, women's attitudes and their social position changed significantly, creating a clash of opinion between those who wanted to restore prewar social values and those who demanded the modernization of society. Women

Otto Dix's "Metropolis" (1927–28) ironically depicts a Berlin nightclub with its "new morality."

seemed more ubiquitous in postwar society, both because millions of men had been killed in the war and because women increasingly did things once reserved only for men—women became journalists, took part in professional sports, flew airplanes, and entered mainstream politics. Women's public conduct became more relaxed, and many now demanded careers of their own. The role of women in the professions and the arts assumed greater importance, and the modern middle-class housewife emerged in the 1920s.

Women changed their physical appearance in a number of ways. In dress, they began to reveal their arms, legs, and shoulders. The length of their skirts was shortened by about twelve inches and sleeves, once wrist-length even in summer, disappeared. Women who thought of themselves as modern adopted varying degrees of male appearance—short, bobbed hair, flattened breasts, and a slim figure, and wore slacks and trench coats. Scanty bathing suits were fashionable, and the ideal of a suntanned body replaced the Victorian preference for pale skin. The cosmetic business grew to a mass industry as millions of women began to use lipstick, rouge, and mascara, items once identified only with prostitutes.

In the 1920s, the gains in employment made by women during the war were generally pushed back. With the coming of peace, many governments encouraged women to return to the home and allow men to take their place in the workforce, a policy that unions and even reform-minded socialists supported. The percentage of women working declined almost every-

where. Some of the women who lost their jobs went back to low-paying work as domestics or in agriculture, occupations in which they could not qualify for unemployment insurance. In Britain, unemployment insurance payments were lower for women than for men and not enough for a woman to live on. The expansion of bureaucracies and the growth of department stores did give many women new job opportunities as office workers or salesclerks, and the spread of the telephone led many women to become operators. In factories, where men sometimes outnumbered women nine to one, women were relegated to the most menial jobs. Only in the Soviet Union, where the desire to industrialize took precedence over everything else, did women constitute a major portion—as high as 45 percent—of the workforce.

In those countries where unemployment was high in the 1920s, women workers suffered more than men. The Great Depression made the plight of working women even worse. As conditions deteriorated, increasing numbers of women were forced out of jobs, in both democratic and authoritarian countries. In 1931, British Labour Minister Margaret Bondfield (1873–1953) excluded most women from unemployment insurance. In Fascist Italy and Nazi Germany, women were encouraged as a matter of ideology to be wives and mothers, not workers (see Part VIII, Topic 4).

Varieties of Sexuality

If women demanded the development of a modern outlook, much of the new mentality focused on sexuality.

In the Victorian era, the prevailing middle-class attitude had been the exercise of sexual restraint for men, virtue for women, and the general repression of overt sexual references in daily life (see Part VII, Topic 13). These conventions began to change with the war, when men and women mingled more freely in an atmosphere of "living for today." Modern medicine and postwar psychology both undermined the earlier emphasis on restraint by stressing the benefits of release and self-expression. Finally, the rise of consumerism led to the discovery of the power of sex as an advertising device, while mass culture, especially the movies, promoted sex symbols on the silver screen.

The struggle against gender tradition inevitably contributed to a more open discussion of sex, but the issue often aroused bitter debate. One of the most controversial figures in the postwar encounter with sexuality was Marie Stopes (1880–1938), a British paleobotanist and birth control advocate. A university lecturer and author, in 1921 Stopes founded the Mothers' Clinic for Constructive Birth Control. She argued that sexual pleasure was an important part of marriage and life in general, and should not be limited to procreation—indeed, the search for physical pleasure, she said, was a woman's right. In 1918 she published *Married Love*, vividly describing the sexual joy that could be attained in marriage. In 1926, she also wrote *Sex and the Young*, which countered Victorian assumptions about the innocence of youth.

The year 1926 also saw the appearance of *Ideal Marriage: Its Physiology and Technique*, by the Dutch physician Theodor von de Velde. The book was one of the most authoritative sex manuals, and became an international bestseller. Its popularity, like that of Stopes' books, was due to the fact that it provided women with detailed practical information.

Europeans not only read such works, but increasingly practiced birth control and abortion. Between 1850 and 1914, Europe's population increased steadily. After the war, however, marriage and birthrates changed in a manner that suggests deliberate efforts to control fertility. The bloody battles of the war, together with disease and undernourishment, killed some 11 million people, or about 3 percent of Europe's population. The war also disrupted the pattern of marriages and births. In the interwar period, mortality rates fell and life expectancy grew, yet the birthrate declined everywhere. A number of factors explain the change: economic hardships and unemployment, especially after the Depression, the diffusion of birth control information, and the changing role of women. In many countries, politicians expressed concern about the population decline, and France, Italy, and Germany passed laws restricting birth control information and abortions. Nevertheless, it has been estimated that perhaps as many as 1 million German women had abortions each year in the 1920s. On the other hand, nations as diverse as France and Sweden, Fascist Italy and Nazi Germany instituted programs to encourage large families.

Sexual minorities also encountered a freer atmosphere in the postwar era. Gays and lesbians came out of the closet in increasingly larger numbers, and many prominent intellectuals and artists made their orientation known publicly. The German psychiatrist Magnus Hirschfeld (1868–1935) founded his famous Institute for Sexual Science, where homosexuals had access to counseling and psychological support in coping with a society that still retained deep hostility toward them. The problem of lesbian identity was directly discussed in the novel *The Well of Loneliness* (1928), by the British writer Radclyffe Hall (1880–1943). Although the book was banned by the government, it appeared in many languages throughout the world.

The Life of the Family
The family as it had developed over the 19th century had also begun to undergo profound changes after World War I, and many of the trends continue to this day. Men and women both postponed marriage longer than ever before, and when they did marry they had fewer children. The average size of the family declined steadily as the number of offspring dropped by almost half.

Within the family, the dynamics of gender moved slowly away from the patriarchal model of the Victorian bourgeoisie. Husbands increasingly shared household responsibilities and became more directly involved in child rearing. Nevertheless, most working-class and middle-class women continued to have major responsibility for managing the household. Technology and consumerism did, however, change the role of the housewife. The 1920s saw the beginnings of modernization in the middle-class home, primarily through the introduction of new machines and the application of technology to household tasks. Electric washing machines and irons transformed those tasks, while the vacuum cleaner came into general use. Such machines made strenuous work less demanding for the average housewife, although some experts have argued that they also raised the standards to which women had to aspire.

The most dramatic change came in the kitchen. During World War I, working women, often without the responsibility of feeding husbands, sons, or brothers, adopted lighter meals that were quick and easy to prepare, and the widespread availability of preservatives and canning after the war encouraged a continuation of such practices. A host of new cookbooks catered to the modern diet, with a new emphasis on nutrition and health. Electric mixers and juicers were introduced, and gas or electric stoves and ovens replaced wood-burning stoves, while electric refrigerators eliminated the need for hauling ice and for daily shopping.

In the mid-1920s, industrial design altered the way in which both home appliances and the home itself looked. The International Exposition of Modern Decorative and Industrial Arts, held in Paris in 1925, presented the first views of streamlined everyday objects and furniture, while the so-called International Style of architecture, developed in Europe by Walter Gropius and Le Corbusier and in the United States by Frank Lloyd Wright, stressed simplicity, modern building materials such as steel, reinforced concrete, and glass, and functionalism (see Part VIII, Topic 7). By the 1930s, a "streamlined modern" style had shaped the design of everything from vacuum cleaners to airplanes to railroad engines and refrigerators, while kitchens became laboratory-like in their cleanliness, organization, and functionalism. The modern household, like the modern family, assumed a new, more progressive aspect.

The social transformations that took place in the 20 years between 1919 and 1939 explain much about how Europeans and others live today. As the West began to emerge out of the industrial revolution and toward the postindustrial world, the composition and status of social classes also changed. The middle classes grew increasingly complex, especially with the growth of the white-collar group, and while the condition of the working classes improved, that of the upper classes deteriorated. The result was a general leveling of society, at least in terms of a more equal distribution of income and standard of living. The social impact of the Great Depression, by threatening the well-being and security of the middle and the working classes, increased class tensions and encouraged the radicalization of domestic politics.

Despite the grim aspects of life between the wars, the era was one of self-conscious modernity, in which many of the repressive features of Victorian society were replaced by values that stressed nonconformity, free expression, and individualism. Women enhanced their social equality, advanced sexual freedom, and won the vote in most democratic countries; in the totalitarian dictatorships, however, the status of women regressed under the impact of a self-

consciously male-dominated ideology. Everywhere, working women experienced a mixture of new opportunities and exclusion from the workforce.

The 1920s especially were an age of hedonism marked by a desire for fast-paced, unconventional public behavior. Behind the glitter of the jazz clubs and cabarets lay evidence of a society bent on excess and overindulgence after the shattering experience of a war that had upset tradition more than any single event since the French Revolution. By the 1930s, a more sober, solemn mood set in as society grappled with the ravages of the Great Depression.

Questions for Further Study

1. What was the impact of World War I on European society? How did that impact manifest itself in the 1920s?

2. What were the chief characteristics of popular culture and leisure time activities in the postwar period?

3. In what ways did postwar society reflect the changing role of women?

Suggestions for Further Reading

Bridenthal, Renate, A. Grossmann, and M. Kaplan, eds. *When Biology Became Destiny: Women in Weimar and Nazi Germany.* New York, 1984.

Cantor, Norman. *The History of Popular Culture Since 1815.* New York, 1968.

Gay, Peter. *Weimar Culture.* New York, 1968.

Grossmann, Atina. *Reforming Sex: The German Movement for Birth Control and Abortion Reform, 1920–1950.* New York, 1995.

Gruber, Helmut. *Red Vienna: Experiment in Working-Class Culture, 1919–1943.* New York, 1991.

Kent, Susan. *Making Peace: The Reconstruction of Gender in Postwar Britain.* Princeton, NJ, 1994.

Maier, Charles S. *Recasting Bourgeois Europe: Stabilization in France, Germany, and Italy.* Princeton, NJ, 1975.

Roberts, Mary L. *Civilization Without Sexes: Reconstructing Gender in Postwar France, 1917–1927.* Chicago, 1994.

Stearns, Peter N. *European Society in Upheaval: Social History Since 1800.* New York, 1967.

Winter, J. M., and R. M. Wall, eds. *The Upheaval of War: Family, Work and Welfare in Europe, 1914–1918.* Cambridge, MA, 1988.

T o p i c   7

CIVILIZATION AND ITS DISCONTENTS: PSYCHOANALYSIS AND THE ARTS

orld War I led many Europeans to question the basic values of their society and culture. Concepts such as patriotism, the glory of war, aristocracy, rationalism and technology, and the notion of progress itself were tarnished by the carnage of the trenches. Profound doubts arose about the ability of Western civilization to survive. Some artists reacted by seeking refuge in frivolity, often combined with a spirit of cynicism. Others sought to understand human motives by exploring ideas that had been developed before the war, in particular psychoanalysis.

Freud's emphasis on irrationality and the nature of the unconscious proved especially fruitful. The French critic André Breton ushered in a movement called Surrealism which affected literature and the visual arts, while the English writer Virginia Woolf used her novels to explore the "stream of consciousness" of her characters. In drama, the American Eugene O'Neill made explicit the Freudian theme of the relations between parents and children.

Woolf was one of the leading members of an intellectual circle known as the Bloomsbury Group, whose members were responsible for many important cultural developments between the wars. In his poem "The Waste Land," T. S. Eliot analyzed the failure of modern civilization. The philosopher Bertrand Russell and the economist John Maynard Keynes also had contacts with the world of Bloomsbury. In painting, the two leading movements represented opposite attitudes. The Dadaists fought against the idea of any kind of meaning, while the Surrealists explored the intellectual implications of the subconscious and the meaning of dreams. Meanwhile, other painters continued to explore the possibilities of Cubism, the style invented just before World War I. The work of one of them, the Dutch painter Piet Mondrian, influenced much modern design.

With the spread of modern urban culture some artists and designers tried consciously to create a style which would be valid in a wide variety of settings. At the *Bauhaus* in Germany, Walter Gropius and his colleagues devised the International Style, which had a great influence on the urban landscape of the 20th century. Bauhaus artists also sought to provide a modernist idiom for all aspects of everyday life.

Artists were profoundly affected by the growing popularity of photography and the movies, and the diffusion of the radio and recorded sound. Among the most widespread influences of the day was jazz, originally a form of music indigenous to America. Jazz became popular among all those with access to a radio or a phonograph. The leading composers of the day, including Igor Stravinsky and Paul Hindemith, incorporated jazz elements in their music.

The interwar years were overshadowed not only by the horrors of World War I, but by the growing realization that further conflict seemed ahead. The Spanish Civil War drove many artists and writers to protest the brutality of fascism. The German novelist Thomas Mann warned against the direction the Nazi regime was taking, before joining other intellectuals in exile. Yet if art could warn, it could not prevent. With the outbreak of World War II, Freud's insistence on the power of the irrational seemed frighteningly justified.

STREAM OF CONSCIOUSNESS: LITERATURE AND PSYCHOANALYSIS

World War I brought into question many of Europe's most cherished values. Some, such as a belief in the inherent superiority and leadership qualities of noble birth, were already being challenged in the 19th century. Others, most notably the importance of patriotism and national pride, retained their potency and their potential destructiveness. Technological progress, the proud achievement of the late 19th century, was now revealed as morally neutral. Its ability to cause good or ill was vast, and depended on how it was used: tanks, planes, and poison gas were responsible for the slaughter of millions of troops.

For some the shock to civilization marked the beginning of the end. The Irish poet William Butler Yeats (1865–1939) spoke for many who were fearful of the future when he wrote: "Things fall apart: the center cannot hold; Mere anarchy is loosed upon the world." The sense that Western civilization was deteriorating permeated *The Decline of the West* (1918–1922), a massive historical study by the German philosopher Oswald Spengler (1880–1936). According to Spengler, history moved in cycles. Western culture, he believed, had passed its high point and was on the way down.

Those of less apocalyptic temperament sought escape from recent memories in the lighthearted, even trivial. The English novelist Evelyn Waugh (1903–1966) caricatured the dizzy world of London's "bright young things" with a mixture of attraction and repulsion. In Paris, Picasso designed sets for a ballet, *Parade*, with music by Erik Satie (1866–1925), which included sound effects such as whistles, automobile horns, and typewriters to evoke everyday life.

The 1920s was the age of the "flappers" (see Part VIII, Topic 6). Elegant young women with broad hats and tight-fitting short skirts, smoking cigarettes in long holders (a sign of their emancipation), spent their afternoons at tea dances, or listening to the latest jazz records from America. For their generation, or so it seemed, nationalism and the wars it provoked were unthinkable. Students at Oxford University debated the notion of fighting for king and country, and voted overwhelmingly against it.

Literature and the Unconscious

Among those to look deeply at the problems of the modern age was Sigmund Freud, who published *Civilization and its Discontents* in 1930 (see Part VII, Topic 21). Freud's work earlier in the century proved an increasing source of inspiration to artists searching to understand the motives for human behavior. By stressing the importance of the unconscious and the inner meaning of dreams, he underlined the power of the irrational to affect apparently rational thought processes.

Exploration of the unconscious was the chief goal of Surrealism, an artistic movement which influenced both writers and painters. The high priest of Surrealism was the French poet André Breton (1896–1966), who published his *Manifesto of Surrealism* in 1924. In his poems he intermingled the everyday and the fantastic, probing the connections between dream and reality, the subjective and the objective. The finest poet of the Surrealist movement, Paul Éluard (1895–1952; real name Eugène Grindel), even turned to various forms of mental alienation as a means of shedding light on hidden mental processes. By the use of mysterious images and fragmentary language, his love poems tried to recreate the dreamlike disorder of the subconscious.

The novels of Virginia Woolf (1882–1941) use the "stream of consciousness" technique to deal with themes of time, change, and human personality. Instead of providing a chronological account of her characters' lives, she moved back and forth in time, describing the effect of the past on present consciousness. In *To the Lighthouse* (1927), the central section of the three parts into which the novel is divided is called "Time Passes." It provides an impressionistic rendering of the effects of the passage of time on people and things. In further

A curtain designed by Picasso for the performance of the ballet *Parade,* with music by Erik Satie, given in Paris in 1917 by Diaghilev's Ballets Russes company.

refining on the techniques of Joyce and Proust (see Part VII, Topic 21), Woolf paid special attention to the experiences of women. Her book *Mrs. Dalloway* (1925) described a single day in the life of the novel's heroine. Woolf's own frustration at the exclusion of women from intellectual life found expression in *A Room of One's Own* (1929), in which she argued that only financial independence and freedom from the demands of family could give women the same possibilities as men. A later polemical work, *Three Guineas* (1938), described a fascist-like world dominated by men, in which individual rights, freedom, and justice were suppressed.

The great American dramatist Eugene O'Neill (1888–1953) used psychology and symbolism to illuminate another of Freud's revelations: the complexity of the relationship between parents and children, and the fundamental importance of early family experience in creating human personalities. In *Mourning Becomes Electra* (1931), ancient Greek tragedy became reenacted in Civil War New England, with Aeschylus' idea of the unavoidability of fate given modern form as psychological destiny.

THE WORLD OF BLOOMSBURY

Amid the confusion of the interwar years, a group of writers and intellectuals in England sought to maintain a coherence of thought and action. They were called after the area of London in which many of them lived and worked, Bloomsbury. The name acquired further cultural resonance from the fact that the Bloomsbury district also contained the British Museum. Virginia Woolf and her husband, Leonard Woolf (1880–1969), were at the center of the Bloomsbury Group. From the basement of their house they operated a publishing company, the Hogarth Press, which circulated works by many of the most influential writers of the time. Among the offerings in Hogarth Press editions were the first complete English translations of the works of Freud, and the first English translations of the German poet Rainer Maria Rilke (1875–1926) and the Italian novelist Italo Svevo (1861–1928; real name Ettore Schmitz).

Eliot and "The Waste Land"

Although an American, and on the periphery of the Bloomsbury circle, the poet T[homas] S[tearns] Eliot (1888–1965) was among the writers the Woolfs published. His most famous work, "The Waste Land," appeared on their list in 1922, and over the following years Eliot acted as informal adviser to them.

After studying at Harvard, Eliot moved to London, where he eked out a living by teaching and writing reviews, and working in a bank. "The Waste Land" placed him immediately at the center of the modernist movement. Its theme was the spiritual and moral chaos of postwar Europe. Abandoning traditional forms, the style of the poem conveys the bleakness of its theme in broken lines and fragmented images. The overwhelming mood of the work is one of alienation and exile, expressing the disillusionment of an entire generation.

In subsequent works, Eliot moved from the despair of "The Waste Land" to an affirmation of traditional culture. The foundation of his growing optimism was Christianity. The most fully worked-out meditation on his Christian faith appeared in the *Four Quartets* (1944). Not only the most widely read poet of his generation, Eliot was also an enormously influential literary critic.

The Influence of Bloomsbury

Bloomsbury's cultural influence extended far beyond poetry. Lytton Strachey (1880–1932) brought new life to the writing of biography by taking an irreverent look at pillars of the Victorian establishment. His *Eminent Victorians* (1918) caught the postwar mood of cynicism by depicting Florence Nightingale as an interfering busybody, and General Charles George "Chinese" Gordon as an alcoholic. In a slightly later work he took on even Queen Victoria herself.

The art critic and painter Roger Fry (1866–1934) was one of the leading champions of Cézanne and the other Postimpressionist painters; the exhibitions he organized of their works helped to inspire public interest and enthusiasm for them. The historical writings and translations of Arthur Waley (1889–1966) introduced Chinese and Japanese culture to a wide audience. Although many of them are now superseded, his versions of Chinese poetry and the great Japanese novel *The Tale of Genji* (written around 1000 by Lady Murasaki) opened up new cultural horizons for many readers.

Other influential figures who maintained links with Bloomsbury included John Maynard Keynes (See Part VIII, Topic 3), a major pioneer in the development of modern economics. The leading philosopher of the day, Bertrand Russell (1872–1970), although not an inner member of the group, was in contact with many who were. Far more closely involved—she had a love affair with Virginia Woolf—was Victoria Sackville-West (1892–1962), whose unconventional marriage to the critic and diplomat Harold Nicolson (1886–1968) illustrated the iconoclastic spirit of the world of Bloomsbury.

MOVEMENTS IN MODERN ART: DADA, SURREALISM, ABSTRACTION

The years before World War I saw a succession of "isms," including Fauvism, Cubism, and Futurism, as artists tried to build on the innovations of their prede-

Marcel Duchamp's famous "defacement" of Leonardo da Vinci's *Mona Lisa,* with an obscene reference beneath (1919).

PUBLIC FIGURES ⬤ PRIVATE LIVES

VITA SACKVILLE-WEST AND HAROLD NICOLSON

Daughter of an eccentric English aristocrat, Vita Sackville-West became one of the most flamboyant and well-known figures of her era. Passionately attached to her family and its ancestral home, Knole, her two absorbing interests were literature and gardening. After meeting her for the first time around Christmas 1922, Virginia Woolf wrote of her: "Not much to my severer taste—florid, mustached, parakeet-colored, with all the supple ease of the aristocracy, but not the wit of the artist." Two years later, under the spell of her infatuation, Virginia described Vita's legs: "Oh they are exquisite—running like slender pillars up into her trunk, which is that of a breastless cuirassier."

In 1913 Vita married Harold Nicolson, an eligible young man in the diplomatic service, whose early emotional relationships included a number of lighthearted homosexual affairs. When they first met in 1910, Vita herself was involved in a romantic crush on another young girl. While maintaining their own independent lifestyles, they brought up two sons and wrote.

Nicolson published literary criticism, including an influential monograph on Tennyson. From 1935 to 1945 he served in Parliament.

Vita's first work, a collection of poems, was inspired by the time she spent in Teheran, where her diplomat husband had been posted. A later long poem, "The Land," won an important literary prize in 1927. She followed this with novels, works on family history, and innumerable articles on gardening. Many of these latter were based on her restoration of the garden at Sissinghurst Castle, which is still visited annually by thousands.

Throughout their marriage, Sackville-West and Nicolson kept diaries, and exchanged a flood of correspondence with one another during their frequent separations. Their relationship has been described, in fact, as one of the best-documented marriages in history. They constantly brooded on their own lives, and on the question of relations between men and women, as well as on the issue of feminism. In 1934, Nicolson recorded in his diary a discussion about women's lives and their approach to freedom: "V says that in every revolution there is a transitional stage. That women have for centuries been suppressed and that one cannot expect them to slide quite naturally into freedom. This saddens me."

Twenty years later, Vita summed up her feelings about her marriage in a letter to a friend: "We have gone our own ways for about 30 years; never asked questions; never been in the least curious about that side of our respective lives, though deeply devoted and sharing our interests. I love him deeply, and he loves me. . . ."

To some extent, the openness of their marriage was facilitated by the well-to-do British social world in which they moved and by Sackville-West's utter indifference to convention. Both of them drew considerable strength and satisfaction from their independent literary work. Nicolson's early pleasure in his political career gave way to a growing sense of not being taken seriously enough, but his diary reveals a keen if somewhat detached interest in diplomatic affairs. Certainly they both took their duties as parents seriously. In a letter to her elder son, in fact, Vita spelled out the oddness and success of an unlikely union: "Two of the happiest married people I know, whose names I must conceal for reasons of discretion, are both homosexual." Their son had little doubt about whom his mother meant.

cessors. The movement of the immediate postwar period, Dada, rejected the past and sought to begin again.

The Dadaists

The Dadaist movement was born out of anger, frustration, and despair. In 1915, as war raged, a group of artists met around a café table in Zurich, Switzerland, to protest the madness of their times. Their response was to reject the past and all its works, and to create meaningless nonsense. The very word "Dada" seems to have been chosen for its similarity to childlike babble. The leading Dada poet, the Romanian-born Tristan Tzara (1896–1963), wrote a manifesto in 1918 calling for the destruction of memory, the end of good manners, and the practice of the spontaneous.

Dada's most original, and iconoclastic, figure was the French Marcel Duchamp (1887–1968). An early proponent of Cubism, he created a sensation in New York in 1913 with his *Nude Descending a Staircase*. Duchamp invented the Dada form of sculpture, the "ready-made," by taking ordinary objects—a snow shovel, a urinal—and putting them on display. ("Ready-made" sculptures enjoyed a revival after World War II; among those producing them was Picasso.) No masterpiece of high culture was safe from his scorn, as his notorious defacement of a copy of Leonardo's *Mona Lisa* vividly illustrated. For all the anger, however, the sheer energy of the Dada movement soon worked itself out. Duchamp abandoned art for chess in 1923, and many Dada artists went on to produce Surrealist paintings.

Surrealist Art

Unlike the Dada pursuit of the meaningless, Surrealism set out to discover the deeper meanings that lay beneath the surface of the conscious mind. According to Breton's Surrealist manifesto of 1924, artists should set out to express "the real functioning of thought without any control by reason." One of the leading exponents of Surrealism, the Spanish painter Salvador Dalí (1904–1989), described his works as "hand-painted dream photographs." Like many others of the period, Dalí was obsessed with the nature of time. His best-known work, *The Persistence of Memory* (1931), has become virtually an icon of Surrealism. The work combines precisely painted detail with melting watches to create a sense of quiet alarm.

Dalí's paintings are often foreboding, even threatening. His Belgian contemporary René Magritte (1898–1967) used absurdity to call into question the nature of reality. His haunting images show familiar subjects, but play tricks with the viewer's expectations; the title of the painting often plays a part in the surprise effect. Thus, his *Man with a Newspaper* (1928) is divided into four identical quadrants, in which the man seen in the upper left quadrant disappears thereafter.

The form of Magritte's painting, with its four separate "frames," reveals one of the sources of inspiration for Surrealist art: the cinema and photography. Dalí worked on a number of film projects, as did the French Surrealist author and artist Jean Cocteau (1889–1963).

Other Surrealist artists adopted a less literal approach. The Swiss painter Paul Klee (1879–1940) once said: "I want to be as though new-born, knowing nothing." His small, beautifully executed works depict a world of pure imagination, avoiding any trace of the realism of Magritte or Dalí. Klee experimented with "psychic automatism," a technique by which the artist set down lines at random, without rational control.

The finished drawings and watercolors (he rarely used other mediums) are subtle and delicate in line and color. The element of humor in Klee's work—an unusual quality in modern art—also appears in that of the Spanish artist Joan Miró (1893–1983).

Cubism After World War I

Both Pablo Picasso and Georges Braque, the coinventors of Cubism, continued to explore the possibilities of the style, while generally moving away from the highly analytical character of their prewar work (see Part VII, Topic 21). In works such as the *Three Musicians* (1921), Picasso still used flat planes, but the figures have a liveliness and color—even humor—absent in earlier Cubist work. One of the chief exponents of this freer, "Synthetic Cubism" was Picasso's fellow-Spaniard Juan Gris (1887–1927), who applied the technique to still life subjects.

By contrast, the Dutch artist Piet Mondrian (1872–1944) moved toward ever greater abstraction. Art, he believed, should have "balance, unity, and stability." Using pure colors and clean lines, he constructed rectangles of varying dimensions that seem almost to be street plans—Mondrian wrote, in fact, that "the new style will spring from the metropolis." The spare, abstract repose of his works had a considerable influence on many aspects of modern design, from fashion to advertising.

BAUHAUS: THE INTERNATIONAL STYLE IN BUILDING AND DESIGN

Mondrian was one of a group of Dutch artists who joined forces in a movement known as *De Stijl* (Dutch for "The Style"). At the end of World War I, De Stijl architects constructed buildings according to Mondrian's principles of geometrical balance. The Schroder House in Utrecht, designed in 1924 by Gerrit Rietveld (1888–1964), has a façade whose severely geometrical lines form the three-dimensional equivalent of a Mondrian canvas. In addition to buildings, Rietveld also designed furniture, using a similar spare geometrical style.

Gropius and the Bauhaus

The most comprehensive attempt to devise an all-embracing design style for modern living developed in Germany in the 1920s. In 1919, the German architect Walter Gropius (1883–1969) was commissioned to organize a German art school. The result, the Bauhaus (Building Institute), became the 20th century's most influential school of architecture and design.

The innovations of Gropius and his colleagues derived from a new attitude to the nature and function

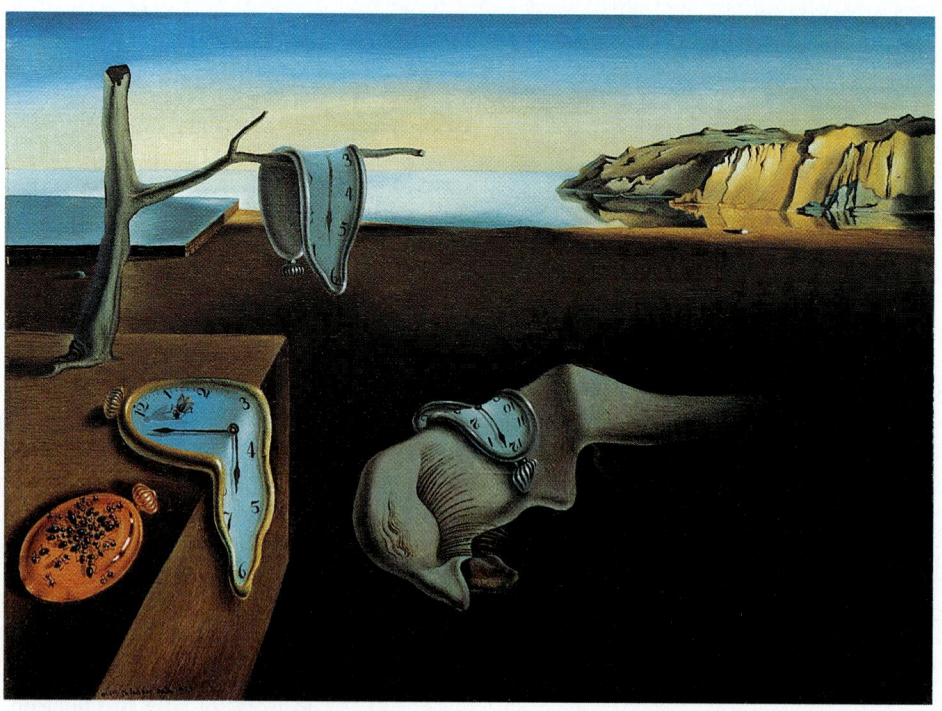

Salvador Dalí's *The Persistence of Memory* (1931), with its distortion of time, is one of the key works of the Surrealist movement.

Three Musicians (1921), a colorful, lighthearted work in Picasso's later Cubist style.

of a building, based on the possibilities of advanced construction techniques. The three principal ingredients were a reinforced concrete base, a structural framework made of steel, and glass panels for walls. By using the principle of cantilevering (projecting beams to support balconies) Bauhaus architects were able to construct upper stories which overhung their supporting bases.

The most visually daring of these elements was the use of glass for walls. Since glass reflects light, as well as transmitting it, changing weather patterns outside a building, along with illumination inside, affect its appearance. At times both inside and outside are visible simultaneously, creating the equivalent of the Cubist effect whereby two different views can be seen at the same time. At other times the glass walls produce a mirror-like effect, reflecting the buildings around. In Bauhaus architecture, in fact, the wall became a decorative rather than structural element, acting as a curtain against the outside environment.

The inventors of the Bauhaus style intended it to serve for constructions in any urban setting. Their "International Style" became widely diffused throughout Europe, and was carried to the United States when Gropius and his colleague Mies van der Rohe fled there in the late 1930s.

One of the first important Modernist buildings, Mies van der Rohe and Philip Johnson's Seagram Building in New York City.

The Bauhaus philosophy of design affected far more than architecture. Its governing principle, that of unadorned utility, characterized the forms of a wide variety of objects and processes. Printmaking and metalwork techniques laid emphasis on clarity of line and ease of production. Mass-produced tubular chairs combined simple comfort and convenient storage capacity. Household appliances were streamlined, and easy to use and to clean.

The characteristically "modern" look of most post–World War II industrial production owed much of its inspiration to the Bauhaus group. Followers of the school praised the clean lines, efficiency, and practical advantages. Others, less convinced, lamented the uniformity and lack of character of the International Style. In architecture, at least, a reaction against Bauhaus simplicity began to develop in the 1980s, when the Postmodernist movement reintroduced elements of decoration (see Part VIII, Topic 14). Yet in the late 20th century the urban landscape of most large cities throughout the world remained firmly conditioned by Bauhaus ideas, and modern design continued to pay homage to the Bauhaus principle: "Less is more."

THE JAZZ AGE: MUSIC, RADIO, AND THE MOVIES

The years after World War I saw the rapid spread of mass communications. Radio, first invented by Guglielmo Marconi (1874–1937) at the turn of the century, became an increasingly popular source of information, culture, and simple entertainment. It linked city and country dwellers, it crossed over national boundaries, it spanned the Atlantic. By the outbreak of World War II, more than 300 million people had access to radio sets. In most European countries, radio networks were state-controlled. Transmissions throughout the 1930s served to reinforce government attitudes, especially in Fascist Italy, Nazi Germany, and Soviet Russia. During World War II, radio broadcasts were used for psychological warfare.

The effect of radio on popular culture, especially music, was to produce a growing standardization of "consumer product," whereby listeners in remote regions or countries could hear the latest Berlin cabaret song or Broadway hit almost as soon as their first local audiences. At the same time, radio also won new listeners for symphonies and operas. In the United States, nationwide transmissions of Metropolitan Opera broadcasts began in 1931. That same year, when Arturo Toscanini (1867–1957), one of the towering figures in European musical life, fled Fascism and went to America, he became the chief conductor of a radio orchestra, the NBC Symphony.

The Movies

Scarcely less revolutionary was the impact of the movies. Like radio, the movies had been around before World War I, but their great age was the 1920s and, with the coming of sound, the 1930s. In the decade before World War II, giant picture palaces sprang up in the big cities, and few rural communities did not have access to a movie theater in a provincial center nearby. Between 1933 and 1942, annual cinema attendance in Germany rose from a quarter of a billion to 1 billion. Over the same period in Britain it remained constant at around 1 billion.

As in the case of radio, movies could and did serve propaganda purposes. Weekly newsreels, feature films, and documentaries poured out of government propaganda ministries. The most notorious examples of film at the service of the state are the works of the German Leni Riefenstahl (1902–1987). Her *Triumph of the Will* (1936) set out to glorify the Nazi party and its doctrines of mass ritual and racial superiority, using highly controlled and sexually charged images of young athletes and physical beauty.

Still shot from the diving sequence of Riefenstahl's film of the 1936 Berlin Olympics, *Olympia.*

The Russian filmmaker Sergei Eisenstein (1898–1948) was more equivocal. His works illustrated Lenin's belief in the high importance of the cinema in winning proletarian support for the Revolution. Most of his films, including his last masterpieces *Ivan the Terrible, Parts I and II* (1944–1946), showed the sufferings of the working class and the inevitability of the class struggle. Yet Eisenstein maintained control over his works; they aimed to teach historical lessons by reference to past events, rather than documenting contemporary politics.

In spite of the politicians' efforts, most people went to the movies for entertainment. With the rise of Hollywood in the 1930s, and the cult of the superstar, the cinema reached new heights of popularity. One of the most successful types of film, the musical, became possible with the improvement of sound techniques and the introduction of color processing.

The first sound film, *The Jazz Singer* (1927), had seemed to many to mark a setback in movie history. The first sound cameras were immobile, and permitted only very limited flexibility. Many of the stars of the silent screen, furthermore, feared the effect of the sound of their voice on their adoring public: adroit publicists cleverly managed to capitalize on this, and turned the first sound appearance of Greta Garbo (1905–1990) into an international event. By the 1930s, however, the movie industry had developed improved methods, and musicals such as *Showboat* (1936; original stage version 1927) played to audiences of millions.

Jazz

It is no coincidence that the movie chosen to inaugurate the new age of sound was *The Jazz Singer*. Not only did it provide even wider circulation for jazz music itself; by casting a white actor, Al Jolson (1886–1950), as a black jazz musician, it illustrated the degree to which a black musical idiom had been appropriated by white America (see Part VIII, Topic 6).

Jazz grew out of the black culture of the southern United States. Complex in rhythm, making frequent use of syncopation (the stress of normally unstressed beats), jazz was at first improvised. It took its mood from the work songs, laments, and spirituals (religious folk songs) of the slaves and black communities of the Deep South; its distant origins were derived from the folk music of Africa. The first organized performances were given by street bands of black musicians in New Orleans and other southern cities around 1900.

In the 1920s, as the black populations of the northern cities began to grow, jazz found a wider audience. Listeners in Chicago, New York, and other centers developed a taste for the blues singing of Bessie Smith (c. 1898–1937), and the trumpet playing of Louis Armstrong (1900–1971). White musicians took up the idiom, often forming big bands that developed a commercialized form of jazz known as "swing." The popularity of bandleaders such as Benny Goodman (1909–1986) or "Count" Basie (1904–1984) would be further spread by radio and phonograph records.

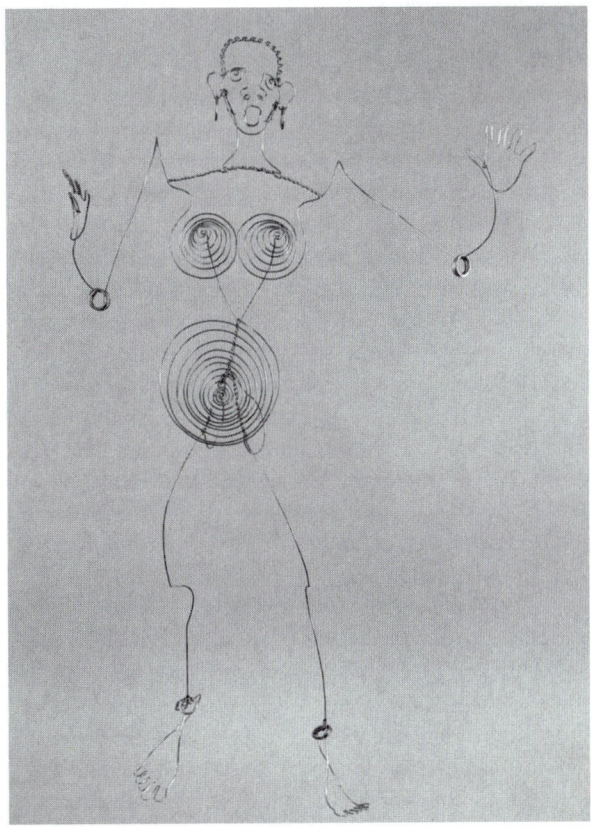

Alexander Calder, *Josephine Baker.* 1927–1929.

In a short time the new music spread to Europe. In Paris there grew up a cult following for *"le jazz hot,"* and one of the jazz world's most celebrated figures, the singer and dancer Josephine Baker, settled there permanently (See Part VIII, Topic 6). She was later to play a part in the French Resistance movement during World War II. Cabaret artists in Berlin included jazz numbers in their acts, and in 1933 recordings by Benny Goodman and his band created a sensation in Britain. So pervasive was the influence of jazz that some spoke of "the Jazz Age," a phrase derived from the title of a collection of short stories by F. Scott Fitzgerald, himself one of the chroniclers of the expatriate American community in Paris.

European composers soon began to explore the possibilities of jazz in their own music. Igor Stravinsky incorporated elements of "ragtime" (one of the early stages in the development of jazz) in his work *The Soldier's Tale* (1918). In the slow movement of his Violin Concerto of 1931, he made use of a blues-like theme. In Germany, Kurt Weill (1900–1950) developed a sophisticated blend of jazz and popular music to create works filled with powerful social criticism. The best-known is *The Threepenny Opera* (1928), the most ambitious *The Rise and Fall of the City of Mahagonny* (1929). (In Weill's later works, written after his move to the United States in 1935, he drew on the Broadway musical tradition.) The French composer Darius Milhaud (1892–1974) traveled to Harlem, New York, to hear the latest jazz for himself. He then incorporated his discoveries in the score for a ballet, *The Creation of the World* (1923).

The most consistent attempt to combine jazz and traditional musical forms occurred in the work of the American composer George Gershwin (1898–1937). His *Rhapsody in Blue* (1924), a piano concerto in all but name, was written for the jazz band of Paul Whiteman (1890–1967); Gershwin himself played the solo part at the sensationally successful first performance in New York. His full-length "American folk opera," *Porgy and Bess* (1935), incorporated jazz and spiritual music. Received with only limited enthusiasm at first, the work enjoyed increasing success at its revivals in the 1970s. By the 1990s it had entered the repertory of such traditional companies as the Metropolitan Opera, New York, and Glyndebourne, England.

COMING SHADOWS

Over the restless energy of the Jazz Age there began to fall the shadow of war. The sense of trouble ahead emerged in the work of a number of European artists and writers. The German satirical artist George Grosz savagely chronicled the corruption and militarism of post–World War I Germany, before fleeing to the United States in 1933. The brutalities of the Spanish Civil War (1936–1939) provoked widespread protests. Among the most eloquent were those of the English poet W. H. Auden (1907–1973) and Picasso—his painting *Guernica* (1937) commemorated the bombing of the small Basque town by German planes fighting for Franco's fascist forces (See Part VIII, Topic 8).

One of the first to warn of the dangers of Nazism was the eminent German writer Thomas Mann (1875–1955). Mann's reverence for the conservative, philosophical, and musical traditions of German culture permeated his first successful novel *Buddenbrooks* (1901), a sensitive and moving picture of German provincial family life. In the 1920s he began to diagnose the sick state of contemporary society; his novel *The Magic Mountain* (1924) used the metaphorical background of a tuberculosis sanatorium to describe the intellectual and moral uncertainties of the postwar years. In 1933, while Mann was abroad, the Nazi regime denounced him and confiscated his property.

Mann settled in Switzerland, from where he continued to issue warnings, some of them in the form of broadcasts to Germany itself. In 1939, on the eve of war, he took up a visiting professorship at Princeton University. Many other leading German and Austrian intellectuals and artists sought refuge in the years preceding and during the war in the United States; they included Albert Einstein and Arnold Schoenberg, both of them Jewish. Mann was one of the few major non-Jewish European figures—Toscanini was another notable example—to protest their country's regime and go into exile.

With the benefit of hindsight, it is clear that the sense of instability that permeated the culture of the interwar years—Dada, Eliot's alienation, the Surrealists' rejection of reality—represented not only a reaction against the values of life before World War I; they reflected a greater sense of doubt. If old political and social realities were dead, there was nothing firm with which to replace them. An understanding of the unconscious proved a difficult foundation on which to rebuild civilization. Nor did Freud's insistence on the power of the irrational provide much comfort for those who had already seen its capacity for destruction.

Thus the arts of the years between the wars reflected the agitated mood of the times. The new freedom from traditional restraints opened up exciting possibilities in painting, music, and fiction. New means of communication created a vast public for art at all levels. Yet for all the vitality and variety of the Jazz Age, its spirited energy failed to hide completely a sense of foreboding. The Great War had shown one terrible direction civilization could take, and a repeat of the "war to end all wars" seemed increasingly likely.

In 1918, a week before the armistice ending World War I was signed, a young Englishman, Wilfred Owen (1893–1918), was killed in action. A year earlier, he had been invalided out of the fighting in France, and spent some time in a military hospital. While there he wrote poems, describing the horror and human sacrifice of war. One of them contains the line: "All a poet can do today is to warn."

Questions for Further Study

1. How did both poets and painters use symbolism and surrealism? What other styles influenced more than one art medium?

2. How did the ideas of Freud influence the arts between the world wars?

3. Is Owen's observation, "All a poet can do today is to warn," a true reflection of the role of the arts in the 20th century? How far is it still true today?

Suggestions for Further Reading

Ackroyd, P. *T. S. Eliot.* London, 1984.

Berman, M. *All That Is Solid Melts into Air: The Experience of Modernity.* New York, 1981.

Cantor, N. F. *Twentieth Century Culture: Modernism to Deconstruction.* New York, 1988.

Hayman, R. *Kafka: A Biography.* New York, 1981.

Hughes, R. *The Shock of the New.* New York, 1981.

Richardson, J. *Pablo Picasso.* New York, 1991.

Topic 8

THE ROAD TO WAR

nternational relations in the interwar period fell into two broad phases. In the first, from 1919 to 1931, the major Western powers put their hopes for peace on the League of Nations and a general spirit of reconciliation; in the second, from 1931 to 1939, Japan and the two fascist powers of Europe—Italy and Germany—unleashed one act of aggression after another, demonstrating the helplessness of the League and testing to the limits the policy of appeasement adopted by Britain and France. The Nazi invasion of Poland in September 1939, coming in the wake of Adolf Hitler's violation of earlier agreements, pushed the West to the wall and triggered war.

In the 1920s, many Western statesmen believed that they could create a condition of permanent peace by simply willing it into existence. International efforts at disarmament and the abandonment of war as an instrument of national policy were well-intentioned, but belied the fact that the 1919 peace settlements had created an imbalance of power in the world. Germany and Italy demanded a revision of the settlements, while France recognized the danger to its own interests but could not convince Britain that alliances rather than the League of Nations were needed.

Appeasement had begun in 1931, even before Hitler came to power, when the West protested Japan's aggression against China but did nothing. Mussolini's invasion of Ethiopia in 1935 was the crucial test case for the efficacy of the League. On the other hand, wars in East Asia and in Africa were not perceived as immediate dangers to Europe. The intervention of the fascist powers in the Spanish Civil War should have been a clearer lesson as to the direction of German and Italian policy, but the ideological nature of the conflict there made Britain and France prefer not to intervene.

When Hitler moved against Austria and the Czech Sudetenland in 1938, the Western powers rationalized his demands as legitimate goals based on the argument of self-determination. Only in 1939, when it became clear that the appetites of the dictators would not be quenched by appeasement, did Britain and France conclude that war was necessary.

THE ILLUSION OF PEACE

The League of Nations (see Part VIII, Topic 1), with which President Woodrow Wilson hoped peace would be permanently preserved, rested on the concept of "collective security," which meant that its members guaranteed each other's security. But the European powers did not find this arrangement sufficient for their purposes, and during the 1920s a variety of separate treaties created the illusion of stability. When the U.S. Senate refused to ratify the Treaty of Versailles and Wilson's commitment to offer the French an assistance pact, France arranged a military alliance with Poland in 1921 and with the so-called "Little Entente" of Czechoslovakia, Yugoslavia, and Romania. In doing so, France had attempted to link the preservation of the peace settlement in the West with that in the East.

The Spirit of Locarno

In the 1920s, Europe entered a period of relative stability and sought alternative ways of guaranteeing security. In 1923, the Draft Treaty of Mutual Assistance came before the Assembly of the League. It stipulated that in the event of hostilities, the League Council should determine the aggressor, and that members were then obliged to offer military assistance. This treaty would have made military sanctions by the League automatic instead of optional. France, worried about future German aggression, was enthusiastic, but Britain opposed it. In the autumn of 1924, Premier Herriot of France and Prime Minister MacDonald of Great Britain met in Geneva and proposed compulsory arbitration of disputes, but MacDonald's fall from power wrecked the initiative.

Unable to strengthen the League, France turned to efforts aimed at securing a guarantee of her border with Germany. This aim succeeded, in part, due to the policies of German Foreign Minister Gustav Stresemann (1878–1929), who sought reconciliation with the great powers. In 1922, Germany had already proposed a mutual pledge with France not to resort to war and had signed the Treaty of Rapallo with the Soviet Union in which each side had agreed to stay neutral in the event of an attack. The Rapallo agreement made the international community uneasy, for it ended the diplomatic isolation of both Germany and the Soviet Union.

In October 1925, Britain, France, Germany, Poland, and Czechoslovakia met at Locarno, Switzerland, and signed a number of agreements. The Treaty of Locarno stipulated that any changes in the French-German and the Belgian-German borders would come as a result of negotiations; meanwhile, France concluded a treaty with Poland and Czechoslovakia that guaranteed the eastern borders. Germany further agreed to submit all frontier disputes to arbitration. The next year, Germany became a member of the League of Nations.

The mood of international cooperation was expanded further with the Pact of Paris. In 1927, French Foreign Minister Aristide Briand (1862–1932) proposed to U.S. Secretary of State Frank B. Kellogg (1856–1937) that each country renounce war as an instrument of national policy. This "Kellogg-Briand" Pact, signed in 1928, was eventually endorsed by all the great powers (except the Soviet Union) and a total of 65 nations. Making war "illegal" did much to foster an illusion of international peace, but did little for its reality.

Significant Dates

The Road to War

October 1925	Treaty of Locarno
1928	"Kellogg-Briand" Pact
1931	Japanese invade Manchuria
October 1933	Hitler withdraws from League
March 1935	German Air Force announced
1935	Mussolini proposes Stresa Front
October 1935	Ethiopian War
March 1936	Hitler occupies Rhineland
1936	Mussolini and Hitler support Franco in Spain
October 1936	Rome-Berlin Axis
November 1936	Anti-Comintern Pact between Germany and Japan
1937	Japanese invasion of China
March 1938	German annexation of Austria
September 1938	Munich conference
March 1939	Germany occupies all of Czechoslovakia
August 1939	Nazi-Soviet Non-Aggression Pact
September 1, 1939	Germany invades Poland

By the end of the decade, a more self-confident Germany had rejoined the community of nations, and many of the conditions imposed on her by the peace settlement had been removed. In June 1930, Allied troops left the Rhineland. By then, France had begun the construction of the Maginot line of fortifications along the frontier with Germany, and in September the Nazis had 107 deputies in the Reichstag.

EUROPE, JAPAN, AND THE LEAGUE OF NATIONS

In the 1920s, few observers anticipated the first real challenge to the League of Nations would come from East Asia. But in 1931, Japan embarked upon a program of deliberate expansion that tested the willingness of the Western powers to stand behind treaty obligations, even when the participants in the dispute were Asian nations.

Japan as a World Power

Japan had burst upon the international scene during the Sino-Japanese War of 1894–1895, when it defeated China in a struggle over Korea. To Europeans, even more startling had been Japan's smashing victory over Russia in the 1904–1905 war. The Japanese eyed China and adjoining territories as a natural sphere of interest. During World War I and the Civil War in Russia, Japan had moved on to the Chinese mainland and captured markets once controlled by the Western powers.

Crown Prince Hirohito of Japan toured Europe in 1921, visiting King George V in London.

Map 8.1 Japanese Expansion

In the 1920s, Japanese factories supplied most of Asia with a host of consumer products, but the foundations of its economy were fragile. Japan had created modern industrial and financial institutions, mainly by large family-owned trusts, but it lacked raw materials. Political economists argued that Japanese power would depend on securing both raw materials and markets.

Japan's government was modeled on the European example. In 1889, a constitution had been adopted and, in 1925, universal male suffrage went into effect. Nevertheless, Parliament's authority was limited, and ministers served at the pleasure of the emperor, whose powers were supreme. Militarism had a strong influence in society and high army officers wielded significant influence in government circles. As in 19th-century Germany, many officers came from the landed nobility, where the code of the Samurai warrior still prevailed.

In the postwar period, Japanese imperialist expansion was widely discussed in military circles. Not only was expansion for economic gain proposed, but some insisted that the future of Asia itself was in the hands of Japan, the only local power capable of freeing it from European influence.

The Manchurian Crisis

The Japanese first turned their attention to Manchuria. Manchuria had been wrested from Russian control in the Russo-Japanese War of 1904–1905. On paper,

The Japanese broke the peace in Asia when they invaded China in 1934. Here Japanese soldiers man a position in the streets of Shanghai, a city they first bombed.

Japan allowed Manchuria to revert to China, but in reality the region became a Japanese protectorate. Border tensions between the Soviet Union and Japan occurred over the years. They culminated in September 1931 in a bomb explosion on the south Manchurian railroad, a few miles from the Japanese garrison at Mukden. The Japanese used the incident as a pretext for occupying strategic points in southern Manchuria. The Chinese government appealed to the League of Nations, and also to the United States under the terms of the Kellogg-Briand Pact. Secretary of State Henry L. Stimson insisted that the matter be settled peacefully, but took no real action. In January 1932, by which time Japan had conquered all of Manchuria, Stimson announced that the United States would not recognize the Japanese gains.

China, otherwise powerless, announced an economic boycott, but Japan responded with a temporary occupation of Shanghai. In March, Japan proclaimed the territory an independent nation called Manchukuo ("Land of the Manchus"), and eventually installed Henry Pu Yi (1906–1967), the last emperor of China, as its ruler.

The League of Nations sent a commission to Manchuria headed by Lord Victor Lytton (1871–1947). The commission's report, in October, condemned the Japanese invasion and exposed the pretense of Manchukuo. Japan, a member of the League, withdrew from that international body and invaded the Chinese mainland southwest of Manchuria. By mid-1935, Japanese had penetrated deep into China. Neither the League nor the United States took any action beyond verbal protests. The League of Nations had been dealt a deadly blow.

In July 1937, after a two-year hiatus, the war between Japan and China was renewed. The Japanese took the cities of Shanghai, Nanking, and Canton and drove Chinese forces under General Chiang Kai-shek (1887–1975) deep into western China. In Nanking, the Japanese troops killed perhaps 300,000 civilians in reprisal for their resistance. The invasion finally came to a halt when the Japanese reached the mountains of western China, while in the north a guerrilla resistance was led by the communists. The Japanese occupation of China proved to be a brutal experience.

AUSTRIA, ETHIOPIA, AND THE AXIS

The failure of the League to stop Japan's aggression in China lent encouragement to European dictators. In 1934, Hitler attempted to seize Austria, but Mussolini prevented him from doing so. The following year,

The coffin of Austrian Chancellor Engelbert Dollfuss passing Vienna's city hall, July 28, 1934.

however, Mussolini himself tested the mood of the powers in the West by his invasion of Ethiopia in October 1935. Before that conflict was over, Hitler had violated the Versailles Treaty by remilitarizing the Rhineland. Again, neither the League nor the Western powers acted. The era of appeasement had begun.

The Austrian Coup and the Stresa Front

Upon coming to power, Hitler began immediately to strengthen Germany's military position. That March, Mussolini had proposed a joint agreement among Britain, France, Germany, and Italy designed both to keep Hitler in check and to prevent a war between Germany and France. In October 1933, however, Hitler withdrew Germany from the League and allowed Mussolini's pact to lapse without signing it. The following year he made his first move toward the creation of his "Greater Germany." In July, the Austrian Nazis, some 100,000 strong, attempted to seize power in a coup supported by Hitler. Chancellor Engelbert Dollfuss (1892–1934), who had befriended Mussolini in an effort to keep Austria independent of Germany, was assassinated, but martial law was proclaimed in Vienna and the coup failed. Kurt von Schuschnigg (1897–1977), one of Dollfuss' collaborators, became the new chancellor and Mussolini sent Italian troops to the

Brenner Pass to dissuade Hitler from invading Austria.

Mussolini later reminded the European powers that he could not always be the one to "march to the Brenner," by which he meant that they too would have to take responsibility for controlling Hitler's expansionist ambitions. In March 1935, Hitler demonstrated his complete contempt for international agreements by announcing that Germany would no longer abide by the disarmament clauses of the Treaty of Versailles. Secret German rearmament had been going on ever since 1933, but now Hitler reintroduced peacetime conscription. Taking their cue from Mussolini, Britain and France met with Italian representatives at Stresa, in northern Italy, and agreed to Mussolini's proposal for common action against Germany. But British and French unwillingness to take the idea of the "Stresa Front" beyond mere words made it useless. Instead, in June, Britain signed a naval pact with Hitler that permitted Germany to build a fleet equal to one-third of British strength. The French felt betrayed.

The Italian Invasion of Ethiopia

In the meantime, Mussolini had been laying his plans for colonial conquest. For this he had been preaching to Italians that Fascism would restore the grandeur of

Ethiopian soldiers, including young boys, fought Italians armed with modern weapons in 1935–1936, when Mussolini invaded the African country.

the Roman Empire and give Italy its rightful position in international affairs. Since the summer of 1934 he had been preparing for the military conquest of Ethiopia (then known as Abyssinia). The country was one of two independent states in Africa. The Italians had tried unsuccessfully to conquer it in the 1890s, but were disastrously defeated by Ethiopian troops at the Battle of Adowra. Mussolini now promised to "wipe clean the stain of Adowra."

In January 1935 Mussolini persuaded French Foreign Minister Pierre Laval (1883–1945) to give Italy a free hand in Ethiopia, but the British balked. In September British Foreign Minister Sir Samuel Hoare (1880–1959) assured the League that Britain would resist Italian aggression. On October 3, Mussolini launched his attack. Ethiopian Emperor Haile Selassie (1892–1975) went before the League and warned that Europe would be next if Mussolini was not stopped. Less than a week later, the League voted to condemn Italy and imposed economic sanctions. The sanctions, however, omitted petroleum from its list of proscribed materials. Moreover, Germany, the United States, and Japan did not participate in the sanctions. Toward the end of the year, Laval and Hoare met in Paris, where they agreed to offer Mussolini a compromise—he could have two-thirds of Ethiopia. When news of the Hoare-Laval Agreement became public, a storm of public indignation broke.

Mussolini, gambling everything on a military victory, proclaimed that Italy would stand alone against the world. In truth, much-needed oil was still flowing to her ports. Hitler, hoping to make Mussolini grateful for his friendship, shipped Italy essential supplies, while at the same time secretly sending arms to the Ethiopians. On May 5, Italian troops marched into Addis Ababa, the capital.

During the Ethiopian War, Hitler had been active. On March 7, 1936, he remilitarized the Rhineland

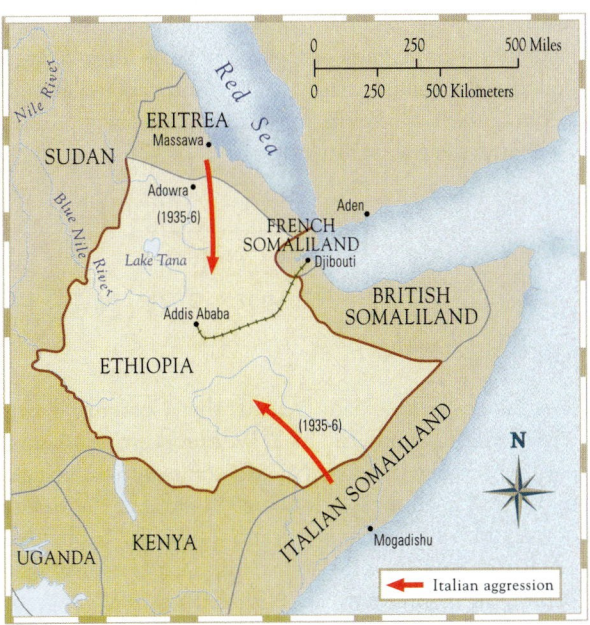

Map 8.2   The Ethiopian War

After Mussolini's visit to Germany in 1937, the *Duce* and the *Führer* were inseparably linked—they signed the military Pact of Steel the next year.

in direct violation of Versailles, and denounced the Treaty of Locarno. In October, Mussolini, who felt at once betrayed by the Western powers and grateful to Hitler, sent his foreign minister, Count Galeazzo Ciano (1903–1944), to Berlin to arrange a treaty with Germany. The result was the signing of an agreement to collaborate on anticommunist propaganda in their foreign policies. Proclaiming this the beginning of a "Rome-Berlin Axis," Mussolini moved increasingly closer to Germany over the next two years.

THE MARCH OF FASCISM: THE SPANISH CIVIL WAR

Ever since Lenin had created the Communist International (Comintern) in 1919, European communist parties had been instructed by Moscow not to participate in political coalitions with bourgeois parties. The spread of fascism, however, gave Stalin pause. In September 1934, the Soviet Union joined the League of Nations. When the Comintern held its 1935 world congress, Italian and French communists suggested that the policy be reversed in order to fight fascism. The result was

that communist parties now joined with socialists and democrats in what came to be known as "Popular Fronts." The most prominent Popular Front government was that of Léon Blum in France (see Part VIII, Topic 5). Over the next four years, the Popular Front concept would be sorely tested in the tragedy of the Spanish Civil War.

The Spanish Labyrinth

The civil war in Spain was a struggle fought on several levels at once: an ideological war between fascism on one side and an international alliance of democratic, socialist, communist, and anarchist forces on the other; an internecine struggle among these antifascist forces; an internal Spanish political struggle for power; finally, as a test of wills between the Axis powers and the Western democracies it represented the real prelude to World War II.

The war broke out in July 1936 and raged on until March 1939. Its origins lay in the political culture of modern Spain. In September 1923, General Primo de Rivera staged a coup d'état and created a military dictatorship, although King Alfonso XIII (ruled 1902–1931) continued to rule in name. In 1930, Alfonso dismissed the unpopular general and in 1931 restored the constitution. In the elections that followed, the repub-

This photograph of a Loyalist fighter carrying a wounded friend to safety, was one of the best known images of the Spanish Civil War.

lican forces won a landslide in the cities and the king, interpreting the vote to be against him, left the country, although he never abdicated. The Spanish Republic was proclaimed on April 14, 1931.

The Constituent Assembly was divided over the policies of the government, from those on the left who wanted social revolution to Catholics on the right who hated the Republic. The new democratic government began to initiate major social and economic reforms, including civilian control of the army, land reform, and regional autonomy. By late 1933, when the first *Cortes*, or parliament, met, the conservative majority under the leadership of the clerical José Gil Robles (1898–

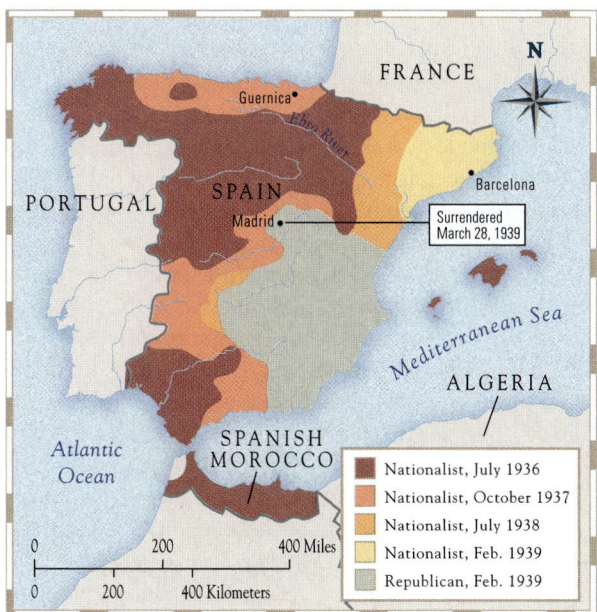

Map 8.3 The Civil War in Spain

1980) began to undo the reforms and move Spain toward fascist dictatorship.

In 1936 the Republicans, syndicalists, anarchists, and communists joined together in a Popular Front to halt the reaction and succeeded in winning power. They immediately began to push for radical change, seizing landed estates and staging revolutionary strikes. Then, after a well-known reactionary deputy was assassinated, the forces of counterrevolution responded. On July 17, a military garrison in Spanish Morocco revolted under the leadership of General Francisco Franco (1892–1975). Other generals on the mainland joined in support. At the end of July, the rebels set up their headquarters in Burgos, in the north, and proclaimed a Junta of National Defense. Franco was named its *caudillo*, or chief.

Franco was a shrewd, calculating man, wedded to tradition and authority but with no precise ideology of his own. He gathered under his leadership nationalists, monarchists, and members of the fascist *Falange*. He also had the support of landowners, business interests, and Catholics. The Popular Front forces were as disparate a group as Franco's, although the left—composed of socialists, communists, a Trotskyite group, and the Anarcho-Syndicalists—dominated.

With the backing of most of the regular army, Franco's forces—known as the Nationalists—quickly hemmed the Republicans into four areas: Madrid, Valencia (where the government had fled), Barcelona, and the Basque provinces. For the next two and half years, Spain was racked by a cruel and bloody civil war that was complicated by foreign intervention.

Intervention and Ideology

Foreign nations quickly took sides in the Spanish conflict. Blum's French government supported the Popular

Pablo Picasso's powerful painting *Guernica* was conceived in response to the German bombing of civilians in the Basque city by that name in northern Spain, April 1937.

Front, while Mussolini and Hitler made common cause with the Nationalists. In November the two dictators officially recognized Franco's government, while the first antifascist volunteers organized by the Comintern began to arrive in the form of the International Brigades. The French Popular Front sent equipment and the Soviet Union fighter planes, equipment, and advisers. Hitler supplied Franco with tanks, planes, and military advisers, while Mussolini sent troops. In March 1937 the antifascist forces won a major moral victory when the International Brigades repulsed the Nationalists at Guadalajara. By the end of 1937, the war had reached a stalemate.

With the Spanish participants more or less evenly matched and deadlocked, foreign intervention became decisive. Portuguese dictator António Salazar (1889–1970) sympathized with Franco, British Prime Minister Stanley Baldwin expected the Nationalists to become the future government, and even Blum was careful not to antagonize the right wing in France by openly supporting the Republicans. As a result, when Blum suggested the formation of a Non-Intervention Committee, Britain readily agreed. The purpose of the committee was to prevent foreign powers from intervening and to withhold military assistance from both sides. The committee, composed of representatives from 27 states, met in September 1936. The League of Nations backed its position.

Despite such appeals for neutrality, volunteers continued to arrive from abroad while the fascist powers poured in men and supplies. In effect, nonintervention meant that the legitimate government of Spain was prevented from purchasing supplies from abroad, while the Nationalists received significant illegal help. Morally, the Axis intervention aided the Republicans, especially after German planes bombed the town of Guernica in April 1937, inspiring Pablo Picasso's famous painting by that name. In September, unidentified submarines—now known to have been mostly Italian—attacked ships carrying goods to the Republicans. When Britain and France called a conference at Lyon to prevent such actions, Germany and Italy boycotted the meeting, whereupon the Western powers jointly patrolled the Spanish waters and the piracy stopped.

By the spring of 1938, Franco—supported by some 100,000 Italian troops—launched a major offensive against the government. Franco had the advantage, especially as the Republican forces had become bitterly divided. Stalin had decided on a policy of no support for socialist revolutions in Spain, in order to reassure Western opinion. It was a cynical policy that persuaded no one and undermined the Spanish left. Before the war was over, communist forces were killing Anarcho-Syndicalists by the thousands and Stalin's advisers had taken command of communist groups.

In mid-1938 the Soviet Union abandoned the Republic, convinced that Britain and France would not help. With the end of Soviet support, Franco succeeded in cutting government holdings in half. In the months that followed, the Nationalists proceeded to take more and more territory and began the systematic bombing of civilian populations. Barcelona fell in January 1939, followed by Madrid in March. The struggle was a particularly bitter one on both sides. The Republicans had killed priests and nuns, and now tens of thousands of

Spaniards met the fate of brutal reprisals from Franco's victorious forces. Many thousands more fled Spain, and Franco imprisoned hundreds of thousands of opponents. When it was over, the civil war had bled the country of perhaps 1 million lives.

The civil war was a devastating blow for the democratic forces of Europe. The defeat of the Republicans became a symbol of fascist victory, and the war deeply divided opinion abroad. Mussolini and Hitler had shown that they could defy international opinion and the Western powers with impunity.

THE PRICE OF APPEASEMENT: AUSTRIA AND CZECHOSLOVAKIA

The year 1938 proved to be crucial. Hitler had been planning for some time to strike at Austria, determined to bring about *Anschluss* (union) with Germany. No sooner was that goal accomplished, than Hitler began working against Czechoslovakia, whose German minority provided the pretext for aggression there. In the case of the Czech crisis, however, the Western powers did not merely stand by—they actively participated in the dismemberment of an independent country.

Even before Hitler moved against Austria, political conditions in Britain and France mitigated against Western opposition. In Britain, the government of Neville Chamberlain (served as prime minister 1937–1940) was doggedly determined to do whatever it could to prevent war. Chamberlain embarked, therefore, on a policy that came to be known as "appeasement," by which the British were willing to make major concessions to Hitler for the sake of peace. The foreign minister, Anthony Eden (1897–1977), was a staunch opponent of the fascist dictators and in 1938 he resigned in protest against appeasement. Thereafter, Chamberlain really conducted his own foreign policy. In France, the resignation of Blum's Popular Front in 1937 eventually brought to the premiership Edouard Daladier (served 1933, 1934, 1938–1940). Claiming that he would prepare France for war, he assumed the defense ministry himself. Yet French resolve, already softened by the fear of war, hinged to a great degree on Britain.

Anschluss

In February 1938, Hitler began to pressure Austria, using the Nazi radio and press to agitate for union with Germany. The Führer insisted that Chancellor Schuschnigg come to Berchtesgaden, his retreat in the Bavarian mountains, where Hitler proceeded to harangue the hapless Austrian leader for hours. After Hitler's bully-ing, Schuschnigg consented to concessions—he would appoint a Nazi as minister of the interior (who controlled the police) and issue an amnesty for imprisoned Austrian Nazis.

Once back in Vienna, however, Schuschnigg's resolve returned and he began to mobilize public opinion against Germany. The chancellor decided to hold a plebiscite to secure public endorsement of his anti-German position. Hitler exploded and sent an ultimatum to Vienna demanding that the plebiscite be canceled. When Schuschnigg refused, Hitler moved German troops to the border. Faced with the prospect of invasion, Schuschnigg resigned. The Germans began marching against Austria even before Schuschnigg's successor, the Nazi Arthur Seyss-Inquart (1892–1946), had invited the Germans into his country, which Hitler then annexed to Germany. In April, a rigged plebiscite registered 99.75 percent public approval.

In Britain, Chamberlain had already written Austria off to appease Hitler, and France was caught between governments. The most interesting reaction came from Italy. In 1934, Mussolini had sent troops to the Brenner to prevent what he now congratulated Hitler for accomplishing. Hitler had not bothered to inform the Duce of his plans, but Mussolini pretended to ignore the slight. In any case, by then Mussolini's Italy was in no position to stand up to the Third Reich. Hitler rejoiced that he had added this strategically important nation to his realm, and no doubt remembered the difficulties of his youthful days spent in Vienna.

Czechoslovakia and the Sudetenland

When the Paris Peace Conference of 1919 decided on the creation of Czechoslovakia as an independent state, it burdened the new republic with a serious problem: the mountainous rim of territory known as the Sudetenland, where some 3 million German-speaking people lived. In truth, Thomas Masaryk, the founder of the Czech state, had insisted on having the area, arguing that Bohemia and Moravia were an historical and economic unit and should not be broken up. Moreover, a border drawn strictly along linguistic lines would have been impossible.

The Sudeten Germans received better treatment at the hands of the Prague government than most ethnic minorities in Eastern Europe. After 1933, however, Nazi agents, led by Konrad Henlein (1898–1945), worked feverishly to arouse German sentiment and to push for an autonomous Sudetenland independent of Czechoslovakia. Nevertheless, most Czechs, including President Eduard Benes, knew that the real intention behind Hitler's rhetoric was annexation.

A week after the annexation of Austria, Henlein's followers inflamed the Sudetenland question. Consultations between Britain and France followed. The French,

Map 8.4 The Dismemberment of Czechoslovakia

open violence, hoping no doubt to provoke German intervention. Czechoslovakia partially mobilized. When Chamberlain actually warned that Britain might have to get involved, Hitler backed off publicly but ordered plans for a military attack on Czechoslovakia. In the meantime, Chamberlain sent a mediator to Prague to arrange a compromise. When the Czechs agreed to Henlein's demands, the Nazi leader broke off the talks. On September 15, a distraught Chamberlain boarded a plane—the first time in his life—and flew to Berchtesgaden to make a personal appeal to Hitler. In a three-hour meeting, Hitler insisted that he would now settle only for outright German annexation of the Sudetenland, and convinced the prime minister to join with France in trying to extract this concession from Prague. Chamberlain was undaunted, not understanding that he was about to be a party to the dismemberment of a sovereign state. He wrote at the time that Hitler "was a man who could be relied upon when he had given his word."

The Munich Tragedy

On September 19, the French and British governments told Benes that he had to concede the Sudetenland, warning that they would not be responsible for the consequences if the Czechs refused. Without the support of the Western powers, Benes had no choice but to give in. Chamberlain flew to Germany again, this time to Godesberg on the Rhine, where Hitler now raised his demands still further, presenting the prime minister with a strongly worded memorandum insisting on immediate occupation of the territories in question. Chamberlain was wounded and disillusioned. On September 24, the Czechs mobilized and the French called up reservists. Four days later, the British Navy was mobilized. Chamberlain wrote to Mussolini and Hitler asking for a four-power conference to resolve the crisis.

who were bound to Czechoslovakia by a defensive treaty, were prepared to come to Czechoslovakia's aid, but Chamberlain announced in the House of Commons that Britain would not commit itself to supporting France in such an event. Chamberlain was convinced that any effort to coerce Hitler would result in war. With support for this position within the French cabinet, Premier Daladier agreed to follow Britain's lead.

In April, Henlein increased his demands for autonomy. When Benes refused, the Nazis erupted in

Munich, September 1938—Chamberlain (left), Daladier, Hitler, Mussolini, and Ciano.

Mussolini convinced Hitler to attend, and the four statesmen—Hitler, Mussolini, Chamberlain, and Daladier—met in Munich on September 29. The Soviet Union was not invited.

The Munich conference was brief. The participants agreed to the terms of the Godesberg Memorandum, but now also to guarantee Czechoslovakia's borders. On September 30, Chamberlain and Daladier presented the terms of the agreement to the Czechs, who had no choice but to accept. Benes resigned as president.

When Chamberlain arrived in England that day, he held aloft a piece of paper on which he and Hitler had indicated that henceforth they renounced war. "This," he declared in one of the most haunting phrases of the age, "means peace in our time."

Chamberlain may have believed his own words, but he nevertheless embarked upon a massive rearmament program for Great Britain. The end came with a kind of numbed disbelief. On March 14, the new Czech president, Emil Hacha (1872–1945), was summoned to Berlin, where he was subjected to six hours of continuous verbal abuse from Hitler and his entourage. When Hermann Goering, one of Hitler's associates, threat-ened to reduce Prague to rubble, Hacha agreed to sur-render his country, and Hitler's troops carved up the re-mainder of Czechoslovakia. Chamberlain was stunned, and British opinion suddenly hardened against the man who could so callously violate a solemn agreement.

The Czech fiasco created a mood of fatalism in Europe, for both sides now began to prepare for war. Hitler clearly did not believe that the Western powers would act, and by the end of March 1939 he was al-ready making it clear that Poland was his next target. A much sobered Chamberlain assured the Poles that Britain and France would protect them, and the next month gave similar guarantees to Romania, Greece, and Turkey. On April 3, Hitler secretly told his generals to be ready for an assault against Poland in September. Mussolini, who had remained an observer of Hitler's triumphs, invaded Albania on April 8. Britain intro-duced peacetime compulsory military service for the first time in its history. On May 22, Mussolini and Hitler concluded a military alliance that Mussolini dubbed the "Pact of Steel." The pact bound each part-ner to render assistance to the other in the event of war.

Map 8.5   The Expansion of Nazi Germany

The Nazi-Soviet Pact

One more shock awaited the Western powers. The Soviet Union now controlled the balance of power in Europe. In planning for the attack against Poland, Hitler wanted to prevent interference from Stalin and thereby avoid the danger of a two-front war. Since the Spanish Civil War, the Soviet Union had suspected that the Western powers would not stand against the fascist dictators. Yet, while talking secretly with Hitler, Stalin also carried on secret negotiations with the West. He insisted that any mutual defense pact include guarantees for the Baltic states, but these nations feared the Soviet Union as much as they did Germany and would have nothing of it.

On May 3, Stalin appointed a new foreign minister, Vyacheslav Molotov (1890–1986), a man with a much narrower sense of Russian national interests than his predecessor, Maxim Litvinov. Because Litvinov was Jewish, Molotov's appointment was a clear signal to Hitler that accommodation was possible. In Molotov's view, an alliance with Britain and France would most certainly lead to war against Germany, but with little advantage for the Soviet Union. Stalin was interested, on the other hand, in reaching an agreement with Hitler to divide Poland, thus providing a buffer between the two countries. In talks with Molotov, the Nazis suggested not only that the Soviets remain neutral in the event of a German war with the West, but that the Soviet Union and Germany divide Eastern Europe between them.

On August 23 Germany and the Soviet Union signed a trade agreement, a ten-year Non-Aggression Pact, and a secret protocol. The news took almost everyone, including Mussolini, by surprise, since communism andNazism had been such deep ideological enemies for so long. The real import of the pact, however, lay in the "Secret Additional Protocol" added to the treaty. The protocol created spheres of influence in eastern Europe. Western Poland and Lithuania were to fall to Germany, while eastern Poland, Finland, Estonia, Latvia, and the Romanian province of Bessarabia would go to the Soviet Union.

If Hitler hoped that news of the pact would frighten Britain and France into abandoning support for Poland, he miscalculated. On August 25, Britain signed a mutual assistance pact with Poland. When German troops invaded Poland at the beginning of September, the Western powers declared war.

From 1931 to 1939, the Western powers remained on the defensive against policies of aggression and expansion by Japan, Italy, and Germany. The repeated violation of the League of Nations charter made a shambles of the spirit of internationalism that had spread in the 1920s and meant, inevitably, a return to power politics. In this circumstance, however, Britain and France were unwilling to see the out-break of another world war, and adopted appeasement as the way to avoid it.

That Britain and France were militarily unprepared for war as late as 1938 added an element of sober logic to the policy of appeasement. In retrospect, that policy appears more foolish and morally reprehensible than it did at the time. Yet in the atmosphere of reconciliation that began with Locarno, European statesmen had begun to accept German and Italian arguments that the 1919 settlements had been unfair. In negotiating with Hitler, Chamberlain tacitly admitted the justice of Germany's demands for union with Austria and the Sudetenland.

Yet Mussolini and Hitler were no ordinary statesmen. They did not believe in the sanctity of treaties or conventional notions of balance of power. In dealing with such men, Chamberlain and Daladier were at a supreme disadvantage in not understanding the ideological imperatives that drove them. After appeasement had given up too much and the dictators were still not satisfied, the realization dawned on the West that war was inevitable.

Questions for Further Study

1. To what extent were the origins of World War II to be found in World War I? In the peace conference?

2. What was the policy of "appeasement"? Was it a logical and credible policy in the 1930s?

3. To what degree was the Rome-Berlin Axis inevitable?

4. Did fascist ideology affect foreign policy? How do you explain the Nazi-Soviet Non-Aggression Pact in light of the ideological clash between fascism and communism?

Suggestions for Further Reading

Burgwyn, H. James. *Italian Foreign Policy, 1919–1940.* New York, 1996.

Divine, Robert. *The Reluctant Belligerent: American Entry into World War II.* New York, 1979.

Hildebrandt, K. *The Foreign Policy of the Third Reich*, trans. A. Fothergill. London, 1973.

Iriye, Akira. *The Origins of the Second World War in Asia and the Pacific.* London, 1987.

Kitchen, Martin. *Europe Between the Wars: A Political History.* London, 1988.

Marks, Sally. *The Illusion of Peace: Europe's International Relations, 1918–1933.* New York, 1976.

Preston, Paul. *Franco.* New York, 1994.

Robertson, E. M. *Mussolini as Empire Builder.* London, 1977.

Sontag, Raymond J. *A Broken World, 1919–1939.* New York, 1971.

Taylor, A. J. P. *The Origins of the Second World War.* New York, 1972.

Thomas, Hugh. *The Spanish Civil War.* New York, 1987.

Ulam, Adam. *Expansion and Coexistence: The History of Soviet Foreign Policy, 1917–1943*, 2nd ed. New York, 1974.

Watt, D. C. *How War Came: The Immediate Origins of the Second World War, 1938–1939.* New York, 1989.

Topic 9

THE SECOND WORLD WAR

he Munich agreements of September 1938 created a sense of relief in British and French opinion that peace had been preserved. A year later the general feeling in those countries had shifted decisively, most citizens now sensing that war was inevitable. The change was due to the dismemberment of Czechoslovakia, which made it clear that Nazi ambitions would not be satisfied by appeasement. By the time Adolf Hitler targeted Poland for his aggression, Britain and France were no longer in a mood to compromise.

The outbreak of World War II in September 1939 brought almost six years of unparalleled death and destruction. Hitler's armies rolled quickly across Poland, which he and Joseph Stalin proceeded to divide between them. Soviet forces then occupied the Baltic states and attacked Finland. Until the spring of 1940, however, no real fighting between Germany and the West occurred. The Nazi *Blitzkrieg* began in April, when the Germans smashed Norway and Denmark, and the following month attacked Belgium, the Netherlands, and France. By mid-June, France had fallen. When months of aerial bombardment could not induce the British to surrender to Hitler, the Axis (the alliance of Germany and Italy) turned toward North Africa and the Balkans and occupied both regions. The high tide of Axis power came in 1941, when Hitler began his assault against the Soviet Union and the Japanese attack at Pearl Harbor brought the United States into the war.

The year 1942 saw a crucial shift in the fortunes of war, as Soviet troops stopped the German advance and American forces struck back at the Japanese in the Pacific. But even while the Allies won some headway, the most horrible of tragedies unfolded: in Germany and the occupied regions of Eastern Europe, the Nazi extermination of the Jews began to take shape. In the course of the war, more than 6 million victims of Nazi hatred were claimed by the Holocaust. By the end of 1942, the Allies had invaded the Axis stronghold in North Africa, and Hitler's armies had been defeated at Stalingrad. In 1943, Mussolini was overthrown by an internal coup and the Allies launched the invasion of Italy. The principal Allied heads of state — Winston Churchill, Franklin D. Roosevelt, and Stalin — met for the first of a series of wartime conferences that determined not only military strategies but the shape of the postwar peace settlements. In June 1944, the Western powers finally opened a second front in Europe by invading France. By the spring of 1945, Mussolini and Hitler were dead and the war in Europe was over.

The war in Asia came to an end several months later. The Allies began to advance in the Pacific in the second half of 1942. American and Australian forces slowly reclaimed the captured islands of the Pacific, and by 1944 U.S. aircraft were bombing mainland Japan. In August 1945, Japan surrendered after the United States dropped two atomic weapons on its cities.

World War II proved to be the most costly conflict in history, both in human lives and in material terms. In response to the tremendous suffering that the Axis powers had caused, the Allies held a series of tribunals in which Axis leaders were tried for "war crimes," and a new international organization—the United Nations—was created in an effort to maintain the peace so dearly won.

FROM BLITZKRIEG TO THE BATTLE OF BRITAIN

By late 1939, the city of Danzig and the Polish Corridor contained the only important German populations still living beyond the frontiers of the Third Reich, and these territories Hitler wanted to add to the Reich. Yet by then no amount of appeasement could have prevented war. On August 11, the Germans informed their Italian allies that Hitler was determined to resolve the Polish question at any cost. Mussolini sought to temper German demands in order to prevent the outbreak of a general European conflict, but German Foreign Minister Ribbentrop declared unabashedly that the *Führer* wanted war, not compromise.

Blitzkrieg in Poland

With the signing of the Nazi-Soviet Non-Aggression Pact on August 23 (see Part VIII, Topic 8), Hitler positioned himself for the assault on Poland: the Soviets had been neutralized and the Poles isolated. The Germans wanted to strike a quick knockout blow before the fall rains limited the effectiveness of their tanks. At dawn on September 1, without a formal declaration of war, the Germans struck against Poland. Britain and France went to war on September 3.

The Polish campaign was the first demonstration of the new German strategy known as *Blitzkrieg,* or "lightning war." Blitzkrieg was the brainchild of Heinz Guderian (1886–1954), a German officer who had experienced the senseless war of attrition on the Western front during World War I. In 1933, Guderian—whose ideas were derived in part from British strategic thinkers—won Hitler over to the idea that the outcome of the next European war would be determined by a combination of rapid-moving, heavily armed armored tanks, supported by aircraft and motorized infantry units. Blitzkrieg involved the close coordination of these three kinds of forces. The armored tank

(*Panzer*) divisions would drive wedges into the enemy's territory and rapidly cut off its troops from behind. The *Luftwaffe* (air force) would simultaneously destroy the enemy's air force before turning against its communications system and infantry troops. The German motorized infantry, moving behind the Panzers, would then secure the overrun territory while the tanks continued to press forward. When the regular infantry had moved up, the motorized troops would rejoin the Panzers.

Panzer divisions under the command of Guderian pushed through Poland ahead of the mobilized units and foot infantry. German dive bombers, called *Stukas,* assaulted civilians not only with bombs and machine guns, but with shrill sirens that struck terror in their victims. Polish military forces lacked modern military equipment, especially tanks, heavy artillery, and transportation units. Hitler's Luftwaffe had ten times more operational planes than the Polish Air Force, and Poland's 39 divisions were no match for Germany's 60 divisions. After a few days, the Germans broke through Polish lines. On September 17, the Soviet Union invaded Poland from the east in conformity with the intent of the Nazi-Soviet Pact and overran the rest of the country.

Warsaw was surrounded by German armies and on September 25 Hitler ordered his bombers to reduce the city to ruins. The capital surrendered on September 27. The next day Ribbentrop and Soviet Foreign Minister Molotov met to partition Polish territory. The Soviet Union occupied a little more than half the country, including a third of the population, while Germany took the bulk of the population and the core of the industrial and farming regions. The western half of the German area was annexed into the Reich along with Danzig, thus pushing the frontiers beyond Germany's 1914 borders. The rest was placed under Nazi occupation as the "Government General" of Poland. Poland ceased to exist as an independent nation. General Wladyslaw Sikorski (1881–1943) formed a new Polish government, first in France and then in London, the first of many such governments in exile.

Significant Dates

World War II

September 3, 1939	World War II breaks out; Blitzkrieg against Poland
April–May 1940	Blitzkrieg in West
May 10, 1940	Churchill becomes prime minister
June 10, 1940	Italy declares war on France
June 22, 1940	Surrender of France
April 1941	Germany occupies Yugoslavia and Greece
June 22, 1941	Germany invades Soviet Union
December 7, 1941	Japanese attack Pearl Harbor
June 4, 1942	Battle of Midway
November 1942	Allied invasion of North Africa
February 2, 1943	German surrender at Stalingrad
May 1943	Axis surrender in North Africa
June 1943	Allied invasion of Sicily
July 5–12, 1943	Battle of Kursk
July 25, 1943	Coup against Mussolini
September 1943	Allied invasion of Italy; Italian armistice with Allies
June 6, 1944	Normandy invasion
February 1945	Yalta conference
April 28–30, 1945	Mussolini shot and Hitler commits suicide
May 7, 1945	Surrender of Germany
July–August 1945	Potsdam conference
August 6, 1945	Atomic bomb destroys Hiroshima
August 14, 1945	Japan surrenders

The Fall of Western Europe

While the Blitzkrieg ravaged Poland in the East, a strange, tension-filled peace known as the "Phony War" prevailed in the West. Hitler, planning to attack Western Europe in the fall of 1939, had moved his troops from Poland to the Western frontiers in October but did not order them into battle. Leading German generals believed that an all-out war with the West at that moment was premature. When Hitler overruled them, a conspiracy to overthrow him evolved in military circles but came to nothing. Bad weather and the

capture of German military plans by Belgian authorities in January 1940 caused a delay in the attack until the spring.

French military leaders expected that their defense system would suffice to ward off any German attack. This Maginot Line consisted of an intricate system of fixed fortifications, built in the 1930s, that ran from the Swiss border northward to where Luxembourg and Belgium joined. Its weakness lay in the fact that it gave the French a false sense of security that retarded military modernization. In any case, it was through Belgium that a German attack was likely to come. British Prime Minister Chamberlain, still hoping for a negotiated settlement, doubted that Hitler would attack in the West. Instead, he believed that the German economy would collapse under the stress of a major war and instituted, together with the French, a naval blockade. Unlike the blockade imposed during World War I, this one did not prove effective because of a far-reaching economic agreement between Berlin and Moscow that provided Germany with essential resources such as oil, grain, and rubber. The British used the respite provided by the Phony War to build up their air force.

Stunned by Hitler's overwhelming victory in Poland, Stalin had begun to worry about Soviet security and tried to create a buffer zone between his own country and Germany. By the middle of October 1939, he had forced Latvia and Estonia to accept Soviet bases and soldiers on their territories. When the Finnish government refused to grant similar concessions to the USSR, the Soviets attacked Finland in late November. This so-called "Winter War" lasted longer than Stalin had anticipated, requiring the use of some 45 divisions to crush the stubborn Finnish resistance, which was led by Field Marshal Carl Mannerheim (1867–1951). Only in March 1940 did the Soviets finally force an armistice, according to which Finland conceded extensive territories and military bases.

The Allies had seriously considered sending help to the Finns, largely because they suddenly grew worried that the mines and strategic location of Scandinavia might make the region a target of German operations. At the beginning of April, Hitler's armies quickly invaded and overran Denmark, whose 15,000-man army collapsed after a day of fighting. Geography made Norway more difficult to take, and the Allies landed troops there to assist the Norwegians. After several weeks, however, Norway fell and Hitler set up a collaborationist regime under the leadership of Vidkun Quisling (1887–1945), a name that became identified with treason.

With Scandinavia secured, Hitler turned next to the Low Countries. The long-awaited war against the West began on May 10 with the invasion of Belgium,

Map 9.1   The Second World War, Europe and North Africa

the Netherlands, and Luxembourg. In terms of troop numbers, the Allies actually enjoyed some superiority. Germany had 136 divisions (42 of which were held in reserve), while the Allies counted 144 divisions—101 French (36 involved in the Maginot Line defense), 11 British, 22 Belgian, and 10 Dutch. The Allies also had more tanks, although the Germans concentrated theirs in armored divisions while the French dispersed them. Similarly, the French actually possessed 4360 aircraft to Germany's 3270, but French air strategy had been so inadequate that when Hitler attacked they could put only a fourth of their planes in the air.

The French proved indecisive against Hitler's Blitzkrieg, but the country's premier, Paul Reynaud

(1878–1966), was a strong-willed leader who had warned repeatedly that France needed to adopt modern military strategies.

The capture of secret German documents in 1939 was partially responsible for Hitler's decision to adopt an entirely new plan for the assault against Western Europe. The original plan provided for a heavy concentration of strength in a northern spearhead that was to push through the Netherlands, Belgium, and northern France, while a support group was to move through southern Belgium and Luxembourg. The revised plan, designed to overcome the possibility of stalemate similar to that of World War I, called for making the southern force the armored spearhead of the assault. Once the southern army group had broken into France, it could push on to Paris, swing behind the Maginot Line, or—and this in the end was the decision—rush to the English Channel in order to cut off Allied forces. Some generals thought this plan too risky, but Hitler overruled them.

Only in recent years has it become known that by the outbreak of the war the Allies possessed the ability to break the German codes. Before Hitler came to power, German engineers had developed an incredibly sophisticated coding machine known as Enigma, capable of creating literally billions of different coding patterns. When the Germans attempted to deliver an Enigma machine to their embassy in Warsaw, Polish intelligence agents intercepted it and, unknown to the Germans, had it reproduced. The Poles then discovered how the machines operated and in July 1939 turned copies of Enigma over to the French and British. Tragically, the French failed to exploit Enigma—although it provided numerous deciphered German messages concerning the new invasion strategy, the generals remained convinced by the documents captured in 1939 that the original attack plan was still operative. The British, on the other hand, created a top-secret intelligence network, known as Ultra, that monitored and decoded Enigma messages throughout the war.

The recast invasion plan worked brilliantly. When British and French forces entered Belgium, they were quickly outflanked and the Germans broke through the French lines at Sedan on May 13. "We are beaten," a tearful Reynaud telephoned to British Prime Minister Winston S. Churchill (1874–1965), who had replaced Chamberlain the very day the German attack began. A week later, Guderian's swiftly moving armored divisions reached the English Channel in order

to encircle the Allies between the two converging German armies. The British Expeditionary Force retreated quickly to the French Channel ports of Boulogne, Calais, and Dunkirk, from where they hoped to evacuate. Guderian drove toward the same destination, but just as he reached the outskirts of Dunkirk he was ordered to halt. Despite the German conviction that such a massive escape was not possible, on May 26, 338,000 Allied soldiers began leaving France. Although Dunkirk proved an amazing success as an evacuation operation, it symbolized an unprecedented military defeat for the British.

Reynaud reorganized his government, appointing General Maxim Weygand (1867–1965) as military commander and the venerable Marshal Henri Pétain (1856–1951) as vice premier. Neither man, however, believed that France could be saved, although Weygand was at least determined to fight to the last. After Dunkirk, the Germans made rapid headway. On June 5, they sent 95 divisions across northern France, with one spearhead driving into Normandy and the other toward Paris.

When Mussolini joined Hitler in the Pact of Steel in May 1938, the dictators bound themselves to provide each other with total assistance in the event of war. But Mussolini had informed the Germans that Italy would not be prepared for full-scale war until 1943. Mussolini had, therefore, remained neutral in 1939, but the dazzling success of Hitler's Blitzkrieg shocked the *Duce* into acting, lest the war end before Italy could claim a part in the victory. Mussolini declared war on France on June 10, 1940, although he did not send Italian troops into battle until a week later. In the meantime, Paris fell to the Germans on June 14 and the government, which fled south, grew deeply divided over whether to continue to resist. Reynaud

A jubilant Hitler hears news of the French capitulation in 1940.

proposed fighting from French possessions in North Africa, but Weygand and Pétain secured the cabinet's support to sue for an armistice. Pétain took Reynaud's place as premier on July 16, and while he awaited Hitler's response to his request for peace terms, the Germans pushed deeper into France and Mussolini's armies attacked in the southeast.

Hitler demanded severe terms for an armistice, which he insisted be signed on the same site in Compiègne, northeast of Paris, where the Allies had forced terms on Germany in 1918. The document, executed on June 22, 1940, provided for German occupation of two-thirds of France, comprising the north and central portions of the country and the city of Paris. Alsace-Lorraine was given to Germany for the second time in less than a century. The remaining southern third of French territory, together with the colonial empire, continued to be headed by Pétain, whose government ruled from Vichy in collaboration with the German authorities. The Third Republic, founded in the wake of the Prussian victory of 1871, now came to an ignominious end.

While Pétain headed a rump state in the name of the humiliated French, national honor was kept alive by General Charles de Gaulle (1890–1970), the undersecretary of war who opposed both the armistice and the Vichy government. De Gaulle had taught military history at the Saint-Cyr military academy, where he himself had been educated. An advocate of tank warfare from whose books the Germans had learned some of their tactics, the strong-willed general had never been popular among his more traditional fellow officers. Refusing to recognize the armistice, he flew to Britain and appealed to the French people to continue the fight under his leadership. In London, he set up a government in exile, the Free French National Committee, and recruited an army of volunteers.

The Battle of Britain

Germany's Blitzkrieg gave Hitler control over as much of Europe as Napoleon had once ruled. Victory was, however, not yet his, for Great Britain remained still at war, although Hitler believed that the British had no choice but to make peace. The British rejected all offers of a settlement. Churchill, the new prime minister, was a pugnacious leader in the face of adversity, a brilliant speaker, and a tireless proponent of British national interests. Out of office for much of the 1930s, he had been a staunch advocate of rearmament and a bitter critic of appeasement.

Hitler saw no alternative other than to force Britain into submission, but he recognized that an invasion would be virtually impossible as long as British air and naval power remained intact. Nevertheless, in July Hitler ordered his strategists to develop an invasion plan, called Operation Sea Lion, which was to begin on September 15. Before the invasion could start, however, German leaders agreed that the Luftwaffe

St. Paul's Cathedral seen through the smoke of the German *Blitz* on London, January 1941.

would have to destroy the Royal Air Force (RAF) fighter planes, after which bombers could destroy British ships, coastal defenses, and ground troops. Reichsmarshal Hermann Goering was supremely confident that his Luftwaffe could not only destroy the RAF but also bomb the British people into surrendering without an invasion. Preparations for Operation Sea Lion were known to the British through Ultra reports.

Goering failed to appreciate the British spirit of resistance and overestimated the strength of the Luftwaffe. The two chief German air fleets consisted of 1200 bombers, which lacked sufficient range and bomb capacity, and 280 Stukas. The latter, which had proved so effective elsewhere, were decimated by British fighters and withdrawn. For daytime missions, the German bombers had to be escorted by Messerschmitt fighters, whose range was equally limited. In all, the two German air fleets had 980 Messerschmitts of various kinds. Because the RAF boasted only 650 Hurricane and Spitfire fighters, its commanders insisted on keeping large numbers of their planes in reserve. Aircraft production soon increased significantly, however, and the British also developed a radar system.

After a month of preliminary bombing of British shipping, the Germans began to attack airfields in mid-August in an effort to destroy the RAF. During the Battle of Britain, RAF pilots engaged in intense aerial combat with the Luftwaffe, losing more than 800 fighters while destroying 668 German fighters and 500 bombers during the first two months. On September 7, Goering began raids on London, but it was soon clear that the Germans could not destroy the RAF. Hitler canceled Operation Sea Lion in mid-September, although the bombing of civilian targets in Britain continued through the spring of 1941. The Battle of Britain cost the RAF some 1265 planes and the Luftwaffe 1882 aircraft.

THE PARALLEL WAR AND BARBAROSSA

When it was clear that the Battle of Britain had proved to be a standoff, Hitler undertook operations against British forces in the Mediterranean Sea. It was Mussolini, however, who forced Hitler's hand in campaigns designed as his own "parallel" war, but that the German leader considered merely a sideshow to a much larger goal: the invasion of Russia.

North Africa and the Balkans

In September 1940, Italian forces in Libya invaded Egypt. The Italian thrust came quickly to a halt at Sidi Barrani, 50 miles across the border, where they wanted to build a supply base. In early December, British

General Archibald Wavell (1883–1950), commanding half the number of troops but with double the tank strength, counterattacked. The British pushed the Italians out of Egypt and across the North African desert, taking huge numbers of prisoners.

The Italian defeat was so sweeping that it forced Hitler to intervene. He sent General Erwin Rommel (1891–1944) to North Africa with meager forces consisting of one light motorized and one Panzer division, information that came to Wavell through Ultra. In March, Rommel attacked, driving the British back into Egypt, but because his supply lines were stretched thin he could not move further. The war in North Africa had turned into a stalemate. In East Africa, however, the British won a clear victory, overrunning Italian possessions in Eritrea, Ethiopia, and Somaliland.

In October, while the North African campaign was under way, Mussolini ordered an attack against Greece—an ill-advised move taken against the opinions of his generals. The attack deeply angered Hitler because it threatened German domination of the Balkans. The Italian invasion met with torrential rains, and the tough if small Greek army fought back fiercely. Italian forces suffered huge casualties as they overextended themselves into the mountains. Churchill also sent some 58,000 troops to help the Greeks. That April, Hitler moved to rescue Mussolini from disaster in Greece, while simultaneously invading Yugoslavia, and by the end of the month had conquered both countries. In late May, these successes were followed by a remarkable airborne conquest of Crete.

Operation Barbarossa

Even as the Battle of Britain began, Hitler had turned his mind eastward to the Soviet Union. He had long regarded Eastern Europe and Russia as providing the necessary *Lebensraum* ("living space") that Germany would require if the Reich was to dominate Europe. For Hitler, the Nazi-Soviet Pact of 1939 had been a temporary expedient. His long-range plans called for the destruction of Bolshevism and the seizure of Soviet oil and food resources. Once he had defeated the Soviet Union, he believed, Britain would be forced to capitulate. The invasion of Russia proved, however, to be a fatal error that would eventually cost Hitler victory.

Convinced that Britain was near collapse and that the USSR was too weak to stop him, Hitler told his generals in July 1940 to plan for "Operation Barbarossa," an attack on the Soviet Union. In this instance, the generals shared with Hitler a gross misconception of the difficulties ahead and sorely underestimated Soviet military strength. The Germans assembled some 145 divisions along the long Russian front, while the Soviets had more than 230 divisions. Hitler disagreed, however, with the generals over strategy: the latter wanted to focus on taking Moscow, not only the Soviet capital but an important industrial and rail center, while Hitler wanted to aim both at Leningrad in the north and the Ukraine in the south. In the end, Hitler approved an ambitious plan that consisted of three army groups, each aimed at one of the targets.

The invasion, which began a month later than scheduled on June 22, 1941, caught the Soviets completely off guard. German planes took off before the start of hostilities and within hours had destroyed some 1200 Soviet aircraft. The northern army group got to within 80 miles of Leningrad in five days, while the center army group captured almost 500,000 prisoners and were 200 miles from Moscow within a month. Only in the south, where the Soviets fought strenuously, was progress slower than expected. In mid-July, however, Hitler overruled his generals and weakened the center army group by shifting armored divisions to Leningrad and the Ukraine. In September, Hitler ordered the siege of Leningrad, which he intended to starve into surrender. The population suffered gruesome deprivations and enormous casualties as it fought with the Soviet army to defend the city. Only in 1944 was the siege finally lifted. In the south, the Germans succeeded in encircling Soviet forces near Kiev and took 600,000 prisoners. At the end of the month, Hitler changed strategy again, this time ordering an all-out drive toward Moscow and a simultaneous push deep into the industrial regions of the Ukraine. Hundreds of thousands of additional Russian soldiers were captured along with vast amounts of material. As the Germans moved forward, Stalin had more than 1500 Soviet factories dismantled and moved to the east of Moscow along with some 2 million workers.

The coming of heavy rains toward the end of October halted the advance of Hitler's armies, which had come as close as 40 miles to Moscow. German supply lines were in serious jeopardy when the winter set in, but, on November 15, Hitler and his generals began what they believed would be the final assault on Moscow. However, extreme temperatures, as low as minus-40, and heavy snows forced the Germans to stop. On November 28, the Nazi armies sustained their first setback when a Soviet counteroffensive in the south forced them to abandon positions. On December 5, Marshal Georgi Zhukov (1896–1974) attacked the German flanks north and south of Moscow, but instead of making a tactical withdrawal Hitler ordered his forces to fight on. It was Stalin's turn now to make a serious error. He overruled Zhukov, who wanted to make an all-out offensive at the Moscow front, and dispersed the Red Army along all sectors, a decision that helped

make it possible for the Germans to resist the counteroffensive.

Both sides suffered enormous losses and the war on the Eastern front, like the war in North Africa, ground temporarily to a stalemate. The failure of the German attack against the Soviet Union resulted in a major shake-up of the German high command, and Hitler himself now assumed the role of commander-in-chief of the army. By the beginning of 1942, victory over both Britain and the Soviet Union had eluded Hitler's grasp.

THE JEWS AND HITLER'S "NEW ORDER"

Hitler's dream of creating a Greater Germany went far beyond any traditional thirst for territory. His aims were determined by the racial concepts that were the basis of Nazi ideology. It is difficult to say precisely what form Hitler's empire would have taken had he won the war, but Nazi policies in conquered territories suggest the fiendish nature of the "New Order" he hoped to create.

Hitler's "New Order"

By the end of 1941, Hitler held sway over as much European territory as any ruler in modern history. In addition to an expanded Germany that included Austria, portions of Czechoslovakia, and half of Poland, his troops occupied northern France, Belgium, the Netherlands, Luxembourg, Denmark, Norway, Greece, part of Yugoslavia, and a vast segment of the Soviet Union. At the height of the war, Vichy France, Italy, Hungary, Romania, Albania, Bulgaria, Slovakia, Croatia, and Finland were allied with Germany. Moreover, much of North African territory was in Axis hands. Spain, Portugal, the Irish Republic, Sweden, and Switzerland remained neutral.

According to Nazi plans, the Germans of the Third Reich were to be the rulers of the new Europe, and Germany its core. The so-called Aryans whom the Nazis extolled as the superior race also included Germanic peoples such as the English, the Scandinavians, and the Dutch, and Hitler hoped one day to incorporate most of them in Greater Germany. At first, Hitler allowed those Germanic states which he conquered to administer themselves, but resistance to Nazi occupation led to direct German control. In any case, the status assigned to each conquered area was only temporary, until victory enabled Hitler the leisure to impose a final settlement on Europe.

Hitler's attitude toward the Latin peoples of Europe, including the Italians, the French, and the

Spanish, was mixed. Although the Latins were not in the élite Germanic category, Nazi ideologues argued that they had some Aryan blood. His admiration and friendship for Mussolini led him to treat Italy with special regard, and after Mussolini adopted anti-Semitic policies in 1938, Fascist theorists there claimed that Italians were an Aryan race.

Despite such gradations, the Nazis generally considered all non-Germans to be inferior, and some—such as the Slavs of eastern Europe, who were low in the Nazi racial hierarchy—were thought useful only as a source of manual labor. The Third Reich regarded the populations and resources of other European nations as German resources. In occupied areas, inhabitants were conscripted into forced labor squads—over 2.5 million Poles and Russians, for example, were brought to Germany as forced workers and industrial equipment and agricultural produce were confiscated on a grand scale. By 1944, some 7 million foreign workers were eventually conscripted to Germany, where they were overworked and treated poorly.

Hermann Goering, who supervised economic policies in occupied areas, announced blatantly, "I intend to plunder, and plunder copiously." Occupation was generally more severe in the East than in Western Europe, where local populations were assessed for the cost of occupation troops but most private property was not actually confiscated. Policies were often confused, for Nazi authorities such as the army, the SS, and the Gestapo often vied with each other for control. Regardless of which Nazi officials ruled, however, their policies were harsh and brutal.

Nazi cruelty engendered resistance almost everywhere. In occupied territories active underground movements sprang up in opposition to German authority. Sometimes resisters engaged in symbolic acts of defiance, but more often they were involved in intelligence gathering, sabotage, and other meaningful acts that helped the Allied war effort. The attack against the Soviet Union pulled hundreds of thousands of communists into the underground, and after 1943 resistance forces became mass movements, increasingly armed by the Allies.

In France, where the resistance forces were generally called the *Maquis* (meaning "underbrush"), a number of groups fought against both Vichy and the Nazis. In 1943, French resistance leaders unified them into a single National Resistance Council and a Military Action Committee, and by the time of the Allied invasion some 200,000 armed resisters were in the field. Yugoslav and Russian partisans achieved significant military successes, and hundreds of thousands of German soldiers were bogged down in antiresistance operations. After Mussolini was overthrown by a coup in the summer of 1943, the anti-Fascist armed resistance played an equally significant role in northern Italy, where perhaps 250,000 partisans fought.

Nazi victims did not all go to their slaughter passively. In Warsaw, the Nazis had herded some 400,000 Jews together into the overcrowded ghetto, where SS-Chief Heinrich Himmler planned to starve and work them to death. In the spring of 1943, however, Himmler tired of the slow process and ordered the ghetto and its inhabitants destroyed. A group of Jewish survivors, led by the youth of the ghetto, fought heroically against the Nazis for 42 days.

The Nazis tried to keep their crimes secret, but word began to leak out as early as late 1941, and by the following year the U.S. government knew about the death camps. Nevertheless, Churchill and Roosevelt decided that the Jewish problem would have to await the opening of a second front. Only when the Allies liberated the camps in 1945 did the full horror of what had happened become public knowledge. What made the horror even more difficult to comprehend was the fact that so many millions of human beings were destroyed with careful deliberation and according to scientific principles by a state whose people had otherwise made such significant contributions to the civilization of Europe.

Map 9.2   The Holocaust

OCUMENTS ON HISTORY

The Destruction of the European Jews

The most horrendous aspect of Hitler's New Order was its policies toward the Jews—policies that resulted in the planned extermination of millions of innocent people. This Holocaust, as the destruction of the European Jews is known, made an already gruesome and inhumane war even more terrible.

HITLER'S PLANS FOR THE JEWS

itler's anti-Semitism had been one of the principal forces in his early development (see Part VIII, Topic 2). During his rise to power he made the "Jewish question" a central issue of the Nazi platform. Although he did not explain the exact nature of his plans for the Jews, he did talk of creating a Germany free of Jews. In an interview as early as 1922, he was outspoken about what he would do once he took full power.

His eyes no longer saw me but instead bore past me and off into empty space; his explanations grew increasingly voluble until he fell into a kind of paroxysm that ended with his shouting, as if to a whole public gathering: "Once I really am in power, my first and foremost task will be the annihilation of the Jews. As soon as I have the power to do so, I will have gallows built in rows—at the Marienplatz in Munich, for example—as many as traffic allows. Then the Jews will be hanged indiscriminately, and they will remain hanging until they stink; they will hang there as long as the principles of hygiene permit. As soon as they have been untied, the next batch will be strung up, and so on down the line, until the last Jew in Munich has been exterminated. Other cities will follow suit, precisely in this fashion, until all Germany has been completely cleansed of Jews."

Quoted in Gerald Fleming, *Hitler and the Final Solution.* University of California Press. Copyright © 1984.

THE NUREMBERG LAWS

nce in power, the Nazis made life difficult for German Jews. Acting on a direct order from Hitler, the Reichstag passed two measures on September 15, 1935, which, together with the Reich citizenship law of November 14, constituted the so-called Nuremberg laws. The laws, selected portions of which follow, stripped Jews of their rights as citizens.

The Reich citizenship law of September 15:

1. (1) A subject is anyone who enjoys the protection of the German Reich and for this reason is specifically obligated to it.

   (2) Nationality is acquired according to the provisions of the Reich and state nationality law.

2. (1) A Reich citizen is only that subject of German or kindred blood who proves by his conduct that he is willing and suited loyally to serve the German people and the Reich.

   (2) Reich citizenship is acquired through the conferment of a certificate of Reich citizenship.

   (3) The Reich citizen is the sole bearer of full political rights as provided by the laws.

The Law for the Protection of German Blood and German Honor:

   Imbued with the insight that the purity of German blood is a prerequisite for the continued existence of the German people and inspired by the inflexible will to ensure the existence of the German nation for all times, the Reichstag has unanimously adopted the following law, which is hereby promulgated:

1. (1) Marriages between Jews and subjects of German or kindred blood are forbidden. Marriages nevertheless concluded are invalid, even if concluded abroad to circumvent this law.

   (2) Only the State Attorney may initiate the annulment suit.

2. Extramarital intercourse between Jews and subjects of German or kindred blood is forbidden.

3. Jews must not employ in their households female subjects of German or kindred blood who are under 45 years old.

4. (1) Jews are forbidden to fly the Reich or national flag and to display the Reich colors.

   (2) They are, on the other hand, allowed to display the Jewish colors. The exercise of this right enjoys the protection of the state.

Quoted in Yehuda Bauer, *A History of the Holocaust*. Franklin Watts. Copyright © 1982.

THE KILLING FIELDS

The systematic destruction of Europe's Jews began to be implemented in the wake of the attack against the Soviet Union. As the German armies moved eastward and some 2 million Polish Jews fell under their rule, Nazi policy makers began thinking about the "Jewish question" on a more far-reaching basis. At first they debated forced emigration to the east. Reinhard Heydrich (1904–1942), head of the SS security service (the SD), organized SS Einsatzgruppen ("special-duty groups"), squads that followed the armies into Poland and later into the Soviet Union. The squads rounded up Polish workers and Russian prisoners for shipment to German slave labor camps and herded Jews into ghettos.

As Operation Barbarossa unfolded and the number of Jews under their control increased, the concentration strategy was replaced by what came to be known as the "Final Solution." Sometime in the spring or summer of 1941, Hitler made mass murder official policy and in July ordered Heydrich to draw up plans for this gruesome purpose. The Einsatzgruppen began to round up and shoot Jews and bury them in mass graves. In all, some 1 million men, women, and children may have been killed in this way. Here an SS colonel reports on the activities of his "Strike Commando" unit in Kovno, which covered parts of Lithuania and Latvia.

Lithuania could be freed of Jews only because a specially selected raiding party was set up under SS-1st Lieutenant Hamann who shared my aims in full and who knew how to cooperate with

continued next page

Lithuanian [anti-communist] partisans and the appropriate civil offices.

The implementation of such actions is in the first instance an organizational problem. The decision to free each district of Jews necessitated thorough preparation of each action as well as acquisition of information about local conditions. The Jews had to be collected in one or more towns and a ditch had to be dug at the right site for the right number. The marching distance from collecting points to the ditches averaged about 3 miles. The Jews were brought in groups of 500, separated by at least 1.2 miles, to the place of execution.

Vehicles are seldom available. Escapes, which were attempted here and there, were frustrated solely by my men at the risk of their lives. For example, 3 men of the Commando at Mariampole shot 38 escaping Jews and communist functionaries on a path in the woods, so that no one got away. Distances to and from actions were never less than 90–120 miles. Only careful planning enabled the Commando to carry out up to 5 actions a week and at the same time continue the work in Kovno without interruption.

Kovno itself, where trained Lithuanian partisans are available in sufficient numbers, was comparatively speaking a shooting paradise.

All officers and men of the Commando in Kovno participated in the major actions in the city. Only one intelligence official was excused because of illness.

I regard the Jewish actions of Strike Commando 3 as virtually completed. The remaining work Jews and Jewesses are urgently needed, and I can imagine that they will still be needed after the winter. I am of the opinion that the male work Jews should be sterilized immediately to prevent any procreation. A Jewess who nevertheless becomes pregnant is to be liquidated. . . .

From photostats of documents in the Institut für Zeitgeschichte, Munich, report of December 1, 1941, as reproduced in Raul Hilberg, ed., *Documents of Destruction: Germany and Jewry 1933–1945.* Copyright © 1971, Raul Hilberg.

AN EYEWITNESS ACCOUNT

Here is the terrible testimony of Mrs. Rivka Yosselevscka, who as a young girl survived one of the innumerable episodes of killings in Russia.

When it came to our turn, our father was beaten. We prayed, we begged with my father to undress, but he would not undress, he wanted to keep his underclothes. . . .

Then they tore the clothing off the old man and he was shot. I saw it with my own eyes. And then they took my mother, and she said, let us go before her; but they caught mother and shot her too; and then there was my grandmother, my father's mother, standing there; she was eighty years old and she had two children in her arms. And then there was my father's sister. She also had children in her arms and she was shot on the spot with the babies in her arms. . . .

And finally my turn came. There was my younger sister, and she wanted to leave; she prayed with the Germans; she asked to run, naked; she went up to the Germans with one of her friends; they were embracing each other; and she asked to be spared, standing there naked. He looked into her eyes and shot the two of them. . . . Then my second sister was shot and then my turn did come. . . .

We were already facing the grave. The German asked "Who do you want me to shoot first?" I did not answer. I felt him take the child from my arms. The child cried out and was shot immediately. And then he aimed at me. First he held on to my hair and turned my head around; I stayed standing; I heard a shot, but I continued to stand and then he turned my head again and he aimed the revolver at me and ordered me to watch and then turned my head around and shot at me. Then I fell to the ground into the pit amongst the bodies; but I felt nothing. The moment I did feel I felt a sort of heaviness. . . . Then I felt that I was choking; people falling over me. I tried to move and felt that I was alive and that I could rise. I was strangling. I heard the shots and I was praying for another bullet to put an end to my suffering, but I continued to move about. I felt that I was choking, strangling, but I tried to save myself, to find some air to breathe, and then I felt that I was climbing towards the top of the grave above the bodies. I rose, and I felt bodies pulling at me with their hands, biting at my legs, pulling me down, down. And yet with my last strength I came up on top of the grave, and when I did I did not know the place, so many bodies were lying all over, dead people; I wanted to see the end of this stretch of dead bodies but I could not. It was impossible. They were lying, all dying; suffering; not all of them dead, but in their last sufferings; naked; shot, but not dead. Children crying "Mother," "Father". . . .

THE FINAL SOLUTION

A t the end of July 1941, Hermann Goering sent the following order to Heydrich:

Complementing the task already assigned to you in the decree of January 24, 1939, to undertake, by emigration or evacuation, a solution of the Jewish question as advantageous as possible under the conditions at the time, I hereby charge you with making all necessary organizational, functional, and material preparations for a complete solution of the Jewish question in the German sphere of influence in Europe.

In so far as the jurisdiction of other central agencies may be touched thereby, they are to be involved.

I charge you furthermore with submitting to me in the near future an overall plan of the organizational, functional, and material mea-

sures to be taken in preparing for the implementation of the aspired final solution of the Jewish question.

The Nazis established death camps in order to murder Jews in large numbers by rational, systematic methods. Camps were built in Auschwitz, Chełmno, Bełzec, Treblinka, and at numerous other sites. These policies were discussed and approved at the Wannsee Conference of high German officials in January 1942. The text of the discussion was carefully sanitized by SS officer Adolf Eichmann (1906–1962), who took the minutes.

Chief of Security Policy and Security Service, SS-Lieutenant General Heydrich, opened the meeting by informing everyone that the Reich Marshal [Göring] had placed him in charge of preparations for the final solution of the Jewish question, and that the invitations to this conference had been issued to obtain clarity in fundamental questions. The Reich Marshal's wish to have a draft submitted to him on the organizational, functional, and material considerations aimed at a final solution of the European Jewish question requires that all of the central agencies, which are directly concerned with these problems, first join together with a view to paralleliz-ing their lines of action.

The implementation of the final solution of the Jewish question is to be guided centrally without regard to geographic boundaries from the office of the Reichsführer-SS and Chief of the German Police (Chief of Security Police and Security Service).

The Chief of Security Police and Security Service then reviewed briefly the battle fought thus far against these opponents. The principal stages constituted

a) Forcing the Jews out of individual sectors of life [*Lebensgebiete*] of the German people

continued next page

b) Forcing the Jews out of the living space [*Lebensraum*] of the German people

In pursuance of this endeavor, a systematic and concentrated effort was made to accelerate Jewish emigration from Reich territory as the only temporary solution possibility. . . .

The disadvantages brought forth by such forcing of emigration were clear to every agency. In the meantime, however, they had to be accepted for the lack of any other solution possibility. . . .

In lieu of emigration, the evacuation of the Jews to the east has emerged, after an appropriate prior authorization by the Führer [Hitler], as a further solution possibility.

While these actions are to be regarded solely as temporary measures, practical experiences are already being gathered here which will be of great importance during the coming final solution of the Jewish question. . . .

In the course of the final solution, the Jews should be brought under appropriate direction in a suitable manner to the east for labor utilization. Separated by sex, the Jews capable of work will be led into these areas in large labor columns to build roads, whereby doubtless a large part will fall away through natural reduction.

The inevitable final remainder which doubtless constitutes the toughest element will have to be dealt with appropriately, since it represents a natural selection which upon liberation is to be regarded as a germ cell of a new Jewish development. (See the lesson of history.)

In the course of the practical implementa-

tion of the final solution, Europe will be combed from west to east. If only because of the apartment shortage and other socio-political necessities, the Reich area — including the Protectorate of Bohemia and Moravia — will have to be placed ahead of the line. . . .

Quoted in Raul Hilberg, ed., *Documents of Destruction: Germany and Jewry 1933 – 1945.* Copyright © 1971, Raul Hilberg.

Eichmann rounded up his victims and used railroads to ship them to death camps in Poland, the largest at Auschwitz. After Jews were killed in the gas chambers, the Nazis processed all usable items, including clothing, gold teeth, eyeglasses, and even human hair, and burned the bodies in ovens. Here is a description of the first testing of gas on Russian prisoners by Rudolf F. Hess, commandant of Auschwitz:

While I was away on duty, my deputy, Fritzsch, the commander of the protective custody camp, first tried gas for these killings. It was a preparation of prussic acid, called cyclon B, which was used in the camp as an insecticide and of which there was always a stock on hand. On my return, Fritzsch reported this to me, and the gas was used again for the next transport. . . . Protected by a gas-mask, I watched the killing myself. In the crowded cells death came instantaneously the moment the cyclon B was thrown in. A short, almost smothered cry, and it was all over. . . . I have a clearer recollection of the gassing of nine hundred Russians. . . . While the transport was detraining, holes were pierced in the earth and concrete ceiling of the mortuary. The Russians were ordered to undress in an

AMERICAN INTERVENTION AND THE WAR IN ASIA

While the war raged for two years in Europe, the United States maintained a guarded neutrality. Isolationism remained deeply rooted in American

public opinion. In 1935 Congress had passed a law that ensured U.S. neutrality during Mussolini's invasion of Ethiopia, and in 1937 an even stronger measure prevented the government and U.S. manufacturers from shipping armaments and vital war materiel to belligerents on any side of a conflict. On the other hand, President Franklin D. Roosevelt was deeply concerned over the dangers of Nazi-

anteroom; they then quietly entered the mortuary, for they had been told they were to be deloused. The whole transport exactly filled the mortuary to capacity. The doors were then sealed and the gas shaken down through the holes in the roof. I do not know how long this killing took. For a little while a humming sound could be heard. When the powder was thrown in, there were cries of "Gas!", then a great bellowing, and the trapped prisoners hurled themselves against both doors. . . . The mass extermination of the Jews was to start soon and at that time neither Eichmann nor I was certain how these mass killings were to be carried out. . . . Now we had the gas, and we had established a procedure.

Quoted in Yehuda Bauer, *A History of the Holocaust.* Franklin Watts. Copyright © 1982.

*A*t his trial for crimes against humanity in Jerusalem in 1957, Eichmann gave this chilling explanation of his "moral" universe:

I did not take on the job as a senseless exercise. It gave me uncommon joy, I found it fascinating to have to deal with these matters. . . . My job was to catch these enemies and transport them to their destination. . . . I lived in this stuff, otherwise I would have remained only an assistant, a cog, something soulless. . . .

I thought it over, and I realized the necessity for it, I carried it through with all the fanaticism that an old Nazi would expect of himself and that my superiors undoubtedly expected

from me. They found me, according to their experience, to be the right man in the right place. . . . This I say today, in 1957, to my own disadvantage. I could make it easy for myself. I could now claim it was an order I had to carry out because of my oath of allegiance. But that would be just a cheap excuse, which I am not prepared to give. . . .

To be frank with you, had we killed all of them, the 10.3 million, I would be happy and say, Alright, we managed to destroy an enemy. . . .

I suggested these words ["Final Solution"]. At that time I meant by this the elimination of the Jews, their marching out of the German Nation. Later. . . . these harmless words were used as a camouflage for the killing.

Quoted in Gideon Hausner, *Justice in Jerusalem.* Herzl Press. Copyright © 1966.

*B*y the end of the war, as many as 6 million Jews—three-fourths of all Jews in Europe—may have been murdered. The Holocaust consumed others as well, including political enemies and resisters, some 200,000 gypsies, and 60,000 homosexuals. Hitler regarded most Slavs, particularly the Poles, with utter contempt, and during the Nazi occupation millions perished as prisoners of war or in labor camps. History as well as aspects of the social and economic structures of modern Germany had contributed to the Holocaust, and Nazi policy had evolved over the years. There is no doubt, however, that by 1942, the Nazis intended to destroy the Jews of the whole of Europe.

Fascist aggression in Europe and Japanese ambitions in East Asia.

The Crisis of American Neutrality

A move away from neutrality first appeared in connection with the Japanese invasion of China in 1937, when the Roosevelt administration came out openly against Japan. The president, in his famous "Quarantine

Speech" delivered in October, asked that the world community oppose violations of international law. There was, he declared ominously, no escaping responsibility through "mere isolation or neutrality."

When war erupted in Europe, most Americans supported the Western democracies but still opposed intervention. Nevertheless, Roosevelt moved to strengthen U.S. defenses and to make America what

Jews from the Warsaw ghetto are rounded up by German troops — and headed toward death.

When the Nazi death and concentration camps were liberated, Allied troops discovered unbelievable horrors — here, piles of corpses at Belsen concentration camp.

he called the "arsenal of democracy." In November 1939, he persuaded Congress to repeal the arms embargo and permit the sale of war supplies to Britain through a "cash and carry" program—the measure did, however, prohibit U.S. ships from transporting the arms so as to avoid German submarine attacks. Congress also approved a huge defense budget and in September 1940 instituted the draft. After he had won reelection that year, the president introduced the Lend-Lease Bill into Congress—Britain was about to exhaust its financial resources, and the law, passed in March 1941, allowed the president to lend or lease arms, with payment to be made after the war. That summer, lend-lease was extended to the Soviet Union.

Under Roosevelt's leadership, the United States inched its way closer to active intervention on the side of the Allies. In January 1941, British and American military officials met in Washington, DC, to develop plans in the event the United States entered the war. In April and July, U.S. military forces took possession respectively of Greenland and Iceland, two Danish possessions in the North Atlantic. In August, Roosevelt met Churchill on a British battleship off the coast of Newfoundland. Despite Roosevelt's suspicions that Churchill was intent on maintaining the British Empire, the two leaders issued an important statement known as the Atlantic Charter. The document described a joint postwar policy that affirmed the right of all peoples to self-government, rejected any territorial acquisition as a result of the war, and called for the destruction of Nazism. For the United States, still a neutral nation, the Atlantic Charter represented a virtual announcement of war goals.

War in Asia

It was Japan, rather than Germany, that actually provoked American intervention (see Part VIII, Topic 8). In September 1940, Japan joined Germany and Italy in a Tripartite Pact, a defensive alliance aimed indirectly at the United States that gave Japanese expansionism the endorsement of the Axis. Japanese leaders now took advantage of the war in Europe to build their own empire in Asia—one that they hoped would reach from Manchuria in the North to embrace all of Southeast Asia, including Indochina, Indonesia (the Dutch East Indies), Singapore, and the Philippines. Japanese strategists, claiming that they would free Asia from Western control, conceived of this empire as the "Greater East Asia Co-Prosperity Sphere," a far-flung economic zone in which Japan's industrial and technological superiority would be combined with the vast resources and labor supply of East Asia.

In 1940, Japan pressed the Dutch government to grant trade concessions and forced the French to cut off supply lines to China through their colony in Indochina. The American reaction was to impose an embargo in July on the export of such items as steel and aviation fuel to Japan. Working against pressure from Japanese military leaders, Premier Fumimaro Konoye (1891–1945), a moderate aristocrat, began talks with the United States in 1941 in an effort to reach a peaceful agreement. When the German attack against the Soviet Union removed the danger of Soviet action in East Asia, Japan overran Indochina. Roosevelt responded by freezing Japanese assets in the United States and announcing a severe trade embargo, including the shipment of oil.

Konoye resigned in October and was replaced by Tojo Hideki (1885–1948), an army general who favored war with America. His colleague, Admiral Isoroku Yamamoto (1884–1943), commander of the Japanese Fleet, believed that such a war could be successful only if Japan destroyed the U.S. Pacific Fleet in a surprise attack. Emperor Hirohito (ruled 1926–1989) insisted that negotiations continue, while Tojo's cabinet decided on war should this second diplomatic effort fail. In November 1941, Washington insisted that Japan withdraw completely from China and Indochina before it would lift economic sanctions. The Japanese considered this an ultimatum and at the end of the month secretly decided on war. The Americans, who had broken the Japanese diplomatic code, knew that war seemed likely but did not anticipate that an assault would come where it did, although debate on the background to the Pearl Harbor attack continues.

The Japanese launched their surprise attack on the morning of December 7. The target was the U.S. naval base at Pearl Harbor, in the Hawaiian Islands. Hundreds of planes from Japanese aircraft carriers caught the Americans by surprise, sinking four out of eight U.S. battleships, three destroyers, and four smaller ships, and destroying 160 planes. The United States, its military strength in the Pacific severely damaged, was at war.

Immediately after Pearl Harbor, the Japanese also struck against the British fleet near Singapore and the U.S. Air Force base in the Philippines. Japan overran Malaya, Burma, the Dutch East Indies, and the Philippines, campaigns made possible by its control of Indochina. Thailand was forced to let Japan use its military bases, and by 1942, Japan had seized most of the islands in the western Pacific. Japanese occupation policies were no less brutal than those of the Nazis in Europe, for the Japanese regarded other Asians with their own attitude of racial superiority. By the beginning of 1942, Japan controlled most of East Asia, and its newly created empire appeared to be invincible.

The Japanese attack on Pearl Harbor, December 7, 1941 brought the United States into the war. Here U.S. battleships are shown shortly after the raid.

TURNING THE TIDE: THE RUSSIAN ADVANCE AND THE ECLIPSE OF JAPAN

With America's entrance into the war in December 1941, the Axis powers now faced an informal alliance consisting of Great Britain, the United States, and the Soviet Union (the three powers were allies only in the European theater, since the USSR and Japan were not at war). From December 22 to January 14, Churchill and his chiefs of staff met in Washington with Roosevelt and American officials to develop a grand strategy. The two nations agreed that the defeat of Germany and victory in Europe would be the first goal, to be followed by the defeat of Japan. The Allies accepted two other essential points: that a second front had to be opened in the West to relieve the Russian war effort, and that a cross-channel invasion of the European continent would have to come. The Anglo-American conference ended with the issuance of a "United Nations Declaration" in which the 26 countries fighting against the Axis endorsed the principles of the Atlantic Charter, accepted the premises of the

Anglo-American conference, and agreed to postpone political questions until after military victory.

The Allies disagreed over both strategy and broader political issues. The Americans believed that victory could be achieved only by a direct frontal assault on Hitler's "Fortress Europe" through an invasion of France. The British, however, feared that a premature landing there would spell disaster, and Churchill pushed for an attack against what he called the "soft underbelly" of Europe—either in the Balkans or in Italy. A compromise was reached, whereby the Allies would first seize North Africa and use it as a base for a campaign against the "underbelly," followed then by an invasion of France.

Strategic disagreements combined with political mistrust, for each of the three leaders came from a totally different political background. Stalin, a lifelong communist, worried that the two Western statesmen were intent on keeping the Soviet Union from sharing in the postwar settlement and from expanding into Eastern Europe. Even Roosevelt and Churchill had doubts about each other—Roosevelt, a Wilsonian internationalist, believed that Churchill was driven by the desire to extend Britain's empire into the Mediterranean basin, while Churchill thought the

U.S. president naive about international politics. Nevertheless, the three men forged an alliance of convenience around the immediate goal of defeating the Axis.

The Soviets Push West

The fortunes of war began to turn against the Axis in 1942, in North Africa, Europe, and the Pacific. That fall, British General Bernard Montgomery (1887–1976) won a decisive victory over Rommel's desert forces at El-Alamein. In November, while the fighting was still raging at El-Alamein, a joint Anglo-American army commanded by U.S. General Dwight D. Eisenhower (1890–1969) landed in Morocco and Algeria, and by May 1943 had captured all of North Africa.

It was in the Soviet Union, however, that Hitler suffered his greatest setbacks, the accumulated weight of which proved decisive. The Führer's decision not to pull back his forces in the winter of 1941–1942 proved crucial in draining his eastern armies. The Germans were fighting the Red Army on a front line that stretched almost 2000 miles. Hitler then decided to abandon the Moscow campaign and concentrate his strength in a huge offensive in the south. The aim of this strategy was to seize the vital oil fields in the Caucasus. The drive began in late June 1942 by attempting to encircle the Soviet forces in the region where the Don and the Volga rivers flowed close to each other, near the industrial city of Stalingrad. The Soviets withdrew toward Stalingrad under the impact of the German attack, leaving Hitler to believe that the Soviet war effort was on the verge of collapse. Yet the strategic withdrawal induced the Germans into dividing their strength in pursuit of several different objectives.

As one German force made its way toward Stalingrad in late August, Marshal Zhukov prepared to defend the city. Stalingrad itself was important primarily as a symbol—Stalin was determined that the city named after him would not fall to the Germans, and Hitler became obsessed with the goal. After the Germans reduced most of the city to rubble, they and the Soviets fought desperately in street-to-street fighting that took a terrible toll on both sides. By November, the Germans held almost the entire city, a success won at the price of having exposed themselves along a dangerously overextended line. The Soviets, who had been steadily building up their forces, counterattacked, and on November 23 they surrounded the city and trapped the entire German Sixth Army as well as a Panzer corps. Hitler refused irrationally to permit a withdrawal—as the situation worsened and the cruel Russian winter set in, he ordered his troops to fight to the last man. Nevertheless, the remaining soldiers of the Sixth Army surrendered on February 2, 1943, the Germans having lost more than 300,000 men. Thereafter, the Germans would be on the defensive in the East. A major turning point in the war had been reached at Stalingrad.

Faced with a significant inferiority in manpower, the Germans were now forced to adopt a defensive posture that involved carefully planned withdrawals at key points along the Russian front. In July, Hitler approved an attempt to eliminate a Russian bulge that extended into the German line at Kursk. Marshal Zhukov, whose intelligence agents learned of the German plans, prepared a defensive position. In the Battle of the Kursk

Stalingrad during the raging battle, November 1942.

Salient, July 5–12, the Russians outnumbered the Germans in all areas: 1,300,000 to 900,000 men, 3300 tanks to 2700, and 20,000 artillery pieces to 10,000. After a week of exceptionally heavy German losses, Hitler ordered an end to the attack. The Germans reeled under heavy counterattacks that fall, and the Soviets began pushing the enemy westward.

Japan on the Defensive

The Japanese position in the Pacific began to weaken in the summer of 1942, when American forces struck two major blows. On May 4–8, U.S. carriers stopped the Japanese advance toward New Guinea in the Battle of the Coral Sea, an engagement fought by aircraft from ships that never made visual contact with each other. Then, in June 1942, the U.S. Navy attacked a Japanese force approaching the American base at Midway, northwest of the Hawaiian Islands, winning a decisive victory that passed the initiative to the Allies in the Pacific.

The war in the Pacific became the primary responsibility of the Americans, assisted by Australia and New Zealand. Roosevelt divided military command between General Douglas MacArthur (1880–1964), the commander-in-chief of Allied forces in the Southwest Pacific, and Admiral Chester Nimitz (1885–1966), who commanded the rest of the Pacific theater. Together they began a costly strategy of "island-hopping," in which they retook the Pacific islands in a continual series of bloody invasions. Beginning in 1943 with battles in New Guinea, the Solomon Islands, and the Bismarck Archipelago, in 1944 they pushed northward, taking Saipan in June. In October, the Americans won a major victory at the Battle of Leyte Gulf in the Philippines, which struck a death blow to Japanese naval power.

In 1945, Americans retook the Philippines, and in February Nimitz launched an invasion of Iwo Jima, a small but heavily defended volcanic island some 660 miles from Tokyo. Iwo Jima was taken after five terrible

Map 9.3   The War in Asia

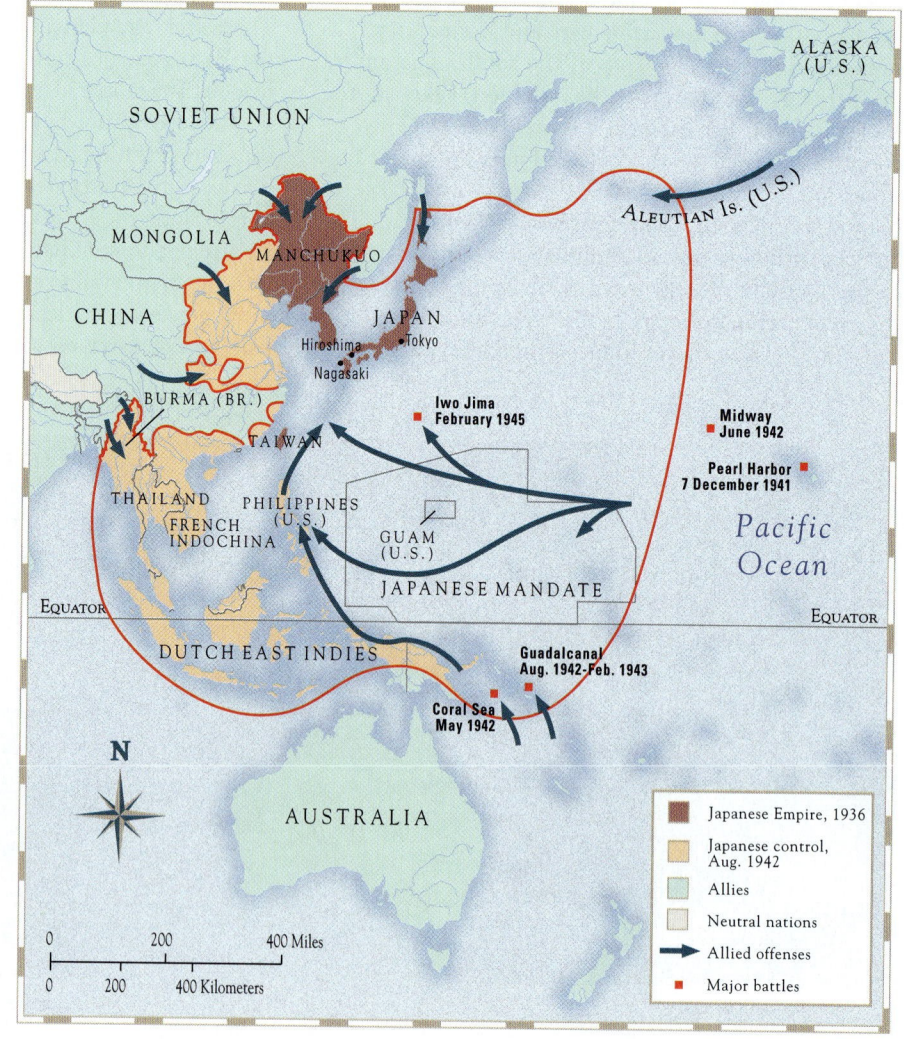

weeks of battle, followed in June by the seizure of Okinawa, which cost 12,000 U.S. lives. In these and other confrontations, the Japanese fought almost to the last man. During the Battle of Leyte Gulf, the Japanese also introduced a new weapon known as *kamikaze*, or "divine wind" ("Kamikaze" was the name for the typhoon that destroyed the Mongol fleet that hoped to invade Japan in the 13th century)—suicide missions in which pilots deliberately smashed their planes into enemy ships. Despite the determination of its military commanders to hold out, Japan's naval power had practically disappeared, its cities had been bombed and gutted by U.S. planes, and its population was on the edge of starvation. By the spring of 1945, Japanese authorities were beginning to probe the Allies for peace terms. The collapse of Japan was imminent.

YALTA, POTSDAM, AND THE DIVISION OF EUROPE

In January 1943, while the campaign in North Africa was still under way, Roosevelt and Churchill held a meeting in Casablanca, Morocco. The two leaders agreed to a cross-channel invasion of France in 1944, and chose Italy as the target for the "soft underbelly" assault in the Mediterranean.

The Fall of Mussolini and the Invasion of Normandy

In June, Eisenhower commanded an Allied invasion of Sicily, and its success led to widespread dissatisfaction among Fascist leaders over Mussolini's conduct of the war. On the evening of July 25, at a meeting of the Fascist Grand Council, a group of dissidents—including Count Ciano, Mussolini's son-in-law—voted no confidence in the Duce. During an audience with King Victor Emmanuel III the next morning, Mussolini was arrested. Marshal Pietro Badoglio (1871–1956) was named prime minister, a position Mussolini had held for more than 20 years. Badoglio opened secret talks with the Allies for an armistice. Hitler immediately sent German troops into Italy and around Rome in anticipation of an Allied assault against the mainland. In September, as the Allies made their first landings on the mainland, Badoglio signed an armistice according to which Italy abandoned the Axis and now fought on the side of the Allies.

Shortly before the armistice, the Führer sent a special mission to rescue Mussolini, who then set up a new Fascist government in northern Italy known as the Italian Social Republic (RSI). The Duce had little autonomy, however, as German military authorities made most important decisions. Over the next year and a half, Italy was cut in two—Mussolini ruled in the region north of Rome, while Badoglio and the king governed the southern portion of the peninsula. In the RSI, hundreds of thousands of armed partisans fought the Germans as well as a bloody civil war with Fascists.

In November, while the Allies pushed their way up the Italian mainland, the foreign ministers of the chief Allied powers gathered in Moscow. They again insisted on the unconditional surrender of Germany and Japan as well as the postwar occupation of Germany. The Moscow meeting was prelude to the conference in Teheran, where Stalin met for the first time with Roosevelt and Churchill. The three leaders agreed on basic aspects of "Operation Overlord," the assault against France planned for the spring of 1944, and Roosevelt announced the appointment of Eisenhower as supreme commander of the Allied forces.

The landings on the Normandy coast on June 6, 1944, were part of the largest sea-to-land operation ever undertaken. Within a week of D-Day, some 300,000 soldiers—three-fourths of them American—and endless supplies had landed and began spreading out through Fortress Europe. On July 20, an unsuccessful attempt on Hitler's life was made by army officers who wanted to make peace. Field Marshal Rommel, implicated in the plot, was forced to commit suicide. Paris was liberated on August 25, and by mid-September, Eisenhower's forces had advanced steadily, pushing the Germans to the borders of France. In December, Hitler ordered a powerful counterattack that struck hard at Allied positions in the Ardennes forest, but at the cost of seriously weakening the Eastern front. This Battle of the Bulge was his last important military offensive.

In January 1945, the millions of Soviet soldiers who were pushing westward overran Hungary, Poland, and Czechoslovakia and entered German territory. American and British forces crossed the Rhine in March, and over the next two months the noose tightened around the Third Reich.

The End of the Second World War

With victory in Europe in sight at last, in February 1945 the three Allied leaders gathered once again, this time at the Black Sea resort of Yalta in the Soviet Union. In a show of unity, they repeated what had now become fundamental Allied policy: unconditional surrender; the occupation, disarmament, and denazification of Germany; and the establishment of the United Nations.

The three great powers were already engaged in a struggle among themselves to win the peace and create spheres of influence in Europe. In this context, the

U.S. soldiers wading toward the beach of Normandy on D-Day, June 6,1944.

controversial Yalta meeting has been viewed by some as a shortsighted capitulation to Soviet demands, but Roosevelt and Churchill had little choice. For one thing, the Red Army had reached eastern Europe, Germany, and the Balkans at the time of the conference. Furthermore, the United States and Britain had already approved a democratic, capitalist government for postwar Italy without consulting the Soviets, and

The Yalta conference, February 1945—Churchill, Roosevelt, and Stalin.

Stalin felt free to act with the same independence in Eastern Europe. Finally, Roosevelt felt he had to make concessions in order to induce the Soviet Union to declare war on Japan. Roosevelt and Churchill therefore agreed in principle to Stalin's demands that portions of eastern Poland be given to Russia and German territory be transferred to the new Polish state. For his part, Stalin agreed to the "Declaration on a Liberated Europe," a purposefully vague statement about free elections and self-determination.

Within two months of the Yalta conference, the war in Europe ended. On April 25, U.S. and Soviet forces linked arms on the Elbe River. Mussolini was captured by Italian partisans and executed on April 28, two days before Hitler committed suicide. Admiral Karl Doenitz (1891–1980) became head of state and officially surrendered to the Allies. Berlin, the capital of the thousand-year Reich, lay in ruins, and Germany surrendered unconditionally on May 7, 1945. Roosevelt, who died on April 12 of a cerebral hemorrhage, did not live to see V-E Day—Victory in Europe.

The war in the Pacific ended after the Big Three had held still one more conference, this time at Potsdam, Germany, in July–August 1945. Of the original leaders, only Stalin remained, for the United States was represented by its new president, Harry S. Truman (1884–1972), and Britain by Clement Attlee (1883–1967), who had replaced Churchill as prime minister. It was at Potsdam that the political divisions between the Soviet Union and its Allies surfaced openly for the first

Map 9.4   Postwar Europe

time, and some scholars have seen in this meeting the origins of the Cold War (see Part VIII, Topic 12). Truman accused Stalin of having gone back on the promises made at Yalta by setting up communist-dominated regimes in eastern Europe.

It was at Potsdam that Truman revealed to the other powers that the United States possessed a powerful new weapon, the atomic bomb. Scientists had been working feverishly on the top secret Manhattan Project since 1942, and the bomb was tested in the New Mexico desert on July 16. That same month, although the Japanese agreed to all the Allied terms of surrender except the deposition of the emperor, Truman approved the use of the atomic bomb against Japan, a much-debated decision. The president himself explained that he and his military advisers believed that the bomb was the only way to avoid massive American casualties during an invasion of Japan. Yet Truman may well have wanted to impress the Soviets with America's new

power. At the same time, he could bring the Pacific war to an end before the Russians declared war on Tokyo and claimed the right to take part in a Pacific peace settlement.

On August 6, the *Enola Gay*, an American B-29 bomber, dropped a five-ton atomic weapon on Hiroshima, reducing the city to rubble and killing a fourth of its inhabitants—almost 80,000 people. Truman warned the Japanese that another nuclear explosion would come if they did not surrender. The Soviets officially entered the war against Japan two days later, and on August 9, the Americans dropped an atomic bomb on Nagasaki. On August 10, Emperor Hirohito ordered his government to prepare to surrender, and declared to his people that they must now endure "the unendurable" pain of defeat. Americans celebrated August 14 as "V-J Day," although the Japanese signed the surrender document officially on September 2 aboard the U.S.S. *Missouri* in Tokyo Bay.

The controversy surrounding the decision to use atomic weapons on civilian populations should be seen in the wider context of the saturation bombing of German and Japanese cities. The Germans had begun bombing London and other British cities in 1940, and by 1942 the British began to respond in kind—that May, hundreds of bombers struck against Cologne, leaving the city in ruins; the next year some 50,000 inhabitants of Hamburg were killed as a result of massive incendiary bomb raids, while as late as February 1945—six months before the dropping of the atomic bombs—British planes killed more than 100,000 civilians in Dresden. In Asia, American B-29 bombers began the large-scale bombing of Japanese cities in late 1944. The atomic bombing of Japan was the last, terrifying, consequence of modern warfare.

Since the Atlantic Charter in 1941, the Allies had demanded unconditional surrender from the Axis powers and the elimination of fascism. In order to ensure that history would not repeat itself, they forced a series of social and political reforms on the defeated enemy states, drafting democratic constitutions and implementing far-reaching changes in the educational systems. They also insisted on purging fascists and militarists from government bureaucracies. As the horrors of the Holocaust became widely known in 1945, the Allies decided that the chief enemy war leaders should be tried and punished for their "crimes against humanity." The Nuremberg Military Tribunal was the most famous of these trials. Among the most prominent fascist leaders, some committed suicide, while others were executed or given long prison terms. Hitler and Mussolini escaped the judgment of the victors, if not of history.

World War II was the most terrible conflict in history. Before it was over, perhaps as many as 50 million people had perished, nations had vanished, and the battles had destroyed property and economic life around the globe.

The great powers fought World War II as a "total war," mobilizing their societies and economies toward the single goal of victory. The war became the focus not only of private industry and farmers, but of ethnic groups, writers, the scientific establishment, the entertainment industry and filmmakers, universities, and every other resource that could be useful to the military effort. As in the First World War, traditional social arrangements were altered and some trends accelerated. Millions of men from all walks of life were drafted or volunteered to serve in the armed forces, while women joined in noncombatant positions or moved to fill assembly line jobs in factories making munitions, tanks, planes, and ships. Rationing, wage and price controls, and government production quotas became the norm. The vast intervention of government in the daily lives of citizens required by this huge effort established the foundations for the welfare state that was to evolve in the postwar period.

Once again, as they had done at the end of the First World War, the winners put their hopes in the idea of an international organization to preserve the peace won with such difficulty. At the Moscow foreign ministers' meeting in October 1943, the Allies had agreed to create a United Nations when the fighting was over. The new body, formally endorsed by 50 sovereign states in July 1945, took the place of Woodrow Wilson's old League of Nations, which had proven unable to prevent aggression in the years between the wars. But although the nuclear superpowers, not the United Nations, would dominate world affairs over the next half-century, Europe was to remember the harsh lessons of the past as it reshaped its future.

Questions for Further Study

1. What were the principles of modern warfare embodied in Blitzkrieg?

2. Can the Holocaust be explained historically? What in your opinion is the explanation?

3. What were the principal contributions of the United States to the outcome of the war? Of the Soviet Union?

4. What factors were behind the expansionist policies of the Japanese?

5. Was the use of the atomic bomb necessary and/or justified?

Suggestions for Further Reading

Ambrose, Stephen. *Eisenhower: The Soldier.* London, 1984.

Boyle, John H. *China and Japan at War, 1937–1945.* Stanford, CA, 1972.

Calvocoressi, Peter, and G. Wint. *Total War.* Harmondsworth, England, 1972.

Costello, John. *Love, Sex and War: Changing Values, 1939–1945.* London, 1985.

Dower, John. *War Without Mercy: Race and Power in the Pacific War.* New York, 1986.

Dziewanowski, Michael K. *War at Any Price: World War II in Europe.* Englewood Cliffs, NJ, 1987.

Erickson, John. *Stalin's War with Germany,* 2 vols. London, 1973–1985.

Gilbert, Martin. *The Holocaust: The History of the Jews of Europe During the Second World War.* New York, 1985.

Harrison, Tom. *Living Through the Blitz.* London, 1985.

Hilberg, Raul. *The Destruction of the European Jews,* rev. ed. New York, 1985.

Lewin, Ronald. *Hitler's Mistakes.* New York, 1986.

Loth, Wilfred. *The Division of the World, 1941–1955.* New York, 1988.

Marrus, Michael. *The Holocaust in History.* New York, 1987.

Milward, Alan S. *War, Economy and Society, 1939–1945.* London, 1977.

Rupp, Leila J. *Mobilizing Women for War: German and American Propaganda, 1939–1945.* Princeton, NJ, 1978.

Weinberg, Gerhard. *A World at Arms: A Global History of World War II.* New York 1994.

Topic 10

THE END OF EMPIRE: DECOLONIZATION AND THE THIRD WORLD

orld War II wrought major transformations around the globe, especially in regions that had been held in the grip of European domination. Nationalist movements for independence had begun to develop in some of the European colonies of Africa and Asia as early as the beginning of the 20th century. With the disruption of the war, and the resulting military and financial weakness of the great powers, the European grip over their colonial possessions was loosened. Political independence for colonial peoples was the result not only of external forces, but of struggles for freedom. World War II had been waged in the cause of freedom from oppression and by 1945 Britain's new Labour government saw imperial domination as neither acceptable nor feasible. Involved in repairing the ravages of war and building a welfare state at home, it was not eager to invest resources in maintaining colonial possessions. India and Pakistan, the chief British colonies in Asia, became independent in 1947. Subsequent Conservative governments continued the process of decolonization, and most of Britain's West African territories were self-governing by 1960. In East Africa, however, resistance by white residents led to protracted negotiations. African rule was not achieved there until the mid-1970s. The major exception was the white minority government of South Africa, which declared its own independence and resisted both internal and international efforts to liberalize rule there.

Postwar French leaders were less willing to give up their empire. Bitter fighting between French troops and nationalist guerrillas continued in Indochina until 1954, and in Algeria, France's principal North African colony, until 1962. In both cases the French finally negotiated a withdrawal. The struggle over Algeria deeply split public opinion in France itself and produced considerable political upheaval.

The withdrawal of the European powers from the Middle East was accompanied by the founding of a new nation there, Israel. In 1947, the United Nations voted to divide Palestine (at the time a British mandate) into an Arab and a Jewish state. The subsequent history of the region has been dominated by fighting between Israel and its Arab neighbors, together with feuding among the Arab states themselves. The volatile situation was further complicated by the conflicting interests of the two superpowers—the United States and the Soviet Union—concerned to preserve their access to a region that contains about half of the world's oil supplies.

Elsewhere in Asia and Africa, former rulers struggled to maintain control. After several years of bloody fighting, the Dutch finally recognized Indonesia's independence in 1949. Alarmed by a series of riots in 1959, Belgium suddenly withdrew from the Congo, leaving a vacuum that plunged the region into a state of confusion threatening Western economic interests there. In spite of substantial guerrilla campaigning, the Portuguese colonies of southern Africa won their independence only in the mid-1970s, when Portugal's authoritarian rule at home was replaced by democratic government.

By the late 20th century, European colonial holdings were reduced to a handful of small territories. One of the first indicators of autonomous politics among developing countries came when a group of nations describing themselves as "nonaligned"—uncommitted, that is, to alliance with either the United States or the Soviet Union—joined together in a loose association. Their aim was to establish a basis for economic assistance on the part of the superpowers and other rich Western countries for the poorer countries of the world, many of which were former colonies.

The problems in providing European and U.S. aid to developing countries were formidable, and the results were mixed. Furthermore, the collapse of Communist regimes in Eastern Europe in the winter of 1989–1990, and the subsequent Western efforts to help economic reconstruction there, threatened to divert resources from other regions of the globe. Nevertheless, by the 1990s it was clearly in the interests of both the affluent and the poorer countries throughout the world to work together in raising living standards and creating stable economies.

THE LEGACY OF EMPIRE: COLONIES IN A CHANGING WORLD

The dismantlement of the European colonial empires in Asia and Africa was hastened by World War II, but long before the war, effective nationalist movements were developing in a number of countries.

Gandhi and Indian Nationalism

The Indian National Congress party, founded in the late 19th century (see Part VII, Topic 18), was led by Mohandas Gandhi (1869–1948), whose policy of nonviolent civil disobedience became an inspiration to liberation movements throughout the world. Born into a wealthy Hindu family, Gandhi studied law in London. He went to South Africa to practice, and discovered brutal discrimination there against Indian laborers who had been imported by the British. In seeking to devise a strategy that would enable weak victims to overcome their oppressors, he organized peaceful protest marches, and nonviolent resistance to police actions.

In 1915 Gandhi returned to India, where his emphasis on the spiritual values of nonviolence exerted a profound influence on sophisticated nationalist leaders and, more importantly, on the Hindu rural masses. His own austere lifestyle (he was known as the *Mahatma*, or saintly one) was combined with the organization of mass demonstrations, at which thousands of peaceful protestors surrounded government offices, or lay down on railway lines. Gandhi himself was frequently arrested, but time after time public indignation, exacerbated by the Mahatma's hunger strikes, forced the authorities to release him.

In 1935, as a result of the demonstrations, the British introduced a new constitution which extended the right to vote to 35 million people, and which provided a limited measure of Indian participation in government. Although Gandhi favored trying out the new system of government, more radical leaders, anxious to obtain complete independence, pressed for continued opposition to Britain. With the onset of World War II, and the refusal of the nationalists to support the British cause, Gandhi and others were arrested. In 1939, India found itself under British military rule and at war with the Axis through no choice of its own.

Although lacking a charismatic leader of the stature of Gandhi, nationalist movements elsewhere in Asia began to agitate for independence. In Indochina one of the chief organizers of the struggle against the French was Nguyen That Thanh (1890–1969), better known as "Ho Chi Minh," the name (meaning "He who enlightens") which he took in 1940. Like Gandhi,

Gandhi leading a protest march in 1930.

he was to play a crucial role in his country's liberation after the war. In response to popular demonstrations and rioting, the French introduced some reform measures, but made it clear that they intended to retain power. The Dutch authorities in their colony of Indonesia similarly tried to discourage nationalist uprisings, but their arrest of popular leaders only led to increased agitation.

Africa Between the Wars

By contrast with their limited concessions to nationalist movements in Asia, the colonial powers in Africa showed few signs of relinquishing their grip. At the same time, however the capital investment that had marked the early years of the 20th century, most of which went to regions north of the Sahara, had almost completely faded. Europeans seeking prosperity abroad after World War I continued to make for North America rather than the African colonies.

In the face of increasing political neglect and economic decline, Africans in many parts of the continent began to form nationalist organizations to achieve independence. One of the first leaders to emerge in North Africa was Habib Bourguiba, one of the founders in 1934 of a liberation party seeking independence for the French Protectorate of Tunisia. Although the authorities imprisoned Bourguiba and banned his organization, his campaigning led to Tunisia's independence after World War II.

In the European colonies of West Africa, increasing numbers of Africans were frustrated by their continued exclusion from political participation in spite of their Western-style educations. In 1918, the West African National Congress was formed to fight for the creation of national parliaments in the British-held territories. These new bodies would replace the existing legislative councils, which generally consisted of British civil servants with a handful of African "advisers."

African leaders in the French colonies strove to advance the cause of black African nationalism by demonstrating the richness of the African cultural tradition. Leopold Senghor (1906–1989), who was to

The Vietnamese nationalist leader, Ho Chi Minh.

become Senegal's first president in 1960, used both poetry and prose to expound the idea of *negritude,* a version of socialism which incorporates black African values.

The efforts of Senghor and other African intellectuals to promote the intrinsic importance of black African culture were reinforced by the development of similar ideas in the United States and the West Indies. The American William E. B. Du Bois (1868–1963) helped to create the National Association for the Advancement of Colored People (NAACP) (1909). His advocacy of Pan-Africanism stressed the common destiny of American and African black people. Marcus Moziah Garvey (1887–1940), born in the British West Indies, founded the Universal Negro Improvement Association (UNIA) in 1914. Two years later, he went to the United States, where he started UNIA branches in Harlem (New York City) and other northern ghettos. Like Du Bois, he preached pride of race and black self-sufficiency, and planned a "Back to Africa" movement to establish a black-governed country in Africa.

Only in South Africa was there no overt sign of a developing nationalist movement. With the discovery of diamonds and gold in the 1870s and 1880s and the growth of mining operations (see Part VII, Topic 18), unskilled African laborers began to live in "shantytowns" on the outskirts of the large industrial centers. By comparison with white workers, the black laborers, ununionized and underpaid, endured unspeakable conditions. Nonetheless, dependent as they were on employment by white mine owners, they were able to accumulate enough money to buy the consumer goods manufactured and sold to them by white South Africans. Thus the industrial development of South Africa created a black urban proletariat politically and economically under the control of the white bourgeoisie.

The white inhabitants, made up of the descendants of British and Dutch settlers (the latter known as Boers), retained complete political control and economic power. By the policy called *apartheid* ("separateness"), legally enacted in 1948, this minority maintained strict racial segregation, with separate and inferior housing, education, and public services for nonwhites. The apparatus of a repressive police state enforced the dominance of the whites. Although those of Asian descent received limited political rights, the black majority remained disenfranchised.

In both Asia and Africa, the end of World War II in 1945 brought renewed demands for national independence. After the years of fighting, most European powers were in no condition to resist for long. Given the importance of reconstruction at home, taxpayers were unwilling to see large amounts of money diverted to support colonial empires. In any case, public opinion, convinced that the war had been fought in the name of freedom and liberation, was less sympathetic to the notion of imperialism. Nor, after the experience of two world wars, could Europeans seriously claim a right to rule on the grounds of moral superiority.

Both of the superpowers encouraged the process of decolonization. The United States favored the granting of self-determination to European colonies, while the Soviet Union (and, after 1948, the People's Republic of China) provided help to revolutionary nationalists in Africa and Asia. Once begun, the drive for independence gained rapid speed: in less than 20 years from the end of the war, almost all the European empires were gone.

THE DISSOLUTION OF THE BRITISH EMPIRE

The Labour government of postwar Britain, faced with the problems of reconstruction, and committed to implementing a massive program of domestic social welfare, was only too eager to avoid further conflict in India. One of the most divisive issues on the subcontinent was the rivalry between Hindus and Muslims, which led to violent rioting. The creation in 1947 of two independent states, a mainly Hindu India and a predominantly Muslim Pakistan, served only to exacerbate tensions. The following year, Gandhi's attempts to conciliate the two sides led to his assassination by a Hindu fanatic who resented his tolerance of Muslims.

British Decolonization in Africa

By 1945, most British politicians realized the necessity of preparing the populations of their colonies for independence. In introducing advances in health care, housing, and sanitation, colonial administrators aimed at social as well as economic improvements. Educational opportunities were also enlarged. As early as 1943, Britain had formulated a scheme to set up universities in the colonies. By contrast, other colonial powers showed less concern for their subjects. Belgian fears that educational advances could be destabilizing led them to invest only in primary and vocational schooling.

The first British colony in Africa to win independence was Ghana, formerly known as the Gold Coast, because of the early coastal trade in gold. In 1945, its American-educated nationalist leader, Kwame Nkrumah (1901–1972), formed a mass political movement with the slogan "Self-Government Now." After a decade of strikes and riots, the British yielded to the inevitable, and Ghana became independent in 1957.

The decolonization of other British West African possessions followed swiftly. Like many former colonies, Nigeria, which achieved independence in 1960, was subsequently beset by rivalries among its many tribal

Map 10.1   Contemporary Asia

Ghanaian wearing a shirt printed with a portrait of Nkrumah, Ghana's president.

groups. Different cultures had evolved in the northern and southern regions of the country. The cultural disparity was compounded by both colonial rule and religious missionaries. In the north the Hausa had been converted to Islam by Mali traders in the 14th century, while the southern and coastal Ibos—Christians and animists—were affected by the fact that their territory contained Nigeria's colonial capital, Lagos. More involved with the British colonial administration, the Ibos were in general better educated and more active in their new country's government. In 1967, tribal hostilities led the Ibos east of the Niger River to secede as the Republic of Biafra. Only in 1970, after bitter fighting, did the central government manage to reincorporate the rebel province into the Nigerian state.

In the British colonies of East Africa, resistance by white settlers complicated the granting of independence. In 1965, as the tide of nationalism swept through Africa, the white government of Southern Rhodesia refused to grant black majority rule, and illegally issued a "unilateral declaration of independence" from British control. Only in 1980, after years of conflict, international pressure, and eventually negotiation, did the country become legally independent, under the name Zimbabwe.

In Kenya, the final years of British rule were marked by the rise of the Mau Mau, a secret society made up of members of the dominant Kikuyu tribe. The aim of the Mau Mau was to drive out the British and all other white settlers, and set up an independent Kenya. After more than a decade of terrorist activity, the movement's aims were undermined by peaceful acquisition of independence. In 1960 Kenya became self-governing, under the leadership of Jomo Kenyatta (1893?–1978).

The Commonwealth

As Britain's possessions obtained their independence, the vast majority chose to retain a link with their former rulers by joining the Commonwealth of Nations. This free association operates without any constitution or specific treaty. Members are linked by common economic and cultural interests and, more broadly, by a shared heritage that includes the English language; they all recognize the British sovereign as symbolic head of the Commonwealth. Nations involved range in size from India (population 800 million) to the tiny Pacific kingdom of Tonga (population 95,000). Commonwealth prime ministers and leaders meet at regular intervals. Their conferences discuss issues of mutual concern, and sometimes succeed in bringing moral pressure to bear as a means of settling differences.

The most intractable problem facing the Commonwealth was political repression in South Africa. Black resistance to *apartheid* was led by the

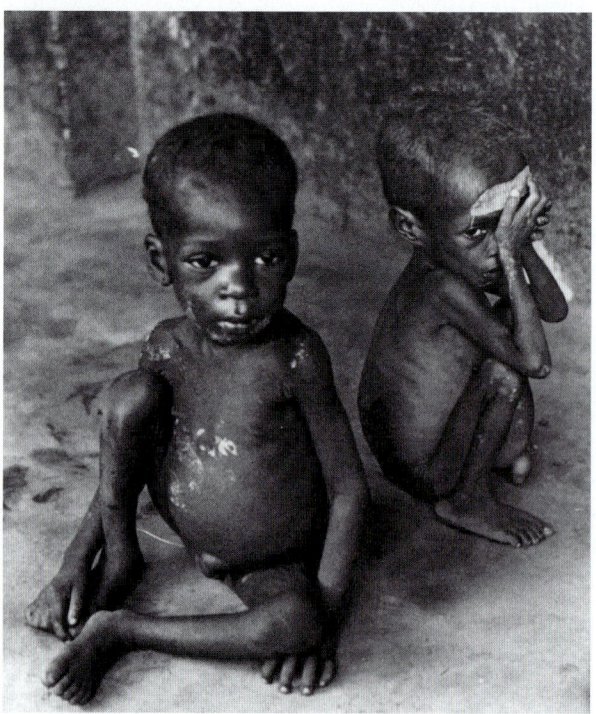

Starving children in Biafra, 1970.

African National Congress (ANC), which was formed in 1912. Throughout the 1950s, the ANC embraced both moderates and radicals, including Marxists, and pursued both political and terrorist tactics, organizing strikes and demonstrations against the government that culminated in the massacres by the police at Sharpeville in 1960. The authorities continued to refuse any form of negotiation with the ANC. They outlawed it and arrested its leader, Nelson Mandela (born 1918).

South Africa withdrew from the Commonwealth in 1961 over criticism of its apartheid policies. Over the years, various commissions of Commonwealth statesmen and resolutions passed at conferences tried to induce the South African government to dismantle its police state and introduce a democratic system of government. A program of economic sanctions was introduced, backed by the European Economic Community and the United States.

Bowing to continual international pressures, the South African government began a fitful dismantling of apartheid. Prime Minister F. W. de Klerk (born 1936), who came to power in 1989, began a new policy of tentative negotiation with the ANC and released Nelson Mandela, leader of the African National Congress, from prison. Economic sanctions by the Commonwealth, the European Community, and the United States seemed to play some part in encouraging the South African government to open the subsequent talks with black leaders. Tribal and racial violence persisted, however, allowing the authorities to maintain their authoritarian controls. Nevertheless, by 1991 most of the laws sustaining apartheid had been repealed, and in April 1994 Mandela was elected president of South Africa.

Last Vestiges of Empire

By the early 1980s, little remained of the British Empire except a few scattered possessions, and nostalgic memories. In 1982, one of these last British holdings, the Falkland Islands in the South Atlantic, served to demonstrate the continuing allure of British imperial power. At the same time the Falkland crisis illustrated the use by the Argentine regime of nationalism and expansionism as a means of bolstering its unpopular dictatorship—a practice not uncommon in the Third World.

When Argentina's military government invaded and conquered the territory (it lies about 500 miles off the Argentine coast), renaming the islands the Malvinas, Conservative Prime Minister Margaret Thatcher sent British troops to drive out the Argentine forces and retake them. Her success in reasserting British rule over the barren, sparsely populated islands won her government massive popular approval. Her op-

ponents claimed that the Falklands War was a cynical diversion, to distract public opinion from problems at home. At all events, the mood of patriotism the war stirred up, enthusiastically endorsed by the press, was in the best—or worst—19th-century tradition.

By the early 1990s, the last British holding of any importance was Hong Kong, a Crown Colony on the South China coast. Hong Kong had been acquired during the 19th century, on terms which foresaw its return to Chinese rule in 1997. A major financial center, and one of the world's busiest ports, Hong Kong is a free trade area, while relying heavily on China for water and food supplies. In 1984 Britain agreed to honor the original agreement and hand the territory over to China in 1997, on condition that it would remain capitalist for 50 years and have a high degree of autonomy. In 1988, the first draft of the Chinese Basic Law for Hong Kong was made public; it suggested that China felt free to interpret "autonomy" as it saw fit. The early 1990s saw increasing waves of business and professional people leaving the colony for Australia, Canada, and the United States. Meanwhile the British government wrestled with the problems, moral as well as practical, involved in denying subjects of Hong Kong (who were technically British) admission to Britain. At midnight on June 30, 1997, Hong Kong returned to China and HMS *Britannia* sailed out of its harbor carrying on board its last British governor, Chris Patten.

THE FRENCH IN INDOCHINA AND AFRICA: THE AGONY OF WITHDRAWAL

Like the British government, postwar French leaders were forced to adjust their imperial ambitions in the light of the calamitous state of the economy. In the hope of maintaining some measure of control over their colonies, in 1946 France created a federation known as the French Union. Some of its members, however, successfully demanded their independence: Syria in 1946, Morocco and Tunisia in 1956. By 1958 the Union had become the French Community, a loose alliance of France itself, its few remaining possessions, and those African nations which formed French Equatorial and West Africa.

Yet in two places—Indochina and Algeria— French pride in imperial rule, coupled with a desire to efface memories of their disastrous defeat by the Germans in 1940, led to prolonged and bitter conflict. Both former colonies obtained their independence only after struggles that were fought not just on the field but in French public opinion.

Sgnificant Dates

Decolonization After World War II

1946	France creates French Union
1947	Partition of India and Pakistan
1948	UN votes to divide Palestine into Jewish and Arab states
1949	Indonesia becomes independent
1954	French withdraw from Vietnam
1955	First conference of nonaligned nations at Bandung
1956	Tunisia becomes independent
1957	Ghana first West African state to become independent
1960	Nigeria and Kenya become independent
1961	South Africa withdraws from Commonwealth
1965	Rhodesia declares unilateral independence
1967	Secession of Biafra
1975	United States withdraws from Vietnam
1978	Camp David accords
1982	Falklands War
1987	Palestinian Intifada begins
1991	Gulf War
1994	Mandela elected president of South Africa
1997	Hong Kong returned to China

The Battle for Indochina

French suppression of independence movements in Vietnam, Laos, and Cambodia was encouraged by the United States, fearful of the spread of communist regimes in Southeast Asia. During World War II, Ho Chi Minh, the founder of the Vietnamese Communist party, had led the resistance to Japanese occupying forces. In 1945 he declared his country a republic, only to see it reclaimed by the French the following year. From 1946 to 1954 the French waged an increasingly bloody and hopeless war against Ho Chi Minh's Vietminh guerrilla forces whose activities were aided by the support they received from the peasantry. The increasing casualties provoked growing protests at home. At the Battle of Dien Bien Phu in 1954, the French Army, besieged for 55 days, lost 15,000 troops to the Vietminh.

Later the same year, at an international conference convened in Geneva, the French formally withdrew from Vietnam. It was agreed to divide Vietnam on a temporary basis: the Vietminh were to take the north, while Vietnamese supporters of the French were to move to the south. Within two years free elections would be held, and the country reunited. The United States refused to sign the Geneva accords, and over the next few years discouraged any attempt at reunification, creating a South Vietnamese state with its own government. The claim that this "independent" state was under attack by equally "independent" North Vietnam served to justify increasing American intervention, leading to the Vietnam War. Only in 1975 did the last U.S. troops leave Saigon, and the following year a unified republic was proclaimed.

Khrushchev, Mao Tse-Tung, and Ho Chi Minh, 1959.

Map 10.2   Independent Africa

The French Settlers and Algeria

With the rest of their former empire melting away, the French determination to hold on to their most important North African colony, Algeria, became increasingly grim. Nor was the issue only one of French national pride. The longstanding community of French residents in Algeria, faced with the possibility of losing their rights and property, became more vocal in urging the government to maintain French rule. Meanwhile, under the impact of growing terrorist and guerrilla attacks, French troops and their commanders resorted to violent countermeasures.

Back home in France, as governments fell over the "Algerian question," intellectuals and socialists furiously protested army brutalities, and called for France to leave Algeria to the Algerians. By 1958, tension between army officers and the indecisive authorities was so high that a group of soldiers staged an insurgency and seized control of Algeria. Both government and rebels turned in desperation to Charles de Gaulle (see Part VIII, Topics 9 and 11). The French National Assembly invested him with extraordinary powers as president for a period of six months (in fact he remained France's leader for ten years).

Although the insurgents believed that the former general would be sympathetic to their revolt, de Gaulle moved quietly to dissolve the rebellion, and began to promote the cause of Algerian self-determination. In January 1961, a referendum in its favor was approved by some 75 percent of French voters. Those army elements most implacably opposed to Algerian independence went undercover in the Secret Army Organization (OAS), and staged a series of terrorist attacks both in Algeria and in France itself. By 1962, however, de Gaulle's firmness put an end to the OAS, and Algeria was declared independent.

ISRAEL AND THE MIDDLE EAST

The Arab states of North Africa and the Middle East, many of which achieved independence after World War II, demonstrated a wide range of political perspectives and systems of government. Yet one characteristic united virtually all of them: implacable opposition to the founding and continued existence of the state of Israel.

The Founding of Israel

The Zionist movement was founded in the 19th century (see Part VII, Topic 16), and grew rapidly after World War I. In the 1930s, increasing numbers of European Jews sought to escape the horrors of persecution by emigrating to Palestine, where they swelled the population of the *Yishuv,* as the Jewish community was called, to almost half a million—a third of the overall population of Palestine. The British, under whose rule the League of Nations had placed Palestine, resisted the

settlement of Jewish immigrants there, as did the surrounding Arab nations. After World War II, mounting violence, and terrorist attacks by both Arabs and Jewish settlers, led in 1947 to a United Nations decision to divide Palestine into separate Jewish and Arab states of roughly the same size. Later that year, the British withdrew. Against a mounting swell of Arab hostility, in May 1948 the Jewish settlers proclaimed the existence of the State of Israel. The new nation's first task was to beat off an attack mounted by the surrounding Arab countries—Egypt, Iraq, Jordan, Lebanon, and Syria—which had refused to accept the United Nations decision. The Israelis' successful campaign, which left them in control of most of Palestine, ensured the survival of their state. At the same time, however, it created the problem which embittered future Arab-Israeli relations and lay at the heart of the unrest in the Middle East: the fate of the Arab refugees displaced by Israel's victory.

Refugee settlements were established, under United Nations administration, in southern Lebanon, on the West Bank of the river Jordan, and in the Gaza Strip. Over the following decades these camps continued to pose political and social problems, while also proving to be the breeding ground for Palestinian guerrilla and terrorist groups. Tension rose further when, in the Six-Day War of 1967, Israel won control of the West Bank and Gaza Strip territories, and thus assumed direct administration of the refugee settlements. In December 1987, frustrated by the lack of progress on the issue of Palestinian independence, and angered by Israeli plans for development on the West Bank territory, Palestinian Arabs launched an uprising, known as the *Intifada,* which won their case considerable attention in Europe and the United States.

Israeli soldiers in the Negev Desert, 1948.

The Camp David peace accord: Israeli Prime Minister Menachem Begin, Egyptian President Anwar Sadat, and U.S. President Jimmy Carter.

Israel and Her Neighbors

The general pattern of unremitting hostility toward Israel on the part of her Arab neighbors, exemplified by another Arab-Israeli war in 1972, was broken in 1977, when the Egyptian president, Anwar Sadat (1918–1981), traveled to Israel and subsequently succeeded, with the help of U.S. President Jimmy Carter, in negotiating an Egyptian-Israeli peace treaty; the agreement, signed in 1978, became known as the Camp David Accords. Apart from a brief reduction of tension, and the return to Egypt of some of the territory captured in 1967, the agreement did little to produce any lasting improvement in Middle East affairs.

Relations with Lebanon, Israel's neighbor to the north, were further complicated by the fact that Palestinian guerrilla groups, notably the Palestinian Liberation Organization (PLO), were using the country as a base. In 1982, Israeli forces invaded southern Lebanon and succeeded in driving the guerrillas out. The result, however, was to produce even greater conflict in Lebanon, a country already racked by religious and political civil war. Multinational attempts at peace-keeping operations, including the sending of French, Italian, and Syrian troops, as well as U.S. Marines, proved fruitless; the international forces withdrew in 1984, and most of the Israeli troops were gone by 1985.

With almost 50 years behind it, Israel's future remained overshadowed by two apparently irresolvable issues: the refusal of most Arabs to recognize the country's right to exist, and Israel's own refusal, on security grounds, to surrender territory won in 1967. In 1988, Yasir Arafat (born 1929), the leader of the PLO, declared that his organization accepted the United Nations resolutions recognizing the legitimacy of Israel; no other Arab leaders followed, and the Israelis dismissed the declaration as a propaganda move. As for territorial concessions, in the late 1980s Israel began moving in the reverse direction, by extending settlements into the West Bank area. With the liberalization of the Soviet Union in the late 1980s, and the revolutions of 1989 in Eastern Europe, Arab spokesmen began to voice fears that waves of Russian and other Jewish immigrants would prove permanent occupants for these new settlements.

Israel's problems were compounded by domestic political divisions. In the elections of 1988, support for the two chief political parties, Labour and Likud, was almost equally divided. The right-wing Likud party managed to put together a government which included support from conservative religious forces, making the prospects of compromise even more remote.

The upheaval of the Gulf War of early 1991, fought under UN auspices to free Kuwait after Iraq had occupied it in August 1990, produced some significant shifts in a situation that had seemed deadlocked for a generation. Hard-line Arab states such as Saudi Arabia and Syria seemed on the verge of following Egypt's earlier lead and recognizing Israel, while Israeli restraint in not responding to Iraq's missile attacks won general approval. Furthermore, American influence in the Middle East was sufficiently strong to allow the United States to play a significant role in working toward a settlement of the Palestinian question. Yet the problem of who would represent the Palestinians in any negotiations leading to such a settlement remained crucial. The PLO had backed Iraq in the conflict, and as a result it lost many of its supporters, not least among the Arab countries that had supported the mission to free Kuwait. In the confusion that followed the Gulf War, however, the Palestinians seemed bereft of any other spokesmen. Secret negotiations in Oslo led to a public reconciliation in 1993 between Labour Prime Minister Yitzhak Rabin and Yasir Arafat, but Rabin's subsequent assassination and the return of the Likud party to power seemed bound to set back progress toward peace.

BELGIUM, THE NETHERLANDS, AND PORTUGAL: END OF EMPIRE

The dismantling of the British and French empires presented a multitude of problems, but most political leaders recognized the irresistible force of nationalism. Other imperial powers were less willing to relinquish their possessions. The Dutch colony of Indonesia was occupied by the Japanese during World War II. At the end of the war, the Indonesian nationalist leader Sukarno (1901–1970) declared his country a republic. When the Dutch tried to reconquer it, they encountered bitter resistance. By 1949, they were forced to withdraw and recognize Indonesia's independence.

Belgium's departure from the Congo was equally violent and even more precipitate. In 1959, demonstrations there in favor of independence developed into violent riots. Within a year the Belgians were gone. The result was chaos. Whereas elsewhere in Africa the British and French had tried to prepare their colonies for independence, the Belgians had limited the education of their subjects, and prevented any African participation in political affairs. The elections held in May 1960, a month before the Belgian withdrawal, were the first ever held in the country. There were no Congolese doctors or army officers, and the only teachers were at the primary school level. The number of African university graduates living in the country totaled 16.

Belgian financial interests assumed that, in the light of such complete inexperience, the citizens of the new Republic of the Congo would leave their old colonial masters in control. Instead the army mutinied; in the growing confusion the mineral-rich province of Katanga broke away from the rest of the country, encouraged to do so by Belgian investors. The Katangese rebellion ended in 1962, but the country returned to stability only in 1965, when Joseph Mobutu (1930–1997; later took the name Mobutu Sese Seko) led an army coup.

Mobutu's rule led to hopes for reform, which were at first fulfilled. The mining production of minerals increased, and the educational system improved. In 1971 Mobutu changed the country's name to Zaire, one of the names for the Congo River, as a symbol of the new spirit of "Africanness." Yet general poverty remained widespread; in 1988, the per capita annual income was $180, 10 percent of that in 1960, and the eighth lowest in the world—in spite of Zaire's considerable natural resources. Meanwhile, the ruling class became notorious for its corruption, and Mobutu himself amassed a fortune estimated at between $3 and $5 billion. The country's economic survival was assured only by massive support from Europe, the United States, and international financial agencies, anxious not to lose access to valuable mineral resources. Only in 1997 was Mobutu finally driven from power by an army led by one of his longtime opponents, Laurent Kabila. Mobutu himself, abandoned by his former Western protectors, died shortly after in exile.

No European country held on to its colonies longer than Portugal. Like the Belgians, the Portuguese exploited their natural assets, while doing nothing to provide lasting political or economic stability. Only a political revolution at home, which ended 40 years of dictatorship, finally brought independence to Portugal's African colonies—Guinea-Bissau in 1974, and Angola and Mozambique in 1975. The lack of any preparation for nationhood led to bitter civil war in the latter two, exacerbated by interference by South Africa.

EUROPE AND THE THIRD WORLD

With the end of European colonial power, many of the new nations in the Third World (the poorer, developing countries of Africa and Asia) faced the task of building politically viable systems against a background of economic instability and social injustice. In response to this need for assistance, Western governments created a number of international agencies whose task was to help developing nations. The International Monetary Fund (IMF), an organization affiliated with the United Nations, began operations in 1947. Led by the "Group of Ten" (Britain, France, West Germany, Italy, Belgium, the Netherlands, Sweden, Japan, Canada, and the United States), its purpose was to provide international credit and stabilize exchange rates. The World Bank, a specialized agency of the United Nations, was established to perform similar functions.

The results of massive loans by richer, industrialized Western nations to the Third World were mixed. The steep rise in oil prices after 1973 prompted heavy borrowing. By the early 1980s, Third World debts amounted to over $400 billion. When rising interest rates combined with inflation to produce a general worldwide recession, many countries found themselves unable to repay even the interest on their loans, let alone the principal. The first government temporarily to suspend payments was Mexico, and others soon followed. Banks and international agencies were forced to renegotiate loans, and impose tough (and often highly unpopular) conditions before extending further credit. The economic hardship these measures created proved dangerously destabilizing in many Third World coun-

Leaders of the nonaligned movement: Egyptian President Gamal Abdel Nasser, Indian Prime Minister Jawaharlal Nehru, and Yugoslav President Josip Broz Tito (1956).

tries. Their difficulties increased in the late 1980s and early 1990s, when the newly democratic countries of Eastern Europe attracted Western capital and investment away from Africa, Asia, and Latin America.

Under the threat of serious global economic crisis, a number of international movements developed. The major Western nations began in the 1970s to hold regular meetings on financial and trade problems. The intention was to coordinate policy on issues such as interest rates and export regulations. Differences between the group's members prevented the agreement on a common policy of economic assistance to developing countries, however, and international development remained largely controlled by banks and private corporations.

The Nonaligned Movement

In the 1950s and 1960s, in response to what they regarded as the inadequate response of Western governments, Third World nations created their own organizations. In 1955, at a conference in Bandung, Indonesia, leaders of countries claiming to belong neither to the Western nor the Soviet bloc met to proclaim their independence. Among the governments represented were those of Egypt, Yugoslavia (Tito had broken with Moscow), and India. The group met intermittently over the following years. In 1960, the Organization of Petroleum Exporting Countries (OPEC) was formed. A more formal alliance, the "Group of 77," was born in 1964, as the result of the United Nations Conference on Trade and Development (UNCTAD), held at Geneva. The organization, which eventually acquired over 100 members, represented the interests of nonaligned countries. When oil prices rose steeply in 1973 as a result of an OPEC agreement, a special session of the United Nations General Assembly was held at which Third World countries, co-

ordinated by the Group of 77, succeeded in passing two resolutions. The first called for a New International Economic Order (NIEO), whereby all nations would be equal; the second called for the transfer of Western technology to poorer countries, and the end of Western exploitation.

In further meetings held in the 1970s and 1980s, the economic imbalance between the prosperous Northern Hemisphere and poorer Southern countries became the subject of intense discussion. A few actual decisions were made: by the Lome Convention of 1975, 46 former European colonies could export their products to the European Community free of tariffs. On the whole, however, prosperous Western nations were unwilling to surrender the advantages of cheap labor and natural resources provided by Third World countries, or to share their own wealth.

At the end of World War II, European domination of world affairs seemed over. Quite apart from the moral responsibility for two global conflicts, the European nations had lost the economic capacity to maintain their prewar power. Many of them—Germany, Italy, France—were faced with rebuilding workable political systems. All, even the most stubborn, eventually withdrew from their imperial possessions.

For most of the new nations born in Africa, the Middle East, and Asia, the euphoria of independence was followed by the grinding problems of political and economic reality. Many of them had been deliberately left unprepared for self-government. For all the talk, furthermore, there was little concerted economic assistance from their former rulers. Relations between the richer countries and the Third World were further complicated by the growing power of the big multinational corporations, which often moved into developing countries as Western governments moved out. The multinationals frequently operated on financial assets greater than the national budgets of the countries in which they set up factories; they exploited natural and labor resources, while being concerned almost exclusively with profit. Not surprisingly their activities drew considerable resentment.

For the Europeans themselves, however, the loss of empire provided the chance to concentrate on rebuilding at home. The economic chaos of the immediate postwar years gave way to an economic rebirth that was slowed only by the oil crisis of the 1970s. By the 1990s, political tensions were lowered by the collapse of Communist regimes in Eastern Europe, and economic expectations raised by the prospect of vast new markets developing there. With its emergence as an economic power potentially as great as the United States or Japan, Europe was in a position to provide vitally needed aid to its former colonies.

Questions for Further Study

1. What part did the United States and the Soviet Union play in the process of decolonization?

2. How did the European powers differ in their handling of independence movements? How far were they motivated by political factors, and how far by economic ones?

3. To what extent have international organizations—the UN, the World Bank, OPEC, the Nonaligned Movement—been able to provide help to developing nations? What are the future prospects?

Suggestions for Further Reading

Adu Boahen, A. *African Perspectives on Colonialism.* Baltimore, MD, 1989.

Davidson, B. *Modern Africa.* London, 1984.

Herring, G. C. *America's Longest War: The United States and Vietnam, 1950–1975.* New York, 1986.

Lockman, Z., and J. Beinin, eds. *Intifada.* Boston, 1989.

Richards, A., and J. Waterbury. *A Political Economy of the Middle East.* Boulder, CO, 1989.

Sampson, A. *Black and Gold.* New York, 1987.

Wolpert, S. *Roots of Confrontation in South Asia.* New York, 1982.

T o p i c   1 1

THE POLITICS OF STABILITY IN WESTERN EUROPE

 aced with the devastation created by World War II, the nations of Western Europe strove to reconstruct political and economic institutions, and—literally—to rebuild cities and industries. With the old guard of European statesmen discredited by the failures of the 1930s, many of the political and financial leaders who rose to power represented a new generation.

The task of reconstruction was complicated in many countries by the need to reject the past as decisively as possible. In Germany, Italy, and Vichy France, an entire ruling class had to be replaced and, in some cases, tried for its complicity in Fascist and Nazi crimes. New, or in some cases renewed, political parties found themselves in unlikely coalitions: in Belgium, France, and Italy the first postwar governments included Communists, Socialists, and liberal Christian Democrats. In Britain, despite the personal popularity of Winston Churchill, his Conservatives lost decisively to the Labour party.

On the international scene, growing tensions between the Soviet Union and the United States polarized European loyalties, and the Cold War came to dominate political life. After the Berlin crisis of 1948–1949, Western Europe and the United States formalized their alliance in the North Atlantic Treaty Organization (NATO), signed in 1949. Among the provisions was the stationing of U.S. troops both in West Germany and elsewhere in Western Europe.

In part to build Western Europe's ability to withstand Communist pressures, and in part to make possible its economic recovery, the United States launched the European Recovery Program, generally known as the "Marshall Plan," which operated between 1947 and 1952. This provided massive financial aid to 17 Western European countries.

In Britain, the postwar Labour government established a welfare state (assistance for the needy), expanding social services and nationalizing key industries. Subsequent Conservative governments continued Labour's social policies, and took Britain into the Common Market. After an economic boom in the early 1960s, chronic inflation and strained labor relations undermined British industrial competitiveness, and brought down successive Conservative and Labour governments. When the Conservative leader Margaret Thatcher became prime minister in 1979, she began to dismantle aspects of the welfare state, to check the power of the unions, and to create a free market economy.

The French Fourth Republic, which lasted from 1946 to 1958, was marked by political instability. It was replaced by the strongly presidential Fifth Republic, created by Charles de Gaulle; the former general left retirement to lead his country for the following decade. Conservative in domestic policies, De Gaulle encouraged an independent French line in foreign affairs, which involved loosening ties with the United States; he also negotiated the French withdrawal from Algeria. De Gaulle resigned in 1969. After another decade of conservative government, in 1981 François Mitterand, a Socialist, was elected president. Apart from the period between 1986 and 1988, the Socialists maintained a majority in Parliament throughout the 1980s.

At the end of the war, the Allies divided Germany into four zones of occupation. In 1949 three of these became the German Federal Republic, and the fourth the German Democratic Republic. Berlin, the former capital of Germany, lay in the Soviet zone but was divided between the Soviets and the other Allies. West Germany's postwar boom, the so-called "Economic Miracle," created under the leadership of the Christian Democrat Konrad Adenauer, saw the country become Europe's leading economic and industrial power. Eventual reunification of the two Germanies remained a long-term West German goal. With the collapse of the East German communist regime in 1989, the dream became a reality. Economic union in the summer of 1990 was the first stage in the creation of a newly united Germany, formally proclaimed in October 1990.

Given its lack of natural resources, Italy's postwar reconstruction was as impressive as Germany's. Under a new republican constitution, introduced in 1948, a series of coalition governments (virtually all of them dominated by the Christian Democrats) sought political stability, while private management developed Italian industry along modern lines. Apart from the deep south, living standards vastly improved. As a founding member of the Common Market, Italy benefited from European economic initiatives.

THE NEW GENERATION IN POWER

The reconstruction of postwar Europe began under the most daunting of conditions. Through a continent whose chief cities were scarred by bomb devastation, there streamed millions of refugees: the former occupants of the Nazi concentration camps, people displaced by wartime action, increasing numbers fleeing from Soviet-occupied eastern Europe. Food supplies were woefully inadequate. The destruction of war had created havoc in rail and road transport. Inflation and economic chaos made cigarettes the most stable currency for buying necessities—when goods were available.

Behind the difficulties of day-to-day survival lay other, more general fears. Already by the last year of the war the Grand Alliance was under a strain, and as the Soviet Union moved toward taking over Eastern Europe, the shadows of the coming Cold War began to close in. To make matters worse, the possibility of renewed conflict threatened horrors even greater than those of the recent past. In the new age of the atom bomb a third world war, played out once again on the battlefields of Europe, might well be the end of the Continent.

A decade or so later, much of Western Europe's industry was more productive than ever. In West Germany and Italy, democratic governments replaced the dictatorships of the years between the wars. British, French, and Belgian transport systems were reconstructed. In most West European countries, more people led more prosperous and comfortable lives than ever before.

One of the paths to solving Europe's problems proved to be treating them, in fact, as broad European issues rather than simply national concerns. Beginning in the early 1950s, national leaders began to work toward European collaboration and cooperation, at least in economic matters (see Part VIII, Topic 15). Here we are concerned with the internal affairs of individual European countries.

New Leaders

Each country faced its own particular set of issues, but many shared certain broad trends. Among the most significant of these was a major change of leadership, both in politics and in other aspects of public life—business, the law, education. For most of continental Europe, politicians, judges, administrators were irrevocably tainted by their wartime actions and collaboration. There were practical limitations to the extent to which it was possible totally to remake society. The Nuremberg Trials of 1945–1949 tried to establish as a principle of international law the fact that individuals are responsible for their actions, but the ordinary business of daily life had to continue. Many card-carrying Nazis and Fascists lost their positions, or even their lives, but many others quietly transferred their allegiances. At the same time, inconvenient aspects of recent history were buried or forgotten. Until 1983, French school textbooks made no mention of the Vichy collaborationist government.

With the coming of peace, those who had been active in Resistance movements, or in fighting against the Axis, came forward to play a part in shaping the freedom they had fought to save. Many of this new generation of leaders came from the parties of the left. Communists served in the immediate postwar governments of France, Belgium, and Italy. Socialists reinforced their position in the Scandinavian countries. In Britain, the election of 1945 brought a socialist government to office. Britain's wartime government had been a coalition one, and the Conservative leader, Winston Churchill, was a national hero. Nonetheless prewar Conservative leaders were seen as responsible for not having prevented the outbreak of war, and for having left the country so unprepared.

The result of the perceptible shift to the left was a new emphasis on technical and leadership skills. The last traces of aristocratic power disappeared from political life and the business world. Noble birth did not prevent a career in public life, but it certainly ceased to guarantee one. At least one British politician gave up his hereditary title rather than abandon his seat in the House of Commons. The doings of Europe's aristocracy—marriages in Monaco or Westminster Abbey—retained their glamour and fascination for many, but almost exclusively as a kind of branch of the entertainment industry.

Efforts to remove the old business families proved less successful. After the war, the head of the leading German armaments producer, Alfred Krupp (1907–1967), spent three years in jail for war crimes, but although the company was reorganized, it still retained most of its original holdings. Nonetheless, in the business world as in politics, expertise in engineering

Konrad Adenauer and Charles de Gaulle, 1963.

or economics became more important than family connections.

Thus, as Europe faced the difficult problems involved in reconstruction, leadership passed to an increasingly broad-based and highly qualified "meritocracy." Most of the new generation accepted a more limited role for their own country and for Europe in international affairs. The only European leader who continued to sound the note of national pride was De Gaulle, one of the few survivors of an earlier generation.

THE POLITICS OF RECONSTRUCTION

The immediate task of postwar governments was a double one: to restore democratic institutions and to reconstruct shattered economies. Following Britain's lead, many countries introduced welfare state programs, which aimed at improving the lives of their less affluent citizens.

The Welfare State

Although a few social welfare programs had been launched in the late 19th century, and then expanded

Prefabricated housing under construction in Bedforshire, 1965.

during the Great Depression, the notion of a complete welfare state did not become common until after World War II. In Britain, the Labour government of 1945 to 1951, led by Clement Attlee (1883–1967), passed legislation to provide virtually free medical care to all, and to expand unemployment insurance and educational opportunities. In an attempt to put basic facilities under the control of all citizens, Labour nationalized the steel and mining industries, and the railways.

By the 1950s, most other Western European nations had introduced similar schemes. Subsidies for housing, financial support for child raising, the provision of education beyond the primary level, all improved the opportunities for poorer citizens. Measures such as these, together with increasing government control of industry, enlarged the power of the state. To offset this, many countries set up "worker councils," groups of workers elected to discuss with management various aspects of working conditions.

Political Parties

European political life after the war was characterized by the development of democratic multiparty systems, in which government generally alternated between two main parties. The chief exceptions were Spain and Portugal, where dictatorships established well before World War II remained in place. Most politicians avoided extremes. The horrors of Fascism and Nazism

had completely discredited the radical right. A small neo-Fascist party remained active in Italy, although it was regarded as "outside the constitutional arc" (not constitutionally legitimate) by the other political forces. Otherwise, apart from a few fanatical terrorist groups, extreme right-wing politics was unrepresented in the decades immediately following the war. By the 1980s, an extremist party began to collect some support in France, campaigning principally on the issue of immigration restrictions. All official conservative parties were fully committed to maintaining democratic government, and rarely dismantled welfare legislation introduced by socialist predecessors. The most notable exception to the latter characteristic was Thatcher's government in Britain in the 1980s.

On the left, no respectable communist or socialist movement in Western Europe publicly advocated extreme views in theory, or tried to put them into practice when in power. Communists never achieved control of national governments, but where they won administration of a city or region they proved no more doctrinaire—and no more or less efficient—than their opponents. The socialists who came to power showed the same concern for individual liberties and the democratic process as their conservative rivals. Extreme differences of ideology and opinion still existed, but no political leader posed a radical challenge to the prevailing system, as Hitler, Mussolini, or Stalin had done.

THE UNITED STATES IN EUROPE

The international background against which the process of European renewal began to unfold was dominated by growing tension between the world's two superpowers and former allies—the United States and the Soviet Union. In the last year of the war, while the Allies began to make plans for the future of Europe, Stalin took advantage of the reigning confusion to move Soviet troops into the chief Eastern European countries. By 1947, pro-Soviet regimes were firmly installed in Bulgaria, Czechoslovakia, Hungary, Poland, and Romania. The Baltic states of Estonia, Latvia, and Lithuania remained under Soviet rule, incorporated into the Soviet Union. In 1945, when the Allies had divided Germany into four zones, the most eastern zone came under Russian occupation. Berlin, the former capital of Germany, lay in the Soviet zone but was divided between them and the other Allies.

If Stalin were planning further aggressive expansion, the "Eastern Bloc" he had created would provide an effective base. At the same time he built a psychological division between two Europes, one free and democratic, the other repressed. The "Iron Curtain," a memorable phrase of Winston Churchill's, left both sides in mutual fear and incomprehension. The nations most likely to be affected by Soviet aggression were those of Western Europe, in particular the western zones of Germany. Yet the Allies had disarmed the Germans at the end of the war, and in any case no European state was in a condition to confront Stalin.

The Marshall Plan

This vacuum was filled by the United States. Regimes that seemed under threat from the Soviets received American backing. In some cases U.S. intervention helped to prevent communist takeovers. In 1947, President Harry S. Truman (served 1945–1952) sent a massive amount of American military assistance to Greece, thereby securing the defeat of communist guerrillas and the installation of a parliamentary system. Elsewhere, as in Iran, American support for regimes that were strongly anticommunist but also strongly repressive embarrassed some Western observers, and led the Soviets to accuse the United States of doing its own empire building. The American efforts to "contain" communism in those areas the United States already controlled came to be known as the "Truman Doctrine."

In a similar vein, the United States introduced its European Recovery Program, which operated from 1947 to 1952; the scheme is better known as the Marshall Plan, after its originator, U.S. Secretary of State George C. Marshall (1880–1959). Seventeen European countries, which formed the Organization for European Economic Cooperation, received some

The Brandenburg Gate, dividing East and West Berlin.

Map 11.1 Europe During the Cold War

$13 billion in money and materials, to help their economic recovery.

The plan was clearly intended to combine humanitarian concerns with a strong dose of self-interest. Its provisions undoubtedly gave vital and much-needed aid to war-ravaged Europe, and brought about improvements in the daily lives of countless ordinary citizens. For the Soviets, however, the help represented yet another case of American economic imperialism. It also created the possibility of U.S. control over its allies' politics. In countries such as France and Italy, where communist parties made a strong showing immediately after the war, governments receiving aid were also under American pressure to "control the spread of communism" in their internal politics. In any case, strong economic growth certainly reinforced the capitalist system, and undercut support for the left among voters. On balance, the Marshall Plan not only provided much-needed financial assistance but became an important element in America's politics of stabilization in Western Europe.

The Berlin Crisis

The confrontation between the two superpowers—the "Cold War"—was most direct at the heart of Europe, in Germany. The three allied zones there soon began to function as a single unit, with local and national elections and a unified economy. The Soviet response to the revival of German strength was to blockade access by rail, river, or road to West Berlin, which was completely surrounded by Soviet-controlled territory. The Berlin blockade lasted from late June 1948 to mid-May 1949. During that period, the United States and Britain mounted a massive airlift to provide the West Berliners with food, water, and other essential supplies. The total number of flights amounted to around a quarter of a million, carrying two million tons of goods, at a cost of $224 million.

By the end of the blockade, the Americans had made their point. They would defend the interests of their allies, at whatever price, but would seek to do so without open conflict whenever possible. In May 1949, a separate West German nation, known as the Federal Republic of

One of the flights of the Berlin airlift.

Germany, was established at Bonn, which became its capital. In response the Soviets formalized the existence of their zone of Germany as a separate country, called the German Democratic Republic, with its capital in East Berlin. East Germany hailed the division of the country as irreversible, while West Germany's leaders at first refused even to recognize the existence of East Germany, and maintained the goal of eventual reunification.

The Creation of NATO

Even before the blockade was over, the Western allies had formed an organization specifically directed at the "threat of armed communist attack in Europe or the North Atlantic or Mediterranean area." The nations that joined the North Atlantic Treaty Organization (NATO) in April 1949 were Belgium, Britain, Canada, Denmark, France, the Netherlands, Iceland, Italy, Luxembourg, Norway, Portugal, and the United States. Greece and Turkey became members two years later, West Germany in 1955, and Spain in 1982. The terms of the treaty affirmed that an attack on any one member would be regarded as an attack on all.

Among the provisions of NATO was that American forces would remain in Europe, both in Germany and elsewhere. The popularity of the American presence rose and fell on both sides of the Atlantic as the intensity of the Cold War fluctuated. In the decade following the end of World War II, the United States' "umbrella" protection, by now nuclear, was widely regarded as essential to the continued security of Western Europe. In the 1960s, as new trouble spots developed outside Europe—the Middle East, Vietnam—complaints began to be heard in the United States about the high cost of European security to American taxpayers. At the same time, some European political movements started to agitate for the closing of U.S. military facilities in their countries. In 1966, De Gaulle actually expelled NATO forces from French territory. Throughout the 1980s, the Greek government threatened to close American bases in Greece. With the apparent collapse of the "Soviet Bloc" in the revolutions of 1989, heated debate began to rage about the future role of NATO and of its Soviet equivalent, the Warsaw Pact (see Part VIII, Topic 12).

GREAT BRITAIN: BEYOND THE WELFARE STATE

British politics following World War II was dominated by alternating Labour and Conservative governments. Other forces included a small Liberal party, and a Social Democratic party (founded in 1981). In the early 1980s, these two groups formed an alliance which seemed at first able to challenge Labour and Conservatives, but by the end of the decade, with the Conservatives in power, the Labour party remained the only real alternative.

The first postwar Labour government, following both its socialist principles and the spirit of the times, began the dismantlement of Britain's former imperial possessions and laid the foundations of the welfare state. Conservative governments followed from 1951 to 1964, continued the granting of independence to colonies, and led the country into a period of economic prosperity. Prime Minister Harold Macmillan (served 1957–1963) used the slogan "You've never had it so good" to win the election of 1959.

Macmillan had become prime minister two years earlier, in 1957, following the resignation of his predecessor, Sir Anthony Eden (served 1955–1957). Eden's departure was the result of the Suez crisis of 1956, which clearly illustrated the limits on postwar Britain's freedom to follow an independent course in foreign affairs. When Egypt's President Gamal Abdel Nasser (1918–1970) nationalized the Suez Canal, hitherto under joint Franco-British ownership, Britain and France invaded Egypt to regain possession. Under strong U.S. pressure, and with UN intervention, the occupying forces withdrew, and the canal reopened under Egyptian control. Eden, who had served earlier as Churchill's foreign secretary, was professionally and physically wrecked by the crisis; at its height, his wife later observed, it felt as if the canal itself were flowing through their living room.

By 1964, Britain's economy was facing serious problems. The government's failure to enable industry to compete in international markets, coupled with rising unemployment and chronic inflation, persuaded the electors to turn to Labour. For the next fifteen years each party in turn failed to solve the country's economic difficulties. In 1971, after years of heated controversy and debate, Britain became a member of the Common Market.

The Trade Unions in Britain

Britain's labor unions played a central role in the existence of the Labour party. Their delegates helped in the selection of parliamentary candidates, while their annual meetings were influential in the shaping of party policy, and their money kept the party going. The issue of relations between labor and management was thus far more complicated a matter than simple negotiation. When a Conservative government undertook to resolve an industrial dispute, it was in effect negotiating with its political opponents. A Labour government was equally, if differently, hampered: the unions expected their own party automatically to support their position.

Much of Britain's industrial and social life was paralyzed by more than a decade of union conflicts. In 1972, with factories opening only three days a week, and London in nightly darkness, a Conservative gov-

ernment introduced a bill to limit the unions' powers. The attempt broke down, creating yet further mutual mistrust, and the bill was repealed by a subsequent Labour government.

Once back in office again in 1979, the Conservatives introduced further legislation to make strike action more difficult. By now the public was generally in favor of greater control of the unions. A coal miners' strike in 1984–1985, which openly aimed to defy the legislation, was marked by violence. It was finally broken by a combination of government firmness and public disapproval of the miners' actions.

The Conservatives Under Thatcher

The Conservative leader from 1975 was Margaret Thatcher (born 1925), who served continuously as prime minister from 1979 to the end of 1990. From the beginning she announced an abrupt change of direction: no concessions. In her first year in office, steel, railway, and national health service workers all struck. All their strikes collapsed. The price was massive unemployment and social unrest.

Thatcher's own personal popularity, dimmed by the disastrous state of the economy, received a sudden boost from the Falklands War of 1982 (see Part VIII, Topic 16). In the following year's election, the Conservatives won the largest number of seats any party had gained since 1935. In part, this was due to the extreme program on which Labour had fought the election. Among other pledges, Labour promised to withdraw from the Common Market, abandon Britain's nuclear weapons (a long-standing cause of furious debate in the party), nationalize more industries, and suppress foxhunting. In large measure, however, the Conservatives' success was helped by the intervention of candidates representing the alliance between Liberals and Social Democrats, than at the height of its popularity.

With her huge parliamentary majority, Thatcher pushed forward to rein in the welfare state and develop a free market economy. The unsuccessful coal miners' strike of 1984–1985 served to reinforce her reputation for getting her way. (The letters of one of her nicknames, "Tina," stood for "There Is No Alternative.") Her admirers praised her firmness; her critics pointed to the increasing gulf between the prosperous and the poor, and to the growing violence on the part of the jobless and hopeless in Britain's big cities.

Reelected in 1987, her government began to run into increasing trouble as the economy went into decline again. Thatcher herself, once the Conservatives' biggest asset, came under increasing fire for her uncaring, confrontational attitude. When in 1990 she insisted on pushing through an unpopular reorganization of the local taxation system—the new method became known as the "Poll Tax"—rioting broke out not only in London but in hitherto firmly Conservative provincial regions of the country.

With her leadership of the party increasingly open to challenge, the annual election by Conservative Members of Parliament (MPs) of their leader was held in December 1990. These contests were generally a formality, and Thatcher herself was out of the country at the time of the first ballot, representing Britain at a Paris summit conference. Amid general surprise, she failed to gain the necessary percentage of votes for outright victory, and after a day or so of uncharacteristic hesitation withdrew her candidacy. John Major (born 1943) became the new prime minister and leader of the Conservative party. Thus a handful of Tory Members of Parliament, voting in secret, brought to an end the Thatcher years.

Postwar Britain, in spite of victory, had to face adjustment to a world position far below that of the preceding centuries. Firmly overshadowed by U.S. policy on the international scene, surpassed as a European economic power by Germany and France, and in the mid-1980s by Italy, Britain's own commitment to a European identity remained less than wholehearted. The left wing of the Labour party continued to fight, unsuccessfully after the 1983 debacle, for a promise that Labour would negotiate Britain's withdrawal from the Common Market. Thatcher for her part had remained deeply suspicious of growing European economic interdependence, and firmly opposed to any form of political union. With her replacement by Major, Britain seemed likely to reverse its anti-European stance and move toward a policy of cooperation rather than isolation, although the Conservative party remained deeply divided. With the victory of Tony Blair's New Labour party in 1997, British official attitudes to European unity became far more positive.

FRANCE IN THE FOURTH AND FIFTH REPUBLICS

By contrast with Britain, France's modern political history has been marked by discontinuity. The 19th century saw a constant alternation of republican and monarchical rule. As a result, by the 20th century, French politics became conditioned by the average citizen's distrust of the state and its agencies. Unlike the British, the French tended to defend themselves against collective action, rather than turning to the state for help. At the same time French political culture held abstract ideology in high esteem, seeking logical and rational solutions, rather than the kind of pragmatic compromises favored by the British.

The Fourth Republic

In comparison with its European competitors, by the beginning of World War II French industry was relatively stagnant. Between 1870 and 1940 German gross national income had increased five times, and British three and a half; that of France rose only 80 percent. Reconstruction thus involved not only repairing war damage, but also strengthening the economy as a whole. The architect of the plan to modernize France, Jean Monnet (1888–1979), began a series of five-year schemes to rebuild basic industries and develop exports. The first Monnet Plan covered the period from 1947 to 1952. Even before it went into effect, the government had nationalized key industries, including electricity, gas, rail transportation, and the Renault automobile plants (their former owner was accused of collaboration with the Germans). Economic reform was accompanied by an extensive program of social legislation, including accident and unemployment compensation, medical care, maternity benefits, and family allowances.

The constitutional framework which governed France from 1946 to 1958 was that of the Fourth Republic, already sharply criticized on its introduction in October 1946. Parliament exercised supreme power, and the conflicting interests of various parties and political groups threw up and then destroyed a continual series of prime ministers and cabinets. Unlike Italy, where the apparently endless series of governments concealed a genuine stability, the 20 different cabinets of the Fourth Republic's twelve years were a sign of serious political uncertainty. In Britain the chief political parties represented, in theory at least, clearly distinct points of view, and electors had some idea of what they were voting for. The French political parties often supported different policies in different parts of the country, and even after an election it was not clear which groups would support—and eventually abandon—which leaders.

De Gaulle and the Fifth Republic

By 1958, the combination of political instability and public agitation over the Algerian crisis clearly indicated the need for major reform. Charles de Gaulle, leader of the Free French movement in exile during World War II, had served as president during the transition to the Fourth Republic and retired from active political life in 1953. Yet because he stood as a powerful symbol of French national determination, in June 1958, at the height of the Algerian crisis, he returned as prime minister, with authorization to prepare a new constitution. De Gaulle remained France's leader until 1969, when he resigned on the failure of a referendum to give him further powers for constitutional reform.

By contrast with the Fourth Republic, the Fifth Republic vested strong powers in the president, who became not only the symbol but the instrument of executive authority. The original constitution of the Fifth Republic called for the president to be chosen by an electoral college, but in 1962 De Gaulle successfully campaigned for presidential election by a direct popular vote. Independent of any political party, presidents have exercised a wide range of powers, including the designation of prime ministers, the dissolution of Parliament, and control of French foreign policy. De Gaulle himself claimed, in fact, that "the President elected by the nation is the source and holder of the power of the state."

Already in the early years of the Fifth Republic the multiple parties of the postwar period began to coalesce into two main groups: on the left, communists, socialists, and radicals; on the center-right, Gaullists and various centrist parties, including the UDF (Union for French Democracy) and RPR (Rally for the Republic). In the early 1980s, the FN (National Front) began to attract increasing attention as a party of the extreme right, campaigning mainly on the issue of immigrant workers.

Under De Gaulle, France pursued generally conservative policies at home, while seeking to maintain an independent line in foreign affairs. Growing resentment of U.S. domination led to France's withdrawal from NATO in 1966. Deeper signs of unrest at the president's paternalistic style of government became manifest in the student and worker uprisings of two years later; 1968 was marked, in fact, by student protests throughout much of Europe.

The following year, when De Gaulle resigned, his former prime minister, Georges Pompidou (served 1969–1974, died in office), won election as president. Both Pompidou and his successor Valéry Giscard-D'Estaing (served 1974–1981) continued De Gaulle's conservative financial policies, while failing to prevent rising inflation and unemployment.

Mitterand and the Socialists

In 1981, for the first time the voters turned to a socialist to head the Fifth Republic. With the Communist party in decline, and the parties of the right divided, François Mitterand (served 1981–1995) won election in May 1981 as president. A month later he called a general election in which the Socialist party won a clear majority and the Communists lost half their members of Parliament.

For many in Europe, Mitterand's victory signaled the beginning of a new era for European socialism. His government began, indeed, by introducing generous new social legislation that increased minimum wages, family allowances, and housing subsidies. After a year, however, it was clear that the program had backfired. The French were spending more and more money on imported goods, imports were increasing while exports lagged. As a result, unemployment remained high.

At the end of 1982, despite union and communist protests, the government changed direction. State spending became lowered, wages were frozen, and state and industrial employees dismissed. The austerity program succeeded in lowering inflation and balancing the budget, but it disappointed, and actually hurt, many who had voted socialist.

The general election of 1986, fought two years before Mitterand's term expired, saw the Socialist party hold most of its strength—it lost 5 percent of the support it had won in 1981. On the right, however, the two major parties, the RPR and the UDF, put together a temporary agreement which gave them jointly a majority of seats in Parliament. The RPR leader, Jacques Chirac (born 1932), became prime minister, facing Mitterand with two years of "Cohabitation" with a premier who was a political opponent. The Socialist president maintained his right to control French foreign policy, while the conservative Chirac began to privatize the economy, selling off state-owned enterprises to private investors.

In 1988 Mitterand's term was up. In the presidential election of that year Mitterand stood again, with

Significant Dates

Western Europe After 1945

1947-1952	The Marshall Plan
1948-1949	The Berlin Blockade
1949	Creation of NATO
1951	European Coal and Steel Community formed
1956	The Suez crisis
1958	De Gaulle returns to power
1961	Construction of Berlin Wall
1968	Strikes and student demonstrations
1971	Britain enters Common Market
1979	Thatcher becomes British prime minister
1981	Mitterand elected first Socialist French president
1982	Kohl becomes West German chancellor
1983-1986	Craxi serves as Italian prime minister
1989	Fall of Berlin Wall

Chirac running as his principal opponent. This time the socialist represented stability and the conservative change. The voters chose the former. Chirac lost and resigned as prime minister. As in 1981, Mitterand called a general election, gambling on the electors returning a socialist majority. In the event the socialists won enough seats to be able to form a government, although by no means by as wide a margin as that giving Mitterand the presidency. While political pundits had a field day interpreting the public mood, Mitterand appointed Michel Rocard, a moderate socialist, as prime minister. On both left and right, candidates began to look toward the presidential election of 1995. The two leading candidates were Jacques Chirac and the Socialist Lionel Jospin. On the final ballot, Chirac emerged as the winner, although—to the surprise of many observers—Jospin won more votes in the first round than any other candidate (although not an absolute majority). Two years later, when President Chirac called a snap general election, the socialists astonished most observers by winning, and formed a government with the support of Communist and Green deputies.

WEST GERMANY: REBUILDING THE INDUSTRIAL GIANT

In 1945 Germany lay in ruins, split among its conquerors. Ten years later, the Federal Republic of Germany joined NATO and attained full sovereignty. At the end of 1989, the communist regime in the German Democratic Republic collapsed; a government installed after free elections in March 1990 began negotiations to prepare for reunification in late 1990.

German Economic Recovery

This astonishing reconstruction of a nation that seemed shattered beyond repair was made possible in part by West Germany's rapid financial recovery. By 1960, West German national income had surpassed that of France; in 1964 it overtook that of Britain; by 1973, German and American workers were paid the same. By the late 1980s the only country in the world to exceed West Germany (population 61 million) in total exports was the United States. At the same time as rebuilding industry, creating jobs, and providing housing, the postwar German government found shelter and employment for over 14 million Germans fleeing from or expelled from eastern Europe. All of these achievements were accomplished against a background of relative social peace, broken only by recurrent bursts of extremist terrorism.

The political scene in West Germany provided a firm and generally tranquil foundation for this rebirth. The two main parties, the conservative Christian Democrats and the left-wing Social Democrats, alternated in power, each on occasion forming a coalition with the much smaller liberal Free Democratic party. Politicians resigned or were removed from office generally as the result of personal scandal rather than for political reasons.

Konrad Adenauer

The tone of German public life, serious and responsible, was set by West Germany's first chancellor, Konrad Adenauer (served 1949–1963). No newcomer to political office, Adenauer had served as mayor of Cologne during the Weimar Republic. Having avoided involvement with the Nazis, he was an appropriate choice to provide his country with authoritative leadership. A venerable figure of lofty dignity, he was 73 when he became chancellor. Adenauer did much to repair Franco-German relations by the cooperative relationship he established with De Gaulle.

American aid in the form of the Marshall Plan certainly contributed to the German economic revival, but other important factors were also involved. Management was efficient and the labor force hard-working. Trade unions concentrated on increasing production rather than seeking to improve conditions for their members. The influx of refugees from Eastern Europe provided cheap and plentiful labor, with a strong incentive to improve their conditions by hard work. German Economic Minister Ludwig Erhard (served as West German chancellor 1963–1966) skillfully balanced a free market economy with welfare programs for the workers and government incentives for management. Unlike Britain, France, and Italy, the government nationalized no important services or industries.

In foreign policy, Adenauer maintained close relations with the United States, while beginning to work toward European cooperation. In 1951 the foundations of the Common Market were laid with the establishment of the European Coal and Steel Community (see Part VIII, Topic 15), of which Germany was a member. In the same year Adenauer addressed the painful issue of German responsibility for the Holocaust. Germany signed an agreement with Israel, pledging to make financial reparation over the following twelve years. As for East Germany, and the "German Question," at first Adenauer's government recognized neither East Germany nor the Soviet Union.

By the mid-1950s, West Germany was ready to assume the status of a fully sovereign state. In 1955 it joined NATO, and the following year the Western

Allies declared the occupation formally over. Later in 1955, Adenauer traveled to Moscow to establish diplomatic relations with the Kremlin. In March 1957 West Germany became one of the founding members of the Common Market. Toward the end of Adenauer's chancellorship, in 1961, relations with the Soviet Union grew tense with the construction of the Berlin Wall—built by the East Germans to cut off their citizens from access to the West.

"Ostpolitik"

Under Adenauer's successors West Germany began to try to improve relations with the governments of eastern Europe. The policy of "Ostpolitik"—politics looking east—was the special creation of the socialist Willy Brandt (1913–1992), who served first as foreign minister and then, from 1969 to 1974, as chancellor. Brandt was especially qualified to open up relations with eastern Europe, for as mayor of West Berlin from 1957 to 1966, he had dealt directly with the problems of isolation. In 1972 a treaty was finally signed between the two German states, which established mutual recognition. Brandt's "Ostpolitik" marked a major step in easing East-West relations, and paving the way for eventual reunification. Brandt himself resigned in 1974 as the result of a spy scandal in his administration.

Under the leadership of Helmut Schmidt (born 1918), Brandt's successor as head of the Social Democrats and chancellor from 1974 to 1982, the German economy remained strong. Beginning in the late 1970s, however, the general calm of German life became increasingly shattered by terrorist outbreaks. The revolutionary Red Army Faction claimed responsibility for a rash of bombings of NATO installations and the murder of prominent industrialists. The other social problem that helped to bring down Schmidt's Socialist government and return the Christian Democrats to power in 1982 was that of the *Gastarbeiter* ("guest workers")—the large and increasing number of foreign workers living in West Germany.

Helmut Kohl (born 1930), chancellor since 1982, favored a move to a free market economy. Under continued opposition from employers and unions, both unwilling to change the status quo, most of his initiatives failed, and by the end of the 1980s the German economy had begun to falter. Growth was slow and unemployment relatively high.

Kohl's most visible initiative was his immediate espousing of the cause of German reunification after the events of November 1989. Leading the East German Christian Democrats' campaign in the elections of March 1990, and appearing at packed rallies where he was hailed as a second Bismarck, Kohl helped his East German counterparts to achieve an overwhelming victory. The effects of this on his popularity in his own country were more difficult to assess, depending as they did on the economic consequences of eventual reunification (see Part VIII, Topic 16).

The booming center of West Berlin (1965), a stark contrast with the poverty of East Berlin.

By the early 1990s, then, after nearly half a century of rehabilitation, West Germany moved toward leading a renewed and reunited Germany. While the United States and West Germany's European allies underlined the need for safeguards, the Soviet Union expressed fears of future aggression. Yet the general realization that the choice of reunification was and should be essentially a German one underlined the degree to which 50 years of responsible leadership had changed the defeated country of 1945. For many years it was said that the key to German reunification lay in Moscow. Now, for the first time, it lay in Bonn.

ITALY'S ECONOMIC MIRACLE

With the collapse of Fascism in 1943, Italy faced the choice of either restoring the monarchy or introducing a republican form of government. In June 1946 a referendum decided by a narrow margin to abolish the monarchy, which had collaborated with Mussolini. The republican constitution which went into effect on January 1, 1948, was based on those of other Western democracies, with two chambers of parliament and universal suffrage. Unlike France of the Fifth Republic or the United States, the president had few powers; the prime minister became head of the government.

Party Politics in Italy
Unlike Britain or Germany, Italian political life was made up of a host of parties, most of which were represented in Parliament as a result of a system of proportional representation. Governments depended on the formation of coalitions, which either made up a parliamentary majority, however precarious, or which could count on opposing parties not voting against them. Since virtually all parties, even the small ones, had internal divisions, the making and unmaking of coalition cabinets became an apparently endless process. Between 1950 and 1980, 35 governments held office, some lasting no more than a few weeks.

Yet, by contrast with the confusion of the French Fourth Republic, the Italian economy was strengthened, major social changes such as divorce and abortion were introduced, and the scourge of terrorism was brought under control. By the 1980s Italy was one of the "Club of Seven," one of the seven most wealthy and industrialized nations in the world. Italian automobile manufacturers controlled the largest share of the European market, and Italian fashion and leather goods were popular throughout the world. A founding member of the Common Market, Italy was one of the countries that pressed most enthusiastically for greater European union.

One important reason for this apparent contradiction was that changes of government did not necessarily produce a change of party. By far the most powerful force in postwar Italian political life was the Christian Democratic party, whose members led virtually every Italian government from 1945 to 1981, with various assortments of coalition partners. A loose association of factions representing shades of opinion from center left to fairly far right, the Christian Democrats confirmed the Italian propensity for individualism, negotiation, and compromise. Although the party was promoted and supported by the Catholic Church, Christian Democratic governments introduced the referenda that legalized divorce and abortion—both vigorously opposed by church leaders.

Italy's second largest party, the Communists, continued throughout the postwar period to attract the votes of almost a third of the country's electors. Although never admitted to any of the national coalitions, they held seats on the important parliamentary committees that administered much of the day-to-day running of the country. They also won control of many city and regional governments. In the mid-1970s the Communist party began a period of rapprochement with center-right forces. The Communist leader Enrico Berlinguer (1922–1984) and the Christian Democrat leader Aldo Moro (1916–1978) began to talk cautiously of the "historic compromise," and in 1977–1978 the Communists supported (i.e., did not oppose)

Alcide de Gasperi, Christian Democratic leader and Italy's first postwar prime minister.

a Christian Democrat government. Then Moro was captured and murdered by extreme left-wing terrorists known as the "Red Brigades," in one of the grimmest periods of Italy's *"anni di piombo"* (years of lead). Talk of cooperation faded. Support for the party began to diminish in the late 1980s.

The Socialist party, the third largest in Italy, began to increase its share of the vote in the late 1970s and 1980s. Its leader, Bettino Craxi (born 1934), was strong enough to head Italy's longest-lasting government since World War II, from 1983 to 1986.

Thus, for all of its political fragmentation, the Italian system permitted a surprising degree of political stability. At the same time it also achieved the intentions of its creators, by never allowing a single individual to attain significant power—the success of Mussolini had taught a grim lesson. It was no accident that Italian politics never produced an Adenauer or De Gaulle, a Mitterand or a Thatcher. Significantly enough, Craxi's fall from popular favor in the late 1980s was due to his being perceived as too strong.

By 1990, Western Europe had enjoyed four and a half decades of peace and prosperity, broken only by the steep rise in oil prices in the mid-1970s. Democratic government was introduced in Spain and Portugal, and Greece's brief period of dictatorship in the late 1960s was over. The success of the Common Market was demonstrated by the number of nations seeking to join it. The challenge of the next decade was to achieve economic unity as painlessly as possible, and, as some believed, to look toward Western European political unity in the future.

Then, in a few weeks at the end of 1989, the division between Eastern and Western Europe, which had seemed permanent, fell apart. The road to a Europe united from the Atlantic to the Urals was infinitely long, and filled with wrong turnings. Many did not want to make the journey. Yet even the remote possibility of accomplishing a small part of it was an indication of the degree of European recovery after two disastrous world wars.

Questions for Further Study

1. How did the major Western European nations emerge from World War II? How did their populations see the role of the state?

2. What part did social protest and mass demonstrations play in postwar political life in western Europe?

3. What were the immediate effects of the fall of the Berlin Wall? What are its long-term consequences likely to be?

Suggestions for Further Reading

Bark, D. L., and D. R. Gress. *A History of West Germany: Vol. II. Democracy and Its Discontents, 1963–1988.* Oxford, 1989.

Bashevkin, S., ed. *Women and Politics in Western Europe.* London, 1985.

Hughes, H. S. *Sophisticated Rebels: The Political Culture of European Dissent, 1968–1987.* Cambridge, MA, 1988.

Mazey, S., and M. Newman, eds. *Mitterand's France.* New York, 1987.

Lewis, R. *Margaret Thatcher: A Personal and Political Biography.* London, 1984.

Spotts, F., and T. Wieser. *Italy, A Difficult Democracy.* New York, 1986.

Topic   12

The Soviet Union and Eastern Europe

ith the end of World War II, the Soviet Union faced the daunting task of domestic reconstruction. In accordance with Stalin's policies, priority was given to heavy industry and weapons production. Governmental bureaucratic decisions controlled centralized state industrial development. In foreign affairs, relations between East and West grew tense and confrontational, as the Cold War dominated international relations.

In the period immediately following the war, most of the governments in Eastern Europe were taken over by Soviet-backed Communists. By 1948, these "Eastern bloc" countries were under firm Soviet control. Only Yugoslavia succeeded in breaking away from Soviet influence. The countries of Eastern Europe were bound to the Soviet Union economically by the COMECON organization, and militarily by the Warsaw Pact, although individual countries developed along different paths.

After Stalin's death in 1953, his eventual successor, Nikita Khrushchev, denounced the crimes of "Stalinism" and assumed sole power in 1958. Khrushchev encouraged the beginnings of East-West détente. Partly as a result, Soviet relations with China became strained and were eventually broken. In 1964, the failure of Soviet agriculture, coupled with the diplomatic consequences of the Cuban missile crisis of 1962, brought about Khrushchev's downfall.

The Soviet Union was ruled from 1964 to 1982 by Leonid Brezhnev. Brezhnev's policies were cautious. Amid intermittent signs of détente, the massive Soviet arms buildup continued. The power of the bureaucracy was intensified, and agricultural and industrial production remained backward.

Both Khrushchev and Brezhnev maintained a repressive policy in Eastern Europe. Soviet troops put down the Hungarian Revolt of 1956 and Warsaw Pact forces intervened to end the attempts at liberalization in Czechoslovakia in 1968. When in the late 1970s, unrest in Poland led in 1980 to the formation of an independent trade union, Solidarity, a Soviet-backed government imposed martial law and arrested Solidarity's organizers.

With the coming to power of Mikhail Gorbachev in 1985, Soviet policy underwent a dramatic change of direction. In an attempt to revitalize the Soviet economy, Gorbachev turned to more open, reformist policies. By decentralizing and privatizing sectors of the economy, democratizing party rule, and encouraging individual creativity, he aimed at raising productivity and improving the lives of Soviet citizens. This program required a reduction in weapons spending, and as a result the Soviet Union proved increasingly flexible in negotiating arms control treaties.

The degree of change in Soviet policy was demonstrated by the freedom with which the countries of Eastern Europe were able to overthrow their governments in the revolutions of 1989. The long-term effects of these revolutions remained uncertain. In the spring of 1990, free elections were held in Czechoslovakia, East Germany, and Hungary, all of which led to center-right, pro-Western governments. Later in the 1990s, many Eastern European countries returned former communist leaders to power. Internal affairs and relations between Eastern European nations, however, remained afflicted by ethnic rivalries, survivals from the Hapsburg empire. Yet it was a sign of the degree of change that throughout the upheavals the Soviet Union, preoccupied with its own ethnic minorities, made no move to interfere.

THE SOVIET UNION FACES RECONSTRUCTION

World War II left havoc throughout Europe, but the problems that faced the Soviet Union were especially daunting. Estimates of the number killed are impossible to confirm, but the figure generally given of 22 million does not seem exaggerated. Innumerable towns and villages were in ruins. Leningrad suffered massive damage during its long siege by the Germans, and many industrial plants elsewhere in the Soviet Union had been obliterated. Living conditions were grim: around 25 million Soviets were homeless, and many of those who did have shelter had to share kitchen and bathroom facilities with other families for decades.

Soviet victory in the war had been due in large measure to the industrialization of the Soviet Union in the 1930s. Furthermore, the German invasion had reinforced Russian fears of foreign interference. Thus, Stalin's top priority in 1945 was to rebuild the heavy steel and iron industries and to step up armaments production: "In industry lies power." The relatively little attention paid to the manufacture of consumer goods meant that the standard of living of most Soviet citizens remained low.

Control of planning and production was kept firmly in the hands of the Communist party, itself subject to Stalin. The system was that of a "command" economy in which all decisions were centralized and carried out by the state bureaucracy. Capital investment, production levels, and pricing, matters that in a free market economy are decided by private industries or even individual factories, remained subject to state control. Multi-year plans, and more detailed annual and even monthly production quotas, were imposed on all industrial enterprises and state collective farms. In practice, however, plans and deadlines were rarely met. The weight of bureaucratic obstructionism and inactivity led to growing inefficiency, and the stifling of initiative and creativity.

Stalinism

By the end of the war, Stalin was able to use the Soviet Union's victory to enhance his image as his country's savior. The purges of the 1930s had removed any chance of serious opposition, but the paraphernalia of a secret police state remained firmly entrenched. Spies and police terror ensured that even his immediate subordinates feared their master, whose bursts of suspicion and sudden changes of mood were notorious. Prisons and labor camps remained the fate for political and intellectual dissidents. Both in the Soviet Union and in the Eastern bloc countries, art, music, and literature served to glorify Stalin's "genius."

In 1949, when the dictator celebrated his 70th birthday, the gifts he received were sufficient to fill a warehouse. Yet, to the end of his life, he remained insecure and untrusting, capable of turning on his closest supporters.

STALIN AND THE SOVIET BLOC

World War II had resulted in German invasion and occupation of Eastern Europe. Bulgaria, Hungary, and Romania became allies of Germany; Poland was divided between the Soviet Union and Germany at the outset of war and subsequently occupied by the Germans. At the end of the war, Bulgaria, Hungary,

Poland, and Romania, together with the Soviet zone of Germany (the future East Germany), all fell under the control of the Red Army. In Stalin's mind, Soviet control of Eastern Europe would guarantee protection against future threats. The governments which were formed there, known as "national fronts," originally consisted of coalitions between local politicians and Moscow-backed Communists. In 1947, however, local communist parties seized power and created one-party regimes.

The postwar Government of National Unity in Czechoslovakia had been made up of both Communist and noncommunist parties, and enjoyed broad popular support. Its program of economic reform included land redistribution. In 1948, however, the Czech Communist party engineered a coup that placed their country also under Soviet domination. The only Eastern European nation to retain its independence was Yugoslavia, where Josip Broz Tito (1892–1980) had led Communist partisan resistance to the brutal German occupation. After the war, Tito suppressed all noncommunist opposition to establish a one-party Communist state, but managed to avoid becoming part of Stalin's empire.

The Stalinization of Eastern Europe

In all of the Soviet Union's Eastern "satellites," the Stalinist totalitarian system of government imposed the Communist party as sole political force, and the Kremlin as leader: all policy decisions and choices were made or at least approved by Moscow. Eastern bloc countries introduced constitutions based on Stalin's Soviet Constitution of 1936, developed élite leaderships, severely restricted individual liberties, including religious worship, established central planning, and imposed Soviet-approved culture. Industries in each of the states were nationalized.

Methods used in the Soviet Union in the 1930s served to suppress all traces of indigenous opposition in Eastern Europe. In the late 1940s and early 1950s, local Communist leaders in Hungary and Bulgaria were purged, tried for "treason," and executed. Other show trials took place in Romania and East Germany. In Czechoslovakia in 1952, fourteen party leaders, eleven of whom were Jewish, were tried; all but three were subsequently executed. By such means Moscow crushed any possibility of autonomous development, and maintained an iron grip on events.

Stalinist control became further reinforced by the creation of a number of organizations. The formation of the Council for Mutual Economic Assistance (COMECON) in 1949 provided a means of subordinating the economies of Eastern Europe to that of the Soviet Union. Since Soviet industry was geared

Cartoon showing the two sides in the Cold War as children.

to the production of armaments, iron, and steel, the Soviet Union came to rely on eastern Europe for consumer and other manufactured goods. These became increasingly traded for Soviet raw materials and energy supplies. In the 1970s, COMECON helped eastern European countries to invest capital in developing technology and equipment for the processing of Soviet natural resources. In its initial stages, however, the organization was chiefly a means for ensuring the dependence of the Eastern bloc on the Soviets.

Soviet military domination of the region was formalized in the Warsaw Pact treaty, signed in 1955, which represented the East European equivalent of NATO. The original members were the Soviet Union and Albania, Bulgaria, Czechoslovakia, East Germany, Hungary, Poland, and Romania. Albania's idiosyncratic Communist regime, led by Enver Hoxha (1908–1985), broke with Moscow in 1961 to form a temporary alliance with Communist China, the Soviet Union's ideological and political rival. The Albanians formally withdrew from the Warsaw Pact alliance in 1968, claiming as their reason the invasion of Czechoslovakia in that year by Warsaw Pact forces.

Yugoslavia: Stalin Versus Tito

In 1945, no East European political leadership more enthusiastically espoused communism than Yugoslavia, where the Communist party's heading of the resistance to the Germans had won it considerable popular support. Tito, the former resistance leader, nationalized the economy and introduced centralized planning, and collectivized agriculture. As Stalin increased his control of the rest of eastern Europe, the Yugoslavian leadership began to emphasize nationalism, and to resist Soviet pressures to conform to Moscow's directives. Stalin is said to have told Nikita Khrushchev in anger: "I will shake my little finger and there will be no more Tito. He will fall."

In 1948, when Yugoslavia was expelled from the Communist Information Bureau (COMINFORM), Tito held firm to an independent line, and began to establish contacts with nations describing themselves as "nonaligned." Strict party control was maintained within Yugoslavia, but communist policy became increasingly modified. By the time of Stalin's death in 1953, the Yugoslavs had introduced "self-management" in factories. In foreign affairs, they firmly rejected Soviet domination in favor of neutrality toward the West.

Tito's success in creating the first nationalist Communist state received official acknowledgment after Khrushchev's denunciation of Stalin in 1956, when Khrushchev admitted that "the ways of socialist development vary in different countries and conditions." Future Soviet actions made clear, however, that the rest of Eastern Europe was to be denied the possibility of trying out variations of their own.

THE SOVIET UNION FROM KHRUSHCHEV TO BREZHNEV

The death of the "Wisest of the Wise" was followed by a power struggle in the Soviet Presidium from which Nikita Khrushchev (served 1958–1964) emerged victorious. The Ukrainian-born Khrushchev was groomed by Stalin to succeed him, and in 1953 became party secretary.

De-Stalinization

At the Party Congress of 1956, Khrushchev began his campaign of "de-Stalinization." For the first time a Soviet leader attacked some of the Soviet Union's most sacred myths. In a fiery speech he denounced Stalin's excesses and "cult of personality," accusing him of crimes against his political opponents. As Khrushchev subsequently moved to take over the premiership, he abandoned two of Stalin's chief doctrines: the notion that the closer the Soviet Union moved to true

Nikita Khrushchev, Stalin's successor, harangues the delegates at the United Nations.

Communism, the more intense the class struggle would become; and the labeling of political opponents as "enemies of the people." Both of these had been important in Stalin's reign of terror. Khrushchev's own rivals, rather than being purged, were dismissed or demoted as "antiparty."

Khrushchev's policies were generally conservative, but the release from Stalinist oppression triggered a period of economic growth. By the 1960s only the United States surpassed the Soviet Union in overall wealth and production. His rule also saw a number of technological breakthroughs. In 1957 the Russians launched *Sputnik I*, the first artificial satellite, and in 1961 they put the first man in space.

Khrushchev's foreign policy, at the same time argumentative and conciliatory, seemed to take its character from his own brash personality. He traveled to Western Europe and the United States, where his much-publicized encounters with government leaders and ordinary citizens served to humanize the Soviet Union's image. The increasing rapprochement with the West was accompanied in 1960 by a diplomatic break with China. The direct cause of the split was a long-standing border dispute between the two nations, but a deeper reason lay in Chinese resentment of Soviet approaches to the West; a Chinese newspaper article of

The Soviet space capsule *Sputnik*, on display at the Brussels World Fair, 1958.

the time referred to the "filthy Soviet revisionist swine." With accusations such as these hurled by both sides, the idea of a united world Communist movement seemed increasingly improbable.

The Cuban Missile Crisis

Amid the general relaxation of tension between East and West, the Cuban missile crisis of 1962 came as a fearful warning of the precariousness of peace in the nuclear age. In 1959, Cuba's revolutionary leader Fidel Castro (born 1926) seized power and set up a Communist state less than 100 miles off the U.S. mainland. The following year, when Castro accepted Soviet military aid, America broke off relations with Cuba and supported an unsuccessful invasion of the island by a band of Cuban exiles.

In October 1962, American intelligence sources reported that Soviet forces in Cuba were constructing nuclear missile sites, from which nuclear warheads could be launched well into the heart of the continental United States. The American president, John F. Kennedy (1917–1963), promised reprisal against the Soviets for any missile dispatched from Cuba against the United States, and blockaded the seas around the island to prevent the delivery of the warheads themselves.

For the week of October 22 to 28, 1962, amid frantic diplomatic activity, the world faced the most serious crisis of the Cold War. While Khrushchev and Kennedy established direct communication by telephone, Soviet actions gave contradictory signals: Soviet ships sailing toward Cuba turned back, but work continued on the missile sites. Finally, the Soviet Union agreed to dismantle the missile launchers in return for an American promise not to invade Cuba. Khrushchev's face-saving proposal that the Americans should also dismantle some missiles of their own in Turkey led eventually to their removal, but as part of an existing United States–Turkish policy.

The appearance of Soviet weakness that the Cuban adventure created did much to undermine Khrushchev's power. Together with the Sino-Soviet split and growing restlessness in Eastern Europe, it reflected an uneasy instability in Soviet foreign policy. Khrushchev's opponents drew further ammunition from the continuing poor performance of Soviet agriculture, where new technologies he had introduced failed to produce significant improvements. The Central Committee and the Presidium voted him out of office in October 1964. His retreat into quiet retirement represented another stage in the Soviet Union's development of an orderly system of transition.

The Brezhnev Era

The years in power of Leonid Brezhnev (served as first secretary of the Communist party 1964–1982; chief of state 1977–1982) were generally a period of stagnation. The Soviet bureaucracy assumed ever-greater powers, and the state continued to throw its most massive efforts into armaments manufacture. By 1981, the Soviet Union was probably the most fully armed power in history. Yet poor agricultural yields continued to create food shortages. In 1972 and 1975, the Soviet Union had no choice but to purchase large supplies of grain from the United States.

In spite of firm attempts to muzzle it, the issue of human rights in the Soviet Union began to create some attention. Soviet Jews, some 3 million in number, were subject to discrimination at home. At times, Jews were permitted to emigrate, although at other times the government arbitrarily removed the right of emigration. One of the most vocal Soviet dissenters was the writer Alexander Solzhenitsyn (born 1918), who was denied permission to leave the Soviet Union to accept the Nobel Prize awarded him in 1970. (An earlier Nobel Prize winner, Boris Pasternak, received similar

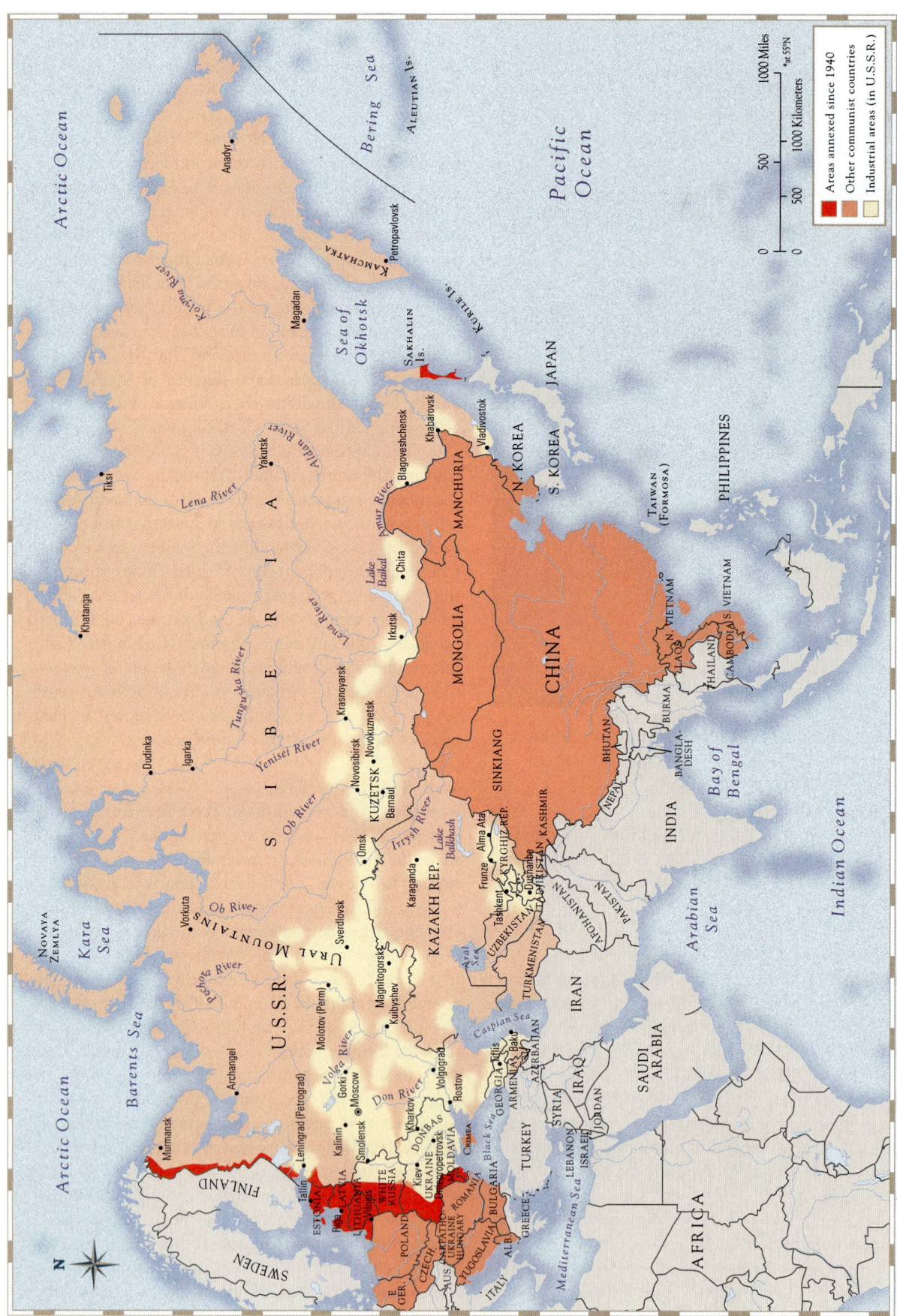

Map 12.1   The Soviet Union in 1988, on the Eve of its Collapse

S **i g n i f i c a n t   D a t e s**

The Soviet Union and Eastern Europe After 1945

1948	Communist party coup in Czechoslovakia
1949	Formation of COMECON
1953	Death of Stalin; Khrushchev in office
1955	Creation of Warsaw Pact
1956	Hungarian uprising
1957	*Sputnik* satellite launched
1960	Soviet break with China
1961	Soviets put first man in space
1962	Cuban missile crisis
1968	Prague spring
1974	Deportation of Solzhenitsyn
1979	Soviet invasion of Afghanistan
1980	Solidarity labor union formed in Poland
1985	Gorbachev general secretary of Soviet Communist party
1989	Fall of Berlin Wall

treatment in 1958.) His *Gulag Archipelago* exposed the brutality of Stalin's labor camps. In 1974, Solzhenitsyn was arrested and deported, and he continued his denunciation of the Soviet regime from his exile in the West.

In foreign policy outside Europe, the Brezhnev years saw the extension of Soviet influence in Africa and Asia. Cuban troops with Soviet arms and support helped to set up a Marxist regime in Angola. Similar forces assisted the revolutionary government of Ethiopia to put down rebellions. The biggest, and most disastrous, Soviet adventure was the invasion in 1979 of Afghanistan, to support a Marxist regime Moscow had installed there. In 1988, after years of fruitless fighting between the Soviet troops and United States–backed guerrillas, the Soviet forces began to withdraw.

REPRESSION AND RESISTANCE IN EASTERN EUROPE

For all the signs of growing détente between the superpowers that intermittently marked the years after Stalin, the Soviet grip on Eastern Europe remained tight. Both Khrushchev and Brezhnev left no doubt that they were prepared to use brute force to remove any government not fully under Soviet control.

The Hungarian Uprising of 1956

Khrushchev's speech to the Moscow Party Congress of 1956 acknowledged that the Yugoslav-Soviet break had been avoidable, and hinted that different forms of socialist development were legitimate. Events later that same year proved the emptiness of his words.

Late in October 1956, mass demonstrations in favor of political change—including withdrawal from the Warsaw Pact alliance—broke out in Poland. The situation was resolved peacefully, when a faction of the official party threw its support behind the reformist leader Władysław Gomułka (served 1956–1970). Gomułka managed to convince the Soviet leadership that the central institutions of party government remained intact, and that Poland intended to keep unchanged its close ties with the Soviet Union and membership in the Warsaw Pact. Throughout the 1960s, Gomułka continued a policy of cautious social and economic reform.

The Hungarians were encouraged by the Polish success. Within days, crowds gathered in Budapest and in Hungary's other big cities, demanding similar changes—withdrawal from the Warsaw Pact among them. The Central Committee of the Hungarian Communist party turned to Imre Nagy (1896–1958). During an earlier period as premier, from 1953 to 1955, Nagy had been openly critical of the Soviets, and was ousted by the Stalinist party secretary. Now he was restored to office. In an atmosphere of considerable nervousness, Soviet troops entered Budapest to keep the situation under control, only to be withdrawn four days later. Nagy and the new party secretary, Janos Kadar (1912–1989), were given the chance to set up a regime acceptable to Moscow, as Gomułka had done a few days earlier in Poland. On October 30, the Soviet government issued a statement affirming the principle of noninterference.

The same day Nagy, perhaps under the influence of his more extreme supporters, declared that a multiparty system would be introduced, and moved to make the Hungarian army independent of the Soviets. A day later, he announced Hungary's intention of withdrawing from the Warsaw Pact. On November 1, he proclaimed Hungary neutral. On November 4, Soviet tanks again entered Budapest. They were met with mass uprisings, which they crushed. With the revolt under control, the troops arrested thousands of Hungarians. Many were executed, others deported to Siberia. As for Nagy himself, the Soviets seized him from the Hungarians and executed him. (In 1989, Nagy was officially rehabilitated, and his remains received a solemn state funeral.)

Soviet tanks invade Budapest, Hungary, in 1956 to crush the Hungarian Revolution.

Kadar, Nagy's former associate, became premier and helped the Soviets eliminate the remaining rebel leaders. He served as prime minister from 1956 to 1958, and again from 1961 to 1965, and remained party secretary until 1988. Although Kadar permitted a certain flexibility—the so-called "goulash communism"—he remained close to Moscow. His death in 1989 came at exactly the same time as the collapse of the Communist regime in Hungary.

World reaction to the brutal extinction of the 1956 uprising was one of shock, but became confused by the fact that the events occurred in the middle of another international crisis, that involving the Suez Canal (see Part VIII, Topic 11). In the course of a few days in the fall of 1956, the two superpowers asserted themselves, albeit by very different means. The United States reined in its allies by opposing the British and French takeover of the Canal; the Soviet Union made it only too clear that it would tolerate no true independence in Eastern Europe.

The Prague Spring of 1968

Unlike Hungary and Poland, Czechoslovakia remained under continuous Stalinist rule. Its president from 1957 to 1968 was Antonín Novotny (1904–1975), a hardline supporter of Moscow. By the late 1960s, however, with the centrally planned economy performing increasingly poorly, dissent began to grow. The Slovaks,

in particular, claimed that Czech regions were receiving preferential treatment. Matters came to a head at the beginning of 1968, when reformers within the official Communist party ousted Novotny, and replaced him with Alexander Dubcek.

As spring approached, Dubcek and his supporters carried out an ever-increasing process of democratization. They allowed independent political movements to develop, reduced censorship, promised to guarantee individual freedoms, and proposed to create a federation giving equal rights to Czechs and Slovaks. A special congress was scheduled for September, to reform the party along democratic lines.

Soviet reaction began with press criticism and escalated in July with Soviet troop movements in bordering countries. In the same month, all the Warsaw Pact members except Czechoslovakia (and Albania, which had broken with Moscow earlier) met to discuss the conditions that would legitimize intervention. These conditions were made public a few months later and constituted the "Brezhnev Doctrine." They stated that "when internal and external forces hostile to socialism seek to reverse the development of any socialist country whatsoever in the direction of the restoration of the capitalist order . . . this becomes a common problem and concern of all socialist countries."

In August 1968, Warsaw Pact forces moved into Czechoslovakia. Dubcek and the others who had tried to introduce "socialism with a human face" were purged, and the staunchly pro-Soviet Gustav Husak was put in charge. Husak enforced rigidly Stalinist policies of state planning which, together with inept management, undermined the economy. By the late 1980s, with Gorbachev's reforms in effect in the Soviet Union, Czechoslovakia remained the only bastion of orthodox Stalinism in Eastern Europe. In 1989, in the regime's last weeks, Dubcek emerged from retirement to play a part in leading the revolution.

Poland and the Birth of Solidarity

In Poland, Gomułka's program of cautious reform failed to prevent food shortages, and a steep rise in the prices of the available supplies. In 1970, Gomułka resigned, and was replaced by Edward Gierek (born 1913). The problem of the scarcity of food remained unsolved, however, and in the late 1970s public unrest led to the creation in 1980 of an independent trade union movement, "Solidarity." Solidarity led a series of strikes to demand lower prices; toward the end of the 1970s, the staggering size of the national debt had forced the government to raise the price of basic supplies to more realistic levels.

After beginning as a protest against the rising cost of living, the Solidarity movement began to press for political reform, including the establishment of independent trade unions. In 1981, Gierek was driven out of office and at the end of the year, under Soviet pressure, Poland's new leader, General Wojciech Jaruzelski (born 1923), imposed martial law and arrested Solidarity's leaders. In the year of their release, 1983, Solidarity's

head, Lech Wałesa (born 1943), received the Nobel Peace Prize for his contribution "to ensure workers' rights to establish their own organizations."

Solidarity maintained a low profile for the next five years. With the beginnings of reform in the Soviet Union, however, the trade union returned to the fray. In 1987, with the economy still in poor shape, the government announced reforms that included a reduction in central planning and wage incentives. For the first time a popular referendum was held to approve the plan. Massive public rejection of the government's proposals, the result of general lack of confidence, led to further rises in food prices. In a mood of widespread hostility, a wave of strikes broke out throughout the country.

In 1988, Solidarity was revived. The movement's leaders sat down with government representatives and other political forces, and negotiated an end to the strikes. Subsequent talks led to the establishment of a noncommunist prime minister—ending the Communist party's monopoly on power—and the holding of free elections. Thus, Poland set the lead in breaking Soviet control of eastern Europe.

THE GORBACHEV ERA: GLASNOST AND PERESTROIKA

The liberalization of Eastern Europe would have been inconceivable in the Brezhnev era. With the death of Brezhnev and his two elderly successors, however,

Demonstrators in Prague, August 1968, rally round the name of their leader, Dubcek.

Lech Wałesa speaking to Polish workers, December 1981.

power passed to a new generation of Soviet leadership. The changes inaugurated by Mikhail Gorbachev (born 1931), general secretary of the Soviet Communist party from 1985 to 1992, produced radical and far-reaching reforms in the Soviet Union, freed Eastern Europe from dependence on Moscow, and began to end the Cold War.

Gorbachev was born in the Stavropol region of southern Russia, and began his political career as party first secretary there in 1970. In 1978, he was called to Moscow to take over the controversial task of running Soviet agriculture. Within two years he was promoted to the Politburo, becoming its youngest member.

Gorbachev's election as party leader in 1985 signaled a dramatic change in direction. The conservatives in the Kremlin, led by Yegor Ligachev (born 1921), continued to oppose the Gorbachev reform program, but most of the Brezhnev generation of political leaders were forced into retirement. The leading figures in Soviet government during Gorbachev's first five years in office—Nicolai Ryzhkov (born 1929), the prime minister, Eduard Shevardnadze (born 1928), the foreign minister—were all supporters of reform. Indeed, Gorbachev's most vocal opponents in the early 1990s were those who felt that the pace of change was too slow; their leader was Boris Yeltsin (born 1931).

The Reforms of Gorbachev

By the mid-1980s the Soviet economy was still stubbornly resisting all attempts at improvement. Sluggish and backward, it was responsible for keeping the quality of life of most Soviet citizens well below that of capitalist countries, and even inferior to that of some East European nations. In the 1950s, the Soviet annual growth rate was around 6 percent; by the 1980s it had fallen to 1.5 percent. Gorbachev's economic reforms were intended to free industry from the stifling hand of centralized state planning by encouraging decentralization, reducing bureaucratic inefficiency, and using market incentives to encourage increased output. At the same time he aimed to modernize Soviet industry by eliminating unproductive labor and introducing the latest technology.

Ronald Reagan and Mikhail Gorbachev in New York, 1988.

He symbolized these goals in two words: *glasnost* (openness) and *perestroika* (restructuring). The first signified an opening up of Soviet society, so that individuals could use their initiative to break through the heavy weight of bureaucracy and general apathy. Glasnost also signaled an openness to comment and criticism. With perestroika, the institutions of the state were to be restudied and, if necessary, restructured.

The Soviet economy was in so desperate a state, and its habits so deeply ingrained, that little progress was visible. Food supplies and consumer goods remained in short supply, and living conditions showed no real sign of improvement. Yet the more general effects of glasnost and perestroika transformed Soviet society and wrought important change in international relations.

Within the Soviet Union, the Gorbachev era brought a degree of genuine freedom for political dissent, and open discussion of problems past and present. Political dissidents, including the distinguished physicist Andrei Sakharov (1921–1989), were released. Artists, musicians, and writers had a new freedom of expression. Heated parliamentary debate accompanied the passage of reform measures. Yet the new democratic spirit had its limitations. By 1990, Gorbachev had assumed virtually supreme power, ruling as the Soviet Union's first president to be "elected" by Parliament. It seemed that, in order to deal with his opponents on left and right, extraordinary powers were still necessary.

In international relations, the need to reduce Soviet spending on armaments produced a new flexibility in negotiations to reduce weapons. A series of summit meetings between Gorbachev and American President Ronald Reagan (born 1911) produced the signing of a treaty to reduce intermediate-range nuclear weapons in 1987. Further arms talks on both conventional and nuclear weapons seemed likely to produce more agreements. Soviet involvement in Africa, Asia, and the Caribbean was reduced, economic aid to Cuba was cut, and in 1988 Soviet troops began to withdraw from Afghanistan.

THE REVOLUTIONS OF 1989

In the last three months of 1989, almost half a century of Soviet and Communist domination in Eastern Europe collapsed. Inspired by the sight of free elections in Poland, increasing crowds of peaceful demonstrators drove their governments from power.

Latvians watch as a colossal statue of Lenin is torn down, 1991.

The Fall of 1989

The long process of negotiating a means of shared rule in Poland ended in August 1989, when Tadeusz Mazowiecki, a Solidarity member, became prime minister; his cabinet included both Solidarity representatives and Communists. Over the late summer months, thousands of East Germans, "voting with their feet," began to pour westward. Many had sought visas at the West German Embassy in Budapest, but needed to find a way out of Hungary to travel through Austria to West Germany. In September, the Hungarians opened their border with Austria to allow them to leave. October, ironically, saw the celebration of the 40th anniversary of the founding of East Germany. As parades marched through East Berlin, at a ceremony attended by an impassively smiling Gorbachev, the stream of refugees became a flood. By the end of the month, East Germany's leader, Erich Honecker (1912–1997), who had had a series of anxious meetings with Gorbachev during the latter's visit, quit as party chief. Meanwhile in Hungary, liberalization was being effected within the party. Already in the previous June the government had signaled its change of attitude by staging the imposing ceremonies that accompanied the hero's reburial accorded to Imre Nagy. Their facilitating the exit of East German refugees was another sign of yielding. Now, as the crisis intensified in East Germany, the Hungarian Communist party changed its name, and announced free multi-party elections for the following year.

In November, the already hectic pace intensified. In a last desperate attempt to deter its people from abandoning their country, the East German authorities began to tear down the Berlin Wall—hated symbol of oppression. As the world watched in disbelief, East and West Berliners danced and drank champagne on the spot where armed guards had patrolled hours earlier. Far from quieting the excitement, the removal of the wall increased the upheaval, as evidence of massive corruption at the highest level of the party began to circulate. Within weeks the Communists abandoned their positions, and a coalition of political representatives began to prepare for free elections early in the following year.

Inspired by success elsewhere, the people of Czechoslovakia began their own mass demonstrations. At first, the government responded with tough police action, but once again the sheer force of events drove the Communist party from power. The weary but jubilant Dubcek addressed the crowds, and the playwright Václav Havel (born 1936) began to emerge as the dominant figure in his country's political rebirth. Again, elections were promised for the following year.

Even Bulgaria, a country with virtually no experience of democratic politics, deposed its aging Stalinist

dictator, Todor Zhivkov (born 1911); he was subsequently accused of corruption.

Revolution in Romania

The only remaining Soviet bloc country hitherto unaffected by the ferment was Romania, where Nicolae Ceausescu (1918–1990) and his wife Elena presided over a bizarre form of Communist dictatorship. Ceausescu's relations with Moscow had been strained for years. In the 1980s, as his country lurched from one economic crisis to another, and against a background of serious food and energy shortages, he poured resources into grandiose construction projects. Much of Bucharest was bulldozed to make space for a new "imperial" capital, with a vast palace, in which Nicolae and Elena were each to have two immense office suites. In the countryside, villages were destroyed, and their inhabitants forcibly gathered together in "collectives." Overseeing all of this was the dreaded secret police, infamous for their cruelty.

At first, the apparatus of repression seemed sufficient to deter protest demonstrations. In mid-December 1989, when protestors began to gather, police fired on the crowd; around 200 people were killed. The violence provoked an immediate reaction. Angry demonstrators stormed through Bucharest. Gun battles broke out between army units sympathetic to the crowds and the secret police force. Ceausescu and his wife fled. Captured by army forces, within hours they received a military trial, were sentenced to death, and summarily executed.

The path toward democratic government in Romania remained fraught with obstacles. Many of those remaining in power were compromised by their complicity with the Ceausescus. The holding of genuine free elections seemed problematic. Yet at least a start had been made on dismantling a regime that—even for Eastern Europe—had found new extremes of repression.

The end of World War II found the Soviet Union and the United States facing one another as opposing powers, anxious to demonstrate their own supremacy, and fearing one another's military capacity. With its political stability and economic dynamism, the United States was able, in a gesture of enlightened self-interest, to help western European reconstruction of economies and democratic institutions. While Stalin consolidated his dominion over Eastern Europe, his natural paranoia was reinforced by the American success.

Khrushchev aimed at achieving recognition of his country's superpower status by a combination of promises and threats. During his rule, the Soviet Union extended its activities to the Third World, which Stalin had largely ignored. Thus, the struggle of former colonies in Africa,

Asia, and Central America for national independence became the battleground for confrontation between the two superpowers.

The same policy was continued under Brezhnev. No less than fourteen Soviet-backed revolutionary movements around the world achieved power in the second half of the 1970s. At the same time, the Soviet Union claimed military parity by building huge numbers of nuclear missiles, while investing unprecedented sums in its naval forces. In Eastern Europe, the Brezhnev Doctrine maintained rigid control until the upheavals of 1989.

Fundamental to Gorbachev's attempt to modernize the Soviet state was the realization that it could not afford massive spending abroad to support friendly regimes, and equally vast sums at home on an armaments buildup. The maintenance of revolutionary movements and governments drained national resources and brought in return little power or prestige. To cut the military budget required better relations with the United States—an end to the Cold War—and a stable and independent Eastern Europe.

To move on so many fronts at the same time inevitably presented enormous risks. In the first place, domestic opposition to the Gorbachev reform plan from both right and left remained an unpredictable factor. Secondly, the very existence of the Soviet Union came under threat, not from outside, but from the growing demands of individual republics for independence (see Part VIII, Topic 16). Thirdly, old rivalries and hostilities between the various eastern European nations and ethnic groups, stifled under the grey weight of Stalinism, soon began to emerge. Yet another complication was the reunification of Germany, with its effect on the balance of power in Europe, and on plans for European unity.

Yet by the early 1990s, many Europeans, both West and East, were more hopeful about the future of the old Continent than at any time in the century. The arms buildup to World War I, the tensions and failures of the interwar years, the grim confrontations of the Cold War,

were replaced by talk of the common house of Europe (see Part VIII, Topic 16). It was at least possible that at some future time NATO and the Warsaw Pact would no longer be needed—or at least would no longer serve their original purpose. The Western European union of 1992 began to appear not as the final stage in European unification, but as a beginning.

Questions for Further Study

1. What were the main stages in the "de-Stalinization" of the Soviet Union? How far was the process reversed under Brezhnev?

2. How did the Communist regimes of Eastern Europe differ in their relationship to the Soviet Union?

3. What factors helped to prepare the countries of Eastern Europe for the collapse of Soviet influence? Were they chiefly political, economic, or social?

4. To what extent were Gorbachev's reforms in the Soviet Union a reaction to a process that could not be halted?

Suggestions for Further Reading

Banac, Ivo. *With Stalin Against Tito: Conformist Splits in Yugoslav Communism.* Ithaca, NY, 1989.

Cohen, S. E., and K. vanden Heuvel. *Voices of Glasnost. Interviews with Gorbachev's Reformers.* New York, 1989.

Davies, R. W. *Soviet History in the Gorbachev Revolution.* Bloomington, IN, 1989.

Garton Ash, T. *We the People: The Revolutions of 1989.* London, 1990.

Hosking, G. *The Awakening of the Soviet Union.* Cambridge, MA, 1990.

Rothschild, J. *Return to Diversity: A Political History of East Central Europe.* New York, 1989.

Selbourne, D. *Death of the Dark Hero: Eastern Europe 1987–1990.* London, 1990.

Wolchnik, S. L., and A. G. Meyer. *Women, State, and Party in Eastern Europe.* Durham, NC, 1985.

Topic 13

MOBILITY AND SOCIAL CHANGE: TOWARD THE CONSUMER SOCIETY

hroughout most of Europe, the postwar years saw the restructuring of society by increasing state support for the lives of large numbers of citizens. Social welfare legislation proved so popular that even when, in the 1970s, national economies began to decline, governments avoided cutbacks as much as possible.

Several groups played a special role in the formation of postwar society. Many intellectuals, who had seen left-wing movements as the only real defense against fascism and capitalist dictatorship, grew increasingly disillusioned with the political alternatives facing them. Some, like the Frenchman André Malraux, chose to play an active role in political life. Others, including the German Heinrich Böll and the Englishman John Osborne, used their novels and plays to comment on contemporary problems. A third category, led by the French existentialist philosopher Jean-Paul Sartre, maintained a broader theoretical concern.

Other groups preferred action to words. Growing dissatisfaction with the direction in which capitalist society was moving led to widespread protests, which reached a head in 1968 with violent student and worker demonstrations. On the whole, the "Spirit of '68" consisted of a release of accumulated tensions without producing any major change of direction. The 1970s and 1980s brought a general relaxation in the polarization between left and right. The only major exception in Western Europe was Britain, where confrontation between government and trade unions continued to influence political life. In Eastern Europe, and in particular in Poland, the trade union movement played a vital role in the transition to more democratic government.

Perhaps the most significant changes in late-20th-century society were produced by the women's movement. As women became an increasingly important part of the workforce, and began to play a part in running industry and government, their traditional role became increasingly questioned and rethought. The battle for equal rights was fought at a variety of levels and few elements of society remained untouched, from campaigns for national office to individual families.

The whole structure of family life in Western society entered a period of considerable turmoil. Greater sexual freedom, coupled with vastly improved methods of contraception, caused many to rethink the institution of marriage. The birthrate declined. Perhaps more significantly, divorce became widespread and by 1980 had more than doubled.

The increase in prosperity created new attitudes and expectations. Urban-industrial society became virtually the only form of life, as traditional food production was taken over by "agribusiness." Within the cities, young workers and professionals—without family responsibilities, and therefore with more money to spend—were barraged by publicity, as advertising assumed ever greater importance for most corporation budgets. Many workers from the Third World, attracted by Western prosperity, settled in Western European countries. Their arrival provided a source of cheap labor for unpopular jobs but also led to an increase in racism and the resurgence of the far right.

By the early 1990s, society in Western Europe was moving into a postindustrial phase. As machines, in particular the computer, revolutionized the processes of industrial production, more and more people were working in service industries rather than in factories. This "new industrial revolution" seemed bound to lead to radical changes in the lifestyles and social roles of both individuals and institutions.

LIFE IN THE WELFARE STATE

The spread of the welfare state ushered in profound changes in the lives of ordinary citizens. Social policy was no longer only a means of improving the lives of the workers, for the expanded concept of welfare aimed to achieve a broad social balance. An all-party agreement in France in 1946 looked to the extension of social security to "promote the solidarity and renewal of French society." The Basic Law of West Germany, formulated in 1948, declared that the state was a "social state" with a "social market economy." Not all these egalitarian aims were achieved in practice. In West Germany, different classes received different treatment: blue-collar workers and white-collar salaried employees had separate insurance funds.

Welfare systems spread rapidly in the 1950s and 1960s. In 1950, the only Western European countries where more than 70 percent of the population were covered by welfare legislation were Britain, Denmark, Norway, and Sweden. By 1975, the only countries where coverage was still below 70 percent were Greece, Portugal, and Spain. Although Eastern Europe dismissed the notion of welfare as a "bourgeois capitalist concept," these governments tended to introduce legislation providing insurance and pensions. These were initially reserved for state employees, leaving peasants and the self-employed uncovered. Retirement age was low—in Czechoslovakia and Hungary 60 for men and 55 for women—but so were the pensions.

The Welfare State and the Family

The welfare state affected life from birth to death. In Sweden in the 1970s, public doctors treated 99.7 percent of all newborn babies, and all parents were required by law to submit their children to a medical checkup when they reached the age of four. Children throughout Western and Eastern Europe went to state-subsidized schools, and then on to public universities. Unlike the United States, there were very few private European universities.

A young couple could generally count on some form of subsidized housing, and help in bringing up their children. Welfare legislation introduced in France in 1946 gave women benefits and maternity leave before and after pregnancy, and provided day care centers and after-school programs. Most European countries followed suit. At work, employees were covered by national insurance schemes, which would allow them treatment by a national health service. On retirement, they spent the last years of their lives drawing a state pension.

Nor did the welfare state cover only basic expenses such as these. The state ran, and therefore controlled the cost of, services such as energy, communications, and transport. Culture and the arts were also subsidized, and most postwar governments in Europe had a Ministry of Culture. One of France's most distinguished literary figures, André Malraux (see below), served in such a post, and ministers of culture played important if controversial roles in East European politics. The notion of state support for the arts continued into the 1980s. In the opera season of 1987–1988, La Scala (Milan) received public funds to cover 74 percent of its expenses; similar grants were 78 percent for the Munich opera, 76 percent for Vienna, and 82 percent for Paris. In the same period, the Metropolitan Opera House in New York could count on 2 percent.

The Welfare Crisis

In 1950 the average proportion of the gross national product devoted by Western European countries to social welfare was 9.4 percent. By 1977 this figure had risen to 22.4 percent. The expense of health care alone more than doubled. At the same time, the average age of the European population continued to rise. Improved medical techniques, which were more widely available, enabled increasing numbers of people to survive to retirement age; on retirement, they began drawing pensions and continued to need state medical care.

The vast rise in costs coincided with the economic recessions of the 1970s. The enormous growth of the 1950s and 1960s turned stagnant, and most western European countries were badly hit by the 1970s oil crises. The welfare state, which had seemed a permanent feature of postwar European life, became subject to agonized debate. Conservatives argued that social welfare was too expensive and too inefficient, and should be dismantled, while private enterprise and individual initiative should be encouraged. On the other side, radical critics claimed that social legislation emphasized material welfare without creating a sense of community.

Throughout the 1980s, both conservative and socialist governments in Western Europe cut back benefit levels. Nonetheless welfare was so integral a part of the lives of millions that most countries continued to devote large proportions of their annual budget to it, hoping to cover the costs with higher taxes and increased production. Only in Thatcher's Britain was there a sustained attempt to shift back the cost of welfare to the private sector. The results produced furious public debate about the consequences for Britain's educational and medical systems, and about the general issue of social justice.

THE INTELLECTUALS' DILEMMA: EXISTENTIALISM OR COMMITMENT

In the euphoria of victory in 1945, the intellectual map seemed easy enough to interpret. Of the two chief movements of the 1930s, the radical right was discredited beyond repair. The left was triumphant, for Communists and Socialists had been among the leaders in resistance struggles throughout Europe, both West and East. Furthermore, the Soviet Union, the supreme Communist power, had been one of the principal architects of military victory.

Yet as the Soviets moved to occupy eastern Europe and set up their puppet governments there, doubts began to arise. Even before the war, some intellectuals had seen the darker side of the Russian Revolution and its consequences. In 1940, Arthur Koestler (1905–1983) published *Darkness at Noon*, a novel which drew on the Moscow purges of the 1930s to indict the excesses of Stalinism.

The Intellectual and Society

As many began to face disillusionment with all forms of social organization, some artists and thinkers turned with increased despair to the search for meaning in a hostile world. The works of the Irish playwright Samuel Beckett (1906–1989) presented an enigmatic vision of a world beyond logic. In his best-known play, *Waiting for Godot*, two bizarre characters wait for an event that never takes place: the arrival of Godot. Is Godot God? Does his nonarrival illustrate the hopelessness of life? At least the two continue their vigil. In other works, Beckett presented a bleaker vision of the possibilities of human communication, and of the significance of existence.

Other intellectuals sought to illuminate aspects of the modern dilemma. The Swedish filmmaker Ingmar Bergman used his films to explore the disappearance of religious faith and the demands of contemporary despair. As knowledge of the atrocities of the Nazi death camps began to come to light, some writers tried to give voice to the experience. In some cases they were actual survivors. The Italian Primo Levi (1919–1985), and the Romanian-born Elie Wiesel (born 1928) both wrote works meditating on their experiences in the camps.

Not all thinkers took so hopeless a view of the possibilities for change. Among the first postwar writers to take an active role in government was André Malraux (1901–1976), one of the most distinguished figures in French 20th-century culture. Although never a Marxist, Malraux had impeccable left-wing credentials. He fought for the Republicans in the Spanish Civil War, was one of France's leading antifascists before World War II, and was active in the Resistance. He served as minister of information from 1945 to 1946, and as minister of culture from 1959 to 1969.

Many on the left accused Malraux of betraying their cause by taking the Gaullist (that is, right-wing) side in the Cold War. Malraux himself insisted that he was defending society against Stalinism. In perhaps his most profound literary work, *The Voices of Silence* (1951), he claimed that art—"the essential, eternal assertion of human freedom over destiny"—transcended history.

In some cases intellectuals used their work to fight for social and political change without actually playing an active role. Few voices spoke out more powerfully or authoritatively about the evils of Stalinism than Alexander Solzhenitsyn (born 1918), who based his descriptions of Stalin's labor camps on his own experiences there. At first suppressed, then expelled, Solzhenitsyn moved from epic denunciations of Stalinism to broader criticism of the nature of modern society.

In Germany, Heinrich Böll (1917–1985) used bitter satire to expose what he saw as the moral vacuum behind the West German "economic miracle." His books saw love as the only mitigator of despair in postwar Europe. Another critic of German society was Günter Grass (born 1927). A committed socialist, Grass explored the nature of human identity, and the moral fragmentation of modern (in particular, German) European society.

In Britain, social criticism became symbolized in the figure of the "angry young man"—classless, disillusioned, rebellious. The archetypal example appeared in *Look Back in Anger,* a play by John Osborne (born 1929), first performed in 1956. Osborne and others bitterly questioned the comfortable assurances of the welfare state and of middle-class society. A more specific issue which a number of writers addressed was that of feminism (discussed below). Sylvia Plath (1932–1963) and Doris Lessing (born 1919) both moved to England—Plath from the United States and Lessing from southern Africa. Their works explore feminine consciousness from a variety of angles.

STUDENTS, WORKERS, AND POWER: 1968 AND ITS AFTERMATH

By the mid-1960s, the driving force of European renewal had begun to run out of steam. After the initial excitement of reconstruction, society began to show deep signs of protest and grievance. The two chief groups to lead demonstrations against the state were students and workers.

The Student Uprisings of 1968

The wave of student demonstrations that peaked in the spring of 1968 was by no means limited to Western Europe. Similar protest rallies took place in Eastern Europe, in Africa, and in the United States; in the latter, there were passionate demonstrations against American participation in the Vietnam War.

The war in Vietnam also figured in the European protests, but there were also more local causes. By the late 1960s, the baby boom of the war years had led to overcrowded classrooms and teaching facilities. Furthermore the increased number of students qualifying meant that job opportunities were becoming scarcer. To some extent the problem became seen in terms of class warfare: few university professors and not enough students were from the working classes.

The disorders in Germany lasted from 1967 to 1971 and their eventual suppression led to the formation of secret left-wing terrorist groups. Similar "revolutionary cells" were created in Italy, where left-wing agitation produced neofascist counterdemonstrations and a revival of the far right. Those killed on both sides were hailed as martyrs to their cause; the chain of reprisal lasted well into the 1980s.

The most spectacular demonstrations occurred in Paris in May 1968. When clumsy police actions tried to prevent student sit-ins and classroom occupations, the situation erupted. Students occupied the main university quarter, and set up street barricades—in the spirit of 1848—to prevent police access. The general goals of the demonstrators remained vague. They felt that society should be changed, but were inspired by no coherent ideology. "Be realistic: demand the impossible!" was one of the popular slogans.

This lack of an overall strategy diminished the long-term effect of the protests. When order was restored, most governments reformed university structures and increased the influence in academic affairs of students and younger faculty members. On the whole, though, the student demonstrations gave voice to a general sense of uncertainty about contemporary society without producing a real change of direction. When, 30 years later, former participants gathered throughout Europe to remember and commemorate the events of their youth, the mood was generally more of nostalgia than of political protest. Many of those involved admitted that they themselves had become as "bourgeois" as those against whom they had protested.

Labor Protests

One direct effect of the student demonstrations, however, was to galvanize workers into protest action. In the inflation-ridden 1960s, wages often failed to keep up with prices. Factory work, with its unending assembly line monotony, provided little work satisfaction. In many countries, trade unions seemed less concerned with the welfare of their members than with waging their own political battles.

The problems came to a head in France in 1968, as workers followed the example of the students and took to the streets; at the height of the protests, some 10 million were involved. A frightened government increased wages. A month later it consolidated its power when De Gaulle and his party swept to victory in a

PUBLIC FIGURES ⊕ PRIVATE LIVES

SIMONE DE BEAUVOIR AND JEAN-PAUL SARTRE

The most overarching attempt to find a path forward for modern society was that of the existentialists. More an attitude than a coherent system of philosophy, existentialism began in the 19th century with the ideas of the Danish theologian Søren Kierkegaard (1813–1855). According to Kierkegaard, individual humans are more important than collective abstractions—"The crowd is untruth."

The most important exponent of the existentialist view after World War II was the Frenchman Jean-Paul Sartre (1905–1980). Sartre's intellectual position was reinforced by his experiences; after being a prisoner of war, he lived through the German occupation of France, and played a part in the Resistance. After the war, his writings served as inspiration to a generation of intellectuals.

In politics, Sartre tried to reconcile two opposed convictions: his belief in freedom and individualism, and his attraction to the ideas of brotherhood and community represented by an ideal Communism. Sartre's own relationship with the Communist party remained ambiguous. While generally approving many of the aims of Marxism, he wrestled throughout his life with the degree to which they justified the means used to achieve them.

His existentialist works tried to come to terms with the problems of living in a world without God, where there is no ultimate significance to existence. People are alone, forced to decide who they are, "condemned to be free." In such a world, it was necessary to come to terms with freedom, and try to devise a system of behavior.

It was typical of Sartre's commitment to intellectual enquiry that he both wrote about and explored in his actual life the issue of feminism. His inspiration in this was Simone de Beauvoir (1908–1986). Together, they became the most celebrated intellectual couple in the postwar period.

De Beauvoir grew up conventionally enough in a Parisian middle-class family. After World War I, when she needed to find some means of supporting herself, against her family's wishes she decided to become an academic. De Beauvoir and Sartre met at the Sorbonne and fell in love. For the rest of Sartre's life, they maintained an intense emotional and intellectual union. Refusing to marry, they also remained independent, often living separately and having other love affairs.

De Beauvoir's most widely read book, *The Second Sex* (1949), dealt with the nature of womanhood, and analyzed the way in which women are locked into gender definitions. For many women, the traditional feminine role had its attractions. The "independent woman," by contrast, preferred the harder but more rewarding life of work, self-definition, and significant interaction with the male "Other."

The Second Sex was widely read, at least in part because of De Beauvoir's relationship with Sartre. Some readers were shocked (or claimed to be) by her frank discussion of issues such as misogyny and lesbianism. Others accused Sartre

of having written the book. His influence on her thought emerged far more consistently, however, in her four volumes of memoirs. Following the existential principles advocated by Sartre, she described her own self-creation by means of her relationships with Sartre and others.

De Beauvoir and Sartre illustrated by the example of their own public lives the possibilities opened up by collaboration between individual men and women on equal terms. (In private, De Beauvoir seems to have been rather more conventionally bourgeois, often abandoning her feminism to cater to Sartre's wishes.) Both of them inspired countless individuals to question the basic premises that underpinned society, and to search for new and more satisfying ways to face the uncertainties of the modern world. De Beauvoir, although criticized by early feminists for underestimating the need for radical change, became in the late 1960s one of the women's movement's most important leaders.

Students rioting at the Sorbonne, Paris, 1968.

general election. Many of those who voted for him, including Communists, were also voting against the radical student protestors who had challenged the values of postwar society.

WOMEN IN A CHANGING SOCIETY: THE CHALLENGE OF FEMINISM

Since the days of the French Revolution of 1789, European women have been active participants in shaping their own lives. Women's movements inspired by a variety of ideologies sought equality for women throughout the 19th and 20th centuries.

After World War II, women gained the right to vote in every European nation except Switzerland and the principality of Liechtenstein. Women have been particularly active in Socialist and Communist political parties, where a long tradition of support for women's rights attracted them. In the 1950s and 1960s, politically active women tended to involve themselves in the great international issues of the day: the dangers of nuclear testing, oppression in Eastern Europe, the Vietnam War.

Beginning in the late 1960s, new feminist groups began to form to deal specifically with the treatment of women. The first international meeting of the new women's movement was held at Oxford, Great Britain, in 1970. By the end of the decade, hundreds of groups throughout Europe debated women's issues from widely different and sometimes conflicting positions. Some of these distinctions were due to the specific situation of women in individual countries.

European Women, East and West
The Soviet Union was the first government in history to include female emancipation in its constitution. Liberal divorce laws, state child care facilities, and legalized abortion also existed. Yet the reality of gender relations there was far from ideal. As late as the 1980s, Soviet women earned only two-thirds of male income for the same work. Almost half of the women in the labor force held unskilled manual jobs. While women held almost a third of all membership cards in the Communist party, they represented only a tiny minority in party or government posts. At home, conditions also remained unequal, for Soviet men generally refused to assume household responsibilities.

In Western Europe, conditions for women were mixed. In 1970, women in most European countries earned little more than half the wages earned by men in equivalent positions. In technical professions, such as medicine and engineering, Soviet women held a significantly higher percentage of positions than American women. Yet legislation favoring equality and women's rights had been passed in virtually every Western nation. Even in southern countries such as Italy, where the influence of the Catholic Church was still pervasive, divorce laws were enacted.

Feminism in West Germany
Women in West Germany faced two problems in organizing themselves as a separate and distinct category. In the first place, postwar German society encouraged conformity, and the avoidance of anything that could be construed as extreme. Secondly, in the very shadow of the Berlin Wall, the Marxist and Socialist origins of 19th-century feminism created instant suspicion.

The first major feminist initiative in West Germany proved, in fact, a failure. In 1971, a national conference of women began a drive to legalize abortion. Not only was the law's antiabortion stance intensified, but proabortion groups became subject to police harassment and those suspected of political activism found themselves without jobs.

One of the consequences of official opposition to the feminist movement was that the most extreme of its leaders took to terrorist activities to fight their battles. Ulrike Meinhof (1934–1976) was one of the leading journalists to promote the feminist cause. In 1970, she helped to found the Red Army Faction, which was responsible for a burst of murder and arson over the next decade. Meinhof herself was captured in 1972, and died in her cell four years later under mysterious circumstances.

Other women found a more congenial setting in the Green Movement, which aimed at defending the environment. Claiming that the destruction of nature represented a negative aspect of male supremacy, they helped the Green party to become a significant force in West German political life. Some women expected the Greens to respond by promoting feminist causes in return. On the whole, however, the predominantly male leadership resisted attempts to become involved in women's issues.

Italian Feminism
The Italian feminist movement had greater success in spearheading reform. In 1945, Italian women were among those least-well-off in Western Europe. They were a source of cheap labor, and had little legal protection. In the 1950s, married women could not apply for a passport or travel abroad without their husband's permission.

The first victory of the Union of Italian Women was the successful campaign to introduce divorce; a popular referendum legalized it in 1970. If West

Women political leaders: Sirimaro Bandaranaike of Sri Lanka, 1971; Golda Meir of Israel, 1973; Indira Gandhi of India, 1977; Margaret Thatcher of Great Britain, 1979; Vigdis Finnbogadottir of Iceland, 1980.

Women demonstrating in Rome against outdated laws, 1974.

German women had to contend with conservatism and fear of communism, Italian feminists were faced with the opposition of the Catholic Church in many of their battles. Only after mass demonstrations, which included women chaining themselves to the gates of the Vatican, did the Christian Democrat government make the distribution of contraceptive information legal. Even more impressive was the success in 1978 of the campaign to legalize abortion.

Women activists were also in the lead in seeking reform of other aspects of society. Throughout the 1980s, feminist groups sponsored demonstrations against the Mafia and other organized crime, pointing to them as extreme forms of *machismo*.

By the late 1980s, the European women's movement was facing conservative reaction. Pope John Paul II reaffirmed the Catholic Church's traditional view of women. In Britain, Margaret Thatcher, the country's first woman prime minister, began to cut social benefits that had given women the possibility of self-support. The scourge of AIDS, a sexually transmittable disease, encouraged monogamous relationships. Originally believed to affect only homosexual males, AIDS also spread by means of heterosexual contact and by the exchange of hypodermic needles used in drug abuse.

Yet the feminist challenge had changed perceptions about gender differences and their effects throughout large sections of Western society. No politician could afford to ignore the "woman's question," or fail to pursue the women's vote. At the humblest level,

American feminist leader Betty Friedan with Indian, Kenyan, and Egyptian delegates, 1984.

few families were unaware that new ways of viewing old stereotypes were in the air. As so often is the case, revolution sometimes brought reaction, but in the last decade of the 20th century the issue of feminism showed no sign of disappearing.

SEX, MARRIAGE, AND THE FAMILY: NEW DIRECTIONS

The postwar period saw a loosening of centuries-old sexual attitudes. Women's fashions emphasized breasts and legs, rather than concealing them. In the 1960s women sunbathers of all ages wore bikinis, and a decade later "topless" sunbathing became increasingly common in Europe. Even Spain, for long under Franco a bastion of conservative social attitudes, permitted the new fashion after the dictator's death. Books, magazines, and films encouraged women to take pleasure in sex and provided them with detailed instructions on how to do so.

In the mid-1950s the appearance of *Playboy* magazine and other similar publications heralded a change in the male sexual image. Instead of emphasizing the man's role as husband and father, they glamorized the attractions of personal gratification and sexual freedom. Partial or even total female nudity became acceptable in publicity posters and images, and sex shops opened up in many northern European capitals.

Attitudes toward "alternative" sexual patterns remained mixed. Sweden decriminalized homosexuality between consenting adults in 1944, as did Britain in the early 1960s. Most Western European countries had never had specific legislation, in fact, that treated homosexuality as a crime. In the 1960s, gay and lesbian activists joined women, blacks, and other groups struggling for civil rights and organized vocal protest movements. Yet in general, although awareness and tolerance increased, homosexuality remained frowned on and a barrier to public office. The appearance and rapid spread of AIDS, at first mistakenly associated exclusively with homosexuality, served to increase prejudice against gays and lesbians.

Contraception and the Birthrate

For both men and women, especially young ones, the appearance of the birth control "pill," and the wide diffusion of other contraceptive methods, meant that more-or-less casual sexual contacts no longer ran the risk of producing unwanted pregnancies. As a result, many began to have sexual relations at an early age. In Scandinavia in the 1980s, the average for a girl was fifteen years, two months; for a boy fifteen years, five months.

The new ease of contraception meant that married couples had even greater freedom in planning their families. Increased numbers of women, freed from the burdens of repeated pregnancies, joined the workforce. The birthrate, which soared during the "baby boom" of the war and the postwar period of the "economic miracle," declined steeply after 1964. In France, the rate of births per 1000 population fell from 22 in 1950 to 14 in 1980; in Czechoslovakia for the same period, the fall was from 18 per 1000 to 12. Even Italy, with its traditionalist family attitudes, and Spain (after Franco's death) followed suit. More permissive legislation on abortion, introduced in most of eastern Europe (1956–1957), Britain (1967), and France (1975–1979), further reduced the rate of population increase.

By the 1980s, the rate became stabilized in most European countries at "zero population growth": the annual number of births equaled that of deaths. The average in Western Europe was 1.7 children per woman, that in Eastern Europe 1.9 to 2.2. One of the chief effects of this was the disappearance of large families. Except for Ireland and Albania, the relative number of third births fell from 15 to 20 percent in 1950 to 9 to 12 in 1980. The two-child family became more than ever the most common family unit.

Patterns of Marriage and Divorce

In the years of renewed prosperity after the war, the rate of marriage rose steeply. In 1950, the proportion of unmarried women in their late 40s was 20.5 percent in Norway and 16.6 percent in England. By 1975 the number had fallen to, respectively, 5.9 and 7. Ireland again proved the exception: in the 1980s, 25 percent of Irish women never married.

Along with the increase in marriage rates went a corresponding rise in divorce. The factors involved were many and complex. With marriages often contracted at an early age, and a higher life expectancy, couples were faced with longer periods of living together, with the increased possibility of friction. In the early 20th century, the average marriage lasted 20 years, before being terminated by the death of one of the partners. By 1980 the average duration of marriages unbroken by divorce was 35 years.

The drastic fall in the birthrate enabled increasing numbers of women to develop their own careers, or at least to contribute to the family income. The consequent rethinking of traditional family roles, encouraged by the women's movement, inevitably changed conventional attitudes. As a result, legal discouragement of divorce, together with cultural disapproval, greatly lessened.

On average in the 1980s, in both Eastern and Western Europe, the rate of marriages ending in divorce was around 25 percent. The highest rate was in

Denmark and Sweden—almost 50 percent—and the lowest in Poland—around 11 percent. Divorce remained difficult in Portugal, and impossible in Ireland and Spain; Italy legalized divorce in 1971.

Thus the phenomena of a high rate of marriage and an increasing number of divorces coexisted in European society. Many of those who ended one marriage contracted another. Others chose to return to a single life, and the number of those living alone rose dramatically. In 1980 over half the households in Paris, Vienna, and West Berlin consisted of only one person; 25 percent of the cities' populations lived alone. In this as in other respects the late 20th century was marked by a strong break with past social habits.

THE AGE OF CONSUMERISM: AFFLUENCE AND ITS CONSEQUENCES

The general increase in prosperity of the postwar years transformed the lives of most of Western Europe's citizens. Some of this, at least, made its way across the Iron Curtain into Eastern Europe: by the 1980s, East Germans and Czechs could buy McDonald's hamburgers and Italian Benetton sweaters. The spread of technology made for more leisure time. Among the ways of passing it was travel, facilitated by postwar developments in air transport and packaged vacations. In the late 1980s, an average summer saw some 400 million Europeans on the move, taking holidays that ranged from a day at the beach to a cruise halfway round the world.

The concentration of society in great cities and their suburbs forced traditional agricultural life patterns into further decline. In part this was due to continued migration from country to city, a tendency especially strong in Greece and southern Italy. An additional cause was the inability of traditional farming methods to provide food for increasing populations. As a result, governments encouraged the development of "agribusinesses"—large corporations that mass produced and marketed food products such as milk, eggs, and poultry.

As goods began to circulate within the Common Market, they crossed national lines. A shopper in a small-town West German supermarket could expect to find olive oil from Spain, Greece, and Italy; chocolates from Belgium; flowers from the Netherlands; tea from Britain; cheese from France; and smoked salmon from Ireland. In some cases the free flow of goods caused resentment. In the "wine wars" of the 1970s and 1980s, French protestors overturned and emptied trucks containing inexpensive Italian wine. The same diffusion of products occurred in Eastern Europe, although at a much lower consumer level. Food shortages became unknown in Western Europe, and increasingly resented in the Soviet bloc countries; they helped in bringing down several governments in the fall of 1989, and remained one of the Soviet Union's severest problems in the early 1990s.

As wages and the number of wage earners rose, young workers and professionals began to attract the attention of marketing organizations. Many young people continued to live at home until they married—far more than in the United States—and thus had considerable disposable incomes. Companies began to direct their products and advertising at this new "youth market," rather than toward the traditional family one.

A resort condominium complex on the French Riviera.

Throughout the 1970s and 1980s, attendance at "family films" declined, while discotheques mushroomed even in small provincial centers.

The "youth cult" led to a new emphasis on physical fitness, and changing eating patterns. In traditionally meat-eating countries such as Germany and Britain, the consumption of red meat fell, and in France the "Nouvelle Cuisine" (New Cooking) provided a lighter approach to the preparation of elaborate dishes. Vegetarian and macrobiotic restaurants became more common. At home, as more family members worked, meals ceased to be an important and extended period for family life and exchange. They shrank in size, and working women turned increasingly to preprepared or frozen food for their families, which microwave ovens—now an essential tool in many kitchens—heated up in a few minutes.

Immigration

As standards of living rose in Western Europe, immigrants began to arrive from Third World countries. Earlier immigration had seen waves of movement from the poorer parts of Europe itself—principally the Mediterranean region—to the richer northern countries. In the late 1940s and 1950s, large numbers of Italians from the rural south migrated to Belgium, where they worked in the mines. By the 1980s, as one of the four most industrialized European nations, Italy attracted immigrants from North and Sub-Saharan Africa, and from the Philippines.

In many cases, immigrants took menial and unpopular jobs as hospital orderlies, road workers, garbage collectors. Many worked illegally, and received less than official minimum wages. On some occasions, local authorities made efforts to allow ethnic groups to maintain some form of identity, while encouraging community participation. The Turkish *Gastarbeiter* ("guest workers" in German) were an example of relatively peaceful integration.

Elsewhere racial tension proved pervasive. Britain, as head of the multiracial Commonwealth, attracted widespread immigration, both black and white. Whereas Australians and Canadians were easily absorbed, Caribbean and Pakistani immigrants often had difficulty in finding acceptance. A generation of immigrants' children born in Britain grew up, regarding themselves as British but often resented by their neighbors. Successive governments introduced legislation to combat various forms of racism. Nonetheless, during the 1970s and 1980s race riots broke out at intervals. In some cases they were provoked by the National Front, an extreme right-wing organization which rose to prominence in the general election campaign of 1979. At other times, ethnic minorities held their own demonstrations, to protest discrimination.

Computer skills are taught to children in a predominantly immigrant neighborhood.

Similar problems developed elsewhere in Europe. A French version of the National Front campaigned in favor of "France for the French." In the 1986 general election, there seemed a possibility, although it remained unfulfilled, that center-right candidates would seek its support. In 1990 Italy, one of the European countries most open to Third World immigrants, was the scene of growing racial tension, as African street vendors were banned from the streets of Florence. Government officials and social workers in most countries remained only too aware of the possibility of increased tensions, but the best that seemed possible was an uneasy truce.

Europe in the Postindustrial Era

By the early 1990s, it seemed that European life, like that of North America, was entering a new phase. The computer technology developed over the preceding decade now controlled most heavy industrial production. Following the example of Japan, industries from automobile manufacturing to printing used machines, appropriately programmed, to make their products. In countries where the trade unions were traditionally powerful, including Britain and Italy, automation led to bitter strike action. Modern day Luddites, however, had no more success than their predecessors in halting technological progress.

In this new postindustrial era, more and more people were working in "service industries." Banking, insurance, communications, entertainment—these and others replaced traditional manufacturing jobs, whether at labor or management level. With the rise of the personal computer, many ordinary tasks—depositing a check, buying a pair of shoes or a plane ticket, registering for school—could be done without leaving home.

Wilder imaginations pictured the 20th-century city as redundant in the postindustrial world. People would live in the suburbs, linked to one another and to the outside world by telecommunications and their computer screens. The office would be at home. Social patterns would be revolutionized. The gap between the late 20th century and the late 21st would become as great as that between the end of the 19th century and the 20th.

Some of the effects of these broad changes were already visible. The ability to work at even the most complex jobs from their own homes enabled growing numbers of women to combine family and career. Yet on the whole the postindustrial revolution had a considerable way to go. As it spread and intensified, it seemed bound to lead to radical changes in social and political life.

In the second half of the 20th century, many long-cherished social institutions came under attack. In public life, authoritarian leadership gave way to a search for consensus. Most European nations made a determined attempt to achieve a consistent standard of social welfare. Women continued to battle for equal rights. At home, traditional roles and gender relationships gave way to a period of uncertainty about the rules and function of family life.

By the late 20th century, two competing tendencies drove society. On the one hand the forces of mass commu-nication, ease of transport, and sheer economic necessity produced a "global village." The search for some form of political and economic unity, or at least community of interests, was accompanied by the spread of social and cultural uniformity. Yet, at the same time, there developed growing pressure toward the assertion of national and ethnic identity, real or imagined. From Wales to Lithuania to Lombardy, Corsica to Croatia, minorities campaigned, often violently, for some form of independence. The long-term effects on society of the inevitable conflicts between the two forces at play remained difficult to predict.

Questions for Further Study

1. What have been the main changes accomplished by the feminist movement since World War II? What has their effect been on Western society?

2. What role has nationalism played in the evolution of postwar European life? How far—if at all—has it been linked with racism?

3. In what ways do western European and American attitudes to politics, society, and culture differ? How do people in former Soviet bloc countries compare with either?

Suggestions for Further Reading

Caute, D. *The Year of the Barricades: A Journey Through 1968.* New York, 1988.

Gillis, J. R. *Youth and History: Tradition and Change in European Age Relations, 1770–Present.* New York, 1981.

Hellman, J. A. *Journeys Among Women: Feminism in Five Italian Cities.* New York, 1987.

Hughes, H. S. *Sophisticated Rebels: The Political Culture of European Dissent.* Cambridge, MA, 1988.

Mead, M. *Culture and Commitment: The New Relationship Between the Generations in the 1970s.* New York, 1978.

Schlesinger, J. R. *America at Century's End.* New York, 1989.

Topic 14

CULTURE IN THE AGE OF UNCERTAINTY

 n the immediate postwar period, with Europe in ruins, American culture assumed a dominating role in Western civilization. Just as the United States, as the Western superpower, led in the reconstruction of the Western European economies, so American ideas, styles, and themes became widely diffused throughout all levels of European life.

The area to be most radically affected was popular culture. The rapid spread of American popular music, movies, and television programs, of Coca-Cola and blue jeans, made an impact that extended from the smallest Irish hamlet to the Greek islands. Over the following decades they even penetrated behind the Iron Curtain, where enthusiasm for American ways and products provided a way of rebelling against conformist regimes.

In the world of painting, American artists led the way in the move toward abstraction of the 1940s and the return to realism in the early 1960s. Painters like Jasper Johns and Andy Warhol invented a vision of "the American scene," and then diffused it. American emphasis on technology encouraged sculptors to use metals such as stainless steel welded into shapes combining weightiness with grace. By contrast, the Englishman Henry Moore—perhaps the best-known sculptor of the 1950s and 1960s—evoked primordial forms in stone figures on a Renaissance scale.

A number of influential European architects had fled to the United States in the late 1930s. The most important of these, Mies van der Rohe, set the style for much urban architecture in the late 20th century. The clean lines and repetitive forms of city skyscrapers spread in both western and eastern Europe, often with deadening aesthetic and human consequences. The Frenchman Le Corbusier opposed the "inhumanity" of such buildings by creating structures with greater variety.

In music, a vast gulf opened up between average music lovers and the avant-garde. Most performers limited themselves to the basic repertory of the Classical, Romantic, and early 20th-century eras. Advanced contemporary composers found their public increasingly shrinking. In the 1980s, minimalist composers began to close the gap, and the works of Philip Glass appealed to wider numbers. In the field of pop music, commercial interests combined with social statement (on occasion, at least) to achieve global circulation. The distribution of music videos, and worldwide telecasts of concerts such as the Live Aid concert of 1987, or the Mandela concert of 1990, reached a public of proportions inconceivable before the late 20th century.

The leading literary movement of the latter part of the century was postmodernism, a term more easily used than explained. The postmodernists generally rejected the modernist preoccupation with alienation and self-analysis. Using unconventional literary forms, they created works containing meanings to be teased out by the reader—the text itself, not the author, was the point.

By the 1990s Europe had withdrawn from the cultural shadow of the United States. Yet popular culture, and in particular pop music, remained under strong American domination. In the arts, however, the age of mass communications not surprisingly produced a constant exchange of cultural influences, which tended to extend increasingly to non-Western culture.

THE AMERICANIZATION OF EUROPE

In the early part of the 20th century, Americans turned to Europe as cultural arbiter. European artists and intellectuals set the pace and style of cultural development, headed American publishing companies and symphony orchestras, and helped American art collectors to build their holdings. French fashions, British automobiles, Italian aristocrats—all represented old world elegance and charm. Even in Hollywood, most quintessential of American settings, many of the most glamorous stars and directors were European: Greta Garbo, Rudolph Valentino, Fritz Lang, Alfred Hitchcock.

By the end of the war, with Europe's leading cultural nations either vanquished and in ruins, or exhausted from the conflict, roles became reversed. A weary Europe looked to America for spiritual recharging. The wide open spaces, the sense of unflagging optimism, the illusion of innocence, attracted a continent war-torn and deeply insecure.

Other, more practical factors helped to reinforce the Americanization of Europe. From Scotland to Hungary, many families had relatives in the United States, and so thought of it as a possible future home. The affluence and plenty of American life, represented by the cigarettes and nylons so freely dispensed by American servicemen, made a special appeal in the bare postwar years. Most importantly of all, American intervention had been decisive in helping the Europeans to put their own house in order; American troops seemed likely to stay around for the foreseeable future to help maintain that order.

As the Marshall Plan helped the western European nations to rebuild their economies, Europe's debt to the United States continued to be cultural as well as financial. With the diffusion of television, American programs and personalities became as familiar to audiences in Manchester, Munich, or Milan as on their home territory. The art-buying market moved from Paris to Manhattan. Success for an opera singer required an engagement at the Metropolitan Opera. American universities attracted the leading scholars in fields as diverse as nuclear physics and art history, while European universities began to offer courses in a new area: American Studies.

The process had, in fact, begun before the war. Many European artists and intellectuals fled to the United States in the 1930s to escape persecution or war. W. H. Auden, Arnold Schoenberg, Thomas Mann, Mies van der Rohe, Albert Einstein—all major influences in modern culture—spent the war in America.

POPULAR CULTURE: THE UNIVERSAL LANGUAGE

The aspect of life most overwhelmingly influenced by American ways was popular culture. In the 19th century, each country sought to develop its own national characteristics in the arts, and nationalism was a powerful force in art and politics alike. In the second half of the 20th century, the lifestyles of Europeans came to follow American models. As prosperity returned to western Europe, blue jeans, T-bone steaks, and supermarkets became the symbols of progress, followed in turn by fast food and disco nightclubs. In Eastern Europe, political and economic realities precluded such open Americanization. American pop music, however, provided at least temporary refuge from the bleakness of life under Stalin and Brezhnev.

The most singular feature of this popular culture was its universality. Never before had personalities, products, and fashions had so wide a diffusion. One

A German McDonald's, 1988. Note the inclusion of beer on the menu, and the punk teenagers.

obvious explanation was the phenomenon of mass communication, in particular television. Although introduced on a limited scale before World War II, television became generally available only in the 1950s. By 1980, one out of every five Poles owned a television set, while in France, Italy, and West Germany the figure was one in three. Its impact was instant. When a few years later space satellites made international telecasting possible, the "global village" became even smaller. The daily lives of countless millions of people, many of them in remote parts of the globe, could suddenly share common experiences. In some cases these were great public events: the Kennedy funeral, royal weddings, the dismantling of the Berlin Wall, the death of Princess Diana. In other cases television coverage contributed, for better or worse, in forming public opinion: the Vietnam War, the Tienanmen massacres of 1989, the Palestinian Intifada. More important, however, was the general sense of a shared culture, operating on the most basic day-to-day level.

The spread of American-style popular culture was not without its critics. Some charged the sheer act of watching television with causing physical damage. In 1964, surveys showed that television-watching habits

in the United States, Britain, and Japan were much the same. A report to the American Academy of Pediatrics released in the same year accused television of causing fatigue, headache, loss of appetite, and vomiting, all of which could be cured only by abstinence. Others claimed that exposure to violence would adversely affect children and adults alike.

More serious critics feared that the relentless Americanization of everything from fast foods to buildings would lead to monotonous conformity, and the loss of individual character. Furthermore, giant United States–based conglomerate corporations came to wield enormous power, especially in developing countries. As the Cold War dragged on, and the United States became embroiled in Vietnam, European critics of America became more vocal. With political disillusionment came cultural doubts, and talk of urban wastelands and "Coca-Cola-ization."

By the 1990s it seemed as if "the American Century," proudly proclaimed in 1945, was drawing to its political conclusion. In the arts, global communications led to a growing internationalization of styles and movements. Yet, in popular culture, American models, promoted by American salesmanship, continued to appeal. The opening of a McDonald's in Moscow at the end of 1989 served as clearly as any summit meeting to proclaim the end of the Cold War.

THE VISUAL ARTS: FROM ABSTRACT EXPRESSIONISM TO CONCEPTUAL ART

Just as Paris dominated the art world at the beginning of the 20th century, so did New York in the years after World War II. Among the factors was the flight to the United States of a number of leading European avant-garde artists, including Hans Hoffmann (1880–1966), Josef Albers (1888–1976), and George Grosz (1893–1959). An important role was played by the American patron and collector Peggy Guggenheim (1898–1979), whose Art of This Century Gallery in New York became an important center for modern art.

Abstract Expressionism

Jackson Pollock (1912–1956), one of the leading members of the New York School, held his first one-man show at this gallery in 1943. The works he exhibited there were in a style that came to be known as "abstract expressionist." The paintings made no reference to recognizable subjects—they were abstract—and sought to express interior states of feeling—as the early 20th-century German Expressionists had.

Pollock's paintings used elements of random dripping, splashing, and pouring to produce intricate webs of color, filled with energy and movement.

Other abstract expressionists devised complex systems of color and image symbolism. Mark Rothko (1903–1970) experimented in using floating blocks of color to capture a sense of mystical transcendence; among his most ambitious works are those he painted for a chapel at Rice University, Houston. By the 1960s, artists were expanding the possibilities of pure color, with no reference to a specific state of mind. Helen Frankenthaler (born 1928) contrasted the liquid quality of her paint with stretches of bare, unpainted canvas.

Pop Art

In the mid-1950s, a new generation of painters was moving in exactly the opposite direction, toward the literal representation of mundane objects. Paintings of the American flag, beer cans, and toothbrushes by Jasper Johns (born 1930) were intended to reject the emotional and intellectual portentousness of abstract expressionism in favor of the symbols of popular culture.

The high priest of the cult of pop art was Andy Warhol (1930–1987), whose depictions of soap boxes and Coca-Cola bottles helped to reinforce the image of American conspicuous consumption. Some claimed that Warhol's apparent high seriousness, especially in his notorious icons of Marilyn Monroe and other celebrities, masked a severe social critic. Whatever Warhol's attitude to his subjects, his deliberately banal paintings and silk screen prints perfectly captured the spirit of an era which they contributed to create.

Faced with the explosion of American talent and interest in contemporary art, a number of important European artists were drawn to the United States. The English David Hockney (born 1937) moved to California, where he produced sunny, colorful works that owed something to the pop art "tradition." Francis Bacon (1909–1989) was an English artist in a very different tradition. His tormented figures and distorted images convey isolation and horror. Both in composition and in actual subject, Bacon's work often made reference to the old masters of the past, especially Velázquez.

Conceptual Art

By the 1970s, some artists were trying to break away entirely from what they saw as the straitjacket of any tradition, old or new. Conceptual artists aimed to cre-

November 1, 1948 by Jackson Pollack, one of the leading Abstract Impressionist artists.

Andy Warhol, *Mick Jagger.*

ate "objects" or experiences that were not intended to be bought or sold, or put in a museum. Their works, often consisting of unlikely materials such as corn flakes or ice, were installed and then dismantled.

The most spectacular environmental artists, Christo and Jeanne-Claude (both born 1935), devised projects involving hundreds of people and vast quantities of material. Their *Valley Curtain* stretched 1 million square feet of orange fabric across Rifle Gap in Colorado. Their major project was the *Running Fence*, 18 feet high and 24½ miles long, which ran through the farmland north of San Francisco in Marin and Sonoma Counties for two weeks in 1976; it had taken four years to bring the project to fulfillment.

Contemporary Sculpture

The sculptural equivalent of abstract expressionism was to be found in the work of David Smith (1906–1965). Instead of carving his pieces in stone or casting them in bronze, Smith constructed them by welding together sections of steel. He claimed that the metal expressed the spirit of the age: "power, structure, movement, progress, suspension, destruction, brutality." Some of Smith's works include objects found in junk-

yards, given new significance by the artistic context in which he placed them.

Pop art's use of the everyday and mundane reached a new degree of realism in the uncannily lifelike figures of Duane Hanson (born 1925). Common-place, dull, ordinary people, pushing a handcart, shopping at a supermarket, became transmuted into powerful criticism of the social forces that had produced them. Painstakingly built of polyester resin and fiberglass, the statues often wear real wigs, jewelry, and clothes. They alarmingly evoke precisely that banality and weariness of the age of affluence which critics of the "American dream" often castigate.

Henry Moore (1898–1986), the grand old man of 20th-century sculpture, drew his inspiration not from the present, but from the remote past. The art of ancient Egypt, pre-Columbian America, Africa, and natural objects—bones, caves, stones—all provided sources for his work. His creation of monumental sculptures for specific locations, often out-of-doors, put him in line with the sculptors of the Renaissance. His themes included the basic stuff of humanity: mother and child, sexuality, death. Moore's own attitude to sculpture—his own and others'—saw the art form as

Christo's work, like this *Valley Curtain* in Rifle, Colorado, uses forms of sculpture to decorate buildings or, as here, natural sites.

still vital in the late 20th century: "The best sculptures are static and strong and vital, giving out something of the energy and power of great mountains."

ARCHITECTURE AND THE ENVIRONMENT

By the nature of their profession, architects are as much concerned with the practical use of their buildings as with aesthetic considerations. In general, the architecture of the second half of the 20th century tried to balance the two not necessarily opposing elements of form and function.

The foundations of much modern architecture were laid in the 1920s by Ludwig Mies van der Rohe (1896–1969) and his fellow members of the Bauhaus, an influential school of design and architecture, founded in Germany in 1919 (see Part VIII, Topic 7). The Bauhaus taught that "less is more," and when Mies fled Germany for the United States in the late 1930s, he brought this approach with him. The austere lines, absence of fussy decorative details, and use of reinforced concrete in works such as the Seagram Building, New York, influenced innumerable skyscraper structures throughout Europe and the United States.

Not all buildings in this "International Style" achieved the elegance and practicality of Mies' best work. Many of his followers' steel, concrete, and glass public and office buildings filled the urban landscape with the same forms endlessly repeated. Nor did they always wear well; as metal discolored and concrete cracked, indifferently built International Style constructions brought their own touch of desolation to eastern European and Third World capitals.

The Swiss-born, French-trained Le Corbusier (1887–1965; his real name was Charles-Edouard Jeanneret) brought a rather different approach to the International Style. Emphasizing function, he claimed that a house was "a machine to live in." Among his most important constructions was a housing complex built in Marseilles between 1947 and 1952. The complex includes both living space and areas for shopping, recreation, and walking. Unlike Mies and his followers, Le Corbusier aimed to place his constructions in green park settings, with the natural world as a background. Colored panels and rough concrete walls provided decorative touches. Like Mies, Le Corbusier was unlucky in his imitators. Much grim public housing copied the general lines of his work, without matching the care for detail and aesthetic effect.

By the 1970s, both architects and public were beginning to be weary of stark concrete piles. The Pompidou Center for Arts and Culture, which opened in Paris in 1977, made a complete break with the idea of less as more. Its architects, Renzo Piano and Richard Rogers, covered the surface of the building with decoration that was also functional—heating ducts, elevators, escalators.

Few architects were prepared to go as far as this in decorating their buildings, but in the 1980s decorative design came back into fashion with the postmodern style (the name is little more than a convenient label). Postmodernist architects continued to build large structures with simple, basic lines, but added decorative elements derived from Classical architecture: arches, columns, pediments.

Thus the late 20th century witnessed a modernist form of neoclassical revival, and a return to greater variety in architecture. Public interest in the effects of construction and reconstruction upon the environment became increasingly vocal. The vast new building plan for Paris, which reached its first stage of completion in time for the Bicentennial of the French Revolution in 1989, was greeted with furious debate. In Britain, Prince Charles became embroiled with the country's leading architects, as he lambasted many of London's new buildings. Not surprisingly, of all the contemporary arts, architecture aroused the most enthusiasm and condemnation.

CONTEMPORARY COMPOSERS IN SEARCH OF AN AUDIENCE

By contrast with architecture, advanced developments in contemporary music left many music lovers and performers bewildered or indifferent. First the long-playing record, then stereo sound, and then digital recording on tape and compact disc made music increasingly available to an ever-wider public. Concert audiences grew, and regional opera companies sprang up throughout Europe and the United States. Yet the music that audiences wanted to hear, and performers to play and sing, was overwhelmingly drawn from the standard repertory of Baroque, Classical, Romantic, and early 20th-century works. A leading contemporary composer accused the opera houses of being only museums, endlessly repeating the same dead works. Certainly few operas written and performed since World War II succeeded in winning themselves a permanent place in the

Renzo Piano and Richard Rogers' *Georges Pompidou Cultural Center* in Paris (1977) broke new ground by using the building's functional tubes and pipes as decorative elements.

repertory. Significantly enough, one exception, *Amahl and the Night Visitors*, by Gian-Carlo Menotti (born 1911), was written for television performance.

In a way that has no parallel with the other arts, the musical world of the second half of the 20th century was characterized by a growing tendency to look back to earlier times, in a series of revivals. In the 1950s, listeners discovered Baroque music, especially that of Vivaldi, and, under the inspiration of the operatic soprano Maria Callas (1923–1977), the world of 19th-century Italian bel canto opera. The 1960s saw the growing popularity of the music of Gustav Mahler, up until then virtually unknown. By the 1990s, the early music and original instrument movement was in full swing, as musicians tried to reconstruct the original performing conditions of works ranging from Bach to Verdi by using authentic instruments.

The Musical Avant-Garde

Viewed from the end of the 20th century, the break between audiences and contemporary music seems to go back to the early 1900s, when Arnold Schoenberg rejected tonality in favor of other systems of musical organization (see Part VII, Topic 21). One of the postwar period's leading composers, the Frenchman Pierre Boulez (born 1925), extended Schoenberg's ordering of pitch to other musical elements: length of notes, volume, method of performance. This total control eliminated any traditional sense of melody, harmony, or counterpoint. The purely abstract structures that resulted deliberately avoided any kind of subjective emotional expression.

In the 1950s and 1960s, as technology came to dominate modern life, composers turned to machines to generate their works. In *concrete music,* everyday sounds were taped and then combined and manipulated in the recording studio. Composers of *electronic music* produced artificial sounds by means of an electronic oscillator; the invention of the Moog synthesizer provided an easy means of combining and changing these sounds. Few of the experiments produced lasting results. The leading composer of electronic music, the German Karlheinz Stockhausen (born 1928), tended increasingly to combine electronic sounds with these produced by conventional instruments. In his massive "seven-day" opera, *Licht* (Light), parts of which were performed in the 1990s, he used singers, dancers, and instrumentalists, as well as electronic equipment.

Faced with the dilemmas of the contemporary musical scene, the American John Cage (1912–1992) produced pieces that seemed to question the very nature of music. Many of his works, in reaction against the rigid ordering of Boulez and Stockhausen (or Bach and Brahms, for that matter), used elements of chance. The performers tossed coins or shuffled the pages of the

A page from Karlheinz Stockhausen's *Nr. 11 Refrain.*

work to determine in what order the sections should be played.

The Minimalists

In the 1980s, several young American composers found a very different solution to the search for a new musical style. One of the first was Steve Reich (born 1936), who built substantial pieces out of the extended repetition of simple chords and rhythms; the use of these basic elements earned the music the stylistic label of "minimalist."

The most successful minimalist composer was Philip Glass (born 1937). Glass was influenced by Indian and West African music, and some of the repeated rhythmical structures in his pieces derive from classical Indian pieces. The seemingly endless repetitions produce either a mood of hypnotic concentration or growing irritation, depending on the individual listener. Glass' best-known works were three large-scale stage pieces—*Einstein on the Beach, Satyagraha,* and *Akhnaten*—performed between 1975 and 1985. His collaborator, the American dramatist Robert Wilson, described their "apparent motionlessness and endless durations during which dreams are dreamed and significant matters are understood." Although enthusiasm for Glass and the whole minimalist school remained

The Beatles.

Popular Music

mixed, performances of his works drew large and generally enthusiastic audiences, a rare phenomenon in the field of contemporary music.

The worldwide appeal and circulation of pop music continued unabated in the decades after World War II. Between 1965 and 1973, "Yesterday"—a John Lennon and Paul McCartney song originally recorded by the immensely popular British group, the Beatles—appeared in some 1200 other versions. By the late 1970s, the Beatles had sold over 100 million record albums and an equal number of singles.

Throughout the 1980s and 1990s, rock music took changing forms, mirroring the mood of the times. Acid rock tried to reproduce musically the experience of hallucinogenic drugs, using advanced electronic sound effects. Performers of glitter rock aimed to challenge all the social conventions by their outrageous costumes and makeup. The bitter violence of punk rock grew out of the hopelessness of the working-class youth in postindustrial Britain.

Other popular musicians used their songs for open political protest. Bob Dylan (born 1941; real name Robert Zimmerman) combined American folk idioms and the blues style. Protest singers were among the first to incorporate non-Western music; by the late 1980s, pop music had absorbed elements from the Caribbean, West Africa, and Latin America.

The internationalization of pop music itself was matched by its ever-wider circulation. With the coming of the video cassette and world television broadcasting,

Punk culture in London.

concerts of pop music became global events. In many cases these were inspired by political, or at least humanitarian, motives. The first was the Live Aid concert of 1987, which was intended to raise money for aid to Third World countries. Among its successors was the Mandela concert, held in London in 1990 to greet and acclaim the recently released South African black leader, Nelson Mandela.

Music has provided the best evidence for the formation of a global culture. The same pop music echoed from continent to continent, while audiences in Europe, America, India, and Japan filled concert halls to hear the great masterpieces of European music. Ironically, at a time when the demand for music had never been greater, avant-garde composers seemed searching for the right direction in which to advance their art.

POSTMODERNISM

By the 1980s, a number of writers had moved beyond the modernist preoccupation with alienation and self-analysis. Critics tended to collect them under the name of postmodernists, although it was not always clear what specific characteristics they had in common. Nor was the term itself exactly helpful in defining the nature of their work, although it served to indicate a change of direction. The postmodernists did not break with their modern past; they built on it.

As far as it is possible to obtain a perspective on their work, the postmodernists seemed less concerned with traditional plot and character lines, and less interested in rational organization. Their visions were more private, and their works created isolated worlds with their own meanings and significance. They often used language in an elaborate, even virtuoso way.

Among the leading writers to be labeled postmodernist was the Italian Italo Calvino (1923–1985), whose works draw heavily on fantasy. He produced science fiction and historical allegory, explored the genre of the folk tale (*Italian Folktales*; 1956, revised 1980), and toward the end of his life wrote experimental fiction (*If on a Winter's Night a Traveler*; 1979).

Other postmodernists reveal a wide variety of influences. The complexity and ingenious wordplay of the American Thomas Pynchon (born 1937) recalls the style of James Joyce. The short stories and novels of Donald Barthelme (1931–1989) evoke a mood of surrealism. The grand old man of postmodernism, the Argentinean Jorge Luis Borges (1899–1986), created his own unique blend of essay and short story.

Although in the 1990s traditional fiction was far from dead, postmodernist writers seemed to be exploring a variety of different directions. Without breaking with the past—an impossible aim, in any case—their work suggested rich new possibilities for future literature.

Western culture in the second half of the 20th century was shaped by two contrasting forces: unity and diversity. Instant communication and ever-advancing technology made possible a global culture, whereby events and ideas could span the world in minutes. People on every continent could watch the same television programs, admire the same sports stars, share the same fashions and food—and they did. Yet the very speed of communication meant that styles and ideas became outdated and were replaced with dizzying speed. The appetite for variety grew as it was fed, and the 200 or so television channels of postindustrial society offered a choice so bewildering as to be no choice at all.

Faced with this homogenized culture, people in many parts of the world found a renewed sense of national or ethnic identity. For many European countries, the 1970s and 1980s were a period of nationalist sentiment and active nationalist movements. Belgium, Britain, Italy, and Spain all saw separatist demonstrations. By 1990, it was clear that the fall of communism in Eastern Europe would lead to renewed tensions between rival ethnic groups.

The battle to promote national identity was often fought with cultural weapons. Welsh nationalists won a notable victory in establishing their right to a fixed number of hours a week of television programs in the Welsh language. The language issue remained a sensitive one in countries as different as Canada and Yugoslavia; it even arose in the United States, as Spanish became increasingly widespread. Virtually nowhere on earth seemed untouched by nationalist sentiments. When in 1990 even remote Mongolia began to liberalize, one of the state's first moves was to reintroduce the Mongolian alphabet, which had been replaced by a form of the Russian one.

Thus by the 1990s Western culture, by now part of global civilization, enjoyed both the advantages and disadvantages of postmodern times: the freedom and constraints of pluralism.

Questions for Further Study

1. In what ways have technological developments— the communications revolution, computers, etc.— changed the nature of Western culture? What are the effects of the speed of these developments?

2. What are the main characteristics of pop culture? What forms do they take in music, the visual arts, and popular entertainment?

3. How does culture reflect the historical experiences of the world after World War II? In comparison with earlier periods, have the role and function of the artist changed?

Suggestions for Further Reading

Burgess, A. *Ninety-Nine Novels*. London, 1984.

Connor, S. *Postmodernist Culture: An Introduction to Theories of the Contemporary*. Cambridge, MA, 1989.

Gianetti, L., and S. Eyman. *Flashback: A Brief History of Film*. Englewood Cliffs, NJ, 1991.

Glass, P., and R. T. Jones. *Music by Philip Glass*. New York, 1987.

Hampton, W. *Guerrilla Minstrels: John Lennon, Joe Hill, Woodie Guthrie, Bob Dylan*. New York, 1986.

Maltby, R. *Passing Parade: A History of Popular Culture in the 20th Century*. Oxford, 1989.

T o p i c   1 5

THE PATH TOWARD EUROPEAN INTEGRATION

n the aftermath of World War II, some European political leaders began to see cooperation, and not competition, as essential to survival. In 1952, the first stage of European integration saw the combining of the coal and steel industries of all the major Western European nations except Britain—France, West Germany, Italy, Belgium, the Netherlands, and Luxembourg.

In 1957, the same nations signed two agreements in Rome: the first was to share nuclear energy research, the second to create an economic unit by eliminating tariffs and trade barriers between member states. This European Economic Community (EEC), founded by the Treaty of Rome, proved so successful that it led to an economic boom in Western Europe. In consequence, more optimistic politicians began to see economic union as the prelude to some future time when Europe could achieve political union.

The only major Western European industrialized power that refused to join the EEC was Britain, in large measure because of doubts about surrendering its sovereignty in a future united Europe. As the EEC continued to prosper, however, Britain's Conservative government opened prolonged and difficult negotiations to become a member. In 1973, Britain and Denmark left EFTA to join the EEC, and Ireland was also admitted.

The EEC soon developed a complex—some said too complex—institutional apparatus, including a dual executive: a Council of Ministers, and the European Commission. A European Parliament whose members are elected directly in their home countries is seen by enthusiastic European federalists as a step toward future political unity. The remaining EEC institutions are the European Court of Justice, and the European Council, which provides a forum for the heads of governments and their foreign ministers to meet at regular intervals.

In 1981, Greece joined the EEC, and in 1986 Spain and Portugal became members. In the same year, the Single European Act was ratified, which listed a series of future goals. The most immediate was the creation by the end of 1992 of a European community with no frontiers or trade barriers.

Relations with Switzerland and Austria were complex. Both, as neutral nations, had avoided participation because of its eventual political implications. In the early 1990s, however, Austria became a member together with Finland. With the revolutions of 1989, the notion of European unity suddenly took on far vaster dimensions.

Thus by the early 1990s, Europe already provided a market and economic force to compete with the United States and Japan. The chances of any form of political union that would be acceptable to all its members still seemed distant, but the divisive and destructive national rivalries that had riven the first half of the 20th century had been replaced by constructive cooperation. As the millennium approached, plans advanced for a single European currency.

THE FIRST STEPS TOWARD EUROPEAN UNITY

For the first four centuries of the Christian era, most of Europe was united under the strong political and legal rule of the Roman Empire. With the decline and fall of the Roman Empire, individual rulers fought over territory, religion, and dynastic questions. The empire of Charlemagne (742–814) imposed unity on a part of Europe, but the authority of his successors in the Holy Roman Empire as leaders of Europe was challenged by the papacy.

Over the centuries, plans for European integration occasionally emerged. The Duc de Sully (1560–1641), finance minister to the French king Henry IV, produced a "Grand Design" for a council of Europe, backed by a European peace-keeping army. A hundred years later, the French political reformer the Abbé de Saint Pierre (1658–1743; real name Charles-Irénée Castel) advocated the creation of a "European Republic," with a European senate; another of his visionary ideas was the establishment of a peace-keeping international organization. All these proposals foundered on the realities of dynastic and colonial rivalries.

Toward European Integration

The modern notion of a Europe united both politically and economically dated back to the troubled years between the two world wars, when some politicians saw a federal United States of Europe as a means of preventing renewed hostilities. Moves were made toward introducing some degree of economic cooperation, but in 1930 the French politician Aristide Briand argued that a limited customs union would not work. Economic union was possible only if each member's security was guaranteed, but security depended on political deci-

sions. Thus, an economic partnership required the setting up of political institutions and structures. With these in place, a "common market" (the term was Briand's own) could be established. The growing nationalism of the 1930s swept away all such notions of cooperation.

During the war, many of those fighting to free Europe from Hitler's "New Order" began to look to the idea of federalism as a hope for the future. *"Libérer et fédérer"* ("Liberate and federate") was one of the slogans of the French Resistance movement, and freedom fighters in the Netherlands, Italy, Czechoslovakia, and Poland developed similar goals. In July 1944, resistance leaders from various countries, meeting in Geneva, called for the creation of a European Federal Union.

After the war had proved yet again the futility and destructiveness of national rivalries, politicians began to talk seriously about the idea of a European federation. One of the leading promoters of the cause of European integration was the French economist Jean Monnet (1888–1979), who became known as the "father of Europe." Another important figure was the Belgian politician Paul-Henri Spaak (1899–1972), author of the report which eventually established the European Economic Community (EEC). The Belgians, in fact, helped to lead the way in demonstrating the possibilities of European cooperation. In 1947, Belgium, the Netherlands, and Luxembourg—the so-called Benelux countries—agreed to form a customs union. From 1948 all tariffs between the three partners were abolished, and a standard tariff became imposed on outside imports.

The chief spokesmen for European cooperation were fervent believers in the ideal of a united Europe, but even Winston Churchill and Charles de Gaulle, strong defenders of national sovereignty, spoke approvingly of federation. During the war, Churchill had proposed a postwar European state, governed by a joint

European Community headquarters under construction in Brussels. With the need to use a bilingual sign within one small country (the top line is in French, the one below in Flemish), Belgium, illustrates the challenge of European unity.

council and with its own armed forces. In 1945, De Gaulle called for some form of all-European association "between Slavs, Germans, Gauls, and Latins."

The supporters of European unification saw that the only way to achieve progress was to advance slowly and cautiously, with the goal of maintaining peace. The industries most vital to a war effort were those of coal and steel production. If countries would surrender control of these to a supranational authority, an important step would have been taken toward making future conflict less likely. In 1951 an agreement was signed to form the European Coal and Steel Community (ECSC); the agreement went into effect the following year. The member states were France, West Germany, Italy, and the Benelux countries. Thus six nations, which only a few years earlier had been locked in bloody conflict, agreed to share their goods rather than fight over them.

Encouraged by the success of the ECSC, the same nations tried to establish a European Defense Community (EDC), for the purpose of creating a European army and establishing a common European foreign policy. In the end, however, neither France nor Italy was prepared to give up control of its defense forces or independent policies. In 1954, the attempt was abandoned.

THE TREATY OF ROME

By 1957, confidence and growing experience led to the next step. On March 25 of that year the Treaty of Rome, signed by the same members, created two new bodies: the European Atomic Energy Community (Euratom), and the European Economic Community

(EEC). (The ECSC subsequently became absorbed into the EEC, which in turn became the European Union.) The ceremonies took place on Rome's Capitoline hill, ancient center of the first and only power to unite most of Europe under a single rule, the Roman Empire.

Euratom was set up to encourage cooperation in research and development of nuclear energy. It proved to have only limited success, mainly because each country had its own attitude to the use of nuclear energy. France soon came to rely on it for a significant proportion of its energy needs; Italy, after an initial investment in nuclear plants, responded to public uneasiness about nuclear energy by drastically reducing its dependence on nuclear power.

The European Economic Community

From the beginning, the EEC proved a success. The long-term goal of the Treaty of Rome was to achieve some sort of political union. Its terms claimed that its purpose was "to establish the foundation of an ever-closer union among the people of Europe." The aims of the EEC, however, were strictly practical, and limited to what could be actually accomplished. It sought to create one large economic market—the Common Market—for its members, by eliminating tariffs and customs barriers between them. Common tariffs and trade restrictions were erected toward nonmembers. Within the EEC, labor and capital could in theory circulate freely (in practice, some countries maintained restrictions), and a Common Agricultural Program (CAP) established equal price levels for agricultural products. Agricultural prices were to become a much-fought-over issue in the future, bringing the farming-intensive countries of southern Europe into conflict with the northern industrial

Many European tariff and customs barriers fell in January 1993, making German beer available to British shoppers in a French supermarket near the Calais ferry docks.

members, which were unwilling to pay huge farming subsidies.

The treaty laid down a timetable for bringing these policies into effect. The first steps to bring the national customs tariffs of the EEC's six members together took place at the beginning of 1961; EEC countries then had until July 1, 1968, to eliminate all customs duties between one another, and establish common tariffs toward outsiders.

Map 15.1   The European Common Market and the Soviet-Led COMECON, c. 1970

BRITAIN AND THE COMMON MARKET

The most obvious absentee from the negotiations that led to the signing of the Treaty of Rome was Britain. For all the British approval of the general idea of a European federation, politicians there were unwilling to embark on a journey whose ultimate destination—however distantly—was political union. Even Churchill had no doubt that Britain was in some important way different from the continental nations. His attitude summed up the position of many of his fellow citizens: "We are with Europe, but not of it. We are interested and associated, but not absorbed."

The possible loss of national sovereignty became a hotly discussed public issue. The nations of continental Europe accused the British of insularity and lack of commitment to the European ideal. The British counterattacked by pointing out that their insularity had saved them from invasion and occupation for hundreds of years. When the foreign ministers of the future EEC met in 1955 to formulate a common policy, they officially invited Britain to take part. The British government refused.

The European Free Trade Association

As the success of the EEC became apparent, Britain and other European nations began to look toward forming a similar organization that could both liberalize trade among themselves and act as a bargaining force with the EEC. In 1959, a group of seven countries created the European Free Trade Association (EFTA); it came into force the following year. The founding members of EFTA were Austria, Britain, Denmark, Norway, Portugal, Sweden, and Switzerland. Finland became an associate member in 1961, and a full member in 1985; Iceland joined in 1970.

EFTA's goals were avowedly completely nonpolitical, and none of its members had any intention of forming a supranational union. This factor was important not only to Britain but also to the neutral nations of Austria and Switzerland. Even in economic terms, EFTA was less binding than the EEC: although tariffs on industrial goods were eliminated between its members, they remained in place on agricultural and fishing products. The provision on fishing was especially important for the Scandinavian members and the British, who often found themselves in fierce competition for the catch and sale of fish.

Barely had EFTA come into being than opinion in Britain began to swing in favor of joining the EEC. The trade barriers that the EEC had erected against outsiders left British trade in a dangerously uncompetitive position. Then, as wartime memories receded, the idea of peaceful cooperation took precedence over defensiveness. No less important a consideration was the fact that France and Germany—under the leadership of the two senior statesmen, Konrad Adenauer and De Gaulle—were tending to dominate the decision making. Both Britain and the other EEC members could see the potential advantage of a British counterbalance in the community.

In 1961, Britain formally applied for application; it was followed by Denmark, Ireland, and Norway. Negotiations began later the same year. The bargaining was hard. As head of the Commonwealth, Britain was concerned to safeguard the reciprocal trading rights existing between itself and the various Commonwealth nations. Nor had the earlier British refusal, followed by the abrupt reversal that led to its application, created a sympathetic atmosphere for negotiating. France, in particular, resented what it saw as the British attempt to obtain "special treatment."

After a period of increasing tension, the French blocked Britain's entry; in January 1963, De Gaulle announced at a press conference that Britain was not yet ready to join the Common Market. Among his reasons was the fear that British membership would undermine the ability of continental nations to control their own affairs. As he put it, with Britain in the EEC, "in the end there would appear a colossal Atlantic Community under American dependence and leadership which would soon swallow up the European Community."

It took ten more years before Britain was finally admitted. In 1969, the year in which De Gaulle stepped down as head of state, the EEC members agreed to reopen negotiations. One of the leading British representatives at earlier sessions had been the

The French statesman, Charles de Gaulle.

Conservative Edward Heath (born 1916). In 1970, he became prime minister, and two years later his government signed the treaty which was to admit Britain. On January 1, 1973, the EEC received three new members: Britain, Denmark, and Ireland. The first two withdrew from EFTA. Norway, which was also offered membership, rejected it in a popular referendum. By 1990, three more states had joined: Greece in 1981, and Spain and Portugal in 1986.

Significant Dates

The Formation of the European Union

1947	Benelux countries form customs union
1951	Creation of European Coal and Steel Community
1957	Treaty of Rome establishes ECC
1959	Creation of EFTA
1963	Britain's application to EEC blocked
1973	Britain, Denmark, and Ireland join EEC
1981	Greece becomes member of EEC
1986	Spain and Portugal join EEC; Single European Act passed

THE ORGANIZATION OF THE EUROPEAN UNION

The devisers of the EU's institutions tried to take into consideration the fact that members would often find their own interests in conflict with those of the EU as a whole. They therefore created an organization that would balance national interests against intergovernmental cooperation. The vast bureaucracy that developed (in 1989 there were 18,000 civil servants—or "Eurocrats"—working for the EU) is a frequent cause of criticism. Jobs and subsequent promotions are assigned on the basis of nationality rather than merit, and Eurocrats can be moved to other positions or dismissed only under exceptional circumstances.

The Executive of the EU

The EU has a dual executive. The European Commission, which meets in Brussels, represents the supranational component. According to the Treaty of Rome, it acts in the general interest of the European Community. Its commissioners, appointed for four years by the member states, must judge for themselves what the interests of the Community are; they cannot receive instructions from the governments that nominate them. The commission can initiate policy and make recommendations; it cannot make policy.

That task is performed by the Council of Ministers, the second half of the executive, which guards national interests. It consists of the foreign ministers of the member states, who are at times represented by other ministers when specific problem areas are under discussion—energy, transport, health, agriculture, and so on. The council meets several times a month; every six months the presidency passes in rotation among the member nations. It discusses measures proposed by the commissioners, and votes either to accept or to reject them.

The voting system whereby decisions are made is a "weighted" one. The larger states have more votes. (In 1990 Britain, France, West Germany, and Italy had ten votes each; Spain eight; Belgium, Greece, the Netherlands, and Portugal five; Denmark and Ireland three; Luxembourg two. Proposals are considered passed if they obtain 54 votes.) If, however, a state feels that its vital national interests are at stake, it has the right to block a decision by vetoing it, even if every other government votes in favor.

The existence of the power of veto remains controversial. In 1984, French President Mitterand pointed out the absurdity of running as complex an organization as the EU "by the rules of the Diet of the old kingdom of Poland, where every member could block the decisions." By the 1990s, there was strong support for a reform to eliminate it, but members failed to reach overall agreement—the countries in favor of retaining the veto were Britain, Denmark, and Greece.

The EU Institutions

The notion of a European Parliament was established by the Treaty of Rome. Enlarged along with the EU, and elected by popular vote since 1979, its powers are limited. It cannot legislate and has no right to control or replace the executive organs. It oversees and expresses opinions on the commission's proposals, and has control over part of the EU budget; the greater part of the funds—71 percent—is under the supervision of the Council of Ministers.

The members of the European Parliament are directly elected in their home countries, by the electoral system in force in each. In 1989, there were 81 members from each of the four largest nations, 60 from Spain, 25 from the Netherlands, 24 each from Belgium, Greece, and Portugal, sixteen from Denmark, fifteen from Ireland, and six from Luxembourg. They take their seats in the assembly not as national delegations, but according to their party—Christian Democrats, Liberals, Socialists, Communists, and so on. A Rainbow Group brings together Greens and other ecologists, as well as a number of smaller parties—one of which is the Danish anti-EU party, the People's Movement against the community.

The Parliament originally met in both Strasbourg and Luxembourg, and Eurocrats spent considerable time and energy in transporting files and records back and forth each month. In 1981, it voted to hold all its sessions in Strasbourg, where it meets about eight times a year for one-week sessions.

The EU's legal arm is the European Court of Justice, composed of thirteen members, which meets in Luxembourg. It oversees compliance with the Treaty of Rome, and makes sure that all executive decisions are in accordance with the treaty's provisions. It hears cases at all levels, from member nations to individual persons.

More broadly, the European Court sought to develop a body of "community law." This chiefly concerns economic, trade, and social issues. Community law applies throughout the member states, and supersedes national law. It thus represents the principal instance to date of the surrendering of national sovereignty to a supranational institution.

Both the Parliament and court were created by the Treaty of Rome. A new institution, the European Council, came into being in 1974. Made up of the

PERSPECTIVES ON HISTORY

Sovereignty, Law, and Unity

Mary Volcansek
Florida International University

The treaties establishing the European Community followed the standard model of modern democratic governments by instituting three separate powers—executive, legislative, and judicial. An underlying assumption was that the judicial arm, the European Court of Justice, would be the more passive, because judges typically, by virtue of age and training, are expected to respect tradition more often than boldly to break new ground. The Court of Justice, hidden away in the Duchy of Luxembourg, has often shattered conventional assumptions about the behavior of courts as its judges defined the limits of national sovereignty and pushed for greater unity through its interpretation of the treaties. The Court, which now hears more than 500 cases each year, has significantly contributed to European integration, particularly in its decisions announcing the supremacy of European law over that of individual member states, the legal rights of individuals, human rights protected by the treaties, and rules that foster economic integration.

The relevance of community law for individual nations was firmly fixed by the Court of Justice in 1964 by its decision in *Costa v. ENEL*. That case stands as the source from which the authority of the court and of community law flows. Flaminio Costa was a lawyer and also a small stockholder in Italy's electric company ENEL, an operation that was nationalized by the Italian government in 1962. He refused to pay his electric bill of less than three dollars and filed a lawsuit charging that the Italian government had violated the article in the Treaty of Rome relating to national monopolies. The Italian judge hearing the case followed Costa's recommendation that he seek an interpretation of that specific treaty article from the European Court of Justice. The European Court declared that community law was superior to the laws in any member state and was absorbed into the legal systems of each nation. Community law was declared to supersede any existing national law or constitution. That stark assertion of supremacy provided a legal basis giving force to all laws passed by the Community and transforming the founding treaties into the "constitution" of the Community.

If the treaties are a constitution and regulations passed by other institutions of the Community are lawful in any nation, how can an individual secure the protections offered by them? The Court of Justice's answer was to create the doctrine of "legal rights of individuals." This concept was first announced in the 1958 case of *Van Gend en Loos* that dealt with duties on imports from Germany into the Netherlands that interfered with free movement of goods. The case involved not only the validity of the customs taxes, but also the recourse of individuals who felt that the guarantees of the treaties were being ignored by a national government. The Court of Justice announced that the European Community constituted a "new legal order," that signatories to the treaties had limited their sovereign rights, and that the treaties conferred legal rights, as well as obligations, on individual citizens. The doctrine of legal rights for individuals was given a more human face in the 1975 decision of the Court of Justice in *Van Duyn v. Home Office*. Ms. Van Duyn, a Dutch citizen, was denied entrance into Great Britain because she would be employed by the Church of Scientology. The court in Luxembourg acknowledged that a citizen of another EC country can be barred from immigrating to a different member state on grounds of public policy, but provided that such an exclusion must be based solely on the behavior of the specific individual. Britain could not, therefore, prohibit Ms. Van Duyn from coming to the United Kingdom simply because the British government disapproved of her employer.

The treaties of the Community include no "bill of rights," though certain economic rights are specifically mentioned. The Court of Justice has, nonetheless, moved far in the creation of a set of rights, both economic and social. The Treaty of Rome, for example, specifically dictates comparable pay for men and women, inclusive of indirect compensation. Gabrielle DeFrenne, a flight attendant on Sabena, the Belgian national airline, challenged a Belgian law that made retirement for cabin crews mandatory at age 40 for women, but not for men. Though Ms. DeFrenne lost her argument that pension schemes are a form of indirect compensation, she did, in her second suit, obtain the satisfaction that back pay could be ordered because gender discrimination was barred by the treaties. The *DeFrenne* cases address economic rights, but the Court of Justice has also recognized other human rights. That there existed "fundamental rights" for citizens under Community law was first recognized in 1974 in the case of *Nold v. Commission*. In the years following that decision, the court has found due process rights, guarantees of respect for private lives, protections against ex post facto laws, and rights against self-incrimination and illegal search and seizure as being fundamental rights of citizens of all EC countries. None of these is specifically mentioned or necessarily implied in any of the treaties.

The European Court of Justice has also been active in removing trade barriers among nations that interfered with the Community's stated goal of a common market. The landmark *Cassis de Dijon* decision in 1979 emerged when Germany tried to halt the sale of a French beverage in Germany because it had an insufficient alcoholic content. The court concluded, as it would again later when Italy refused the sale of German pasta, that "if it's good enough for a Frenchman, it is good enough for a German." The equation is the same for any two or more nationalities within the Community. That single legal principle was able to sweep away thousands of restrictions that had been erected to halt imports among the member states. Imports from sister countries could, thereafter, be barred only on grounds of public health or safety.

Proponents of greater economic and political integration in Europe have applauded the bold initiatives of the European Court of Justice. The judges in Luxembourg have been hailed for assuring integration of the markets of western Europe and for "democratizing" the Community through their handling of human rights. The court has, in fact, been in the forefront of integration.

Some commentators on both sides of the Atlantic have criticized the court's extreme activism or its willingness to exceed the legal tradition's norms of simply applying the law objectively and impartially. These critics note the court's tendency to create law that comports with the judges' personal notions of how things *ought* to be and accuse the court of usurping legislative powers. They argue that when judges exceed their mandate of interpreting law and make forays into lawmaking, the legitimacy and efficacy of the judiciary may be jeopardized. This line of argument says less about the outcomes of specific court decisions or their policy implications and more directly focuses on the traditional role of courts and judges in Western democracies. Another criticism addresses the policies that the court has pursued. That analysis targets the political agenda of the judges, who, as the argument goes, have allowed their enthusiasm for the European experiment, not the treaties or other relevant laws, to guide their decisions. The European Court of Justice, like other Western courts, is undoubtedly politicized, but whether that should be viewed as positive or negative is likely dependent on the political persuasion of the observer.

The European Community entered a new era with the passage of the Single European Act with its goals for the end of 1992. Before that deadline arrived, the leaders of the member states had already made a commitment to amend the founding treaties to achieve monetary union and

continued next page

to explore closer political union. A reconsideration of the division of powers of the Parliament also received implicit agreement. These developments may well transform the role of the European Court, as may the sheer size of the Community, as the number of countries seems likely to swell beyond fifteen to eighteen or even more. What will not change, however, is the significant contribution that the European Court made in defining sovereignty and forging unity in the first 35 years of community history.

heads and foreign ministers of the member governments, it generally meets three times a year at highly publicized "European Summmts," held in appropriately picturesque settings. The Council is the only EU body that has some jurisdiction in all fields. Since its meetings permit direct confrontation of government leaders, they are often stormy. At the same time, they sometimes manage to resolve thorny problems by hard bargaining.

THE FUTURE OF THE EUROPEAN UNION

Throughout the 1970s and 1980s, public opinion in Europe varied widely on whether membership of the EU was a good thing. In a poll taken in 1985, 72 percent of Italians polled were in favor of EU membership, and only 4 percent against. At the other extreme, only 29 percent of Danes, and 37 percent of Britons favored the organization, and 31 and 30 percent respectively were against it.

The Single European Act

Meanwhile in 1986 the EU moved another stage forward with the passage of the Single European Act. The most immediate new goal the act set out was the completion by the end of 1992 of a unified European internal market. By that date there were to be no more trade barriers between members. All frontier and border formalities would disappear for European Community citizens. Labor and capital could circulate freely. There

The Parliament Building for the European Community, Strasbourg, France.

The Euro, intended to be valid in all countries of the European Union.

would be further progress toward economic and monetary union. More generally, members would work together to improve the environment, and to establish a common plan of social legislation. These last two aims met with less than unanimous approval; some states, most vocally Britain, felt that the ecological and social plans were unrealizable, and represented interference in domestic affairs.

The late 1980s were marked by bursts of frantic activity as the various nations began to prepare themselves for the end of 1992. With no forms of restriction in effect, each individual firm and company would be in direct competition with the whole of Europe. This had increasingly been the case for manufacturers and traders since the EU's early days. After 1992, however, it applied to a host of service industries, such as banking and insurance, that in many cases had been protected by government regulations. Portuguese or Irish investors looking for the best interest rates could send their money to Germany. Car owners in Italy, where insurance rates are high, could insure their vehicles with French or Belgian companies. Many insurance and other service firms began to open branches in countries other than their own. American and Japanese firms, hitherto discouraged by protectionist legislation in individual European countries, also began to eye the vast new market with interest.

On the other hand, for all the difficulties it presented, European economic unity could create a bloc strong enough and independent enough to stand up to the United States and Japan. Already by 1987, in fact, western Europe was the world's largest trading power,

although not, of course, a unified power in the political sense; it handled 37 percent of global trade, more than that of the United States and the Soviet Union combined. The Western European nations also held a third of the world's monetary reserves, and contributed 36 percent of the world's development aid—all this with only 6 percent of the world's population.

New Members for the European Union

As the EU prepared to face 1992, it had to grapple with a new problem: whether to admit new members. Switzerland, a member of EFTA, signed an agreement in 1977 to abolish tariffs on industrial products for EU partners. Its neutral status, and its unwillingness to allow free movement of labor, meant that it would not seek membership in the foreseeable future.

Austria and Finland, however, presented different issues. Neutral since the end of World War II, they theoretically served as bridges between East and West. Even so, by 1987 around half of Austria's exports went to EU countries, principally West Germany, and only about 12 percent to the Soviet Union and eastern Europe. Finland's position was similar. With the collapse of the Soviet bloc's communist regimes in 1989, and the imminent end of the Cold War, the status of these two countries inevitably changed. The interests of European economic unity, as well as their own interests, led both Austria and Finland to become full members in 1995.

The application of Turkey presented more formidable problems. Although only a small part of Turkey lies on the European continent, the Turkish government contended that the country's economy was basically linked with that of Mediterranean Europe. Morocco, in informal approaches to the EU, made a similar argument. In addition, as a leading partner in NATO, Turkey plays an important role in European defense.

Several factors combined to make it unlikely that the Turkish application would be accepted in the near future. In the first place, government rule in Turkey did not correspond to the broadly based democratic systems and traditions that operated in most of the EU member countries most of the time. Secondly, political instability in Turkey would make negotiations difficult. Thirdly, years of implacable animosity between Greece and Turkey—intensified by the Turkish invasion and annexation of northern Cyprus in 1974—made a Greek veto likely. Finally, the admission of Turkey would create a precedent with far-reaching consequences. The European Community began as an association of partners sharing a common history and culture; divergence from that principle could prejudice the chances of a later political union. When Turkey renewed its application in 1997, members' reactions

An anti-fundamentalist demonstration in Istanbul, 1993.

continued to be negative. On the other hand, Cyprus—providing that it achieved unification—was encouraged to apply.

The EU and Eastern Europe

It was precisely the idea of a shared history and culture, however, which made the liberalization of eastern Europe a potential milestone in the EU's history. Countries such as Czechoslovakia, Hungary, and Poland had played a key role in European history, and produced some of the leading figures in European intellectual life, literature, and music. Furthermore, access to the EU's rich markets would help them rebuild economies worn down by years of Stalinism. As a final touch of enlightened self-interest, if the EU members helped to reconstruct the eastern European economies, they would be creating a future market for their own products.

One Eastern bloc country—East Germany—was assured entry by the unification of East and West Germany. Most of the others began negotiations as soon as new governments had been installed. After the spring elections of 1990, Hungary and Czechoslovakia made their initial approaches. Czechoslovakia signed an agreement of economic cooperation with the EU, and began the process of adaptation that membership would require. Hungary, whose economy was in a healthier state, looked to joining the EU at an earlier date. Poland seemed an-

other future applicant, and Bulgaria also signed a treaty of economic cooperation in 1990. At the 1997 meeting which rejected Turkey's renewed application, the slow process of admitting Hungary, Poland, and the Czech Republic (the richer half of the now divided former Czechoslovakia) began. All these should become full members by 2002.

By the early 1990s, the cause of European economic unity had done much to heal the scars of half a century earlier. The countries of Western Europe weathered the economic slumps and political uncertainties of the 1970s, to emerge as a leading world economic force. By committing themselves to the 1992 deadline, they hastened the further process of unification. Few claimed that 1992 would be less than traumatic; it was clear that the pressures of competition would strain each country's resources and run the risk of adversely affecting the lives of countless ordinary citizens. Yet the process was by now irreversible.

Many factors remained vague. Monetary union, the next stage if any form of political union was to be achieved, fiercely divided the EU membership, with Britain resisting anything that could be construed as a loss of national sovereignty. By the spring of 1998, it was decided that most of the members would proceed to monetary union beginning January 1, 1999. The economies of Greece and Portugal were judged too weak to participate, and Britain and Denmark chose not to join the single European currency, the Euro. The plan was for participating members to phase out their national currencies over three years, leaving only the Euro in circulation by 2002.

The landscape of European history seemed permanently changed. As a tumultuous and often cataclysmic century drew toward its close, the Old Continent, whose economic strength and moral standing had been shattered in 1945, once again began to emerge as a leading world power.

Questions for Further Study

1. How successfully does the political and administrative structure of the European Union compensate for national differences among the various members?

2. Which are the most likely candidates for new members by the early 21st century? What effect would their joining have on the EU?

3. What are the arguments for and against monetary union?

Suggestions for Further Reading

Daltrop, A. *Politics and the European Community.* New York, 1987.

Frey-Wouters, E. *The EC and the Third World.* New York, 1980.

Kerr, A. *The Common Market and How It Works.* Oxford, 1983.

Mayne, R. *Postwar: The Dawn of Today's Europe.* New York, 1983.

Padoa-Schioppa, T. *Efficiency, Stability and Equity: A Strategy for the Evolution of the Economic System of the European Community.* Oxford, 1988.

Wallace, H., W. Wallace, and C. Webb. *Policy-making in the European Community.* London, 1983.

Topic 16

Epilogue: Facing the 21st Century

y the 1990s, with the prospect of economic union in sight, Europe had regained an independent position in world political and economic affairs. With the end of Soviet control in Eastern Europe, and the relaxation of the tensions of the Cold War, European nations began to look toward a status that did not lock them into an unconditional alliance with either the United States or the Soviet Union.

The generation of political leaders of the late 1980s saw a series of European figures attain international standing. The conservatives Margaret Thatcher and Helmut Kohl, and the socialists François Mitterand and Felipe Gonzalez, all represented around a decade of continuity in their respective countries—Britain, West Germany, France, and Spain. In Italy the Socialists, under the leadership of Bettino Craxi, became key members of the ruling government coalition. The Greek Socialist leader Andreas Papandreou finally lost power in 1989, when a series of scandals brought down his government.

In Eastern Europe, the Czech Václav Havel became one of the most articulate spokesmen of the "new politics." Above all, the rise of Mikhail Gorbachev in the Soviet Union produced a thaw in East-West relations, and made possible the abrupt dismantlement of the Soviet-supported regimes in eastern Europe.

A number of new problems began to excite public attention. The oil crisis of the 1970s had led many countries to explore the alternative of nuclear energy. The Three Mile Island accident in the United States of 1979, followed by the much more serious accident at Chernobyl in the Soviet Union in 1986, raised widespread doubts about dependence on nuclear power. General concern about damage to the environment became focused in the growing strength of the "Green" movement. In several countries, most notably West Germany and Italy, the Greens became a political force of some significance.

The general mood of political stability continued to be overshadowed by terrorist activities on both right and left. In some cases, such as Northern Ireland and Spain, terrorism was related to specific local issues, often nationalist in origin. In West Germany and Italy, terrorists tried to bring down political and social systems on ideological grounds. A third category of terrorist attacks was related to issues outside Europe, most notably the Palestinian problem.

As the nations of Eastern Europe began to rebuild their governments, and Western Europe prepared for European monetary union by 2002, some visionary politicians began to talk of Europe's "common house," a single continent stretching from the Atlantic to the Urals, which would combine differing social and political systems in a single family. Yet, at the same time, the divisive issue of nationalism continued to create frictions in both East and West. Conflict between the two opposing tendencies dominated the last decade of the 20th century.

BETWEEN EAST AND WEST: THE SEARCH FOR EUROPEAN INDEPENDENCE

The two world wars brought to an end centuries of European dominance in international affairs, and left most European countries unable to rebuild their economies without aid from one of the two superpowers: the United States and the Soviet Union. In the case of Western Europe, U.S. assistance was offered and accepted; in Eastern Europe, the Soviet Union imposed Stalinism. The result in both cases was to create alliances that left Europe divided, and locked into virtually unconditional support for their respective patrons.

Europe and Nuclear Weapons

After 1945, a few strong European leaders asserted their right to independence, including Tito in Yugoslavia and De Gaulle in France. For the most part, however, Western Europe welcomed the "Atlantic Alliance," seeing the American military presence as essential to European security. European leaders, most notably West German Social Democratic leader Helmut Schmidt, supported the installation of medium-range American nuclear missiles on NATO bases in West Germany, Britain, Italy, Belgium, and the Netherlands. The "Two-Track Decision"—to continue arming and negotiating at the same time—was taken late in 1979; it provoked widespread demonstrations and protests in the countries involved.

The missiles were installed in response to the Soviet deployment of nuclear weapons on eastern European soil, in particular in East Germany. Thus, by the mid-1980s each superpower possessed the ability to wage nuclear war in Europe without using weapons located in its own territory.

In 1985 the growing economic crisis in the Soviet Union, and the arrival on the scene of Mikhail Gorbachev, led to the renewal of détente. As Gorbachev sought ways to reduce the burden on the Soviet economy of defense spending, he proved increasingly willing to negotiate significant arms reductions. The American position under Ronald Reagan—that negotiation required a further armsbuildup—became moderated. In 1987 the two superpowers signed a treaty to reduce medium-range nuclear weapons. Thus, at the end of the 1980s both sides began to dismantle their European armaments.

Although the medium-range arms were under American control, they formed part of the NATO forces. Two countries, Britain and France, maintained their own independent nuclear forces. The French continued a program of nuclear testing in the Pacific. In 1985, when the Greenpeace environmental movement threatened to send its boat, *Rainbow Warrior*, to interfere in the tests, the French Defense Ministry had the vessel sunk; one person was killed. Public protests in France forced the resignation of the defense minister and the head of foreign intelligence operations. Nonetheless, France continued to maintain its nuclear capacity, and in 1987 embarked on an expensive and ambitious five-year rearmament plan. In 1996, to a barrage of international protest, the French carried out a series of underground nuclear tests in the Pacific. Similar outrage greeted the nuclear tests of three non-European powers—those of China in 1996 and of India and Pakistan in 1998.

Britain's aging nuclear force became the focus of fierce public debate in the late 1980s. The Thatcher government announced its intention of replacing the old Polaris submarines with updated craft, capable of firing American-made Trident missiles. Thatcher's opponents argued that, in addition to the vast expense of the change, the easing of tension between East and West made an independent British nuclear deterrent increasingly irrelevant.

The process of détente continued through the end of the 1980s, and was rapidly accelerated by the liberalization in eastern Europe of 1989. As politicians and generals alike began to rethink the future role of NATO and the Warsaw Pact alliance, it seemed possible that by the 21st century European security would be in predominantly European hands. The role of the independent British and French nuclear forces in a European defense plan would depend on government decisions and on public reactions. In 1983 an opinion poll in Britain showed eight out of ten people in favor of an independent British deterrent, but this broad support began to shrink.

Nuclear disarmament demonstrators gather in the rain, England, 1981.

By 1997, as NATO prepared to consider applications from a number of former Soviet allies, including the Czech Republic, Poland, and Hungary, NATO leaders signed an agreement with the Soviet Union: the "Partnership for Peace." The occasion signaled reluctant Soviet acceptance of the enlargement eastward of NATO.

POLITICAL LEADERSHIP IN THE LATE 20TH CENTURY

Although the progress in disarmament of the 1980s was due principally to the improved relations between the United States and the Soviet Union, European nations and their leaders continued to play a part on the international scene. French and Italian troops joined the U.S. Marines in an unsuccessful attempt to stabilize conditions in Lebanon between 1982 and 1984. In 1987, with Iraq and Iran locked in violent conflict, British and American ships swept the waters of the Persian Gulf to protect neutral ships from underwater missiles.

New Leaders in Britain and West Germany

The chief political leaders of the 1980s remained in power for most of the decade, although by 1990 several seemed to be losing popular support (see Part VIII, Topic 11). In Britain and West Germany, conservative parties governed. The British prime minister for the entire decade was Margaret Thatcher—Britain's first woman premier—who was elected in 1979. A firm advocate of transatlantic cooperation, she helped U.S. forces to make an air attack on Libya in 1986 by providing the use of British landing and refueling facilities.

By 1990, with Britain's fundamental economic problems still unsolved, there was a growing feeling that a new leader should take the Conservatives into the next election. In the routine leadership election of December 1990, Thatcher failed to win the necessary percentage of votes on the first ballot and withdrew. John Major subsequently was elected Conservative leader and became prime minister. After narrowly winning the general election of 1992, the Conservatives were finally swept from power by a Labour landslide in 1997. In the intervening years, Labour's popular new leader, Tony Blair (born 1954), succeeded in replacing his party's old working-class image with one of efficient modernity.

Helmut Kohl became chancellor of West Germany in 1982. Like Thatcher's, his chief support came from the prosperous middle classes. Less divisive than his British equivalent, he used his exuberance and glowing optimism to promote party unity and present the most favorable image possible of West Germany's international standing. He strengthened ties with eastern Europe and the Soviet Union, while remaining a strong ally of the United States. Indeed, by the end of the decade the American–West German relationship seemed about to supersede the American–British as the cornerstone of the United States' ties to Western Europe.

Domestic problems—unemployment, immigration, pollution—were beginning to erode the Christian

Democrats' popularity, when German politics were suddenly shaken up by the fall of East Germany's communist regime. From the very start, Kohl led the drive for a reunited Germany. In the East German elections he campaigned widely and visibly for the East German Christian Democratic party, promising that West Germany would guarantee the value of the East German mark as equal with that of the West German currency. The West German mark was, in fact, worth around ten times the value of its East German equivalent. His promise, which cost West Germany an enormous amount of money and led to inflation and unemployment there, was implemented a few months later with certain provisos.

Kohl's wholehearted support helped the East German Christian Democrats to win the election and become the country's leading political force. Back in West Germany, however, the economic strain of reunification began to create doubts about the wisdom of Kohl's speed. The Social Democrats, while endorsing the goal of eventual German unity, advocated a slower pace. In regional elections in May 1990, the Social Democrats made significant gains, and the Christian Democrats lost control of one of the houses of Parliament. As both parties prepared for national elections in December 1990, it seemed that West Germans were as concerned with their pocketbooks as with the notion of a reunited Germany, yet the speed of events was irresistible: on October 3, 1990, Germany became reunited. With the approaching end of the century, optimism at the end of 45 years of division became tempered, however, with preoccupation at the financial price of reunification. Voters' worries about the German economy—in particular the replacement of the German mark with the proposed standard European currency, the euro—threatened Kohl's bid for reelection in 1998.

Socialist Leaders in France and Spain

The socialist leaders of France and Spain, François Mitterand and Felipe Gonzalez, came to power respectively in 1981 and 1982. By 1990, both were undergoing a fall in popularity, in part because of their jettisoning of socialist principles in an attempt to solve economic problems.

By the early 1990s, with the political parties preparing for the presidential elections of 1995, the Socialists began to divide up in support of various potential candidates. In consequence, Mitterand's legendary skill at political maneuvering was tested to its limits. Nonetheless, Mitterand's own standing as a senior European statesman allowed him, together with Kohl, to coordinate a European response to the issue of German reunification. His lofty dignity and air of sibylline wisdom also served to resolve differences at

fractious European summits. The 1995 election saw the victory of Mitterand's old rival Jacques Chirac, with a strong showing by the socialist candidate, Lionel Jospin. Two years later, in May 1997, Jospin led his socialists to victory in a surprise general election, thus inaugurating five years of "cohabitation" with a right-wing president.

For most of the 1980s, the moderate and pragmatic Gonzalez presided over Europe's most popular socialist government. Before his election in 1982 he opposed Spanish membership in NATO. By 1986, the year in which Spain entered the EU, he had changed his mind; he was sufficiently convinced of the importance of continued membership to call a popular referendum. To the general surprise, he won victory by a wide margin. An avowed internationalist, Gonzalez did much to facilitate Spain's return to European affairs after the Franco years of isolation.

Like his colleagues elsewhere in Europe, Gonzalez proved less successful in solving domestic economic problems. His mildly conservative policies of wage restraint and monetary caution failed to halt rising inflation, while angering the unions and his left-wing support. Widespread demonstrations led to a decline in Socialist power. By 1990 the Socialists were still in control, and Gonzalez a popular figure, but neither party nor party leader could afford to ignore their supporters; the honeymoon had been a long one, but it was over. In the spring of 1996, a conservative government came to power, although only with the support of smaller regional parties.

Government Crises in Italy and Greece

In Italy the usual creation and collapse of coalition governments dominated by the Christian Democrats was briefly interrupted in 1981–1982, when the Republican leader Giovanni Spadolini (1925–1994) formed two center-left governments of short duration. The Socialists provided a more consistent interlude, when Bettino Craxi led a left-center government which lasted from 1983 to 1986—three and a half years, a record in postwar Italian politics.

Craxi's rise to prominence in Italian political life began with his election as Socialist leader in 1976. Over the following decade the Socialists slowly increased their share of the votes, rising from 9.6 percent in 1976 to 16.8 percent in the regional elections of 1990. (The same period saw the Italian Communist party in precipitous decline, falling from 34.4 to 24.4 percent.) Craxi's own combative and aggressive personality proved a mixed blessing. There was a general feeling that his government was efficient and "got things done." On the other hand his histrionic oratory and tough political style, coupled with an unfortunate resemblance to

Mussolini—both leaders bald and portly—led to doubts. In cartoons and television satirical programs, Craxi became regularly portrayed as Italy's late and unlamented *Duce*.

The fall of the Craxi government was followed by another long-drawn-out period of instability, during which the country's economy continued to boom. Carlo de Benedetti, a leading industrialist, was heard to remark that, with all the confusion in Rome, he and his colleagues could get on with running Italian business successfully and uninterruptedly. By 1988, however, government was firmly back in the hands of the Christian Democrats, under the leadership of Giuliano Andreotti (born 1919). The coalition's chief partners, Christian Democrats and Socialists, continued to bicker as Craxi alternately threatened and cajoled. As Italy entered the 1990s, its eccentric political system seemed likely to continue relatively unchanged.

Yet in the spring of 1993, a series of investigations began to unfold that implicated a high proportion of Italy's ruling class in massive bribery and corruption. The scandal came to be known as *"Mani Pulite,"* or "Clean Hands." The base of operations was Milan, and one of the chief investigating magistrates, Antonio di Pietro, rapidly became a popular hero. In a matter of months, many of Italy's leading politicians, most notably Craxi himself, were driven from office. After a period of caretaker governments, and seven months during which Silvio Berlusconi, one of the leading business men in Italy, served as prime minister, elections in April 1996 brought a center-left alliance, the Olive Branch, to power for the first time in Italian history. The largest single party, the Democratic Party of the Left (PDS), consisted of the majority of the former Italian Communist party, but the alliance also included former Christian Democrats: its leader, Romano Prodi, had served as a state bureaucrat under Christian Democratic rule.

Greece spent the 1980s under socialist government. In 1981 the Panhellenic Socialist Movement (PASOK) won an electoral victory whose size was unparalleled anywhere else in Europe. Their leader, the charismatic if controversial Andreas Papandreou (born 1919), instituted a wide-ranging program of reform. His government liberalized the divorce laws, restructured agriculture, and began to move from a pro-Western position in foreign affairs to an independent nationalism: among the recurrent causes of tension between Greece and the United States was the presence of American forces on Greek territory.

The Greek economy remained in bad shape. The Socialists did little to modernize industry or introduce new technologies, and the country remained dependent on foreign aid. In 1988, a personal scandal involving Papandreou—he announced plans to divorce his wife and marry his mistress—shook his party. Subsequent revelations of widespread corruption in government circles, which also involved Papandreou directly, led to his fall from power. A period of inconclusive elections finally ended in May 1990, when a conservative government was returned to office with the narrowest of margins—one seat. By the late 1990s, with the Socialists once again in power, the economic problems facing Greece's new rulers were formidable: rampant inflation, growing unemployment, and increasing foreign debt.

THE DISSOLUTION OF THE SOVIET UNION

The two years from 1989 to 1991 dramatically transformed the entire situation in Eastern Europe as well as the nature of global politics. The revolution of 1989 (see Part VIII, Topic 12) had brought an end to Soviet hegemony over the nations behind what was once called the "Iron Curtain." Then, in 1990–1991, the Soviet Union itself collapsed under the stress of the fundamental changes that had been wrought by Gorbachev.

New Leadership in Eastern Europe

With the revolutions of 1989, virtually all countries in Eastern Europe underwent a change of leadership. In some cases this was more apparent than real. The new regime in Romania, under the leadership of Ion Iliescu (born 1930), retained a suspicious number of those politicians who had served under Ceausescu. Bulgaria, too, moved slowly in replacing the old guard. Hungary, East Germany, and Czechoslovakia, however, all elected new noncommunist leaders, who in turn nominated new heads of state.

One of these, the Czech Václav Havel (born 1936), began to emerge as one of the leading representatives of the new order in Eastern Europe. A playwright and intellectual, Havel became president of Czechoslovakia in 1990. Traveling widely in Eastern and Western Europe, and to the United States, he spoke eloquently and feelingly of the needs of the new democratic nations, and of the urgency of reconciling old hatreds. Even his influence, however, could not prevent the country from splitting into two independent nations, the Czech Republic and Slovakia.

In Poland, the beginning of 1990 saw the beginnings of a split in the hitherto united Solidarity leadership. As Polish Prime Minister Tadeusz Mazowiecki (born 1927) introduced unpopular economic reforms along generally liberal lines, Lech Wałesa, Solidarity's most prominent leader, began to press for more conservative policies. Wałesa had been prepared earlier to hand over the business of government to his colleagues and occupy a symbolic leadership position, but there were signs of coming conflict. Wałesa and Mazowiecki both ran for election as Poland's president. Wałesa won. By the time of Poland's next presidential election in 1995, however, disillusioned voters rejected Wałesa and turned to a former Communist politician.

The End of Soviet History

By 1990, the greatest of all changes in post–world war history had been wrought by the leader whose own position seemed least secure: Mikhail Gorbachev (see Part VIII, Topic 12). Almost as striking as the actual achievements themselves was the change in the character of Soviet leadership, symbolized by the prominent role played in Soviet public life and visits abroad by Gorbachev's wife, Raisa.

Among the qualities brought by Mikhail Gorbachev to his position was an awareness of the importance of "image" in a world of global communications. His predecessors had done nothing to relieve the monolithic uniformity of Soviet leadership or its secrecy. Gorbachev took part in much-publicized "walk-arounds," on which he met people in the street. Outside the Soviet Union these mainly consisted of opportunities for passersby to shake hands with the famous man; the public relations sessions blocked traffic in most of the cities Gorbachev visited. On home ground, the "walk-arounds" often led to lively debate, with Gorbachev listening to complaints and arguing back. Early in 1990, when the possibility of Lithuania breaking away from the Soviet Union seemed increasingly likely, Gorbachev made an unsuccessful attempt to prevent the move by going there and presenting his case against independence.

Soviet leaders after Stalin severely discouraged the "cult of personality." Little was known about their private lives or families—Yuri Andropov's wife made her first public appearance at her late husband's funeral in 1984. Furthermore, although women were officially equal to men in Soviet society, very few played any part in public life.

From his first visits abroad, Gorbachev was accompanied by his wife Raisa (born 1932). Like an American president's wife, the Soviet first lady played an important role in humanizing the lofty affairs of state. Indeed, Raisa's role seemed modeled on the American system. While her husband held meetings with President Reagan on his visit to the United States in 1987, she visited the White House; a less than friendly encounter there with Nancy Reagan led to a distinctly cool relationship between the two wives.

Gorbachev's power clearly remained dependent on the success of his economic reforms, and not on his public image. In the winter of 1990–1991, as food supplies grew increasingly short in the Soviet Union's principal cities, Boris Yeltsin, elected president of the Russian Republic in 1989, stepped up his hostile criticism of Gorbachev's program. The issue of whether individual republics could break away from the Soviet Union became the cause of widespread demonstrations and protests.

Early in 1991, Soviet troops used tanks to block demonstrators in Lithuania who were threatening to take over a radio station. Worldwide disapproval of the bloodshed focused on the timing of the move, which came as the crisis in the Persian Gulf turned into open war (see below), and many feared that events in the Middle East would distract international attention from the Baltic, as the Suez crisis of 1956 had from Hungary (see Part VIII, Topic 12). Gorbachev himself condemned the use of force, and claimed that he had not been consulted in advance. In any event, the political future of the Soviet Union remained shrouded in uncertainty. A referendum held in the spring of 1991—which was boycotted by a number of the republics—gave Gorbachev a majority in favor of maintaining Soviet unity. Nevertheless, although the central government in Moscow continued to direct defense, foreign policy, and currency matters, the individual republics assumed considerable power over internal regional affairs. Gorbachev then stunned party followers by dropping Marxism-Leninism as the nation's official doctrine. Other changes followed rapidly. By 1991, Moscow had begun to abandon the state-directed economy in favor of a market-driven system. Russian voters also backed Yeltsin's proposal of popular election for the Soviet president.

Yeltsin's standing became further enhanced when he led the opposition to an abortive coup by a group of conservative hardliners in the fall of 1991. As huge crowds filled Moscow's streets in protest against the coup, Yeltsin's public defiance made him the hero of the moment. In the ensuing confusion, a discredited Gorbachev stepped down and Yeltsin was elected president. In spite of recurrent bouts of ill health, he ran for reelection in 1997 and won. It was thus under his leadership that the Soviet Union dissolved into Russia and a series of independent republics, and the complex process of negotiating the terms of new relationships began. The new loosely linked confederation became known as the Commonwealth of Independent States.

The Gulf War

Events in the Middle East clearly demonstrated the collapse of Soviet power. On August 2, 1990, Iraqi troops

Map 16.1   The Middle East, Mid-1980s

invaded the neighboring oil-rich state of Kuwait. Over the following weeks, a consensus gradually emerged at the United Nations to impose economic sanctions on Iraq, while 29 nations began to send troops and supplies to the Persian Gulf to form an alliance under UN auspices. By far the largest contingent—almost half a million participants—came from the United States, but other members of the alliance included Britain, France, and Italy. Egypt and Syria were among the Arab states to participate.

As the months passed, with no sign of concessions from Iraq's increasingly belligerent dictator, Saddam Hussein (born 1937), at the urging of the United States the United Nations issued an ultimatum: if Iraq failed to withdraw from Kuwait by January 15, 1991, the coalition forces would take military action. The Soviet Union sent no forces to the Persian Gulf, and launched a number of independent peace initiatives, but in the end supported UN action.

The deadlock was broken when the allied forces duly began massive aerial bombardments of Baghdad and other Iraqi cities and military installations. Among Iraq's responses was the shelling of

Israel—itself not a member of the UN coalition—in the hope of provoking Israeli forces into action, and thereby detaching from the coalition states such as Syria, traditionally hostile to Israel. For the first time in its history Israel did not respond to provocation, and the allied forces remained intact (see Part VIII, Topic 10).

After a month of bombing had crushed Iraqi powers of resistance and morale, allied victory in the ground campaign took only a few days. Iraq and the allies signed a cease-fire agreement which restored Kuwait's sovereignty. Iraqi forces withdrew, leaving Kuwait devastated with many of its oil wells in flames. Iraq itself plunged into civil war, with the remaining forces of Saddam Hussein battling with Kurdish and Shiite rebels.

Among the terms of the cease-fire was a proviso that Iraq would dismantle and destroy its stockpile of chemical weapons, and UN inspectors were given the task of overseeing the process. Seven years later, in the winter of 1997–1998, tensions again flared when the Iraqis refused to open certain "Presidential Palace Compounds" to inspection.

THE ENERGY CRISIS AND THE NUCLEAR DILEMMA

Europe's industrial rebirth after World War II was heavily dependent on imported oil supplies. Unlike the United States, there are only scanty oil deposits on European territory. In 1960, the Organization of Petroleum Exporting Countries (OPEC) was founded by the world's main oil producers: Iran, Iraq, Kuwait, Libya, Saudi Arabia, and Venezuela. Membership subsequently extended to Qatar, Indonesia, United Arab Emirates, Algeria, Nigeria, Ecuador, and Gabon. As the industries of many countries came to rely on oil supplies, the power of OPEC increased dramatically.

In 1973, OPEC quadrupled world oil prices, and in the years between 1974 and 1980 the price of oil tripled again. In the 1980s, OPEC's ability to control the market began to decline, as its members failed to agree on production limits, and non-OPEC members started to produce oil and natural gas. Nevertheless, the industrial world had received a severe shock. The booming years of the 1960s gave way to a period of economic crisis, as energy costs began to absorb production profits.

Nuclear Energy

One solution to steeply rising energy costs was to introduce conservation measures. A more attractive, and less stringent, answer seemed to lie in the development of nuclear energy programs. The heat generated by the process of nuclear fission within a reactor can be used to produce electricity. The disposal of radioactive waste from the process presented problems; at first, it was stored in concrete vaults lined with stainless steel.

For many European countries, lacking their own natural energy supplies, the production of artificial energy seemed an ideal solution to the problem of outside suppliers and their demands. In France, government sponsorship encouraged the construction of a network of nuclear plants that was to provide more than 60 percent of the country's energy needs. By 1985, West Germany was producing a third of its energy by nuclear processes.

The potential dangers of this new energy source were the difficulty of storing increasing quantities of waste, and the possibility of a major accident at a nuclear energy plant. The cost of such a disaster, it was clear, would be immense in both human and financial terms. As early as 1957, the U.S. Congress passed the Price-Anderson Act, limiting insurance company liability for nuclear disasters to a small fraction of any projected claims. Yet the construction of nuclear plants continued throughout the industrialized world, as businesses sought to cut their dependence on imported energy, and governments saw an easy way to meet their needs.

The first serious nuclear failure occurred in 1979, at the Three Mile Island site, near Middletown, Pennsylvania. As a result of a failure of the reactor's cooling system, it began to emit "puffs" of radiation. Hasty action prevented the meltdown of the reactor's core and the explosion of a hydrogen bubble that had formed inside.

Far more disastrous was the accident at Chernobyl, near Kiev, in the Soviet Union. On April 26, 1986, one of the reactors there exploded, scattering radioactive debris over thousands of miles. One hundred thirty-five thousand people living in the region were evacuated, and food products throughout Europe

A meeting of OPEC.

Atomic power station at
Calder Hall, England.

were contaminated—from Welsh lamb to Parmesan cheese. The burning reactor was eventually buried in concrete.

The Environmental Movement

The dangers of nuclear pollution would be added to the list of causes that environmental movements were waging throughout western Europe and the United States.

The effects of nuclear fallout had, of course, been all too clear at the end of World War II, with the bombing of Hiroshima and Nagasaki. During the 1950s public preoccupation about human interference with nature continued to mount. In 1962, an American biologist, Rachel Carson (1907–1964), published *Silent Spring*, a dramatic account of the dangers of other forms of pollution, in particular pesticides.

Pollution from oil shale ash, Estonia.

By the late 1960s, environmental groups—the "Greens"—were drawing attention to crisis situations in many parts of Europe. In the heart of the continent, industrial plants in Austria, Switzerland, West Germany, France, and Holland were discharging ever-greater quantities of industrial waste into the river Rhine. The Mediterranean was so polluted in places that swimming in it was dangerous. In many cities exhaust fumes and traffic vibrations were damaging historic buildings and monuments; they included the Gothic cathedrals of northern Europe and the Parthenon in Athens. Industrial cities, both in Europe and in North America, were plagued with smog, a form of air pollution produced by factory and automobile fumes.

The Greens roused considerable public support. Britain set up a Department of the Environment in 1970, and France followed a year later. In 1972 a conference meeting in Stockholm established a United Nations Environment Program to deal with issues on an international basis.

The Environmentalists and Nuclear Energy

In West Germany, the Greens developed into a significant political force. Part of their success was due to the grave problem presented by the condition of the country's forests: between a third and a half of them were at risk of dying of pollution, much of it caused by acid rain (the result of air moisture combining with chemicals emitted by factories and automobiles). The Chernobyl disaster galvanized the Greens into action, and increased their public support. In the election of 1987 they won 8.3 percent of the votes, a notable improvement over their 5.6 percent in 1983.

The protests led by the Greens forced the West German government to cut back its nuclear energy program. The building of plants and waste disposal facilities was halted, often blocked by angry crowds of demonstrators. As a result, West Germany was forced to import increasing quantities from abroad. In 1988 it was the highest per capita importer of energy of any major industrialized country.

In Italy, also, public protests led to the suspension of a nuclear energy program. As a country particularly poor in natural energy resources, Italy had welcomed the chance to produce its own nuclear resources. Three plants were constructed, and plans were made to increase the number. With growing concern, however, fueled by the Chernobyl disaster, the Socialists and other parties sponsored a referendum that allowed the public to express its opinion: no more nuclear energy. Work at the existing plants was phased out, and new construction suspended. The Italians turned for energy supplies to natural gas, to be supplied by two pipelines, one from the Soviet Union and one from Algeria and Libya. Both projects were inaugurated in 1982, and work was stepped up in the late 1980s.

France was too dependent on nuclear energy to be able to eliminate it. Although Mitterand's Socialist government briefly suspended new plant construction in the early 1980s, by 1986 two-thirds of the country's electricity was generated by nuclear plants. Britain's coal supplies, together with natural gas from under the North Sea, made the provision of nuclear energy less vital. Nonetheless, by the 1990s nuclear power provided 13 percent of electricity there.

The European country most dependent on nuclear energy was Sweden, in spite of strenuous efforts on the part of environmentalists to block the building of new plants. In 1980, a referendum produced a compromise. The government would complete twelve plants, to be functioning by 1985, but all of them would be shut down by 2010. No Swedish political party opposed a nuclear phase-out, although it presented huge problems, and the future of the country's energy supplies remained in doubt.

Demonstration poster of the West German ecological party, the Greens.

In Search of Safe Nuclear Power

The dilemma presented by the dangers of nuclear energy dominated the planning of individual governments, but also crossed national boundaries. As Chernobyl showed, radioactive fallout could spread over thousands of miles. One solution was the construction of safer reactors. In the late 1980s, the Swedes started to pioneer the latest nuclear technology in their Process Inherent Ultimately Safe Reactor (PIUS).

The invention of a process to manufacture energy by nuclear fusion, rather than by fission, offered the hope of a more long-term solution. Fusion would require only small amounts of fuel, and none of the by-products would be radioactive. Research into methods of generating energy by fusion led to the construction of particle accelerators in Western Europe and the United States. In 1988, the U.S. Energy Department announced the building of a "Supercollider" near Dallas, at a cost of $6 billion.

By the last decade of the 20th century efforts were stepped up to find an alternative solution to the problem that faced countries in all parts of the world: the advantages of nuclear energy—clean, capable of being produced in quantity—were overshadowed by its dangers.

TERRORISM AND THE POLITICS OF VIOLENCE

One of the problems that continued to plague the world in the latter part of the 20th century was terrorism. In a reaction to the general political stability of the major Western democracies, groups supporting a variety of causes used violence—or the threat of violence—for political ends.

Terrorism and Nationalism

In a number of Western European countries, nationalist groups or regions claimed the right to independence. The Basques, a people of unknown origins, inhabit the Pyrenees area of southwestern France and northern Spain; there are around 100,000 in France and 600,000 in Spain. In the Spanish Civil War, many Basques fought against Franco's Falangists, and the region was subsequently subdued. In 1952, a Basque nationalist movement was formed, which soon split into a militant and a moderate wing. The moderates stood for election; the militants turned to the gun. Both wings demanded local autonomy.

The 1970s and 1980s were marked by a string of assassinations, for which ETA (the militant Basque organization) claimed credit. The moderates, condemning the use of violence, became an increasing force in local politics. In the 1986 regional elections, Basque nationalist parties won two-thirds of the seats. The government made concessions, giving the Basques the right to raise their own taxes, and to replace the national police and the Civil Guard with an all-Basque police force. The moves reduced support for the terrorists, and cooperation between French and Spanish antiterrorist forces produced a higher level of arrests. Nonetheless, the assassinations continued sporadically, and discouraged foreign investors in the region, one of Spain's most industrialized areas.

Similar separatist violence scarred Corsica and the German-speaking region of northern Italy. Europe's most bitter terrorist campaign, however, was that waged by the Irish Republican Army (IRA) for control of Northern Ireland. In 1922, the island had been divided, with the lower 26 counties forming the independent, predominantly Catholic Republic of Ireland. The northern, mainly Protestant part rejected "Home Rule" (independence), and remained part of Britain, although with its own parliament, Stormont.

British soldiers with 1,000 pounds of homemade fertilizer explosives which were found in an abandoned van on the grounds of Belfast Castle, 1997.

Relations between Protestants and the Catholic minority in Northern Ireland were soured by centuries of mutual mistrust and hate. In 1969, peaceful street demonstrations led to open violence. By 1972, the British government felt obliged to disband Stormont and govern the region directly, seeking to satisfy the Protestant majority while protecting Catholic interests. Over the following decades the IRA battled against a string of illegal paramilitary Protestant groups in their campaign to drive out the British and assume control. Between 1969 and 1998, some 3000 people were killed in bombings and street fighting.

The British tried a series of ways to reduce the bloodletting and restore local government. After the death of ten IRA hunger strikers in prison in 1981, a new Northern Ireland Assembly was elected in 1982, but dissolved four years later. In 1983 a law was passed granting pardon (or at least lenience) to "informers" in either the Protestant organizations or the IRA; it led to a dramatic increase in the number of arrests. Yet at the end of the same year, IRA terrorists exploded a bomb outside London's Harrod's department store in the middle of Christmas shopping crowds, and in 1984 blew up a hotel in Brighton at which a Conservative party conference was taking place. Further IRA and paramilitary Protestant bombings continued throughout the late 1980s, some of them aimed at British troops outside Northern Ireland, on bases in England and West Germany. An IRA cease-fire, announced in 1994, lasted only a little more than a year. With the exclusion from all-party talks of the Sinn Fein movement, widely seen as the political wing of the IRA, there

seemed little hope of progress, although the arrival in power of Tony Blair's "New Labour" party offered the possibility of a fresh start to negotiations. They resumed in the winter of 1997–1998, with both Sinn Fein and the leading Protestant groups represented at the conference table. Discussions were overshadowed by a series of acts of violence by extremists on both sides. Nonetheless, agreement was reached in April 1998, and its terms were approved by a large majority a month later in a referendum held in both Northern Ireland and the Republic of Ireland. As preparations began for the selection of a Cross-border Council later that year, the mood seemed cautiously optimistic.

International Terrorism

Terrorist activities elsewhere in Europe were inspired by ideological rather than nationalistic issues. In West Germany and Italy, extreme left-wing groups tried to destabilize the established social and economic order, as a prelude to political revolution (see Part VIII, Topic 11). Italy was further plagued by extreme right-wing violence. The worst single incident was the bomb explosion in Bologna's railway station in August 1980, at the height of the holiday season; more than 80 people were killed. Although those responsible were never caught, they seem to have been part of a far-right terrorist group.

As investigators throughout Europe and the Middle East began pooling information and working more closely in collaboration, a picture began to emerge of links between the various terrorist groups. The IRA, the Italian

Aftermath of a terrorist car bomb explosion in Paris.

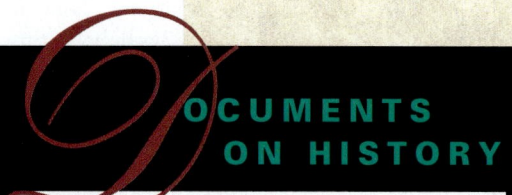

Analyzing Terrorism

Two of the leading terrorist organizations operating in Europe after World War II were the Irish Republican Army (IRA) in Northern Ireland and the Red Army Fraction (RAF) in Germany, both of which accompanied their campaigns of violence with barrages of propaganda. The first two selections below consist of an objective description of the RAF and an example of their propaganda. Then follow a statement of intentions of the IRA and a counterstatement from an opposing Protestant extremist group. Perhaps the most notorious terrorist operating in the last 20 years has been Abu Nidal, whose career is described in a "portrait" first published in the *Washington Post*. Finally, Walter Laqueur, one of the world's leading authorities on terrorism, places the phenomenon in perspective.

TERRORISM IN GERMANY: THE RAF

The description of the RAF reprinted below comes from a longer article by Hans Josef Horchem on terrorism in Europe. It is followed by a section from one of the RAF's propaganda statements, which sets out the organization's notion of the "urban guerilla."

The RAF is the oldest and most dangerous German terrorist organization. In June 1980 the RAF took over the remaining cadre of the second German terrorist group, the "Movement of 2nd of June."

The RAF retained its structure and its system of organization after the unification with the "Movement of 2nd of June." Hierarchical order does not exist and decisions are made collectively. In an attack every member has to fight unto death.

The commando unit includes only 20 people. The attack against Hanns Martin Schleyer was made with only 20 members of the RAF, in spite of the fact that extensive logistic preparations were necessary.

The commando unit is living underground and depends on the "legal environment," which includes approximately 200 people. In the seventies the legal units were organized in "Anti-Fascist Groups" or in "Committees against Isolation-Torture." These names don't exist anymore. But the supporters of these groups compose a reservoir for illegal activities in the future.

Enough money is available. The "war booty" of the "Movement of 2nd of June" after the kidnaping of the Austrian industrialist Palmers in November 1977 is now in the hands of the RAF. Of the original 4 million Deutschmark the RAF has spent about 2 million Deutschmark.

The RAF propagates only one thing, that is armed conflict, and tries to win comrades-in-arms for this. "The armed campaign is the highest form of class struggle." The leading force and the avant-garde of the class-struggle is not the working class but the "revolutionary intelligence."

Already in 1971 the RAF said in its publication "Close the Loop-holes of the Revolutionary Theory—

Build up the Red Army": "It is not the organizations of the industrial working class, but the revolutionary sections of the student bodies that are today the bearers of the contemporary conscience." The industrial proletarians inside the developed capitalist countries have changed into an "aristocracy of workers." Therefore a true revolutionary cannot rely on them anymore.

The long-range strategy of the RAF was then and is today aimed at "U.S. imperialism" and its chief ally in Europe, the Federal Republic of Germany.

From Horchem, H. J. "European Terrorism: A German Perspective." Terrorism: An International Journal, Vol. 6, no.1. Copyright © 1982.

If we are correct in saying that American imperialism is a paper tiger, i.e., that it can ultimately be defeated, and if the Chinese Communists are correct in their thesis that victory over American imperialism has become possible because the struggle against it is now being waged in all four corners of the earth, with the result that the forces of imperialism are now fragmented, a fragmentation which makes them possible to defeat—if this is correct, then there is no reason to exclude or disqualify any particular country or any particular region from taking part in the anti-imperialist struggle because the forces of revolution are especially weak there and the forces of reaction especially strong.

As it is wrong to discourage the forces of revolution by underestimating their power, so it is wrong to suggest that they should seek confrontations in which these forces cannot but be squandered or annihilated. The contradictions between the sincere comrades in the organizations—let's forget about the prattlers—and the Red Army Fraction, is that we charge them with discouraging the forces of revolution, and they

suspect us of squandering the forces of revolution. Certainly, this analysis does indicate the directions in which the fraction of those comrades working in the factories and at local level and the Red Army Fraction are overdoing things, if they are overdoing things. Dogmatism and adventurism have since time immemorial been characteristic deviations in periods of revolutionary weakness in all countries. Anarchists having since time immemorial been the sharpest critics of opportunism, anyone criticizing the opportunists exposes himself to the charge of anarchism. This is something of an old chestnut.

The concept of the "urban guerilla" originated in Latin America. Here, the urban guerilla can only be what he is there: the only revolutionary method available to what are on the whole weak revolutionary forces.

The urban guerilla starts by recognizing that there will be no Prussian order of march of the kind in which so many so-called revolutionaries would like to lead the people into battle. He starts by recognizing that by the time the moment for armed struggle arrives, it will already be too late to start preparing for it; that in a country whose potential for violence is as great and whose revolutionary traditions are as broken and feeble as the Federal Republic's, there will not—without revolutionary initiative—even be a revolutionary orientation when conditions for revolutionary struggle are better than they are at present—which will happen as an inevitable consequence of the development of late capitalism itself.

To this extent, the "urban guerilla" is the logical consequence of the negation of parliamentary democracy long since perpetrated by its very own representatives; the only and inevitable response to emergency laws and the rule of the hand grenade; the readiness to fight with those same means the system has chosen

continued next page

to use in trying to eliminate its opponents. The "urban guerilla" is based on a recognition of the facts instead of an apologia of the facts.

From Rote Armee Fraktion (RAF). *The Concept of the Urban Guerilla*, April, 1971.

THE IRA AND THEIR PROTESTANT EXTREMIST OPPONENTS

Both the IRA and the extremist Protestant groups in Northern Ireland who oppose them have used propaganda as well as violence in their campaign for public support. For all the extreme divergences in their positions, they perceive a common enemy in the British government, as the following two excerpts from their declarations make clear.

The effect of the IRA bombing campaign can be gauged in many different ways. Firstly, they have struck at the very root of enemy morale, confining and tying down large numbers of troops and armored vehicles in center city areas, thus relieving much of the pressure on the much-oppressed nationalist areas. In terms of direct financial loss (structural damage, goods, machinery), also in the crippling of industrial output and perhaps worst of all in the scaring-off of foreign capital investments, IRA bombs have hit Britain where she feels it most—in her pocket.

England always found unfortunate soldiers quite dispensable and to a certain extent replaceable, but she always counted in terms of cost to the Treasury. Any peace through the granting of freedom emanating to rebellious colonies from London came by means of calculation—the cost of occupation. Since 1969 a bill of warfare running to at least a conservative 500,000,000 pounds has not gone unnoticed

back home in Britain where recent opinion polls showed that over 54% of the ordinary people wanted the troops withdrawn forthwith.

Already some 1,500 troops have left Northern Ireland never to return. In many cases death certificates have been issued as for fatal road accident victims to the unsuspecting next-of-kin of soldiers killed in action in a heartless attempt at cooking records and hiding telling manpower losses. Suddenly Northern Ireland has become England's Vietnam. In the knowledge that the will to overcome of a risen people can never be defeated by brute force or even overwhelming odds more enlightened politicians have seen the light and are themselves thinking along Tone's famous dictum: "Break the connection!"

Great Britain too, of course, has suffered losses other than bomb damage and loss of personnel. Her prestige and credibility in terms of world opinion and world finance have been severely shaken; her duplicity and selective sense of justice have been seriously exposed; her puerile hankering after "holding the last vestige of the Empire" has marked her as a recidivist nation, psychologically vulnerable, unstable, and mentally immature.

From *Freedom Struggle* by the Provisional IRA.

We are not good at propaganda and not good at extolling our Virtues or admitting our faults. We just stick to our points of view, bow our heads, and pray for it all to die down for another fifty years or so.

Gradually, however, we have come to realize that this time other factors have come into the age-old conflict of the Scots-Irish versus the Irish-Irish, or if you prefer it that way, the Protestants versus the Catholics in Ireland.

Traditionally the English politicians let us down—betrayal we call it. The Catholics try to overwhelm us so we are caught in between two lines of fire. Second-class Englishmen, half-caste Irishmen, this we can live with, and even defeat, but how can we be expected to beat the world revolutionary movement which supplies arms and training, not to mention most sophisticated advice on publicity, promotion, and expertise to the IRA?

The British army in Ulster has good soldiers who are being set up like dummy targets. The orders of the politicians are tying both hands behind their backs. The British public says: "Send the soldiers home." We say: "Send the politicians and the officers home and leave us the men and the weapons—or, why not send the soldiers home and leave us the weapons and we will send you the IRA wrapped up in little boxes and little tins like cans of baked beans."

The politicians who rule our lives from England do not understand us. They stop the army from defending us properly and stop us from defending ourselves. We do not like these flabby-faced men with pop eyes and fancy accents. . . .

From statement of Protestant Extremist Group, Dublin *Sunday World*, June 9, 1973.

ABU NIDAL: A PORTRAIT

One of the features of terrorism over the past 20 years has been the link between terrorist campaigns in various parts of the world. The Palestinian Abu Nidal, who has operated in Europe and throughout the Middle East, is a powerful and frightening symbol of international terrorism.

Abu Nidal left a calling card last fall in an interview with the German magazine *Der Spiegel*. "I can assure you of one thing," he said. "If we have the chance to inflict the slightest harm to Americans, we will not hesitate to do it. In the months and years to come, the Americans will think of us."

Americans may indeed be thinking of Abu Nidal following recent events. His real name is Sabri Khalil al-Banna, and he is one of those on

whom Libyan leader Muammar Khadafy will most likely depend to carry out his campaign to attack American interests. It is clear that the Libyans are supporting Abu Nidal, and he is linked to last December's bloody attacks at the Rome and Vienna airports, only the most recent example of the mayhem that he has made his life's work.

Here is a snapshot of the man who describes himself as America's enemy: His politics are those of revenge and revolution on a grand scale. He seeks through terror a retributive and perfect justice that can never be achieved. He moves through a shadowy inter-connected world of international and Arab terrorist networks that have given him a mystique larger than life. And yet through all of this there is something very ordinary, small and marginal about him—something that seems to reinforce the fact that terror, no matter how brutal, is only a symptom of a failed cause and of the frustrations of a desperate man.

Perhaps even more frightening than the man himself is his relationship to those Arab regimes willing to tolerate his excesses. In a world where assassinations and violence have become legitimate tools of political struggle, Abu Nidal and those like him provide important services in the never-ending fight for influence and power. He is not simply a product of the Arab-Israeli conflict but of an intra-Arab struggle in which ideology is subordinated to regime survival and personal vendetta. How else can we explain that a man who in 1976 tried to kill the Syrian foreign minister could be operating out of Damascus seven years later?

Who is this elusive figure and what is the nature of the environment in which he operates? Is he simply the hired gun of state-sponsored terrorism, or is he the genuine revolutionary he claims to be?

One of the most frustrating aspects of dealing with Abu Nidal is that so little is known about him. Even in the murky subterranean world of international terrorism, he is a mystery.

continued next page

Despite two recent interviews, rumors still abound that he is dead or incapacitated and that his operations are run by committee. In a recent interview, Abu Nidal claimed that he had undergone plastic surgery. His interviewers usually ask him for some proof of his identity and wonder themselves whether he is who he claims to be. During one interview, Abu Nidal reportedly ripped open his shirt to show an inquisitive journalist scars from a much rumored heart operation.

His method of operation only enhances his reputation as a secretive shadowy force likely to appear anywhere at any time. The entire Abu Nidal organization is tightly compartmentalized and may not number more than a few hundred. The structure of the organization further obscures the links between operations and the master command. Capitalizing on the shadowy terrorist network in Europe and the Middle East, Abu Nidal further covers his tracks. Thus, in the Rome and Vienna operations, the terrorists could have been trained in Lebanon, acquired Libyan confiscated Tunisian passports, and obtained weapons in Europe. . . .

The lessons drawn from studying Abu Nidal and his world are not heartening ones. Indeed the consistency and effectiveness of his operations lead to the conclusion that his brand of terrorism is likely to remain a permanent feature of the Middle East's political landscape. Even more sobering is the recognition that Abu Nidal's terror has become very much a permanent fixture of shifting rivalries between Arab regimes. He remains effective because he is willing and able to provide services for a variety of patrons.

Nonetheless, in the end there are limits to what Abu Nidal can hope to achieve. He represents no constituency with any real power, he can never achieve anything positive for Palestinians. He can only destroy and intimidate until he himself is destroyed. More like him may follow, but their legacy will not be any more enduring.

From Miller, Aaron. "Portrait of Abu Nidal," *Washington Post,* March 30, 1986. Reprinted with permission of Aaron Miller.

REFLECTIONS ON TERRORISM

he following extracts come from an article by Walter Laqueur, chairman of the International Research Council of the Center for Strategic and International Studies in Washington, DC, one of the leading experts on terrorism in all its forms.

Fifty years hence, puzzled historians will try to make sense of the behavior of Western governments and media in the 1980s vis-a-vis terrorism. Presidents and other leaders have frequently referred to terrorism as one of the greatest dangers facing mankind. For days and weeks on end, television networks devoted most of their prime-time news to terrorist operations. Publicists referred to terrorism as the cancer of the modern world, growing inexorably until it poisoned and engulfed the society on which it fed, dragging it down to destruction.

Naturally, our future historian will expect that a danger of such magnitude must have figured very highly on the agenda of our period—equal, say, to the danger of war, starvation, overpopulation, deadly diseases, debts, and so on. He will assume that determined action was taken and major resources allocated to the fight against this threat. And he will be no little surprised to learn that, when the Swedish Prime Minister was killed in 1986, the Swedish government promised a reward for information leading to the apprehension of his killer that amounted to less than 10% of the annual income of an investment banker or a popular entertainer—not necessarily of the front rank; that the French government offered even less for its terrorists; that West Germany was willing to pay only up to $50,000 "for the most dangerous." The United States, always a great believer in the effectiveness of money, offered up to $500,000, again not an overwhelming sum considering the frequency of the speeches about terrorism and the intensity of the rhetoric. . . .

On the basis of these and other facts, our historian will lean towards revisionism. He may well reach the conclusion that there was no terrorism, only a case of mass delusion—or that hysteria was deliberately fanned by certain vested interests, such as producers of anti-terrorist equipment perhaps or the television networks which had established a symbiotic relationship with the terrorists, providing them with free (or almost free) entertainment for long periods.

These are, of course, the wrong conclusions. The impact of terrorism is measured not only in the number of victims. Terrorism is an attempt to destabilize democratic societies and to show that their governments are impotent. And if this can be achieved with a minimum effort, if so much publicity can be achieved on the basis of a few attacks, there is no need to make greater exertions. It is also true that there have been ominous new developments such as the emergence of narco-terrorism and of state-sponsored terrorism on a broader level than before. If terrorism was never a serious threat as far as America was concerned, let alone other major powers such as Russia, China or Japan, it is also true that in certain Latin American countries, but also in places like Turkey and Italy, it was for a while a real danger.

In short, there has been (and is) a terrorist menace in our time. But the historian of the future will still be right in pointing to the wide dis-crepancy between the strong speeches and the weak actions of those who felt threatened. And he must be forgiven if he should draw the conclusion that the "age of terrorism" perhaps never understood the exact nature of the threat. . . .

How to eradicate terrorism? Moralists believe that terrorism is the natural response to injustice, oppression, and persecution. Hence the seemingly obvious conclusion: Remove the underlying causes which cause terrorism and it will wither away! This sounds plausible enough, for happy and content people are unlikely to commit savage acts of violence. But while this may be true as an abstract general proposition, it seldom applies to the real world, which is never quite free of conflicts. The historical record shows that while, in the nineteenth century, terrorism frequently developed in response to repression, the correlation between grievance and terrorism in our day and age is far less obvious. The historical record shows that the more severe the repression, the less terrorism tends to occur. This is an uncomfortable, shocking fact, and has, therefore, encountered much resistance. But it is still true that terrorism in Spain only gathered speed after Franco died, that the terrorist upsurge in West Germany, France, and Turkey took place under social democratic or left-of-center governments, that the same is true with regard to Peru and Colombia, and that more such examples could easily be adduced.

Terrorism has never had a chance in an effective dictatorship, but hardly a major democratic country has escaped it. There is a limit to the perfection of political institutions, and however just and humane the social order, there will always be a few people deeply convinced that it ought to be radically changed and that it can be changed only through violent action. . . .

From Laqueur, Walter. "Reflections on Terrorism," *Foreign Affairs*, October 1986.

Red Brigade, and the West German Red Army Fraction all used similar weapons, often Soviet made. Libya provided training camps for would-be terrorists. There were even connections between groups in Europe and Japanese terrorists.

The threat of terrorism was intensified by the activities of groups from outside Europe. The Palestine Liberation Organization (PLO) and its various splinter factions were all active throughout the 1970s and 1980s; their operations provoked Israeli reprisals and counterattacks (see Part VIII, Topic 10). Iran, Iraq, and Syria were accused of harboring, if not encouraging, terrorists. A string of airplane hijackings and bombings culminated in the explosion over Lockerbie, Scotland, of a crowded Pan American flight bound for the United States a few days before Christmas, 1988. Suspicion fell on Iran or Syria as the base from which the bomb planting was organized; experts later discovered that the plastic explosive responsible was manufactured in Czechoslovakia, a claim subsequently confirmed by Václav Havel, Czechoslovakia's new president.

By the 1990s most governments were resigned to the fact that only a drastic and unacceptable curtailment of their citizens' liberties could lead to a serious curtailment of terrorist activities. They turned instead to increased security measures, international police collaboration, and diplomatic pressure to limit the damage. The last years of the 20th century continued to be marked by outbursts of terrorist violence.

A space photograph of Earth—humanity's "common house."

FROM THE ATLANTIC TO THE URALS: EUROPE'S "COMMON HOUSE"

As national governments and international bodies wrestled with the day-to-day problems of environmental pollution and political violence, more visionary leaders began to look to a distant time when the geographical unit of Europe would achieve some form of union. Mikhail Gorbachev wrote of a "common house," in which members of the family might live at peace, all in their own ways.

Gorbachev's image implied a continuing political and social diversity, but economic developments and the communications revolution increased the speed with which conformity spread. The revolutions of 1989, furthermore, were waged by people anxious to share in the benefits—as they perceived them—of capitalism. Hungarians, Czechs, and Poles of the last decade of the 20th century tried to build societies modeled on those of Western European nations.

Perhaps in reaction against the tendency toward broad supranational groupings, nationalism continued to create friction in both East and West. In Western Europe, the various separatist movements continued to agitate. Attempts to establish order in the new Eastern European democracies were challenged by ethnic divisions going back to the Hapsburg and Ottoman empires. The country most dramatically affected was the region of the former Yugoslavia known as Bosnia, where conflict raged between Serb, Croat, and Muslim groups. An international peace-keeping force, led by U.S. troops, tried to impose the settlement terms negotiated in the "Dayton Accord," a peace plan negotiated in 1995. The peace-keepers were originally scheduled to withdraw by the summer of 1998, but by the beginning of that year it became clear that they would need to remain in place to prevent further conflict.

Europe faced the 21st century with new hopes and old fears. The burying of old national rivalries, the end of the Cold War, the search for increased cooperation and eventual union—all these held out possibilities of peace, and an improvement in the material conditions of millions.

Yet many problems remained unsolved, and are probably incapable of solution. The consequences of a transition to a postindustrial society in the West and the breakup of the Soviet Empire in the East were unpredictable. The nuclear energy issue demonstrated all too clearly that technological progress was a two-edged sword. Most importantly, the ability of the European family members to live peaceably with one another in their respective parts of the "common house" was going to be sorely tested.

Questions for Further Study

1. How have events since 1989 changed the global political landscape? What are their consequences likely to be for the early 21st century?

2. On the basis of the experience of the past half-century, how successful is terrorism as a means of producing radical change?

3. What are the major environmental issues of our times, and how great is their threat? Is uncontrolled population growth more or less dangerous to the quality of human life?

Suggestions for Further Reading

Alexander, Y., and C. K. Ebinger, eds. *Nuclear Terrorism: Defining the Threat.* New York, 1986.

Kidder, R. M. *Reinventing the Future: Global Goals for the 21st Century.* Cambridge, MA, 1989.

Lovenduski, J. *Women and European Politics: Contemporary Feminism and Public Policy.* Amherst, MA, 1986.

Maier, C. S., ed. *In Search of Stability: Explorations in Historical Political Economy.* Cambridge, MA, 1987.

Schlesinger, J. R. *America at Century's End.* New York, 1989.

Spretnak, C., and F. Capra. *Green Politics.* Toronto, 1986.

Abbreviations: Ancient Art & Architecture Collection (Pinner, UK): AA&A. AP/Wide World Photos (New York): AP/WW. Archiv fur Kunst und Geschichte (London and Berlin): AKG. Art Resource (New York): AR. Bibliotheque Nationale (Paris): BN. Bildarchiv Preussischer Kulturbesitz (Berlin): BPK. Bridgeman Art Library (London and New York): BAL. Corbis-Bettmann (New York): C-B. The Granger Collection (New York): GC. Hirmer Fotoarchiv (Munich): HF. Hulton Getty Collection/Tony Stone Images (Chicago): HGC. Mary Evans Picture Library (London): MEPL. Réunion des Musées Nationaux/Cliché © RMN (Paris): RMN.

Page   Credit

Part Opener VI, p. 571 Tate Gallery, London/AR
Part Opener VII, p. 707 Museo del Prado, Madrid
Part Opener VIII, p. 1003 Copyright © 1998 Artists Rights Society (ARS), New York/ Demart Pro Arte, Paris. Photo copyright © 1998 The Museum of Modern Art, New York
693 Hervé Lewandowski/RMN
694 top GC
694 bottom C-B
695 Giraudon/AR
703 SuperStock
710 Giraudon/AR
712 Giraudon/AR
713 Oesterreische Nationalbibliothek, Vienna
714 Giraudon/AR
717 Novosti/Sovfoto/Eastfoto
722 GC
728 GC
730 GC
731 J. Freeman/Barnaby's Picture Library
732 Mansell/Time Inc.
733 Mansell/Time Inc.
734 Musee Carnavalet/photo J. E. Bulloz, Paris
740 J. E. Bulloz, Paris
741 GC
743 BN/photo J. E. Bulloz, Paris
748 Giraudon/AR
749 top C-B
749 bottom J. E. Bulloz, Paris
751 C-B
759 National Gallery of Art, Washington (Samuel H. Kress Collection)
761 Louvre/BAL
762 C-B
763 C-B
764 Museo del Prado, Madrid
766 Scala/AR
768 HGC
773 GC
774L Brown Brothers
774R GC
776 C-B
777 Museo del Prado, Madrid
779 © Hervé Lewandowski/RMN
780 HGC
787 HGC
788 BN
789 Andrew Haslam/National Trust Photographic Library
790 Mansell/Time Inc.
791 GC
793 Collection J. Kugel/Lauros/Giraudon
794 GC
805 G. Blot/C. Jean/RMN

806 AKG
808 top By permission of the Houghton Library, Harvard University
808 bottom Staatliche Museen zu Berlin
810 RMN
811 Giraudon/AR
812L GC
812R GC
814 RMN
819 MEPL
820 C-B
821 Photographie Bulloz
822L C-B
822R MEPL
823 GC
826 Harlingue-Viollet
831 MEPL
832 HGC
833 HGC
834 HGC
836 HGC
837 GC
840 GC
843 David King Collection, London
844 GC
845 Sovfoto
846 C-B
851 HGC
852 MEPL
853 Culver Pictures
854 HGC
862 bottom GC
862 top GC
866 Brown Brothers
869 Culver Pictures
871 Mansell/Time Inc.
873 Deutsches Museum, Munich
875 Fogg Art Museum, © President and Fellows, Harvard College, Harvard University Art Museums
876 top HGC
876 bottom GC
881 GC
883 Keystone Mast Collection/California Museum Photography/University of California, Riverside
884 GC
886 James Helme/Royal Photographic Society
888 MEPL
889 Culver Pictures
891 Culver Pictures
896 GC
898 Culver Pictures
899 Print Collection, Miriam and Ira D. Wallach Division of Art, Prints and Photographs, The New York Public Library, Astor, Lenox and Tilden Foundations
902 © 1993 Beth Bergman, New York
903 top Bequest of Mrs. H. O. Havemeyer, 1929. Photo © 1985 The Metropolitan Museum of Art
903 bottom BAL
904 Presented to the Amon Carter Museum, 1990, from the Modern Art Museum of Fort Worth through grants and donations from the Amon G. Carter Foundation, the Sid W. Richardson Foundation, the Anne Burnett and Charles Tandy Foundation, Capital Cities/ABC Foundation, *Fort Worth Star-Telegram*, the R. D. and Joan Dale Hubbard Foundation, and the people of Fort Worth.
909 GC
910L GC
910R GC

911 HGC
913 MEPL
914 HGC
917 UPI/C-B
923 Wilhelm Gause/Historisches Museum der Stadt Wien/Erich Lessing/AR
925 C-B
926 Sovfoto
929 Culver Pictures
931 MEPL
932 GC
936 GC
937 UPI/C-B
938 Culver Pictures
941 Collection, Brandywine River Museum (acquisition made possible by Beverly and Ray Sacks)
943 top National Portrait Gallery, Smithsonian Institution/AR
943 bottom Brown Brothers
950 India Office Library
951 India Office Library
957 Bowring Collection/India Office Library
958 MEPL
959 SuperStock
961 HGC
963 C-B
964 GC
967 Sovfoto
968 Culver Pictures
969 HGC
971 C-B
973 Culver Pictures
974L INDEX/Pizzi
974R Culver Pictures
981 MEPL
982 HGC
984 C-B
985 GC
986 Thomas Gilcrease Institute of American History & Art, Tulsa, OK
987 ILN Picture Library
988 MEPL
991 Richard Wagner Museum, Triebschen-Luzern, Switzerland
992 GC
994 GC
996 bottom Copyright © 1992 Munch Museum, Oslo
996 top Cincinnati Art Museum (John J. Emery Endowment, 1928)
997 Museum of Modern Art, New York (acquired through the Lillie P. Bliss bequest). Copyright © 1998 The Museum of Modern Art, New York
998 Copyright © 1998 Artists Rights Society (ARS), New York/ADAGP, Paris. Photo by David Heald/© The Solomon R. Guggenheim Foundation, New York (PN 54.1412)
1000 Brown Brothers
1009 Robert Hunt Library
1010 Robert Hunt Library
1017 top MEPL
1017 bottom Bilderdienst Suddeutscher Verlag, Munich
1019 UPI/C-B
1021 AKG
1022 Topham Picture Source
1025 GC
1026 UPI/C-B
1031 UPI/C-B
1036 MEPL
1038 C-B
1040 top UPI/C-B
1040 bottom UPI/C-B

Page numbers in italics refer to illustrations and maps.